UNCOMMON ARTISTRY

UNDERSTANDING BAKARE, OJO RASAKI'S
DANCE, DRAMA AND THEATRE

SPM PUBLICATIONS
London

SPM Publications
Unit 136, 113-115 George Lane, South Woodford,
London E18 1AB, United Kingdom
www.spmpublications.com
in conjuction with the Department of Theatre and Media Arts
Federal University Oye Ekiti, Nigeria.

First published in Great Britain by SPM Publications – an imprint of Sentinel Writing & Publishing Company Limited in October 2014.

Copyright ©2014 Rasheed A, Adeoye, Uche Nwaozuzu, Solomon Ejeke, Etop Akwang, and the contributors.

Rasheed A, Adeoye, Uche Nwaozuzu, Solomon Ejeke, Etop Akwang, and the contributors have asserted their moral rights under the Copyright, Designs and Patents Act 1988, to be identified as the editors and authors of this work.

ISBN 978-0-9927055-3-4

All rights reserved. No part of this publication may be reproduced, stored in or introduced into a retrieval system, or transmitted, in any form, or by any means (electronic, mechanical, photocopying, scanning, recording or otherwise) without the prior written permission of both the above-named copyright owner and the publisher.

Set in Times New Roman.

UNCOMMON ARTISTRY
UNDERSTANDING BAKARE, OJO RASAKI'S DANCE, DRAMA AND THEATRE

Editors

AbdulRasheed A. Adeoye, Ph.D.
Uche-Chinemere Nwaozuzu, Ph.D.
Solomon Ejeke, Ph.D.
Etop Akwang, Ph.D.

Contents

Foreword | *10*
Acknowledgments | *13*

PART ONE: Dramatic Theory and Criticism on the Works of Bakare, Ojo Rasaki

Code-Switching and Code-Mixing In Bakare, Ojo Rasaki's *The Gods and The Scavengers* by Michael, A. Abiodun. | *15*

Tropes of Pax - Nigeriana and Pax - Yorubania in the *Selected Plays of Bakare, Ojo Rasaki* by AbdulRasheed, A. Adeoye, Ph.D. | *28*

Human Violence as a Political Ideology and its Import in Bakare, Ojo Rasaki's *Rogbodiyan* by Stephen, E. Inegbe, Ph. D and Anietie, Francis Udofia. | *48*

Text and Textuality in Bakare, Ojo Rasaki's *Rogbodiyan* and *The Gods and The Scavengers* by AbdulRasheed, A. Adeoye, Ph.D., and Oludolapo, Ojediran Ph.D. | *68*

Between and Betwixt the Constellation of Voices: Towards a Theory of Dance Rasaki by Uche-Chinemere, Nwaozuzu, Ph.D. | *82*

Disciplinary knowledge, Narrative Surplus, and Cognitive Boost in Bakaresque Dramaturgy: an Archaeological Study of *Rogbodiyan* by Etop Akwang, Ph. D | *97*

Dramatic Techniques in Ojo Rasaki Bakare's Once *Upon a Tower* by Joseph, O. Umukoro, Ph.D | *118*

Intimations of Social Dysfunctionality in The Plays of Bakare, Ojo Rasaki by Afolabi, John Adebayo, Ph.D. | *124*

Drama in its Social Context and the Kaleidoscope of Oppression in Bakare's *Once Upon a Tower* by Jide Balogun, Ph.D. and B.J. Balogun. | *138*

Political Theatre and the Leadership Question in Nigerian Drama: Statements in Bakare, Ojo Rasaki's *This Land Must Sacrifice* by Mbachaga, Desen Jonathan, Ph.D. | *150*

Womanist View and Political Stance in Bakare, Ojo Rasaki's *Selected Plays* by Oludolapo Ojediran, Ph.D. | *162*

Destiny as Aesthetic in Bakare's *Rogbodiyan* and *The Gods And The Scavengers* by Aliyu-Ibrahim, Foluke R., P.h.D. | *176*

Systemic Problems and Self Preservation in Institutions of Higher Learning in Nigeria: Lessons from Bakare Ojo *Rasaki's Once Upon a Tower* by Ekweariri, Chidiebere, Ph.D. | *187*

Bakare On The Decadence In The Ivory Tower: A Commentary On Bakare, Ojo Rasaki's *Once Upon A Tower* by Ubong, S. Nda, Ph.D. | *203*

Bakare, Ojo Rasaki's *Drums Of War* and the Hermeneutics Of Women Emancipation in Mark 7: 23 -34. By Ojo, Olanrewaju Paul, Ph.D. | *215*

Political Gansterism and Materialism in Bakare, Ojo Rasaki's *The Gods and The Scavengers* and *Rogbodiyan* by Ekweariri, Chidiebere S. Ph.D. and Uzondu Ifeyinwa | *229*

Reflection of Nigerian Tertiary Institutions in Bakare Ojo Rasaki's *Once Upon A Tower*: Metaphor For Social Transformation by Umukoro, M. Oghenevize and Iyamah, C. Yankson. | *244*

Òjóism: Bakare's Artistic Tendencies in Comparison with the African Masquerade by Adeoye, Aderemi Michael. | *258*

Shadow Over The Promised Land: Effects of Attitude On Quality Of Education In Tertiary Institutions as poyrayed by Bakare, Ojo Rasaki by Ezinne Igwe | *269*

Revolutionary Aesthetics in Contemporary Nigerian Theatre: A Study of Bakare Ojo Bakare's Once Upon a Tower by Obiora Ekwueme. | *282*

Heuristic Appraisals Of The Works Of Bakare Ojo-Rasaki As Quintessential Choreographer And Dancer by Obasi, Nelson Torti. | *295*

Marxist Radical Playwriting in Bakare, Ojo Rasaki's *The Gods and The Scavengers* by Christopher, Elochukwu Unegbu. | *307*

Change and The Role Of The Playwright in Bakare, Ojo Rasaki's *Once Upon A Tower* by Chukwukelue, Uzodinma Umenyilorah. | *324*

Voices Of Power And Echoes Of Moral Decadence In Bakare Ojo Rasaki's *Rogbodiyan* by Oluwatoyin, Olokodana. J | *336*

Leadership And Insensitivity In Nigeria: The Example of Bakare Ojo Rasaki's Drums Of War by Fanyam, Joel Avaungwa And Gbilekaa, Richard K. | *350*

Nigerian Ivory Tower And The Human Development Dilemma: Bakare, Ojo Rasaki's *Once Upon A Tower* Paradigm. By Joseph Agofure Idogho. | *360*

Corruption Syndrome In Nigeria, A Thematic Analysis Of Bakare, Ojo Rasaki's *Once Upon A Tower*: Challenges For The Director And Designers. By Kingsley, Oyong Akam. | *375*

Factional Insurgency in Bakare, Ojo Rasaki's Drums Of War And Rogbodiyan. By Idogho, Joseph Agofure. | *393*

Satirical Reflection Of Social Stasis And The Reader/Audience Interpretation Of Dramatic Text: An Examination of Bakare Ojo Rasaki's Rogbodiyan. By Ozobeme, Cecil. | *404*

The Playwright And Commitment: A Study of Bakare, Ojo Rasaki's This Land Must Sacrifice And Rogbodiyan. By Ekpenisi, Kingsley And Iyamah Chijioke Y. | *417*

The Aesthetics Of Performative Trinity For Audience Engineering: A Study of Bakare, Ojo Rasaki's Directorial Device. By Asuquo, Nsikan Bassey. | *426*

Language Use and Semiotic Appraisal of Bakare Ojo Rasaki's Rogbodiyan. By Inegbe, Miriam Stephen . | *441*

PART TWO: Dance and Music in the Works of Bakare, Ojo Rasaki

Music And Songs In Bakare Ojo Rasaki's Rogbodiyan And Drums Of War. By Solomon, Ikibe, Ph.D. and Gabriel, Ojakovo, Ph.D. | *453*

Break and Mould the Dancer: Bakare Ojo Rasaki's Technique of Training. By Suru, Cyrus Damisa, Ph.D. | *467*

Body Rhythmicity And Bakare Ojo Rasaki's The Deformed Can Also Dance: Democratizing Dance Practice In A Democratized Nigeria. By Ifure, Ufford-Azorbo Ph.D. and Ikike, Inieke Ufford. | *478*

A Synergy of Musical and Theatrical Works as Exemplified in Bakare Ojo Rasaki's Once Upon a Tower. By Ekong, E. Grace, Ph.D. and Ukeme A. Udoh. | *490*

Functionality Of Music And Dance In Bakare Ojo Rasaki's The Gods And The Scavengers. By Ifure Ufford-Azorbo, Ph.D. and Tam Gordon Azorbo, Ph.D. | *518*

The Choreographer as a Teacher: Analyzing Bakare Ojo Rasaki's Impartation Method. By Onyemuchara, E. Casmir. | *527*

The Choreographic Style And Techniques Of Dancerasaki. By Dosumu–Lawal, Yeside. | *539*

Dance Practice and the Choreographer's Creative Role through Bakare Ojo Rasaki's view lens. By Peter, Adeiza Bello. | *548*

Postmodern Dance In Bakare, Ojo Rasaki's Drums Of War And Rogbodiyan by Olalusi, Kehinde Adedamola. | *558*

PART THREE: Performance and Design Aesthetics on the Works of Bakare, Ojo Rasaki

Reconstructing The Democratic Environment In The Dramaturgy And Performance Of Bakare Ojo Rasaki's Drums Of War. By Olympus, G. Ejue, Ph.D. | *568*

Artistic Direction and Directorial exploration in Bakare Ojo Rasaki's The Gods and the scavengers and Once upon a tower. By Arinde, Tayo Simeon, Ph.D. | *594*

Interrogating Dance Drama as a Total Ensemble: A Study of Bakare Ojo Rasaki's Production of The Voyage. By Nnamdi, c Mbara. | *613*

Theatre Design in Bakare Ojo Rasaki's Drums of War: An Evaluation of Nigeria's Diversity. By Adeoye, Aderemi Michael. | *625*

Jagunmolu: Dance Battle In Nigeria And The Triumphant Dancerasaki. By Victor, Thompson. | *634*

Aesthetics Of Body And Floor Patterns In Bakare Ojo Rasaki's Choreography: The "Sai Ka Yi Aiki" Example. By Tume, 'Tosin. K. | *644*

Multi-Dramatic Aesthetics In Bakare Ojo Rasaki's Rogbodiyan And The Gods & The Scavengers. By Adenekan, Lanre Qasim. | *657*

Riddles And Ripples In Bakare Ojo Rasaki's Works: A Directorial Perspective. By Ugala, B. Best. | *670*

The Abuja Carnival and Bakare Ojo Rasaki's Directorial Imprint. By Isijola, Oluwatayo. | *684*

PART FOUR: Bakare, Ojo Rasaki on the Marble of History

Interview I: *Abinibi and Ability:* An Incussion Into Nature And Nuture In The Art Of Bakare, Ojo Rasaki. By Adeseye, Bifatife Olufemi, Ph.D. | *698*

Interview II: How to Develop Nigeria's Culture – Bakare, Ojo Rasaki. *By Balogun, Olusola Kayode.* | *717*

Interview III: Bakare, Ojo Rasaki in the Spotlight: In Conversation with Agozie Ugwu by Agozie, Ugwu | *725*

Notes on Editors and Contributors | *739*

Foreword

In the career of anyone growing through the University system in Nigeria there are four interlocking traditions which are celebrative, commemorative, exhibitionistic, and tributary i.e conferring of honours.

The first is the tradition in which parents and family celebrate with the prospective university student on Matriculation Day. After such a day the ambitious student undergoes a period of training and study at the end of which he has stepped into the second tradition.

The second is the tradition of graduating, going into National Youth Service as a patriot, and then convoking on Convocation Day. On that day he is robed, decked out, garlanded as an achiever. He may undergo altogether three such convocations if he wishes to pursue an academic career, steps which take him through Master's and Doctoral Degrees. Thereafter he embarks on a scholarly professional career, still within it, now fully steeped in the dyes of the Ivory Tower, he reaches tradition number three.

That third is the tradition of earning and being installed into a chair in the professional area in which he has demonstrated irrefutable expertise. He now has a profession he "professes", and is titled, "Professor", an authority and specialist in a defined, socially and culturally palpable area. There he makes his mark, shares socially revolutionary and status-changing ideas and theories with many within his Nigerian borders as well as beyond those borders as his publications join in the global battle for the minds of the young, old, and established thinkers and doers of the world.

It is at this stage, in the third tradition, that the man has what I want to call, "the festive commendation stage" - a Festschrift is organized in his honour.

Festschrift-ism is the fourth tradition. In it, as in this book, edited by four well-entrenched fellow scholars and friends, there is a celebration – of the subject's birth, career achievements, highlights of controversies and contributions, underscoring the solidity and reflectiveness of the man's entire career.

A remarkable achiever has been taken through these traditions, and his name is Rasaki Ojo Bakare.

The joy this writer has in presenting this monumental theatre studies Professor goes beyond the joy of parents and family celebrating at Matriculation or Convocation, or Enthronement into a chair at which time the man gives the justification for earning a Chair with an Inaugural Lecture. My joy is that fuller because Rasaki Ojo Bakare has been under my personal, non-biological parental periscope for more than twenty-five of his fifty years: he was my undergraduate student; I assessed his suitability for professorial chair; I adjudicated Abuja Carnival Festive Events for him, when he was the Festival's Director; I supervised him as theatre director, as dance and choreography specialist, as playwright and writer of such jubilee marker plays as This Land Must Sacrifice, Once Upon A Tower, and mightily, The Drums of War. Nigeria, with the vagaries of its evolution as a country has been his homeground, in the way England was for Shakespeare, scientific Norway was for Henrik Ibsen, and socialist Russia was for Anton Chekhov.

Though a mere 50 years of age, Rasaki Ojo Bakare by this celebrative, encomiastic, and assessing picturization by this theatre and drama scholar to veaguos classmates, peers and parents has joined the ranks of those who come to limelight in this profession, as Soyinka demonstrated winning the Nobel at 52, and Esiaba Irobi underscored by winning the NLNG Prize at 50, and Sam Ukala joining at about the same age range.

It is a pleasure to invite you, dear readers, to share this book on "Rasaki Ojo Bakare At 50". You will be inspired, motivated, challenged. The contributors have given you an all-round, rounded character treasure beyond the stage. Relish it.

Kalu Uka
Professor of Theatre Arts, UniUyo

Acknowledgments

The editors would want to acknowledge the subject of this book, Professor Bakare, Ojo Rasaki for graciously giving us the nod to embark on this scholarly labour. Our thanks also go to his amiable wife who helped facilitate the acquiescence of her husband for us to carry out this project.

In writing a book like this, many debts are incurred, not least to the friends and colleagues of Bakare who have over the years harassed us into clarity and made us sharply conscious of the need for a reliable guide to approaching the man and his works. Particular thanks are due to all scholars and artists who contributed articles here.

We would also like formally to thank those without whose cheerful friendship, professional conversation and generous assistance we would not have started, let alone finish. In this regard, heartfelt thanks go to members of the 'Bakare at 50' committee. Staff and students of Faculty of the Humanities and Social Sciences, Department of Theatre and Media Arts, Federal University Oye-Ekiti, Ekiti State, The secretarial staff amongst whom are Taiwo Olusola, Niyi Adeosun, Sunday Abatan, Catherine Oloni and Felicia Richard. We cannot end without recognising those individuals and scholars who have in one way or the other worked with Professor Bakare, Ojo Rasaki in sustaining and furthering the universe of performing arts in Nigeria.

AbdulRasheed A, Adeoye, Ph.D.
Uche-Chinemere Nwaozuzu, Ph.D.
Solomon Ejeke, Ph.D.
Etop Akwang, Ph.D.

PART ONE

DRAMATIC THEORY AND CRITICISM ON THE WORKS OF BAKARE, OJO RASAKI

Code-Switching And Code-Mixing In Bakare, Ojo Rasaki's *The Gods And The Scavengers.*

By
Abiodun, A. Michael, Ph.D.

Introduction

Code-switching and code-mixing are common phenomena in a language contact situation. When a person has access to two or more codes, he/she unconsciously (consciously at times) makes use of the different codes in normal speech. These two phenomenon have interested sociolinguistics and scholars in other fields of study that include Anthropology, Literature, Sociology and many others such that a very robust literature exists on the phenomena. The phenomena is not limited to oral speech, it extends to written works. Ugorji and Osiruemu (2001) and Owoeye (2011) have reported this in the creative works of literary writers. Hodge (1979), Olumuyiwa (2013), Ahmed (2009) have also reported the use in written advertisements on bill-boards, leaflets and handbills.

This paper focuses on the manifestation of these phenomena (code-switching and code-mixing) in one of the plays of Bakare Ojo Rasaki: *The Gods and the Scavengers.* As will be shown in the body of the work, there is a robust injection of linguistic elements from the three major Nigerian languages and two of the nations 'minor' languages, Efik and Ibibio and also from Nigerian Pidgin English into the play. The injection, apart from being for aesthetics, is to affirm strongly the setting of the play, and also to create a strong psychological link between his readers and the message of the play.

The paper is divided into seven sections. The first section is the introduction, section two presents a review of the major concepts in the work code-switching and code-mixing. Section three presents some of the existing works related to the use of different codes in literary texts while section four presents s short exposition of the text under study. Section five contains the data for the work and section six contains an analysis of the data. Section seven is the conclusion.

Code-Switching and Code-Mixing
As already mentioned above, both code-switching and code-mixing are consequences of language contact. Languages are said to be in contact when two or more languages are used within a geographical area, and speakers of the different languages interact frequently without inhibition, (Weinreich 1953, Vogt 1954, Alvarez 1998, Poplack 1980, 2001) Nigeria is a good case of a nation where languages are in contact. Apart from the English language, which is the official language of the nation, there is Pidgin English which is a form of English with simplified grammar and vocabulary. Wardhaugh (2006:61) defines pidgin as "a 'reduced' variety of a 'normal' language, i.e. with simplification of the grammar and vocabulary (of the normal) language, considerable phonological variation, and an admixture of local vocabulary to meet the special needs of the contact group". Apart from English and Pidgin English, there are close to four hundred Nigerian languages of which three are classified 'major' languages and others minor languages. One must, not forget to add French and Arabic as contact languages in Nigeria. With this scenario, bilinguals and multilinguals are bound to arise, and in normal speech, code-switching and code-mixing become the norm in everyday speech.

Scholars are unanimous in their observation and claims that both code-switching and code-mixing involve the use of different codes (languages or dialects) within a speech context. They, however, differ as to the accurate definition of the terms. Poplack (1980) for instance distinguishes the two terms in his work when he says that code-mixing should be regarded as the "mixing of two or more languages within a sentence while code-switching should be regarded as the switching between two or more languages at the clause level of discourse", other scholars that share this view of distinguishing the two terms include Sridher and Sridher (1980), Alveres (1998), Crystal (2008) and some others. Other scholars, however, contend that the terms are synonymous, and can be used interchangeably. Weinreich (1953), Kachru (1978) Muysken (2000) and some other scholars share this view. The issue of inter or intra-sentential should not count as far as these latter scholars are concerned. The main issue is the link between contact languages in normal speech. There is no doubt that phenomenon of written the context of language contact for the purpose of this study, the two terms are captured under code-switching.

Review of Relevant Works
There is a robust discussion in the literature on the features of code-switching and code-mixing in the works of creative writers, particularly, writers of prose and drama. Scholars that include Obafemi (2006), Ugorji and Osiruemu (2007), Owoeye (2011) and many others have described the influence of Nigerian indigenous languages and Pidgin English on the use of English in (creative) literary works. Owoeye (2011: 4) is apt in her remarks about some creative writers in Nigeria that there works "are neither expressed absolutely in indigenous languages nor in perfect Queen's English." She goes on to say that with some writers their works "are written in domesticated English, otherwise referred to as Nigerian English, coupled with an indiscrete mixture of Nigerian Pidgin English and items of Yoruba language".

Ugorji and Osiruemu (2007) look at the injection of Esan an Edord language spoken in Edo State in one of the works of Ahmed Yerima – *Dry Leaves on Ukan Trees*. These scholars noted "the infusion of Esan language vocabulary, i.e. loan from Esan' into the work, they equally note "the skillful weaving of indigenous cultures into English expressions ... the patterning of constructions follows the patterns of Esan, but the lexicalization is English. Owoeye (2011) writes on the influence of Yoruba in the works of Ola Rotimi and Femi Osofisan. Just like Yerima's work demonstrates a discrete mixture of Esan vocabulary, proverbs and figurative expressions, so also are the works of these creative writers. Owoeye brings copious illustrations of

Yoruba vocabulary, folktales, folksongs, proverbs and figurative expression from the works of the writers".

There are a number of works that have discussed the influence of one Nigerian language or the other in works of Nigerian writers. One very interesting thing in the works of Bakare that is the focus of this paper is the creative ingenuity of bringing the three indigenous languages of Nigeria – Hausa, Igbo and Yoruba into his work. Whereas other writers like Yerima restricts himself to Esan, Rotimi and Osofisan restrict themselves to Yoruba, Achebe (Chinua) also restricts himself to Igbo (cf Nwachukwu, 2004), Bakare appears to be a writer 'without linguistic border'. He is a native speaker of Yoruba, but he injects vocabularies and folksongs from the three major and 'minor' languages not just for aesthetics, but, as will be shown in this work, for a better understanding of the generalisation of the setting of his work, and an attempt to create a psychological link between his works and his readers.

The Context of *The Gods and The Scavengers*
The play mirrors the social disconnection between the rulers and their subjects In the society. It is a reflection or an exposition of a society held in the 'jugular by corruption arising from unbridled greed, injustice, insensitivity and uncontrollable criminal tendencies of rulers. Anago, the Honourable Chairman of the Council, his adviser and the Councillors are the rulers in the text while the market women, the artisan and the middle class workers (the Scavengers) constitute the subjects.

Anago at the onset gives the impression of a ruler that would be upright, sincere and people friendly. He meets the market women and speaks eloquently about equality, justice, and social development. He says:
>......We shall not only tar the roads but jail criminals a well. Amenities shall not only be provided tax evaders shall also sweat in the dungeon. And as for the powerful ones who

> would prefer to live and let other dies, this
> season shall be nemesis (p. 11).

As the play unfolds, however, Anago shows his inability to live above board, a major characteristic of leaders and rulers in a developing world. He shoes this in his effort to forcefully and fraudulently acquire a piece of land for the expansion of his personal business. When cautioned by Andy, his adviser, and reminded that "tongues are wigging", he retorts

> Talk like a politician. The plot of land is strategic and my business will thrive there .... If anybody has problem with his tongue he should visit a surgeon, as for me I day Kakaraka (p. 20)

The Councillors do not pretend about their greed, sense of injustice, insensitivity, and criminality. They show this by insisting on the collection of royalty from the market women and their inability to account for the money they collect for the development of their respective 'wards'. Mallam clearly reflects this:

> Wallahi tallahi, I no even know wetin I do with
> my own money, but I know say de money don
> finish (P. 29).

The criminality is reflected in the killing and maiming of their people in a bid to counter the Honourable Chairman's outbust and threat.

The play is not only about bad leadership, it is also a 'call to duty', a wake-up call for the subjects to put their destinies in their hands and fight collectively for equality and justice. The text is aimed at reminding the society that the gods will only show the ways and means of achieving peace, equality and justice in the society, the gods will not physically participate in correcting the errors and ills of the society. They onus of doing this lies solely on the oppressed of the land. Andy put this fact succinctly in the text when he says:

> I have not denied the existence of the gods, but we do a lot and we shout "the gods" My people. He that created us gave us brains. Anago was manufactured by the connivance of the ruling class ... (pp. 49-50).

In another instance he says:

> But people, we make our destiny. We are what we choose to be. We are the final deciders of whatever happens tous. (p. 50).

Finally, the text is a reminder that in every hopeless situation there is always a redeemer. A character emerges to lighten up the dark tunnel and shows the way to prosperity. Andy represents the redeemer in the text, he mobilises the oppressed, the market women and the scavengers to action, to save themselves from the hands of their oppressors.

The Data

As earlier mentioned in the introductory part of the paper, the concern here is not about Nigerian English, rather the paper focuses on the use of elements of the three Nigerian major languages in the text, and the use of Pidgin English. The work will not describe and discuss the patterning of constructions in the Nigerian languages that manifest lexicalisation in the English language. Thus our data will be purely linguistic elements in Hausa, Igbo and Yoruba, and Pidgin English.

Folksongs

Several songs are rendered in the text. They are illustrated below:

Hausa

(i) **Akwai wata gari Ana Samu zinamya
Wai Suna ta e e Wai Suna ta Gidan dei
dei (2x)** (pg. 7)

(ii) **Ina za muje 2x**

Ina zamu koma yar uwa ina za muje
  Anche duniya badu dadi
  Anche lahira kuma da zafi
  Ina zamu kema jar uwa ina zamu je (p. 15)

Igbo
(i) Unu abiala
  Madu nile ndi biara n'ebe a
  Unu abiala
  Ngozi na ekele diri unu n'ile
  Unu abiala (p.8)

(ii) Ebee ka anyi na a gaa
  Ebee ka anyi n'ejee e
  Ebee ka anyi na agaa o nwanem
  Ebee ka anyi n'ejee e
  Elu uwa adighi uto
  Elu igwe dikwa oku
  Ebee ka anyi na – gaa o nwanem
  Ebee ka anyi n'ejee (p. 15-16)

Yoruba
(i) Ile kan mbe to san fun wara ati oyin
  Ile kan mbe to je ile ileri
  Ero to nlo ero to mbo (p.8)

(ii) Tani lawa o ni baba
  Kai ani baba
  Honourable **baba wa**
  Kai ani baba (p. 13)

Pidgin English
(i) We no go gree o
  We no go gree
  Sam sam sam sam
  We no go gree (p. 17)

Sentences
Apart from songs, whole sentences, phrases and lexical items are found within English utterances.

Igbo
Chief Madunagu: **Mechie onu!** Are you asking me? When last did you send your royalty to the Honourable …. (p. 14)

Chief Madunagu: **Gini?** What can't you understand? Okay … (p14)

Hausa
Hadiza: **Haba Mallam! Mai ya faru? Ram ka dede** Just left this place. (p15)

Mallam: **Mai ki ki nufi?** What do you mean? Am I lying? Okay. **Shi kenan…..** (p15)

Yoruba
Chief Olowokere: What am I talking about? **Wo! Ti n ba gba e ni igbakugba.** I am talking about the royalty meant for the Chairman and you feign ignorance. (p13)

Chief Olowokere: **Oya!** Man the gate. **E ti le kun gboingboin.** They must not be allowed to enter (p. 23)

Pidgin English
Iyaloja: **All dis one way una de talk, una just day scratch the body of the coconut with fingernail. If dis market extend go reach Kafachan, make roads big so tay five elephants day waka side by side the same time** …. (p10)

Papa Ononu: **Ehen? Dat one no concern our people now. It them go finish themselves make them finish themselves.** (p. 38)

Woman: **E concern us oo. E concern us well well because as them shoot stab each other them day made mistake shoot and stab out people.** (p. 38)

Discussion
One of the major pre-occupation and interest of an artist, particularly a creative writer, is to get his /her message across to readers. To achieve this, the writer looks for simple and fascinating ways that will arouse the interest of readers and their power of imagination. He or she strives as much as possible to make his work comprehensible and appealing. Thus, his theme, characterisation, setting and language must be part of the experience of the readers for them to comprehend and appreciate the message of the writer.

Bakare, in *The God and the Scavengers*, shows his clear understanding of the multilingual nature of the Nigerian nation and the language policy that recognises three out of the over four hundred Nigerian languages as 'major' and others as 'minor'. He understands the relevance of Hausa, Igbo and Yoruba in the socio-political landscape of the nation. Part of his understanding is the appeal that Nigerian Pidgin has in the linguistic landscape of the nation. Unlike Nigerian indigenous languages that each has regional native speakers, Nigerian Pidgin has no regional native speakers, its influence cuts across the nation, (Elugbe and Omamor 1991, Elugbe 1995, Fracalas 1996, Egbokhare 2001). To get his message across to a large section of the Nigerian community, Bakare deploys the use of the major and minor Nigerian languages and the Nigerian Pidgin English. Using folksongs, names and grammatical sentences from the indigenous languages and background side by side with the English language, the writer is able to draw his readers to appreciate and understand the setting of the play. The strategy has a psychological undertone; a great effort designed to appeal to the emotion of the readers to be interested in the message of the text.

Language is a major tool in the business of mobilisation, when a person reads or (hears) grammatical elements from his or her language, the person becomes more alert and more sensitive to his environment. The sense of inclusion in the reader is aroused, and he or she gets interested in the text or events around him or her. Bakare is mindful of these, he strives to get his message to every part of the Nigerian community by using indigenous languages and Pidgin. The folksongs in Hausa presented in the play have the power of arousing and motivating the Hausa speaker, those in Igbo have similar effect on Igbo speakers and the same goes for Yoruba speakers.

The demonstration of code-witching in this play has further reinforced the place of indigenous languages in written literature, even when they are written in foreign languages. The folksongs in the text would be hard to comprehend if translated into the English language. Their originality and the cultural undertone would have been lost, a situation that would have rendered the work unappealing to the native owners of the songs.

Conclusion
This work has brought to focus, the role of indigenous languages in the creative works written in English. The paper reveals the psychological implication on code-switching from a literary perspective. It is argued in the paper that a writer has the potential of appealing to the emotion of readers by injecting into his or her work linguistic forms from the local languages of his or her target audience. The paper has particularly shown the literary ingenuity of Bakare to take his message to all corners of the Nigerian nation by deploying very extensively linguistic forms from many indigenous languages of the nation.

References

Ahmed, S. O. (2009). *Code-switching English and Hausa in Advertising: A Strategy for Mass Communication.* Ms.

Alvarez, C. (1998). From 'Switching Code' to 'Code-Switching': Towards a Reconceptualization of Communicative Codes. In Auer, P. (Ed.). *Code Switching in Conversation: Langua ge Interaction and Identity.* (pp 29-48). London: Routledge.

Bakare, O. R. (2013). *The Gods and The Scavengers.* Abuja: Topklass.

Crystal, D. (2008). *A Dictionary of Linguistics and Phonetics.* Malden: Blackwell Publishing.

Egbokhare, F. (2001). The Nigerian Linguistics Ecology and the Changing Profiles of Nigerian Pidgin. In Igbohanusi, H. (Ed.). *Language Attitude and Language Conflict in West Africa,* (pp104-124). Ibadan: Enicrownfit Publishers

Elugbe B. (1995). Nigerian Pidgin: Problems and Prospects. In Bamgbose, A., Banjo, A. and Thomas, A. (Ed.). *New Englishes: A West African Perspective,* (pp 284-299). Ibadan: Mosuro Publishers and Booksellers.

Elugbe, B. and Omamor, A.(1991). *Nigerian Pidgin: Background and Prospects.* Ibadan: Heinemann educational Books.

Fracalas, N. (1996). *Nigerian Pidgin.* London Routledge.

Hodge, C. R. (1979). Code Switching as a Strategy for Marketing in Malaysia. *Journal of Asian Studies.* 9, 4: 154- 171.

Kachru, B. (1978). Code-mixing as a communicative Strategy in India. In Alatis, J. E. (Ed.) *International dimensions of Bilingual Education,* (pp 107-124). Washington DC: Georgetown University Press.

Muysken, P. (2000). *Bilingual Speech*. Cambridge: Cambridge University Press.

Nwachukwu, A. (2004). *The Culture and Philosophy of Igbo in the Works of Chinua Achebe*. Ms.

Obafemi, O. (2006). The Languages of Post Colonial Literature: The African Experience. In *Refereed Proceedings of the 23rd Annual Conference of the Nigeria English Studies Association*, pp17-21.

Olumuyiwa, T. (2013). The Use of Code Switching/Code Mixing in Olusegun Mimiko's Political Billboards, Ondo State, South-West Nigeria. *Canadian Studies in Literature and Language,* Vol 6,No1: 26-34.

Owoeye, O. K. (2011). Yoruba Based Nigerian English in the Drama of Ola Rotimi and Femi Osofisan. *Journal of West African Languages*, 38, 2: 3-19.

Poplack, S. (1980) Sometimes I'll Start a Sentence in English y termino en espanol: Toward a Typology of Code-Switching. *Linguistics*. 18, 581-616.

Poplack, S (2001). Code-Switching (Linguistics). In Smelser, N. and Baltes, P. (Ed). *International Encyclopedia of Social and Behavioural Sciences*. (pp 2062-2065). Amsterdam: Elsevier Science Ltd.

Stridher, S. N and Stridher, K. K. (1980). The Syntax and Psycholinguistics of Bilingual Code-Mixing. *Canadian Journal of Psychology,* 34(4), 407-416.

Ugorji, C. U. C and Osirueme, E. O. (2007). Nigerian English in *Dry Leave on Ukan Trees*. *Journal of West African Languages*. 34, 1: 3-23.

Vogt, H. (1954). Language Contact. *Word*. 10(2-3), 365-374.

Wardhaugh, R. (2006). *An Introduction to Sociolinguistics 5th Edition*. Malden: Blackwell Publishing.

Weinreich, V. (1953). *Language in Contact*. The Hague: Mouton.

Tropes of *Pax - Nigeriana* and *Pax - Yorubania* in the Selected Plays of Bakare, Ojo Rasaki

By
Adeoye, AbdulRasheed Abiodun, Ph.D.

Introduction
There is no need for unnecessary mingling of suspense with illusion in a linear plot structure: Bakare, Ojo Rasaki is an important archetype in the Nigerian postcolonial theatre and culture. Our initial rationalism on Bakare, Ojo Rasaki is as a result of his critical investment in dance, music and drama, responding frequently to the trope of total theatre. Within the third generation of Nigerian playwrights and theatre practitioners, Bakare's new vision and admirable courageous exploration are also expanded to acting, theatre management and cultural administration. Bakare, Ojo Rasaki; the ebullient pacesetter of the Nigerian postcolonial theatre storms the Nigerian stage to redefine, very materially and critically too, our inept live performance of the early 1990s by daring to challenge existing themes and tendencies.

Certainly, the conspiracy of the West and its clearly defined hegemony of globalisation and high culture drove the African cultures into the state of comatose. In this state, we live the culture of hybridism by borrowing from the Blackman's culture (our culture) which nature has endowed us with and partly too, we are in cloud nine with various imported cultures from Asia, Europe and America. What is at play in this type of state is the gradual extinction of our culture and ideology. It is this parlous state that most plays of Bakare, Ojo Rasaki appear to celebrate the oxymoronic multicultural culture of Nigeria and the connectivity of Yoruba culture within other cultures in Nigeria. The Nigerian ideology that defines this essence are also celebrated in most of his plays. With Bakare, Ojo Rasaki, the polemics, paradoxes and contradictions in culture have been used as interfacing and interacting factors in our changing Nigerian societies.

Flowing from the above, this chapter examines the thematic and dramaturgical essence of *Pax -Nigeriana* and *Pax – Yorubania* in the selected plays of Bakare, Ojo Rasaki. The selected plays are *Drums of War* (1995), *Once Upon A Tower* (2001) and *The Gods and The Scavengers* (2013). Our pedagogical style in this chapter is to examine culture and the dramatist's obsession with it, to explore the theoretical tropes of *Pax – Nigeriana* and *Pax – Yorubania* within cultural divides, and importantly, to examine the culture of *Pax – Nigeriana* and *Pax – Yorubania* in the selected plays of Bakare, Ojo Rasaki.

The Pre-text, Text and Post-text of Culture
Since the establishment of the first University in 1088 AD at Bologna in Italy (Umukoro, 2011, p. 137), culture has been intellectualised and theorised. Several scholarly perspectives have also been advanced to foreground the essence of culture. Beyond the clear transmission of culture in the Universities and other institutions of learning, the home has always served as the place whereculture is placed on a canvass of reality. It is at home that objections to culture and objections tocultural detractors are hemmed down. In a discourse on culture, there is no abstraction - the codes, ethics, mores, values, and institutions that define its inclusiveness are not matter of conjectures. In fact, there is no subliminity on a discourse on culture.

Culture is a pillar of our corporate essence but why are we always hysterical about culture? Theconvivial nature of culture has opened to us, rooms of possibilities but why are promoters of culture seen as ethnic champions? Culture is a pillar that guides the totality of our way of life, a golden symbol that tells us our dos and don'ts. But why are we dragging our feet to accept our own culture and quickly too, we run cap in hands, compete and even attempt to undo one another as we embrace foreign cultures? What is our collective mantra on our culture? How do we re-live our good but forgotten cultures?

Certainly, we do not have all the answers to the questions above, but we should note that we need culture so that we can re-order our disordered society. We need culture so that our people may not go into extinction. We need culture so that our people will not be enslaved by living the culture of other people. We need culture so that our people will be role models to others. We need culture so that we can cure deceit and tame the flourishing culture of disrespect among us. We need culture so that we can fight corruption and tame people who love materialism targeted towards territorialism.

Wallace (1970, p. 16) also captures the positive organic values and the positive symbolic values of culture to celebrate the inevitability of culture in the social process:
A. Positive organic values
1. Eating and drinking
2. Sleeping, rest, relaxation, absence of discomfort or bodily tension
3. Sexual satisfaction
4. Optional temperature maintenance
5. Elimination of wastes
6. Breathing
B. Positive symbolic values
1. Testimonials of love, administration, and respect from human objects
2. Enactment of behavior-sequences satisfying "in themselves", or satisfying because they are instrumental to other values
3. Presence of objects associated with organic and symbolic consummations (including human and non-human objects)

Adhering to one's culture may be seen as obeying the clarion call of nature. Accommodating other people's cultures without allowing them to swallow or destroy one's culture is the reality of the postmodern age which should be embraced.

Advancing the concept of culture, Aime Cesaire, the prodigious Martinician poet and politician in (Ojo-Ade, 1989, p. 252) says that "culture is everything. Culture is the manner of dressing, of carrying one's head, of walking, it is the manner of tying one's tie – it is not just the fact of writing books, of building houses. It is everything". The metaphor of culture as everything that we do is not an exaggeration but the true reflection of culture in our life. We should, therefore, strive to guide our culture jealously instead of pointing to the superpowers as responsible for the state of inertia in which most African cultures are.

As we attempt to fight back, and write to re-locate our dislocated cultures or decolonise the decolonisers of our culture, let us not be afraid of the charges of Afrocentricism as we also come home to appropriate Post-Afrocentricism. As a passing comment, Afrocentricism is the Blackman's revolutionary weapon of seeing slavery, colonialism and re-colonialisation as responsible for our underdevelopment or the 'seizure of our own technological development'. Those who, therefore, invest their energies to proclaim the reality of the Africans as pacesetters in arts and in the sciences, and the race as the beginning of the universe are thus seen as Afrocentrics by Americans and Europeans. On the other hand, Post-Afocentricism is a satiric jibe for us in Africa to move and think beyond slavery, colonialism and re-colonialism as we empower our people and charge them to stop dancing like whether beaten chickens to history that has happened, and that we can only learn from that history and move on. We are in support of the main themes and tendencies that Post-Afrocentricism offer.

The nature of culture and it proximate doctrine of dynamism has made it incumbent on researchers to rethink the link between the pre-text (the very formative period of any culture), text (the current wave of culture) and the post-text (the expected place of culture in the future).

Foregrounding the Tropes of *Pax – Nigeriana* and *Pax – Yorubania*

The ideology, strategy and nationalism that define Nigeria as a nation have great import on the definition of Organization of African Unity (OAU) and the redefinition of the African Union (AU). In spite of our diversities, the Nigerian initiatives are pillars that have sustained our dominant role in Africa. This acknowledged atmosphere of "Big Brother" has indeed made other African nations to accept our unique identity and even attempt to allow our initiatives to define African political ideology and diplomatic direction.

The brief profile above is to foreground the essence of Nigerian culture in the social, political, economic and religious directions of most African nations in the tropes of *Pax – Nigeriana* and its new creation by us, the *Pax – Yorubania* which has been tactically entrenched in the Nigerian socio-political landscape.

Arguably, the Yorùbá people are the most urban, cosmopolitan, communal and homogenous ethnic group in Nigeria. We, therefore, speak now of the symbol of *Pax - Yorubania*. This is not to foist Yorùbá cultural hegemony on the Nigerian nation. It is not an attempt to claim that the Yorùbá culture is superior to other cultures in Nigeria but to defend the material and immaterial elements, and features of the Yorùbá culture. To preach Yorùbá concepts of peace, custom, tradition, ethics, mores, proverbs and to stop the race from losing her heritage. *Pax – Yorubania* is aimed at negotiating the Yorùbá ideology, vision and mission within the Nigerian multicultural and multi-religious society. Also, *Pax – Yorubania* is a creation from *Pax – Romana*, *Pax – Britannia* and *Pax – Nigeriana* which Bolaji Akinyemi has written extensively on. In fact, the concept of *Pax – Nigeriana* in the view of Akinyemi (2005, p. 1) does "not imply the imposition of a Nigerian peace on non-Nigerians" but that the search "for norms of behavior to guarantee peaceful relationships" among people of Africa. Hence, *Pax – Yorubania* is a critical factor as we re-invent the Nigerian nation. Also, to bring our cultures home is to counter "the boredom of Western culture, a refuge from its hyper-technological posture" (Ojo-Ade, 1989, p. 248).

Our culture is our pride and we have spoken about *Pax-Yorubania* in this sub-heading to energise us to defend our lost cultures. We should also add *Mutatis mutandis* for the Nigerian and Yorùbá cultures. *Mutatis mutandis* for Africa is "the desired African renaissance...the transformation of the people or peoples of each African country into upstanding and modern societies" (Babalola, 2002, p. 10). *Mutatis mutandis* for the Nigerian and Yorùbá cultures should be seen as calculated attempt of seeing to the development of our old culture within the reality of the postmodern age.

Tropes of *Pax – Nigeriana* and *Pax – Yorubania* are friendly cultural aesthetics that allows for negotiation, re-definition and emulation of good things in Nigeria by other African countries and the acceptance of the beneficial concepts and ideas of the Yoruba people by the rest of Nigerians. The symbolic relationship between *Pax – Nigeriana* and *Pax – Yorubania* is linked to the inspiration and the open agenda of any culture to learn from the other and without the fear of foisting and imposition.

Tropes of *Pax – Nigeriana* and *Pax – Yorubania* in the Selected Plays of Bakare, Ojo Rasaki
One clear dramaturgy used by Bakare, Ojo Rasaki in the three plays selected for this study is his Prologue – Movement style. For example, *Drums of War* has a Prologue and Four Movements, *Once Upon a Tower* has a Prologue and Nine Movements while *The Gods and The Scavengers* has a Prologue and Nine Movements. Curiously, the text of this kind of style has hitherto defines the modern theatre. This choice is a rebellion within the laid down artistic conservatism which Bakare is known for. The tropes of Prologue – Movement is in itself the poetics of free will which Bakare has made use of in his essential postcolonial theatre to define the place of *Pax – Nigeriana* and *Pax – Yorubania* tropes in the larger umbrella of a well – made play which William Shakespeare and few others are reputed for.

Bakare, Ojo Rasaki's pedagogy of *Pax – Nigeriana* can be found in his *Drums of War*. Beyond the tragic vision of the play, *Drums of War* is a critical celebration of multicultural identity which is one of the main hubs of *Pax – Nigeriana*. Multiculturalism is the main metaphor of many cultures living together under one nation. The import of this to other African nations is that we should imbide the culture of tolerance, give and take and the ubiqutiousness of the entire world as a global village. In *Drums of War*, the twenty-two songs used in the play are from Hausa, Igala, Yoruba, Edo, and Ibira ethnic groups. This makes the discourse on the setting of the play a controversial one. However, this controversy is unique because it is a setting that can be described as 'Nigerian multicultural setting' which is articulated on the trope of *Pax – Nigeriana*, the clear preaching of using different ethnic songs to arrest the attention of the mix – grill Nigerian theatre audience. The playwright script is unique because he allows one ethnic song to dovetails into the other as subject of war and the counter – discourse to it are celebrated and expanded in the play.

For example, songs 7, 8 and 9 in the play are moralisers for Nigerian unity and a clear sermon that other African nations should emulate:

A song in Igala
Nigerian cho okete kane oo (2ce)
We only have one Nigeria (2ce)
Ukwe Hausa ukwe doma
Dagba kechi igbo kpa
No matter your tribe
Yoruba and tongue,
Chio-okete kane
Nigeria is only one.

A song in Hausa
Nigeria daya ne muke dachi,
We only have one Nigeria (2ce)
Nigeria daya ne muke
No matter your tribe
Da, koke bahaushe and tongue,
Ko Igala, ko Iyamirin
    Nigeria is only one.

>Ko beyerbe, Nigeeoo
>Eee Nigeria daya ne
>Muke da.
>*A song in Yoruba*
>Nigeria kan n lomi wao   We
>only have one Nigeria (2ce)
>Nigeria kan n loniwa   No
>matter your tribe
>Hausa ni e tabi   and
>tongue,
>Ibo Yoruba ni e tobi
>   Nigeria is only one.
>Idoma. Nigeria ooo
>Eee, Nigeria kan
>Nio ni wa (p. 80).

Songs 10, 11, 12 and 13 in the play are also placating. They are meant to tame the rebellion and the war mongering King in the play. These types of placating songs have the emotional essence of changing the heart of listening leaders notwithstanding the disaster that the King in *Drums of Wars* leads himself and his people into.

The protagonists of war (King, Akogun in the beginning of the play and Orighoye) and the antagonists of war (Beleku, Gbeje, Jeje and the Women) also reflect the oppositional stance between the breakers and makers of Africa. The play, *Drums of War*, has shown that most African leaders fight to support territorialism using all forms of tricks and deceits available to them while the script, succeeded admiringly to celebrate feminism and the collective power of women that can lead to success in any course of action that they believe in. The conversations below and the attendant cross-fires drive home the fact that collective struggle, even if crafted under the yoke of monomaniac heroism will still succeed:

>Akogun: (*A sarcastic but hysterial laughter*) We thought those we gave guns to were

men, we thought we had human beings whose heads were full of brain, whose chests shelter strong hearts pumping with the rhythm of patriotism, whose bodies could boasts of tough muscles with which to defend the integrity of our father land. I never knew how we deceived ourselves until now that the truth has stared us in face. Have your brains vacated their abodes for rotten tomatoes that you can no longer put your heads to use? Have your hearts become so tendered that they can be melted so easily by women? Like the plantain tree that kisses the ground before the bluntiest matchets, have your bodies become so hallow that you allow the bastards of Ibuji to go back unhurt? Is it unforgiveable that not a single matchet of yours has tasted blood?

1st Woman: Go and quench the thirst of your matchet with your blood, Akogun. We put you there, the chiefs and the king, to be our light, to lead us aright and make the world a better place. But what do you do as our leader? You set us against our neighbours and make us fight senseless wars, instead of concentrating our effiorts on meaningful development. We wake up every morning suspecting our neighbours, preoccupying our minds with the next strategy to use in bringing our so called foes on their knees, we live in perpetual fear, our hearts now live in our throats, we live in perpetual fear because we know not who the next arrow will hit. Akogun, go and tell your

	king and his chiefs that we, the people of Abakpa say we no longer want war.
All:	Yes
1st Woman:	What we now demand is peace and love with our neighbours and meaningful development for our land.
All:	Yes! Yes! Yes!... (pp. 60-61)

As a smart General of Abakpa's army, Akogun accepts the will of his people in a clear demonstration of loyalty although this later cost him his office. In Liberia, Sierra-Leone, Rwanda, Somalia and other troubled spots in Africa, women are always the major victims of war and they shared most, in the unmitigated disaster that wars have caused. Sharing their resolve to put an end to war as shown in the play is Bakare, Ojo Rasaki's *Pax – Nigeriana* of peace as the drums of war roll incessantly.

The observed *Pax – Yorubania* in *Drums of War* has to do with the playwright's use of Yoruba proverbs, idioms and metaphors and their relevance in the larger multicultural setting of the play. These linguistic icons contribute to the overall success of the play. Some are: "water from the snail's shell..." (p. 58), "smearing dungs at the pride of our land...", "opening their mouth like he-goats when savouring their mother's urine", "bleating like sheep with pepper in their mouth" (p. 59), "the dog loves breast feeding its child, but also loves devouring the child of the grass-cutter", "the son of the lion must have claws", "the chick explores the thorny bush and returns home unscathed", "the eye of the battle" (p. 72) and the King's diplomatic oratorical display that drives home the wise saying of Yoruba people as important factor in the larger Nigerian society:

>King:...This is Abakpa. Defend its people, restore its honour... Chiefs, go with Origboye and at once and recruit more soldiers to join the ones already at the battlefield. Get them immediately to resume the war immediately. If they refuse, cajole them, if they say no convince them. If they are

> stubborn confuse them: If they refuse to be confused, confront them. Give me words in few courses... (p. 73)

Names of characters in the play such as; Akogun, Eriokan, Gbeje, Jeje, Origboye also have deeper meanings that bother on courage, conscience, peace, war, patience, royalty and power that eventually celebrate the main themes and sub-themes of the play. *Pax – Yorubania* through the above is the agelong perspective of art in culture and culture in art. In fact, Johnson (2014, p. 30) concludes that "art and culture are inseparable. It is often used synonymously. For example, the art of the people is the culture of the people showcased".

In *Once Upon A Tower* by Bakare, Ojo Rasaki; death is used as a purgation of emotion in the fictious but familiar story of Marrapinto University. This is a play in which a dialogue is instituted by a playwright for his other colleagues lecturing in Nigeria and elsewhere to face their works and avoid engaging in destructive tendencies such as bootlicking, recruitment of incompetent and unqualified staff, admission racketeering, corruption and profiteering. In content and context, the play historicises the glorious past of our university education in Nigeria and also, dramatises its destruction.

The point of connection between this play and *Pax – Nigeriana* has to do with the fact that the Nigerian University system of the 1960s to 1970s remains the pride of Africa. The song below which is in the Prologue of the play, *Once Upon a Tower* captures the past success and of course, the present decay in our universities:

> <u>Once Upon a Tower</u>
> Solo: Once Upon a Tower
>   In our country Nigeriana
>   the tower upon an ivory
>   on a gold on the mable000

Chorus:	Later but later ... the tower on the silver eee
	Later but later the tower on the bronze/x2 a
Solo:	Once upon a' tower
	the Ivory upon the marble
	na the citadel of learning
	a place for civilization
Chorus:	Small by small the tower
	on the stone ee little by
	little the tower on the wood/x2ce
Solo:	Once upon a tower
	the Ivory upon the gold e dey
	shine e dey glitter
	a place for the high and mighty
Chorus:	Now but now the tower
	in the dust eee now but
	now the tower in the mud.
	The high and the mighty
	they are crawling they are sleeping...(p.1)

Universities of Ibadan, Lagos, Benin, Nigeria, Ife and Ahmadu Bello, represent the best legacies of the Nigerian intellectual power in the 1960s and 1970s. This was a time that education was taken serious by all (the students, the university administrator and the government at all levels). This culture of total education made some African universities to adopt the University of Ibadan model in teaching and learning and it was a period that foreigners set serious foundation for studies in Education, Arts, Sciences, and Medicine. Their Nigerian colleagues were also creative as names such as Wole Soyinka, Chinua Achebe, J.P. Clerk, Ola Rotimi, Femi Osofisan and others indeed made lasting statements to foreground the culture of scholarship in literature. This success extended to almost all the existing fields of studies then. It was a period of fairness, equality and justice. It was a period where religion and state of origin or ethnic background had no place in placement, staff recruitment and admission.

Once Upon a Tower reveals the crisis of confidence between Professor Kurumbete who remains the genius of intolerance, pride, and the academic gadfly to intellectual weaklings such as Drs. Yemi and Ugolo in the play. His antagonist, the radical and brilliant Dr. Akitikori also reveals his search for freedom and disrespect for elders in the revenge tragedy. The following carefully selected lines indeed celebrate Kurumbete's pride and dictatorship:

- ❖ But I have instructed him that you must not fail the course (p. 17)
- ❖ Impunite insubordination!... Okay, don't worry, I am the Provost here. My command must hold… (p. 17)
- ❖ Be sorry for yourselves. The Vice – Chancellor cannot even talk to me this way. The VC, even the VC prostrate for me each time I enter his office… (p. 20)
- ❖ Impunite insubordination! If a University can take you back on contract three different times after retirement, then you are a genius… I am a genius… yes… God has created very few geniuses into this country… and I am one of those few. And all of us, we were created between 1935 and 1954. Since then, God has never created any genius, so small boy Akitikori I wonder the source of your confidence… (p. 20).

In counter-reactions, Dr. Akitikori also shares in the same pride that he accuses Kurumbete of. He is impatient and rash. Though he is oppressed and obiously, Akitikori fails to understand that in Africa, the patient dog eats the fattest bone. Now, Akitikori's infantile and counter reations in *Once Upon A Tower* deserve to be considered:

- ❖ No way, if you lilly–livered blokes have nothing to say, I Akitikori ona ofun ogbeegun eja, have something to say...
- ❖ Don't Kitikori me Mr. Head of Department. And you Prof. if you have rats and roaches as staff members, I am definitely not one of them... (p. 19).
- ❖ Yes Kurumbete's dog I will go on. Prof... if a university has given you contract appointments three different times after retirement, it shows two things. One is that the place has decayed and two is that you are a local champion... (p. 21).
- ❖ In spite of his pathological dullness, and despite scoring a shameful 200 in JAMB, Professor Kurumbete ensured his admission... (p. 26)

The narrative of the rise and fall of the Nigerian university education system has also drawn the attention of Jacob Kehinde Olupona, the Harvard double Professor of African and African American Studies and African Religious Traditions when he concludes rather paradoxically that:

> Countries that once looked up to our higher educational institutions as models to emulate are now places where our children flock to receive their education. It is certainly becoming a national disgrace and international embarrassment... (Olupona, 2013, p. 14).

The Nigerian university education before was indeed dependable for it to pass the acid test of *Pax – Nigeriana* and for now, it has lost that sport and this paradigm shift dwarfs the initial revolution as the essential Bakare, Ojo Rasaki reflects in *Once Upon A Tower*. Again, the play integrates in its dramaturgy, the muse of *Pax – Yorubania* through the magical wand of spine metaphors of names – Kurumbete, Akitikori senator Ikeanobi and other hidden Yoruba treasures of diplomacy, love, courage and law of revenge.

The Gods and The Scavengers is Bakare, Ojo Rasaki's manifesto for deconstruction and Marxist dialectics. This play is also allegorical and didactic, hiding scavengers who are professor, healer, farmer, technician and agent of multi-religiousity (the fifth scavenger). One other remarkable factor that defines this play is the aesthetics of hiding and deception, two skills that the playwright used successfully in the play. The two aesthetics lead to heroism and anti – heroism in a play about the gods and the destruction of the belief in them. For example, Anago, the Local Government Chairman and his Councilors start as heroes and end as anti – hero. The scavengers start as anti - heroes and end as heroes. This oppositional stance to their purported intention is what can be aptly described as the aesthetics of hiding and deception.

The Prologue of the play sets the deconstruction of the gods rolling through a song from the Lead:
> Why do we shout Gods as if He never gave us brain? Why do we shout the devil like we are zombies? In the scriptures all things were put in our hands. When we do nothing the gods do nothing (p. vi).

There is another refrain from the scavengers that takes the gods to the cleaner and insists that we make them and that we should be able to decide their fates. The gods here are the corrupt political class. The refrain goes thus: "We make them our gods and they loot our treasury" (p. 2-3).

Linked to the above common refrain is the need for us to smoke the gods out of our hearts. Therefore, the conversation between Scavenger 4 and Andy, the repentant and principled Political Adviser to Anago, the Local Government Chairman should be instructive:

> SCAV 4: Exactly, the gods will be angry if we fight their anointed…
> ANDY: We chose Anago with our votes and prayers. Leave the gods out of this. We never ask them to give us who they desire. We limited the options and prayed specifically for

> Anago. We made the gods and they gave us the desire of our heart (p. 48).

Bakare, Ojo Rasaki's anger against seeing the gods as the final deciders of our fate also comes to the fore in the play through his deconstruction of Ola Rotimi's *The gods are not to Blame* in which he makes a choice for Odewale in his *The Gods and The Scavengers* other than Odewale's initial fatalism:

> ODEWALE: Who wanted those things to happen?
> CROWD: The gods
> ODEWALE: Why then do they blame me for an act plotted by the gods? The gods are to blame, not the son of man. I choose to live and reign and be happy. Hold the gods responsible for your ailments. I choose to be free and I'm free indeed (p. 54-55).

The last conversation is still from Andy who ventilates his anger in the play and calls us to think and condemn the gods:

> ANDY: Damm the gods, screw their will. When our ignorance, slot, greed, and inertia hold us captive, we mutter "the will of the gods". We are either victims of our choices and thinking or the gods are mere robbers whose pre-occupation is to kill, maim and destroy. And let brothers and sisters tell one another that when men think right and rise in action, their lives are affected and miseries flee. I say dam the gods, and choose to be free (p. 61).

The *Pax – Nigeriana* in this play is the fact that Nigerians should jettison the contraption of fatalism to embrace self determinism.

Doing is to reflect dogmatism in religion, the battle cry of Scavenger 5 in the play and to once again, appropriates Marxist dialectic of seeing religion as the essential "opium of the masses". In the postmodern age, fatalism will lead to docility where men will resign to fate by refusing to query maladministration, injustice, corruption and social vices. In spite of our differences, the Nigerian democracy since 1999 has indeed offers us the platform for us to query maladministration, injustice, corruption and social vices that have attempted to pull us down.

The alluring reality of most African cultures is the dominance of the concepts of scapegoatism, ritual, sacrifice and godliness which are contradiction to critical thinking. The myth – culture cauldron should therefore be seen as a negation of the realistic assessment of men in culture, and the place of culture in man. No doubt, this play has accepted the notion that culture is real, the gods are in us and that "historical and politico – economic factors conditioned the evolution of African theatre" (Nwosu, 2014, p. 106). Interestingly, the appropriation of *Pax – Nigeriana* in *The Gods and the Scavengers* is a call on all African nations to think – out – of the box and come to term with the fact that we are the ones who should take our destiny into our hands. Indeed, there are several gods and the ultimate god is the god of the choice that we make.

Pax – Yorubania in *The Gods and The Scavengers* is a confirmation of social realism of *Pax – Nigeriana* in the play. In fact, the Yoruba gods such as Osun and Yemoja in the play indeed express their own limitations as well. Yemoja, the half fish, half human goddess says it all:

>YEMOJA: The best of men, all soaked in filth. The best men cast stone if never your beaks sucked where your wings scatters no grain. Anago, you are the chosen one. Your past you have paid for, your

	present we shall perfect and your future ye shall determine.
ANAGO:	Determine, how?
YEMOJA:	The experiences to come depend on how faithful you are from now on, not who you were. Anago, the cries of my children ring in my ears and I have chosen you to bear their burden. Your cheeks are rosy, add rose to theirs too (pp. 42-3).

We make the gods what we want them to be and the above is a reminder to other ethnic groups in Nigeria not to invest their destiny in the hands of their gods but rather to deconstruct and appropriate them within the reality of critical thinking and postmodernity.

Conclusion

The core of *Pax – Nigeriana* is the restoration of peace and order in sister African countries. It is the emulation of the gallantry, industry and efficiency which are noticeable attributes through the Nigerian spirit. These attributes cannot be divorced from the Nigerian cultures especially, the communion of multiculturalism and the literarisation of such in prose, poetry and drama.

Peace and order will lead to democratic order and democracy will produce good leaders and development will be envisaged. It is important to return to Bolaji Akinyemi once again as he gives examples to illustrate his own definitive notion of *Pax – Nigeriana*:

> The most spectacular exercises in *Pax – Nigeriana* occurred in the 1990s when Nigeria led the forces of ECOWAS (the ECOMONG troops) into Liberia first to restore peace and to help re – start electoral democracy. The final result were elections in 1997, which returned Charles Taylor to power for a while in 1998, Nigeria more unilaterally took on the army in Sierra Leone,

which had overthrown the elected government of the president. Nigeria reversed the military takeover and restored the constitutionally elected government... It is arguable that one of the first exercises of *Pax – Nigeriana* occurred in Tanzania in 1964... it is arguable that the beginnings of *Pax – Nigeriana* lie in a voluntary partnership between Nigeria and what later became Tanzania" (Akinyemi, 2007, pp. 12-3).

Pax – Yorubania cannot be a rigid imposition of Yoruba culture on the larger Nigerian cultures. This is impossible. It is, however, the flexible and systematic preaching for the acceptance of Yoruba positive ideas and concepts of love, peace, order, democracy and civilisation by other ethnic groups in Nigeria. The acceptance of *Pax – Nigeriana* and *Pax – Yorubania* is indeed the re-appraisal of the fundamentals that define the Nigerian and the Yoruba nations.

The tropes of *Pax – Nigeriana* and *Pax – Yorubania* in the three plays of Bakare, Ojo Rasaki discussed in this study has thus brought to the fore, the need for cultural negotiation and re-negotiation of the African and the Nigerian nations. Bakare's plays within the tropes of *Pax – Nigeriana* and *Pax – Yorubania* are indeed texts that have moved beyond mythology and fatalism to celebrate the need for cultural harmony, religious tolerance, social cohabitation, peace, love, democracy and development in Nigeria and Africa. Certainly, the moral therapy and social context of the three plays cannot be ignored. In fact, Nigerian and African nations, citizens, followers and leaders will learn greatly from Bakare, Ojo Rasaki's experiment and innovation in his plays crafted on the tropes of *Pax – Nigeriana* and its new creation, *Pax – Yorubania*.

References

Akinyemi, B. A. (2007). *Nigeria: The blackman's burden*. Lagos: Center for Black and African Arts and Civilisation.

Babalola, A. (2002). African renaissance: Making the new culture grow well out of the old. In: Steve Ogude (Ed). *Toward an African renaissance*, pp. 1-54. Ibadan: the Nigerian Academy of Letters

Bakare, Ojo Rasaki. (1995). *Two plays*: *Rogbodiyan* and *drums of war*.

Bakare, Ojo Rasaki. (2000). *Once Upon a Tower*. Uyo: Afahaide Publishing Company.

Bakare, Ojo Rasaki. (2013). *The gods and the scavengers*. Abuja: Roots Books and Journals Nigeria Limited

Johnson, Etim Effiong. (2014). *Re-positioning Nigeria's cultural industries for economic empowerment and social security*. Lagos: National Institute for Cultural Orientation (NICO).

Nwosu, Chukwuma Canice. (2014). *Postmodern and paradigm shift in theory and practice of theatre*. Onitsha: Eagleman Books.

Olupona, Jacob Kehinde. (2013). *Rethinking higher education in contemporary Nigeria: Reforms, challenges and possibilities*. Ilorin: Center for International Education.

Umukoro, M. M. (2011). *The art of scholarship and the scholarship of art: A collection of critical essays*. Ibadan: Ibadan University Printery.

Wallace, A.F.C. (1970). *Culture and personality*. New York: Random House, Inc.

Human Violence As A Political Ideology And Its Import In Ojo Bakare's *Rogbodiyan*

By

Stephen E. Inegbe, Ph.D and Anietie Francis Udofia

Introduction

> There is in man the perennial quest for freedom and self-actualization and this lies at the root of the urge to destroy oppressive institutions and unjust arrangements and re-create in their places a humane society which allows for freedom, for freedom alone is the ultimate precondition for meaningful creativity (Irele, (1993: 1)

Democracy is a universal political concept. However, it is manifested in varying forms in different parts of the world. Like the amoeba, each society has its capricious form of democracy depending on the orientation from which that society acquires its political doctrine. From its very essence, democracy was fashioned to be a government occasioned by the voice of the people, a populist form of governance which, expectedly should administer to the needs of the people that ensured its realization in the first instance. A peep into the primordial echoes of the famous Athenian democracy where the concept is believed to have evolved reveals that

> Democracy functioned on the idea that all full citizens, the *demos*, were sovereign... Athenian democracy was to prove an inspiring model... it demonstrated that a large group of people, not just a few, could efficiently run the affairs of the state. In Athens, democracy was a form of government in which, in theory, poor men as well as rich enjoyed political power. (McKay *et al*, 129)

This historical Athenian paradigm for selecting citizens to represent the diverse communities in the different offices of the

Athenian Greek state by the citizens themselves has lost its bearing in Nigeria. Recent political unfoldings have shown that if democracy is utopian in other societies, it is a different political ball-game in Nigeria. It was understood differently in June 12, 1993, when the Babangida administration squandered the hope of Nigerians by leading them through a turbulent eight-year "democratic pregnancy" fully conscious of the fact that a political abortion was certain to be birthed ultimately. The annulment of the June 12 election in Nigeria, therefore, has brought to the sensibility of the average Nigerian citizen a new awareness of the democratic process, a negative one at that. The late Nigerian dictator, Sanni Abacha attempted to achieve what Babangida could not by making himself the only eligible candidate to vie for the office of the president of the Nigerian nation. But for divine intervention, he would have succeeded as all the political parties in existence then came to a "democratic" consensus that they had all adopted him as the only candidate to stand election. In this kind of situation, the masses are often left with no alternative but to make violent change inevitable. It is this break-away from the spirit and letters of democracy that underlies Nigerians political alertness today. In the words of Emmanuel, therefore, "violence then becomes the acceptable means of expression in human relationship" (109) In Nigeria's electioneering process, violence appears to be the basic ingredient for eligibility into political offices. The above-expressed views have found discursive significations in Ojo Bakare's *Rogbodiyan*, a drama text. This literary masterpiece has straddled the strangle-hold of contemporary Nigerian political mentality with its expression of human violence as a *sine qua non* to achieving political power. The play dissects as it were, the various forms of aggression which the political class often unleash on the masses in their drive towards wielding and holding on to political power.

Dipo Irele's assertion which opens this essay is of paramount importance at this stage. Every man wants to be free. Every man wants to be a success story. As long as society does not provide an enabling environment for that, man's quest for societal mutations will always be ignited and brought about through violence.

Theoretical Framework

In a study on the spectrum of violence associated with political struggles in colonial times, Irele, (1993, 1-17) identifies two parallel forms of violence on which other variants of violence are based. These two parallel forms of violence are identified in his work, *The Violated Universe: Fanon and Gandhi on Violence*, as the *violent approach* and the *non-violent approach*. Beaming his critical stethoscope on Franz Fanon.s *The Wretched of the Earth*, Irele argues that Fanon's theory on violence concedes violence as the only reality in the effectuation of societal mutation and this finds its justification on two fronts; the fact that every form of imposition (colonialism inclusive) is as a result of violence, and therefore, to either return to the *status quo* or ensure a better, harmonious society, violence is the only antidote, and secondly, that "violence is regenerating and spiritually purifying" (Irele, 3) After the intents of violence must have been achieved, a new man with a new mentality is created. From Fanon's disputations, Irele is able to decipher three types of violence and these are Physical violence, Structural violence and Psychological violence. Although Irele argues that this tripartite categorization of violence "may give rise to confusion and ambiguity when it comes to employing it for empirical purposes" (7), the categorization serves the need of this essay as it is on this premise that we intend to examine the layers of violence in Bakare's *Rogbodiyan*.

Any form of violence that directly affects the human body, be it an injury or inflictions, falls within the realm of Physical violence. An extreme manifestation of physical violence is the resultant death to the individual or individuals concerned. Since, in most cases, the agents of governments "speak the language of pure force" (Irele, 4) it then becomes necessary to match force with force if the desired change must be realized.

Structural violence finds its manifestation in acts of deprivations and injustices meted out to people who, naturally should be the beneficiaries of the abundance of their resources as well as their labour. The widening and yawning gap between the rich and the poor, therefore, constitutes structural violence. In the same vein, the unconcerned attitude of the powers-that-be in providing certain basic amenities to the electorates or the masses is also an act of structural violence.

The realm of Psychological violence includes "the injury or harm done to the human psyche" (Irele, 5) Elaborating more on Psychological violence, Irele cites Jinadu as insisting that Psychological violence "includes brainwashing, indoctrination of various kinds and threats, all of which not only serve to decrease the victims' mental potentialities but also constitute 'violence that works on the soul' " (Irele, 5) Psychological violence is also referred to as "psychic alienation" (irele, 6), the type of alienation that emasculates the victims and turns them to inferior beings, no longer certain of themselves, their values and belief system.

All these layers of violence find expressions in Bakare's *Rogbodiyan* and it is the intention of this paper to examine them with copious textual illustrations.

ROGBODIYAN – A BRIEF SYNOPSIS

This is a political drama, showcasing Adebunmi, the regent, announcing to hand over power to eligible citizens. Adebunmi pre-adopts Asagidigbi and Gbadegesin, two fallible characters, and imposes them on the kingmakers to choose from. Asagidigbi emerges through violence. In his personal weaknesses, Asagidigbi dares the gods: he forces his way to the seclusion room and ravishes Arugba Oge in her sacred confinement. The gods punish Asagidigbi with blindness while maladies pervade Ilu Koloju following his atrocities. According to the oracle, it is only a sacred water which is in the land beyond that of the spirits that can heal the land. Asagidigbi alone is qualified for this journey because he wears the royal garb but he is now blind and cannot go. Adegbani volunteers to go but he must wear the full royal regalia to have free passage through the land of the spirits. Adegbani takes over power after her mother by exemplary sacrifice.

PERSPECTIVES OF HUMAN VIOLENCE IN *ROGBODIYAN*

Human violence would be considered in this section in levels and in response to the cognitive temperament of democratic blocks within the Nigerian society of today. The rulers, the delegates, and the masses embody these peculiarities of human blocks/violence in Bakare's *Rogbodiyan*. Human violence would be treated within the nature and standpoint of its occurrence in the text. By its nature of violence revolves around human actions that involve haptic and bodily contact using objects or human fist to register wrath or let off steam of ire in aggressive hit. It also includes those verbal insinuations and non-verbal significations evinced to dissipate and cow citizens. Finally violence involves aggressive acts of self realization and forceful thrust of ego that confound others in the society. The diverse disputations above envision the reducability of violence into physical violence, emotional violence and personal violence respectively.

Human violence, as dramatized in Bakare's *Rogbodiyan*, becomes the basic quality of endearment to the populace in Nigerian societies. Primitive rigours of selecting leaders by basis of credence in character and popularity thrust which characterized the Athenian idea of democracy has metamorphosed to newer models in contemporary Nigeria. Leadership quality significations are fundamental aggressive potentials that can trigger off "psychological trauma, mental torture, to physical abuse and battery, involving sometimes complete dehumanization and loss of human dignity" (Nnenyelike:117). These are the qualities in the average Nigerian psyche that can make for a volatile colossus against opposition. It is only the violent colossus that is viable in the consciousness of Nigerian electorates of today. *Rogbodiyan*, portrays Nigeria's democratic electioneering, "where the main electorate is a single body – one person, the incumbent leader alone. He elects his successor as he realizes his qualities of aggressiveness have been toned down by time. This reflects that the power of "incumbency" supersedes any other source for effecting democratic change Adebumi, (Regent) who occupies the seat of power, in her generosity, single handedly selects her successors. Regent, Salotin and woman establish a background for change in this conversation.

Regent: I want others to be given the chance to rule the land. The land does not prosper when it is one man that does the tilling.

Salotin: (*Stands up*) your Royal Highness, we hear you, and judging from the reactions here, we are happy with what you have said. But Oyibo people say "once bitten, twice shy." With all due respect, your highness, why may we believe you this time? (Pg:9)

Regent: I have decided to choose two candidates who are not from my lineage and out of these two candidates, the kingmakers shall chose one and announce to the people…(pg:10).

The regent single handedly decides the democratic responsibility of the people. This amounts to a perforced imposition of her personal candidates upon kingmakers, who must conform without scrutiny. Regent's action is a thrust of ego, as Crooks and Baur note, "it bleeds personal violence" (224) and "these violent tendencies are nurtured in words and action" (Dzurba:31). They form personal violence.

In the same vein, Salotin retorts immediately after that his leader is a lier. This act by a kingmaker before his leader emphasizes the dark side of the leader. "Those social mores that are not seen as harmful, and derogatory comments are what constitute emotional violence" (Wodak:44) and this is evoked in Salotin's seemingly harmless response.

The two thrusts of human violence between the Regent and the kingmaker as shown above is a perfect portrayal of the squabble between the executive and the legislature in Nigeria. Extreme verbal insinuation is also a level of human violence.

The last rung of the democratic force in Nigeria is represented by "Woman" and "All."

Woman:	(*Furious*) With all due respect, I am baffled by what is going on, your Royal Highness
All:	(*Reproachfully*) Eehn!
Woman:	(*Defiantly*) yes. I insist on being heard! I must speak my mind. How can anybody wake up one morning and impose two candidates on us just like that? Aren't there established procedures for this sort of thing? Are we people without tradition? Wonderful things are happening in this land. (pg:10).
Regent:	I refuse to take your words in anger. As far as this issue is concerned I have spoken. And so it shall be... (pg:11).

The above lines canopy the state of minds of the Nigerian citizens. Bakare uses "Women" to reflect the psychological state of the Nigerian citizen. The citizens only express their feelings in their minds. They rave and complain but never change anything. In other words, the citizens only loath their leader in concealed wrath. "this instinct constantly generates hostile impulses that demand release. We release this hostile impulses by aggression against others" (Michener; 273). The general orientation for effective democratization is portrayed in *Rogbodiyan* as an interplay of human violence.

Personal Aggression as a Perspective of Human Violence.
Personal aggression is the thrust of self, or better still, an imposition of ego by violent assertion of personal conviction to the hurt and dissipation of another. This is the violence that

Fanon, says is "non-violent yet, can cause destruction and pain" (8) according to Osaghae, "it tends to lay too much emphasis, however, on manifestly political variables which obviously cannot sufficiently explain acts of criminal violence" (2). In *Rogbodiyan*, personal violence flourishes through unnecessary self exaltation and bragging right. This in turn, portrays the levels of political campaign and demagogue in Nigerian societies today of which the interest and response of the populace lie in the pungency of the candidates aggressive thrust and prospect for demolishing opposition alone.

>Asagidigbi: (*Stands up with pride*) I am Asagidigbi. Hun. You know the meaning of the name "the Big Eagle", you know the eagle is a powerful bird. That is what you want for a king- a powerful man who has the stamina to withstand the rigours of government. That is why I am your natural king. My honourable friend calls himself the horse. Yes, the horse. Now we all know a horse is a stupid animal...
>All: Asagidigbi ooo: (pg:12)

Asagidigbi's manifesto is an extreme thrust of self, a beyond-the-spirit-of democracy verbal attack. Asagidigbi's demagogue is a direct attack on opposition, "but an incidence of violence and horror that directly affect a few people can nonetheless have a direct psychological impact on millions" (Territo; 6).

>Gbadegesin: (*Starts moving round amongst the people*). Elders and children of Ilu Koroju, I salute you.
>All: ooo
>Gbadegesin: My people, it is sure that the eagle is a bird with strength. But what does he do with it... the eagle uses his strength to oppress... the horse uses his strength to serve the people. The horse is a helpful and serving animal; that is what I am. The eagle is an oppressive and predatory bird, that is what he is (*pointing to Asagidigbi*). He is like the eagle and

>   like the eagle he shall oppress and reap where he does not sow.
> All (cheer) Gbadegesin ooo.
> Regent: Now that you have heard from both men, I hereby order you kingmakers to chose the next king (pg 13/14).

By what *Gbadegesin* says, it is easier to deduce a counter defamation and a thrust of ego beyond human civil bounds. In today's political candidacy, subjugation of opposition is laced in aggressive verbal attack attempting to tarnish the opposition's worthiness before the people while the people take delight in the hurtful utterances that can attenuate opposition. Nevertheless, political consciousness simmers from the social tempos of a time while man remains a mere recipient of social consequences. The harbingers of democratic consciousness in the system are the ruling class as reflected in Regent commanding kingmakers to "adopt" her choice. Personal decision does not even spring from the recesses of human psyche anymore. It is what the social wind blows and what the political wind vane redirects that occupy the mind of the Nigerian citizen. That is why Mgbeke says; "society now controls man, not man society. Action adapts, albeit in rational ways to externally given circumstances and values" (9). Such external circumstances as the imposition of orders in the network of ego signification summarizes Mgbeke's talk. It is not surprising why "All" in *Rogbodiyan*, which represents the Nigerian citizenry applaud anyone that has the political wherewithal to intimidate the other. Asagidigbi speaks, they support him; Gbedegesin speaks they support him. All these, as Cohen, in *Attitude Change and Social Influence*, observes are at variance with the spirit and letters of democracy, even their conscience:

> It is obvious that all of them, for one reason of inducement or another, are saying or doing something contrary to their private attitudes... we should therefore expect all of the people mentioned to engage in some cognitive modification aimed at reducing the dissonance

between their attitudes and their behaviour. It is this push to reduce dissonance that results in attitude change in situations of enforced discrepant behaviour (82).

Another instance of personal violence is the verbal interplay and exchange in Agogo, king and Akigbe's speeches. The custom forbids the king to go into extreme debauchery, but Akigbe remains silent while the king, Asagidigbi wallops from one immoral spree to another. The conversation between Agogo and king is an encapsulation of personal violence.

Agogo: Shut your mouth lest the flies enter… you are a disgrace to the grey hair on your head. We have been advising kings even before my lord; the new king was born, so we expect you to know better than leading a king in seclusion to a late night revel. The people…. (pg 30)
King: (*cuts in*) Agogo, enough of your rantings. I have had enough of your insults and….
Agogo (*cuts in*) I am not insulting you, my lord….

These congerie of aggressiveness between the king and one of his advisers is an imprint of personal violence. Asagidigbi further unleashes his wrath in verbal aggression.

King: No wonder the last three reigns were unmitigated disasters
Agogo: And may yours not be more disastrous, with the way you are starting now (pg. 31).

Personal violence is inalienable in Nigerian political scenario today. Threats counter threats to sustain the efficacy of influence. Threats have made life unbearable in today's Nigeria and "the issue of hostile environment has become the subject of considerable debate both in courts and in the general public" (Scaefer: 280).

In Nigeria, powers rotate within the confines of initiates and line up of groups. Devolution of powers in a mere eye-pleasing overture. This is done in Nigeria by practically swinging party's tickets to fallible candidate who would falter so that national conscience would be circumvented to the cardinal member and pre-adopted candidate.

Asagidigbi copulates with Arugba Oge who, by custom is purified to carry the land's sacrifice and lead the procession to the shrine festival day. He also breaks the tradition tenet of going into seclusion for seven days to prepare for the Oge festival. Disaster stalks on Asagidigbi but he refuses to see. Malady pervades every home; deformities rock Ilu Koroju. The people yearn for survival. The diviner that the land brings says the reason why the entire kingdom suffers is consequent upon the transgression of one person; the leader. The option now remains that the people should drink water from a sacred river; only that can cure the citizens. Quite like the Nigerian situation, the transgressions of Nigerian leaders always toll on the citizens. The tragedy of the leaders squirts and soils the fingers of the led; but the satisfaction of the leaders is confined within the structural network of their hegemony. Leaders abuse social anchors and truncate values to please themselves. They corrupt history and tincture the purity of scared relics. They demolish social strongholds in an attempt to sustain the orderliness of the people. No one group clone on the political annals of the other to hasten development; rather, a new phase would be set so that the project would be named after the incumbent leader. Leaders never abridge the past and future of the society by their present deeds. Ironically, Guobadia says:
> Human tendency to think solely in terms of
> prevailing conditions and to belittle what was
> done in the past, without any regard to the
> conditions that then existed would not mean our
> starting from the scratch, "ground zero", (65).

Adegbani, son of the predecessor to Asagidigbi, volunteers to go and bring the sacred water. He wears the royal gears of the king so that he can pass the land of spirits unscathed. Personal violence resurfaces when Adegbani returns with the sacred water.

Adegbani: Don't come near me.... Asagidigbi brought you disaster, but I, Adagbani, have brought you the healing water. Who may, therefore, rule the land? (pg.49).
salotin: (*To the regent*) Adebunmi, you were the regent that handed over to our king, Asagidigbi.... Adegbani has seized the throne (50).
Adegbani: Enough of all this nonsense. You and I know that you cannot do without the Adeakin lineage. When power is given to you, what do you do with it? you squabble among yourselves and mess up. You cheat and lie and play games. And we of the Adeakin family, have to come and clean after you. Shut up. Where will you be without us.

Personal violence simmers through the thrust of ego, and attempts to register the prominence of one's value. This violence finds expression in bragging, scolding, chiding and even in tentative hit. But personal violence most reflects through extreme verbal threat. "It is nurtured in words and action" (Dzuba:31)

Emotional Violence as Perspective of Human Violence.
Emotional violence builds from social mores and queer attitude towards people. It is intended to emphasize the dark side or negative side of people. This violence develops from verbal insinuations and nonverbal remarks that torment and destabilize harmony in the psyche of persons it is directed to. To Wodak, emotional violence encapsulates.

Behaviours society commonly portray as innocent and harmless, such as street remarks and so called compliments.... In actuality serves to harass and to create a context for more overt act of violence (44).

There are many instances of emotional violence enhancing political consciousness in *Rogbodiyan*. Some of these are captured in the conversation between Asagidigbi and Aloba:

Aloba: Thanks for your concern for my pocket. But one thing is certain that I, Aloba, son of Layemi shall not be tongue-tied. I refuse to sell my conscience to anybody…. The oracle is against the choice of any of you, that I shall tell the people.

Asagidigbi: A cockerel which has been visited by the long knife cannot crow at dawn. (pg.32).

Emotional violence also surfaces in Agogo's words addressing Akigbe before the king.

Agogo: Shut your mouth, lest the flies enter. Keep your breath to yourself (pg 38)

Agogo's expression accentuates the dark side of Akigbe. Akigbe is stirred to emotional aggression instantly for hearing his dark side cast to all by vociferous Agogo. "Emotional violence causes serious mental torment" (Oyeshola:88) Another instance is the king abusing soothsayer.

Fadele: But Kabiyesi, Ifa has revealed to me why we are suffering. And he said I should tell the people before….

King: *(Cuts in sharply)* tricks, tricks! You don't want to talk because your mind is not clear, hen?...

Quite like the Nigerian society, leaders use harsh words to weaken and attenuate their rivals. "Emotional violence includes verbal abuse like words that hurt". (Nnenyelike: 178) As part of the politically evinced phenomenon in Nigeria, Nigerian citizens experience and exert emotional violence upon others. All actions by words or gestures that emphasize the stark side, the weakness, the ugly side or debased nature of characters in the play are emotional violence. The following lines in *Rogbodiyan* reveals emotional violence as aspect of human violence in the play.

Adegbani: people of Ilu Koroju, use your heads. I have the knife and I have the yam. I have already taken out of the water and I am healed. It is you who now need the water and unless I am pronounced the new king, I will break this gourd and pour away the water and you shall go to your graves with your various deformities (pg. 50).

Every emotional violence is laced with contemptible undertone to dissipate the opponent

Physical Violence as Perspective of Human Violence. Physical violence involves the direct contact by way of hitting slapping, kicking, flogging or even killing another person by the aggressor. Physical violence underscores an instant act that damages. Ruddick considers physical violence as "an act or policy that is primarily designed to destroy without recompense" (164) "physical violence involves bodily injury inflicted on human beings, the most radical manifestation of which is the killing of an individual" (Irele: 4) Oyeshola lists the basic human acts that entail physical violence. To him,

> Physical aggression includes slapping, drowning, grabbing, hair-pulling, punching, arm-twisting, pushing, kicking, handcuffing, typing up with rope, chocking, threatening with a knife, biting, breaking or throwing objects (73).

Stabling and even killing with any object also constitute physical violence.

Physical violence occurs in *Rogbodiyan* on several occasions. These are instances of physical violence in the play;

Aloba feigns he will not collect bribe in a conspiracy with other kingmaker to make Asagidigbi king. Asagidigbi orders his heavy-chest thugs to slit his throat. Aloba lays motionless and yields to Asagidigbi's coercion. Though it is a mock and tricky show to trap other gullible kingmakers so that they will not grasp that Aloba is even the mouthpiece for Asagidigbi. This is a reference to Nigeria's political psychophants, the scheming in political drama that consolidates the illegal extension of tenure in office of political leaders.

Agogo insists that Asagidigbi should conform with the requirements of the culture by staying in seclusion for seven days. Asagidigbi views his utterance as a challenge of ego. The following conversation highlights the conversation as tending towards physical violence.

King:	(*Cuts in*) Enough of your ranting I have had enough of your insult and….
Agogo:	(*Cuts in*) I am not insulting you, my Lord. I am only doing what the people of this town pay me for.
King:	And what do they pay you for?
Agogo:	Advising the king
King:	No wonder the last three reigns were unmitigated disasters.
Agogo:	And may yours not be more disastrous, with the way you are starting now.
King:	(*Throws a punch at Agogo*) you can't get away with this! (*Agogo falls heavily*). I will…

The above lines capture the scene that leads to Agogo stabbing himself to death. Asagidigbi's blow and Agogo stabbing himself to death are indications of physical violence.

Adegbani disguises as a king to sneak through the land of the spirits. They spirits detect him. As he makes to cross their land, they string their hands. This act of barricading Adegbani amounts to physical violence.

Asagidigbi compels Arugba Oge to copulate with him. This act against the will of the land and the will of Arugba Oge is also tantamount to physical violence.

Asagidigbi commands his thugs to seize Gbadegesin who has been his opponent, drag him to the stake and cut off his head, though the supernatural forces intervene. The scenario is an act of physical violence.

Adegbani, after claiming the crown, orders his own hefty men to drag Asagidigbi and the kingmakers away. This scuffle and dragging is a portrayal of physical violence.

All the incidents discussed above are portrayals of the political squabble in today's Nigeria. Every act to show power ends in brutality. Suicide bombing is physical violence now in Nigeria. Kidnapping is physical violence; assassination and other outlets of eliminating opponents are indications of democratic lots in Nigeria. Politics in Nigeria is a game of survival of the fittest where the winner takes it all.

The people's government where majority should rule for the respect and response of minority right, has swerved to the storm and tide of exuberance of threat, perpetration, suffering and death by fellow brothers and sisters of the same Nigeria.

It is by exuberance of aggression that worthiness to contest for leadership position exudes. It appears that Nigerian leaders have imbibed the negative aspect of political theories.

Such theories as that of Niccolo Machiavelli, would not be spared for saying that:
> Political life revolved around conflict over scarce resources. Rulers concentrated on securing, maintaining, and expanding political power. The ruled showed insatiable desires for power, wealth, property and status... political

> leaders needed a collective cause that would dampen interest conflict... National salvation became the major collective cause that would curb mass desires, instill discipline, and promote self sacrifice (Andrain and Apter:105/106).

Even as conflicting with the spirit of democratization as Machiavelli's postulate seems, one can easily deduce that Machiavelli was condemning nonchalant attitude to political issues. He was decrying feudal glory, political indifference and extreme piety of the citizen to divine providence. Machiavelli preached National salvation. In today's Nigeria, is this winner-takes all veiled in fierce aggressions the "National salvation" that Niccolo Machiavelli talked about? Is this national damnation in vain glory the essence of national togetherness? Back to *Rogbodiyan*, Adebunmi (Regent) and her son, Adegbani, are models overtly portrayed in "politiricking". Asagidigbi and Gbadegesin are at polar end yet, another model to reckond with. The political graph of Regent and Adegbani her son is symbolic of the absoluteness of incumbency and godfatherrism in today's Nigeria. Asagidigbi and Gbadegesin themselves are the same, portraying the intellectual waste-bins and never-do-wells churned out of schools into the "empty space" called politics. They reflect brain-washed fools who act on theories they never have full grasp or insight of. They exude violence instead of making an effort to quell its furnace by squirting the chill stream from the fountain of their conscious academy flow upon the citizen for national salvation. They seer the mire of human violence; they have indoctrinated the people's minds goading citizen towards national damnation. But as wilks in *Talking about Tomorrow: A New Radical politics*, observes about pretentious generosity of incumbency and violent thrust of individualism, he decries that:

> Both have a doctrine, based upon an extremely simplified view of society. That is why they are easily understood and why both of them have a certain aesthetic beauty about them... that is

> why both are so seductive to very many clever people. Unfortunately, they are wrong (8)

Human violence has permeated every Nigerian psyche following daily occurrences in the system. In religion, it is the violent that taketh; in economics, it is the violent that acquires; in education, it is the violent that triumphs – In all sectors of the national economy, the violent taketh by force. Violent therefore becomes the original identity for survival quite like animals where mere instinct of semblance prevents them from killing one another. Human beings will soon eat, if not are already eating human beings, for power.

> An innate inhibition prevents most animals from killing members of their own species... Human beings never develop this inhibition, probably because with neither lethal claws nor sharp teeth, they are unlikely to inflict serious damage on the other. Today, however, our guns and bombs make us the most dangerous of all living creatures... the situation is worsened by social norms that suppress our fighting instinct, thus causing our aggressive urges to build up to the point that they are sometimes explosively released in acts of extreme violence (Crooks and Stein: 574).

Conclusion
In a society where upheaval is reaching crescendo as daily ritual, what then is expected as the guiding principle in the lives of citizens than adherence to sublime aesthetics of violence? Who wants to be last? Let such a one take on his cross and trek to heaven alive. Nigeria has been dragged by political circumstances to rank in world most violent sovereign states. Even in the most solemn ritual for the most peaceful god in Nigeria, violence becomes the vehicle to speed up the sacred diet to the supernatural so that as usual, everything that is borne out of human violence remains futile.

Works Cited

Apter, David and Charles Anadrain. *Political Protest and Social Change: Analyzing Politics* London: Macmillan Press Ltd., 1995.

Bakare, Ojo. *Rogbodiyan*. Zaria: Tamaza Publishing Company Limited, 1994.

Crooks, Roberts and Karla Baur. *Our Sexuality*. Balmont: Wadsworth, 2002.

Crooks, Roberts and Jean Stain. *Psychology: Science, Behavior and Life*. New York: Holt, Richard and Winston Inc., 1992.

Cohen, Arthur. *Attitude Change and Social Influence*. New York: Basic Books, Inc., 1964.

Dzurba, Akpenuun. *Prevention and Management of Conflict*. Ibadan: Loud Books Publishers, 2006.

Emmanuel, Usen "Human Violence in Tony Morrison's *Sula*" in Egharevba, Chris (ed). Uyo Journal of Humanities: vol 11 Uyo: Candid Resources, 2006.

Guobadia, Abel. *Reflections of Nigerian Electoral Empire*. Benin: Mindex Publishing Co. Ltd., 2009.

Irele, Dipo. *The Violated Universe: Faron and Gandhi on Violence Ibadan:* Critical forum, 1993.

Mckay, John: Benneth Hill and John Buckler. *A History of World societies – 4th ed.* Boston: Houghton Miffling Company, 1996.

Mgbeke, J. *Public Policy Implementation in a democratic Governance Society: A Road Map to Empowering*

Citizen Participation: an – Empirical Study. Bloomington: Author House, 2009.

Michener Andrew; John Delamater and Daniel Myers. *Social Psychology-5th Edition*. Balmout: Wadsworth, 2004.

Nnenyelike, Nwagbo. "Violence Against Women in Ahmed Yerima's *Otaelo*" in *Atakpo*, Uwemedimo and Stephen Inegbe (eds*). Making Images, Re-Making Life: Art and Life in Ahmed Yerima.* Uyo: Modern Business PRESS, 2007.

Osaghae, Eghosa. "urban violence in South Africa" in Osaghae, Eghosa; Ismail Toure, Ngusaan Kouame, Isaac Olawale and Jinmi Adisa (eds). *Urban violence in Africa* Ibadan: IFRA, 1994.

Oyeshola, Dokun. *Conflict and Context of Conflict Resolution.* Ile-Ife: University Press Ltd, 2005.

Ruddick, Sara. *Matenal Thinking Toward a Politics of Peace*. Boston: Beacon Press Book, 1989.

Schaefer, Richard. *Sociology: A Brief Introduction (Sixth Edition).* New York: McGraw-Hill, 2006.

Territo Leonald; James Halsted and Max Bromley. *Criminal Justice in America*: A Human Perspective. New York: West Publishing Co., 1989.

Willks, Stuart. *Talking About Tomorrow*: *A New Radical Politics*. London: Pluto Press, 1993.

Wodak, K. *Gender and Discourse.* New York: McGraw-Hill, 2003.

Text and Textuality in Bakare, Ojo Rasaki's *Rogbodiyan* and *The Gods and The Scavengers*
By
AbdulRasheed, A. Adeoye, Ph.D.,
and Oludolapo, Ojediran Ph.D.

Introduction
The play-text is the specially created guiding document and the engine room of aesthetically loaded performance. Right from the time of Thespis to Aristotle and all through the evolution of international playwrights like Aeschylus, Sophocles, Euripides, Aristophanes, Shakespeare, Chekov, Brecht, Soyinka, Ngugi and so on; the prescription, description, logicality and reasoning essence necessary for the making of the play-text has been theorised and illustrated upon.

The profile, content and context of what the play-text should look like have also be examined within various diversified poetics and in the word of Nwabueze (2012, p.v), "no text without intertext". The intertext serves as the strategies, ingredients, forms, links and determinants of a play-text. In this type of creative endeavour which is speculative, the voice of the playwright in his play remarkably celebrates the intention and the mission of the dramatist. Whether the style of writing or the dramaturgy pleases one or not, the tension of rejection and the confrontation of critic can only lead to the play to be re-written. The first edition of the text, if not re-written remains creative words on the landscape of dramatic enactment. As we regulate our behaviours through our obedience to rules and regulations so also, there are rules and regulations (not imposition) guiding the text and the expanse of textuality in the theatre profession. Like Nelson Mandela's Torch of Freedom recently auctioned, the torch of a good text lies in the hand of the playwright who is expected to have carried out a serious research as he puts pen to paper to create a work of art that has been described as personal, subjective and emotional.

As much as we appreciate the usefulness of various organic rules guiding the postcolonial and postmodern plays, we are quick to add that the postmodern theatre has no respect for writing rules. The centre is being broken to accommodate the periphery and the periphery moves closer too to the closet to celebrate the tension of the postmodern age of terror, violence, illogicality and opposition. Consequently, this study examines text and textuality in Bakare, Ojo Rasaki's *Rogbodiyan* (2004) and *The Gods and The Scavengers* (2013). The study also discusses the issues that define the success and challenge of the two plays.

On Text and Texuality
The outlay of a play and what it takes to write a good play has been set by Aristotle. These features are universal standards except that the tension and dynamic with those standards have led to arguments and center-arguments. To Aristotle in his *Poetics (the unabridged dover edition)*:

> Every tragedy, therefore, must have six parts, which parts determine its quality – namely, plot, character, diction, thought, spectacle, and song. Two of the parts constitute the medium of imitation. And these complete the use. These elements have been employed, we may say, by the poets to a man; in fact, every play contains spectacular elements as well as character, plot, diction, song, and thought (Aristotle, 1997, p11).

Technically, these prescriptions can only be used for and to write tragedy. This challenge is a sign of insufficiency in the Aristotelian postulation because there are several tragic plays whose content and context deviate radically from the Aristotelian projection. For example, as crucial as a plot is to a play, the post – Aristotelian perspective and Betiang's (2001, p. 30) observation is that

> …in many modern and contemporary plays, especially of the 'avant garde' tradition, plots are not necessarily resolved in the Aristotelian tradition. Apart from being in the episodic form, more like screen plays, most plots prefer to pose questions for individual resolutions.

> Some plots like Brecht's *The Good Woman of Setzuan_* 'resolve' the play with a 'deus – in – machina'…

The sense of plot illogicality is not peculiar to tragedy alone. In fact, "some comic plots have some peculiarities in structure designed to entertain, or tide man to respond through what only man can do, laughter." (p.31). The important point here is that there are several winning ways in the construction of the text and textuality which have rubbished Aristotelian dramatic principles. Literally, text is seen as "a written record of the words of a speech, lecture, programme, or play" (Rundell, 2007, p. 1545). In literature, the generic form of drama, which is a play, will essentially inform its structure. In the reality of writing, the text is given life through verbal creeds and linguistic colouration all housed by accessible or, as others may claim, inaccessible language which often extends to semiotics.

Text and texuality assume critical dimension in performance because the text may have one story (linear plot structure) or assemblage of stories (episodic plot structure) and this may essentially limit or make textuality to be expanded. In fact, Jenkeri Zakari Okwori has written on the limit and expanse of textuality to celebrate the fact that the text is limited and can as well be critically expanded by the theatrical author. On the limit of textuality, Okwori (2004, p.154) reflects that:

> I begin to address this by first cautioning against the myth of text. A myth deriving from the notions of stability and security based on the 'civilisation of the sign'…Textuality is not limited to the printed word alone. And to promote the written above other forms of textuality is to narrow the expansive and creative implications of concept. Performance itself is by implication text stored in the human body and in this inscription written text may even be a limiting rather that an enabling factor in performativity.

The text that is limited in performance can also be expanded within the polemics of "the expanses of theatricality". Certainly, "performance...has been honoured with dismantling textual authority, illusionism, and the canonical actor in favour of the polymorphous body of the performer" (Diamond, 2000, p. 68). The text must be accountable to some standards and it is when this is achieved that we can be talking of expanding its limit and re-orders its wrong or illogical arrangement.

In the postmodern theatre, the structure of the text is changing. Some texts have accommodated the successful style of Henrik Ibsen's dramatic technique which "is patterned after the method of exposition – situation – discussion which constitutes the three – act structure" (Nwabueze, 2011, p. 102) to embrace the "subversion – containment dialectic which has been a central concern of new historicist critics..." (Abrams and Harpham, 2012, p.249). In fact, some texts cannot even be placed or categorised – they simply deconstructed existing structures known about the text. In this type of situation, examining text and texuality in the dramatic enterprise should be encouraged. Hence, the desire to examine text and textuality in Bakare, Ojo Rasaki's *Rogbodiyan* (2004) and *The Gods and The Scavengers.* Certainly, the endless nature of creativity has made the text to wear chamelonic garb and this proximate dynamism makes the theatre, the confirmed house of truth and reality.

Text and Textuality in Bakare, Ojo Rasaki's *Rogbodiyan* and *The Gods and The Scavengers.*

In *Rogbodiyan* (2004), textuality is not just the written words, rather, the word in context and the readers' interpretation of what has been written. As Bakare employs simple and beautiful language, dynamic characters and deft skill to keep his readers/audience interests, it is the interpretation of the text that appeals to people's imagination. This reality cannot be overemphasised.

In Bakare's text, *Rogbodiyan*, he shows a sense of real society experience whereby the people suffer for no just course due to bad leadership. Apart from the Prologue, the play consists of 9 Movements which revolves round the actions and the abundant suspense which is aesthetically handled by Bakare. This also gears the imagination of his audiences/readers. In the Prologue, the playwright discusses the people experience through a narrative song below:
Rogbodiyan, oo, ee Rogbodiyan oo (twice) Trouble has come oo, ee, Trouble has come oo Rogbodiyan tide oran sele, ijangba ti de oran Trouble has come, problem has arrived sele, Iluoo roju kotun raye, awa bere ooo, eee Confusion has visited, chaos fills the land
Awa bere oo kini ka ti se? (p.6)
We are asking, what shall we do? (p.6)

Bakare starts this play with a rhetorical question which none of the people could answer. The king and his chiefs are portrayed has novice because when trouble strikes, nobody is said to be intelligent. As the narrator explains what the people of Koroju are experiencing and seeing the entry of the physically deformed people, it is vivid that the problem is more catastrophic than it appears ordinarily:

Narrator: . . .Yes, catastrophe brought upon oneself by oneself. When the child does what he is not supposed to do, his eyes see what he is not supposed to see. They are now victims of self-inflicted disaster because he people dine and wine with injustice, Koroju, a land where merit is thrown to the winds, Koroju, an entity controlled by nonentities, Koroju, abode of religious hypocrites and political sycophants, Koroju, where intelligence means nothing and academically brilliant is a political pauper. Koroju, a land where truth has been hindered and falsehood exalted. Ladies and gentlemen, a land of corruption where material and political wealth are worshipped and

> the false acquisition of them is encourage is bound to be stricken by Rogbodiyan (p.7)

The Narrator's words have summarised all that is expected in the play. He gives the background information, details and establishes the setting of the story the readers/audiences are expecting. Koroju, meaning 'No Solution' reveals a society filled with corruption and retarded growth. Bakare succinctly explores the socio-political, historico-economic and religious situations amongst many other problems in Koroju. The Narrator's words show a creative artist whose intension is to expose the irregularities of a society through an entertaining medium. Like most contemporary playwrights who do not want to lose focus of contemporary social, economic, political, religious issues, Bakare tries to keep track of what is happening in his own society by presenting a political situation which relates to social conflict and social disorder.

In Movements 1 to 8, corruption becomes the main issue in the play. Although several plays such as Femi Osofisan's *Who is Afraid of Solarin?*, Wole Soyinka's *Madmen and Specialists* and *Kongi's Harvest*, Ayo Akinwale's *This King must Die,* AbdulRasheed Abiodun. Adeoye *The Killers* (*a social drama*) have discussed corruption at large. Bakare's *Rogbodiyan* sees corruption from the traditional cum political end where political leaders are imposed on the people without asking for their input. Njoku (2014, p. 267) observes that corruption has many forms. Many writers have grouped corruption into such forms/types as political, bureaucratic, judicial and electoral. Others are: bribery, nepotism, favouritism, embezzlement, extortion and so on. Njoku's observation summarises Bakare's play, *Rogbodiyan*, whereby people deviates from the standard codes of conduct to deliberately do what is unacceptable for their own selfish end. Although no one knows the criteria which the Regent used in picking Gbadegeshin and Asagidigbi as opponents, it later becomes clear how these two wanted power by all means. The conversation that takes place at the palace shows the people's unwillingness to go along with the Regent whose imposition of two candidates sounds awkward:

Regent: That has been taken care of. I have decided to choose two candidates who are not from my own lineage and out of these two candidates, the Kingmakers shall choose one and announce to the people in four days time while three days after the announcement, coronation shall take place…

Woman: (Defiant). Yes. I insist on being heard! I must speak my mind. How can anybody wake up one morning and impose two candidates on us just like that? Aren't there established procedures for this sort of thing? Are we people without tradition? Wonderful things are happening in this land (pp.11-12).

The Regent is not bothered by the people's interests; rather she authoritatively speaks of her two choices. Bakare depicts these two opponents as people who want the throne at all cost and will do anything to be crowned. Despite the Ifa priest, Fadele's warning that none of the two candidates is suitable for the position; the people are left with no other choice. As the two opponents bribe their ways through the Kingmakers (except for Aloba who rejects their offers), Asagidigbi emerges as the winner. Although Aloba calls to the conscience of other Kingmakers, but their poverty level will not allow them think.

While there are lots of sacred moments that must be observed after coronation to make the community free of problems and calamities, Asagidigbi, flouts many of them because he cannot do without what he calls 'enjoyment' at the detriment of the people. Despite Agogo's several warnings to the King not to defile the young maiden, Arugba Oge, he rejects this warning and goes ahead to defile the Arugba. This brings affliction to his people:

Agogo: Good advice, indeed. I know I am the one who gives you bad advice. That is the way of our

> leaders. God advisers are quickly sent packing because they tell the truth. Bad ones get promoted because they are professional sycophants. Hnn, I remember my childhood friend, the former Second-in-Command. Good trees don't live long in the bush. Kabiyesi, may Akigbe not lead you astray (p.38).

At the end, Akigbe leads the King astray and collaborates the meaning of his name which his opponent, Gbadegesin, summaries during their manifestoes that "the eagle is powerful but is it just? Ask the mother hen what she did to the eagle when it clawed her chick away. The eagle uses its strength to oppress . . . . The eagle is an oppressive and predatory bird, that is what he is". (p.15).

Movement 9 can be assumed to be the epilogue and the resolution of the play. The playwright presents a solution to the existing problems of the people who are introduced at the prologue. As the prologue is used in capturing the interests of the readers, so is the epilogue as readers are interested in knowing the end of a leader who is incorrigible and the Kingmakers who are ingrained in corruption. Nevertheless, Bakare employs Adegbani as the resolution to the play. He pretends to be the saviour of the people, but he is a saviour with a hidden agenda through his suggestion:

Adegbani: Listen to my own suggestion first. People of Ilu Koroju, let us fool the dead by making me wear the costumes of a king. I shall wear his agbada and sokoto, put the king's beads on my neck and wrists; but most of import of all, I shall wear the crown on my head. Then I shall go for the healing water. When I get to the land of the dead, their leader will believe I am the king and will allow me cross their land. In less than two days from now I will be here back with the water and

> then I will return the king's property back to him (p.49).

The question Bakare raises at this point is that 'Can anyone deceive the gods?' Who is fooling who in this context? Adegbani's lines mirrors Ogunsiji (2013, p. 30) view that man is a political animal, man uses language as part of his instrument to achieve and sustain his political ambition. Ironically, Adegbani's spoken language serves as his manifesto, but unknown to the people, he navigates his way through to the end while he convinces the king and the people that he intends to do them a favour. Although the gods are aware of his actions, he is accused when he gets to them:

Ara Orun: You bear this task not because of your people but because of yourself. But by helping your selfish self you may as well be helping your people. Do not forget what you have prom-ised us. We will allow you to pass for your bravery, confidence and readiness to give unto the Dead what is theirs (p. 51).

This shows that no one can fool the gods. They understand the lies, selfish interests and gains Adegbani is after, but because he will also help his people out of their problems, the gods decide to help him cross the land of the Dead. Bakare exemplifies what Gowon (2005, p. 469) observes about Brecht that readers should identify with the helpless heroes on stage and advocates that they should think, compare, question and see the implication of the play as it affects the environment.

The Gods and The Scavengers (2013) has a Prologue and 9 Movements. The one page Prologue is the exposition that summaries the central theme of the play. In this particular Prologue, the deconstruction of the gods in the Marxian mode becomes central. In fact, the lyrics of the first song of the play from the Lead and the Chorus points to the need to begin afresh, think of a new dawn as we are informed in the to note that:

Lead: Why do we shout God as if he never gave us brains? Why do we shout the devil like we are zombies? In the scriptures all the things were put in our hands. When we do nothing the gods do nothing (p. ivi).

Prologue in some play-texts serve as the muse of introduction but in this particular play, the Prologue serves as exposition and a critical resolution of what to expect in the play.

Movement 1 of the play is a continuation of the Prologue. Here, the gods are further satirised and the Scavengers in the play bemoan maladministration and leadership failure. This style moves closer to the episodic text form and this also embraces the subversion – containment dialectic earlier discussed.

The rising action of the play is engraved in Movements 2 to 6. These Movements allow the Protagonists and the Antagonists in the play to pull the tension of conflict which is the soul of drama through camp following, deception, betrayal, deceit, emotion and distraction. For example, Chief Anago anatomises the unpredictability in man through his deception while his Councillors plan a dangerous coup that throw the community (now Nigeria) into religious, ethnic and political strives. In fact, Chief Olowokere, a leading member of the corrupt Councillors expands the deception nexus:

Chief Olowokere: Chairman, there is problem in the land. Big problem. People are just maiming and burning. People are just killing one another shaa. Let me go. I don't even know whether they are now in my house (p.40).

The above is the situation of the play that makes the text, a good material for performance. Movements 7 and 8 represent the climax of the play. This climax also contains the main themes and tendencies of Movements 2 to 6 except that Movement 7 an 8 take a swipe at fatalists as the grand plans of the activists or freedom fighters come to the fore. Andy leads this pack and the 5 Scavengers are his instruments. The Movements serve as the dramatic time for action as it also historicises man's failure to take his own destiny in his hand. Yet, the supposed bad people (Andy and Scavengers) now transform into the defenders of the people, agitating for a new dawn contradicting a play of destiny and fate as seen in Ola Rotimi's *The gods are not to Blame*.

Movement 9 is the resolution of the play and to us, an obvious anti-climax. We should not forget that in anti-climax, discussion continues. Interestingly, this Movement gives a clear direction to the Nigerian society through Andy who insists that:

Andy: …I am not suitable to lead you either. Those of us who clamour for a kind society may not be exactly kind ourselves. Among you are capable leaders. Go home, search for leaders among yourselves and give them your mandate to lead…(p. 62).

Therefore, the play has a clear open ending in terms of thematic concern.

Conclusion
Bakare, Ojo Rasaki's is a success in text and texuality. This is because the two plays analysed in this study: *Rogbodiyan* (2004) and *The Gods and The Scavengers* (2013) have shown flexibilities and complexities that are the hallmarks of the postmodern drama and theatre. In the two plays; the explosion – situation – discussion and the subversion - containment dialectic are unknowingly accommodated. At the same time, Bakare's uniqueness in prologue – movement – discussion – resolution style cannot be ignored. His language is apt while his description of place and event should not be overemphasised especially by budding dramatists as they create to change the society.

In conclusion, Bakare, Ojo Rasaki has celebrated the success of the text in the two plays studied and at the same time, he has opened a wide gap for creative re-invention of texuality especially to artistic directors who may want to direct the two plays. To direct the two plays studied in this work, future artistic directors are admonished that dramatic theory and criticism (in this present case, the text and texuality) of the two plays should be appraised as they direct creatively and as they interpret imaginatively.

References

Abrams, M.H. and Harpham, G.G. (2012). *A glossary of literary terms.* Australia: Wads worth. Language Learning.

Aristotle. (1997). *Poetics (dove edition).* New York: Dover Publications, Inc.

Bakare, Ojo Rasaki. (2013). *The Gods and The Scavengers.* Abuja: Roots Books and Journals Limited.

Bakare, Ojo Rasaki. (2004). *Rogbodiyan.* Zaria: Tamaza Publishing Company Limited

Betiang, Liwhu. (2001). *Fundamentals of dramatic literature.* Calabar: BAAJ International Company.

Gowon, A.D. (2005). Theory, criticism and the sustenance of film production in Nigeria: An exploration of Brechtian concept in the film 'Yesterday'. In: Oni D. (Ed.). *Nigerian theatre journal,* volume 8, No.1. Lagos: Concept publications limited. pp. 468-477.

Njoku, Juliana C. (2014). The theme of corruption in James Alachi's The gods are to blame: A clarion call for change. In: Ododo, S.E. & Mbachaga, J.D. (Eds.) *Theatre and sociocriticism: The dramaturgy of James Alachi.* Maiduguri: Society of Nigeria Theatre Artists (SONTA). pp. 264-279.

Nwabueze, Emeka. (2012). *The Polemics of the dramatic text.* Enugu: ABIC Books and Equip. Ltd.

Nwabueze, Emeka. (2011). *Studies in dramatic literature.* Enugu. ABIC Books and Equip. Ltd.

Ogunsiji, Ayo (2013). The power of language. In: Ogunsiji, A., kehinde, A., Odebunmi, A. (Eds*.) Language, literature and discourse.* Ibadan: Stirling Horden publishers Ltd. pp. 23-37.

Okwori, J.Z. (2004). The Nigerian nation in crisis: Examining the expanses of theatricality and the limits of textuality in Daynight. *Nigerian theatre journal.* Pp. 152 – 170

Shovel, Martin. (2007). *Macmillan English dictionary for advanced learners.* Oxford: Macmillan Publishers Limited.

Between and Betwixt the Constellation of Voices: Towards a Theory of Dance Rasaki

By
Nwaozuzu, Uche-Chinemere, Ph.D.

Ojo Rasaki Bakare is a Nigerian playwright, scholar, choreographer, play director and instrumentalist. He has taught Dance and Theatre at the University of Calabar (1991-92), Ahmadu Bello University, Zaria (1992-97) and Obafemi Awolowo University, Ile Ife (1997-2000). He was also the choreographer and technical adviser to National Troupe of Gambia between 1994 and 1996, and served as senior lecturer in the Department of Theatre Arts, University of Uyo. His previously published works include *This Land Must Sacrifice* (1991), *Drums of War* (1995). *Rogbodiyan* (1995), *Rudiments of Choreography* (1995). *The Artist –Intellectual: Sony Oti on Stage* (1998). *Once Upon a Tower* (2000). Bakare equally moved to the University of Abuja where he served as Associate Professor and Head of Department of Theatre Arts for many years. While in Abuja, the Federal Government appointed him Artistic Director of the yearly Abuja Carnival, and he has anchored the carnival since 2009.

Our subject of inquiry here, who is presently a Professor of theatre aesthetics and choreography at the Federal University Oye-Ekiti, has remained one of the most visible and astringent voices in the practice and scholarship of dance in Nigeria. Our labour in this paper is to attempt a theoretical construct of the artistic vision and temperament of this scholar and perhaps situate it within a knowing framework that would aid us in approaching his art. Our task here will be restricted to Bakare's vision of dance, we say this bearing in mind that we are dealing with a scholar whose creative rubrics spans the genres of playwriting, administration, directing, design dramatic theory and criticism. His works on dance and choreography constitute some of the profound and abiding treatises in contemporary Nigerian performance universe. Even among colleagues who dispute some of his views on theatre practice in Nigeria, there is still that disposition of acknowledging the sound fundamentals and polemics associated with them. Some of these include his discourse on national cultural policy, the carnival theatre, tourism, the place of dance and choreography as genuine fields of scholarship in the Universities among many others.

The title of this paper is evocative for us on several levels. Firstly, whereas the modernist and avant-gardist theatre of the late nineteenth and mid-twentieth centuries conceived of their works in terms of innovations in dance, subsequent postmodernist innovations have resulted from a reconsideration of the nature of the activity that takes place and classified as dance, and the development of dance art, in which artists from non-theatrical backgrounds have brought divergent sensibilities to bear on the art.

Secondly, the title perhaps evokes developments and debates within the Nigerian academia surrounding the evolution of dance studies and practice as a genuine and studious discipline within the larger spectrum of the theatre scholarship. Our title here ultimately tries to capture with some measure of objectivity, the creative temperament of one of Nigeria's finest theatre scholars and art innovators. The basis of our analysis will be to theorise his contribution to the development of dance scholarship and practice in Nigeria. From this perspective we will take dance to be an articulation of an important aspect of theatre studies and not just a revolutionary or outsider way of approaching theatre studies. In fact, in the African context, it may not even be possible within our performance nexus to think of theatre without thinking of dance. We shall pause a little, to briefly dwell on the universal nature of dance

Universal Nature of Dance

Throughout the world, people dance to express themselves, and have done so for thousands of years. This happens in a range of contexts and takes many different forms. Dance through its expressive and communicative qualities, allows us to be more conscious of ourselves and of the world around us in a unique way. It gives us opportunities to celebrate diversity, enhances our understanding of the individual, the group or community and strengthens the feeling of belonging. By the same token, much has been written about the centrality and primacy of dance within the corpus of traditional African performance. We shall cite few instances here. Olaudah Equiano, the eighteenth century Nigerian freed slave posited that his indigenous society was one where most social activities were immersed in dance. Also, Kalu Uka, in discussing drama, observes that virtually every social activity in traditional society terminated in dance, songs and festivity (137). Arnold Udoka sees dance as a tool for cultural integration and social development (276) and Ojo Bakare concurs by positing that "Dance is a language which expresses the geographical locations, biological temperament, religious beliefs, political and historical experiences, social practice and economic peculiarities of the people that own it (76).

The numerous discourses on dance in Nigeria have not expressed a kind of uniformity of outlook, but expresses a kind of lively debate that borders on form, practice, theory and growth. Perhaps it is this frustration that has led practitioners such as Arnold Udoka to prescribe what he terms the Trans-ethnic dance format in an attempt to perhaps orchestrate a national dance ideology. Our concern in this paper however, will revolve around the creative visions of Ojo-Rasaki Bakare who is one of the most cerebral dance scholars in Nigeria.

Bakare's idea of dance is one that conveys, energy, enthusiasm, knowledge and expertise which are communicated to his artists in order to stimulate, challenge, provoke and encourage them to reach their full potential. His style enhances creativity and spontaneity that allow his students to flourish and develop. In practical terms Bakare comes across as someone who is able to get the best out of people and expect them not to give anything less than their best. Demanding the highest standards and quality which are achievable, his method imbues his artists with an enthusiastic response that urges every one of them to put in his best. He does this through a system of sensing and responding to individual needs and nurturing each individual. These ensemble methods instill a sense of group as well as individual awareness and in the process build a team working towards the common goal.

In handling traditional material, Bakare's method is informed by a deep sense of honesty, freshness, reliability, sense of humour, consistency, perceptiveness, imagination and creativity Having given a brief vignette on style of our subject, we shall go further now to articulate a theoretical framework on which to situate the art of this artist and scholar.

Theoretical Framework On Bakare, Ojo Rasaki

Over the years, scholars such as Peggy Harper (1978), Zikky Kofoworola (1984), Ossie Enekwe (1991), Meki Nzewi (1981), amongst others, have passionately debated the role that critical paradigm should play in the study and interpretation of dance in Nigeria. Some have argued against the importation of theories into dance as if art has no theories and does not need it. Some scholars such as Joel Adedeji (1981), Edith Enem (1981) and Nnabuenyi Ugonna (1981) Isidore Okewho (1979) embraced formalism and the often rather narrow historicism and resisted the examination of such issues as production and reception raised by Marxist, psychoanalytic and semiotic lines of investigation among other schools of thought.

Engaging in a theory of Bakare however, is not about what is trendy or what other people, scholars, practitioners are doing. It is about Bakare's own intellectual, artistic and creative commitments and endeavours, and about searching out and developing critical paradigms that would aid us in approaching and expanding his works. My aim here is perhaps to make us think better about our subject, enlarge our perspective on him and maybe formulate a critical template to appropriate his works. Our endeavor here is in form of a discourse or a web of many intersecting discourses and as such is not neutral or universal but rather, impartial in its attempt at constructing a theoretical design to approach the creative vision of a man whom we have come to regard as a restless spirit. In interrogating Bakare as a scholar and artist, we shall use a language that is not innocent or neutral. This is because the scholar who is the focus of this study has constantly chosen sides, redefined and reaffirmed it. In this regard, we shall approach our discourse on him as meaningful communication that expresses and shapes cultural ideas and practices.

Various writers and scholars present specific ideas and views of the world. By the same token, given theories emerge from different places and times in response to particular events. It subsequently circulates, and is used and developed or expanded by scholars with particular motivations, working in particular places and time, with peculiar creative temperament. Ojo Bakare's exploration and journey into dance within the Nigerian academia and larger public space is cast within the same scholarly crucible highlighted above. His vision of dance can best be elucidated in these words of the scholar were he posits that,

> The arts eventually come to do just one thing; express that which has already been internalized. This is spiritual because what the artist expresses is even beyond him, but invariably art is all about expression. What the poet cannot paint, he sings in his poetry and what the sculptor does not have word for, he simply carves in wood. What the dancer cannot write or spell in words, he demonstrates using some dance steps. (interview with Sola Balogun; 2013).

To start with, we may tentatively classify the subject of our inquiry as an artist provocateur in the sense of bringing about change. In this context he could be said to also be a positivist. Our polemic however, deviates from the positivism associated with traditional evolutionary or relativist tendency which has often informed a lot of dance criticism in Nigeria to orchestrate a variant of post structuralism, mediated by formalism. We carefully thread these paths bearing in mind that most formalistic dance history, usually do not identify itself as such (eg; Enekwe's *theories of dance in Nigeria*). Often, they claim to be more real, or more factually grounded, than theoretically informed dance study; this is significantly at bay with the post structuralist ideals of indeterminacy and 'death' of the of the creator as advance by scholars like Derrida and Howells.

The problem with applying formalism alone in our theoretical construct lies in the feature that it sometime sets up an unfortunate opposition between theory and fact, as if the two do not go together. In fact, any aspect or fact of a work of art could form part of a theoretically informed interpretation. For example, Kalu Uka's contention that modern choreographers are still battling to capture in symbolic notation, and make permanent for the purposes of teaching and instruction African dance forms (137). This line of thought obviously highlights the need to theorise form but is suspect, in its assumption that African dances cannot be theorised in their present forms except when subjected to externals such as Western notations. In this paper, we advance for a progression from what is to what probably ought to be. There is a decided positivist image here, a hope that traditional African dances as we have them now may still need to, and will surely develop along the lines occasioned by prevailing performance needs and idioms of the present day. Ojo Bakare seems to bring this theoretical cum experimental tendency to fruition in his works when he avers,

> I am a natural carrier of the seeds of all the art forms. I am an amalgam. I am an inter-generational link so to say. I am a bridge between two templates and for me that is the joy of hybridism; you are a blend of the different cultures that made you (interview, 2013).

A lot of the polemics raised by him in his approach to contemporary theatre informed dance in terms of context reception, dance institutions, power and ideology, relations of production have roots in indigenous African performance orature even if some of the idioms may have fallen into disrepute in present times. His views on dance however, seem not to argue against detailed contextual or visual analysis which are both essential in appreciating the art. To him, the facts themselves are not the problem but the way they are presented. What they are used for, and vice-versa. Simon Shepherd and Mick Wallis seem to reecho the views of Bakare on performance and society when they observe that "In a different relationship between institution and social practice, the value of facts may derive from their application in rather than separation from social practices" (41). Bakare believes that the idea that a presentation of facts is not shaped by 'intellectual' position is an illusion, because even the absence of a conscious application of theory in itself bears the mark of a style. As Terry Eagleton puts it, "Hostility to theory usually means an opposition to other people's theories and oblivion to one's own" (vii-viii).

From Bakare's works, we evince an ideal that employs a theoretical approach to the study and practice of dance as a means of channeling visual and contextual analysis into a more focused inquiry around a particular set of issues. Instead of starting from the general question of "what is this dance expressing through its movement and rhythm", he asks "what does this dance tell us about puberty or social relations in the nineteenth or twenty-first centuries". We see this design in some of his works such as *Adanma, Voyage, Parable of the Beads* and *Sarakin Yaki*. In confronting the relativists, he contends that, "protectionist has made relativist theorists and their sympathizers to consider the activities of contemporary choreographers in Nigeria as dangerous to the preservation and survival of the traditional Nigerian dances" (67). Tackling Ahmed Yerima who advances a measure of the evolutionist view, Bakare contends that Yerima's declaration does not recognise the true personality of the contemporary choreographer whose role as purely a creative thinker has conferred on him the right, freedom and license to use the traditional dances as his raw materials and make them yield new statements (68). He goes on to lament that the cultural policy of Nigeria is such that approaches dance from a static and archaeological point of view. In this regard, they are almost seen as artifacts that should be preserved wholesale without the mediating agents of change and development. Using traditional African performance as an example, he contends that,

> The theatrical context of the traditional African rituals which qualifies them as performances comes to the fore when such rituals are extricated from their efficacious context. All forms of artistic practices that avail in Africa are approached from the form and content perspectives. Africans did not use their art for only aesthetic reasons, but it centred on their entire life. It is a combination of form and content. This is why African art is often regarded as "art for life" unlike European art which is regarded as "art for art's sake." (NICO, 2013).

A careful reading of his views above betrays the measure of rejection of the evolutionist paradigm of Echeruo and the relativist bias of Enekwe. Rather, he charts a course which sees no need to be pretentious over the strength and weakness of African performance in their true forms, but rather sees African traditional performance forms as organic sculptures which should grow in accretion with the people and their society.

Another issue that Bakare highlighted is the proclivity by some scholars to sometimes classify dance sorely as part of popular culture often not worthy of serious academic interest given to other areas of performance such as playwriting, acting, theory and criticism among others. Some feel that the only way to remedy this perception of dance is to apply or appropriate the norms of these other elements of the theatre in the study of dance. It is in this regard that Bakare urges persistence practice, study and research. We could concur with his hindsight when taken in accretion to a similar circumstance where the application of his ideal has yielded positive result. His persuasion is perhaps akin to Bernth Lindfors polemics for the preservation of the originality of African literature and allow them grow organically. Using the case of Amos Tutuola's *The Palm-Wine Drinkard* which was initially not accorded the same status with the works of peers among the literati, Lindfors argues that such a work inhabits and prescribes its growth and audience (145-146). History, it would appear, vindicated Lindfors given the visibility that Tutuola's work went on to command later on. We can cite another instance like this from John Storey. Storey in his articulation of popular culture observes that, "William Shakespeare is now seen as epitome of high culture yet as late as the nineteenth century his work was very much a part of popular culture" (6). We have chosen to highlight these issues of critical persistence, practice and study because it is our view that Bakare's theoretical vision is anchored on these important scholarly attributes.

In the same vein, one could also argue that his theoretical inclinations are rooted within an ideology anchored on studiousness and informed by the dynamism of change and fluidity of form. His recourse to this ideology however, could be termed to be subversive verging on a kind of attempt at unmasking distortions, or concealment in theatre practice in Nigeria. In various instances, Bakare has articulated the tendency of officialdom and bureaucracy to obfuscate the growth and practice of theatre in Nigeria. To him, this ideology that conceals the true reality and universe of the artist is the dominant form that has come to inform policies and administration of art in Nigeria, and as it concerns our focus here, has shaped the path of the growth of indigenous dance in Nigeria. At first, this feature may not seem so obvious because most scholars have pursued it from the praxis of inevitable evolution, immune to bureaucratic officialdom of the government and meddlesomeness religious bodies. Despite these challenges, a lot of these dance forms however, have changed and continue to change adapting to the contemporary audience, artistic nuances and socio-political realities of our time. It will be equally futile to situate them within the framework of artifacts whose survival depends solely on conscious and deliberate fusion of different styles considered contemporary yet arbitrary. By the same token this ideology does not admit a romantic allusion to their pristine state which should remain sacrosanct and untouched. This dominant ideology yields a theoretical framework on which we make bold to situate the works of Ojo-Rasaki Bakare. Our thoughts here derive from certain assumptions about the circumstances of the creation, production and reception of his works. It argues that Bakare's works of art such as dance, and music are super-structural reflections, or expressions of the power of relationship within a given society. This theoretical framework shares certain genetic correlation with aspects of post-structuralism such as fluidity, several levels of signification and indeterminacy which are the antithetical to the structuralist forerunner.

Post-structuralism questions not only the premises of structuralism and its approach to interpreting works of art and culture but also, more broadly, the basic certainties and assurances of Western ways of thinking that dates back to antiquity. Like most post-structural works of art, Bakare is often less interested in unified and systematically arranged works which lend themselves easily to structuralist and highly coherent readings. By rejecting the self sufficiency of cultural structures Bakare seems to agree with scholars such as Christisna Howells, Wole Soyinka, Sean Gaston and Ian Maclachlan who advance the system of the binary oppositions that constitute those structures. Just like in post-structuralist approach to textual analysis where the reader replaces the author as the primary subject of inquiry, in a displacement often referred to as 'destabilising' or 'decentering' (Spivak, Preface *Derrida of Grammatology*...) Bakare replaces the near statis of structuralism with the knowing tension and indeterminacy of social change in his theory of choreography and traditional African dance. He replaces the 'genie' who 'created', 'fashioned' or 'taught' the dances in their primordial forms in the various indigenous societies with the contemporary choreographer. Here, social change and emergent realities form dynamic catalysts which give the choreographer the impetus to tinker with the traditional forms thereby orchestrating artistic development. The development here as envisaged by Bakare does not in any way share the hue or value of the evolutionist but rather is a progression bothering on self-sufficiency and the need to survive and remain relevant. He also believes that rather than study the underlying structures in cultural products in this case dance, emphasis should be placed on the logical and scientific nature of its end-result often occasioned by the dynamics of change. Thus he concludes by observing that any form of dance that fails to accept this reality and waits on the efficacies of relativism or evolution is doomed to go extinct. Bakare's thesis has a great measure of credibility when subjected to the development of dances in other climes. This is more so given that by our post-structuralist paradigm, history and culture condition the study of underlying structures both of which are subject to biases and misinterpretations that emerge organically. It is important to state however, that by organic development we do not mean popular culture but high culture. While the former is informed by mass-production and commercial value, the latter is the result of an individual act of creation.

It is important to note that Bakare's creative vision shares certain homology with the critical opinion of some of his peers and colleagues such as Liwhu Betiang and Wole Soyinka, (*Towards a True Theatre...*). For instance, Betiang's incursion into post-modernism and national integration in Nigeria argues for the promotion of disparate forms that would coalesce into a national colossus. In his opinion, "In examining what role the theatre discipline can play in the resolution of the national question in Nigeria, the aesthetic dimension of postmodernism has to merge with its political dimension in true postmodern tradition which decompartmentalizes knowledge" (68). There is a correlation between Betiang's adoption of the postmodernist paradigm and our post-structuralist criteria in this paper. His critical ideals share a bias for fragmentation which in this instance is a kind of looking from the inside-out of a phenomenon. His thesis however, deviates from our argument where he envisages the 'strengthening of the local' and ' live and let live'. This design significantly puts at abeyance, Bakare's ideal of progress orchestrated by conscious response to social change. In this regard, our traditional orature is no longer a specimen isolated for mere study or plastic manipulation. Rather, It is a material, a phenomenon on which humans mediate consciously on to make relevant and dynamic. It is not inferior as the evolutionists argue or in need of synthetic tinkering as the evolutionist demand.

Conclusion
The study of dance in Nigeria has benefitted from numerous scholars of which the highlights include Sam Akpabot, Ossie Enekwe, Meki Nzewi, S.O.O. Amali, Harry Hagher, Arnold Udoka among many others. Much of the discourse like we highlighted done by these scholars translate into highly descriptive accounts of dance forms, including their formal qualities, history, symbols and motifs, and their utilitarian values. Often such detailed description of dance was presented either as an argument against theoretically driven interpretation or as a necessary work prior to engaging in interpretation revolving around legitimacy, form and growth. What we have done here is to isolate one voice; Bakare, Ojo-Rasaki for investigation. In doing this, we have tried to encapsulate his creative effort within a framework of theory of post-structuralism. His contribution to dance scholarship in the country evokes the pioneering works on literary criticism done by the likes of Oyin Ogunba, Emmanuel Obiechina, Abiola Irele... and their peers. He and his colleagues have had to contend with the same issues of relevance and form that confronted the early efforts in theorising African literature as legitimate products of academic inquiry and scholarship. Some of the issues tackled by these scholars included, but were not limited to the creative and critical nature of the emergent form of African literature. Despite these pioneering efforts, African literature at its infancy as serious scholarly enterprise, suffered the reverses which dance practice and scholarship contends with in Nigeria today. The early writers and critics disputed over issues such as language, the concepts of contemporaneity, modernity and form. It will thus not be out of place that in our investigation of dance

scholarship, to share the deductions of Abiola Irele, one of the visible voices of this era,

> Traditional African culture and society are in fact contemporary, and traditional literature is all around us, alive, growing, and transforming itself and still, therefore available to our modern writers. Its impress on their works is far from negligible. It shows itself both directly in their conscious assimilation of its forms and of its conventional symbols, and indirectly in the way if influences the manner in which our writers construct their works, in the way in which they give a formal pattern to their sensibilities, and present a certain order of imagination (18).

We shall conclude by echoing Irele's final views on African literature "Our criticism must grow with our literature, necessarily adjusting its concepts, seeing itself essentially as the exploration of a new territory which provides familiar signposts, but which is none the less new, demanding respect for its integrity and specificity" (15).

The subject of our analysis in this paper, Bakare, has found himself in the forefront of a similar battle as that highlighted above in his efforts to elevate dance scholarship to a profound and fitting pedestal within the complex of theatre scholarship. In doing this, his voice has been quite astringent within the constellation of his peers who are in the fore of raising critical and intellectual awareness on the importance of dance in the corpus of our national development.

Works Cited
Bakare, Ojo-Rasaki. Interview with Sola Balogun. *The Sun Newspapers*. October,5, 2013
_____. "Theatre in Pursuit of Peace". Lecture Delivered at the NICO, July, 23, 2013.
_____."Beyond Command Performance: An Overview of Current Trends in Theatre Practice in Government Circles". Paper Presented at the Olu Obafemi International Conference on African Literature and Theatre. 2- 4th April, 2010, University of Ilorin Nigeria.
Bakare, Ojo-Rasaki. "The Contemporary Choreographer in Nigeria: A Realistic Culture Preserver of a Harmful Distortionist". In *Critical Perspectives on Dance in Nigeria*. Ahmed Yerima et al eds. Ibadan: Kraft Books Limited, 2006. (64 – 75).
Betiang, Liwhu. "Post-Modernism as a Paradigm For National Integration in Nigeria". *Nigerian Theatre Journal*. June, 2004 (55 – 71).
Derrida, Jacques. *Of Grammatology*. Gayatri Chakravorty Spivak trans. Baltimore, Maryland: The John Hopkins University Press, 1997.
Eagleton, Terry. *Literary Theory: An Introduction*. Oxford: Blackwell, 1983.
M. J. C. Echeruo. "The Dramatic Limits of Igbo Ritual". In *Research in African Literatures*. Vol. 4, No.1, 1973 (29-30).
Enekwe, Ossie. "Myth, Ritual and Drama in Igboland". *Drama and Theatre in Nigeria: A Critical Sourcebook*. Yemi Ogunbiyi, ed. Lagos. Nigerian Magazine, 1981 (149-163).
_____. *Theories of Dance in Nigeria*. Nsukka: Afa Press, 1991.
Equiano, Olaudah. *The Interesting Narrative of the Life of Olaudah Equiano or Gustavus Vassa the African*. Paul Edwards ed. London: Dawsons, 1969.

Howells, Christisna. *Derrida: Deconstruction from Phenomenology to Ethics.* Cambridge: Polity Press, 1999.

Irele, Abiola. "The Criticism of Modern African Literature". In *Perspectives on African Literature.* Christopher Heywood ed. London: Heinemann, 1982 (9-30).

Lindfors, Bernth. "Towards a Nigerian Literary Archive". *Nsukka Studies in African Literature.* No.3, 1980. (145-152).

Shepherd, Simon and Mick Wallis. *Drama, Theatre, Performance. The New Critical Idiom.* New York: Routledge, 2010.

Storey, John. Cultural Theory and Popular Culture: An Introduction. London: Pearson Longman, 2009.

Soyinka, Wole. "Towards a True Theatre". In Yemi Ogunbiyi ed. *Drama and Theatre in Nigeria: A Critical Source Book.* Lagos: Nigerian Magazine, 1981. (457 – 461).

Udoka, Arnold. "Dance in Search of a Nation: Towards a Sociopolitical Re-definition of Dance In Nigeria". In *Critical Perspectives on Dance in Nigeria* (276 – 292).

Uka, Kalu. "The Place of Drama As a Medium of Mass Expression". In Nigeria. In *Nigerian Writing.* A.G.S. Momodu and Ulla Schild eds. Benin City: Bendel Books, 1976, (137-148).

Disciplinary knowledge, Narrative Surplus, And Cognitive Boost in Bakaresque Dramaturgy. An Archaeological Study of *Rogbodiyan*
By
Etop Akwang, *Ph. D*

Introduction

The pivotal enterprise of this study is to excavate the trio of recurring dramaturgic rudiments that have become, apparently, idiosyncratic of the plays of Rasaki Ojo Bakare - *This Land Must Sacrifice, Rogbodiyan, Drums of War, The Gods Are Sharp-Shooters* - herein also referred to as Bakaresque dramaturgy. They are: Disciplinary Knowledge, Narrative Surplus and, by extension, Cognitive Boost. These textual verities are embedded, not so much in the variegated tapestries of dialogue but, in the most part, in the lucid and grandiose landscaping of his stage directions (by which token it has constituted the property of Bakare's texts to focus upon in this study using *Rogbodiyan*). Stage directions are not preposterous properties of the playtext as some readers are wont to think. Nick Wallis and Simon Shepherd have noted, sadly, how after reading the portions of a play containing dialogue the readers' eyes would "skate over the other bits, which seem less relevant. In particular, they often leap completely over the bits in italics, which seem to be instructions only of relevance to actors and designers. The bits in italics are described, and usually dismissed, as stage directions" (4).

The injection of detailed narrative passages or stage directions is a strategy of inscription that Bakare shares with most other modern masters of drama such as George Bernard Shaw, Eugene O'Neill, Henrik Ibsen, or Wole Soyinka because, as W. B. Worthen enthuses, they are "useful to a stage director and set designer, but they principally fill in a kind of novelistic background for the reading audience who will experience the play only on the stage" (2). While establishing themselves as distinctive textual auras cresting Bakare's dramatic texts, the narrative passages or stage directions equally simulate a syntagm of what Dana Polan describes, in the context of film studies as transmitting the "moral force or aesthetic value-of modern society" (2). Whether this is done self-consciously, that is, from prescient, routine praxis or from what Karlis Racevski calls, in respect of Michel Foucault's 'Genealogical Analysis', "aleatory deployment of forces that work to shape events" (233), Bakare leaves so much subterranean knowledge about theatre, cultural anthropology, sociology, politics, religion, directing, acting, choreography/kinaesthetics and design cores in his stage directions that it is acquiring the reputation of a discernible and abiding stylistic certitude, even outside this particularized application in *Rogbodiyan*. This divulgation of core professional knowledge in spaces, as unlikely and strange as stage directions, is what we refer here to as 'Disciplinary Knowledge'; their impressive plenitude is here referred to as 'Narrative Surplus', while the possibilities within this strategy to promote a proper understanding of the texts by young directors is what we mean by 'Cognitive Boost'.

Yet our focus on stage directions does not diminish or even underestimate the profundity of *Rogbodiyan*: the Regent of Ilu Ikoroju summons her citizens and informs them of her intention to relinquish the responsibility of ruling the land which she has done for seven years since the demise of Adeakin, her father. She acknowledges the willingness of her Adeakin lineage to withdraw from ruling the land which they have done with near perpetuity. She initiates this transition by appointing two people from two equally ruling dynasties in Ilu Ikoroju, namely; Asagidigbi (meaning eagle), and Gbadegesin (meaning horse). The kingmakers are advised by the Regent to consult with the oracle quickly as a prelude to choosing one of the two candidates that had been superimposed by the Regent. The oracle disapproves the two candidates on the ground of corruption, but the Kingmakers are content with giving the crown to the highest bidder. Through the sheer size of his gratifications, the Kingmakers settle on making Asagidigbi king.

But Asagidigbi does not hallow the taboos respecting his office. He hastily and untraditionally appoints the Arugba Oge, the virgin who would carry the sacrifice to the gods during the Oge festival and sends her to the palace instead of remaining in seclusion in the palace for seven days to communicate with the ancestors. After a while, Asagidigbi gets drunk, approaches the Arugba Oge and defiles her against all protestations by Agogo on the ground that the virgin is equally in seclusion. In anger, Asagidigbi commands his psychophants to slay Agogo. The Oge festival commences and the Arugba Oge and the King are thunderstruck as the Arugba oge advances to take the sacrifice and the King becomes blind while the citizens are afflicted with infinitude of deformities. The reason for this calamity would be found out by the oracle. Instead, of taking responsibility for the evil that has struck the whole community the King accuses Gbadegesin who narrowly escapes being lynched by the crowd.

The oracle insists on the King being held responsible for his actions by asking him to cross the land of the dead to River Awogbaarun to fetch healing water for the cure of the land. The King abdicates his responsibility and would rather have a volunteer instead, in the person of Adegbani, of the lineage of Adeakin, who would go to fetch the healing water across the land of the dead disguised as the King. Adegbani faces a stiff opposition from inhabitants of the land of the dead who refuse him entrance because he is not the *de facto* of the people. He promises to give them sacrifices if he is allowed to cross the land of the dead to fetch from River Awogbaarun and bring cure to his people. Adegbani is granted the leeway to go across the land of the dead because of how the adventure set out on the basis of selfish interest would be of benefit to the whole community. Following his successful expedition, Adegbani demands that he be made the new King since he has the panacea to the problem of the society. When the people would remind him that his lineage had sworn never to come back to power, Adeakin threatens to break the gourd or calabash containing the efficacious water. For fear of being left with their deformities, and since he is the person with the cure for the land, the citizens of Ilu Ikoroju now makes Adeakin king.

Theoretical Foundation

Since this study entails an investigation of what John McCall interrogates, in the circumstance of Nollywood films, as the integration of "the unintended" (2), a study of this sort would, necessarily, extrapolate from Michel Foucault's Archaeological Criticism or Analysis. According to Wikipedia, "The point of a genealogical analysis is to show that a given system of thought was the result ... of contingent turns of history, not the outcome of rationally inevitable trends". Thus, while Bakare sets about to write dramatic texts for pure literary enjoyment, he ends up writing technical theatre, social anthropological, design and directorial thesis, howbeit not by design but by an accidental discharge of creative energies which we are now trying to contain within a recognizable capsule or taxonomy called playtext. Equally, those who come to receive these potent theatre catechism derivable from studying *Rogbodiyan* or other Bakaesque drama never set out to learn about stage lighting such as follow spots and floodlight, or stage blocking but to engage themselves in a literary adventure. They have arrived at their enlightenment quite by chance.

Usually, an archaeological project sets itself to uncover knowledge, ideas and experiences that are not formed or arrived at through deliberate and recognizable investigative or research procedures. An example could be found in parishioner who determines to sing worship songs every morning for one week, but at the town square, as a part of evangelization only to discover that he or she is developing friction in his/her throat, possibly caused by the early morning cold conditions experiences. The knowledge of how cold causes harshness to the throat is not what our over-zealous devotee set out to affirm. That knowledge is an archaeological knowledge, a knowledge embedded or discovered in a quite distinct knowledge regime, unintentionally. The materials that are used to establish such knowledge systems are experiences or "discourse that exist in the sedimented layers of our past, accumulated in an 'archive'" (Racevskis, 230). Thus Racevskis describes the Archaeological

Method as "a science that goes beneath the surface of a traditional history to find objects of knowledge and to reconstruct the processes through which human subjects have made themselves into objects of knowledge" (230).

Foucault extends these thoughts in a book he published in 1975 called *Discipline and Punish* as the basis for a new hermeneutic strategy he calls 'Genealogy', and in which he hints at the fact that people learn something of the ancient practice of torture by looking at the "gentler" modern ways of imprisoning criminals. While he sees them as containerizing aspects of proper reform, yet they imply the knowledge of complete control. That is, "to punish less perhaps; but certainly to punish better" (Wikipedia). The knowledge of a stiffer punishment is buried underneath the practice a gentler one. .

DisciplinaryKnowledge

Ellen Messer-Davidow, David R. Shumway, and David J. Sylvan have examined "what makes for disciplinary knowledge as such" (7), that is, "the basic operations of disciplines (the rhetorics they employ, the rituals they perform, the characteristic spaces in which they operate); and their 'socializing practices' (how they choose, train, and credential their practitioners)" (Polan, 3). According to this triumvirate:

> Disciplines…work to constitute a field of study (what objects to attend to, what methods will be legitimated in that attending); to produce practitioners (i.e., they and then credential those deemed to have properly demonstrated effective mastery of disciplinary skills); to produce value (e.g., they create jobs, they bring in funding, they build up marketable prestige); and to construct … "the idea of progress" (i.e, they outline which kinds of knowledge are allowed to become objects of study for the discipline, and how the discipline's survey of knowledge

grows and gains in ever-greater effectiveness) (9).

Thus, by disciplinary knowledge we mean the various aspects of the theatre arts discipline or profession that burst upon the readers of Bakare's plays at the earliest contact. The opening tableaux of *Rogbodiyan* at the "Prologue" outlined below bears this fact out:
([i] **Darkness in the theatre. A voice rings**). **Voice:** R-o-gb-o-d-i-ya-n.
([ii] Follow spots pick townspeople coming from the audience [iii] in different directions. They are all deformed, carrying all sorts of physical deformities, e.g. blindness, paralysis of the arms, legs, hunchbacks, etc. those who are blind are led by those who are lame or bunchbacked. The entire picture is nightmarish and horrible yet, somehow, it is grotesquely funny. They sing to the accompaniment of music as they come on stage.
[iv]Their movement is rhythmic to the music though it cannot be said that they are dancing...
.[v] They continue singing as they
[vi] approach the stage. [vii]They take their different positions on the Stage Floor.
[viii] Narrator appears in the audience. [ix]Follow spot picks him.
[x]He picks his way through the audience as he speaks) (Rogbodiyan, 5). Note: Emphases and numbering mine.
The numbering represents moments in the text where disciplinary knowledge and technical jargons punctuate the narrative verve of the stage directions, namely;

"Darkness in the theatre. A voice rings" canalizes a semiotics of communication between the play director and his/her audience. This nodule of enlightenment is a potent bullet that is shot at the ignorance of readers who enjoy the consumption of dramas only as literary commodities without the experiential exposure to the performance of the same dramatic texts. Such readers learn from *Rogbodiyan* the theatrical culture of darkening the stage as a pretext for the commencement of the performance proper. It is common knowledge to theatre – goers that, once the house light is put out, the performance is about to begin. That is, whether the director or the rapporteur comes to announce it or not. Of course, the use of darkness to signify the temporal boundaries of individual scenes or the moment of finitude of a performance is part of what Susan Bennett describes as, "a sign or sign-cluster intended to locate audience focalization on that aspect of the drama" (160). Thus, in his elaboration of what he calls "theatrical codes", that is, "accepted and understood norms of operation that allow the theater to function as a special aesthetic place" (9), Jon Whitmore enumerates the use of *darkened auditorium* among several others of such codes as ingredients that avail the theatre-goers "a sophisticated understanding of theatrical conventions" (9).

Of course, the darkened auditorium is the virtual inheritor of the possibilities suffused in the previously used curtain to signify to the variegated audiences of modern realistic theatres in industrial cities with disparate cultural frontiers either the beginning or an end of a scene or play. .To an experimental director, there are equally potentials ignited in the notion of a *darkened auditorium* for counter-semiotic, counter-aesthetic and counter-discursive subversions. This is the indicative rhetorics in Peter Shaffer's production of *Black Comedy* in which the normal light code is reversed. According to Whitmore's testimony, "when the stage is in complete darkness, the performers whom the audience can hear only move about the stage speaking and acting as if they are in full light. Later, when the lights come on onstage, the performers who can now be seen by the audience act as though they are in a completely dark environment" (9-10). This capsizal of well-established, conventional theatrical signifier disrupts or attenuates predictable representational boundaries.

In the same vein, Keir Elam refers to them, simultaneously as *"dramatic"* and *"theatrical* subcodes" (53). According to Elam,

> Such conventions as the aside, the informative monologue, the tragic peripeteia (or reversal) and the marriage at the climax of romantic comedy are clear instances of *dramatic subcodes....* *Theatrical* subcodes include the once ubiquitous proscenium arch as an

architectural constraint, the rising and falling of a curtain to mark temporal boundaries of the performance, and the use of distinctive kinds of exaggerated movement, make-up or voice projection (which in practical terms ensure visibility and audibility but come conventionally to connote 'theatricality') (53).

"A voice rings out" collocates, equally, with Elam's *theatrical subcodes* relating to "the use of distinctive kinds of exaggerated movement, make-up or voice projection (which in practical terms ensure visibility and audibility....)" observed above. Other forms of technical suggestions in our chosen stage directions that collocates with the above *theatrical subcodes* include numbers iv, v, vi, vi, and vii where it is stated: ***[iv]Their movement is rhythmic to the music*** *though it cannot be said that they are dancing....****[v] They continue singing as they [vi]approach the stage. [vii]They take their different positions on the Stage Floor***. Rhythmic movement to music entails and conveys a range of physical, emotional and motor responses such as joy, anguish, pain, shrieks, bodily contortions and aerobic regimes that periscope aesthetically satisfying bodily pluriforms. Music, dance and rhythmic components, in the context of African performance, co-constitute "a mechanism of psychic release and vicarious euphoria" (Kerr, 16). The choreography of swaying somatic units chanting together as a lumpy choric mass suggested in this opening tableaux approximates Wole Soyinka's pontifications, with respect to Yoruba ritual drama, as "familiar weird disruptive melodies" which "unearths cosmic uncertainties which pervade human existence, reveals the magnitude and power of creation, but above all creates a harrowing sense of omnidirectional vastness where the creative Intelligence resides and prompts the soul to futile exploration" (148).

Taking ***"different positions on the Stage Floor"*** conveys intimations of disciplinary knowledge relating to the stage as a spatial core of performance, and stage geography, and body positions. A theatrically inducted reader or a prospective director would halt at this moment to ask questions about the kind of stage intended by the playwright, since it is not suggested by the text. What kind of stage would the actions conveyed in this stage direction support or suggest? Traditionally, there are four generic physical stage arrangements and they are devised for the performer-audience relationship, namely;

(i) *The Proscenium Arch Stage* – which has the acting areas placed toward one end of the house space while the audience members are required to sit at the opposite direction facing it

(ii) *The Thrust Stage* – in which the acting area is circumscribed by the audience on two or three sides

(iii) *The Arena Stage* – in which the audience surrounds the acting area, omnidirectionally

(iv) *Adaptable Spaces* – which allows for a flexible and unconventional relationship between the audience areas and the acting areas.

According to Oscar G. Brockett and Robert J Ball, "theatrical space creates an environment that influences the theatrical experience" (284). The stage itself is, conventionally, seared into a multiplicity of acting areas and planes. Alexander Dean and Lawrence Carra note that, "The stage is divided into three definitive parts by two equidistant imaginary lines running from downstage to upstage and perpendicular to the curtain line. These parts are designated as right, or R; center, or C,; and left, or L" (62). As a rule, these positions are actor-oriented, that is, reckoned from the actor's position and not from where the audience or the director stands or sits. Moreover, areas of the stage have their emotional and mood values which has resulted in validating centrestage as being very strong because it constitutes the centre of focus; whereas upstage left or right are regarded as a weak position due to the fact that the audience sees only very little of the actions taking place in those stage areas. Equally, the downstage areas are the strongest because, according to Lisa Abel, "actors are closest and most visible to the audience" (178). This arrangement of stage can further be divided into six major areas with their designations if one draws a line parallel to the curtain line across the three parts. This is normally done to achieve exactitude and precision in area placement.

In addition, the stage is further divided into an indefinite series of imaginary lines parallel to the apron called planes. The critical value of a plane, that is, its strength or weakness is determined by the immediacy or distance of the figure to the front edge of the stage (downstage) or to the rear wall (upstage). It is estimated that relative spatial strength of a figure on stage diminishes as he or she withdraws upstage. Closely related to the idea of planes is that of stage levels. Levels relate to the relative height of the actor above the stage floor. Beginning with the weakest, Dean and Carra enumerates "the relative proportion of strength of levels", namely; " lying on the floor; sitting on the floor; sitting in a chair; sitting on the chair's arm; standing; standing on one step, two steps three and so on, until reaching the height of a stairway or high platform. Ordinarily, the higher the level of the figure the stronger the position" (64). Thus, the town's people of Ilu Ikoroju now sprawling on the stage floor are in a weak level.

Furthermore, bodies of performers on stage always acquire specific positions, continuously, relative to the stage area and to the audience. Relative to the audience, as a phrase, means the various positions on stage that actors could possibly take, ranging from facing the audience directly to turning full back on it. Accordion to Dean and Carra:

(i) Full front position is very strong
(ii) One-quarter turned-away position is still strong but less so than the full front.
(iii) The profile, or one-half turned, position is less strong.
(iv) The three-quarter turned-away position is weak- the only really position.
(v) The full-back position is as strong as profile but, other things being equal, not so strong as a one-quarter turn (61).

It is apparent from the stage directions here under consideration, which portray a disheveled community with physical deformities strewing the stage floor, that the playwright suggests the use of varying body positions, divergent planes, and stage areas. The audacity to bring his characters to the stage from various points through the audience is agonistic – a direct African interrogation of the logic which creates water-tight compartmentalization in Europhile stage architectonics between the performer and the audience. This cultural aggression or aesthetic resistance by Bakare that would communalize performers and the audience in a unique fusion of space is further intensified by numbers ii, iii viii, ix, x, where *([ii] Follow spots pick townspeople coming from the audience ([iii] in different directions…. [viii] Narrator appears in the audience. [ix]Follow spot picks him. [x]He picks his way through the audience as he speaks)(Rogbodiyan, 5)*. The spatial literacy here betrays Bakare's aesthetic espousal of African total theatre aesthetics which prefers arenaceous, possibly open-air, settings; while the Narrator gives vent to the mythopoeic antecedents and propensities of pre-colonial African oral narrative arts. Bakare equally introduces strong visual contrasts here between a *mise en scene* filled with bodies, as in [ii] and [iii], and one with a solo performer as in [viii] and [x], leaving the reader with a strange and frightening impact within an envelope of darkness in the house that is only vitiated with the stealthy intrusion of follow spots.

These ideas transmit instances of rich disciplinary knowledge of theater histories and cultures by Bakare; an awareness that his postcoloniality as an artist must negotiate the contingent cultural spaces and sites opened up by the hegemonic discourses of the Empire, and his own quest for self-reclamation. For, as Greg Denning asserts, "History is not the past, it is a consciousness of the past used for present purposes" (170). If this scenario has the definitive temperament of a reclamatory project, then Bakare is self-consciously announcing his disruptive identitarian polemics of retaining or performing his essential Yoruba (African) self in an imperial space in which he privileges the local over and above the foreign. Characteristically, reclamatory projects, among various other strategies, preponderate "the reinstatement of interest groups who have been left out of official records because they were victims of prejudice or punishment, or because they were denied an opportunity to speak" (Gilbert and Tompkins, 118). It also involves, crucially, "staging self-reflexive interventions into theatrical representation itself. Such interventions commonly involve some kind of stylistic feature, narrative structure, and/ metatheatrical device designed to denaturalize the histories performed and to foreground their ideological functions" (Gilbert and Tompkins, 120). In this sense, the aesthetic composition of *Rogbodiyan* exemplifies what Eugene Redmond portrays as the "clash of historical myth and revolutionary intellectual modernity" (17).

Follow spots following and picking performers and the narrator, the way the moon, or firebrand torches follow story tellers in African story-telling sessions, suggest something profounder than Bakare,s cultural immersion. It does, equally, divulge his interest in and knowledge of technical effects in the theatre. Judging against the pervading darkness that surrounds the house, the use of follow spots here is meant to idealize what Duro Oni calls "aesthetic considerations in stage lighting" in which the aesthetic materiality of stage lighting far outweighs its conventional illumination imperatives in order to achieve "both psychological and physiological effects on the performance" (33). The follow spots are also used here, presumably, for "the composition of stage picture, evoking the mood for the psychological reaction of the audience, and re-enforcing the theme to support the action on the stage" (33).

The foregoing indicate that Bakare, as a playwright, does not leave behind kernels of his robust theatre scholarship at the moment of dramatic creation, but injects their particular qualities or values into the aesthetics and poetics of his dramaturgic explorations. There are basic rudiments of the theatrical arts, here referred to as "Disciplinary Knowledge", that are encapsulated into these opening stage directions, as it is done in much of the text, to grant a modest liberal education on performance to the readers. In that short extract of the play, we can syringe directorial, acting, design, and choreographic values of performance, namely, "instructions regarding facial expression, vocal delivery, gesture and basic actions, costume, 'kinesics' (moving about the stage), 'proxemics' (blocking-positioning of characters), space and props" (Wallis and Shepherd, 11).

Yet Bakare goes a little more than providing merely "a kind of novelistic background" since he is propelled by what Wallis and Shepherd call "a design-led approach" (14) to playwrighting. A "design-led approach" to playwriting "conceives of sound and light and the visual organization of the stage as having their own coherent shapes, following a logic from one scene to another, manipulating the audience's response to what they experience on the stage, if not actually making meanings in their own right. In other words, sound and visual organization are, as much as words, texts" (15). This is hardly the crux of concern of many a late modern playwright of whom Ronald Hayman says "feels no need to provide reminders.... He may only catalogue the relevant points: it is for us to form them carefully into a vivid mental picture that will stay with us throughout the ensuing dialogue" (13).

Narrative Surplus
As was mentioned previously, Narrative Surplus is a reference to the sheer prodigality of aesthetic data accruable to the reader from Bakare's playtexts, in this case *Rogbodiyan*. Our phrase derives from Karin Barber who has used the terminology in two separate studies, "Popular Arts in Africa" and *The Generation of Yoruba Plays: Yoruba Populist Life in Theatre,* to periscope a representational temperament in African popular arts/artists to communicate through a combination of media and styles "through the dress and behavior of the performers as well as through the stylistic choices in musical or dance form" (*Popular Arts in Africa,* 2) that grants depth, eclecticism, and enriching varieties to their products. According to Barber: "Many African popular forms make their effects through a combination of music, dance, costume, mime, song, and speech. In these forms the meaning cannot be extrapolated from the words alone but is conveyed by all the elements in combination". This is to say that, "discrete items — a song, a sketch, a comedy routine, a dance —

which in some way, nevertheless, communicate a coherent attitude" are, always, easily brought together. Barber feels that, even in extreme cases, "meaning is communicated simply by the fact that the performance takes place at all — in very repressive regimes, simply continuing to come together to perform and participate is a statement of identity and defiance" (*Popular Arts in Africa*, 2).

Barber's studied deduction is that, "Texts generate 'surplus'-:meanings that go beyond, and theatre may subvert, the purported intentions of the work. Thus, never wholly under the artist's control, they have the capacity to pick up subterranean currents of thought that society itself may be unaware of" (*Popular Arts in Africa, 3-4*). Deriving instantiation from Yoruba plays, Barber indicates that:

> The theatre consolidates its moral credibility in an expansive and demonstrative mode. Characters project themselves through their own words, actions happen before the audience's eyes, and this full, rich embodiment of hypothetical situation in fact generates a huge surplus, so that what we see goes beyond what the closing homily tells us we have learned (*The Generation of Yoruba Plays: Yoruba Populist Life in Theatre*, 268-269).

This is the indicative attitude, of saying or suggesting more than what had originally been intended, in the stage directions found in Bakare's *Rogbodiyan*. Some of the details inherent in portions of the stage directions previously studied contain something of surplus which, if viewed polemically, can pass for what Elam calls "overcoding", that is, where "units of the subcode segments … are more extensive than the base units of the constitutive code" (53-54). Our "subcodes", in this case, are the stage directions while the "constitutive codes" are the complex layers of dialogue. Consider the fastidiousness of a playwright who leaves insights to the readers on what happens to the house lights before the play begins, what kind of theatre light should be used, in this case follow spot, amongst diverse generic classifications of stage lighting; a playwright who tells the reader, or the would be director, the location (*the audience*) from which the townspeople should enter the stage and in how many directions they should do so (*in different directions*), the visual impact of their appearance (*nightmarish and horrible yet, somehow, it is grotesquely funny*), the nuances of physical action that betoken their entrance (*Their movement is rhythmic to the music ...the are dancing*); body positions and planes on the stage floor that they should assume (*different positions on the Stage Floor*) which suggests variously that some should seat, stand, lean forward, sideways, and/or backward thereby creating divergent levels and planes. It equally suggests that they would assume various body positions such as full-front, profile, one quarter turned-away, three quarter turned away, full-back turned away positions, etc. The playwright also suggests in the stage directions the location where the narrator should make his appearance. At the end of the "Prologue", Bakare leaves a suggestion on how he should leave the stage (*Storms out as the song and music pick up again, Rogbodiyan, 7*).

Indeed there is a plenitude of occasion where Bakare demonstrate knowledge of stage dynamics by writing it into his stage direction. Some of them are:

Movement 1a: *Agogo, the King's Adviser/Messenger* **enters from the left crash door. Follow spot is on him. He is holding a gong. He sings.** (p. 6)

Movement 1b: **the song is being chorused by the orchestra twice. He walks across the front of the auditorium as he speaks** (p. 7)

Movement 1c: **He strikes the gong and dances out through the right crash door. The song and music pick up once more and** stop. **Blackout** (p. 7).

Movement 2a: *The palace.* **Townspeople enter from various entrances. They sing and dance as they enter the palace** (p.7).

Movement 2b: **Music and song continue in the palace until the Regent enters.** *She is greeted* (p. 8)

Movement 2c: ***she responds by shaking her horse tail. She sits on the throne while the people sit on the floor*** *(p. 8)*. Note that the emboldened portions are explicatory of our claims.

For instance, Movement 1a, has specified an entrance for Agogo to take as *"**the left crash door**"* and that his entrance should be attended by ***follow spot***. The prop required for his office is also specified as *"**a gong**"*. It is equally suggested that he *"**sing**"s* and, I dare say, dances. In Movement 1b, the playwright specifies that **the song** by the King's Messenger, be **chorused by the orchestra twice**; he also specifies his movement, that is, walking *"**across the front of the auditorium as he speaks**"*. Movement 1c recommends that Agogo *"**strikes the gong and dances out**" **through the right crash door. The Messenger** * who has just danced in to deliver a message from the King, should strke the gong again before dancing out; and that he should use the crash door. Thereafter he tells the reader director that **song and music** should *"**pick up once more and** stop"* before ***"Blackout"***. The position of our paper is that some of these spatio-temporal specifications are surplus narratives, that is, putting in so much about a character's props and accessories (and what to do with them), specific kinds of stage lights, particular dance movements, entrances and exits, and the intensity of the orchestral accompaniment.

They are seen as surpluses because the reader is being provided with not only the ethical imperatives of the storyline and a linguistically ambitious dialogue but also how to contemplate the theatre as a space-time industry. Much of the information here belongs not to the literary continuum of textual codification but to a directorial/ producerly mode of codification commonly found in Prompt Books. This is simply an activity of writing that seems as though one is involved in directing the text for the reader, or would-be producer. It appears that what a would-be producer of *Rogbodiyan* needs to produce it on stage are financial endowment (where he cannot sponsor it) and a menagerie of cast required to sustain the production. A playwright does not need to record that the crowd should enter the King's Palace from various entrances and exits, and that they should do so singing, as in Movement 2a; and that the crowd should not stop singing until the Regent comes in, as in Movement 2b; and that the Regent should carry a horse tail which she should wave in acknowledging her subjects' greetings, or that the people should sit on the floor while the Regent sits on the throne, as in 2c. If not for Bakare's generousity, all these recommendations belong to, and require the thoughtful, critical permutations of the Artistic Director and those of the Technical Director working in tandem. A copious attempt by the playwright to serve as a surrogate director, or consultant – at – large, for the reader is betrayed in the opening stage direction of Movement 3, where the emboldened italics are my emphasis to indicate pastiches of surplus or meta-textual significations, thus:

> *Floodlight in the auditorium. A group of people-Gbadegesin's supporters-storm the auditorium through the left crash door. Gbadegesin is carried shoulder high. They sing: Asagidigbi ojoba (2ce) Nile yi ko o nile bomiin ni, Asagidigbi ojoba. As they are about to make their exit through the right crashdoor, Asagidigbi's suppporters enter the auditorium (through the same door). The two group meet. A little clash and rowdiness. He is carried shoulder high too. They sing: Ta ni pawa oni baba kai ani baba. Asagidigbi Baba wa kai anibaba. Gbadegesin's group later exit through the right crash door while Asagidigbi's group exit through the left crash door. Blackout.* (p. 15).

Here, the floodlight is used for different effects as opposed to the follow spots that dominate the first two scenes. In addition, the dialectical relationship between the Asagidigbi and Gbadegesin is choreographed and heightened by suggesting a faction between the two. Of course, there are other possibilities for writing a scene like this without appearing to block it. One of it is to indicate that the supporters of the two contestants clash in an attempt to outwit one another, without fixing the hues of the action.

Similar instances of clarification of the stage picture for the reader are found in Movements 6 and 9 where the playwright suggests how people should be ranged for aesthetic effect. At the coronation scene (Movement 6), the emphasized portions of the opening stage direction show the spatial distribution of bodies to achieve equipoise during staging: *"....They are in a festive mood. They take their positions **forming a big arc on stage**.... Asagidigbi, the king-elect, is led by the elders. The crowd applaud. **He takes his place at the apex of the arc. Behind him is the throne**"* (25-26). The stage picture forming before the reader is an arched, as opposed to a triangular formation, with the king-elect at its apex. At the scene of the Oge Festival in Movement 9, another textual blocking by the author is orchestrated to unclutter the stage picture, thus: "…. ***The king stands up** and **takes his position behind Arugba, chiefs line up behind the king** while **others line up behind them in two lines***" (p. 36).

Cognitive Boost:
It is Stanley Vincent Longman that has remarked that, "Reading a play script is generally not quite as easy as reading a short story or a novel. The reason is that a novel is complete. It is all there, and you experience it on the terms the novelist intended you to experience it" (5); whereas, when we read plays, it is possible for us to "run the risk of missing most of the atmosphere and the emotional impact that the scene can make" (Hayman, 12). Therefore Longman presents the playwright as having quite a different vision, as one who "puts words on paper with an eye to what will eventually happen on stage. The playwright intends for you to experience the play there, not on the page" (5). He is of the view that "the reader must bring to it some sense of how the page relates to the stage and to the world beyond" (1).

Thus, the foregoing simplifications and clarifications made on the challenges of unraveling the mystery of the text whilst yet constituting it as a piece of literature are meant to supply something of a cognitive boost and psychological incentive to the readers some of whom would contemplate the text for stage production. Bakare's creative strategy finds ratification in Richard Gill's assertion that, "Theatrical language is distinctive because it invites performance. Gestures, actions, use of props, grouping and emotional states are implicitly present in dramatic language" (94). According to Worthen,

Treating the play as a design for the stage forces us to make commitments, to articulate and defend a particular version of the play, and to find ways of making those meanings active onstage, visible in performance. As readers, one way to develop a sense of the reciprocity between stage and page is to think of the play as constructed mainly of actions, not of words.... Another way to enrich the reading experience of drama is to imagine staging the play: how could the design of the set, the movements of the actors, the pacing of the scenes affect the play's meaning, make the play mean something in particular. (2-3).

Conclusion

Our essay has sought to celebrate Bakare's approach to the sublime that has allowed him to preponderate on knowledge sharing by shading abundant light on the technical requirements of producing his play, *Rogbodiyan,* among others. Bakare appears aware of the emotional involvement, and the psychological rigours of staging plays. Thus, to eliminate all roadblocks to understanding and, by extension, presentation on stage, Bakare recuperates technical verities belonging mostly to the rehearsal floor and Prompt Book as ingredients to be included in the published versions of his works including *Rogbodiyan*. By this token, Bakare prepares his readers for the next stage of involvement with his plays which is stage production. It is expected that this kind of simplification would grant Bakare's plays – *This Land Must Sacrifice, Rogbodiyan, Drums of War, The Gods Are Sharp-Shooters,*- in due course, mass appeal and high readability.

References
Abel, Lisa. *Theatre Art in Action*. Lincolnwood, Illinois: National Textbook Company, 1999.
Bakare, Ojo. *Rogbodiyan*. Zaria: Tamaza Publishing Company 1994.
Barber, Karin. *The Generation of Yoruba Plays: Yoruba Populist Life in Theatre*. Bloomington: Indiana University Press, 2000.
……..."Popular Arts in Africa". *African Studies Review, Volume 30, Number 3*, 1987: 1-78.

Bennett, Susan. *Theatre Audiences*. New York: Routledge, 1990.
Brockett, Oscar G. and Robert J. Ball. *The Essential Theater. Eighth Edition*. Belmont: Wadsworth/Thomson, 2004.
Dean, Alexander and Lawrence Carra. *Fundamentals of Play Directing. Fifth Edition*. New York: HOLT, Rinehart and Winston, Inc., 1988.
Denning, Greg. *Mr Bigh's Bad Language*. Cambridge: Cambridge University Press, 1993.
Elam, Keir. *The Semiotics of Theatre and Drama*. London: Methuen, 1980.
Gilbert, Helen and Joanne Tompkins. *Postcolonial Drama: Theory, Practice and Politics*. London: Routledge, 1996.
Gill, Richard. *Mastering English Literature. Third Edition*. London: Palgrave Macmillan, 2006.

Hayman, Ronald. *How to Read A Play*. London: Eyre Methuen, 1979.
Kerr, David. *African Popular Theatre From Pre-colonial Times to the Present Day*. London: James Curray, 1999.

Longman, Stanley Vincent. *Page and Stage. An Approach to Script Analysis.* Boston: Pearson Educational, Inc. 2004.

McCall, John. "Nollywood: The Good, the Bad and the Unintended". Paper Presented at the International Conference on Nollywood Films Entitled 'Nollywood in Africa, Africa in Nollywood', at the School of Media and Communication, Pan African University, Victoria Island, Lagos, Thursday, 21st July – Saturday, 23rd July 2011. 1-33.

Messer-Davidow, Ellen, David R. Shumway and David J. Sylvan. Eds. *Knowledges: Historical and Critical Studies in Disciplinarity.* Charlottesville: University Press of Virginia, 1993

Oni, Duro. *Stage Lighting Design: The Nigerian Perspective.* Lagos: Concept Publications Limited, 2004.

Polan, Dana. *Scenes of the Instruction-The Beginings of the U.S. Study of Film.* Berkeley: University of California Press, 2007.

Racevskis, Kalis. "Genealogical Critique". *Contemporary Literary Theory.* Eds. G. Douglas Atkins and Laura Morrow. Amherst: The university of Massachussetts Press, 1989. 229-245.

Redmond, Eugene B. "tess onwueme's soular system: trilogy of the she-kings-parables, reigns, calabashes". Tess onwueme. *Three plays.* Detroit, Michigan: Wayne State University Press, 1993.

Sharp, Daniel. "Foucault's Genealogical Method". Available at: http://philforum.berkeley.edu/blog/2011/10/17/foucaults-genealogical-method/. Accessed August 3, 2014.

Soyinka, Wole. *Myth, Literature and the African World.* Cambridge: Cambridge University Press, 1976.

Wallis, Nick and Simon Shepherd. *Studying Plays. Third Edition.* London: Bloomsbury Academic, 2010.

Whitmore, Jon. *Directing Postmodern Theatre. Shaping Significations in Performance.* Ann Arbor: The University of Michigan Press, 2012.

Wikipedia. Michel Foucault. http://plato.stanford.edu/entries/foucault/#4.4

Worthen, W. B. *The Wadsworth Anthology of Drama.* London: Wadsworth / Cengage Learning, 2004

Dramatic Techniques in Ojo Rasaki Bakare's
"Once Upon A Tower"
By
Umukoro, O. Joseph, Ph.D.

Introduction
The social task of art and the artist is to help us make life bearable. In order to understand the social and dynamic significance of modern dramatic art, it is necessary to ascertain the difference between the functions of art for art's sake and art as the mirror of life. Art for art's sake pre-supposes an attitude of aloofness on the part of the artist toward the complex struggle of life. The modern drama, as all modern literature, mirrors the complex struggle of life. This is the social significance which differentiates modern dramatic art from art for art's sake. The task of art and the artist towards achieving a sense of harmony and stability is an accepted function and model for all literary creativity. To achieve this, several facilities are open to lift the work of a playwright beyond mere plain, and ordinary or common techniques. Dramatic techniques, as used by playwrights, are to enhance meaning and understanding amongst the audience. Thus, dramatic techniques are methods used during a dramatic scene to create tension, an impact or a certain atmosphere. In general, it is what makes a scene more interesting to watch. These include dramatic irony, open-ended conclusion, proverbs, poetry, symbolism, soliloquy, flashback, song motives, among others. It is against this backdrop that this paper focuses on dramatic techniques in *"Once Upon A Tower"* written by Bakare, Ojo Rasaki.

Thematic Issues
The overriding idea in Bakare Ojo Rasaki's *"Once Upon A Tower"* is the rot in the academia, right from the top-vice chancellor, the lecturers and students, to the bottom. The play is divided into twelve movements and a prologue. In the process of showcasing the dangerous politics in the university system and its terrible consequences on the society at large, various issues come into play as represented by different characters. To this end the

discussion between the Vice Chancellor, Chairman of Council and the Chancellor is quite explicit and revealing on the issue of hypocrisy.

V.C.: I must congratulate you your Royal Highness and you too Chief and of course my humble self for yet another successful convocation ceremony (7).

Chief: Mr. Vice Chancellor, I have tremendous joy for the way everything went smoothly.(7).

Emir: I too. In fact, by the time the president reads those beautiful worded speeches of ours in the newspapers, I am sure he will give us another term. He will believe we are doing the job well. (7).

This is characteristic of most Nigerian leaders including university administrators who are more interested in securing their position than the welfare of their subjects. The incessant strike by university lecturers is equally given attention by Pedro in his words as follows.

Pedro: Now Mr. Vice Chancellor, listen. I came into this university in 1985, to study medicine, although I graduated ten years later, due to no fault of mine. Mind you, I never repeated a class, I was admitted with perfect results. Eight distinctions in my G.C.E. O/Level and a jamb score of 319. So, I came here a real gem. But how does one graduate in record time with these incessant strikes, demonstrations and the attendant closures? (14).

The adverse effects of this on students is no more than producing a half-baked graduate. Nobody cares about the system. It is therefore not surprising that many decide to send their children out of the country for university education. Prof. Kurumbete expresses this negative attitude of people towards university system thus:

Kurumbete: To hell with the system suffering. I hope you are not fooling yourself thinking, that you can help the system? Can't you see nobody cares about the system? Everybody is a hanger-on just looking for how to survive via the system. Those who are in a position to make fat monetary rip offs from the system do so. It is a merchandise. The system is not only suffering already but bleeding. So what difference will another kick make? The system has seen nine hundred and ninety nine to hell with a millennium. (36 – 37).

Pedro happens to be a victim of a half-baked graduate hence his decision to come back and stage a protest against the system. He expresses his determined spirit as follows:-

Pedro: And… make no mistake about trying to play smart. We have completely taken over the security machinery of this campus. Our itinerary was well-planned. Nothing and I repeat, nothing will-foil our mission until we have accomplished all we came for. So you just listen and obey (9).

Such is the extent of exposé of the processes of systematic crippling of the educational system, and its consequence on the new generation of Nigerians.

Language/Style and Techniques
Linguistically, *"Once Upon A Tower"* is lucid and simple as the characters; though an attempt is made by the playwright to explore the use of pithy proverbs as exemplified during the conversation between Khadijat and Senator, her father:

Khadija: You are up Dad? Unusually early for a Saturday isn't it? Good morning. (49).

Senator: Morning. You see, my late father used to say that when you see a rat running in the day time, if it is not pursuing something, something is definitely pursuing it. My rat is definitely pursuing something this morning so don't be surprised that Dad is not still clutching his pillow. (49).

In his foreword to the play, Aderemi Bamikunle acknowledges the impressive nature of the dramatic techniques in the play. It is observed that the central action – the VC Council members, Provost and lecturers being made to confront and pay for their crimes takes place within one or two hours on the day of convocation. Thus, what appears to be a normal plot is a cunningly wrought plot using various dramatic techniques such as song motives, flashback, non-verbal communication, mime and dance movements. The play opens with a prologue of song motive titled *"Once Upon A Tower"* while the set – a university building is being constructed in the full glare of the audience. This is quite reminiscent of the theatre advocated by Bertolt Brecht in his use of Alienation effect (A-effect or "Verfremdseffekt" technique). Movement eight, for example is purely enacted in mime and dance movements. With the exception of movements, one, two, ten and twelve, other movements (three-nine, and eleven) are in form of flashbacks. Dramatic irony is also employed during a conversation between V.C. and Pedro.

V.C.: Evil men… leave my office. Stop treating honourable and well-meaning citizens like commoners.

Pedro (Laughs): Oh! You… you people, honourables? Well-meaning citizens? You rogues and dangerous schemers? (To Maito and Bobo Razor). They are honourables give them honourable treatment.

I leave you to imagine the honourable treatment for these honourable and well-meaning citizens!

Conclusion:
The dramatic techniques are used as tools by Bakare to create suspense, manipulate the plot and characters, to express fundamental concepts and themes and dictate the actions of the characters. Within this the playwright is able to put together what the university system is doing to the potentials of new generation students. Though, the play ends in death, it is however, not a tragedy, as rightly observed by Aderemi Bamikunle in his foreword to the play. Indeed, the dead characters deserve what they have got and society can breathe a little better. One can therefore conclude that the play has meted punishment to whom it is due.

References

Bakare, Ojo Rasaki (2000). *"Once Upon A Tower"*, Afahaide Publishing Company, Akwa Ibom State, Nigeria.

Bamikunle, Aderemi (2000) "Foreword" in Bakare Ojo Rasaki's *Once Upon A Tower*, Afahaide Publishing Company, Akwa Ibom State, Nigeria.

Bamidele, L. O. (2001). *Literature and Sociology*, Stirling – Horden Publishers (Nig.) Ltd; Oyo State, Nigeria.

Emasealu, Emmanuel, C. (2006). "A Study of Bakare Ojo Rasaki's *Drums of War* as Text and Performance" in *The Crab* – Journal of Theatre & Media Arts, Emmanuel Emasealu (ed.), vol. 1, No 2, Department of Theatre Arts, University of Port-Harcourt, Nigeria; pgs 81-109.

Johnson, Effiong E. (2000). *Playwriting: The Fundamentals,* Concept Publications Limited, Lagos, Nigeria.

Taylor, John Russell (1970). *The Penguin Dictionary of the Theatre*, Penguin Books Ltd; Great Britain, pg. 12.

Intimations of Social Dysfunctionality in The Plays of Bakare, Ojo Rasaki
By
Afolabi, John Adebayo Ph. D.

Introductions
Sociology of Art foregrounds the reality of perpetual inextricability of social realities and artistic representations. This is because Art is not existent in a vacuum. It is conditioned by prevalent socio-economic and political realities of the society in which it is based. The artist, in order to be relevant is compulsorily obliged to reflect this in his or her creative endeavour. This is because all arts are geared towards appreciation by audiences, readers and connoisseurs. The artist is successful only when his or her patrons appreciate and accept his creation. The patrons will, however, usually respond positively only to those things they are familiar with, things they believe to be plausible or possible. This could be as a result of previous experience of such things or a belief in the probability of such things, based on experiences, cosmology, traditional mores, norms and values of the society. Society, therefore, serves as source of the raw materials with which artists produce their work. In terms of thematic and stylistics, society must be able to relate to an artistic work. Society must see itself reflected in the work before it could appreciate the artist's preoccupations and accoutrements of aesthetics. This is so, irrespective of the socio-political commitment or non-commitment of an artist. Every art is committed to one thing or the other, whether in the functionalist school where art is seen as a weapon for social upliftment and development or in the school of Aesthetics where artistic quintessence is the watchword. Whichever school an artist or the work of an artist belongs to, he still chooses his samples, models from life in society.

Many artists believe in functionality of art, in the inherent capabilities of art to practically raise society to better and higher levels of existence. The functionalist school believe art should not be created just for aesthetics sake. It believes that it must impact on society. It must have functional roles in ameliorating and obliterating anomalies in society and promote society to quintessential levels. To Niyi Osundare, a highly cerebral and reputable icon of the functionalist school, "art that is shorn of human touch is art for ass sake"

This is a symbolic and metonymic reference to stupidity, as embodied in the ass. To the functionalists, any art that is not reflective of, and practically useful to society is a stupid art. To them, in the words of Niyi Osundare "the writer" must be a "righter" – a corrector of wrongs, who puts wrong things right in society.

Bakare, Ojo Rasaki is a Nigerian scholar, choreographer, playwright and theatre director who believes in the tenets of the functionalist school of art, as evident from his plays, some of which are examined in this presentation. A Nigerian from Ekiti State, Bakere cuts his milk dentition in the world of the performing arts as an apprentice under the great doyen of Nigerian theatre – late Chief Hubert Ogunde, a pioneer of Nigerian theatre. He was also at a time under the tutelage of another great traditional theatre practitioner Jimoh Aliu. He complements these traditional trainings with academic tutelage in theatre arts with first, second and Ph.D degree. This background is important in shaping the personality of this great practitioner who has lectured in six Nigerian universities at one time or the other between 1991 and 2014 and was at a time the Choreographer and Technical Adviser to the National Troupe of Gambia. For some years now, he has been the Artistic Director of the annual National Festival of Arts – called the Abuja Carnival in Nigeria. He is, therefore, quite experienced in his field, practically and theoretically, in both traditional and modern forms.

Although Bakare engages in other forms of artistry – poetry, dance, instrumentation etc, we are only concerned here with his endeavours as a playwright and play director. For this purpose, we have examined three out of his six published plays in order to examine his thematic focus and the aesthetic devices he utilised to achieve his aims. We have been opportuned to know the playwright's personality very well, as colleagues in the same Department at Obafemi Awolowo University between the years 1997 and 2000. We have, therefore, seen him at work as a lecturer, director and playwright. We have also seen him in the social sphere, in the various activities in which he is engaged.

There is no gainsaying the fact that he is a very hardworking academic, an adroit goal – getter and highly industrious scholar. Principled and ready to die defending his convictions, Bakare believes that one does not need to be as big as an elephant before one becomes relevant in society; and that societal relevance he seeks passionately.

In his personal convictions, Bakare is often traumatised by social dysfunctionalities that are prevalent in his nation, Nigeria. This is reflected in most of his writings and is a leitmotif in most of his plays. In his plays, he clinically X-rays the prevalent miasma in the human society, bringing them to ridicule and public opprobrium. He not only criticises but often offer solutions to the problems X-rayed. Most of the time his solutions to the problems are radical and revolutionary, that of patriotic rebellion. Generally, he seeks the prevalence of justice and a normalisation of every anomaly. In this, vice is punished and virtue rewarded. Bakare is a man who is highly intolerant of anomalies and very impetuous about slow paces of amelioration to injustice. He is a man who believes in his rights and will quickly move away from where his rights are being denied to where his rights would be granted.

In *Rogbodiyan*, a parody of the Nigerian socio-political milieu, there is crisis in a society as a consequence of the misdemeanor of political leaders in the society". "Rogbodiyan" itself is a term in Yoruba language that means crisis or problem situation.

The play is dedicated "to the Sojas who go and come" – an obvious reference to the recurrent military administrations that plagued the Nigerian political landscape from 1966 to 1979. The play opens in a crisis situation – a very bizarre picture of townspeople who are physically deformed singing to the accompaniment of music, in rhythmic movement that cannot be regarded as dance (p. 6). They sing about the prevailing situation and ask what is to be done. The narrator then comes in from the audience and addresses the audience, stating what is obviously the thematic preoccupation and motive of the play – to entertain the audience and most importantly, to make the audience meditate and reflect on the woes of a nation, with a view to finding solutions to the problems x-rayed in the play. The narrator identifies the problems as self-inflicted. The townspeople are victims of self – inflicted disaster because they wine and dine with injustice. Part of the injustice identified by the Narrator includes throwing of merit to the winds in order to allow mediocrity to prevail, allowing nonentities to control society, religious hypocrisy and political sycophancy. In the society, intelligence and academic brilliance are guarantees to pauperisation, truth is hindered while falsehood is exalted. Corruption is an entrenched hydra-headed monster while there is a worship of material wealth which guarantees political wealth and status. These are instances of social dysfunctionality which the playwright highlights directly.

Other forms of dysfunction could be seen ingrained in some of the accoutrements of dramaturgy deployed by the playwright to project his political schemes and manipulations is a parody of the antics of a Nigerian military President who announced that he wanted to leave the office for politicians, but actually planned to perpetuate himself in office. He set up two political parties – one a little to the left (socialism), the other a little to the right (Capitalism). The symbol of the "left" party is a horse while that of the "right" party is an Eagle. This is what Bakare emblemises in this play as the two contestants to the throne – Gbadegesin (one who puts on a crown to rides a horse) and Asagidigba (the big Eagles). The Kingmakers in this parody are the masses who are supposed to vote in one of the two candidates. As protested about by the only Woman in Movement 2, the choice of two candidates is an imposition on the people, contrary to the prevalent political convention, but Regent insisted on his decision, since he has the military might to coerce the people. The way the electorate is bribed shows the complex nature of corruption in the Nigerian society, as both contestants employed corrupt means to bribe the Kingmakers. The traditional diviner is called to ask Ifa oracle to choose the right candidates and the oracle adroitly states that none of the two may rule, as they are both bad. Ifa asks the community to search for "a king who is honest and true". As the kingmakers are considering this, Asagidigbi (one of the two contestants) bursts in to bribe the kingmakers. The Kingmakers all proved to be corrupt and we are told that even the diviner (divine or not) has a price. One of the Kingmakers Eto is made to emblemise the average Nigerian citizen in politics – ever changing, not principled, subject to the whims and caprices of the corrupt politicians. This is seen in Eto's constant change of opinions, to support what profits him materially. This is confirmed by another kingmaker Abere:

> Abere – You fool. Can't you see nobody cares for this land! The issue is simple: your pocket is empty. Are you going to do something about it or not? (p. 26).

Having bribed his way, Asagidigbi is crowned as king. He starts misbehaving and oppressing the people. He defiles the traditions of his people, the consequence of which is the epidemics that burst out in the society. To solve the problem, the King has to make an epic journey through the land of the dead to Ite Esumare to healing waters of Awogbaarin (curer of two hundred diseases). This is what will cure all the diseases that have spread in the land. Since this is a very dangerous journey, the King arranges for someone to impersonate him to Ite Esumare by decking him with his kingly robes and crown, to deceive the ancestors in the land of the dead. After Adegbami's departure, Ifa oracle reveals that the sickness in the land is caused by the fact that Arugba Oge, the virgin ritual carrier has been deflowered before her task, an abomination in the land. Without any conscience, the king who is the culprit immediately accused is rival to the throne, Gbadegesin as being responsible. He orders him to be tied and beheaded, but before this could be done, the thunder god 'intervened in a form of deux ex machina'. When the diviner informs him that Ifa has revealed him to be the culprit, he accuses the diviner of complicity and directs that he should be beheaded. In fear of Sango's anger, the Akigbe could not carry out the instruction but rather confesses that he knows about the king's commitment of the offence. Amidst the melee, Adegbami returns with the curing water and snatches the kingship from the incumbent. He justifies his action by stating that it is the king who willingly abdicated the throne by offering him his crown and robes. Since he has the miracle water that would heal the towns peoples' infirmities the people are forced to accept him as king. This less of power is a kind of nemesis designed by the playwright for the errant monarch.

There is no gainsaying the fact that the anomalies x-rayed in Ilukoroju (Yoruba – a town that is not at ease) are those inherent in the playwright's country. He has exposed these things in order to wake up his compatriots from an acritical stage to a stage of critical consciousness. It portrays the problem of dearth of good, honesty, altruistic and incorruptible leaders in the Nigerian nation – state and how leaders misbehave in office, bringing the entire citizenry into poverty, suffering and opprobrium. Rather than accept their faults, the leaders (as seen in the case of the King of Ilukoroju) often blame the usually traumatic effects of their misdemeanor on supposed enemies and opponents. The play showcases how they seek to cling perpetually to political power, how insensitive they are to the plight of the pauperised masses of their nation and how very hedonistic they are in office.

In *Once Upon A Tower,* the playwright's searchlight is on the nation's ivory towers and the various atrocities being committed there on a daily basis. It seeks to expose how the main objective of setting up tertiary institutions are being truncated by the actions and unactions of selfish, egocentric and megalomaniac academics and corrupt university administrators. The main focus is on the activities of academic staff of tertiary institutions and the administrators. Embellished with a live band on stage that encapsulates much of the thematic thrust of the play, the play centres on an ex-student of a university who suffered serious calamity as a result of the poor quality education he was given. He returns to the university to deal with those who ill-equipped him for life. Thus the lecturers, the vice chancellor, provost of the medical college and the university council members who are celebrating the success of convocation ceremony are rounded up by an armed gang of ex-students to answer for their crimes. Issues in the Nigerian educational system that are revealed to be already dysfunctional include corruption and embezzlement of university funds, intimidation of younger academics by their senior counterparts, admission rackets, sexual in decency among staff and students, recruitment of incompetent academics to teach, simply because they have godfathers, how lecturers plan and scheme against their colleagues who choose to be incorruptible, sometimes using female students like Julie (p. 34-35) to frame up such disciplined lecturers like Dr. Akitikori. Prof. This is typical of the attitude of some corrupt senior academics (Prof. Kurumbete) whose up – and – coming younger and junior colleagues as threats to their academic hegemony. There are clinical details of how the academic system is destroyed and how those in positions of trust and responsibility do not care, if the system collapses, as long as they have their own benefits reaped and ripped off the system. This is manifest in the series of conversations between Prof. Kurumbete Provost, college of Medicine and Dr. Ugolo, Head of Gyneacology Department.

At the end of the play, Pedro, a victim of quack university training recounts what is poor training has caused him – the death of his lover who happens to be the daughter of the senator who cornered university contracts that he knew nothing about, and diverted funds that are meant to purchase medical training equipments. Thus, the senator in a law of Karma suffers for his evil acts. At the end, three critical villains and destroyers of the educational system are shot dead before the police comes in to arrest the avengers. Those who died include Dr. Yemi, Prof. Kurumbete and Senator.

From the conclusion of this play, it is obvious that Bakare is a revolutionary who believes in the socialist realist concept of utilising the revolutionary violence of the oppressed masses, to counter and obliterate the reactionary violence of the oppressor, so that all the anomalies inherent in the human society could be quickly terminated and the society brought back to the path of sanity.

This is also the prevalent of attitude in Bakare's *The Gods and The Scavengers* where the bourgeoisie represents the Gods and the proletarians represent the oppressed masses. The play proper starts with a pedagogy of the oppressed masses, a conscientisation, to mobilise them from their acritical stage, to a stage of critical consciousness. The play opens in a refuse dump, with four hungry looking, gaunt and unkempt. In a song, "we are the Scavengers" the four unkempt men state the dysfunctionality in their society: that though they are the workers who develop the economy of the society, they are the wretched of the earth. This is so because instead of taking action, they had slept:

> We are the scavengers, we the main men. Though we sweat like God's beings we feed from bins. How does one explain this?...
> ... Our land is sold to gods that we made with our votes. So, cheat and shit and beans in bins have become our lot because we sleep. (p. 2)

A cursory self-introduction of the Scavengers reveals that they are very professionals, on which the destiny of a society would normally hinge – a professor, a medical doctor, a farmer and a technician. That such professionals could be marginalised is indicative of the level of degeneracy in the society. In the personality of the fifth Scavenger who is an embodiment of the Christian, Islamic and Traditional religions and in the song that is a mimicked version of the second verse of the Nigerian National Anthem, the playwright seems to deviate a bit from leftist conventions in evaluation of societal problems. This is because contrary to leftist conventions that abhor religious sentiments, the playwright made the scavengers kneel in prayer to the gods and seem to pin their hopes on their intervention.

The local government chairman (Anago) is portrayed as emblematic of the typical Nigerian politician – proud, vainglorious, boastful and full of promises – even those promises he has no control over.

This portrays the pathological unseriousness of many Nigerian politicians who promise to do the impossible when they seek votes from the masses. Although Hon. Anago seems determined to serve the masses with honesty and dedication, he is surrounded by lieutenants who are vicious human wolves with corruption deeply ingrained in them. This is typical of the experience of the few honest politicians in Nigeria. Since a tree does not make a forest, they are often frustrated by the corrupt activities of the people who work with them. The playwright shows that corruption cuts through all the ethnic nationalities that make up Nigeria, hence we have Chief Olowookere representing the Yoruba tribe, Chief Madunago representing the Igbo tribe and Mallam representing the Hausa tribe. All these are corrupt councillors with whom the honest chairman has to work.

In the third movement of the play there is an expose of how political leaders operate by embezzling funds meant to cater for the welfare of the electorate. There is a protest by the market people and the chairman is seen trying to enforce sanity even among his councillors. However, as self-righteous as the chairman is, he too has skeletons in his cupboard, as his special adviser makes us to know. The question then is, is the playwright saying that there is no single political leader in Nigeria who is totally free of corruption? The chairman's special adviser seems to encapsulate the dilemma of Nigerian leaders who make laws that they themselves find difficult to obey:

> Andy: Anago, why do you make laws that you yourself cannot keep? No law is obeyed if the maker is a rogue. Those

>who come to equity must come with
>clean hands. (P. 28).

The conspiracy of the councillors against the chairman is typical of the schemes and machinations of politicians to destroy those opponents who stand against their efforts to diversify the nation's resources. As is the case here, such meetings are held late in the night "when the town sleeps" (p. 31)

The forceful relocation of the Scavengers, from a refuse dump to a desert land is symbolic of the degeneration of the socio-economic status of the Nigerian masses from a bad to a worse situation:

>Scave 2: There, at least, there were crumbs to munch, but here the palm Kernel is our saving grace. There at least, we drank from the well but here we dig the rock in search of water (p. 33)

The "digging of rock to search for water" portrays how difficult living has become, among Nigerian proletarians Using the different things that separate the citizens – religion, tribe, language and class, the councillors arrange a civil disorder, setting one tribe against another. This leads to arson, murder, looting and a general chaos. This is very emblematic of how detractors and political opponents sponsor religious crisis, stir up strife and anarchy, often leading to a national disasters, just to discredit a ruler or to make the country ungovernable for him. Nigeria indeed has witnessed many of this.

Andy's mobilisation of the Scavengers is a conscientization of the masses, to teach them that the gods have very little or nothing to do with human affairs; man's destiny is indeed in his hand. His reference to the events of Ola Rotimi's *The gods are not to blame* is a radical rejection of fatalism; of man's destiny being in the hands of the gods. As is in the case of Anago, most of the time claims of empowerment by the gods/divine intervention are fake and an organized subterfuge to deceive the masses. The playwright stance is obvious: man should reject any negative positioning of his position by a so –called transcendental order, assert his own authority and do those things that will make his life meaningful. Whereas King Odewale in Ola Rotimi's play, following the example of the Greek original Oedipus Rex (Oedipus the King) accepted his forlorn fate and submitted to the will of the gods, Bakare's Odewale absolved himself of any blame and planned to continue living his life meaningfully.

In Andy's pedagogy of the oppressed masses, he outlines some of the strategies used by corrupt politicians to appease the electorate, give them fake hopes and subject them to perpetual inertia, doing nothing about their situation. At the end, the Scavengers decide to stop scavenging and take their destiny in their hands. In the last scene, they arrest all their oppressors and put them in chains. The pedagogy then moves to all those present and a solution is suggested – the people should forgive and forget all the evils they have done against each other, abandon superstitions, look for honest leaders among themselves and take their destiny in their own hands. Like Bakare's radical King Odewale and Besija (an obvious allusion to Jabesh in the Bible) they should reject any fatalistic prognostication that is evil and chart a pragmatic, meaningful life for themselves.

In an opening song by two sonorous voices, the playwright encapsulates his main thematic projection in the play. The song states that it is the dawn of a new morning but that the promised land is still far away (p. VI). The song goes on to mobilise: ''… our destiny is in our hands, we must rise up now or else we perish.''

In line with the revolutionary stance of the playwright, the song advocates civil strife and confrontation with the oppressors, in order to normalise the anomalies in the society. Like the Marxist stance that sees religion as the opium of the masses, this song advocates that God be left out of the crisis while the masses take their destiny in their hands:

Lead: Why do we shy away from civil struggle? The heavens help those who help themselves. Our destiny is in our hands. This is the time to fight all our oppressors. (p. VI)

Lead: Why do we shout God as if he never gave us brains? Why do we shout thedevil like we are zombies? In the scriptures all things were put in our hands.When we do nothing the gods do nothing (p. VI).

Conclusion
There is no gainsaying the fact that the playwright is concerned with the welfare of the human society and has gone to great lengths to expose the anomalies in his society. This he does, in virtually all his plays. Confronted with the prevalent crises in his nation that often lead to wars and the attendant decimation of human lives, he wrote the play titled, *Drums of War*. It is a play that x-rays the often selfish stupid and megalomaniac motives that inspire some leaders of society into declaring wars. Like Euripides who wrote *The Trojan Women* to seriously lambaste Athenian leaders for their role in the Peloponesian war in which the Island of Melos was raided by Athens in a very brutal expedition, Bakare too castigates political leaders who go into wars for stupid reasons. He shows that to jaw – jaw is better than to War – war. In the play, he shows that women have roles to play, in promoting understanding and preventing wars and chaos in society.

Like the dancer, musicologist and choreographer that he is, Bakare's plays are usually infused with a high level of music and dance. In most cases, these not only serve as embellishment to the plays, but often also carry important messages of the plays. His plays are usually action – packed and there are usually no dull moments throughout the duration of productions. His plays come alive more on stage than in script form. It appears that like the Attic theatre guru Euripides, Bakare pays attention to practical productions than to the scripts that engender them. In the script you, may find faults, typographical mistakes and technical hitches, but when they come up on stage, the errors disappear into oblivion. Sometimes, actions which appear over-romanticised, idealistic and not plausible in the script, come up realistically and convincingly on stage, in Bakare's theatre. Sometimes too, traditional songs from some ethnic sources are used, without the playwright bothering to translate them, in the script. As discussed earlier on, since songs in Bakare's plays are usually complementary to the dramatic actions and not mere embellishments, a greater understanding would be achieved if the traditional, ethnic songs are translated or transliterated into English. This is more so since the scope and horizon of the plays could be worldwide.

Works Cited

Bakare, O.R. *Once Upon A Tower.* Uyo: Afahaide Publishing Company, 2000.

---------------------- *Rogbodiyan* Zaria: Tamaza Publishing Company Ltd, 1994.

--------------------- *The Gods and The Scavengers* Abuja: Roots Books & Journals 2006.

-------------------- *Drums of War.* Zaria: Tamara Publishing Company, 1994.

Breyten Breytenbach "The Writer and Responsibility". *Endpapers: Essays, Letters, Articles of Faith, Workshop Notes.* New York: Farrar, Straus & Giroux, 1997.

Brocket, Oscar. *The Essential Theatre.* New York: Harcourt Brace College Publishers, 1992.

Euripides. *The Trojan Women.* (Revised edition) London: Oxford University Press, 2008.

Osundare, Niyi. *The Writer as Righter.* (The African Literature Artist and his social obligations) Ibadan: Hope Publications, 2007.

Sidney, I. Landau and Ronald, J. Bogus *The Illustrated Contemporary Dictionary.* Chicago: J.G. Ferguson Publishing Company, 1978.

Wa Thiong'o, Ngugi. *Writers in Politics; A Re-engagement with issues of Literature and Society.* Oxford: James curry publishers, 1997.

---------------------- *Devil on the Cross.* London: Heinemann Publishers, 1987.

Whiting, Frank. *An Introduction to the Theatre.* New York: Harper and Row, 1969.

Drama in its Social Context and the Kaleidoscope of Oppression in Bakare's *Once Upon A Tower*
By
Balogun, Jide, Ph. D. and Balogun, B.J.

Introduction
There is no gainsaying in the fact that drama has become part and parcel of the Nigerian state. This genre of literature emerged using the approach of satirising the management and managers of the Nigerian political, religious, social and economic affairs. Nigeria in its chequered history particularly since independence has witnessed diverse challenges ranging from the unfaithfulness of her leadership in the daily running of her affairs symbolised in the features of man's inhumanity to man, dog eating dog, economic failure, and the institutionalisation of corruption by the political class.

The impact of all of this, is social disintegration. In the midst of this, the writer defies what Kolawole refers to as "the depiction of society from an aesthetic distance" (Kolawole; 1994:223) and concentrates on the redemption of society from its pontificates. This in the words of Gugegelberger (1989: 35), it is:
> The justification of the normative prescription of the artist as conscience to society is anchored on the functional integration of the traditional African artist to his society.

The Context of Drama and Sociology
The preoccupation of drama is the value it adds to the social frame. This is not from the perspective of,
> the study of audiences, nor does it by definition always involve number-crunching and file filling positivistic, or scientific, methodologies. Second, the idea that a sociological approach to performance, is defined by its reference to dramaturgical theories of society is woefully anachronistic. (Shevtsova, 2009:211)

Rather, the concept of drama and sociology promotes and enhances utilitarianism of drama in society. This hinges on the belief that art of drama ennobled, brings sanctity to society bedeviled by all kinds of social menaces resulting from the insensitivity of the leaders to the condition(s) of living of the led. The ability of drama to probe social disorders explains the affinity of literature and society. The Brechtian theory of didactic theatre concisely explains the social implications of drama. It further posits that the relationship between literature and society is expressed when:

> The stage began to instruct, oil, inflation, war, social struggles, the family, religion, wheat, the meat packing industry, became subjects for theatrical portrayal. Choruses informed the audience about facts it did not know. (1968:680)

Perhaps in a way, the sociological drama could take shelter in what is referred to as "the popular theatre and radical aesthetics (Bhadmus, 2008:231). His reference to popular theatre and radical aesthetics suggests the use of drama to discuss various issues in the social strata.

Kaleidoscope in Literature

If art were to influence society, its promotion of the aspirations of the people should be its concern. It is obvious that those aspirations are apparently impeded by certain forces. The Machiavellian paradigm might be very useful in this connection. Machiavelli identifies certain variables such as "Modern Absolution, Machiavelli's Interest, Moral Indifference, Universal Egoism and the Omnipotent Legislator" (Sabine and Thorson, 1973:311-330) as the factors inhibiting the accomplishment of people's social aspirations. We may not necessarily go into the details of the Machiavellian theory, but it suffices to sum up the same, that social contracditions are a product of individual interest aggregating in what Kolawole refers to as "the crux of leadership failure in Africa" (1994:224). According to him, this failure is inevitable when leaders could neither accurately nor faintly give account of their stewardship to their subjects, what he refers to as the "violation of the Stewardship theory" (224). The Stewardship theory is also parallel to the Dependency and Interdependency theory in which context, certain segments of society would naturally fall into the category that rely on leadership for direction and directives which should not make them victims. By the same token, other segments are there to provide leadership which should also not make them tyrants. More often than not however, what we find in this supposed plausible interrelationship is the bastardisation of the whole framework particularly by the leadership category. This is prosecuted through kaleidoscope of methods symbolised in oppression. This kaleidoscope manifests in alienation, corruption, monopoly of all kinds, terrorism, insurgency of various types, hypocrisy, economic diversions, opportunism, etc.

In summary, kaleidoscope in literature is a deliberate attempt by the writer to expose the multi-faceted degrees of complexities in social relationships regarding the desired individual and corporate advancement.

The Kaleidoscope of Oppression in *Once Upon A Tower*
Visible in this play is oppression as a central motif upon which other issues of thematic concern are raised. *Once Upon A Tower* published in 2000 is crafted into Twelve Movements through which the playwright consciously exposes the downward trend of the social frame using the University system which was once a tower but now a thrower (destroyer) as a setting. One may wonder how versatile could the use of the University system as a platform to discuss vital social and economic problems be? But the result is soon revealed in the fact that products of the system would inadvertently become the managers of the affairs of society. Besides, as evident in the play, the University is structured is such a way that it sybolises a microcosm of the larger society. In addition, the University universally is known to be the ivory tower, the peak of learning, and learning is acquired to manage society. Hence, any default in that critical sector of social economy is the beginning of a major set-back in society as exemplified in the relationships of the characters in the play.

Pathetically, characters in these plays embody what Machavelli refers to as universal egotism as each of them failed woefully to fulfill, the needful. Six levels of conflicts are represented in the play. Each level has its intrigues resulting in the birth of a social structure falling from grace to grace metaphorised in the literal expression "Once upon a tower" (Bakare, 2000:1)

Corruption which is one of the strongest levels of the conflicts that pervaded the play, is openly associated with the VC and his team of looters. The assessment of the success of the convocation ceremony ignited by the VC himself is a further display of the negation of the supposed 'hope' of that generation. There is nothing worthy of congratulations in the convocation. The products of that episode leading to the ceremony represented by Pedro neither added any value to themselves nor society. Rather they became nuisances to and destroyers of society, in which the council members sooner or later had their own share of the nemesis.

The Emir's remarks, "I am sure he will give us another term. He will believe we are doing the job well"(7) "Doing the job well" is a metaphor to describe these characters' versatility and incongruity in looting. There is nothing inside the setting to reflect the literal doing the job well but rather all indications reflect their failure in the provision of leadership model to the in-coming generation. Furthermore, the gullibility of these characters is shown in their quest for another term in office. Again, the rhetoric, "Another term to do what?" This quest for another term to perpetrate further evil receives an instant disapproval as "three hard-looking gun wielding half masked men briskly enter the office in various forms of jumps". (7 & 8)
The appearance of this terrorist group showcases the climax of the conflicts in the play. Two interesting but instructive scenes are worthy of evaluation. The first is that of the celebration in the office of the VC and the second is the appearance of the terrorist group to mete judgment on the looters and to confirm that "for whatsoever a man soweth, that shall he also reap" (Galatians

6.7b, Holy Bible, King James Version). Let us assess the dialogue below:

VC:	What … what for God's sake is going on here? What are you people and what are you looking for here?
Pedro:	*Leader of gang.* You and them. But I can see the main culprit is not here – Professor Kurunbete Ijakadi the Provost of the Medical College … and we strategically chose today and this hour for this operation … why others not here especially the Provost – not here?
VC:	*Moves towards Pedro confidently*: Can you now leave since your target is not here? (*Maito-one of the gun men-gives the VC a powerful feet –sweep-kick from the rear. VC falls heavily. Maito places the nozzle of pistol on his ear*)
Maito:	No we are not leaving Mr. VC. You will do yourself some good if you don't behave like a hero here. We are here for business. Feel this … it is no toy (7&8)

The episode here is a complement of retributive judgement. The boys including Pedro brought up by the system rose up to fight it. That kind of fight was avoidable if the right had been done earlier. Little did the culprits know that the result of their maladministration would soon be released. The ill-treatment given to these heavy weights' by those hoodlums, validates the philosophy of the negation.

The VC and his team as the trainers of Pedro and the anonymous others were negative and not nebulous in their dealings with their students. The VC as the head of that institution all through was too indifferent for comfort in the affairs of students and staff to the point that inside his domain, he was not able to control the excesses of the lecturers in his employment. This criminal apathy was deployed by the VC in order to give room for his trade of looting, notwithstanding the state of the students under his tutelage. The devastation he and his council members including the lecturers that were tricked into the scene by the gunmen were subjected to, was deserving. It is so, because that was a pay – back and in a more violent way. The instruction given and acted on the stage is a validation of the Brechtian archetype of didacticism.

From the middle of Movement Two to its end, the playwright with clarity of purpose cleverly makes all the major players in the misrunning of the affairs of the University have a taste of their mismanagement and this was with hardness and great psychological and physical trauma.

Another level of conflicts that is quite germane to our understanding of the intrigues in the play is the hostile relationship that existed between Professor Kurumbete and Dr. Akitktori. The Professor who is also the Provost of the Medical College, believes in his life "provost-ship" of that arm of the institution. Besides, he sees himself as the only career gynaecologist that-ever existed and that would ever exist. He vehemently and openly resists Dr. Akititori's ambition of becoming a gynaecologist. The Professor sees this as a threat. To forstall the realisation of Dr. Akitikori's unexpressed ambition, the Professor puts a lot of pegs on his way with the principal being intimidation and brutalized him.
Prof.

Kurumbete: (*Addressing these members of staff who have by now, taken their seats*)
I am definitely not going to stand
akimbo and watch you rats turn
that department into lawless place.
Remember, that as the first gynaecologist
scholar and consultant this country
has produced I founded that department

> when I came back from Europe after
> my studies ... otherwise I will
> make you cocky and opinionated
> fools, pay for your stupidity. Now
> good day and leave my office. (18)

The above is a display of tyranny, egoism and self aggrandisement to the full. The effects of all of the self praise in the above address were not said to promote the existence of the College, but rather were meant to perpetrate oppression and dominance over his colleagues. The sharp reaction of Dr. Akitikori to the Professor's address is the beginning of the trouble that the former had with the latter. and that negatively affected so many occurrences in the play. Indeed, the making out of Pedro as an eminent and out spoken individual has its root in this incident. Consider this again:

Akitikori: No way, if you lily-livered blokes have nothing to say, I Akitikori Ona Ofun Ogbeegun eja, have something to say. Prof. I object to your approach to this matter...But all you could do was to riot acts to us like babies, insult us, call us names and send us out of your office. (18)

One may not want to sympathise with the Prof. for receiving this kind of response from his surbordinate simply because he let loose the cat from his hiding. He ought to have presented his case more maturely and decently to his professional colleagues and that would have earned him a better recipe from them. He would have behaved better than that, however, his ego got the better of him. Leadership it is said, is earned and not won. Any attempt by the Prof. to force leadership on his junior officers received further resistance.

The emergence of Professor Bola, a senior member of staff of the College brought a kind of comic relief to the whole scenario between the trio of Professor Kurumbete, Dr. Akitikori and Dr. Ugolo. As a progressive senior colleague of Dr. Akitikori,

Professor Bola fulfilled the leadership role desirable in an ideal social setting. He told Akitikori about the conference and workshop sponsorship for Mid-Level Colleagues in his area (24). This on its own brought succour to Akitikori and doused the tension that has pervaded the scenario in the play from Movement One to Four.

Unfortunately, this delight soon became a lamentation as Akitikori fell victim of a set-up of a purported rape that eventually sent him out of his job. The narrator says captures it thus,

Dr. Akitikori's office. He is marking some scripts. A knock on the door.
Akitikori: Yes come in (*Miss Julie enters. She is gorgeously dressed*).
Julie: ….. So I decided to come in and borrow one of your books.
Akitikori: Which book is that?
Julie: Yes Sir
Akitikori: Okay (*As Akitikori stands up turns towards the self to bring the book*) Julie grabs his trousers from behind and pulls it downwards with a great force leaving the belt and zip torn… Before Akitikori could recover, Julie had torn her own blouse and skirt as she shouts):
Julie: Hee!... everybody help…… help this man wants to rape me oo – help (etc) (35)

This was the beginning of the end of the road forAkitikori. Afterwards, the security men rough – handled him and he is thrown out of job.

Pedro confirms this as he says:
   So that way, the hand that was to mould me was
   cut off. Akitikori was thrown out of the

University. You empty head (*Yemi*) became my major teacher and in your complexities of ignorance you taught me the nonsense that has now ruined my life (37).

The final level of conflicts through which the complexities in society are portrayed in the play is the one that featured Senator Abdul Rahaman Ikeanobi, the gluttonous, greedy and gullible father of Khadijat.

The complications found in this level of conflicts are masterminded by Senator Abdul Rahaman Ikeanobi and prosecuted by Pedro. The whole episode started with the oppressive father of Khadijat who attempted to force an husband on her against her wish. The reason behind this was purely economic.

Senator: …You are now grown up, graduate just finishing the youth service programme. The only thing remaining, my dear is to entrust you into the hands of a capable husband.

Khadijat: (*Screams*) Daddy, save me this heartache please. You mean you are actually going ahead to force a man on me? A man I had never met?

Senator: Khadijat don't screem at your father. This man is not completely unknown to you. It is the same man I have always talked to you about, Chief Ogbuefi Alexandra Chukwuma.

Khadijat: (*Screams*). Daddy… stop it. I have told you I have made my choice (43).

The above is just a demonstration of the oppressor syndrome characteristic of the capitalist motif. Irrespective of the affinity that exists, the oppressor would always want to have his way.

The real motif behind this scenario is what Khadijat herself exposed as she says:

> You lie Dad, you lie. Your insistence that I marry that fool is not to give me any quality future though that is what you have always said. But I know your real agenda (*Faces the audience*). Ladies and gentlemen please be our judge. My Dad here is the Chairman House Committee on education at the Senate. He uses his position and his party affinity with the minister to corner ninety percent of the contract awards on education matters. But because of his position as Senator he cannot operate as a contractor openly. So he uses a dummy called Chief Ogbuefi Chukwuma as a front. And they share the proceeds fifty-fifty. My father feels cheated that a mere front is collecting as much as fifty percent, but could not dislodge Ogbuefi for political and security reasons. That is why he wants me to marry Ogbuefi so that part of the fifty percent Ogbuefi collects will still recycle into my father's pocket. (44)

The above highlights the ulterior motive that informs the pursuit of Senator Abdul Rahaman. The question that often comes to mind is that in the context of the Senator, what does he want to make of all the economic accumulation. The family is sizeable enough to be run with minimal funds. Again, Khadijat, the only child whom he should work to see to her success is destroyed by the inordinate ambition of this deadly father. His uncontrolled insatiable ambition leads to the tragedy that befell Khadijat. That tragedy was unnecessary if the man was sincere even in his dealings with his only daughter.

Conclusion
We shall conclude this paper by applauding the craft of the playwright in using various literary devices to great aesthetic effect. There is a heavy deployment of musical accompaniment, particularly songs by the playwright in form of satire to catch the

attention of the audience on the need to have a proper perception of the thematic concern in the play.

Right from its take-off, Bakare introduces music to echo all the happenings in the play. The import of this music as a crucial element of culture could not, but appeal to the sensibility of the people in matters that affect them.

Once Upon a Tower is a dramatic piece that has come to be part of the band – wagon of literary tradition classified as "the popular theatre" (Bhadmus, 2008:231), whose aesthetic concern is to use drama to evoke social transformation.

Works Cited

Bakare, O.R. (2000). *Once Upon a Tower*. Uyo: Afahaide Publishing Company.

Balogun, P.O. and Balogun, B.J. (2013). Olu Obafemi's *Ogidi Mandate* in the Historical Recreation of Anti-Imperialist Drama. *The Performer Ilorin Journal of the Performing Arts 15*

Bhadmus, M.O. (2008). The popular Theatre and Radical Aesthetics of Femi Osofisan: in Aderemi Raji – Oyelade, and Oyeniyi Okunoye (Eds.) *The postcolonial Lamp: Essays in Honour of Dan Izerbaye*

Gugelberger, M. G. (ed.) (1989) *Marxism and African Literature*. Trenton, N.J.: Africa World Press.

Kolawole, G. (1994). The Censorious Use of Drama in Africa. In Olu Obafemi and Bayo Lawal (Eds.) *Issues in Contemporary African Social and Political Thought Volume 2*. Lagos: Academia Publications.

Obafemi, O. (2010). *Ogidi Mandate*. Ibadan: Kraft Books Limited.

Sabine, G.H. and Thorson, T.L. (1973). *A History of Political Theory Fourth Edition* New Delhi: Oxford &IBH Publishing Company.

Shevtsova, M. (2009). *Sociology of Theatre and Performance* Italy: Edizione.

The Holy Bible, King James Version. (2008) Texas: JET MOVE PUBLISHING INC.

Weiss, S.A. (1968). *Drama in the Western World 15 Plays with Essays*. U.S.A. Raytheon Education Company.

Political Theatre And The Leadership Question In Nigerian Drama: Statements In Bakare, Ojo Rasaki's *This Land Must Sacrifice*

By

Mbachaga, Desen Jonathan, Ph.D.

Preamble
The trouble with Nigeria is simply and squarely a failure of leadership. There is nothing basically wrong with the Nigerian land or climate or water or air or anything else. The Nigerian problem is the unwillingness or inability of its leaders to rise to the responsibility, to the challenge of personal example which are the hallmarks of true leadership. (Achebe, 1).

Abuse and misuse of power and authority by Nigerian rulers have not been largely due any national lack of capacity for good governance. Nigerian leaders have not been ineffective and tyrannical because they are incompetent or ignorant. Neither has the lack of administrative or intellectual expertise to formulate and properly execute growth enhancing policies been the major problem. Quite simply, Nigerian leaders have acted in their own selfish interests in total disregard to existing rules and laid-down procedures (Tunde, 3).

Political and economic failings in the polity of African states give credence to the above statements. Consequently, despair, frustration, fear, hunger and diseases' are the daily companions of the generality of the masses in third world countries who look up to their leaders for basic amenities and lively hood through responsible governance. Suffice to mention that, while we can say a level of political growth has been achieved over the last few decades, development eludes us on the continent. This is because economic deprivation and disparities between those that have and those who can barely afford a meal are so glaring that one does not need a fairy to know the existence of this chasm. Gbilekaa captures this situation as one in which; "the underprivileged are choking under the firm grip of the comprador bourgeois pen – robbers, avaricious politicians who would first emancipate their pockets and those of their families before the nation and contractor – army – officers" (63). This odd sore still stares us in the face as the ordinary people – poor masses wait for a deliverer.

Another salient issue within leadership challenge among African leaders is the issues of legitimacy crisis in leadership where leaders usurp power and select themselves and or influence endorsement from stakeholders or king makers either by coercion or by the gun. This completely removes the principles of democracy in governance that emphasizes the ability and freedom of franchise and participation in politics to elect credible leaders that will represent the collective will of the people and not just a select few. It is against this backdrop that this paper looks at Bakare, Ojo Rasaki's play with a focus on highlighting issues of political exploitation, inept leadership and socio – political dysfunction.

An Overview of Political Theatre and the Leadership Question in Nigeria

Nigeria as a state is faced with several challenges that are leadership induced. The list ranges from decadence, dictatorial governance, religious riots and killings that are induced by aggrieved political elite, corruption, untold hardship and poverty.

The contest for power and expression of same is better enunciated through art and of all art forms theatre is the most lucid form through which issues of life are engaged. Tola Adeniyi writing on Theatre and Politics in Nigeria submits that; "from its folk origins to its modern manifestations, theatre and or drama has always reflected the tensions and visions arising from politics… the development of theatre has always followed closely the contours of the evolution of our political systems" (iii).

It is, therefore, not out of place to say that Nigerian theatre addresses these issues by reflecting socio-events, and issues affecting Nigeria. Playwrights have placed their searchlight on the inadequacies of the political leadership beginning with the plays of Hubert Ogunde, *Strike and Hunger, Bread and Bullets, and Yoruba Ronu.* The topicality of his plays shows a dramatist with a flair for social criticism for which the then political powers looked at with bad taste. His plays were tailored towards the resistance of oppression and promote social order and humane existence. In a similar frame, Wole Soyinka in his works *Dance of the Forest, Mad Men and Specialists, Kongi's Harvest, The Road, etc* explores critical issues of nation building. His incision is precise as it is blunt because he says the truth in a situation where the voices we hear are voices of sycophants' and praise singers who worship the very oppressors in awe.

The same applies to Femi Osofisan, Ola Rotimi, Bode Sowande and more recently, Bakare, Ojo Rasaki's whose plays expose political tyranny and oppression of the masses. Their artistic creations as dramatists strongly project the economic and social issues within the Nigerian society. Images of this abound in their works - *Once upon four robbers (1980), Kurunmi* (1971) *If: Tragedy of the ruled, The midnight Hotel, Red is the freedom Road (1999), Birthdays are not for Dying, Rogbodiyan (1994), The gods and the Scavengers(2006),* just to mention a few.

This crop of plays on the Nigerian scene, seriously enunciate the dismal situation in Nigeria where politics has become a cheap means of amassing wealth to the detriment of the ruled. More so, these dramatists preach against state crimes and advocate the virtue of truth, responsible governance that is sensitive to the plight of the masses and above all, they protest against the oppressive political class.

The core issue here is the sense of obligation or commitment to a cause whereby a writer puts himself up to become the society's conscience by using his writing to preach transformation. In the words of Gbilekaa;
> The 'committed' writer preaches the changeability of old achaic institutions, demystifies capitalist myth by attacking the status quo, educates the people, creates hope in

them in such a way that they become confident of making changes (52).

Herein, the writers concern is the need to make society a better place than it is. Thus, his writings become a reaction to a situation or issues in his society. His responsibility here goes beyond merely providing commentary on social issues that are prevalent in his time but he also provides solutions to this ailing problems. Suffice to mention that a writer's work is the eye through which the reader sees his world, his predicament and the social reality around him.

Ngugi corroborates this when he submits that; "Seen in this light, the product of a writer's pen both reflects reality and also attempts to persuade us to take a certain attitude to that reality. The persuasion can be a direct appeal on behalf of a writer's open doctrine or it can be an indirect appeal through influencing the imagination, feelings and actions of the recipient in a certain way towards certain goals and a set of values, consciously or unconsciously held by him" (7).

The above clearly establishes the responsibilities of the writer and artiste to his society and readers/audience. This responsibility here takes the writer from a docile or passive social commentator to a promoter of justice, peace, equity and above all to remold society to be more humane and in this instance the issue of leadership as it connects the challenge of leadership and good governance in Nigeria attracts our focus.

Leadership Challenges in Nigeria: Finding Meanings in Bakare, Ojo Rasaki's *This Land Must Sacrifice*

Nigeria, like other third world countries, continues to grapple with what seems to be an elusive goal of development despite her vast natural wealth and human resources. As such, Nigeria as a nation can be described as a country of extreme paradoxes because of its widespread poverty among its citizenry in the midst of plenty because, the clutches of poverty run through the length and breadth of the country and citizens suffer untold hardship due to bad governance.

Bakare in this play makes firm political statements that deal with contemporary social problems in Nigeria with the aim of projecting the decadence within the polity. In the opening of the play, Ebubedike who is one of the residents of Okalogun community where the play is set laments over the state of affairs in the community. In his words;

> **Ebubedike:** These paddlers of our canoes are to my mind not up to the task. We ought to have reached the Promised Land since we started the journey. See, the lifeless swinging of their arms and the canoes crawling like crabs. They are too weak for the task. Their arms feeble as they paddle… (*This Land Must Sacrifice*, 9).

The above statement, questions the capability of the leaders, as well as their vision and invariably projects the wave of discontent among the citizenry which is reminiscent of contemporary day lamentations of average Nigerians. Why does the fourth wealthiest country in Africa, second wealthiest in sub-saharan Africa with enough manpower and natural resources have a human development index that is lower than the SSA average? Why do the great majority of Nigerian citizens lack access to electricity, clean and safe water, and other basic amenities? Why is unemployment rate on the increase among our teeming graduates? These questions are pressing questions that demand urgent answers from our leaders. Bakare in this instance throws these questions at our political elite who lead us without a defined vision because it seems that despite the various development plans over the years, the economic development of Nigeria as a nation state is disappointing.

Suffice it to say that, mismanagement, ineptitude as well as massive corruption among our political leaders and top officials continue to be the bane of the day. As such, within a larger part of the population there is disillusion in the nascent democracy.

As the play develops, we see the old one who urges the people to select someone to lead them. Here, we see the influence, a replay of the Nigerian independence struggle and that of the colonial masters finally giving way for Nigerian Independence.

The interaction hereafter is the hope for a better future that having gained freedom from the colonial masters things will be better and the need for electing leaders who will represent the masses genuinely and selflessly as can be seen in the words of Ebubedike,

> Here we are in the promise land, hoping to make things better for all. The journey to the future starts today. This is why we must look before we leap…we must choose capable leaders who can work for the masses. If we must be under those who will not eat until our stomach is full, leaders who will not drink until our throat is wet and those on whose laps our problems shall sleep… (*This Land...*, 18)

In this dialogue, we see the yearning and commitment of the people towards having leaders that are committed to protecting the interest of the people they are leading by committing themselves to creating a new order in the interest of the present generation and generations yet unborn. The core issue here is that the present generation of political elite has failed to deliver the dividends of democracy as it is called because the masses continue to be alienated from participating in governance or benefiting from the freedom that democracy ought to bring because there has been so much clamour for civilian rule and now that we have tested civil rule and are still running in circles, the cry is a call for the military to come back because the masses cannot see the expected benefits of the 'New Nigeria'.

The cry herein is the cry for 'saviours', men of integrity who are courageous to serve the country selflessly and bring about tangible socio-economic transformation that transcends empty political promises and mere rhetoric's or propaganda in the media. In essence, Nigerians continue to wait and hope for a 'Messiah' or 'Messiahs' who are to come. For each passing regime we wait for another and another and another?

The dimension of greedy Leaders in the Nigerian polity is another issue treated by Bakare. Nigeria as a nation over the years has been saddled with greedy leaders that have nothing to impact positively on this country or its citizens. As such, the product of the kind of leadership that comes from these leadership misfits has had no gainful impact on the teeming millions of Nigerians. Rather, we are faced with a kind of leadership that is only concerned about itself, self-serving leadership, a leadership bereft of ideas and ideals that can lead to the desired change, growth and progress in this country.

The conversation between Itong and the other chiefs succintly captures this;

Anyaoku: ...don't mention my name o'gini? You Itong that is talking, how did you spend the money you were given for farmers to buy chemicals from the white man's land? Wasn't it you spent during your father inlaws funeral ceremony?

Itong: You cant blame me for that, afterall, I gave Kabiyesi his own share before I spent it. I am not as greedy as both of you.

King: That is it. That is it. Itong is the best of you all. He always remembers to grease my palm whenever things come out fine. But you and you, you eat with all your fingers and soil your mouth like a pig that has just fed from faeces.

Anyaoku: It is not true. The day Okoro gave me Twenty Thousand for giving him the contract of supplying chairs for the village community school, didn't I come here to drop your own share?

This argument between the chiefs and the king in the world of the play depicts a picture where the people who are elected to serve the people forget the very people – the masses that voted them in. The only thing they do not forget is paying themselves bogus salaries and allowances from government coffers. The playwright like what is seen in his other plays – *Once Upon A Tower, The Gods and The Scavengers, Rogbodiyan* ripostes visionless, corrupt political leadership in Nigeria who thrive on kick backs from contracts and diversion of public funds to enrich themselves. His dramaturgy focuses on discussing issues of governance and dysfunctional leadership which the modern political elite dish out to Nigerians. A crop of leaders who deliberately turn their backs on the genuine needs and concerns of Nigerians. The leadership that has not only become a leadership burden too difficult to bear but also a burden of leadership that is meant to run this country down by all means. Over the years, it has been a long standing culture, if not tradition, that the Nigeria leaders have neither been accountable and responsive to the yearnings and aspiration of Nigerians nor have they been responsible to the collective wish of the people.

One notices a conscious effort by the playwright to redirect the negative vision of the King and his circle of Chiefs through the words of the diviner who represents the yearning and aspirations of the people. He reechoes the suffering of the people in the hands of the rulers:

Diviner:	My Lord, Ifa has spoken.
King:	Any answers to my request?
Diviner:	Your people are dying of hunger, poverty, starvation, joblessness and all the ailments that plague the innocent common man.
King:	Really? ... But I have not seen anybody die of hunger.
Diviner:	for the problems of this land and those living in it to be alleviaited, then this land must make a sacrifice.

King:	What sacrifice?
Diviner:	Your Highness, everything must change in this land. We must leave our present way of living … to another one, that is the sacrifice.
King:	You speak in tongues. Be direct.
Diviner:	Ifa says everybody must be equal in this land. … there must be equality in the distribution of of our wealth. …. It is the freedom given to everybody to have as much as he can acquire that plagues the unfortunate ones called masses. Everybody wants to build his mansion in the moon, so they continue cheating the innocent ones. The oracle says this must stop… (*This Land*, 27-29).

Redefining the quality of life of the less privileged is the concern of the playwright here. The struggle here is the inter – class relationship and power relations between the political elites in relation to the less privileged. Suffice it to say that, in Nigeria, where capitalism is crudely practiced in a manner that the average Nigerian masses are completely silenced. Invariably, Bakare proposes a violent destruction of capitalist structures that perpetuate the status quo because it is the unequal distribution of wealth as well as social inequality in a capitalist structure that breeds these problems.

The penchant to accumulate wealth by those in power to the detriment of the people they rule is emphasized. To Bakare, societal degeneration is as a result of people's selfishness. The plight and suffering of the masses does not matter where issues of wealth and property accumulation by the King and his chiefs are concerned. These are people who operate the system and the diviner's call for change is aimed at bringing about total reform because existing structures do not cater for the needs of the people. As such, the communist manifesto is strongly echoed as Bakare emphasizes the need for an egalitarian society where the needs of the masses are taken into consideration by the rulers.

Bakare's penetrating portrayal of social reality in the Nigerian polity ends on a revolutionary note as the youths in reaction to the problems in the play take up arms and eventually besiege the palace of the king and dragged the king out where he is stabbed to death. To the youths, removing themselves from the bondage of the oppressors and exploitation requires removing the very people who perpetuate it. This, they achieve through collective action what Obafemi refers to as 'comradeship of the down trodden'(180). A comradeship that arises from political awareness of events in an unjust socio – political structure. Bakare choose the revolutionary aesthete as a means to show his audience the need and possibility of establishing a new order in the society as such, his plays often portray several instances of people taking up arms to fight oppressive systems and overthrow same. Bakare's theatre can therefore be termed a theatre that aims at egalitarian socio – political restructuring of society.

Conclusion
The political and economic challenges facing Nigeria as a nation after fifty years of nationhood, of which fourteen years have been spent on steady democracy, are enormous and hydra headed. From religious riots we have graduated to religious bombings, and various ugly vices that stare us in the face daily.
There is no gainsaying that the biggest problem facing this country today is the dearth of selfless and transparent leadership. A leadership that is accountable, responsive, transparent and responsible to Nigerians in dealing with the country. Nigeria needs leaders that are upright and true to the Nation's quest for growth and development. Trust worthy leaders who have the nation state at heart as well as genuine concern for the well being of Nigerians. Bakare uses his dramaturgy to realistically engage socio – political issues that bother on the repression and

alienation of the masses and underprivileged in the Nigerian society. His clamour is a cry for a mass awareness to oust this condition by all means. It is needful to say that as dramatists, we must continue to vibrantly use our art to interrogate and engage the ruling classes with a view to challenging our governments regarding issues that bother on political, social and economic reforms.

Works Cited

Bakare, Ojo Rasaki *This Land Must Sacrifice*. Enugu: New Age Publishers. 1991.

Achebe, Chinua *The Trouble with Nigeria*. Enugu: Fourth Dimension Publishers. 1983.

Obafemi, Olu *Contemporary Nigerian Theatre: Cultural Heritage and Social Vision*. Lagos: Centre for Black and African Arts and Civilization. 1996.

Gbilekaa, Saint *Radical Theatre in Nigeria.* Ibadan: Caltop Publication (Nigeria) Limited. 1997.

Adeniyi, Tola "Theatre and Politics in Nigeria". In *Theatre and Politics in Nigeria*. Jide Malomo and Saint Gbilekaa (Ed). Ibadan: Caltop Publications (Nigeria) Limited, (pp. iii-ix) 2006.

Obadina, Tunde "Africa's Crisis of Governance" Acessed from http://www.afbis.com/analysis/crisis.htm on 12/08/2011

wa Thiong'o, Ngugi *Writers in Politics.* London: Heinemann Publishers. 1997.

Womanist View and Political Stance in Bakare, Ojo Rasaki's Selected Plays.

By
Ojediran, Oludolapo Ph.D

Introduction

As a Nigerian male playwright, Bakare epitomizes a writer whose works have consistently explored the beauty of language, culture, economy and politics in all aspects of creativity. He intertwines all these in most of his plays to showcase the economic deterioration, moral decadence, and social decline in his described country system. Bakare exposes the abuse of power, gender, class and position to discuss the wastefulness of what life entails and how human beings handle it and never want to let go.

His use of language reveals that language is a powerful phenomenon in creativity. Thus, this creativity expresses the most important people in the society, i.e the middle class and especially the lower class who are unable to cater for themselves. While the lower class engage in menial jobs and can hardly feed, clothe and provide for their dependants, the middle class see themselves as sophisticated beings who ride on the sufferings and poverty level of the people they are meant to help. In one of the selected plays, The Gods and The Scavengers, Bakare calls these low class people 'The Scavengers' and refers to the middle class who govern them as 'The Gods' in pursuit of their individual selfish interests.

In the plays under analysis, language helps to develop situations that call for further investigation which readers/audiences see and feel vividly when reading or watching a dramatic piece. This mirrors what Morosatti (2009, p.317) observes about Osofisan's writings that

> if we follow Osofisan's argument that a truly autonomous, independent and democratic society should have moments of collective

> discussion to its logical conclusion, then we may be led to a conclusion simple yet of immense importance; that, beyond the literariness of any given genre, drama alone may ultimately be considered a socially-relevant form of expression whereas fiction and prose, based as they are mostly on individual enjoyment, may on the contrary unintentionally become weapons of a society that is more closed, rigid, and isolated.

Although, this is Morosatti's summary of Osofisan's dramatic works, Bakare's works also lends from this point of view. While Bakare is an internationally recognized dancer and choreographer, he writes plays that are challenging, dramatic, entertaining and educating to gain the attention of his audience in order to highlight the democratic values, economic standard and patriarchal view that exist in the country showcased by the playwright. This democratic values and economic standard is evidenced in the scavengers' opening song

> We are the scavengers, we the main men. When
> those rogues eat their beans, we comb their bins.
> They cheat, we lift their shit. We are the
> scavengers, we the main men.
>
> We are the scavengers, we the main men.
> Though we sweat like God's beings, we feed from
> bins. How does one explain this? We are the
> scavengers, we the main men.
>
> We are the scavengers, we the main men.
> Our land is sold to gods that we made with our
> votes. So, cheat and shit and beans in bins have become
> our lot because we sleep (1).

The song reveals the marginalisation, dehumanization and humiliation of voters who elect their leaders, yet cannot boost of any progress in the country in question. Rather, these voters are left at their own mercy without food, clothes, jobs, social amenities and health care facilities, security amongst many other necessities of life. The unavailability of these things makes the scavengers' lifestyles a living hell in a country endowed with more than enough to satisfy its citizens. This also mirrors Agboola's (2012, p. 125) observation of Ayo Akinwale's play, This King Must Die, that

> the nation's political leaders engage in a lot of activities which smacks of a people afflicted with mental illness. Nigeria's numerous problem, particularly the ones paraded in This King…unemployment, prostitution, corruption, bribery, drug peddling, drug addiction, vote rigging (p.70) are products of political elite (man-made problems) which are borne out of selfishness and greed.

Going by what is portrayed in Bakare's The God's and The Scavengers, society does not to depreciate in a day, but accumulation of bad leadership, bad government and egocentricism contributes to the gradual drifting apart of a society.

Also, Bakare's second play, Adanma, presents a young beautiful lady that is admired by many especially Mohammed and Ezego. Ironically, Bakare shows Adanma as a lady who is marginalized in the patriarchal system she lives in. While a woman's beauty is a thing to be appreciated, it can also be a cause of downfall to a woman who is ignorant or boastful of such. In the African context, a woman's beauty is appreciated with different physiques, behaviours, attitudes, cultural heritages and others such attributer which could be evidenced through her shape, teeth, neatness, buttock, breast, eye, complexion, etc. One of the songs rendered by Adanma's friends in the play expresses this perspective of African beauty that

Ada Anna nwamma (2x)	Ada Anna fine girl
Ntutu di n'isi	Hair on her head
Ala di n'obi o	Breast on her chest
Nekwa Ada n;azu o	Look at her behind
Nekwa efekefe efe	Look at her yanga (style)
Ada Anna nwa mma o (2x)	Ada Anna fine girl (p. 20)

However, Adanma is not only deceived by the men in her life, but also, she is misled by her fellow women without using her own woman is gall to discover what is at stake. As the main objective of this paper is to discuss the womanist aesthetics and political view in Bakare's two selected works, the role of women within a patriarchal system is analysed in line with Alice Walker's view of womanism. Walker's (1994, pp. xi-xii) four-partite definition of womanism is useful in analysing the two plays:

> ...the black folk expression of mothers to female children, you acting womanish, i.e. like a woman...usually referring to outrageous, audacious, courageous, or wilful behaviour. Wanting to know more and in greater depth than is considered 'good' for one...(A womanist is also) a woman who loves other women sexually and/or nonsexually. Appreciates and prefers women's culture . . . and women's strength. Sometimes loves individual men, sexually and/or nonsexually . . . committed to survival and wholeness of entire people, male and female. Not a separatist . . . Womanist is to feminist as purple is to lavender" (xi-xii).

Walker depicts the potential for the oppressed in the society to grow out of their situation. Her four-partite definition seems to suggest multiple uses of womanism. These multiple uses are very different, but all of them have a common denominator – they show a link with black women's past in relation to their gender and race and the collaboration that exists within the black society.

Hence, the adoption of womanism in this paper is to see men as working partners rather than foes of women as the western feminism portray them (separatist nature of western feminism).

Women in Bakare's Selected Plays

Women in African society are usually grouped into two different categories. Women can be active participant or passive participants in a society. This elaborates the issue of power and powerlessness, vocal and quietness, confidence and jittery as represented through the presentation of different female characterizations in the works of many African writers. When it comes to male writers, their representations of female characters vary. While many male writers do not show the positive side of womanhood except to present them as, silenced, uneducated, unintelligent, amongst other things, some male writers still present a balanced image of womanhood.

Bakare expresses female voices from a marginalized 'other' view, exploring different forms of womanism which at the end show them as silenced beings. While Walker (1984, p. 256) explores the relationship between men and women, and why women are always condemned for doing what men do as an expression of their masculinity, why men are praised for engaging in the same activities as women who are referred to as "tramps" and "traitors", the selected plays lend credence to this assertion and also create avenues for change. As noticed in Afolabi (2002, p. 131), he agrees that properly coordinated feminism could be a very useful weapon in obliterating human oppression, and in advancing society to higher realms of understanding, tolerance and peace. Afolabi's view shows that barbaric and invaluable traditions, system and laws could be eradicated by women themselves, through women and for women.

Increasingly, one notices that the plays under analysis tend to depict the characters especially women as metaphor for colonial exploitation which makes the writer examine character stereotypes with damaged self-image and inferiority complexes trying to correct the assumed imperfection of their gender. Alabi and Akpa (2003) as quoted by Lucas (2009, p.117) see that

> as a result of historical mistakes of colonialism and forced amalgamation, women have continued to be disadvantaged and discriminated against in all spheres of life ranging from family to political and social places of society. The life of a woman in the social setting is that of a slave or at best a third class citizen.

This shows that the female characters as created on the page and embodied on stage, rather than become the mouthpieces for their own stories through which they can redress traditional and contemporary situations, communal memories and experiences, the social, cultural and gender induced issues, they become dormant, ignorant and inexpressive (third class citizens). Readdressing female issues might not seem as easy as it sound in any patriarchal system where men take charge of public sphere except the domestic sphere and reproductive issues. This is because the male gender is given full support religiously, culturally, socially, politically and economically. It is assumed that even when women in this system navigate themselves, try to be vocal and audible, engage in different things to prove their worth, the fact remains that the patriarchal system is a gendered system that mostly benefits the men. In Ezego's self-worth words, he sees himself as someone who can have anything he wishes for

Ezego: Nkem, Nkem, Nkem, Everybody knows that it is the beginning of a new moon and I have to change blanket. Everybody knows that this one is becoming very old. Look Nkem this world is all about cooperation. If Ada enters this house, the two of you will cooperate inside my bedroom. If she do for Monday you will do for Tuesday or you want to do for the whole week? *Leading her into the bedroom)* (p. 19).

Ezego's words see women as gullible beings who can put up with any situation they find themselves in. While he had promised the assumed last wife (3rd wife) that there will be no other woman after her, he discovers Adanma, whom he sees as the prettiest of all women. The first wife who wants to please her husband, seeks all ways to convince Adanma to agree with her husband's love proposal. She lures Adanma into visiting Ezego. While the playwright presents Adanma as unintelligent "Don't mind my small brain" (p.26), her actions in the play also attest to it. On the one hand, Adanma believing what Ezego's first wife whispered into her ears, trusting her friends especially Nkechi, following Ezego into the bedroom to be disvirgined shows the opposite of what Walker's womanism advocates for women. Walker sees that women are intelligent, supportive and capable. On the other hand, the womanist spirit of wanting to know more than is desired is seen in Adanma when she enters the room with Ezego to confirm what his first wife has said

Adanma: (*coming out and crying after been deflowered*) So they deceived me. They deceived me. Ezenwanyi herself, she told me that Nna-ayi was not complete and with my tiny brain I believed her. I believed her oo (*cries for sometime then goes still. She rises slowly with laughter*) But, he is a man, a real man (*Indicating with her hand*) (p. 27).

Readers might imagine Adanma is raped. Rather than being sober throughout her monologue, she consoles herself that Ezego is also man enough to handle her sexually after the promise of getting her a 'Toyota Cecelia' (p.27). This is a crime committed against Adanma's body, a patriarchal system that should condemn such act, but rather prepares Adanma for marriage. This mirrors Rudin's (2009, p. 191) observation that rape and sexual harassment are traces of oppressive foci that perpetuate women's marginality and *reification*. Women's survival act to have access to economic resources and freedom in the light of patriarchal system is an important issue that makes most women fall victim of rape. Until recently, most patriarchal societies see rape as part of manliness, or do not even consider it as rape or violation of a woman's body. However, since democracy returned to Nigeria in 1999, rape has been seriously considered as breaking of fundamental woman's right.

Ignorantly, Mohammed is the only man in the play that rejects Adanma's marriage to Ezego. Mohammed's love for Adanma explores the expectation of Walker's womanism which explains the accommodationist nature of the theory as observed by Ogunyemi (1996, p. 55) that womanism believes in the freedom and independence of women... wants a meaningful union between black women, black men and black children in order to eliminate the sexist stance that exists.

Bakare's Women and their Political Stance

Moody (1970, p. 58) asserts that the urge to convey one's needs effectively to the other people is one of the fundamental origins of language as it becomes successively more complex as the individual develops and human affairs become more intricate. . . Language may of course be used for the promotion of both worthy and unworthy causes, using either valid or invalid methods, and the use of language for persuasion should be attended by rational critical consciousness. Nevertheless any mastery of a language must include the capacity to marshal facts and arguments in such a way as to gain maximum attention to them.

Moody explains the use of language amongst human. Language could be used persuasively or unpersuasively but most importantly, before one can effectively use it. One must master the language to marshal one's point and argument, that is, the language=code, person speaking=code and person receiving the message=code all have to understand the language before an effective communication takes place. However, persuasive language goes beyond trying to pass across information; rather it is used to gear people's psyche in order to convince them. Such words are mostly used in political settings whereby politicians need to sell their 'products' to the citizens in question. This is the situation in Bakare's The Gods and The Scavengers where the politicians used their persuasive languages to gain the needed votes and at the end exploit the people. Iyaloja in turn uses her own political stance and knowledge to negotiate between the people and the politicians. She speaks of hope instead of hopelessness

IYALOJA: Yes, that the hoodlums in the name of councillors try to perpetuate irregularities, fraud and long throat should not make us hopeless. We have hope in our Chairman, we have a chairman that listens. If our spokesmen and representatives are not happy with the wind of change that is blowing across the land, they can die and roast in pieces. Let us rise and complain to our Honourable. He has ears he will listen. My people, my people, this is not the time to sit and mourn, this is the time to rise and act (p. 16).

Ignorantly, Iyaloja presents a diplomatic view of an African woman who is interested in change and prosperity of her people. Nevertheless, to an African woman, the persuasiveness in the womanist theory that seeks a meaningful union in a patriarchal society seems to be more appropriate in the analysis of women's experiences. While women such as Olufunmilayo Ransome-Kuti, Efunsetan Aniwura, Emotan, Queen Amina, Charlotte Olajumoke Obasa, Omu Okwei, Nana Asma'u, Olaniwun Adunni Oluwole, have been technically and unapologetically involved in wealth creation, fighting of wars, empowering other women and taking up social works at different levels, historically most of the women who took these fore fronts have been neglected and forgotten. This is observed, in Obadiegwu (2009, p. 110) that women have always seen their socio-political involvements in human society as attempts at gender balance rather than calls for their contributions to the development of the society only. The role of Iyaloja in The Gods and The Scavengers clearly reveals this.

IYALOJA: Long live the Honourable. We are here to register our displeasure concerning the way your councilors come to the market to raid us on daily basis. Honourable Chairman you already told us you have stopped the collection of royalties by councilors. But these your councilors (pointing at the councilors seated) still come to the market to forcefully take royalties from us. Secondly, you blame us for evading payment of taxes and revenues. But the truth is we pay our taxes and revenues to the councilors who head our constituencies.Honourable, does it then mean that we suffer lack of basic amenities because our representatives don't bring you the taxes and revenues we pay? Chairman sir, save us from the hands of some of your men who insist milking us dry in spite of the commitment of your regime to abetter life for all and sundry. My people, I never talk una mind? (pp. 24-5).

Iyaloja means mothers of the market. She is often the female head of each community group apart from the Iyalode who is among the chiefs. Iyaloja serves as the mouthpiece of the market women who engage in buying and selling. They are the ones who bear the brunt of the economic deterioration, political instability and social degradation of the society. Bakare presents Iyaloja as an out-spoken and independent minded woman whose persuasive language speaks on behalf of others, both women and men. Just like the women listed above that made political influences, Iyaloja speaks for the survival of her people, prevents them from being exploited, exposes different levels of corruption among the commissioners who are meant to serve the people. While the Honourable Chairman, Anago, is dishonest, he claims to be what he is not by promising heaven on earth to the people. For example,

ANAGO: Let me put it this way. The poor shall become rich in my time as long as the poor work hard. In my time, the rich will remain rich as long as they do honest business. And by the grace of my ancestors, in my time the rich who has been cheating the masses and the land will become poor. I am sure you understand the signs of the season (pp. 11-12)

The chairman's inhuman nature comes up with him at the end when the scavengers who are evicted from their assumed houses return with the chairman's decamped special adviser, Andy, who could not cope with the lies, fraud and unconcerned behaviour of his boss. Andy calls for a true democratic system amongst the Scavengers. However, what readers notice in Bakare's works is summed up by Awuawuer (2009, p. 336) that Nigeria is said to be politically and economically dominated by men who dictate its political affairs and manipulate it to their advantage. Women are perpetually left behind in the political arena, and only a negligible insignificant number are allowed in, to partake in the politics of the nation under the tutelage of men. Ironically, women writers have always neglected the role of women in democratic politics; rather, they often discuss women's positions in socio-cultural, economic and traditional settings, but Bakare's work exposes how men control politics, negotiate themselves in politics and how men make politics their own rights.

Also, diplomatic persuasive language is explored in Adanma. Ezego's first wife uses these words to lure Adanma to her husband. The role played by Ezenwenyi is the same role exhibited by Sadiku in Wole Soyinka's The Lion and the Jewel. Ezenwenyi and Sadiku portray elderly women who are ready to satisfy their husbands' urges in different patriarchal societies, not minding the effect it will have on the younger generation of women. Rather than helping these young women grow out of their inhibitions in societies that view women as men acquisitions, they played along with their husbands to cajole these innocent young women to becoming the latest 'properties'.

Nevertheless, the present writer sees Bakare's playwriting skills in Musa (2002, p. 46) view that the playwright is a creative artist who is often guided by inspiration or the environmental condition of his society when writing. He is also a visioner artist and a creative person, an observer of things- an iconoclast.

Conclusion
Although, more work needs to be done on women and their political stance in democratic societies, women in the selected plays question the low level of women's involvement and commitment in the politics of the patriarchal system, economic injustice and social development. However, Bakare's portrayal of women can be said to be balanced. While he portrayed Iyaloja as vocal and outspoken, speaking for others, Adanma on the other hand is seen as a gullible woman with little or no intelligence. Although, these two women characters are of different age groups and backgrounds, Bakare shows elderly women (Iyaloja and Ezenwenyi) in the plays as people with womanist visions who want the collaboration of men and women in the society, unlike the younger generations (Adanma, Nkechi, Third wife) who want to remain where the patriarchal society dictates for them.

Works Cited

Afolabi, J.A. (2002). Of womb-men, we-men, and woe-men: Feminist aesthetics, heater practice and the democratic process in Nigeria. In: *Theatre and Democracy in Nigeria.* (Eds.) Yerima Ahmed & Akinwale Ayo. pp. 43-52. Ibadan: Kraft Books.

Agboola, M. O. (2012). A dramatist's search for a sane society: A study of Ayo Akinwale's this king must die. In: Adeoye, AbdulRasheed Abiodun (ed.) The dramaturgy of a theatre sociologist: festschrift in honour of Ayo Akinwale. pp. 121-135. Ilorin: University of Ilorin press.

Awuawuer, T.J. (2009). Negotiating gender equality and equity for women empowerment in the 21st century Nigeria: A critique of Irene Salami-Agunloye's more than dancing. In: *Feminist aesthetics and dramaturgy of Irene Salami-Agunloye.* Emmy Unuja Idegu (Ed.). pp. 335-355. Kaduna: TW press & publication.

Bakare, O. R. (2006). *The gods and the scavengers.* Abuja: Roots books & journal limited.

Bakare, O. R. (2008). Adanma. In: *Splitting images and other Nutaf plays from the WELL.* Kafewo Samuel A. & Okwori, Jenks Z. (Eds.) pp. 1-46. Lagos: Dats and partners.

Gbilekaa, S.A.T. (2002). Drama and national politics: The example of Ola Rotimi. In: *Theatre and Democracy in Nigeria.* (Eds.) Yerima Ahmed & Akinwale Ayo. pp. 43-52. Ibadan: Kraft Books.

Lucas, J. M. (2009). The drama of women exploitationand victimization in Irene-Salami-Agunloye's sweet revenge. In: *Feminist aesthetics and dramaturgy of Irene Salami-Agunloye.* Emmy Unuja Idegu (Ed.). pp. 114-134. Kaduna: TW press & publication.

Morosetti, T. (2009). Gone with the western wind: popular genres in the essays of Femi Osofisan. In: *Emerging perspectives on Femi Osofisan.* Akinyemi Tunde & Falola Toyin (Eds.). pp. 297-320. Trenton: African world press.

Musa, A. A. (2002). Sustaining Nigeria's nascent democracy. Playwrights and the need for constant reappraisal. In: *Theatre and Democracy in Nigeria.* (Eds.) Yerima Ahmed & Akinwale Ayo. pp 43-52. Ibadan: Kraft Books.

Okonjo-Ogunyemi C. (1985). *Womanism: The Dynamics of Contemporary Black female Novel in English.* Lagos: Guardian Books.

Rudin, S. (2009). The poetics of woman's survival: Nava Semel's and the rat laughed. In: *Feminist aesthetics and dramaturgy of Irene Salami-Agunloye.* Emmy Unuja Idegu (Ed.). pp. 190-200. Kaduna: TW press & publication.

Walker, A. (1984). *In Search of Our Mothers' Gardens: Womanist Prose.* Berkshire: Cox & Wyman Publishers.

Destiny as Aesthetics in Bakare's *Rogbodiyan* And *The Gods And The Scavengers*

By
Aliyu-Ibrahim, R. Foluke, Ph.D.

Introduction

African philosophical thought is one of the major influences on Nigerian playwrights. This influence is exhibited in the themes and forms of the written works and cuts across all the generations of Nigerian playwrights. Nobel laureate Wole Soyinka for instance is inspired by the paradox of the qualities of creativity and destruction inherent in the Yoruba mythical god Ogun. Ola Rotimi's *The Gods Are Not to Blame* (1975) which is modeled after the Western concept of tragedy is suffused with forms of African oral literature such as proverbs that are indicative of the origin of the playwright. Those that are referred to as socially-conscious playwrights such as Femi Osofisan and Olu Obafemi are no different as they employ myths and oral histories and many other African oral forms to relay their messages. Younger playwrights such as Ododo and Bakare have continued this trend of borrowing from their rich oral culture.

Bakare Ojo Rasaki is Ekiti, one of the various nationalities that make up the Yoruba. Therefore, it would be natural to assume that he would be influenced by some aspects of Yoruba philosophical thought and culture with which he had no doubt come in contact in some way or the other. This aim of this paper is to investigate Bakare Ojo Rasaki's deployment of African philosophical thought with reference to the Yoruba concept of destiny in his *Rogbodiyan* (1994) and *The Gods and the Scavengers* (2006).

Yoruba Concept of Destiny

Destiny in Yoruba is referred to as 'ori-inu' i.e. 'inner head' and conceptualised as 'spiritual head' (Balogun, 2007; 117); the head is thus the seat/symbol for destiny. As agreed to by scholars such as Hallen and Sodipo (1986) and E. B. Idowu (1996), 'ori' in

Yoruba cosmology is one of the components that make up the human being. The other two being the body (ara) and the life giving force (emi). Ori, symbolized by the physical head, is the bearer of destiny and is representative of an individual's personality (Idowu, 1962: 170). The Yoruba believe that there is a Supreme Being who has planned the course of each individual's life; that this is destiny and as such whatever happens follows this course.

Several myths abound as to how an individual acquires his/her destiny. Idowu (1962: 173–174) and Morakinyo (1983: 72) recount the myth of 'ayanmo' where the individual has his/her destiny thrust upon him. Another way of acquiring one's destiny is by kneeling before the Supreme Being and choosing one's own destiny i.e. 'akunleyan' while in the third, the individual kneels down and receives his/her destiny, i.e. 'akunlegba' (Idowu, 1962: 174). All these methods of acquiring destiny, 'ori', are done subconsciously such that by the time the individual comes into the physical world, he/she has forgotten his/ her destiny. In spite of stating that once chosen/received/thrust upon, destiny cannot be changed the Yoruba also believe that after consultations by the Ifa priest who confirms the destiny of the individual/ or a people, an individual's (a people's) destiny may be altered in two ways. The first is through the appropriate sacrifice, 'ebo'. Another way of changing destiny is through 'ese', which means decisive and determined action or struggle like hardwork. (cited Balogun, 2007: 120).

There is a lot of debate on the Yoruba concept of destiny, also called ori, in scholarship. While agreeing on some issues, these debates have however created other controversies. The points of agreement include the meaning, relevance and reality of ori among the Yoruba. One area of controversy concerns the interpretation of destiny i.e. whether the Yoruba belief in ori is fatalistic or not. A critical analysis of these ways of acquiring destiny at first glance implies some implicit contradiction. That is, while there is free choice in 'akunleyan' and 'akunlegba', there is no such freedom of choice in 'ayanmo.' Contributing to the issues in this debate is beyond our scope in this paper. However, our position necessitates a commentary, albeit a brief one, on the matter.

Scholars of Yoruba studies like E.O Oduwole (1996: 48), Taylor (1983: 52) and Idowu (1962) interpret the Yoruba concept of destiny as fatalist arguing that sacrifice (ebo) and struggle or hardwork to change it would be useless in the case of an individual who has been given/ or has chosen a bad destiny. For the purpose of this paper, we align ourselves with the interpretation offered by Abimbola (cited in Balogun, 2007 : 120 2014) and Balogun's (2007) soft deterministic view that destiny among the Yoruba can be altered. This view negates fatalistic interpretation.

Adopting Abimbola (cited in Balogun 2007) and Balogun (2007) enables our analysis of Bakare's deployment of destiny in the two play texts under study. We however re-interpret or extend Abimbola's 'ese' to mean attempts to challenge the perceived course of destiny in the life of an individual or of a people. Therefore, in Bakare's *Rogbodiyan* (1994) and *The Gods and the Scavengers* (2014), we intend to locate these attempts at challenging perceived destinies of individuals or groups of people.

Destiny as Aesthetic in *Rogbodiyan*
A rough translation of 'rogbodiyan' gives 'crisis' or 'disaster'. In *Rogbodiyan* (1994) Rasaki satirises a community, Koroju, which falls into crisis as a result of leaders who impose themselves on the people without going through the laid-down process of selection of leaders. All subsequent page references in parentheses only refer to this edition. The play is a parody of the events happening then in Nigeria during the regime of former military President Ibrahim Babangida and the endless transition to democratic governance. As Rasaki (2013) says in an interview with the Sun Newspapers:

> I wrote the play Rogbodiyan during my Post graduate days in Calabar. I slept and had a

dream. I saw the Military refusing to hand over power. I saw a people's struggle as lead by MKO and there was bloodshed. I woke up and dramatically presented what I saw. A year later political events in Nigeria took the exact dimension. What I wrote happened exactly as I had written it. Those who had read and watched the play started calling me prophet. ("I'll Remain a Restless Artist " Sunnewsonline).

Sadly, to any observer of events in Nigeria today, nothing seems to have changed as the process of choosing the crop of the nation's leadership continues to be mired in crisis and violence. No doubt this is responsible for the poor performance by government at all levels. Therefore, Rasaki's *Rogbodiyan* remains relevant twenty years after its publication. Consider the prophetic words of Narrator in the text:

Koroju, a land where merit is thrown to the winds, Koroju, an entity controlled by nonentities, Koroju abode of religious hypocrites and political sychophants, Koroju, where intelligence means nothing and the academically brilliant is a potential pauper. Koroju, a land where truth has been hindered and falsehood exalted. Ladies and gentlemen, a land of corruption where material and political wealth are worshipped and the false acquisition of them is encourage (sic) is bound to be stricken by Rogbodiyan. (p. 7).

For seven years Koroju has been searching unsuccessfully for a king since the last king, Adeakin, died. The play opens with Regent in a meeting with the people on efforts to crown a new king.

The first indication of an attempt to challenge the course of events happens not too long after the play begins. Note the defiance of Woman, one of the people of Koroju who insists on stating her objection of Regent's unilateral and undemocratic imposition of two candidates on the people. The character defiantly asks: "Aren't there established procedures for this sort of thimg? Are we people without tradition?" (p. 12) However, Regent is successful in bringing forth two candidates who are not from her lineage out of which the kingmakers will choose one as king.

It may be argued successfully that the undemocratic stance of Regent is responsible for the corrupt process which we see in MOVEMENT 4 and which produces Asagidigbi as king of Koroju. This is evident in the kingmakers' disregard of Diviner Fadele's admonition that: "…none of the two candidates may rule this land…Put any of them on the throne and the problem of the land continues." (p. 24).

Agogo is another character who attempts to challenge the king. The king is in seclusion but does not have the discipline to curb his sexual appetite. He wants carnal knowledge of Arugba Oge, the maiden who bears the sacrifice to the shrine on the day of the king's coronatoion. She also has been in seclusion but against Agoro's advice, Asagidigbi sleeps with her. The king thus commits an abomination and brings disaster onto himself and his people as they are stricken with different physical and mental disabilities. The king for instance goes blind, his aide is hunchbacked (p. 42) and even Fadele is not spared as he loses one leg (p. 43). This recalls Ola Rotimi's *The Gods Are Not to Blame* (1975).

It is in the solution provided by the gods that we see Bakare's deployment of the concept that a bad destiny can be challenged and course of the tragic events playing out in the text are halted. Ifa's instruction that someone wearing the crown be sent to bring water from River Awogbaarun as the sacrifice that should be done for the destiny currently playing out to be altered. To gain access to this river, the land of the Dead must be crossed.

It is in the reluctance of the king to go to the land of the Dead is again used by Bakare to present the second way in which destiny is altered. Adegbani offers to go in place of the king by wearing the costumes of the king in order to fool the inhabitants of the land of the Dead. The Yoruba believe that land of the Dead is a different world entirely and it is assumed that one who goes there will probably not return, since no one has died and ever returned to life. It therefore takes courage for anyone to decide to do this as this translates to suicide. Adegbani strives hard through and is rewarded in spite of the fact that his real motives are not hidden to the inhabitants of the land of the Dead:

Ara Orun: You bear this task not because of your people but because of yourself. But by helping your selfish self, you may as well be helping your people. Do not forget what you have promised us. We will allow you pass for your bravery, confidence and readiness to give unto the Dead what is theirs. (p. 51).

Before Adegbani returns however, the truth as to the person responsible for the disaster of deformities and the corruption in the process that produced the king are revealed. Woman, with the support of the people, insists on Fadele revealing the truth. In the middle of this, Adegbani returns and blackmails the people into making him king.

It may be argued that with this ending, Bakare provides no real solution to the problem of the land; more so as Adegbani is said to be no better than Asagidigbi and the kingmakers (p.56). Furthermore, one questions the type of leadership that will be provided by someone who is ready to break the calabash of spiritual water thereby condemning his people to perpetual deformity. However, if one applies the logic in our interpretation of the deployment of destiny as aesthetic, one realizes that Bakare asks the reader to look beyond this ending and rather look at the lesson implied by the challenge of Asagidigbi first by the people and later by Adegbani. If Asagidigbi can be thus successfully challenged, it follows that if Adegbani does not perform, he also can be removed.

Destiny as Aesthetic in *The Gods and The Scavengers*

In *The Gods and the Scavengers* (2006), Bakare aesthetically deploys destiny in a more obvious, though not simplistic, manner. All subsequent page references in parentheses only refer to this edition. The play text presents the same scenario of a group of leaders who is insensitive to the needs and wishes of the people it governs. Consequently, the people have become scavengers as evident in one of the songs:

We are the scavengers, we the main men. When these rogues eat their beans, we comb their bins. They cheat, we lift their shit... Though we sweat like God's beings, wefeed feed from bins. Our land is sold to gods that we made with our votes. So cheat and shit and beans in bins have become our lot because we sleep. (pp 1-2)

Bakare equates the leaders to gods to serve the purpose of his deployment of destiny as aesthetic. Scavenger 5 refers to the song that chronicles the sufferings of the people as being the result of bad leadership as "blasphemies" and shouts on the others:

Stop condemning those the gods have chosen as our leaders. Don't you know that it is the gods who put the kings on the throne and we must respect them no matter what? Don't rise up against the gods' own elect otherwise they will be angry and our situation will grow worse. (p. 4).

Here, Bakare reveals the belief of the people that bad leadership seems to be their destiny since the leaders are the representatives of the gods of the land and to challenge them will be to challenge the gods themselves.

At first meeting, Anago, the Chairman of the Council, seems to be an honest and caring leader as he rolls out people-oriented plans, prevents the market women from giving him produce from their farms as is the normal practice and attempts to halt the corruption in his officials. However, his adviser, Andy asks him: "...why do you make laws that you yourself cannot keep? No law is obeyed if the maker is a rogue. Those who come to equity must come with clean hands." (p. 28) While Andy resigns, his other officials plan to remove him from office for their own selfish purposes and this leads to chaos as the different nationalities that make up the nation are set against each other, killing and maiming one another.

Anago's attempt to give food to the people he had banished to the desert is not the sacrifice thatis needed to halt the bad destiny. This is because the people, led by Andy reject it. Rather, we interpret Andy's resignation as the sacrifice needed to be carried out for the destiny of the people to be changed. As Special Adviser, Andy is part of the corrupt government and as he confesses was also one of those who "hired a trickster whom we costumed to appear like a goddess…who spoke in guttural voice that Anago is the choice of the gods…because we belived our salvation rested in his hands." (p. 49) He consciously sacrifices a life of comfort, albeit ill-gotten, and strives to alter the destiny of the people. Just like we have in *Rogbodiyan,* it is not a task for just one man; the people must be involved as a collective.

Therefore, Bakare uses Andy to show that destiny can be altered and that this can only be done at the behest of the people themselves: "But people, we make our destiny. We are what we choose to be." Andy's story of a hiring a trickster to confer authenticity on Anago's government is not believed because the people wonder how the gods could allow that happen. We interpret this to mean that the gods allow Anago to be in government because that is the destiny of the people. Bakare graphically presents this through literary allusion by re-constructing on stage, a scene from the story of Rotimi's *The Gods Are Not to Blame* (1975). Besija's defiance of his destiny seems to have taught Odewale that his initial acceptance of his bad destiny was faulty. Consequently, Odewale rejects his destiny and blames the gods for his actions. As Odewale puts it: "The gods are to blame, not the son of man. I choose to live and reign and be happy. Hold the gods responsible for your ailments. I choose to be free and I'm free indeed." (p 54-5) The story of

Odewale has the required effect; people alter their destiny themselves and apprehend their leaders. While Andy urges the people: " I say damn the gods and choose to be free", Scavenger 1 summarises it thus: "If the god mean to force us into the destiny of Odewale we should say no and refuse to die."(p. 61).

Responding to a question on the reasons for writing *The Gods and the Scavengers,* Bakare says:
I have used *The Gods and The Scavengers* as a clarion call on all citizens to wage war against corruption. They should wage war against the gods in the Presidency, in the Senate and House of Reps, in the Governor's offices, in the Local Government circles, In the Banking sector, in the Educational sector, in the ministries and parastatals, on the pulpit and anywhere they are. We should wage bloody wars against these gods who have made the rest of us Scavengers. Ordinary Nigerians should stop killing one another because of differences in tribe and religion, we should come together and fight the common enemy. That is my message in the gods and scavengers. ("I'll Remaina Restless Artist" Sunnewsonline)

Summary
African writers do not write in a vacuum as they use their works to attempt to change their societies for the better. Thus Bakare employs destiny to teach his readers that their fate lies in their own hands. One way of ensuring that this reaches the people is by using aspects of their culture which they believe in. Bakare says that the arts "express that which has already been internalised" and stresses the importance of culture thus:

We need to align culture with the national ideology and philosophy. Today, apart from the current state of insecurity, almost every other social problem we have is because our culture has crashed in the first instance. What culture does is to mould humanity, to mould the human being in you. There is no cultured man that would carry a gun and kill his fellow human Being in the first instance – or throw bombs. ("I'll Remaina Restless Artist" Sunnewsonline).

Conclusion

The paper investigated Bakare's deployment of destiny in his *Rogbodiyan* and *The Gods and the Scavengers*. We were able to trace his concept of destiny to that of the Yoruba people from whom the playwright descended. We adopted the interpretation of the concept of destiny as alterable when certain conditions are carried out. These include the carrying out of sacrifices and the conscious effort through hardwork. Our analysis attempted to interpret the two texts along these principles. Our conclusion was that Bakare employs this concept of destiny to serve some of the main the purposes of the arts which include to educate, inform and transform.

Works Cited

Bakare, Ojo Rasaki. *Rogbodiyan.* Nigeria: Tamaza Publishing Company Limited, 1994. Print.

Bakare, Ojo Rasaki. *The Gods and the Scavengers.* Abuja: Roots Books and Journals Nigeria Limited, 2006. Print.

Bakare, Ojo Rasaki. "I'll Remain a Restless Artist" *Sunnewsonline.* Daily Sun, 5 Oct., 2013 Web. 8 September, 2014.

Balogun, Oladele. "The Concepts of Ori and Human Destiny in Traditional Yoruba Thought: A Soft-Deterministic Interpretation." *Nordic Journal of African Studies 16(1)* (2007): 116-130. Web. 8th September, 2014. *http://www.njas.helsinki.fi/pdffiles/vol16num1/balogun.pdf*

Hallen, B. and Sodipo, J.O. *Knowledge, Belief and Witchcraft.* London: Ethnographical, 1986. Print.

Idowu, Bolaji. *Olodumare: God in Yoruba Belief.* London: Longman, 1962. Print.

Morakinyo, O. "The Yoruba Ayanmo Myth and mental Health-Care in West Africa." *Journal of Culture and Ideas 1(1),* 1983: 68–79. Print.

Oduwole, E.O. "The Yoruba Concepts of 'Ori' and Human Destiny: A Fatalistic Interpretation." *Journal of Philosophy and Development* 2 (1&2), 1996: 40–52. Print.

Rotimi, Ola. *The Gods Are Not To Blame.* Ibadan: University Press Plc., 1975. Print.

Taylor, R. *Metaphysics.* New Jersey: Prentice Hall Inc., 1983. Print.

Systemic Problems and Self Preservation in Institutions of Higher Learning in Nigeria: Lessons from Ojo Bakare's *Once Upon a Tower*

By

Ekweariri, Chidiebere, Ph. D.

Introduction

Every artist is imbued with creative energy to explore cultural, political, religious and social problems ravaging man in the society. As a rebel "born of the spectacle of irrationality, confronted with an unjust and an incomprehensible condition" and action, he becomes the mouth piece of the people. For daring to talk or write about these problems, such insinuations as 'mad', 'drunk' 'insane' and 'revolutionary' as tags are bequeathed to artists" (Johnson 20). That notwithstanding, the primary essence of daring the uncertain and dicey, is not only to make these problems manifest but to also provide a platform where they are theatricalised thereby ridiculing and lampooning the perpetrators of such problems. As social crusaders whose works are "more imaginative than practical" according to Brustein (8), they bring their work to bear on the need to improve societal values, uphold justice and fair play, enthrone democratic principles and equity, canvassing for equal opportunity for all, and above all ensuring that man lives in a just society. Rasaki Ojo Bakare's plays encapsulates all these and as a third generation playwright with obvious disenchantment on the way things happen in Nigeria, he creates dramatic scenarios with them thereby providing an enabling environment for people to assess the dangers inherent in perpetrating evil. His plays include but not limited to *Drums of War* (1995), *This Land Must Sacrifice* (1991), *Rogbodiyan* (1995), *Adanma* (2003), *Once Upon A Tower* (2001), *The gods and the Scavengers* (2006) etc. However, the focus of this paper is on *Once Upon A Tower*. In other words, the paper is concerned with the task of assessing the impact of systemic problems and self preservation in institutions of higher learning in Nigeria using *Once Upon A Tower* as a case in point. Other issues that may help to explain the topic under investigation shall be discussed within the context of the study.

Higher Institutions as Ivory Towers

Human beings are imbued with one talent or the other and this talent is such that flourishes when properly nurtured. Apart from the peer group, family and environmental influences that may positively or negatively affect one's talent development, it is only in institutions of higher learning that such talents are harnessed for the benefit of the individual in particular and the society in general. Therefore, the establishment of universities, according to Nwamuo.

> exist to promote the life of the mind, to create and discover new knowledge through reflection and research. They also exist to transmit to each generation a high culture, to make men and women civilized, and to teach matters of intellectual importance and societal concern to their students.(30)

He went further to say that in Nigeria, universities exist to "seek the truth, teach the truth and preserve the truth. They are therefore committed to playing a dynamic and vital role in the significant task which faces the country of which they are part." (30) Regrettably, there appears to be a crack in the pursuit of these goals which has cast a doubt on the true meaning of the word, Ivory Tower. Inyang supports the above statement when he argues that:

> ..., instead of an exemplification of the above virtues, what the ivory tower in Nigeria today presents is a picture of negative academic mentality, brazen display of inane corruptibility, administrative inefficiency, neo-military power juggling, absolute hatred of descent in intellectual opinionation and other vices least expected in the body of Nigerian "men of letters (88)

Various opinions abound as to the precise meaning of the word, Ivory Tower but all tend to adduce and adumbrate the fact that

Ivory Tower as a term is synonymous with academic environment. Historically, the term originates in the Biblical Song of Solomon (7:4) and was later used as an epithet for Mary. From the 19th century it has been used to designate a world or atmosphere where intellectuals engage in pursuits that are disconnected from the practical concerns of everyday life. It usually carries pejorative connotations of a wilful disconnect from the everyday world; esoteric, over-specialized, or even useless research, and academic elitism. In American English usage it is also used as shorthand for academia or the university, particularly departments of the humanities
(http://en.wikipedia.org/wiki/ivory_Tower).

Furthermore, given the calibre of persons in the environment, Institutions of Higher Learning are regarded as Ivory Towers where the highest level of thinking and theorizing takes place. It is a place where everything seems to be perfect. Unfortunately, the title suggests otherwise as the system is now taken over by quarks, reactionary and disapproving minds and people with questionable characters. The tower as used in the play is figurative and indicates vestigiality, decay and deterioration, rottenness and disintegration.

Systemic Problems and Self Preservation in Higher Institutions: The Play Contextualized

The play tells the tale of self centeredness, internal rancour and ramblings amongst lecturers, corruption and the problems of half baked graduates in the Nigerian University system. It specifically talks about the "seeds of discord, unhealthy rivalry, outright wickedness, dangerous envy and satanic politicking which often manifest in blackmail, intellectual conspiracy, infuriating arrogance, name-calling, destructive gossips and subjective criticisms" (Bakare 3-4. *The Artiste-Intellectual...*) that pervade our tertiary institutions. This view is also shared by Euan and Joern when they argue thus:

> .... More and more universities and academias are working in a culture that is untenable and cracks in the ivory tower have already begun to

appear...the work environment is now characterized by high levels of competitiveness and witch hunting...most university employees would argue that their work place has shifted its focus from education outcomes to one increasingly driven by economics...like the oliver twist, this shift has seen an ever increasing focus on more more grant income, promotion and other personal aggrandisement. (http://theconversation.com/cracks-in-the-ivory-tower-is-academias-culture-sustenable-8294).

The play also reveals the processes of systematic crippling of the educational system, and its consequences on the new generation of Nigerians and at the same time, creates an uncomfortable ambience where the central action – the VC, Council members, Provost and Lecturers are made to confront and pay for their crimes. Pedro, an exceptionally brilliant part four medical student had his future jeopardised by the nature of knowledge inculcated in him by his lecturers, especially, Yemi, after the hand that was to mould him (Akitikori) was cut off. After Akitikori was framed and thrown out of the system, Yemi was assigned the responsibility of nurturing his talent. However, after mistakenly killing his girlfriend with an over dose of Anastasia, he went on retributive justice and not only humiliated those who made a mess of his life, but made them to pay the ultimate price which is death.

There are different manifestations of systemic problems that pervade all aspects of the university system. Academicians have become predators in an otherwise serene environment and devour each other especially those suspected to be audacious, fearless, outspoken and intelligent, and more importantly, those perceived to be genuine contenders in various academic positions for which some of them are already occupying. This can be gleaned from the assertion of Pedro when he says thus:

Pedro: .... you have the conscience to refer to me as an eminent gynaecologist when you murdered the 'eminence' even before I graduated from the university? When you three (*referring to Prof , kurumbete, Drs Yemi and Ugolo*) connived and aborted my eminence before it could be hatched? When you, you and you, because of fear, and threat to your professional monopoly resorted to dangerous politicking and scuttled my competence... you have made me look empty and fake in the eyes of the world (14).

The metaphor on the front cover of the play is symbolic in various ways and tends to justify the earlier assertion. Dogs, apart from being voracious animal also tend to be aggressive whenever bones are thrown at them. They also repel and attack other dogs, especially, the lesser ones whenever they are in sight, except the ones they are in good terms with. Bearing this and other nagging factors in mind, Mcquain Bruce is of the opinion that, "the proper metaphor for the university is no longer the "ivory tower", a shining refuge for daily life that promotes creative thought – if it ever was. A better metaphor is something down-and-dirty. (http://www.quando.net/?p=13627). In this context therefore, Prof Kurumbete could be likened to a dog because of his proclivity and propensity to attack and subdue the younger ones. In the play, he made every undesirable effort to remove Dr. Akitikori from the system. Though he succeeded albeit surreptitiously, but his sins finally caught up with him.

The decline in the quality of education today in our tertiary institutions is as a result of the highhandedness and attitudinal behaviour of some lecturers. Expertise and intelligence have been sacrificed at the altar of selfishness and personal goal. Mediocrity, pathological dullness and shambolic nothingness are now celebrated. The following conversations ensued between Prof. Kurumbete and Dr. Ugolo:

Ugolo: Ha... Prof... Yemi is too weak academically. He is not a material to replace Akitikori.
Kurumbete: Who cares? Is he going to teach your child? Look my dear; make no mistake about allowing your

> child to study in this country. If you don't have enough money to send your children to Europe for university education, then send them to Ghana. I know we only compensated Yemi for being a long serving junior staff of ours that was why we got him into the M.B.B.S programme. But if his becoming a lecturer will be the way out to deal with a boy who is a potential threat, then why not? And don't forget... people like Yemi will pose no threat to us. He knows he is weak so he will be gentle, submissive ask no questions and continue to be our boy (37-38).

This is exactly the state of things in most tertiary institutions in Nigeria. Regrettably, even when it is obvious that the system is suffering, the perpetrators of these heinous crimes against humanity seem not to be perturbed. Ugolo and Kurumbete speak thus:

Ugolo: True Prof. But who takes over from him? He is too good in his area. If we get him out, the system will suffer, our students will suffer.

Kurumbete: to hell with the system suffering. I hope you are not fooling yourself thinking that you can help the system? Can't you see nobody cares about the system? Everybody is a hanger-on just looking for how to survive via the system. Those who are in a position to make fat monetary rip offs from the system do so. It is a merchandise. The system is not only suffering already but bleeding. So what difference will it make? The system has seen nine hundred and ninety nine to hell with a millennium (36-37).

Because the system has been corrupted with bad elements whose stock in trade is to make money, the system itself keeps deteriorating. Vice Chancellors have left their primary function of managing the material and human resources of the institution to begin to look for contracts and how to perpetuate themselves in office. They have become politicians over night and end up becoming praise singers as well; refusing to criticize the powers that be when they misappropriate funds meant for the system. In **Movement Two**, after the convocation, the following discussions took place between the VC and his cohorts thus:

V.C: I must congratulate you your Royal Highness and you too chief and of course my humble self for yet another successful convocation ceremony.
Chief: Mr. Vice Chancellor, I have tremendous joy for the way everything went smoothly.
Emir: I too. In fact, by the time the president reads those beautifully worded speeches of ours in the newspapers, I am sure he will give us another term. He will believe we are doing the job well.
V.C: This calls for celebration.... (7)

Another system problem that is ravaging tertiary institutions in Nigeria is the predilection of senior academicians to sit on the promotion of the junior ones. This has so become rampant to the extent that most lecturers are known to have spent seven to eight years in a particular position even when they are overdue and have the requisite qualification for the next step. To some people, promotion has become politicised and if you don't have a godfather, it may take years before you are promoted. Even the issue of international conferences has become an exclusive reserve of the senior lecturers. This was the case of Akitikori in the play. Out of anger, bitterness and frustration, he poured out his heart to Kurumbete thus:

Akitikori: .... you even became a Professor after five papers... but some of us with twelve publications are still lecturers 1 for the fifth year. Yet you wouldn't allow us breathe with the noise of your genuisness. You threaten us younger colleagues and frustrate our promotions. Haba! Kurumbete!

> Kurumbete!! Kurumbete!!! Your arrogant
> selfishness strangulates us (24).

Because of this and so many other factors, people no longer have confidence in our tertiary education and perceive it as a place where un-academic activities take place. That is why the quest to study abroad amongst Nigerians is on the increase even with its attendant monetary implications. The incessant strike action and the attendant closure of tertiary institutions in Nigeria make learning a difficult exercise. The rush to meet up with the academic calendar when the system eventually resumes normal academic activities has its own implication on the quality of graduates produced. Research has it that more than 60% of Nigerian graduates are unemployable not necessarily because they are nonentities but partly because of the corruption and other debilitating self imposed problems in the system.

Presently, cliques have become the order of the day in our tertiary institutions. Nowadays, one finds the coming together of two or more to form allies. Lecturers who are not in this fraternity are termed enemies and marginalized, threatened and sanctioned at any slightest opportunity. Students are usually the worst hit because more often than not, they are used as escape goats in their quest for personal retribution. Merely seeing a student discussing or entering the office of the person in another camp is enough to fail him/her in ones course.

Desperation and cheap blackmail have also permeated the system. They have become cancer worms that have eaten deep into the fabrics of our tertiary institutions. Professors now date their female students (not that it is new) and use them as a pun to deal with their enemies in the department. Kurumbete succeeded in his quest to remove Akitikori from the department because he used his girlfriend to set him up. During lectures, half of the time is used discussing and casting aspersions on other lecturers. Most of them usually destroy the ladder(s) with which they climbed to their present position, all in an attempt to prevent people from catching up with them. All these are salient points raised in the play.

In a similar development, self preservation is another problem bedevilling the academic system in Nigeria. As a matter of fact, all the actions and inactions in the play centre on this ubiquitous problem. For instance, the Vice Chancellor's refusal to speak out and rather turn blind eye on certain wrongful acts in the system is because he wants to perpetuate himself in office thereby guaranteeing the largesse that come with the portfolio. The Senator's insistence that his daughter marry Chief as a third wife (even when he knows their age difference) is not only to strengthen his dubious relationship with him, but to also create an enabling environment where the booties they loot from the educational sector will find its way back to his family through his daughter. This is captured by Khadijat thus:

Khadijat: you lie Dad, you lie.... i know your real agenda... my Dad here is the chairman House Committee on education at the senate. He uses his position and his party affinity with the minister to corner ninety percent of the contract awards on education matters.... so he uses a dummy called Chief Ogbuefi Chukwuma as a front. And they share the proceeds fifty-fifty. My father feels cheated... and wants me to marry Ogbuefi as a third wife so that i will function as a conduit pipe through which money will be siphoned from Ogbuefi's pockets into his pocket.... (52)

In the play, Kurumbete epitomises this problem. What is striking about him is not only his arrogance and over bloated pride, but also his penchant for self preservation. He wants to be the last man standing and abhors any atom of competition. This he is willing to defend even if it means using any devilish means. Perhaps, the conversations between him and Ugolo will help to throw more light on this:

Kurumbete: Sit down. How is the troublemaker in your department?

Ugolo: You mean Akitikori?

Kurumbete: Who else?

Ugolo: Em... Prof. between you and me, he is not a troublemaker. Just that he is a downright non-conformist. He is too bold and vocal, can die for justice and never wants to be cowed. But the young man knows his job.

Kurumbete: You are only confirming the fact that he is dangerous. When a bold, justice-loving, non conformist also has the advantage of intelligence and professional relevance, then he is too dangerous. Look, that boy is dangerous to my future. He is in my area of specialization, well positioned to break my monopoly. He is also dangerous to your future. Brilliant and active, he is a threat to your long stay as the head of Department. We have to get him out of the system fast (36)

Even if it impinges on the academic development of students, he doesn't give a hoot about it. In a similar discussion, the following argument ensued.

Ugolo: Remember the extra-ordinary brilliant part 4 student, Omowaye, Pedro – whose genius we hope Akitikori will help to specially develop. Yemi will definitely not be able to offer the kind of stuff a brain like Omowaye needs to blossom.

Kurumbete: there you go again. Who tells you I even support the idea of a well enriched special training programme for Omowaye Pedro? That wizard? Even without any special training, he is already competing with part six students. People like him should be intellectually disempowered if we must own the future. And don't call me evil, I see nothing evil in what I am saying. Self preservation, they say, is the first human instinct (38).

Ironically, academic institutions have a long history of turning up their noses at things like selling products, making profits and building personal platforms (http://finance.yahoo.com/news/academic-entrepreneur-save-ivory-tower-230000296.html:ylt=) and the play under study is a typical example of how the system has misplaced its priority. More often than not, when opportunities are giving the Head of Department to employ new hands, he ends up recruiting junior staff that are likely to be under his perpetual control. Akin to this is the current trend of having both parents and either daughter or son lecture in one institution. Nothing may be said to be wrong in it especially if they are qualified, but experience has shown that they leave much to be desired and are all geared towards self preservation.

Lessons Drawn
The play *Once Upon A Tower* has a lot of lessons to be drawn from it, especially in view of the catastrophe that befell the offenders at the end of the play. In the foreword to the play, Aderemi Bamikunle argues that:
> the play ends in death but it is not a tragedy. The dead characters deserve what they have got and society can breathe a little better. Without being sentimental, the play has meted punishment to whom it is due.

The perpetrators of the act thought they were having a filled day without a modicum of idea that disaster awaits at the end. Fate played a part on those who escaped, possibly to give them another chance to change for good and be the voice of the voiceless because according to Soyinka, the man died who in the face of tyranny and oppression refuse to say or do anything. Furthermore, the emotional trauma of having escaped death by whiskers is enough to last them for a life time.

The society is bad today partly because of the calibre of people churned out as graduates. The story of Pedro and Khadijat is only but one of numerous stories that abound in Nigeria. That is why when it comes to first class Medicare and proper education, Nigerians pitch their tent and resort to going over sea. Unfortunately, those who study abroad will still come back home to meet a beleaguered society inundated with one problem or the other. Since they cannot work in isolation, they will still need to work with the available ones on ground. Therefore, a corrupt university system breeds a corrupt society and its cataclysmic effect, as we have already seen in the play, is something we are not ready to go through.

There are also lessons to be drawn from the activities of the Senator and his cohorts. He least imagined that his unscrupulous antics of siphoning the money meant for the development of the educational sector through a third party is going to have a devastating telling effect on his daughter, and by extension, his family. Perhaps, if the money had been put into proper use and the equipment and other teaching paraphernalia procured, the system would have been better for it and what befell the daughter may have been avoided. Although Pedro knew the legal implications of his action(s), it was a risk he was willing to take. When the chips were down, he freely surrendered, though with a sense of fulfilment of having dealt with those who aborted his 'eminence' as he echoed on page 4.

There is always a payback time no matter how long it takes. Incidences in the play should be a very big lesson to all concerned especially, academicians. He, who seeks justice, must go with justice. Akitikori was unjustly dismissed from the system for no fault of his and those who thought they won ended up being the loser. He, indeed, had the final laugh.

Conclusion
Once Upon A Tower, provides first class information on the rot and decay in the university system and written by a great academician who may have experienced this in his budding

artistic/academic career. The quantum of knowledge in the academia is such that no one person should be seen as an island, and all academicians, irrespective of rank and affiliation is a stake holder in the task of building the system. The spirit of live and lets live should be imbued in us. Therefore, let each become what he/her was created, capable of being. Both exceptional, semi exceptional and dull students should be encouraged and given equal opportunity to learn in a conducive environment devoid of rancour and bitterness. According to Jane Adam as quoted by Gamut, "one generation after another has depended on its young" (166) and if we must depend on our generation, we must do well to teach them properly. Morgan Holmes and Bundsy's view as quoted by Ihentuge (63) is quite instructive here. They say that:

> When an atomic missile hits a target and explodes, it makes a tremendous difference in all the landscape thereabouts. But an atomic missile is not the only force whose power may make a big difference. When a complete and generous programme of education hits a nation and takes holds, it also makes a tremendous impact in all the area that it touches. Education works in a quicker way than a bomb, but its power reaches further and goes deeper. (63)

The reverse is the case when a wrong education is given to a child. I had earlier argued in another paper that if "quality is compromised and sacrificed at the altar of greed and selfishness, the result is usually catastrophic on both parties" (Ekweariri, 5) as we have already seen from the play.

Therefore, all hands must be on deck to salvage the academic system from this near comatose situation otherwise we may end up experiencing worst things than the ones that happened in the play in the near future. Some have argued that academics are strongly positioned to be the thought leaders of the 21st century, to help cure cancer, identify new energy sources and enhance the human experience with smaller, faster and better technology but couldn't do so because of unnecessary bickering and lack of focus. We need to prove these doubters wrong by being committed in our teaching and shunning negative tendencies that will portray us in bad light.

Works Cited

Bamikunle, Aderemi. "Foreword" Once Upon A Tower. Uyo: Afahaide Publishing Company, 2000.

Bakare, O. Rasaki. The Artiste-Intellectual: Sonny Oti on Stage. Ed. Ibadan: Jofel Books, 2004. Pp.1-10.

Once Upon A Tower. Uyo: Afahaide Publishing Company, 2000.

Bruce, MCquain. Academia: Ivory Tower or "The New plantation?" (http://www.quando.net/?p=13627) Accessed 19th July, 2014.

Brustein, Robert. The Theatre of Revolt: Studies in Modern Drama from Ibsen to Genet. Chicago: Ivan R. Dee Publisher, 1991

Can the Academic Entrepreneur Save the Ivory Tower? (http://finance.yahoo.com/news/academic-entrepreneur-save-ivory-tower-230000296.html) Accessed 18th June, 2014.

Ekweariri, Chidiebere. "Quality Assurance and the Business of Teaching Creative Arts in Nigeria" paper presented at the 2013 SONTA Conference. (print).

Euan, Ritchie and Joern, Fischer. Cracks in the Ivory Tower: Is Academia's Culture Sustainable? http://theconversation.com/cracks-in-the-ivory-tower-is-academias-culture-sustenable-8294.html Accessed 19th July, 2014

Gamut, Veronic. "Peace Education and peer Mediation" Introduction to Peace and conflict Resolution in West Africa. Ed. Shedrack Gaya Best. Ibadan: Spectrum Books Limited, 2006. Pp. 164-183.

http://en.wikipedia.org/wiki/ivory_Tower

Ihentuge, Chisimdi. "Beyond Passing Examinations: A Critique of the Choice of Drama texts for Secondary School Syllabus in Nigeria" IMSU Theatre Journal. Vol. 2, No. 1. 2012. Pp.48-65

Inyang, Ofonime. "Performing the Identity of the Academia: A critical Analyses of the Production of Ojo Rasaki Bakare's Once Upon A Tower" ABALABALA. No. 2. 2003. Pp. 82-93.

Effiong, Johnson. "The Tale of the Hawk and the Chicken: Leadership Paintings on the Canvas of Literature" THE PARNASSUS. Vol. 4. 2008. Pp. 19- 44.

Nwamuo, Chris. The Faces of Nigerian Theatre. Calabar: Centaur Publishers, 1990.

Soyinka, Wole. The Man Died. Ibadan: Spectrum Books Limited, 1972.

Bakare On the Decadence In The Ivory Tower: A Commentary on Bakare, Ojo Rasaki's *Once Upon A Tower*

By
Ubong, S. Nda, Ph. D.

Introduction

Bakare, Ojo Rasaki's *Once Upon A Tower* bemoans the poor situation in Nigerian universities where hero worshipping, self-aggrandizement, high level of corruption and nepotism have replaced objectivity, commitment to teaching and learning. These virtues have been replaced by favouritism and sorting, leading to the churning out of some graduates who are not worthy in character and learning to be products of universities in Nigeria.

One of the issues that the play readily brings to mind is on the standard of education in the country. This is a highly debatable topic. Once in a while, one comes across some highly-endowed people who are brilliant products of the Nigerian educational system and one quickly questions the talk about the falling standard of education. Again, one knows of some graduates of Nigerian education that are doing exceptionally well in foreign countries. But one also comes across graduands of the system that makes one ashamed of having anything to do with Nigerian education. These are poor copies of the educational system that tend to swallow-up the earlier-mentioned brilliance exhibited by products of the same system. Bakare is not focally concentrative on the debate of whether the standard has fallen or not. He is rather presenting a vista of truth: that the system is falling and might degenerate into one where a medical doctor might not be able to hold his own in a committee of his fellow professionals. What with a situation where some libraries may not know of new books and journals for some two years. What kind of students could be graduated out of a system where the laboratories have old bunsen burners that have never lighted, and crucibles that have never held metals. These are happening in the midst of huge budgetary allocations to education, the impact of which do not trickle down to the end-users; the teachers/lecturers and the student. Bakare, a widely travelled academic, fittingly endeavoured to capture the situation where our graduates could become monks without hoods and false wearers of the academic gowns they don on graduation.

Synopsis of The Play

The play is set in a typical university in Nigeria. In spite of the huge budgetary allocation for the education sector, the Minister of Education and the Chairman, Senate Committee on Education have sat on it, only allowing small particles of the allocation to trickle down to the university system, where it is then scrambled for by the Chairman of the Governing Council and Vice Chancellor/Chief Executive. Moreover, one of the professors, in a Faculty of Medicine, Kurumbete, sees his position as a birthright and refuses to recruit anyone he suspects will not be his puppet while on the job. Kurumbete ensures that no lecturer of independent mind is allowed to be employed in the Faculty of Medicine. He even goes on to employ a former Laboratory Assistant in the Faculty, who went through a seamless medical training, to become a lecturing staff so as to increase his pool of yes-men. He finds one of his lecturers, Dr. Akitikori a tough nut to crack. Akitikori is able to see through his antics and is not ready to be part of sycophantic antics of others, so he earns a bitter hatred from the 'only-cock-to-crow' professor and eventually gets dismissed through a set up.

Pedro, a young medical student, graduates as a medical doctor filled with the 'faux-pax' of medical practice stuffed in his head. Following a successful elopement with the daughter of the Senate Committee Chairman for education, who would have wished the daughter to marry a business partner to accentuate their business tie, Pedro camps with his wife in the house of a friend. She gets pregnant and he successfully cajoles her into an abortion, giving her more pills than she needed and this leads to her death. Pedro is imprisoned and while in prison he contrives a 'sweet revenge'. He holds the Vice-Chancellor, Pro-Chancellor, Professor Kurumbete, the lecturer who taught him the wrong dosage, hostage, after a convocation ceremony, and eventually exacts his pound of flesh by killing some of them. With them too is his corrupt father-in-law, the Senate committee chairman on education, and he is about dealing with them when the police interrupts the killing spree.

Salient Societal Facts In The Play

The situation in the Nigerian institutions of higher learning gives room for great concern. *Tell Magazine* of January 20, 2014 reports of

> decaying infrastructure, inadequate facilities, moribund laboratories and obsolete equipment, unsightly toilets and hostels generally poor learning environment (45).

The magazine was conducting an x-ray into the tertiary education system that led to the strike by Academic Staff Union of Universities (ASUU) strike in 2013. It came away with the impression that the state of the universities was appalling

> … it is clear that no single Nigerian public university, whether state or federal is free from the rot or the other whether with respect to lecture halls or hostels, laboratory and equipment, roads, pipe borne water or even academic manpower (52).

The graduates of that type of system could hardly become strong. Thus, the future of young persons is being dastardly bastardised because those who are put in charge of the system are hurting it, instead of aiding its growth. Such a graduate

> … apart from being a product funding is also a reflection of the level of corruption, social and intellectual decay within and outside the system (52).

Let us now attempt a sectoral dissection of the problem associated with the academia in Nigeria as treated in Bakare's *Once Upon A Tower*.

Corruption

Corruption is one of the endemic problems of the Nigeria's socio-political and economic system. Amnesty International, the global body that monitors the international level of corruption in various countries, have for some years now, rated Nigeria very high in the corruption index. Various attempts have been made by pro-governmental forces to play down on the issue, but corruption gets moving from mere crawling in the sixties, to walking majestically in the streets of the country in the 1900s and 2000s. That the situation has permeated almost every facet of societal life is no exaggeration. The university system, popularly known as ivory tower, has been seriously plagued as revealed in the play. Omowale Pedro laughs at the V.C.'s feeble protest that Pedro was disturbing honourable men 'and treating well-meaning citizens like commoners'. (p.10). To this Pedro laughs, and retorts in response:

> Oh! You ... You people, honourables? Well-meaning citizens? You rogues and dangerous schemers?...

Khadijat, Pedro's lover unveils her father thus:

> My Dad here is the Chairman House Committee on education at the Senate. He uses his position to corner ninety per of the contract awards on education matters. But because of his position as Senator he can not operate as a contractor openly. So he uses a dummy called Chief Ogbuefi Chukwuma as a front. And they share the proceeds fifty-fifty (52).

She goes on to reveal the nefarious scheme of her father, decked in his attempt to marry her over to his friend, Chief Ogbuefi Chukwuma.
> My father feels cheated that a mere front is collecting as much as fifty percent, but could not dislodge Ogbuefi for political and security reasons. That is why he wants me to marry Ogbuefi so that part of the fifty percent Ogbuefi collects will still recycle into my father's

pocket. He wants me to marry Ogbuefi as a third wife so that I will function as the conduct pipe through which money will siphoned from Ogbuefi's pockets into his pocket... (p.52)

Tin-Godism

One of the ills of the ivory tower in Nigeria, is that some of those that have made it to the top, end up seeing themselves as a some kind of tin-gods, some kind of sectoral totems upon which life in the institution revolves. Pedro refers to it as 'professional monopoly' (14). Such successful academics see their departments as fiefdoms which must be protected from others. Anyone they know will be so self-opinionated to stop worshipping them, are not good enough for the academic system. Professor Kurumbete insists:

> ... Remember, that as the first gynaecology scholar and consultant this country produced I founded that department when I came back from Europe after my studies. And remember too, that before I retired and came back on contract appointment, I had functioned as the Head of that department for many years. (p.20)

He harbours no patience for independent opinions. Hear him more:

> Otherwise I will make you cocky and opinionated fools, pay for your stupidity... (20)

As an only 'cock to crow', he ensures that no one else rises to the rank of professor so as not to rub shoulders with him. Any attempt to argue with him on any issue only tries to look down on him. To any such persons, he reminds of his pedigree:

> You talk to me like that?...You mean you talk like that to Professor Kurumbete Ijakado, first graduate of Gynecology in Nigeria, Fellow, World Institute of Gynecology, three times recipient of the Willie's Award, Former visiting Professor to Oxford and Birmingham, a biographer of who is who in world Gynecology,

the first African to be appointed life Provost of a Medical College, even on a contract retirement (22).

He describes himself as 'Primus Interpares' claiming that:

> Even in Europe, they know that I am an institution, and that everything about me is institutionally instituted.
> ... See what the eye of a renowned scholar is seeing in common Africa (22).

All these are emissions that come as responses to Dr. Akitikori's remark challenging the holding of opinions contrary to his own.

> ... And you Prof... what is your qualms with people who are opinionated in the department? Is it a crime to hold opinions? This is a university. It is meant for people who have opinions (21).

It is this hatred for other people's opinions that has made Professor Kurubete to only recruit people who will not argue with him on any issue. He makes Yemi a lecturer even when he knows Yemi is academically weak to be a lecturer.

Akitikori says to the tin-god, Kurumbete:
> You even became a Professor after publishing five papers... but some of us with twelve publications are still lecturers I for the fifth year...you threaten us younger colleagues and frustrate our promotions. Haba! Kurumbete! Kurumbete!! Kurumbete!!! Your arrogant selfishness strangulates us (24).

It is natural that such 'one and only' geniuses look for places where they would be lone voices so that their places in such professional areas would be secured. Akitikori asks Kurumbete:

> Why don't you put your so-called genius on sale in the world out there and stop running back to your

colony here to breathe down the neck of mere babies... (25).

It is not surprising that Kurumbete grants approval for the ploy by the Head of Gynecology Department, Dr. Ugolo, to set a trap for the principled Akitikori. Dr. Ugolo is a weak-minded lecturer who may have climbed to his position as Head of Department through the process of licking the boots of persons like Kurumbete. He therefore does not like people like Akitikori, with their penchant for the observance of human right provisions like freedom of expression and freedom to hold opinions.

Wherever students freely gossip lecturers to fellow lecturers, then there is no doubt that societal norms are breaking down. The involvement of students in such escapades could only be promoted by academics who are desirous of building academic empires around themselves. And the admission process gets compromised as such tin-gods like Kurumbete would be busy recruiting students who would sustain the prevalent state of sycophancy. Akitikori says this of Yemi's admission:
> Inspite of his pathological dullness, and despite scoring a shameful 200 in JAMB, Professor Kurumbete eased his admission. Now that he is hearing graduation. Yemi is ambitious (31)

Victimisation

The issue of victimisation is another issue that acts seriously against the smooth flow of academic progress in our institutions of higher learning. Some lecturers have vowed against their academic progress of some of their students because of some perceived wrongs. Some, who are now in the habit of making sexual demands on students, use their courses as blackmail weapons. Inspite of the system's war against such attitude, there is no doubt that it still exists. That is why Akitikori says to Remi
> ... I have always told you it is not my ambition to stop you from becoming a Medical Doctor ... (34).

Thank God for lecturers like Akitikori but one dares

to say that it is all lecturers that look at their students in the face and say so (34).

Lack of Love for The System

Some practitioners in the educational system lack genuine love for the process of impartation of knowledge. They do not care for the type of examples they present to the young ones they are supposed to mentor to maturity. That is why some of them do not attend classes regularly and behave like Pharaohs when students fail to pass assignments, even by ten minutes. They fail in their duties of teaching with flimsy excuses and do not care if the students understand their courses or not. It is a shame when a high ranking academic like Kurumbete replies thus when Dr. Ugolo reports that getting Akitikori out of the system will affect the students adversely:

Ugolo: … If we get him out, the system will suffer, our students will suffer.

Kurumbete: To hell with the system suffering. I hope you are not fooling yourself thinking that you can help the system? Can't you see nobody cares about the system? Everybody is hanger-on just looking for how to survive via the system. Those who are in a position to make fat monetary rip-offs from the system do so. It is merchandise. The system is not only suffering already but bleeding… (37).

One would have thought that an academic of Kurumbete's standing would be interested in the progress and upliftment of the system. There is no wonder therefore where he interest lies when he desires the ousting of a brilliant lecturer like Akitikori and suggests his replacement with someone he adjudges to be very weak.

Crave for Another Term in the Nigerian Political Space
The crave for another term is another serious problem of the Nigerian political position. Almost every official would want to course the elongation of their tenures in office even in spite of the shoddy performances put up by them. And this has seriously permeated the academia. It is in a bid to curtail this that some tenures has been pegged within a number of years. If not for these provisions, it would not have been out of place to hear of Presidents for life, (like it is still happening in some Africa countries) Governors for life, Vice-Chancellors for life and so on. Various attempts are made for the concretisation of the bid for sit-tighting which could be seen in various spheres of rational life. The Chancellor of Marinpinto University, Nigerian, says to the V.C:

> Infant by the time the President reads those beautifully worded speeches of ours in the newspapers, I am sure he will give us another term. He will believe we are doing the job well (7).

There is no doubt such presidents must also be nonentities for not seeing through the sycophantic antics of their appointees.

Extreme Love for Material Wealth
It is only a society that has lost a sense of reasoning that allows an unbridled crave for material wealth to thrive and could use it as a judgment for people's worth. It sounds ridiculous, but it is a hard fact that some parents are looking for suitors like Ogbuefi for their daughters. These are ploys either to get their families out of the throes of poverty or attempts to stay within illegitimately – found status of the rich. Khadijat is a medical doctor but the father, a Senate Committee Chairman in charge of education, does not hesitate wanting her to marry an illiterate money-bag like Ogbuefi, who does not know what an electorate means. To him everything revolves around money.

> I will fire the entire village and caterpillar all the roads. I will also water all the nook and cranny of the village... hook come into my heart of heart and chop my money with me (56).

Unfortunately Khadijat refuses to be impressed and calls him a 'flat-bellied toad'. It is rather sad that many parents are still wishing their daughters were in such marriages so as to brighten the family's financial fortunes.

General Observation

One cannot fail to observe the general use of songs in the play. Bakare had been brought up in the Ogunde Concert Party tradition where songs are integrated into the scheme of plays to accentuate the message. Song is one of the elements prescribed by Aristotle as a needed component of a playscript. Although it is still debated till today what the ancient philosopher meant by it - was it a rendition of relevant songs or mere rhythmised poetry of the lines in the diction. This playwright has effectively, used songs in the play. For instance, the prologue has the following:

Solo: once up on a tower
        the Ivory upon the marble
        on the citadel of learning
        a place of civilization

Chorus: small by small the tower
        on the store ee little by little
        the tower on the wood…

        now but now the tower
        in the dust eee now but
        now the tower in the mud… (1-2)

The play also employs simple English, making is possible for an average literate person to understand its direction and message. Notable playwrights like Ola Rotimi has recommended the employment of 'simple words but potent with that poetically biblical effect so reminiscent of folk speech. It makes the easy comprehension too … helpful in bringing the work closer to a people with moderate literary background'. (51) And another strong practitioner in the Nigerian playwrighting scene, Ahmed Yerima warns that ' the …playwright must be aware of the fact that the clarity of the language contributes to how well the audience understands his play(s)' (78).

Conclusion
Once Upon A Tower is a product of an experienced academic whose love for the profession could be seen in his blowing the whistle lest it deteriorates more than it has already done. It is a warning by a patriot that the situation in the academics, if allowed to fester more and more, is capable of creating graduates who are only churned out to ruin themselves and the society.

Works Cited

Akaeze, Tony. 'The Ivory Towers of Rot' in *Tell Magazine* of January 20, 2014. p.52.

Bakare, Ojo Rasaki. *Once Upon A Tower*. Uyo: Afahaide Publishing Company, 2000.

Gown, Ama Doki; Ako, Ali Sule. 'The Theatre and the Rebranding Crusade in Nigeria' In: Nigerian Theatre Journal. A Journal of the Society of Nigerian Theatre vol.10 No.1 of 2010 p.45

Rotimi, Ola "Interview with Bernith Lindfors" In: *Playwriting and Directing in Nigeria*. Efiok Bassey Uwatt. London: Etherton, M and Mayer, 1981. p 51.

Tell Magazine of January 6, 2014. Published by Tell Communications Limited, Kilometre 22, Lagos – Ibadan Expressway, Ojodu, Lagos.

Yerima, Ahmed *Basic Techniques in Playwriting* Ibadan: Kraft Books, 2003.

Bakare, Ojo Rasaki's *Drums Of War* and the Hermeneutics Of Women Emancipation in Mark 7: 23 -34

By
Ojo, Olanrewaju Paul Ph. D.

Introduction
Appropriating the title of Bakare's play *Drums of War* merely serves as a metaphor on the need for women to rise above the shackles of bias and oppression. In a postmodern age of information overload, the mass media is awash with images of war occasioned by self-serving politicians, religious bigots and shylocks of global capitalism. Of special interest in this preliminary prognosis is the portrayal of women by men under the cultural garb as mere consequences of existence and also as appendage. The reversal of which has become a war in its own. Bakare's woman in the *Drums of War* is involved in a war that is multidimensional in nature and content, among which is that of self-worth, power role and dignity in the Nigerian society. This war is executed through different fronts and acronyms such as: women's emancipation, women liberation, gender equality, feminism etc. This warfare has attracted many interpreters and interests from different fields such as the sociological, the political, the economic, the legal, and the theological fields. This paper adopts the theological dimension in developing a recipe for the emancipation of women in Africa. It is an intercultural hermeneutic (Manus 2003) method that employs the interface between the African traditional, religio-cultural background with the scriptures in its interpretative scheme to arrive at a theological position that is both enriched with the traditional, cultural setting, and also biblical ethos.

It is of note that, contrary to the denial of the voice, wisdom and personality of women in Bakare's Drum of War, the citizens of every nation contribute fully to its development. A nation that uses its full workforce or available manpower will rise above all other nations (Mnenea, 201: 479) thus incurring less waste and more development. African nations have deprived themselves of this advantage when it frustrates its women, and that is why the tag 'undeveloped' has been levied upon them. The women are even more promising in their contribution to nation building, as in the past when women were the most utilized potentials of all nations. At the moment, the story is different as the overriding focus on women by many women writers entails a new definition of women's role and position. Awareness is being created in them towards being participants in all works of life rather than staying in the kitchen and bearing children.

Some common factors which have inhibited this societal awareness are either cultural, or societal, some religious and at times just downright selfishness in the men's part to maintain the status quo (Aina, 1995:2). Politics has served as an inhibiting factor also. In this 21st century, there are deliberate efforts by women emancipation advocates to sensitize the women to become more holistically conscious.

Given the fact that every society has a bedrock of ideas and norms upon which it is built, these shared values and beliefs are referred to as the people's culture. They manifest themselves in both material and non-material components, bringing about changes.

It is in the face of these changes that intercultural hermeneutics and quest for women's emancipation has cropped up. This is important since most of the roles defined for women are gender based and favour men against women. Infact, Ekong (1997:20) believes the male nature has been used to connote virility, force, aggression, efficacy, intelligence and superiority, whereas, the female nature has been used to symbolize weakness, dependence, passivity, docility, ineffectuality, ignorance and inferiority. This means that women's biological identity is used to determine their destiny. In limiting the women's physical and mental capability, and marginalizing them from social polity, most cultures expect men to develop aggressive impulse and females to thwart theirs or turn them inward. This makes male dominance perhaps the most pervasive culture in human nature, as this is evident in the military, technology, finance, science, industries and political offices (Manus 2003). The most indelible source for this dominance is religion. The basis for this work examines the socio-religious garb underlining the neglect and rejection of the woman in the *Drums of War* viz-a viz Mark 7:23-34 a Christian religious text in order to uncover and enunciate appropriate steps towards the emancipation of women in Nigerian society.

There is no doubt that in the heart and mind of an objective and critical reader of Bakare's *Drums of War*, questions such as these arise: why is there a seemingly less important role given to the woman generally? and why traditional, socio-religious and cultural reasons have been advanced for the position of women in the society? To profer some answers to this questions, a biblical hermeneutics model that seeks to interprete issues within a given social context will be employed. We shall begin by giving a brief insight into Bakare's *Drums of War*.

From the beginning, it is women who have gathered to sing, and to denounce the war between Abakpa and Ibuji communities. Unfortunately these harbinger of peace- the women- were taunted and dismissed. No one gave a listening ear to their reasons. Their existence in this circumstance was not valued. They were scorned as being weak; because war was a show of strength.

The most hideous denouncement of their value and existence was at the palace. The overall symbol of the women is Otubu, the Queen, *(Olori)* who on a normal note, is a person that should have the ears of the king, who is the symbol of authority. The masculinity of war was displayed by the king who in all vehemence, shouted at the queen, "woman be silent". This line defines the power, role, authority and value as enshrined in the tradition of the land which also has the backing of the gods whose vicegerent is the king. It was a scene that epitomized the supposed actual identity of the woman in governance, decision making and society at large. The authority of the king is derived from the culture and tradition of the land.

This concept of kingship, rulership, warfare, and the setting of the plots of Bakare's *Drums of War*, has an African and most especially, the Yoruba socio-cultural milieu as its background. It is this background that will serve as the interpretative material or socio-cultural context within which the Quest for women's emancipation will be discussed. The Biblical context will serve as the entry point and hermeneutical tool in positing a recipe for the contemporary women's quest for emancipation and possible attainment in Nigerian context.

The ensuing task amongst many others, is to highlight the status of women in Africa especially among the Yoruba viz-a-vis their involvement in the society, and how that contributes to development or under development. In doing this, we shall look at women from this cultural perspective in order to gain an understanding of their socio-political realities with a view to determining their developmental potentialities.

In Bakare's plays, the Queen is quite vocal in approaching a matter which was considered the perogative of men.

Kings wife: Your Highness, could I make bold to advice you over this issue, listen to your people, let this war stop and …..
King: Quiet woman! Who talks and you wag your tongue? How dare you show such boldness in our presence? Retire to your room at once. (the wife leaves quietly…there is tension in the air… (Chiefs of our land…(Bakare, 1994:71)
There is no gain saying the fact that this is a drama that has won the admiration of many, especially the depiction of the characters; the men, the warlords, the young men and the women. The futility of war and the necessity for peaceful coexistence of all human is the thrust of this piece.

She urges for caution from her husband who had the power of life and death. As we shall try to highlight, she shares marked similarities in terms of orientation, focus and motivation as the syrophoenician woman. They are both driven by the desire to attain goals which they consider genuine and altruistic. Although both characters inhabit different climes and epoch, they exhibit the knowing nuances of our hermeneutics critical to paradigm which seeks to challenge the norm created and fostered by male dominated world to chart a more inclusive one where women are given a presence and a voice.

Re-reading Mark 7: 23 - 34, The Syrophoenician Woman and Her Quest for the Deliverance of Her Daughter
A Highlight on Woman in the Bible

Women have had to struggle harder than men do for everything they have got. And what women have gotten, they usually got well after men had had it (Harris, 3). There still remains a multitude of things available to men which are as yet unavailable to women. Even where there are declarations of availability or supposedly equal opportunity, reality often reveals marked unavailability and vast inequalities based on a supposed qualitative gender difference. In speaking of 'man', the Bible speaks of male and female [Gen 1 1:27}. As male and female together, they were given authority to 'subdue' the earth and to 'rule' all other living creatures. Male and female together reflect God's image, not the male without the female, or vice versa. God made them different, just as He made male and female different in other species of His creatures. The distinction between men and women is an inbuilt characteristic of humankind as God created it (Prime, 25). Equal but different is the proper understanding of the male and female created in the image of God.

It is a well-known fact that women in Judeo-Christian societies have been, since the beginning of recorded history up to the very recent past, second-class citizens. This is not unique to Judeo-Christian societies as there are other societies where women have fewer rights, freedoms and options; and within Judeo-Christian societies things used to be a great deal more unfavourable for women than they are now (:2) Though, women in some churches today cannot exercise the functions of leadership involved in the work of a priest, Akintunde Dorcas observes that women are not passive in church activities; rather they contribute to the renewal of the church combining experiences with commitments to new ecclesial structures in Christendom (:17). In most of the indigenous churches in Nigeria, mainly Pentecostals, women as well as men can be appointed by the church to occupy the position of pastor, teacher, apostle or any other leadership position in the church. However, in some other churches the pastoral care of women and children is the main responsibility of women in the church. However, they are not permitted to use their spiritual gifts and talents to benefit the church as a whole or the society at large. Like the Syrophoenician woman, they must not give in when faced with rejection or intimidation. We shall reference the case of this woman to illustrate our thesis,

> "And from there he arose and went away to the region of Tyre and Sidon. And he entered a house, and would not have any one know it; yet he could not be hid. But immediately a woman, whose little daughter was possessed by an unclean spirit, heard of him, and came and fell down at his feet. Now the woman was a Greek, a Syrophoenician by birth. And she begged him to cast the demon out of her daughter. And he said to her, "Let the children first be fed, for it is not right to take the children's bread and throw it to the dogs." But she answered him, Yes, Lord; yet even the dogs under the table eat the children's crumbs" And he said to her, "For this saying you may go your ways; the demon has left your daughter". And she went home, and found the child lying in bed, and the demon gone". (Mark 7:24-30 RSV).

Though there have been arguments by scholars about the true position and intentions of this account by the gospel writers, the most important point in the text however is that a gentile woman's witty reply wins from Jesus what a plain request had failed to obtain. This story of the Syrophoenician woman therefore is a further proof that neither race nor gender, makes one unclean or unfit for the grace of God. Mark 7 brings to a climax Jesus relation to conventional ideas of the "unclean"

> The syrophoenician woman is unclean on three counts, as a woman: as a gentile; as one who has a

daughter possessed by a demon. She was a gentile woman, of Greek heritage and Syrophoenician by birth (born in the region of Syria Phoenicia). Marks reference to the woman as a Greek, racially a Syrophoenician implies a Roman audience, because such a designation would be most understood by Romans, who distinguished Phoenicians from Carthage and those from Syria. She was of the wrong sex, the wrong ethnic status and the wrong religious background (Minor 1991:134-135)

Matthew called her a Canaanite (a racial term with unsavory religious connotations to the Jews) to stress her racial origin in a people who were regarded as the most dangerous of all Israel's enemies. The inclusion of this story in the Gospel in spite of its uncomplimentary view of Jesus as one who called the Gentile woman and her daughter "dogs", who should not eat the food offered to the Jews, is largely because of the need of the early church to emphasize Jesus' mission to the Gentiles, those outside the Jewish community. It implies that the Gentiles' needs would be met after those of the Jews had been satisfied. The Syrophoenician woman stepped beyond the prescribed male boundaries to seek out Jesus for the sake of her daughter. She was bold, courageous, assertive and persistent. The persistence and ingenuity of love shown in this mother's appeal for her afflicted daughter is significant. She wanted Jesus to cast the demon out of her daughter and would stop at no rebuff. And when he refused, she persisted.

She refused to accept her society's judgment that neither she nor her daughter was worthy of Jesus' time or attention (135). She is portrayed as an unusually strong woman. She disregarded Jesus' need for privacy and entered a (presumably) Jewish house. She also disregarded the Gentile-Jew difference between her and Jesus and the fact that she had no male sponsor. According to Thurston, women had no right to speak directly to male leaders, whether in religion or politics; they had to ask their husbands or fathers or brothers or sons or uncles to intercede on their behalf. But this woman was more concerned over the health of her daughter than over the social expectations of both Jews and Gentiles of her society' (:66)

The woman's address to Jesus was very humble. She was very specific. She humbly, gently fell down in supplication before Jesus. Her request was strong as implied by the *hrwta* — she urged him. Ringe argues that the woman ministered to Jesus, first by witnessing to his ability as a worker of miracles. She addressed him as "Lord", the only time he is so addressed in Mark, and second, by engaging with him in a way that allowed him to move beyond taboos and boundaries' (67)

Jesus' response to her in verse 27- "Let the children first be fed, for it is not right to take the children's bread and throw it to the dogs" is one of the most troubling Christological verses in the synoptic Gospels. It portrays the human Jesus. It reflects the contempt of the Jews for "heathens" and depicts Jesus as a thoroughly racist, typical Jew (Bonnie :38). He had entered a house hoping to be left alone, but this woman came disturbing him, hence he responded sharply. Also, while Jesus was on, earth, his mission was in the first place to Israel. Matthew included it in his account of the same event that "I am not sent but unto the lost sheep of the house of Israel", to emphasize the point that Jesus' earthly ministry was to the Jews.; (Carson :963). Mark however puts it more mildly, "Let the children first be fed..." the adverb "first" implies that there was some mercy reserved for the Gentiles, they were not totally out of the plan of God, but the Jews had to have the first offer.

Gentiles are likened to "dogs" in comparison to God's chosen people (the Jews). That which was intended for the Jews should not be thrown to those who are not of God's family, who have no knowledge of God, and who have no interest in the God of Israel. As "dogs", the Gentiles are vile and profane in contrast with the chosen Israel. The Gentiles snarl at them, spite them and are ready to worry them.' Jews were not pet-lovers, to them "dogs" were dirty, unpleasant and savage animals which roamed the streets in parks, scavenging for food' (1984:417) The apparent harshness of Jesus' reply has perplexed many commentators. Numerous attempts have been made to tone down the seeming rudeness of the saying by suggesting that Jesus spoke in half-jest: that He wanted to test the woman's faith etc. It is believed that the statement in Mark is of doubtful authenticity as a word of Jesus, and that Matthew's account "I was sent only to the lost sheep of the house of Israel" (15:24) is more faithful to ancient tradition and probably Jesus' very own words' (Anderson: 190). The use of the term dogs' was an insult and does not speak well of a Saviour of the whole world. It must have been an addition on the part of Mark and seems to reflect the demeanour of a church that is acquainted with the Gentile mission and with the stand point, 'to the Jew first and also the Greek' (Roman 1: 16).

As a model for contemporary Nigerian women, the woman raised an important issue in her conversation with Jesus which has been described as "the hermeneutical privilege of the poor". She set out to convince Jesus of the importance of healing "nobodies" like her daughter. She responded to Jesus in wisdom. She reasoned with Christ that it is God's purpose for Gentiles to receive blessings indirectly when he blessed Israel (Stamps:1495). She witnessed to Jesus about the need to broaden his ministry of hospitality to those outside the house of Israel: "Lord, even the dogs under the table eat of the children's crumbs". Having been taught to remain silent, hidden, and obedient all through her life, she only heard from Jesus what she is used to hearing (Kinukawa, 58). She cleverly reasoned with Jesus and moved him into healing her daughter by claiming the right to at least the crumbs under Israel's table. Having taught that customs or traditions should not stand in the way of helping those in need (Mark 2:23-28; 3:1-6), Jesus recognized the accuracy and wisdom of the woman's response and effected her daughter's healing.

The contrast between the children of the household at the family table and the dogs waiting anxiously outside for the scraps, as implied in Jesus' statement, is similar to the situation between men and women in many churches today with regards to church leadership. Church leadership is often seen as men's territory and women are not expected to come near it. Women who ventured to be church leaders are equally viewed as "dogs" today just as the Syrophoenician woman.

They are seen as being out of place, unclean, unfit and unwelcome intruders, trying to steal what really belonged to the "children of the household' — the males. Other women in some churches, like the Syrophoenician woman, have accepted the reality that they are not expected to sit at tables of decision-making or on the pulpit with men, but as "dogs" they are ready to stoop under the table (of male hierarchy) to receive the crumbs that fall from the table. Thus, positions of assistant pastors, deaconesses, Sunday school teachers are reserved for them.

Though Jesus granted her request, it was because she was able to point out the absolute necessity of doing so. The Syrophoenician woman moved Jesus to heal, to transcend the racist and sexist boundaries of his society (Ringe 71). Rather than feeling offended by the woman's wit and strange boldness, Jesus was won over by the persistence and intelligence of the gentile woman. Jesus' willingness to talk with and help this foreign woman is proof of his rejection of certain Jewish teaching concerning discourse with women. The woman who was expected to be invisible becomes visible, and her action was not condemned by Jesus. Rather Jesus endorsed her indomitable spirit by healing her daughter.

This is a challenge to contemporary church leaders; Jesus' readiness to change his mind and attitude from that of rejection to affirmation and appreciation should serve as a fitting example to the modern church to be more inclusive and accommodating.

Conclusion
The action of the Syrophoenician woman and her conversation with Jesus shows that women need not be less daring and daunting in pointing out to church leaders and the society at large, the absolute necessity of an inclusive church ministry. She

withstood the test even in the face of rejection. What is remarkable about this woman, like all other women Jesus encountered, is not who she was but what she did. She acted as a faithful seeker. The focus shifted from the fact that she was a woman to the fact that she demonstrated great faith. In the book of Mark, the woman's faith is implicitly indicated by the fact that she believed Jesus when he said her daughter was healed and went home to meet it so. While Matthew explicitly stated, "O woman, great is your faith" (Mathew 15:28), Mark suggests through this story that what happens here is the same as in previous instances in which Jesus responded to women. There is a transformation of the person which corresponds with a shift in perception as to that person's worth. Women must demand their distinctive roles in the church and carefully articulate their aspirations in church and society.

Women in Yoruba land have a pervasive role in the society as they constitute an indispensable element in society. They have been described as "Heaven's best gift, man's joy and pride in prosperity and his support and comfort in affliction". The question is, what would have happened if women failed to be fertile or refused to contribute to societal good? Many people would have to give up life and wind up while society would grind to a halt. Indeed, at the beginning of all great things, there is a woman. These show that women are indispensable. Perspectives from females' studies in Nigeria have shown that during the pre-colonial days in Nigeria, men and women had their own operational space in the political arrangements in most of our societies.

Unfortunately, colonial and post-colonial periods affected women in Nigeria. Colonialism denied women access to a level playing ground as it transferred to Nigeria the gender discrimination that was the norm in the Western world then. It imposed on the society a situation of non-involvement and the inability of women to complement the efforts of their men in the society. It was generally believed that women have inferior brains, intelligence and communicative skills just because of the gender biases created in the society. Badger (1981) reports that in a society that differentiates between roles purely for gender reason, the individual behaviour consequently will be determined by what is seen to be appropriate on the basis of the sex of each person.

If Nigerian women remain undaunted, despite all the odds that are informed by traditional, socio-cultural and religious bias and teachings, and also remain persistent in their quest for equality, inclusive participation in body polity, the feasibility of a gender sensitive and gender free society is on the horizon in Nigeria and Africa at large. Then the *Drums of War* will become the Trumpet of Peace, and Bakare's prophetic pen will be much more celebrated, as the war would have been won by the women's wealth of wisdom, quality and doggedness and not the self-centered swords of the men.

References

Abuku, Mnena (2013) Drama and Women Education in Contemporary Society in E Inegbe *Arts, Culture & Communication in a Postcolny: A FESTSCHRIFT FOR LAWRENCE OLANLERE BAMIDELE*, London: Alpha Crowners Publishers.

Aina, Olabisi (1998) *Nigerian Women in Society and Development*, Ibadan: Dokun Publishers.

Akintunde, Dorcas Olu (2003) "the Impact of Women in Nigerian Society" *Biblical Studies and Women Issues in Africa; A Publication of NABIS.*

Awe, Bolanle (1989) Nigerian Women and Development in Retrospect in Parrat J. *Women and Development in Africa A Comparative Perspective* New York: University Press.

Bakare, Ojo Rasaki (1994) *Rogbodiyan & Drums of War,* Zaria: Tamaza Publishing Company Limited.

Carson D. A. and France R. T. (1994) *New Bible commentary 21st Century Edition,* Leicester, England: Intervasity.

Dufton Francis (1989) 'The Syrophoenician Woman and Her Dogs' in *Expository Times, 100.*

Harris Kevin (1984) *Sex Ideology and Religion,* Sussex: Wheatsheaf Books.
Kinukawa Hisako (1994), *Women in Mark A Japanese Feminist Perspective*, MaryKnoll : orbis

Manus C U (2003) *Intercutural Hermeneutics in Africa, Methods and Approaches, Kenya* : Acton Publishers.

Minor Mitzi (1991) "The Women of the Gospel of Mark and Contemporary Women's Spirituality" *Spirituality Today Vol. 43 no 2*

Olabintan Akinrinade (1987) *Economic Development in Africa*, London: Rinter Printers

Prime Derek (1992) *Women in the Church*, Great Shelford: Crossway Books.

Ringe Sharon (1984) '' A Gentile Woman's Story in Letty Russel *Feminist Interpretation of the Bible,* Philadelphia: Westminster.

Russel Letty(1993), *The Church in the Round*, Louisville: John Knox Press

Stamps Donald (1992) (ed) *Full Life Study Bible*, Michigan: Zondervan Press

Thurston Bornie (1998) *Women in the New Testament Questions and Commentary*, New York: Cross Raod.

Umoh Ekong (1997) *Women and Socio-Economic Engineering of Nigeria*, Uyo: Remlink Printers Anderson Hugh (1981) 'The Gospel of Mark' in *New Century Bible Commentary,* Grand Rapids: Wm B Eerdmans

Political Gansterism and Materialism in Bakare, Ojo Rasaki's *The Gods and The Scavenger* and *Rogbodiyan*.

By
Ekweariri, Chidiebere S., Ph. D. and Uzondu, Ifeyinwa.

Introduction
Politics, they say is a dirty game. It is not bad in itself but those who play the game bring about the dirtiness in it. One negative attribute of politics in the Nigerian polity and indeed other developing countries is gangsterism. Political gangsterism is an age-long problem that has affected countries of the world. Gangsterism in the political terrain of Nigeria did not emerge out of the blues. It has been there all the while. From history, it actually had its tap-root during the First Republic where politicians sought the help of thugs to help scare the living daylight out of their foes and also protect them from unwarranted physical attacks of the opposition (htt://www.osundefender.org/?p=14853).
Political gangsterism has become a pain, a sore spot, a malignant tumour and a thing of shame in the Nigerian political arena. Nigeria as a country still bears the scars of this ugly trend in all aspects of development and is gradually threatening our nascent democracy.

Apart from social commentators who discuss these on the pages of newspapers and the electronic media, no other person(s) does it better than the literary and dramatic artistes (poets inclusive). One person who has devoted most of his time discussing the complexities of these terms in his dramatic works is Bakare, Ojo Rasaki; a man of many parts and an artiste of great proportion. A careful examination of *The Gods and The Scavengers* and *Rogbodiyan,* plays he published in 2006 and 1994 respectively, and other of his published plays, one is inclined to rightly conclude that he is a reformer; and that he uses his art with the hope of changing the state of affairs in his ailing Nigerian society. It is in this light that he can be described as a political writer. He totally agrees with the postulation of Chinua Achebe as quoted by Tracie Utoh that:

> ... an African creative writer who tries to avoid the big social and political issues of contemporary Africa will end up being completely irrelevant like that absurd man in the proverb who leaves his house burning to pursue a rat fleeing from the flames (10)

One of the qualities of a creative writer is that he reads others and in doing so, he equips himself further to create since nobody creates out of nothing (Duruaku, 82). Therefore, following the footsteps of committed African playwrights such as Ngugiwa Thiong'o, Wole Soyinka, Chinua Achebe, Kalu Uka, Ola Rotimi, Emeka Nwabueze, Chris Nwamuo, Effiong Johnson etc, Bakare uses his creative artistry to expose the socio-political trauma of a nation, Nigeria. This paper is, therefore, designed to take a foray into Bakare's plays, specifically, *The Gods and The Scavengers* and *Rogbodiyan* and examine the impacts of political gangsterism and materialism in the Nigerian polity. As earlier stated, materialism as a concept has multiplicity of meaning but in this context, it will, at its simpler level, focus on material "things" as opposed to that which is spiritual or intellectual in nature.

Artiste, Drama and Politics
The theme of politics has always been on the front burner and a major preoccupation of Nigerian writers. This seemingly ubiquitous term with its concomitant effects on the socio-political and religious landscape of a growing nation such as Nigeria, has made many a nation unstable. Like all other writers, dramatic artistes have not relented in lending their voices on this. Unlike the sculptor or the painter who seeks to gratify his artistic ego, the dramatist in our society has always endeavoured to fulfil definite socio-cultural (and political) functions beyond the primary objective of entertainment (Umukoro 15). Furthermore, in the words of Ngugiwa Thiong'o, "every writer is a writer in politics, the only question is what and whose politics" (21). Though a dramatic artiste does not play the kind of politics associated with rascality, but as a "concerned member of the

society which he tries to protect... he is equally a politician" (Kafewo, 93). This is also premised on the fact that all theatre is necessarily political and all the activities of man are political and theatre is one of them (Boal, ix). The dramatic artistes have, therefore, continuously and persistently too (even at the risk of being molested, beaten up and possible imprisonment) exposed the dangers inherent in politicians quest for personal aggrandisement at the detriment of the poor masses.

In all the ages, drama has been a veritable tool for conscientisation. It is the working instrument in the hand of artistes, to socially, religiously, culturally and politically educate the masses. Drama and politics are inter-woven. Ngong (1) writes that "... it is difficult to separate drama from politics; politics being a science that deals with the state and the condition of the human society" (http:/www.antiessays.com/free-essay/drama-And-politics-150515.html). The history of art and the artiste's commitment to politics is as old as the classical period. Aristophanes, notably one of the visible artistes of Ancient Greece engaged his society and the authorities in his satirical plays. As cited in Boal's *Theatre of the Oppressed*, Aristophanes thought that the dramatist should not only offer pleasure but should, besides that be a teacher of morality and a political adviser (vii).

The artiste is "often regarded as a conscious political element, whose product makes pungent remarks and comments about the life of men individually and collectively and also the state of affairs in the country" (Fosudo, 115). He paints the picture of the good, the bad and the ugly in every society, Nigeria inclusive. He "reports through his creative acumen those situations that catch his fancy either in the area of governance or politics, economy, education, infrastructure or any other area that is worth reporting" (Ekwearir and Onyemuchara, 361).

Politics is life and man being a political animal finds himself inextricably linked to the political discourse of his generation. Since drama is a mediator of life, political drama has come to characterise contemporary theatre of the modern era (Uzoji, 49). He recaps further to that:

> drama or theatre is an arena where human beings are presented in a cosmic totality, acting and reacting to forces around them and within them, perceiving and being perceived by those interacting with them, and by those in the audience who experience with them the enigma that is common to humanity (49).

For Osofisan (7) in *Playing Dangerously*..., the artiste's involvement in politics is as unconscious as blinking the eye and "everywhere, whether in the close intimacy of domestic life, or the expanse space of social being, no hegemony is sacrosanct to the probing impertinences of art." Therefore, the training of an artiste gives him the latitude to delve into and explore every aspect of human endeavour and this he does through the impartation of knowledge embedded in the dramatic text. More so, literature has always visited the terrains of politics and leadership probing and questioning the basis upon which politicians do what they do (Ogbonna, 35).

A Contextual Analysis of Political Gangsterism and Materialsim in Bakare, Ojo Rasaki's *The Gods and The Scavenger and Rogbodiyan.*

The Gods and The Scavengers deals with the intrigues in a political system. Anago, through a trickster costumed to appear like a goddess, deceitfully, conspiratorially and fraudulently emerge as the chairman of a local government and when he decides to play the politics of self-enrichment without commiserate consideration of his allies, coupled with his refusal to take advice from his special adviser, Andy, a gang up ensued which ultimately led to his removal. Apart from other noticeable themes, the play is characteristically built on two convergent themes; political gangsterism and materialism. From the chairman to his security aids, down to his councillors and his special adviser, Andy, the story remains the same. The councillors saw their position as that which should guarantee wealth and affluence. They argue:

> **Mallam**: But *Ran Ka dede*. The man who works by the altar also eats by the altar.
> **Chief Olowokere**: In our homes we are comfortable. Likewise as the people's eyes here we want to preside over plenty not poverty. (26)
> **Chief Abasi**: Exactly! Are we made councillors so that we may die of hunger?

Because of these materialistic tendencies, they threw caution to the wind and persistently intimidated the market women, using brute force to extort them in the process. Even when the Chairman decreed otherwise, they found it difficult to keep to that directives and plotted to divert his attention. The level of desperation on materialism in the play is at its highest peak to the extent that genocide was engineered by the elders. In their conspiratory tone, they discuss:

> **Chief Madunagu**: That is not the issue, the truth is that as the people's eyes we deserve to live in affluence. If it means misapplying the money meant for the construction of the market for us to live in a manner befitting the people's representatives, so be it....
> **Chief Abasi**: We cannot underrate Anago, it could prove fatal
> **Chief Madunagu**: Then sort him out!
> **Chief Olowokere**: Exactly!
> **Mallam Maiangwa**: Come closer (*they come closer while he whispers something into their ears*). (29-30).

This is the level men are willing to go for materialism. This is also a reflection of the kind of things found in the Nigerian polity where politicians are ready to kill, maim and destroy in order to acquire personal wealth.

On the part of the Chairman, he appears saintly before the market women and won their respect. He also speaks sternly against dishonesty, insincerity, greed, love for wealth, love of power and desire to amass wealth at all cost before his councillors and he later reneges. This sums up the opinion of Somalian writer, Nuruddin Farah, who painfully laments the situation of the Nigerian politician in the following words. "the African politician is a blind man; he moves only in one direction – towards himself" (11). In the play, the Chairman unsettled the wretched of the earth (Scavengers) from where they pick crumbs from the dust bin because of his desire for materialistic things. When he was confronted, he replies carefully but frankly:

> **Andy**: Didn't I advise you not to relocate the scavengers? I told you that your decision to clear the refuse dump and relocate those pauperized fellows who feed from the dump just because you want to use the land to build a personal filling station would be unpopular... now tongues are wagging.
>
> **Anago**: Take it easy... talk like a politician. That plot of land is strategic and my business will thrive there.... if anybody has problem with his tongue he should visit a surgeon, as for me, i dey kakaraka.

The Chairman is a chameleon and because of this chameleonic tendency, his special adviser, Andy, disgusted with antics to pursue personal goals speaks to him thus:

> **Andy**: Anago, why did you make laws that you yourself cannot keep? No law is obeyed if the maker is a rogue. Those who come to equity must come with clean hands. (*Hands over an envelope to Anago*). This is my letter of resignation... (28).

Andy himself is not left out of this materialistic hook. He also exhibited traces of it when he severed relationship with the chairman. One may have thought that his resignation was to maintain the sanctity and inviolability of his personal self, but contrary to it, it was because he was not getting what he wanted.

In one of his meetings with the Scavengers, he made the following statement:

> **Andy:** …Anago ascended the throne as a result of conspiracy. However, he has disappointed us. We insisted on him getting there by all means because we believed that our salvation rested in his hands. But Anago has come out in his true colour and so the people must show him the path to disgrace (49).

This is also predicated on the fact that he never denounced corruption allegation levelled against the councillors and even when one of the security men was arraigned before the Chairman on offence of bribery and corruption, he never altered a word. Rather he admonished the Chairman for speaking sternly against it and later tendered his resignation, presumably because of his disappointment on the chairman's position. In substantiates the above statement when he says that:

> **Andy:** …I want the road to poverty properly blocked once and for all and today we shall rise and sing a new song (55).

This is one of the problems ravaging the Nigerian political system. Personal advisers and aids see their position as an opportunity to better their lots and make money and when such is blocked, politics of calumny usually sets in.

Another problem in the Nigerian political system is political gangsterism. Political gangsterism in the Nigerian polity has been an age long thing. Skirmishes, disagreement between rival parties, in house fighting, gang up and other retrogressive political motives have always hold sway. In spite of its antithetical and negative attributes, politicians have always explored it to achieve their desired goal. In the play, *The Gods and The Scavengers,* the case is not different. First of all, the

Chairman used it to dislodge the scavengers from their natural home. Secondly, it became a handy tool for the councillors to manipulate with and use it to register their displeasure over the Chairman's ruling method and the need for them to be left alone.

Rogbodiyan also shares some thematic attributes with *The Gods and The Scavengers*. It deals with the problem of leadership and the political manoeuvring to acquire power. A particular family/lineage (the Adeakin's) have ruled the people of Ilu Koroju for nearly twenty tears and suddenly decided to hand over to a new king. Modalities for this were set out by the Regent on how this is to be achieved but due to selfishness, quest for power and corruption; even against the wishes of the oracle, Arigidigbi was crowned as the new king. Soon after this, political sycophancy, circumvention of rule of law and due process, political banditory and Gangsterism became the order of the day. He defiled the *Arugba Oge*, the virgin chosen to carry the sacrifice to the gods on the day of the *Oge* Festival, thereby causing calamity to befall the land. Though remedy came through Adegbani, the son of the former Regent, Arigidigbi, not only lost his throne but was rounded off alongside his cohorts.

Here, all the actions in the play are tied to materialism. The kingmakers sold their consciences because of materialism. From the onset, some of them were already swayed by the wealth of Arigidigbi and eulogised him. Although Aloba (the head of the kingmakers) made efforts to live up to the expectations of the people, but at the long run, it was found out to be a premeditated arrangement to fool his colleagues. This is gleaned from the following discussions.

>**Aloba**: Have they gone?
>**Arigidigbi**: Yes. Gone with their... (*they both laugh again*)
>**Aloba**: I got your message. Your men brought the money to my house. (*a bit seriously*) Yeah... I am worried about the diviner. We are

> ordinary mortals. But nobody can buy the diviner.
>
> **Arigidigbi**: Nobody can buy the diviner, eh? Every man, divine or not, has his price. Every man can be 'settled'.... (27-28).

Similar to this is the circumvention of due process in the bid to acquire this material wealth. In Ilu Koroju, there are procedural ways of doing things including the selection of a new king and other activities that go with his coronation. Due to some persons' quest for materialism, they tried to circumvent this due process to achieve their selfish desire. Abere (one of the kingmakers) was afraid of losing out if the oracle is consulted to decide who their next king is going to be and vehemently opposed that idea, insisting that they themselves can successfully do the selection. He argues thus:

> **Abere**: (*stands. He is dead serious*). You see what I mean. Elders of our land, for how long shall we continue to leave our fate in the hands of the oracle. Can't we as leaders put heads together and choose he that wears the crown? Elders of our land, this is a job for humans; forget about the oracle. Let us assess these two candidates ourselves, let us discuss their merit and take decisions. Let us consider every considerable consideration and choose a king. After all the voice of men is the voice of the gods.
>
> **Eto**: It is true, Abere. I support you, (19).

Akin to this is the issue of sycophancy that pervades the entire play. This also has relationship with materialism because the intentions of those who paid lip service to the King and wrongly advice him is not only to be in his good book but to also share in the largesse that may come from him.

In Movement 8, the case of political sycophancy repeated itself. When the King, Arigidigbi defiles the tradition and leaves the chambers of the oracle where he is supposed to be meditating with his ancestors before the *Oge* festival, his new acolyte, Akigbe, instead of advising him rightly, sings his praises to the consternation of Agogo. This is probably because he lacks the courage or afraid of him, but his sycophantic tendencies led the king to ruin. In one of the occasions he eulogises thus:

> **Akigbe:** Arigidigbi oo, the mighty elephant with the bravery of a lion, the suppleness of a serpent and the beauty of a young antelope in the sun, the great tree that protects all. Oh! Beloved king, director of all noble affairs. Oh! Great Oba – beyond which none greater lives on the surface of the earth; who can determine the minds of the gods. Your treacherous enemy, the horse, is like Ashori, the great tree, so poisonous that no plant may grow under it....(33).

There is also political Gangsterism in the play. In **Movement 3** of the play, prior to the commencement of the selection process, the two contenders (Arigidigbi and Gbadegesin) and their supporters' clash in a show of power and supremacy. Furthermore, when Fadele, the Chief Priest implicates the King as the culprit and in his attempt to extricate himself, he accuses Gbadegesin, his opponent in the election, and ordered his thugs to seize him and tie him up. He specifically orderes that:

> King: ... (to Akigbe and Obembe) Seize him and tie him to *mogun*. I want his head to dance to his drum of down fall (53).

As a matter of fact, not only intimidate people but also cow them into submission. This is in absolute agreement with the opinion of Nwabueze (26) that "our politics has variously been described as hypocrisy, and Africans appear to wallow in indiscriminate abuse of power." However, what is intriguing is the alacrity with which these thugs go about this business. Their zeal and resoluteness to placate their boss can be compared to nothing. In the Nigerian political scene, many of these political thugs have ended up becoming bosses themselves as compensations for their loyalty, thereby perpetuating political Gangsterism in the system.

General Observation
The two plays under investigation are quite specific about the kind of actions expected of us. While *The Gods and The Scavengers* agitates for a revolution as can be gleaned on page 60, that of *Rogbodiyan* encourages us to rise up and look for solution instead of wallowing in self pity. Kelechi Ogbonna writes that... his art (the artiste is a statement of advocacy, a cry for change and where necessary, a violent resolution of the conflict that bad leadership has entangled the masses with (36). In a similar vein, Femi Osofisan, "whose whole dramaturgy is one panoramic journey of intense masses empowerment" (Ngozi Ogbonna 198) opines that "our problems are physical and not spiritual and consequently can be altered through well co-ordinate physical action" (25). The playwright agrees with the two postulations and recommended same in the two plays.

The quest for material possessions always leads to disastrous consequences. The two plays implicitly and explicitly hampered on it. The Chairman and his Councillors in *The Gods and The Scavengers* are disgraced while the Kingmakers in *Rogbodiyan* are rubbished, all in the full glare of the villagers.

Political gangsterism is an ill wind that blows no one any good. Although those who employed it in the two play achieved their goals albeit momentarily, they are later humiliated through the same means.

Emmanuel Ngara contends that the rift in independent Africa is neither vertical nor ordained, but a rift between the haves and the have-nots (35). This is what Ngugi refers to as a horizontal rift dividing the leader from the abroad masses of the people (24). The two plays, especially, *The Gods and Tthe Scavengers* make clear statement on that.

Conclusion
The bane of Nigerian nascent democracy owe partly to the above problems. In civilised politics, there is no room for violence but unfortunately, we are yet to grapple with these ubiquitous problems. Some claim that politics is investment but that has been disabused and squashed in developed countries. Political gangsters are political criminals whose primary objective is to loot the national treasury and politicians are no better than gangsters if they resort to violence to defend honour (*http://www.themalaysianinsider.com/ malaysia/article/bersih-raps-muhyiddin-says-no-room-for-gangsterism-in-democracy*).

The Nigerian political system cannot make any meaningful progress if these problems are not nipped in the bud. Politics should be made as a part time arrangement and the attraction of political positions should be drastically reduced. The 2015 general election is at the corner and there should be zero tolerance to political Gangsterism. Declaration of assets before elective positions should be vigorously pursued, verified by independent body and followed up at the point of exit. Those found culpable should be severely punished as deterrent to others. The removal of the immunity clause as recommended by the on-going National Conference should be welcomed by all well meaning Nigerians so as to stem the tide of political gangsterism and materialism that are already ravaging the Nigerian polity.

Works Cited

Boal, Augusto. *Theatre of the Oppressed* (Translated by Charles 4 & Maria Odills leal McBride). London: Pluto-Press, 1979.

Duruaku, ABC. "Teaching Drama for Appreciation in the Nigerian Learning Space: Strategies to Consider " *nka: a Journal of the Arts*. No. 13. 2011. Pp. 81-91

Ekweariri, Chidiebere and Onyemuchara Casmir. "Creative Arts as Vanguard for Good Governance in Nigeria: A Critical Review." *The Humanities and Good Governance*. Eds A.B.C Chiegboka et.al. Nimo: Rex Charles and Patrick Ltd. 2012. Pp. 357-365.

Ezeajugh, Tracie Utoh. "Dramatising a People's History as a Parable for a Nation in Search of Peace: Alex Asigbo's Duology as a Paradigm" *Theatre Experience*. Vol. 2, No. 1. 2003. Pp. 10-17

Farah, Nuruddin. "The Creative Writer and the African Politician" *The Guardian*. Lagos: September 9, 1983. 11.

Fosudo, Sola. "The Artiste as a Democrat: A Case Study of the Text and Production of Osofisan's *Many Colours Make the Thunder king*" *Theatre and Democracy in Nigeria*. Eds. Ahmed Yerima and Ayo Akinwale. Ibadan: kraft Books limited.

(htt://www.osundefender.org/?p=14853)
http://www.themalaysianinsider.com/malaysia/article/bersih-raps-muhyiddin-says-no-room-for-gangsterism-in-democracy

Kafewo, A. Samuel. "Theatre, Culture and Politics: The Paradigm of Sonny Oti's Look Back in Fury." *The Artiste-Intellectual: Sonny Oti on Stage*. Ed. Bakare, Ojo Rasaki. Ibadan: Jofel Books, 2004. Pp. 92-106

Ngara, Emmanuel. *Art and Ideology in the African Novel*. New Hampshire: Heinemann Educational Books, 1985.

Ngong, T. Kelvin. "Drama and Politics: A study of Bate Besong's *Beasts of no Nation*. http:/www.antiessays.com/free-essay/drama-And-politics-150515.html. Retrieved 27th July, 2014.

Nwabueze, Emeka. *In the Spirit of Thesis: The Theatre Arts and National Integration*. 14th Inaugural Lecture, University of Nigeria, Nsukka. *http://unn.edu.ng/files/inaugural* lecture documents/arts/14th inaugural. Retrieved 7th April, 2012.

Ogbonna, Kelechi. "Nigerian Stage and Revolutionary Aesthetics: Lessons from Alvan Theatre's Performance of Ojo Bakare's: *This Land Must Sacrifice*" *IMSU Theatre Journal*. Vol. 2, No. 1. 2012. Pp.32-47.

Ogbonna, Ngozi. "Chris Nwamuo's Theatre and the Dialectics of Social Responsibility" *The Drama of Liberation and Survival: Festschrift Essays on Chris Nwamuo's Scholarship*. Eds. Esekong Andrew and Babson Ajibade. Calabar: University of Calabar Press, 2009. Pp. 194-200.

Osofisan, Femi. *Playing Dangerously: Drama at the Frontiers of Terror in a Post Colonial State*. Ibadan: University of Ibadan Press, 1998.

Osofisan Femi. *Insidious Treasons*. Lagos: Concept Publications, 1992.

Thiong'o Ngugi Wa. "Language and Literature" *Literature and Society: Essays on African Literature.* Ed. Ernest Emenyonu. Oguta: Zim PAN African Publishers, 1986.

Thiong'o Ngugi Wa. *Writers in Politics.* London: Heinemann, 1981

Umukoro, Mathew. *The Performing Artist in Academia.* Ibadan: Evans Brothers Limited.

Uzoji, Emmanuel. "The Prophetic Power of Drama: Nigeria's Elections and Soyinka's Beatification of the Area Boy" *Nigerian Theatre Journal.* Vol. 11-1. 2011. Pp.49-64.

Reflection of Nigerian Tertiary Institutions in Bakare Ojo Rasaki's *Once Upon A Tower*: Metaphor For Social Transformation

By
Umukoro, M. Oghenevize and Iyamah, C. Yankson

Introduction

The Arts, also referred to as the Humanities, are the foundation for social transformation, growth and development in any society. Ukala (2012) citing the United States Rockefeller Commission on the Humanities notes that:

> Through the humanities, we reflect on the fundamental question: What does it mean to be human?... They (humanities) review how people have tried to make moral, spiritual and intellectual sense of a world in which irrationality, despair, loneliness and death are as conspicuous as birth, friendship, hope and reason.

Ukala also avers that the major focus of the arts is to produce cultivated human beings that are broadly educated, cultured and refined, well-bred, having refined manners and tastes. Ekoko (2012) is also of the above view. He posits that the Humanities cultivate and develop minds that can mediate and channel changes and challenges; and that they also equip people to contribute meaningfully towards the attainment of national goals and satisfaction of national needs.

In order to achieve the above, the artist relates with his society and creates from the residue of materials society thrusts at his disposal. In other words, the artist creates from the sensibilities of his environment, and not from a void. The Nigerian environment with its complexities and absurdities gives verve to many dramatists and artists generally to create; hunger in the mist of plenty, irate corruption, educational and moral decadence, ethnicity, religious vagrancy, insecurity and cut-throat politics are but few societal maladies that have often find expression in the works of Nigerian artists.

Just as art reflects society, so too, every educational system is a reflection of the society that gives it vitality. The rot in the Nigerian citadel of learning, which Bakare, Ojo Rasaki aptly captures in *Once Upon A Tower* has its root deeply entrenched in the soil of corruption, maladministration, unaccountability and the godfather-syndrome in our national polity. If the conception of education as light that illuminates the darkness of the mind is anything to go by, then, the universities, which are the pinnacle of formal learning, could be taken to be the brain-box of society. This is probably why, in modern world, for one to hold a sensitive position, he must be a graduate.

Apart from the above, the tertiary institutions are public space where the activities of government are x-rayed. From the Shehu Shagari through the Babaginda and the despotic regime of Abacha till date, dons in the tertiary institutions have been in the front burners in the vortex of criticism against the government with a view to achieving accountability and good governance. Despite these noble roles, the deluge of corruption in the larger society have enmeshed the environment of the tertiary institutions so deeply that it has become a re-occurring thematic discourse amongst Nigerian playwrights, whom themselves are (were) in the educational system. Sam Ukala's *The Last Hero*, Esiaba Irobi's *Hangmen also Die* and *The Other Side of the Mask* as well as Bakare, Ojo Rasaki's *Once Upon A Tower*, all chronicle the internal and external chaos that have helped to plummet downwards, the educational sector, especially the tertiary institutions in the country.

This paper takes a look at how Bakare, Ojo Rasaki comments on the rot in the tertiary institutions in Nigeria through his play, *Once Upon a Tower*. The paper advances that Rasaki did not just look at this issues to make the audience laugh or cry, but to draw the attention of society to the need for social transformation.

Conceptual Overview on Social Transformation
The term "social transformation" is used to describe positive societal changes, especially towards development. It refers to the

change of society's systemic characteristics in all its social strata be it economic, political cultural and technological restructuring. It is a perceived movement from a current level to a more desired one. John Brennan, Roger King and Yann Lebeau (2004) summarized the following as the areas that require transformation in a society:

- the economy: the formation of human capital;
- the polity: the creation and sustenance of state and civil institutions; the selection and socialisation of political and social elites;
- the social structure: the basis of social stratification, the extent and mechanisms of mobility for different groups;
- the culture: the production and dissemination of ideas, exerting influence upon and providing critique of the above.
- The individual: the basis of all transformations. Attitudes, expectations and behaviours of individual in society.

The last point above is perhaps the most crucial of all because social transformation in economy, politics, and culture is only achievable where the human mind has been properly cultured. Bakare, through *Once Upon A Tower* advocates for quality education and quality leadership in the nation's tertiary institutions as sin-qui-non for social transformation. Quality education according to Grima (2008), is one that is meaningful, worthwhile, responsive to individuals and social needs. Quality education in this regard as Bakare argues in *Once Upon A Tower* is one that provides the basic learning needs to the learner as well as equip them with ethical traits vital for societal advancement. Regrettably, as Bakare reveals in *Once Upon A Tower* neither are the needed facilities for the learner to gain quality education provided, nor positive ethical orientation they can garner from their tutors.

By zeroing on the problems plaguing the country, Bakare is invariably calling for the overhauling of not just the educational sector of the country, but the entire nation. *Once Upon a Tower* is thus a clarion call for social transformation.

A Discourse on *Once Upon A Tower*

Once Upon A Tower is a play that captures three principal acts: the romance between the high echelon in the tertiary institutions and the big-wigs in the corridors of power to short-change the institutions of the much needed funds and quality leadership, the in-fighting or backstabbing within the tertiary institutions and finally, the consequences of the above two. In weaving his plot, Bakare employs the use of dramatic songs. In drama, dramatic songs are songs that capture the essence or theme(s) of the play. They run social commentary on the on-going action and re-enforces the thematic concerns of the play. *Once Upon a Tower* is thus an operatic play with copious thematic songs. The play opens with "Once Upon A Tower" song, which at once sets the pace and tone for the proceeding action. The song chronicles the gradual degradation of the ivory towers in the country; plummeting from gold to silver; from silver to bronze and from bronze "small by small" to stone and dust. This is metaphoric; the golden age of the tertiary institutions in Nigeria was the period when the nation's tertiary institutions produced globally acclaimed scholars, the Wole Soyinkas, the Chinua Achebes, the Chike Obis, the Ola Rotimis, to mention but a few. It is not a surprise therefore that during the brain-drain saga of the 1980s occasioned by the insensitive and despotic military regimes, the international community warmly open their gates for these academics to help contribute to their nation's development. Regrettably, today, the opposite is the case as newspapers burlesque graduates that Nigerian tertiary institutions churn out yearly, who cannot write their names. Madike (2011) comments on this ugly situation:

> The rot in the Nigeria's education sector set in a long time ago with almost everyone watching the decay like a movie. The result is what is believed to be a decline in standards… The university (of University of Ibadan) equally produced scholars, who ranked among the best in the world in their fields. It was

such a global champion that scholars from all over the world came to teach, study and do research there...Although other Nigerian universities soon emerged (with equally glorious outputs). But today, that glory is gone; to say that it is fading, according to Special Adviser on the Media to the President, Reuben Abati, is to be charitable.

This is probably why Rasaki avers that the once glorious tertiary education in Nigeria that was initially imprinted on a marble of gold is now engraved in "dust". Little wonder therefore that no Nigerian university is ranked among the best 200 universities in the world (Madike, 2011). Akitikori, in the play refers to the output from the universities as "empty, stinking hypocrite" (29) and the band sees them as "dem brain na tomatoes" (2).

More so, in the play, Bakare, Ojo Rasaki advances some reasons for the down-turn in the quality of output from the Nigerian tertiary institutions; one of these is that the students, themselves have become indolent and lazy to face their academic work as all they do is:

> to waka corner corner
> when exam don come dem
> go do anything to get marks (2-3)

The playwright again suggests that the lukewarm attitude towards standard education in our tertiary institutions is because the nation has decided to mortgage excellence for mediocrity. In the song "When Omowaye De Convoke" the band says:

> half education is better than none
> na de philosophy of our universities now (5)

In other words, our tertiary institutions have resigned to fate, as they no longer aim at excellence. That is now left for their anthems and slogans. Interestingly Rasaki prophetically cautions against this trend, that:

> Half blindness is risky
> katakata dey for front (5)

The "katakata" Bakare cautions against is quite obvious: our recourse to "half education" now produces medical doctors who cannot distinguish a stethoscope from a thermometer; theatre arts graduates that have never touched a video camera nor seen a gelatine sheet and pharmacists that cannot distinguish paracetamol from multivitamin tablets. Bakare is invariably warning that we are now living in an academic doomsday.

Other reasons for the degradation of tertiary education are also captured in the song "When Omowaye De Convoke":

> Government go dey careless
> Vice Chancellor go turn contractor
> The council go chop money
> Senate confusion galore. (5)

The song is self-explanatory; the Nigerian government continues to give cosmetic attention to the needs of the education sector. One may not be too ambitious to point out that Nigeria is about the only country where the entire tertiary education sector can be almost totally shut down almost at the same time. While it takes the government six months to attend to some of the problems plaguing the Nigerian universities, it takes her another thirteen months to attend to the polytechnics and colleges of education. A proactive and sensitive government would have realised that as it is attending to one arm of the tertiary institutions, as far as it borders on the funding of education it should attend to all. According to Ukala (2014), the Committee on Needs Assessment of Nigerian Public Universities after visiting 61 out of the 74 public universities in Nigeria submitted among others, the following report as its finding in 2012:

- Many laboratories and workshops are old with inappropriate furnishing
- Power and water supply problems
- Scanty and broken furniture
- Equipment and consumables are absent, inadequate or outdated.
- Kerosene stoves used as Bunsen burners in some laboratories
- Science-based Faculties running "Dry Lab" for lack of reagents and tools to conduct physical/real experiments

- No laboratory, workshop or library ranks among 1000 in the world
- Where major equipment exists, the ratio to student, in some universities, is as high as 1:500

The decay in infrastructure in the country is so much that Okebukola, (2009) hinted that if the country must make a headway in its Vision 20:2020 drive then it must be prepared to spend the sum of $510 billion over the next ten years to upgrade its dilapidated infrastructure. Unfortunately, when the government is mentioning infrastructural development, as Okiy (2012) puts it, the nation's tertiary institutions are not deemed to be part of it. Regrettably too, while this infrastructural decay looms, Nigerian spends as much as N137 billion in just two years to acquire education in Britain and United States alone (Okiy, 2012). At this ICT age, Nigerian tertiary institutions are still using outdated chalkboards. Also, for lack of adequate chairs to seat, students still lean on windows and many of them (including some lecturers) are yet to know where the start button on a computer is. The much needed facilities may have been budgeted for and "supplied" on paper as Bakare reveals in *Once Upon A Tower*, but in reality, they are lying deep in the bank accounts of those that be.

While the first line of the stanza of the song cited above reveals government's insincerity towards the advancement of education in Nigeria, the other parts of the stanza reveals the internal rot in the educational system itself. Some of the heads of the various tertiary institutions in the country have turned contractors who are more interested in the welfare of the roads leading to their bank accounts than the actual needs of their institutions. In other to achieve this, sensitive positions in the institutions are given to their loyalists as well as the stooges of those who put them in power. This ugly situation is well captured in Sam Ukala's *The Last Heroes* where the Vice-Chancellor appointed Dr. Danbaba as Deputy Vice-Chancellor because he has connections in high places;

PROF: ...You set the university ablaze, Obiora, by appointing a nitwit as your deputy.

VC:	It's the power game of this country, Bayo. You must appoint into your management team someone who is well connected with the central power block if you want to get things from government. So I was advised.
PROF:	Now look what you've got. Every moment of the day (*mimics*)… "The Minister said, the Minister said. I warned you that a university is not an all-comers political party, not a union of touts (88).

The above scene is also captured by Bakare in *Once upon A Tower*:

Chief:	Mr. Vice Chancellor, I have tremendous joy for the way everything went smoothly
Emir:	I too. In fact, by the time the president reads those beautifully worded speeches of ours in the newspapers, I am sure he will give us another term. He will believe we are doing our job well. (7)

In other words, the tertiary institutions are filled with leaders who are more concerned with what they get out of the system than what they put in. Little wonders therefore why the President of the country Dr. Goodluck Jonathan avers that:

> Given the amount of funds invested in the tertiary education system, I firmly believe that the problem of this sector is not so much the problem of lack of funds or human resources but rather the problem centres on human factor. No amount of finances can turn around our higher educational institutions if the people managing them are not committed, transparent, accountable and place high premium on ethical values. (Ukala 2014).

Also, in order to be in the good book of the Vice-Chancellor, Rector, or Provost as the case may be members of the institutions' Senate or Academic Board become "ayes" men who will never oppose the Vice Chancellor, Rector, or Provost. Those who oppose them are branded as "rebels" or "non-conformists" and punished either by unduly delaying their promotions or denying them recognition for their lofty achievements. This scenario becomes the crux of Esiaba Irobi's *The Other Side of the Mask*. In the play, Jemike, a sculptor and lecturer is denied recognition severally. Professor Njemanze, a member of the selection team secretly admires Jemike's ingenuity, but will not openly admit it.

Njemanze: Why are you so hysterical?

Jamike: Prof., it is because nobody appreciates my work. It is because nobody knows my worth. Even after I have pawned my muscles and my glands as a price for my garlands… Are you not the chairman of the panel that gives out the national awards in sculpture? Are you not the hand that denies me my destiny? Is yours not the face that shrivels in disdain when my work is mentioned for the award?

Njemanze: Look, you must understand that every prize, every laurel, every award has its own politics of acceptance…

Jamike: What is your own politics of acceptance?

Njemanze: …and you must know that because a work wins an award does not mean it is better than all other works submitted. In fact it does not even mean that it is a great work of art or meaningful contribution to society, humanity and …

Jamike: Do you then give awards to mediocre works? (59-65)

Ironically, the same works rejected in Nigeria due to corruption, fetched him international recognition in France. This is exactly what is going on in our country; a man with some money to throw away visits a traditional ruler and picks up a title for himself. It does not matter if he has questionable character. Those who do not have political godfathers cannot win elections in Nigeria. It is however highly regrettable that this ugly trend is metamorphosing in our ivory towers that are supposed to be seats of wisdom. Bakare, Ojo Rasaki also captures these vivid images of suppression and oppression in *Once Upon A Tower:*

Prof. Kurumbete: V.C. Sir, this was the Youngman who won the best graduating student's award in medicine four years ago...Christ! What is an eminent gynaecologist doing with a gun?...

Pedro: Eminent gynaecologist? You have the conscience to refer to me as an eminent gynaecologist when you murdered the "eminence" even before I graduated from this university?...(12)

The theme of godfatherism, which is captured by Ukala in *The Last Heroes*, Irobi in *Hangmen also Die* and *The Other Side of the Mask* did not escape the searchlight of Rasaki in *Once Upon a Tower*. Thus, just as Dr. Danbaba is appointed Deputy Vice Chancellor that he did not merit in Ukala's *The Last Heroes*, just as other cronies are awarded the laurels merited by Jamike in *The Other Side of the Mask*, so too, Pedro is hunted for his genius while Yemi is mentored and given undeserved position in Bakare's *Once Upon A Tower:*

Ugolo: Remember the extra-ordinarily brilliant part 4 student, Omowaye Pedro – whose genius we hope Akitikori will help to specially develop. Yemi will definitely not be able to offer the kind of stuff a brain like Omowaye needs to blossom.

Kurunbete: There you go again. Who tells you I even support the idea of a well enriched special training programme for Omowaye Pedro? That wizard? Even without any special training, he is already competing with part six students. People like him should be intellectually disempowered if we must own the future.

Ugolo: I agree with you completely sir. (32)

Metaphor of Social Transformation in *Once Upon A Tower*
Once Upon A Tower is a call for action vital for social transformation. That Bakare beams his searchlight on the nation's tertiary institutions is not to say that the plethora of decadence he satires in the play are peculiar to the education sector alone. They are common decimal plaguing the very fabric of the Nigerian society. The higher institutions are used as microcosm and special focus because they are expected to be homes to the intellectuals who become the moulding or creative energy that shapes the brains that could propel social transformation. The National Policy on Education (1998) is very clear on education becoming a portent tool of transformation as it specifies that "university education will make optimum contribution to national development by intensifying and diversifying its programmes for development". It is therefore not a coincidence that Rasaki and other playwrights have beamed their searchlights on the activities of tertiary institutions in the country.

An uninformed or ill-informed mind cannot positively affect social change; therefore, the tertiary institutions, which are the major instrument for the enlightenment of the human mind, are deemed to be above board.

Regrettably, the Nigerian society is so bedevilled that corruption is innate and congenital in us, that even those dons in the system that cry foul against government, once they are handed the seats of power turn the other side in matters that they once hold strong. Bakare, Ojo Rasaki as well as other playwrights who have zeroed their searchlights on these maladies is not doing so for mere entertainment, but for how the society we live could be rejuvenated for better human living.

However, whether the educational sector could contribute towards social transformation depends on its focus as well as the society that gives it vitality. Durkheim (1951) once rejected the idea that education could be the force to transform society and resolve social ills. His argument is that "education can be reformed only if society itself is reformed since education is only the image and reflection of society. Durkheim's argument is very cogent because it is what a society puts into education that it gets out of it. If the educational system of a society is failing in its mandate to contribute to social transformation, it is because the society that gives it vitality is also failing in that direction.

What the above presupposes is that a society determines how much its educational system can contribute to social change. It is practically impossible for a society to achieve any meaningful progress without developing and imbibing positive values. Thus without arming its educational system the right values, without arming its labour force the right values, to work honestly, a corrupt society will produce a corrupt educational system, which in turn will produce corrupt graduates. A nation where the President is corrupt, the Senate is corrupt, the Judges are corrupt, the State Governors are corrupt, the Local Government Chairmen and their Councillors are neck deep in corruption cannot expect the Vice Chancellor of a university or the Rector in a polytechnic or the Provost in a College of Education to be saints and produce saints that will transform the society. The product from the education in such a society will definitely be involved in such negative tendency and it will be a continuous ugly circle. This is why it was earlier argued that corruption is becoming congenital in us.

Conclusion
Attitudinal change is a prerequisite for social transformation in any society; this is what Bakare, Ojo Rasaki is advocating for in *Once Upon A Tower*. It is important to note once again, that the

university environment, which is the setting of the play, is but a microcosm for the larger society. Therefore the change that is desirable to transform the Nigerian society is all encompassing. It is hoped that artist will continue to expose societal ills for, as the saying goes, a problem identified is half solved.

References
Bakare, O. R. (2000). *Once Upon A Tower.* Uyo: Afahaide Pub. Co.

Durkheim, E. (1951). *Suicide: A Study in Sociology.* New York: Free Press.

Grima G. (2008). "What is Quality Education" *http://www.Timesofmalta.Com /Articles/View/ 20081128/ Education/What-Is-Quality-Education.234848*

Irobi, E. (1989). *Hangmen also Die.* Enugu: ABIC Books and Equipment Ltd.

Irobi, E. (1999). *The Other Side of the Mask.* Enugu: ABIC Books and Equipment Ltd.

John Brennan, Roger King and Yann Lebeau (2004) *The Role of Universities in the Transformation of Societies.* London: Centre for Higher Education Research and Information.

Madike, I. (2011). "The Fading Glory of Nigerian Universities". *National Mirror*

Okebukola, P. (2009) Education Reform Imperatives for achieving Vision 20:2020. *The Guardian.* April, 29.

Okiy, R. B. (2012) Towards Accelerated Development of Academic Library Services in Nigeria for National development in the 21st Century. http//unlib.uni.edu/ipp/

Ukala, S. (2007) *The Last Heroes.* Ibadan: Kraft.

_____ (2012). "The Humanities and the Humanization of Africans for Security" *Abraka Humanities Review.* 19-38

_____ (2014). "Democracy, Good Governance and Functional Education in Nigeria". Being the text of Convocation Lecture delivered at the 14th Convocation of College of Education, Agbor.

Òjóism: Bakare's Artistic Tendencies in Comparison with the African Masquerade Aesthetics

By
Adeoye, Aderemi Michael

Introduction

This study is an attempt at finding meanings to the fundamental realities of indigenous experiences. It is an attempt to test the findings of a decade-long investigation of the *"Òjóism"* concept. An indigenous concept based on Ekiti performance and linguistic traditions, this concept is characteristically exemplified by the traditional masquerade, whose styles and performative modes have also been observable in the artistic tendencies of Bakare, Òjó Rasaki, as a skilled dancer, poet, dramatist, lyricist and, arguably, a visual artist. Ayoola justifies this approach as "graphology," which he notes,

> is a visual communication creating impacts by representing reality in various formats of writing. It is a concept that has become widely accepted in all walks of life, and thus is appropriate for the exploration of ..." Bakare's performative semblance of the African masquerade (25).

In corroboration with Ayoola's viewpoint, the opinion of De la Croix and Tansey, R.G. also validate the indigenous focus of this experiment as an attempt to make meaning and truth into functions of instrument and language by intellectualising such instruments to obtain the knowledge of the physical world while insisting that such knowledge is mediated by specialised linguistic computation (889). Hence,

> The success of experimental science has had everything to do with making meaning and truth into functions and of instruments and languages. Our knowledge of the physical world is obtained by the manipulation of instruments, and the specialized language of mathematics mediates that knowledge. Thus, the meaning, truth, and reality of scientific

experience– that is, scientific knowledge–are contained in its media and inseparable from them. This is also true of the arts in this age of science and mechanism." (Croix and Tansey, 889).

Consequently, this study intends to validate Bakare's practice and scholarship as *total theatre* as obtainable in his swift handling of the major areas of the arts; vis-à-vis performance, visual and oral traditions, strong emphasis is laid upon the art of dance as the theoretical and philosophical entry points through which Bakare sees the world. McFee agrees that philosophy holds a prominent position in the understanding of dance, because, "the tools used to investigate the understanding of dance are drawn from philosophy" (1). Therefore, *Òjóism* in its *form* indentifies with Esotericism, but in its content and concern, it passes as a philosophical concept of performance, owning to the valid opinion that esotericism is not just a single tradition but also a vast array of often-distinct figures and institutions.

The Esoteric perception, on the one hand, relates to the nominal or titular value of this concept because *Òjó* is first a *name* or a *title*, with divine or celestial origin, but which also has semiotic and mythological readings, that may be hitherto obscure or unknown to scholarship. On the other hand, however, the *Òjó* concept holds a valid linguistic interpretation as an indigenous Ekiti-Yoruba connotation of the *dancer,* hence, *Ò - jó,* meaning "one who does dance or someone who dances" i.e. *Ò + jó = Ò* (One or someone or the person,) + *jó* (do dance or does dance or simply dance) while *ijó* is dance. This also bears relevance to morphological typology, often referred to as a way of classifying the languages of the world. The Yoruba language can thus be classified as tonal, inflectional and sometime, analytical especially when it conveys grammatical relationships without using inflectional morphemes. "*Òjó*" has two morphemes: "*Ò*" (a bound morpheme, signifying the "doer" of an action-) and "*jó*" another bound morpheme, signifying the "action," "to dance." The relative influence of indigenous languages on reality has been stated, thus:

> in our time, 'meaning' and 'truth' join 'reality' as problematic and relative terms. The reduction of truth from absolute, transcendental, and eternal to public, relative and debatable makes our acquisition of it conditional on language. And ordinary verbal language is ambiguous.(Croix and Tansey, 889).

Performance, as deducted from the submissions of De la Croix and Tansey, is a form of art, which ordinarily leverages on the transcendental interaction with language as an element of the visible social environment and experience, but the Esoteric and transcendental freedom evident in all the arts demands a worldview "beyond the reality of visible things (889). Creative manipulation of indigenous phenomena as well as concepts has thus been advocated for in art because no phenomenon would make any sense all on its own except if artistically manipulated. Therefore,

> Maurice Dennis insists that before a picture is *of* anything it is simply a flat surface covered with *colours* arranged in a certain way. By a similar reduction, a poem is only a sequence of sounds. A dominant modern view defines art as consisting of the free manipulation of such elements in arrangement that need not refer to anything outside themselves– that need not *represent* anything. The arrangement is complete and self-contained; one cannot find its message by demanding that it point to something recognizable beyond itself. The modern artist, like the scientist, "experiments" with his medium, investigates, its possibilities, and discovers or invents new forms. But unlike the scientist, for new uniformities and regularities, most modern artists seek the singular and the unique" (Croix and Tansey, 889).

In the argument above, it is clear that while the sciences seek universal uniformities, art is all about making singular and unique impacts. The attempt to bring the *Òjó* concept into limelight becomes valid by virtue of the foregoing authorities. As further confirmation of the innovative import of this indigenous and intellectual exploration, by De la Croix and Tansey, while relying on Klee (2) also recalls, "we used to represent things visible on earth ..." (889), but considering the need for a creative approach to tradition, they advocate for innovation in the appreciation of the world around us. Hence, as cited by De la Croix and Tansey, Klee (2) states

> Now we reveal the reality of visible things, and thereby express the belief that visible reality is merely an isolated phenomenon latently outnumbered by other realities. Things take on broader and more varied meaning, often in seeming contradiction to the rational experience of yesterday... In the end, a formal cosmos will be created out of purely abstract elements of form quite independent of their configurations as objects, beings, or abstract things like letters or numbers.

The view of Klee (2) above empowers the extension of scholarship to hidden traditional and indigenous concepts and opinions such as the focus of this study, especially for the purpose of intellectualising and managing indigenous performance data towards broader social (or international) acceptance. Asserting this, Olorunyomi looks at the traditional masquerade from the interconnected slant of the duo of Esotericism and performance, using linguistics as a paradigm. He thus interprets the transcendental aphorism of the *Okun*-Yoruba masquerade; *"idan pa, Ohin Oye mu,"* as "A confounding experience this; yet the buffoon hollers: a mere harmattan haze" (xxxi). *"Idan"* is an *"òjóistic"* paradigm in traditional Yoruba parlance, because it emanates from a mysterious ritual background into a spectacular performance context. However, *"idan,"* as a linguistic term literally meaning an extreme circus show or magical spectacle, is extricable from its cryptic background into the pure milieu of performance thus bearing strict semblance with the masquerade *theatre* in its eclectic form.

The problem of this study, however, is the gap, which exists between scholarship and tradition, with a view to bridging this gap by focusing on the experimental exploration of *òjóism* thus justifying it as a valid indigenous theoretical principle. In the process of this study, Bakare's genre of performance shall be synonymous to *òjóism;* an indigenous consideration of performance as multimedia and an Esoteric institution of spectacle, will be subjected to operational, etymological and linguistic analyses. The artistic orientations of Bakare Ojo Rasaki and those of the traditional African masquerade aesthestics are also juxtaposed as twin guinea pigs to test the validity of this emerging theory of performance.

Bakare and the African Masquerade Aesthestics: A Comparative Analysis

There have been many scholarly views on the performative genius and multimedia art of the African masquerade aesthetics. The most important of these views is that the African masquerade is an art in totality because it "depends on music, dance and costuming for its real vitality" (Croix and Tansey, 507). While art and the masquerade are inseparable, of particular importance to the masquerade is the art of dance. Bakare also considers rhythm as a major principle, involved in the creation of dance, which of course, has to do with timing as the mental conception of space. This is probably why it is possible for the masquerade to relate rhythmically to space. He identifies time and space as the prominent keys in the multimedia definition of the physical image of a dancer, a quintessence of which is the traditional African masquerade (12). Hence, "as the prevalence of the multimedia art of masquerade suggests, dance may be the artistic medium most important and expressive to native Africans" (Croix and Tansey, 508). Dance is an important feature of the traditional African masquerade because it is an indication of its greatest creative ingenuity. However, the dance art as packaged by the masquerade is surrounded and embellished with other forms of art. This is why the African masquerade with calculated rhythm, logicality of motion and proximate essence of the self within the lore is often referred to as *total theatre* or *total art.*

The African masquerade, particularly as found among the Ekiti-Yoruba of West Africa commands great respect because of

multimedia aesthetics and sacredness in the indigenous society. Akande states that the masquerade is known in Ado–Ekiti as
> **Okiribiti, Amugbosule, Aba Eyindi'** – otherwise known as 'eegun' or 'egigun' (masquerade) He resides spiritually outside the city gate walls. He sometimes comes into the city camouflaged. The belief in Ado classifies masquerades as reincarnated beings. The common belief is that both the young and the old who died are in heaven. Similarly, both young and old masquerades revisit Ado-Ekiti generally on annual basis. The elderly ones are rightly referred to as 'ABA EYINDI'; they include Ede, Moowo, Eegunire etc. (60).

Man has cultivated art via the masquerade media to propitiate his ancestors. "Art," as observed by Nwoko (1) "is also accepted as the most exalted of human activities as it transcends pure materialistic valuations. This makes art "man's worthiest gift to the supreme beings that he worships and to dear memories of his dead ancestors". The masquerade is man's artistic expression in oral, performance and plastic modes. "In this way, man is presented with an opportunity of the cultural manifestation which fulfils the demands of the spiritual part of him which, according to Nwoko (1), 'sorts the mysteries of nature and the unknown into an order that will permit life in his society to be run with some order and stability" (Adeoye, 17).

The Performance Context and Meaning of *Òjóism* and Esosericism

Òjóism is an indigenous conception of performance, which hinges on the syntactic, semantic and semiotic exploration of the Esoteric depth of "*Òjó*," a term ordinarily taken for granted as nominal description of a category of people, believed to have been divinely identified, named and sent on a special mission by the ancestor. The ancestor is often represented by the *masquerades,* who sometimes *come* into the city camouflaged as a reincarnated being. (Akande, 60) Various categories of children are born with different divine or congenital insignias. One of them is the *Òjó,* born neck-laced with his umbilical cord, the others being *Àìná* (a female *Òjó*), *Dàda* (born with dreadlocks, believed to have spiritual affiliations with *Sàngó*, the Yoruba thunder-god), *Olúgbódi* (born with six fingers in each or one of the hands), *Ìlòrí* (born without noticing initial symptoms of pregnancy), *Ìgè* (born in breech position). Others are *Talabi and Oke* (who are born with light membranes covering them). These are traditionally believed to be incarnates of the divine ancestors while the ancestors themselves take the ancestors bear the physical appearance of the masquerade. However, the focus here is on the *Òjó* as a bona fide ancestor-incarnate, whose name incidentally carries thought provoking tone, syllable, syntax and semantics that directly connect him with the art of dance.

The semiotic implication of *Òjó's* connection with the ancestors, who are traditionally believed to have given him a divine identity, is obvious in the tripartite Esoteric connection between the *Òjó,* the ancestor, and the masquerade. It thus appears logical that the masquerade represents the ancestor who, in return, sends– or reincarnates as– the *Òjó*, hence the verisimilitude of the *Òjó* in question and the African traditional masquerade, in fact, Akande holds the opinion that

> the masquerade represent an Ekiti man's attempt to " respect, adore and revere the invisible spiritual powers governing the city – represented by our Lord Jesus Christ, Prophet Mohammed and the traditional gods like '*Obasitu,*' '*Elefonparakutaku,*' '*Umole kan judi i an,*' through festivals like '*Oitado,*' '*Aeregbe,*' '*Ogun,*' '*Ade,*' '*Odede,*' '*Esunsu,*' '*Olorunborun,*' which has been modernised to '*Udiroko.*' We believe in the powers and supremacy of the Divine Providence, which forms the basis of our different modes of worship (60).

During colourful festivals, the masquerades are presented as embodiments of visual crafts ranging from colourful textile, plastic and vegetable or fibrous costumes to large effigies, masks and props, to remember the ancestors. Nevertheless, the semiotic communication of the masquerade goes beyond the visual aesthetics because intangible symbolism, philosophical rhetoric and traditional poetry are tied together in the art of dance, as presented by the masquerade. The masquerade is a master dancer. Dance is the yardstick for measuring the quality of the masquerades as well as the standard for categorizing them, hence the saying in Ado-Ekiti: *"Àbòràngi b' Edè i p'òyì, Eégún Ire b' Edè ijó."* This means "the *Aborangi* never joins issues with the *Edè* when it comes to acrobatic spinning while the *Eégún Ire* also maintains refrain against a duet dance performance with the *Edè*."

Esoterism, otherwise known as Esotericism "signifies the holding of esoteric opinions or beliefs, that is, ideas preserved or understood by a small group or those specially initiated, or of a rare or unusual interest." It is said to be related to the Greek "esoterikos," an extension of the word "eso" which means "within" (http://www.atanha.com/esoteric-metaphysics.). This theoretical principle applies in this study to justify and therefore mainstream such marginalised alternative philosophies, beliefs, practices and experiences as ojoisn into institutionalized traditions. The validity of this emerging theory therefore lies in the nature and context of what the traditional African holds in lieu of performance, which runs deeper than the nominal appreciation of *performance* especially in Western thinking. For instance, the word, *Òjó* relates with divinity as much as with the mystery of *Awo,* of the Yoruba traditional religion being Esoteric sub-genres of performance, therefore extending the contextual limits of performance beyond the ordinary. According to tradition, *Òjó*, refers a divine nomenclature of some exclusive incarnates of the gods usually generously endowed with such gifts as humour, wits, dancing and singing, great sense of self-worth and self-determination. An *Òjó*, therefore, belongs to the Esoteric conclave of unusual performers under a mysterious titular category.

Conclusion
While doing justice to the titular or linguistic appreciation of the term, *Òjó* which constitutes considerable scholarly challenge, it is

imperative to dig up and validate its actual metaphor and hidden truth for "developing the humanistic studies," which, as noted by Mount, "have, however, lagged behind those of political, economic and socioreligious aspects" (xiii). Mount holds this position against the backdrop that, "great transformations have taken place during the past fifty years in Black Africa. Changes in the political, economic, social, and to an extent, in the religious institutions have been investigated considerably by various "on-the-spot" groups from both Europe and America (xiii). Therefore, there is also considerable justification in looking into the relevance of tradition in a changing society. Tradition, in the opinion of this study should be constantly revisited, readapted into the transformation process of society, since "traditions already weakened by long contact with Western ways have been broken down further by the goals of independence and nationalism" (Mount, xv).

This study takes advantage of the values of indigenous instrument and language in order to obtain the knowledge of the physical world. This is also an attempt at establishing the validity of such a field as the Esoteric, which has no single underlying historical thread. As an Esoteric institution of spectacle, Bakare's genre of performance, being classified here as *òjóism;* an indigenous view of performance as multimedia, is hereby subjected to operational, etymological and linguistic analyses. Given the artistic orientations of Bakare Ojo Rasaki and those of the traditional African masquerade, which are founded in deep indigenous philosophies, there is a huge challenge in finding an appropriate Western theoretical pedestal on which to balance it. It, therefore, becomes illogical to attempt juxtaposing an indigenous African behavioural or performative mode with a foreign theoretical standard. Most often, the sub-contents or formative principles the indigenous tradition and those of the foreign artistic theories are never equivalent.

Scholarship should be creatively extended towards intellectualising indigenous performative ideas and artistic data because it is valid, from the tone of this study, to seek relevance for indigenous artistic traditions in a fast growing world. This would lead to a better understanding and knowledge of the immediate physical world around us. Constant theoretical engagement of the perfomatives, in no small measure, would contribute to further advancement of the fields of theatre design as well as the entire humanities and social sciences.

Òjóism as an indigenous theoretical principle has emanated from the attempt to make meaning from indigenous performative thoughts, as well as linguistic and design modes of the *Òjó* and the traditional masquerade, with a view to leveraging truth and social reality. The impact of this special masquerade style on Bakare's artistic mode could probably be assigned to an early followership as an acolyte-initiate of the Ado-Ekiti masquerade cult, to which all males in the local naturally belonged in his formative years, in addition to which he has divine endowments as an *Òjó*.

Òjóism holds the core assumption that "all areas of the arts; performance, visual and technical aesthetics as well as oral traditions are interdependent and interdisciplinary creative faculties in which one single artist may possible be endowed". Thus, Bakare's art is adopted as a benchmark for reviewing and validating the total-theatrical genre. It also could be logically deduced that *Òjóism* is synonymous to *total art* and the *Òjó, a total artist*. Therefore, *when a single individual is endowment with the creative gifts of dance, music, drama, visual design, poetry and the likes, as they sometimes would be, such individual is a total artist; an Òjó.*

Works Cited

Adeoye, M. A. *A Semiotic Analysis of Ogboni Figures in Ekiti.* Ibadan: Institute of African Studies, U. I. (Master's Thesis). 2010.

Akande, O. M. U. *The Cultural Values of Ado-Ekiti, Our Cradle.* (Unpublished paper delivered at Udiroko Festival, Ado-Ekiti) 1997.

Ayoola, M. O. Graphology and Meaning; a Grapho-stylistic Explication of Selected Poems in *The Mines of His Mind: Critical Reflections on the Works of Tayo Olafioye*. Vitanen, B. L. and Owolabi, S. (Ed.) Trenton and Amara: Africa World Press, Inc. pp. 24-35. 2008.

Ayisi, E. O. *An Introduction to the Study of African Culture.* London: Heinemann Educational Books Ltd. 1972.

Bakare, O. R. *Rudiments of Choreography.* Lagos: Dat and Partners Logistic Ltd. 2004

De la Croix, H. and Tansey, R. G. *Gardener's Art Through the Ages.* San Diego: Harcourt Brace Jovanovich, Publishers. 1986.

McFee, Graham. *Understanding Dance* London and New York: Routledge. 1992.

Nwoko, D. Art and religion. *New Culture: A Review of Contemporary African Arts.* 1979.1.8: 1-3.

Olorunyomi, S. *Afrobeat! Fela and the Imagined Continent.* Ibadan: IFRA 2005. Esoterism source: http://www.atanha.com/esoteric-metaphysics. date retrieved 31/07/2014.

Shadow Over The Promised Land: Effects of Attitude on Quality of Education in Tertiary Institutions.

By
Ezinne Igwe

Introduction
Incompetence is a state of inability to properly function or occupy a position; a lack of ability or skill to do a job adequately. Incompetence occurs as a result of no qualification or training to do such work right. So many other things add up together to cause incompetence. Negligence is the quality of being inattentive to duty or responsibilities. Negligence towards academics on the part of lecturer or students brings about incompetence on the part of all concerned.

Since 1996, as rightly reported by the World Bank and UNICEF, education, specifically university education, has become rudimentary to the growth and development of any given society and the knowledge bank of such society. Education has become indispensable as it is a tool which guides or informs opinion generation and decision making in an individual, group of individuals and organisations. Education distinguishes a person and sets him apart, being thoroughly informed of a situation or field and prompts an efficient response. All developing nations of the world need sustainable quality education in order to reach that mark of excellence and level of development which they aspire to reach someday. It's indisputable that countries which are presently still rated 'developing' are undergoing serious problems with the quality of education offered, especially at the university level. In Nigeria for instance, following the 2012 webomatric ranking of world universities, the University of Benin, the nation's number one university ranks 18th in top 100 African universities and 1,639th in the world. The nation's second best institution, University of Agriculture, Abeokuta did not make Africa's top 100, but came 2,266th in the world. University of Ibadan, the nation's 3rd best, was Africa's 53rd best university and the world's 2,515th (Baiyemu, 10). Because education does not just meet an individual's basic needs, but most importantly, his strategic needs (Oladipo et al, 109), the essence and purpose of education ought not to be overlooked and so, quality needs to be greatly emphasized.

This paper intends to examine the effects attitude has on quality education in Nigerian universities, using the department of Theatre and Film Studies, University of Nigeria, Nsukka as a case study. This research assesses a live situation with the artistic recreation of similar circumstance in Ojo Rasaki's *Once Upon A Tower* in order to draw plausible conclusions on the likely consequences of such attitude towards education. The essence of this study is to bring to limelight the consequences of our attitude towards education and the implication of such attitude on the quality assurance of education in our institutions. In this study, the reaction of both staff and students of the department of Theatre and Film Studies, to a short film titled *15 Minutes* is measured and analysed to see how this impacts on the quality of education obtained, how attitude impacts on quality assurance, how this situation relates to Rasaki's work of art and how the sad end of this piece could be ours if certain issues remain unaddressed. It is needless to re-emphasize that a country like Nigeria, considering recent happenings, needs to make quality education a priority as it is a critical element of development which nurtures democracy and promotes peace within an organisation. Little wonder countries like the United States, Japan, United Kingdom, Canada, Norway, Israel are doing so well, being among the countries of the world 'with the most educated people' (Baiyemu, 10).

Interestingly, thousands of students are enrolled into the 103 universities in Nigeria annually and several thousands are equally graduated annually. The shocking truth however, remains that the quality of graduates available now cannot be compared with the quality of graduates there were, say in the 1990's. What is diminishing the quality of our educational system? Is it the economic, political and social ruins we are facing in the country? Or is it as a result of insecurity, misplacement of priority or lack of oversight on issues that concern our curriculum? Curriculum can hardly be the problem since it serves only as a guide to teaching. Clark and Lampert opine that 'the curriculum as published, is transformed and adapted in the planning process by additions, deletions, interpretations and by teacher decisions about pace, sequence and emphasis' (28). Curriculum which has three main dimensions; the intended, offered and received (Bush & Bell, 2002), only guides the teacher in making decisions about what to teach, and how long to apportion to each topic. Prof. Abdullahi A. Zuru, also argued that the problem Nigeria faces in the education sector is not as a result of poor curriculum, but instead, the big problem of attitude; attitude towards education by students, teachers and parents and educational facilitators. Corruption which spreads like wildfire in the country has crept into the educational sector, hence the rot. When morality and dedication which serve as backbone to education have been diseased, there will definitely be a meltdown in the quality of both service and education.

The above just serves to reference the state of University education in Nigeria. We shall go further to make tentative statements on Bakare's *Once Upon A Tower*. Nothing can be more disastrous than turning fine academics into political rivals and animals. Rivalry in an academic institution does not just affect the lecturers involved, but destabilizes innocent students who would be caught in the tangles of the web. In a dialogue between Professor Kurumbete and Dr. Ugolo in *Once Upon A Tower*, this is played out.

>Ugolo: Em... Prof., between you and me, he (Dr. Akitikori) is not a trouble maker. Just that he is a downright non-conformist. He is too bold and vocal, can die for justice and never wants to be cowed. But the young man knows his job.
>
>Kurumbete: You are only confirming the fact that he is dangerous. When a bold, justice-loving, non-conformist also has the advantage of intelligence and professional relevance, then

he is dangerous. Look, that boy is dangerous to my future. He is (in) my area of specialization, well positioned to break my monopoly. He is also dangerous to your future. Brilliant and active, he is a threat to your long stay as the head of department. We have to get him out of the system fast (30-31).

In *Once Upon A Tower*, by Ojo Rasaki explores the complications which can be birthed by poor attitude towards education both staff and students. Dr Akitikori, a bold, intelligent, justice-loving, fast rising academic meets the opposition of Professor Kurumbete, an arrogant, self-asserting professor of gynaecology who has an exaggerated sense of self worth. Dr Akitikori's crime lies in his outspokenness, intelligence, love for scholarship and his aversion to corruption and empty pride. Bowing to the instructions of the provost, Prof. Essor Kurumbete, the head of department, Dr Ugolo joins in the war against Akitikori and ploy towards the eventual sack of the young gynaecologist. He is duly replaced by Yemi, a hypocrite, a junior staff turned lecturer, an academically weak man who is no match for his sound consultant, Dr Akitikori. But this does not seem to matter. Prof Kurumbete explains

    Kurumbete: Who cares? Is he going to teach your child? ...make no mistake about allowing your child to study in this country. If you don't have enough money to send your children to Europe, ...then send them to Ghana. (32)

He is not concerned about the younger generation, the future of the nation and the effect on quality education in the country. Rather, his interest is in the fact that 'Yemi will pose no threat to us. He knows he is weak so he will be gentle, submissive, ask no questions and continue to be our good boy' (32). Their plans fall through. But while all is seemingly well with them and their career, the students suffer, emerging ill taught and 'professionally malnourished' (58). And they would be future leaders of the nation.

In the Theatre and Film Studies Department of the University of Nigeria, Nsukka, a group of students produced a short film titled *15 Minutes*; it tells the story of the dilemma of a psychologically traumatised graduate student, struggling to maintain balance on his personal and family life and still be able to complete his PhD programme which disorganizes him totally. In a bid to escape from his misery, compounded by his unyielding, bossy supervisor, the young graduate student, only recently married, soaks himself in alcohol. Under the influence of alcohol, he returns home to a worried, pregnant wife whom he roughly pushes out of his way. He sleeps, only to dream that his unbending supervisor murders his wife. Upon waking, he slowly recalls the circumstances surrounding his eventful return. Realising he is responsible for his wife's death, he calls the security whose arrival was being awaited as the short ends.

15 Minutes was well written, directed, acted and harmonised with beautiful sound. It is not altogether flawless as it had some minor acting, aesthetic and technical faults. We shall attempt to trace the correlation between this short film and Bakare's play. The film ran for two nights, during which only three out of a total of 16 academic staff members of the department of Theatre and Film Studies were in attendance; no technical staff member was there. There is no gain saying that the students feel highly honoured when their lecturers attend to any business which they (students) take very seriously.

A survey was taken amongst some staff and students of the department in order to effectively, without bias, analyse the implications of the attitude of both staff members and students towards the short film. It had so many implications, but emphasis would be placed on the impact this has on the quality of education. From the students, the researcher tried to find out if they felt a need to invite the lecturers to the premiere, how many of them they were able to invite, how many honoured the invitation and what implication the absence or presence of lecturers had on their educational progress. From the lecturers, the researcher wanted to know how and when the students' invitation got to them, if they honoured the invitation and how the attitudes of the students and lecturers affect the quality of education they were getting.

Analysis
Out of the 'about six' lecturers from the department of Theatre and Film Studies who were invited to the premiere, only two were able to attend the event. Although the students involved acknowledge that the invitation, apart from being informal, was also given very late (few hours from the first night of premiere), they still felt 'disappointed, but used to' the fact that lecturers did not turn up. On the other hand, majority of the lecturers in the department were not aware of the premiere. Those who were aware of it were invited to the event too late, so that they were not able to make out time from their busy schedule. Some claimed that had they been given at least two to three days notice, they would have been happy to grace the event. Being that it was a very informal invitation, the invited lecturers, some of who saw the purpose of the event as more economic than academic and some who did not understand the nature of the event, gave priority to other things they had lined up for the evening. To them, it was a way of teaching these students to learn to attach greater importance to things they consider relevant. One of the interviewed lecturers insisted that the students ought not to feel disappointed that lecturers did not turn up because it would be wrong for the lecturers to barge or intrude into student activities unless they are involved.

Another lecturer observed that what happens within the academic institutions is a reflection of the larger society where just about anything goes and no one bothers about doing things right. Also, the clandestine attitude which may people adopt, believing that their neighbour will be the cause of their downfall, results in students waiting till the last minute before they let even their lecturers know what they are doing. Unfortunately, the institutions cannot be isolated from the society. Whatever happens in the society will inadvertently be obtainable in the academic institutions. There is so much disorganisation and lack of adequate planning in the society and these are just about the problems students have. One of the interviewed students agreed that the late invitation happened because they did not plan well. Besides, a major feedback provided by one of the lecturers present at the premiere has not been put into consideration till the time of this research because the involved students were 'disorganised' and would not 'co-operate'.

While students argue that the motive behind *15 Minutes* and its premiere is solely academic and passion, lecturers disagree judging from their attitude towards the event. Some lecturers link the output to economic gains; others explain that students are becoming more distracted than ever. The idea of red carpet which they see on television distracts them so much that they lose the focus of their objective, misplace priorities and lose emphasis on very vital issues.

Students claim that lecturers are not committed to their students to the point of following up and showing interest or concern in students' progress, but these same students shut off their teachers and make them irrelevant outside and oftentimes even in their academic life. In the premiere of *15 Minutes*, for instance, judging from the attitudes of the students, many lecturers concluded that since their output was not tied to academic pursuit, they never bothered to inconvenience themselves to attend. "Being an educational theatre, the idea of a premiere is a misnomer", Nwaozuzu explained. If the students had organised a preview instead of a premiere, they would have been exhibiting the desire to know more. However, they did not give the impression of a desire to learn. A preview is the showing of a film, to selected, critical audience or spectators, before it is officially open to the public while a premiere is the first showing of a film or play to an audience. Premiere connotes or signifies that a product is finished, one that is ready to be pushed into the market for the consumption of the audience. Unlike a preview, the premiere of *15 Minutes* did not end in an interactive session which provided experts and critics the avenue to make critical and professional comments, ask questions and point out areas that are either commendable or need some more work. And indeed whatever feedback or observations that were provided on that day was definitely lost as the film was not taken back to the work table (Interview 2014).

In *Once Upon A Tower*, this same insouciant attitude towards education is displayed in Miss Julie, the medical student who is not challenged to make effort towards passing the course, Gynae 307, because 'it is too tough' for her (16). She resorts to bribery and buying of grades. But since the lecturer in-charge is the principled, non-push over Dr Akitikori, she allows herself to be used as a agent in the eventually dismissal of the best hand the department had in gynaecology. It is left to the imagination of the audience how such a student will end up in the larger society upon her graduation if brilliant students like Omowaye Pedro could make life threatening mistakes due to lack of infrastructure and expert coaching. The nuisance that the bright Pedro turned into as a result of the bitter circumstance surrounding his affair with Khadijat will bring less pain when compared to the fate of the nation in the hands of half-baked graduates who know nothing about honesty, challenges and hard work. *Once Upon A Tower* paints a certain and futuristic picture of what fate the nation and her people will be facing if attitude towards education does not improve.

Who has the greater blame in the rise of these anomalies that adversely affect the quality of education in our institutions? While students blame it on lecturers who do not have a sound personal relationship with their students, the students themselves cannot be altogether exonerated. Most times, they abuse such relationships. Lecturers on the other hand agree that being too extreme with the students either in the negative or positive light, affects the students and impacts on their attitude towards work. Lecturers are advised to be neither too critical nor too soft with students. Discipline when too relaxed or too hard could make negative impact.

Quality education is that education which can be used to better the society. It is the education that has a motive, a problem solving education. Quality education takes a stance in the society and fills a lacuna; it meets a pressing need in the society. Standard of education has fallen, yes, but so has the standard of everything else, Ndubaisi Nnanna argued (interview 2014). One reason for the fallen standard, a lecturer says, is that the quality of an output can only measure up with the quality of the input. Lecturers cannot give what they do not have. Staff development is hardly spoken about and very few people derive satisfaction from their work. Job satisfaction brings about satisfactory job output.

Lack of sacred values in our education, worsened by our national attitude to life, a life of impatience that lacks expertise has crumbled education in the country. The problem of education in Nigeria is hardly structure or infrastructure as many people cry about, but attitude of people, leadership and management. There is also the problem of checks, balances, evaluation and maintenance.

Summary, Suggestions and Conclusion
At the crux of this research lies the fact that the quality of education in the country can be basically improved when both teachers and students put up a positive attitude to work. Students, just like the teachers, are also major contributors to school decisions on learning and teaching (MacBeath, 1999; Rudduck et al., 1996). Education ought not to be just the process of learning. Quality education goes beyond that. It should be a need based education, an education that meets a need in the society. When teachers are empowered and trained in certain fields to meet a specific need, it becomes easy for such teacher to impact on the students. And when students know that they are needed to solve certain problems in the society, they take up the opportunities that will better equip them.

The state of the society is a huge problem on its own. When people study one field and end up in another, entirely different from the one they studied, they become aware that what is of utmost importance is the certificate, not the qualification. Hence, they endure the years of academic grooming, without interest in what they are being taught. This compounds the confusion they face in differentiating between passion and hobby. Also, parents must understand what their children want out of life. Pushing them into something they do not want to be or do, detracts the student, leaving him with no option but to do just about anything to bring glory home. Like Ojo Rasaki noted, parents should 'let each become what he or she was created capable of being' (63). Teachers need to be encouraged to embark on, and provided with opportunities for career development and self development. Self development is achieved when there is job satisfaction. This creates an avenue for more sacrifice and zeal to work harder. As a standard, it is part of a teacher's duty to foster healthy relationships with school colleagues, parents and organisations in the larger society so as to foster students' learning and development. It is the sort of development that, out of zealousness, students seek on their own, and at the long run, they either make mistakes and lose focus or end up being exploited.

Bakare's *Once Upon A* Tower highlights the fact that the problem of leadership, maintenance and management has to be addressed. Incompetent leadership leads to bad management and this results to the employment of individuals who are incapable or incompetent of doing the job for which they are paid. A sound teacher is one who is reflective and evaluates the effects of his/her choices as well as actions on others (Richards, i). He/she is that person who strives to grow professionally. Professional growth brings about improved standard.

Bakare in his play also suggests that the problem of job dissatisfaction and unavailability of basic amenities must be addressed. Equal opportunities should be given to everyone for development. When students' needs are adequately met and they are exposed to the right people, opportunities and organisations, they would learn to value their teachers and involve them more in their activities.

References.

Arends, I. Richards. *Learning to Teach.* New York: McGraw-Hill Companies. 2009.

Baiyewu, Leke. *Nigerian Varsities Fail to Make Top 1,600.* Punch. http://www.punchng.com/news/nigerian-varsities-fail-to-make-top-1600/ accessed22/04/13, posted 12/02/12.

Bakare, Ojo Rasaki. *Once Upon A Tower.* Uyo: Afahaide Publishing Company. 2000.

Bush, Tony & Less Bell. *The Principles and Practice of Educational Management.* London: Sage Publications Ltd. 2002.

Clark, C.M. & Lampert, M. The Study of Teacher Thinking: Implications for Teacher Education. *Journal of Teacher Education*, vol. 37.(pgs 27-31). 1986.

El-Kurebe, Abdallah. *Problem of Nigeria's education is delivery not curriculum* – Prof. Zuru. The Vanguard, http://www.vanguardngr.com/2013/03/problem-of-nigerias-education-is-delivery-not-curriculum-prof-zuru/ accessed 22/04/13, posted 14/03/13.

MacBeath, J. 1999. *Schools Must Speak for Themselves.* London: Routledge/Falmer.

Nnanna Ndubuisi. Personal Interview. 26/04/14.

Nwaozuzu, Uche. Personal Interview. 26/04/14.

Oladipo, Adebayo et al. *Quality Assurance and Sustainable University Education in Nigeria.* http://aadcice.hiroshima-u.ac.jp/e/publications/sosho4_1-09.pdf accessed 6/04/13. (109-125).

Pavis, Patrice. *Analyzing Performance: Theatre, Dance and Film.* Michigan: University of Michigan Press. 2003.

Rudduck, J., Chaplain, R. & Wallace, G. 1996. *School Improvement: What Can Pupils Tell Us?* London: David Fulton. Wandia 'How do we define "quality" education' in *Daystar University Academic Blog* http://www.daystar.ac.ke/academicblog/?p=352 accessed 29/04/13, posted 14/02/14

15 Minutes. Dir. Ebuka Njoku. DVD. 2013.

Revolutionary Aesthetics in Contemporary Nigerian Theatre: A Study of Bakare, Ojo Rasaki's *Once Upon A Tower*.

By
Ekwueme, Obiora

Preamble
A work of art is either a reflection of the society that produces it or nothing (Bakare, Ojo Rasaki).
The term 'revolution' is very common in various disciplines in the Social Sciences and Humanities especially in the Performance Arts and so on, which denotes the demand or need to effect basic or fundamental changes in the academia and society at large. Revolutionaries tend to be special kind of people because they identify a threatening issue in the society and goes further to device appropriate strategies in tackling such issues. They propose new strategies and create new realities that is more than personal in handling tensions in the society and by so doing creating a new way of life. This could be likened to the vision of radical theatre which has metamorphosed into 'Popular theatre' and 'Theatre-for-Development' (TfD) as the case may be. African scholars, critics, and practitioners like Wole Soyinka, Femi Osofisan, Ola Rotimi, Bode Sowande, Saint Gbilekaa, Ojo Bakare believe that revolutionary theatre should not only be seen from the perspective of ensuring rapid and sweeping changes but also effecting such changes at the grass root level in order to ensure effective, efficient, and even development of the society. According Gbilekaa (82) posits:

> The fundamental Marxist sense of going to the roots, the basic and primary causes underlying the situation here is informed of dialectical methods, and refers to the theatre that adopts the principles of socialist realism.

The revolutionary tendencies of the theatre here are targeted at the upliftment of the standard of life of the grass root masses, by arousing their social consciousness. Revolutionary Theatre took up so many forms in order to meet its target; like the Theatre of pedagogy, liberation and revolution and so on, underlined by

Marxist revolutionary aesthetics. Dramatic texts were not written and produced for entertainment purposes alone, majority of them were to express certain ideological positions, or to condemn threatening socio-political, ethno-cultural, religious and economic practices.

Theatre scholars and practitioners did not just fold their arms and watched, they played an active role in bringing the desired change required in the society by writing and producing works that confronted the threatening issues, delving into the grass roots and exposing the economic, ethno-cultural and social heart of the key issues. As a result, a different kind of revolutionary drama and theatre was born, a synthesising process of transforming composite mixture of cultural renaissance, post-colonial disillusionment and protest into a revolutionary weapon to confront man with the fundamental consciousness of his own existence. A revolutionary aesthetics that de-emphasises the forces of fate and predestination and places the myth-making history of the individuals into the hands of the renaissance man in the society. This movement gave birth to the emergence of great playwrights and practitioners of our time like Femi Osofisan, Bode Sowande, Kole Omotoso, Ola Rotimi, Emeka Nwabueze, Ojo Bakare and others.

These bands of revolutionary playwrights, critics, and practitioners developed a deep passion in the art through the production of works that reflects the concerns, needs and aspirations of their immediate society. Their viewpoints and creative comments became the encapsulation of their proposed solutions for truth change and freeing the African man from neo-colonial oppression and policies. Ngugi Wa Thiong'O in classifying revolutionary writers, scholars and practitioners, maintains:

> ... a writer has no choice. Whether or not he is aware of it, his works reflect one or more aspects of the intense economic, political, cultural, and ideological struggles in a society. What he can choose is one or the other side of the battlefield: the side of the people

or the side of those social forces and class that try to keep the people down. What he or she cannot do is to remain neutral. Every writer is a writer in politics. The question is what and whose politics (204).

These Nigerian revolutionary writers of the oppressed people's politics filled the yawning gap for a combative theatre that could confront the ruling class bravely, and unmask their knaveries and compradorial nature and collaborative stance with the capitalist bloc, particularly, in their dealings with the governed.

Methodology
The study employed the historical and literary methodologies in analysing and critically interpreting data used in the work. Sam Ukala, in *Manual of Research and of Thesis Writing in Theatre Arts* states that, historical methodology "entails the investigation of documented sources, such as books, journals, reports, films, video and audio tapes, archival materials...as well as oral sources" (12). He explains that this method is used to ascertain facts and occurrences in definite places and time. Literary methodology on the other hand, according to Ukala "focuses on written and printed library and archival sources, especially books, journals, theses, reports, literary works, such as plays, novels and poems" (13). These methods are necessary and are employed in this study because of their relevance to the topic.

Theoretical Framework
The evolution of revolutionary theatre in Nigeria followed the growth and development of the nation socially, religiously, economically, and politically. This movement had resultant effect upon arts as reflected in the works of creative artists of the time. The responses of Nigerian creative artists were evident in the varying degree of issues highlighted in their works as it affected their immediate society. According to Achebe,
> An African creative writer who tries to avoid the big social and political issues of contemporary Africa, will end up being completely irrelevant like the

> absurd man in the proverb, who leaves his house burning to pursue a rat fleeing from the flames (54).

Therefore, revolutionary theatricians found the art not only an effective weapon in raising the consciousness of the people towards effective and efficient nation building, but also as an ideal medium of sharing national vision with the populace. They went all out in seeking viable alternatives to handle, combat, and subdue pressing and threatening issues against the society. Theatre Revolutionaries through drama and theatre gave such pressing life threatening issues adequate attention, not only through writing, and dramatisation rather solutions are proffered as how such could be solved or eliminated. According to Enna and Anyagu, Gbilekaa posits:

> The adoption of the socialist vision in their creative works on the Nigerian situation entails a rejection of the animist philosophy and metaphysical profundities which seek to provide answers to man's nature, problems, fate, and social conditions from the metaphysical perspective (84).

Majority of the works of earliest theatricians especially playwrights, and critics share a common theme, and ideology with regards to oppression and class inequality in the Nigerian society. They therefore believe that only the oppressed Nigerians can determine to free themselves from being mere spectators, and become actors (key players) in issues relating to the progress of the nation. Theatre revolutionaries were bent on freeing the mind of the renaissance Nigerian man, so he can take up a part and play an active role (protagonists) in the policies and decisions of the state.

Nigeria's current democratic environment yarns for new values, and national rebirth. The nation is witnessing an upsurge in social disaffection throughout the length and breadth of the nation. The strong united peace-laden nation is unconsciously heading towards disintegration and anarchy with the current wake of insecurity and political jingoism from all the ethno-cultural corners of the country. There is a great need to explore this revolutionary potency of drama and theatre in tackling this menace that threatens the unity of Nigeria. This could be achieved through adequately addressing the emergent religious, ethno-cultural, socio-political and economic challenges plaguing the unity of the nation. Some practitioners of the popular theatre tradition like Gumucio-Dagron believes that such ideologies could be result-oriented if artists can conscientise its audience and,

> Transform the passive receiver of messages into a critical, reflective and active participant in the communication process. The educational objectives would not be complete if in the aftermath, the individual or the community did not have any means to communicate, to speak their own thought, to appropriate a language and explore the possibilities of developing an expression of their own. The bottom line is that the individuals have become subjects of their own development, and not just passive objects (37).

Synopsis of Ojo Bakare's *Once Upon A Tower*
Once Upon A Tower

The play, opens on a celebratory mood. The Vice Chancellor - Prof. Chikwuka, Chief Nosa, and the Emir of Dogon Wayo – Alhaji Sabo Abdella Katonga are celebrating a successfully concluded convocation when they are ambushed by Pedro and his gang. The gang demands that the Vice Chancellor call in Prof. Kurumbete, the Provost College of Medicine, Dr. Ugolo and Dr. Yemi to his office without a clue of what is happening. On getting there, they discover they are all being held hostage by an ex-student whose career they destroyed. It is then discovered that Pedro graduated four years ago as the best student in gynaecology and that the Provost College of Medicine, the first gynaecologist in the country, who is on contract appointment three times after retirement feels threatened by the brilliance of Pedro and that of Dr. Akitikori, another brilliant staff of the College who is bold enough to stand Prof. Kurumbete and wouldn't be subdued. Hence, the Provost and the Head of department, Dr. Ugolo planned to frame Akitikori up and then have him expelled so that they could have Yemi take over his position even though they know Yemi is unqualified and has nothing to offer. Yemi is a former laboratory attendant who was employed by Prof. Kurumbete, when Prof first came back on contract after retirement from the university, calls and asks Yemi to seek admission into the college so that he could transform him from a laboratory attendant to a medical doctor. Years later, Senator Abdulraham's (chairman house committee on education at the senate who uses his party's affinity with the minister to syphon contract funds awarded on education matters) daughter Khadijat, falls in love with Pedro at her father's disapproval. They elope and she gets pregnant. Pedro carries out an abortion on her and she looses her life in the process due to wrong dosage of 'ketamine hydrochloride' which is meant to be given at 1 to 4.5mg per kilogram of body weight but Pedro administers it at 14.5mg per kilogram as a result of the wrong teaching he received from Dr. Yemi. He (Pedro) is jailed for seven years for murder but managed to escape after two years for revenge. He blames the Vice Chancellor and Senator Abdul for not making available the chemicals needed for practicals and instead, familiarizing them with dry practicals, he also blames the Provost for the half-baked education he got. The play ends with the death of Dr. Yemi (while trying to escape), the Provost and the Senator and the police arresting Pedro and his gang.

Reflections on *Once Upon A Tower*
The play essentially harps on the dangerous politics in the University system and its terrible consequences on the society at large. The play exposes some of the havoc politics amongst academics is wrecking in the university educational system and its resultant adverse effects on the graduates. With close reference to the text, the playwright through the character, Pedro says;

Pedro: The will of Allah? Is it also the will of Allah that a professor who has supposed to nurture my growth should play politics with my future as a result, stuff me with ignorance? Professor Kurumbete (points to him) wouldn't mind whatever becomes of the future of an innocent student as long as his professional monopoly is permanently guaranteed and his imagined professional enemies ruined (13).

One may begin to wonder what becomes the fate of our generation when the teachers, whose responsibility it is to impact knowledge on the next generation of leaders are that corrupt, to the level of joking with the impartation that will make the future and development of our society better. This could be a threatening reality for revolutionary theatricians to reflect on. And as we have stated earlier, According to Achebe,

> An African creative writer who tries to avoid the big social and political issues of contemporary Africa, will end up being completely irrelevant like the absurd man in the proverb, who leaves his house burning to pursue a rat fleeing from the flames (54).

The adverse effect of diversion and misappropriation of funds and grants meant for the purchase of educational equipment and materials, training of staff, erection of structures and updating of facilities, and the general development of university education in a given nation. The writer exposes such degree of degradation in the system when unworthy privileged academics are in position of authority, they see themselves as indispensable, in the conversation between Prof. Kurumbete and Dr. Akitikori.

Prof. Kurumbete: Impunite insubordination! If a university can take you back on contract three different times after retirement, then you must be a genius. I am a genius … yes … God has created very few geniuses into this country… and I am one of those few. And all of us, we were created between 1935 and 1945. Since then, God never created any genius, so small boy Akitikori I wonder the source of your confidence that …

Dr. Akitikori: … Prof … If a university has given you contract appointments three different times after retirement, it shows two things. One, is that the place has decayed and two, is that you are a local champion. Why don't you put your so-called genius on sale in the world out there and stop running back to your colony here to breathe down the neck of mere babies? Good day (exists) (20-21).

Pedro in the last scene makes some social comments, in his final words before they (Pedro and his gang) surrender to the police:

Pedro: …Now Mr Senator. I need no psychiatrist. You were not my teacher, but you constrained my teacher from teaching me properly. Tell me, what you know about contract? What do you know about chemicals … what do you know about laboratory equipment that you cornered a contract meant for their being supplied to this university? Of course, you diverted the money into your bank account and supplied noting. After graduation, I was still a stranger to some facilities I should have been familiar with even as a student. Do you know that was partly responsible for my using the wrong stuff to sedate your daughter and she died in the process? The reason for which I was sent to seven years imprisonment. Well … I will save you the seven years! And you Professor Kurumbete you became paranoid with ambition and engineered dangerous scheming to ensure the young does not grow. Have you forgotten what the sage said? "Let each become what he or she was created, capable of being". But no. No, you must contradict the natural principle of creation and regeneration just because you wanted to be the unrivalled Provost for life… (63).

The playwright buried the soul of the play in the lines above; it became a principle action to the entire text (the climax). The writer here exposes the rot in the educational system, and the corruption prevalent at the government level. According to Bakare, as published in Literary Review of the *Sun* News online, *http://sunnewsonline.com/new/?p=39967*:

> Art is a social apparatus, which means it is not isolated from the society. It cannot be hidden if it is good, so the society must enjoy it. Even in the traditional era, the artist held a strong position among his people. The essence of the academia is towards the object of common social good.

In one of the playwright's interview with the *Sun* News online, he (Bakare) reflects that:

Bakare: Balance is an artistic phenomenon whether symmetrical or asymmetrical; but it also has a sociological function too, excellence is a habit not just an act, so you are what you do and there is no running away from the truth. If it is baloney, however you cut it is still meat because life is like a boomerang, it keeps ricocheting when the evils are ripe. Bad trees cannot produce good fruits. An excellent medical system in the next ten years goes beyond a mere dream check out what is happening at the Colleges of Medicine in our various universities; what goes around comes around.

As a revolutionary artist, the playwright is burdened with the passion of bringing the desired changes needed to have an efficient and effective educational system in Nigeria. A system that has been accused for the production of half-baked graduates, thereby, seeing the artist as a restless artist who could strive until his or her dreams are brought to live, like the **Joshua that will bring the Israelites to their promised land**. According to *Sun* News online, Bakare believes:

> Above all, I am an amalgam. A product of many arts rolled into one. From childhood I have often felt this aggressive urge to express; I see forms in the space (even in an empty space) and I simply relate with it. I

don't know if you understand me but the layman sees the firmament and think it is empty. The truth is that the space has never been empty; it only takes the artist to see what others would not see. Michelangelo got a virgin piece of marble left unused by a marble seller and said, "I can see an Angel imprisoned in it and I shall set him free."

The arts eventually come to do just one thing; express that which has already been internalised. This is spiritual because what the artist expresses is even beyond him, but invariably art is all about expression. What the poet cannot paint, he sings in his poetry and what the sculptor does not have word for, he simply carves in wood. What the dancer cannot write or spell in words, he demonstrates using some dance steps. From a prodigious age of seven, I had felt I was going to burst if life would not give me a chance to express myself. There had often been something in me that would not let me rest; art. So talk about music, drama, dance and even the plastic visual arts; they are all informed by the same content, though the differences only rest with the forms. Remember your form and content theory.

As a revolutionary who has produced more than one master pieces (dramatic text) challenging the oppressive powers of the rulers against the ruled, questions some socio-political structure, and highlights religious hypocrisy by the leaders of a given society.

Music could be used to advance the theme and revolutionary thrust of a dramatic text. The playwright being known for music, dance, and so on, employs the potency of music in form of well-thought out songs in the structuring of *Once Upon A Tower*. The play uses a total of eleven (11) songs to bring out the emotional appeal of the story. It helps the reader achieve that emotional transport, appeal, and satisfaction an audience craves for. The songs are carefully selected and employed in language suitable to evoke the emotions of appreciation which is the ultimate goal of any creative art.

Conclusion
The revolutionary movement of the contemporary Nigerian is aimed at conscientising the grassroot masses, and awakening the renaissance man of his right of recognition and opportunities to shape their own destinies, by showing the people that they are the makers of history and masters of their own fate, responsible for the creation of all that is materially or spiritually valuable in their immediate environment. According to Gbilekaa, Gugelberger notes, literature, "… should use whatever is useful, modernist and/or realist, experimentation or its opposites, if it is successful in promoting the struggle for change" (198).

Let us state categorically that revolutionary theatre strives toward solving the immediate topical and contemporary social problems of its environment. Revolutionary drama or theatre sets out to present a critical perspective on the present social order. It aims to lay bare the structures of power and privilege and to show how they permeate everyday life, limiting and curtailing opportunities for self-realisation and social change. It also probes the idealisations and rationalisation that justify the present order. It challenges taken-for-granted assumptions and prices open the gaps between ideological promise and institutional performance. According to Gbilekaa,

> Osofisan regards revolution as, "a seminal biological necessity. It is organic and capable of regenerating itself". Revolution is fissionable. An artist who devotes his work to the emancipation of his people will not wither, he will be renewed. The artist never dies when the ideas he sought to propagate live after him (82).

It is evident that Bakare's theatre, in its subject matter, aesthetics, and structure is geared towards creating awareness to the general socio-political depravity, educational degradation, cultural vices, and religious hypocrisy with the intention of showing the necessity and process for s social, religious, and educational revolution that will usher in an alternative society.

Works Cited

Achebe, Chinua. "Thought on the African Novel". *Morning Yet on Creation Day*. London: Heinemann, 1981.

Bakare, Ojo Rasaki. *Once Upon a Tower*. Uyo: Afahaide Publishing Company, 2000.

Enna, Dauda, Victor Anyagu. "The Nigerian Radical Theatre Movement and the New Democracy". *Theatre and Democracy in Nigeria*. Ed. Ahmed Yerima & Ayo Akinwale. Ibadan: Kraft Books Limited, 2002.

Gbilekaa, Saint. *Radical Theatre in Nigeria*. Ibadan: Caltop Publishing Nigeria Limited, 1997.

Gumucio-Dagron, Alfonso. *Popular Theatre in Nigeria*. Lagos: UNICEF, 1994.

wa Thiong'O, Ngugi. *Writers in Politics*. London: Heinemann, 1981.

Ukala, Sam. *Manual of Research and of Thesis Writing in Theatre Arts.* 2nd Edition. Ibadan: Kraft Books Ltd., 2006.

http://sunnewsonline.com/new/?p=39967 Accessed 30 July, 2014.

Heuristic Appraisals Of The Works Of Rasaki Ojo Bakare As Quintessential Choreographer And Dancer

By
Obasi, Nelson Torti *and* Ezeh, Jonathan Chidi

Introduction
Rasaki Ojo Bakare has become a household name in Nigerian theatre administration particularly in the area of dance and choreography. His versatility and deep-rooted incursion into these fields of theatre practice has earned him the nickname – dancerasaki. Far back in the 1980s, he had joined the Yoruba Traveling Theatre group under the tutelages of Chief Jimoh and late Chief Hubert Ogunde, the acclaimed doyen of professional theatre in Nigeria.

Rasaki Ojo Bakare is a man of many feathers, jack of all theatrical trades and enviably a master of most of his chosen trades. As a theatre director, playwright, designer, songwriter, instrumentalist, arts and culture administrator, dancer and, indeed, a choreographer par excellence, Bakare is perhaps the leading Nigerian dance scholar, the most sought-after Nigerian choreographer and dance trainer and a respected dance adjudicator who has worked directly with and influenced most Nigerian dance practitioners, taught and trained many of those who teach and intellectualize dance and choreography in Nigeria at present. Creditably, his numerous choreographed works are found in the repertoires of most dance troupes in Nigeria and beyond.

The Ideology of Dance and Choreography
Dance can be art, ritual or recreation. It goes beyond the functional purposes of movements used in works or athletics in order to express emotions, moods, or ideas. Dance tells a story, serves religious, political, economic, or social needs or simply be an experience that is pleasurable, exciting, or aesthetically valuable.

Suzanne Youngerman who has written extensively on dance describes it as, "the patterned and rhythmic bodily movements, usually performed to music and serves as a form of communication or expression" (1 of 3). Dance is the transformation of ordinary functional and expressive movements into extra-ordinary movement for extra-ordinary purpose. To this end, Youngerman believes that, even a common movement such as walking is performed in dance in a patterned way, perhaps in circles or to a special rhythm, which occurs in a special context.

Dance entails a language of special nature, that could be delivered literarily or without words. It is an avenue of factual information and for entertainment. Louis Eldeft maintains that the words that dance speak are movement phrases expressive of a choreographer's design (1). Dance is a statement, an expression in movement containing some comments on reality that endures even after the dance is over. It also occurs through purposeful and controlled rhythmic movement. The resulting phenomenon is what is recognized as dance both by the performer and the observing members of a given society.

Dance is natural to man. In this vein, Idis Enem writing on *Nigerian Dances* submits that, "dance is hardly indulged in for its own sake but is always consciously cultivated to some social, religious and aesthetic reasons. Dance is a vibrant art-form that is indispensable from man (68). Every society has its own dances and each dance has its own music, movements, and costumes, and most fundamental of all, each dance, according to Warren, has a function and a motivation that is understood by all members of that society. Each community has its own dances for a particular use at a specific time, for a special event (3).

Dance can be spontaneous or performed in established movements. It can tell a story, explore an emotion, or serve as a form of self expression. Many people dance as a career, but anyone can dance simply by moving in rhythm. Dance is one of the oldest human art forms which many people in modern society enjoy based on its entertainment value. *The World Book*

Encyclopedia notes that, each generation creates new dance as an expression of its own sense of life and fun (25).

A society is scrutinized to understand its art and examine its art to understand that society. Jacques Lipschitz buttresses that this dual approach applies to African dance, for dance is intermeshed in many aspects of life; whatever the style and flow of movement, whatever the tempo, characteristics of a particular movement. Dance serves as a mirror for African life, and at the same time, as a support in the framework of its culture (5). Lipschitz submission reveals that dance is interwoven with people's culture and people's cultural identity can easily be found in their dances. Lee Warren supports this view and emphasizes that, "every dance has a heritage which reflects the ideas of its time. Each society, each group of people, develops its own set of rules by which the structures of the dance are defined. Those rules must be strictly adhered to. Each society uses the body in specific ways. As each culture has its distinctive vocabulary, so it is in dance, where different parts of the body – eyes, hands, feet, neck, shoulders, belly, ribs, and toes may be emphasized in distinctive movement (26).

Dance, therefore, can either be spontaneous or performed in established movements. It can tell a story, explore an emotion, or serve as a form of self expression. It should therefore be noted that the culture of the people is embedded in their dances. Dance, so to say, is as old as man and the motive behind its origin is adoration, imitation and fertility. The implication, therefore, is that dance, since the history of mankind is closely connected with the magical and religious rituals of indigenous people.

Dance has for long been used as a tool for social, political and economic mobilization in both the traditional and modern societies. In this respect, Marion Gough asked as well as answered "Why Dance?" Respondingly, he says, "we have chosen dance because it may be the primary, most immediate form of expression for us. The expressive and social nature of dance gives us legitimate ways in which to invent, explore, solve problems and have fun" (Introd.).

A story told is a story danced. Therefore, dance has been used extensively in the traditional societies, especially in African communities as a tool of expression, representation and re-enactment of heroic past achievements.

In his submission on *Making Dance Expressive,* Madalena Victorino (1997) says that a dance movement may be competently performed and well-executed, but may be meaningless unless expressively executed. By expression it means the memory of things lived (45). It is about communicating, revealing, and defining the intention of the movement. Such expression has to be understood by the dancer and be clear to an observer. It may be simple as a stretch – but the intention of stretching and all the meaning that the stretch entails must be communicated. By expression, the efficacy of the dance could be realized such as image, emotion or feeling reflecting tenderness, loneliness and aggression.

For dance to be expressive too, Jochen Schmidt believes that, "it needs to be performed with integrity and truth. Expression to him is not how people move, but what moves them" (45). Choreography on the other hand, is the art of arranging dance performances. It is also used to arrange any sort of performance which requires organized movement (WiseGEEK, 1). The practice of choreography is ancient. It emerged from Ancient Greek word meaning, "dance writing." Over time, the term has come to be used as "dance notation" as a reference to the notation used to record choreography. Choreography has been described by Microsoft Encarta as the art of composing dances or the movements and patterns of a dance composition (1). It can also mean the anonymously created patterns of folk dance and non-Western classical dance; most typically the term refers to specially composed theatrical dance.

Choreography has been part of dance performances since time immemorial. However, modern dance can be more challenging than the traditional forms and it is less bound by set routines; modern dance equally blends in elements from other styles such as African dance, and it is common for speed and rhythm to change suddenly and unpredictably (Burklyn Ballet Theatre, 1). Choreography is probably most famously linked with the field of dance, where it is viewed as a critical part of the performance. It can be used in essentially any sort of performance which requires organized movement. It can also be used to arrange staged fights for film and theatre, in which case the choreographer is known as a "fight choreographer."

A dance performance faces arduous challenges that a musical or opera does not because it is necessary to communicate themes, ideas, and even a story to the audience without using words. The only way, according to Burklyn Ballet Theater, to pass on this information is through the movements of the dancers. It takes skill and care to achieve this and such skill belongs to the choreographer. Like the theatre director, when people watch a performance, it is the actors or dancers they see, and it is easy to forget that behind the scene lies hours of meticulous planning by the choreographer. Therefore, a choreographer must understand the techniques and idioms behind the movement of his dance. Familiarity with dance styles and other body movements is germane to the skill such as acrobatics, pantomime and gesture, motion of fighting, and athletics.

Choreographers themselves vary widely in their specific procedures, according to Microsoft Encarta. Some formulate the dance fairly completely before working with the dancers; others create most of the dance by guiding and observing dancers' improvisations while trying out ideas; still others develop a general structure and then decide on specific combinations of steps by working them out using the dancers' bodies; some use extensive notes, drawings, and dance notation; some have a mental plan; others work by instinct and improvisation; some study musical scores, while others simply listen to the music.

However, the physique and skills of a particular dancer suggest certain movements. Once the dance composition has been formulated, the choreographer must then teach it to the dancers – demonstrating by watching as the dancers imitate.

Rasaki Ojo Bakare: The Quintessential Choreographer and Dance Scholar

The history of dance and choreography in Nigeria will be incomplete without the likes of Rasaki Ojo Bakare. The Aramoko-Ekiti born Professor has been nicknamed "Dancerasaki" by close friends and the academia for his numerous contributions to the art of dancing. As a leading Nigerian dance scholar, a most sought-after Nigerian choreographer and dance adjudicator and trainer, Bakare has contributed immensely to the field of dance in theory and praxis. He has also received so many awards for the same feat both within and outside the country.

Jedidiah Court, therefore, believes that Rasaki Ojo Bakare first love is dancing and the prized first Nigerian Professor of dance has practiced and taught dance since 1981. As a playwright, a choreographer, a play director and instrumentalist, he practically lives dance. According to Solomon Tai Adetoye, Dancerasaki has lived all his adult life being involved in one form of performance or the other and that when the retired General Yakubu Gowon-led Commonwealth games 2014 bid committee needed a man to put together a cultural package to showcase Nigeria's cultural heritage to influence the decision makers in the United Kingdom, Bakare was picked. Adetoye is of the view that, "Bakare is a widely-traveled and experienced scholar and dancer of repute" (1).

According to Akeem Lasisi, Rasaki Ojo Bakare is an astute believer in the cultural heritage of his people. As Bakare explains himself, "we need to align culture with the national ideology and philosophy." Today, apart from the current state of insecurity, almost every other social problem we have is because our culture has crashed in the first instance. What culture does, according to him, is to mould humanity, to mould the human being in us. Bakare insisted no cultured man, would carry a gun and kill his fellow human being in the first instance, or throw bombs" (2). He is of the view that government is not deliberately planting culture in the consciousness of everybody in the polity even as culture will play a major role in the rebuilding of the human mind. Bakare, therefore, believes that his return from the University of Abuja to Federal University, Oye Ekiti was an opportunity to join hands with the authorities to empower the institution culturally.

Culturally, Bakare berates the over-indulgence of some critics, especially Africans about everything western as being the ideal. Citing Julius Nyerere (1968) Rasaki Ojo Bakare, writes that, as a cultured man, "we must take our system, correct its shortcomings and adapt to its service the things we can learn from the technologically developed societies of other countries" (64).

The implication of the above is that every culture emphasizes certain features in its dance styles as well as uses it to serve its own purpose. Through dance, one can easily notice where one comes from. Bakare has done justice to culture through dance and choreography.

Dance is, in many ways, all about freedom. It is a way of expressing emotions through movement. Depending on the style, that freedom may be limited by many rules. This is because dance has very strict guidelines about acceptable movements (Contemporary dance.org.SBI 2010 – 2014).

As a dance and choreography practitioner, Bakare has used both medium to speak on the state of the nation. In his play, *This Land Must Sacrifice*, he picks on topical issues which he presents in the radical traditions of the likes of Wole Soyinka and Ngugi wa Th'iongo by speaking against the establishment if things go awry. As a matter of fact, his messages through dances and choreographic aesthetics are meant to ignite the masses and call the leaders to order.

In his play *Rogbodiyan*, Bakare also speaks on the state of the nation through a sonorous song that is danced. Using the community of Koroju as a metaphor, the song relives a catastrophe brought upon oneself by oneself. Rogbodiyan satirizes the dilemma of Koroju, a fictional community jinxed with the agony of self-imposed leadership.

Song: (English translation)
Conflict, oo, ee calamity oo
Calamity has come and left a message.
Trouble has come and left us a message
There is chaos everywhere
We are asking, we are asking
What shall we do? (6).

Rasaki's theory of Dance

As a dance theorist, Bakare sees dance as, "a language that expresses the geographical locations, biological temperament, religious beliefs, political and historical experiences, social practice and economic peculiarities of the people that own it" (76). His works are either focusing on the socio-economic problems in the society or on the injustices perpetrated by those in authority as exhibited in most of his dances.

On definition, Bakare defines dance as "the rhythmic movement of the human body in space and time to make statements" (3). From the above, it could be inferred that the essential elements in dance are rhythm, human body, space, time and communication. The greatest tool of dance, according to Bakare, is the human body. Not every body movement is qualified to be called dance. Rhythm is the underlying beat that animates movements. The fundamental reason why dance take place is to make a statement; to communicate; put across a message; and expresses thought. Bakare is of the view that, all arts, no matter the nature and form have something to say and the purveyor of such message is the dancer (Bakare 2004:4).

As a quintessential choreographer, Rasaki Ojo Bakare has done extensive work on choreography. In his book, *Rudiments of Choreography*, he describes this art as the structuring of movements in time and space to make statements while the person who undertakes this responsibility is the choreographer (1). He believes that, whatever the mind of the choreographer is capable of conceiving can be actualized in dancing. But his ability to effectively communicate these thoughts without confusing his audience depends on his experience and dexterity.

According to Rasaki Ojo Bakare there are two genres of choreography – traditional and modern or contemporary and that their respective practitioners are divergent but both are also legitimate (68). Whereas the traditional choreographer is largely engaged in a spiritual activity, the contemporary choreographer is engaged in the business of making personal statements in line with the social, theatrical and aesthetic demand of his contemporary audience.

In a sharp drawn battle between the traditional or relativist theorists and the modern or contemporary theorists, the traditionalists consider the activities of the contemporary choreographers in Nigeria as dangerous to the preservation and survival of traditional Nigerian dances. They argue that, because of their western orientation and the level of acculturation resulting from their academic and professional exposures, they have become alienated from African cultures. Thus, their roles in the Nigerian performance arts have become that of a destroyer of the people's culture. Their tampering with traditional dances, according to Ahmed Yerima, spells doom and such attempts often distort or destroy the essence of the African in traditional dances (67).

In his own wisdom and patriotism for contemporary choreography, Bakare allays the fears of the likes of Ahmed Yerima and states that, the declaration of Yerima does not recognize the true originality of the contemporary choreographer whose role is purely a creative thinker who by his role has been conferred the right, freedom and license to use traditional dances as his raw materials and make them yield new statements. Bakare emphasizes that what the modern choreographer has done could be equated with what famous Nigerian playwright, Femi Osofisan did with the myth of Moremi in his play *Morountodun* by borrowing from Yoruba folklore/myth and in the process diffused and demythologized such myths for aesthetic and ideological reasons (68).

In defence of contemporary choreographer, Bakare argues that, the choreographer is engaged in a legitimate activity within the purview of his artistic performances by trying to give the art more impetus – flesh and blood.

Conclusion:
From the foregoing, it is noteworthy that Rasaki Ojo Bakare has contributed immensely to the growth of dance and theatre practice in Nigeria. As one of the contemporary theorists of choreography, he has by way of theory and practice taken the two art forms (dance and choreography) to an enviable level as well as using them to make critical statements on the state of the nation. His contributions, so far, as a dance trainer, quintessential choreographer, theatre director, playwright, designer, songwriter, instrumentalist, arts and culture administrator, scholar and Professor of Theatre aesthetics, according to him, is like scratching the surface as more is to be expected from him in the coming years.

Works Cited

Adetoye, Tai S.: "Archive for the Nigerian arts' category: Dancing around the globe." *The Nation*, August 02, 2007, p. 1.

Bakare, Ojo Rasaki: "Towards a choreographic theory of indigenous West African dance movements." In: *Critical perspectives on Dance in Nigeria.* Ed. by Ahmed Yerima, Bakare, Ojo Rasaki, and Udoka, Arnold. Ibadan: Kraft Books Limited, 2006.

_____: *Rogbodiyan.* Nigeria: Tamaza Publishing Company Limited, 1994.

_____: *Rudiments of Choreography.* Lagos – Nigeria: Dat and Partners Logistic Ltd., 2004.

Burklyn Ballet Theatre: "Directing the dance: Summer Dance Intensive." Edinburgh: 2014.

"Choreography." Microsoft Encarta 2009 (DVD) Redmond, WA: Microsoft Corporation, 2008.

Contemporary dance.org.SBI 2010 – 2014. accessed online July 2014.

Court, Jedidiah: "Archive for the Nigerian arts' category: dancing around the globe." *The Nation*, 2nd August, 2007, p. 1

Eldeft, Louis: "Choreography and dance." In: *Basic Choreography and Kinesthetic*, 1996.

Enekwe, Onuora Ossie: *Theories of dance in Nigeria: an introduction.* Introd. by Carol Ann Lorenz. Nsukka: Afa Press, 1991.

Enem, Idis: "Nigerian dances." *Nigerian Magazine*, Festival Issue. 115 – 116.

Gough, Marion: *Knowing dance: A guide for creative teaching.* Cecil Court, London: Dance Books Ltd, 1999.

Lasisi, Akeem: "Ojo-Rasaki awakes the stage in Oye-Ekiti." *Punch*, May 7, 2013.

Lipschitz, Jacques: In: *The Dance of Africa: an introduction* by Lee Warren. Englewood Cliff, N. Y.: Prentice-Hall, Inc. 1972.

Schmidt, Jochen: Pina Bauch Wuppertal Dance Theatre, 1987, 45 – 49.

Victorino, M.: "Making dance expressive." In: Marion Gough. *Knowing dance: A guide for creative teaching.* Cecil Court, London: Dance Books Ltd., 1997.

Warren, Lee: *The Dance of Africa: An introduction.* Englewood Cliff, N.Y.: Prentice Hall, Inc. 1972.

WiseGEEK: *This day in History.* Anaheim, California: July 17, 1955.

Yerima, Ahmed, Bakare, Ojo-Rasaki, and Udoka, Arnold: *Critical perspectives on dance in Nigeria.* Ibadan: Kraft Books Limited, 2006.

Youngerman, Suzanne: "Dance." Microsoft Student 2008 (DVD). Redmond, WA: Microsoft Corporation, 2007.

Marxist Radical Playwriting in Bakare, Ojo Rasaki's *The Gods and The Scavengers*

By
Christopher Elochukwu Unegbu

Introduction
Beyond entertainment purpose, the art of playwriting beyond entertainment purpose basically tends to tilt towards correcting certain obvious social malaise within the immediate society of its creation or that which hosts it. The inter-related nature of scholarship now accentuates the ideological basis of plays which could have been hitherto ignored. While some scholars believe in sustaining the existing superstructures of every society, some contend that change remains the only way to utilise power to the benefit of the suffering majority hence the origin of ideas like Marxism. Most published plays supporting the ideas of Marxism are by theatrical scholars whose mode of communication tends to impede the desired effect since the people who deserve to be conscientised via the plays end up losing the message or being confused by the creative but ambiguity of the play-scripts due to style. Therefore, this piece examines the general nature of the concept of Marxism as it influences radical playwriting of Bakare, Ojo Rasaki in Nigeria with the aim of establishing the extent to which the Marxist radical ideals have been clearly communicated to the larger society in a less ambiguous manner when compared to the previous attempts by some "radically-oriented" Nigerian playwrights.

Synopsis of *The Gods and The Scavengers*
This play of nine movements aptly captures the fate of a mercilessly governed people in the hands of a deceitful and corrupt leader (Honourable Anago) and the band of unscrupulous councillors that serve as interface between him and the people. Like the title of the play suggests, these depraved leaders pose as gods while unjustly forcing down supposed divinely predestined (but actually humanly orchestrated) judgement on the governed through exploitative policies aimed at

enriching their already affluent purses. The helpless citizens keep pleading for divine intervention that never come until they get politically organised for a revolt by a defacto political adviser(Andy), of this depraved leader. They (masses) resolve to challenge the existing corrupt status quo of their leaders that set them (unsuspecting followers) against each other so that the culture of perpetual corruption entrenched would be overthrown. When they successfully dethrone the corrupt leadership thereby returning power to the people, the play ends with a clarion call for man to ignore the supposed opinion of the gods and believe in his humanistic ideals to better the society while the blood of the corrupt leaders would be shed to cleanse the land they actually desecrated.

The Text and Context of Marxism
The ideological postulation that champions Marxism is named after a renowned philosopher, Karl Marx. His view is a product of sociological research whose economic impact could not be overemphasised when he believes that the whole societal functionality is tilted towards the few privileged (bourgeois) whose ability to own the means of production prompts to tactically abuse the proletariat and peasants into labouring for them and their success at the expense of the latter. Hence, the classification of the society into *"haves"* and *"have nots"*. This form of oppression, Marx believes, should be overthrown for the workers and less privileged to have freedom to enjoy their labours rather than enriching the already affluent bourgeois that employed them in exchange for meagre wages and salaries not comparable to their invested labour.

In analysing this view, Cox(1998,p.7) opines:
> Human beings are social beings, we have the ability to act collectively to further our interests. However, under capitalism, that ability is submerged under private ownership and the class divisions it produces. We have the ability to consciously plan our production, to match what we produce with the developing needs of the society. But under capitalism that ability is reversed by the anarchic drive for

profits. Thus, rather than consciously shaping the nature, we cannot control or even foresee the consequences of our actions.

The above literally sums up the diverse possible patterns of interpreting and analysing the Marxist ideology which is a vital part of this piece. From the foregoing, it becomes evident that the Marxian dictum alongside its cohorts like Engels are merely reacting to a previous *status quo* which is found to have been encapsulated in the classical opinion of Feudalism where land ownership decided wealth of the lords as a result of the number of serfs under their fiefdom. This is a view popularly influenced by the scholarly endeavors of philosophers like Aristotle and his cohorts like Hegel who sees the society as being in a state of harmony, thereby, shifting to favour the oppressional superstructures of the *neo-feudal* system christened capitalism. Therefore, it becomes imperative at this point to state the obvious truth that the Marxian postulations and agitations are reactionary tendencies triggered off by the universally defined patriarchal views evident in capitalist production process. The concept of class has greater explanatory ambitions within the Marxist tradition than in any other tradition of social theory and this, in turn, places greater burdens on its theoretical foundations. In its most ambitious form, Marxists have argued that class-or very closely linked concepts like "mode of production" or "the economic base"- was at the centre of a general theory of history, usually referred to as "historical materialism". This theory attempts to explain within a unified framework, a very wide range of social phenomena; the epochal trajectory of social change as well as social conflicts located in specific times and places, the macro-level institutional form of the state along with the micro-level subjective beliefs of individual, large scale revolutions as well as sit-down strikes. Expressions like "class struggle is the motor of history" and "the executive of the modern state is but a committee of the bourgeoisie" captures this ambitious claim of explanatory centrality for the concept of class.

Marxist class analysis is ultimately about the conditions and process of social change, and thus, five concepts are particularly relevant for this purpose. They are: class interests, class consciousness, class practices, class formations and class struggle.

- Class interests: These are the material interests of people derived from their location-within-class-relations. "Material interests" include a range of issues-standards of living, working conditions, level of toil, leisure, material security, and other things. To describe the interests people have with respects to these things as 'class" interests is to say that the opportunities and trade offs people face in pursuing these interests provides the crucial theoretical bridge between the description of class relations and the actions of individuals within those relations.
- Class consciousness: The subjective awareness people have of their class interests and the conditions for advancing them.
- Class practices: The activity engages in by individuals, both as separate persons and as members of collectiveness in pursuit of class interests.
- Class formations: The collectivities people form in order to facilitate the pursuit of class interests. These range from highly self-conscious organizations for the advance of interests such as unions, political parties, and employers association, to much looser forms of collectively such as social networks and communities
- Class struggle: Conflicts between the practices of individuals and collectivities in pursuit of opposing class interests. These conflicts range from the strategies of individuals workers within the labor to reduce their level of toil, to conflicts between.

Revisiting Radical Playwriting
In this aspect of the research it should be noted that in a bid to avoid oversimplification of critical terminologies, the researcher stuck to evaluating previously existent views since the definition of playwriting seem to agree that this entails writing of new, adaptation and or any form of modification geared towards the

realisation of a new play either stageable or not. Whereas, the redefinition of radical within this context could best be summed up as meaning the tendency to rectify or correct. Therefore, any playwright whose work is entrenching the obvious change could best be termed, a radical playwright.

This aspect of the research would best be further exemplified by recalling the opinion of Wa Thiong'o (1997, p.68) thus:
> The way power in society is organised can affect writers and their writing in several ways. The writer as a human being is a product of history, time and space. As a number of society he belongs to a certain class and he is inevitably a participant in the class struggle of his times.

This view perfectly captures the pivotal position of the modern Nigerian playwright whose scripts that are to be staged, is a reflection of an inglorious past, almost chequered present and seemingly unpredictable future of a country whose greatest woes emanate from the dichotomy of the material, social, cultural political, religious, and academic polarisation of *"haves"* and *"haves nots"* otherwise known as capitalism and the reactionary agitation of returning power in the means and process of production to the more populated proletariat and peasant class emasculated by the minority capitalists. Lending credence to this view, wa Thiong' o (1997, p.68) further reaffirms that:
> A writer subject matter is history, the process of a people acting on nature, changing it, and in so doing acting on and changing themselves. The changing relations of production, including power relation is a whole territory of concern to writer. Politics is hence part and parcel of this history.

Worthy of note is to highlight the fact that the affluence of the capitalist orchestrated past (history) retold in a harmonic pattern courtesy of the cathartic and resolution impact of the patriarchal Aristotelian dictum (poetics), does not encourage change but sustenance of the status quo .This remains the basis of the theatrical pattern of the post 1960s, as further propagated by the post-civil war era in Nigeria. From the foregoing, it becomes pertinent to reaffirm the basic truth which stems from the facts that radical playwriting as a pivotal art of the theatre, requires selfless dedication since the practitioner will likely collide with the prevalent forces that sustain the existing status quo. Since politics is vital to the radical playwright's modus operandi, Bakare's works are most likely to contradict the existing status quo as is evident in the plays-cript under review. Thus, under the Aristotelian dictum, would be discouraged since the capitalist superstructures of the status quo would defeat a man who believes in change. The cathartic and revolutionary provision of the Aristotlean poetics which is a manifestation of capitalism ideologies tends to discourage revolt. But, this, the radical playwright does not believe in. Rather, he insists on returning power to the people by encouraging them via his art to rise up against all forms of oppression as Gbilekaa (1997, p.38) sums it thus:

> When therefore the 'peripeteia' combine with anagnorisis and catastrophe to produce catharsis, the spectator is intimidated. He is intimidated by a deliberate conditioning of his mind to accept the value of the superstructure, where the idea, views, concept and of a finished world are imposed on him by the ruling class in the cathartic experience. thus he delegates his power to think and act, purge the spectator of the tragic flaw, the harmatia. Thus, catharsis was the most important functions of the Greek tragedy because as a purifier of a spectator it disarmed him from any alternative dissenting views that were of changing the society.

It is easily deductible from the foregoing that the conflicts in such a theatrical endeavors are majorly product of what Gbileka terms "excessive exhibition of their cherished values" (1997:p.31) usually aimed at usurping the place of the rightful repositioning of the common man. This is the result of the seeming endless divisions in the society where the bourgeoises employ virtually every possible means to sustain the propagation of oppressive policies. As Wright observes, Marxist tradition occurs "as an adjective, the word class modifies a range of concepts, class conflict and class consciousness. (2014, p.11).

Therefore, the playwriting style geared towards agitation had always been part of Nigerian theatrical practice over the years but the major impediment lies in the fact that majority of the works had good intents but vaguely communicated as a result of scholarly experimentation and or unnecessary use of extremely elevated figures of speech especially metaphor which makes it physically available but communicatively inaccessible. While analysing the Nigerian theatre, Kerr (1997: p.117) upholds this view thus; "The problem with such methods of making plays relevant is that the theatrical allusion demand techniques of decoding which tend to be far more accessible to educated elites than to popular audiences". By implication, the plays with the thematic preoccupation under this genre of Marxist thematic preoccupation has been in existence but in most cases not easily discernible e.g Femi Osofisan's *The Chattering and the Song*, whereby the predator- prey relationship of a typical capitalist system is reduced to a mere insect characterisation. How many readers will understand this concept? This means that the playwrights should endeavour to consider the uneducated, less educated and the elites as to provide a meeting point for them all. The essence of this basically is to avoid either ambiguity of form creation and or its rendering. The error would emanate from limiting the playwriting language and style, without considering its implication, to strict ivory tower exercise since according to Osofisan (2001, p.63):

> The university is an ivory tower, very deliberately separated from the town, blissfully unaware of an and untarnished by the band realities of quotation life among the people: the teacher who leave and work on the campus .....and those that they teach, are too sheltered away on their campuses, to be able to comprehend, let alone sympathize with the palpable agonies on the street.

But contrary to such unnecessarily elitist assertion as above, the playwright whose play-script is under review tactfully created with the simplest of language and other artistic channels, a work within the ivory tower context, that captures the mood of the average helpless majority in a country of witnessing untold hardship; this same work could still be staged for any class of audience (elitist or not), and the revolutionary messages of the work would neither be lost nor misrepresented since the playwright avoided all forms of ambiguity. This simple but precise means of communicating this creative enterprise, being one that can be easily deciphered by all classes of prospective readers and audience alike, when compared to certain previous works of some prominent playwrights that attempted a Marxist radical playwriting adventure, explains the essence of this study.

Bakare, Ojo Rasaki's *The Gods and The Scavengers* in the Light of Marxist Radical Playwriting.

Basically, the attempt of the playwright to create a new Marxist radical play-script spurred him to creatively use, amidst several elements, devoid of ambiguity to communicate the message of the play to his large audience. These vital elements would be examined under the following points:
- Simple language
- Rhetorical/revolutionary songs
- Play-within-a-play
- Imagery

Simple Language
In exemplifying the agitation of the less privileged against oppressive superstructure, the playwright uses simple but carefully chosen language. The playwright, contrary to some previous works of other Marxist radical playwrights, made use of very easily discernible language devoid of all forms of ambiguity. In this context, no idea tends to communicate a contrary meaning . The playwright spiced up the script under review with languages of both the elitist and non-elitist class of prospective readers /audience members. This basically carries even the stark illiterate along in the meaning-making process. The playwright

makes use of simple language embellished with easily intelligible figures of speech. His dialogues are not subject to any decoding process since they are aptly self explained in the critical evaluation of the existing exploitative superstructures of the politics of the day. The message of revolution would be totally lost if the playwright should use language(s) that would not be easily intelligible to his readers and or audience. Few examples would help exemplify his use of simple language. He clearly communicates the message of oppressive leadership through a simple approach as seen in Movement One thus:

LEADER: You people are stubborn goats. The Honourable Chairman, in his magnanimity, gave you a whole one month notice to pack yourselves, vacate the town and relocate to somewhere of your choice, far away from the glitters of the city which your rage litter unduly. But no, you refused to leave. You refused to leave with respect. Now you will leave by force, with ignominy.

SCAVENGER 1: But why are you people treating us this way? We are not disturbing anybody here. We built our tents here and we make it our abode because when you've had your fill in your homes, this is where you come to dump your leftovers.

SCAVENGER 2: We are satisfied with your litters. We ask that you leave us here in peace.

SCAVENGER 3: We say half bread is better than none. Why do you want to relocate us to a desert where nothing exists at all?

LEADER: Enough of your rattling. (*To his aides*) Okay boys, obey the last order. Move these idiots into the waiting van and ferry them into the jungle. Move! (2013, pp.5-6)

While seriously considering the less educated in his choice oflanguage he communicated the revolutionary element of a Marxist radical theatre thus in movement two through a revolutionary character thus:

IYALOJA: All dis one wey una dey talk, una just dey scratch the body of coconut with fingernail. If dis market extend go reach Kafanchan, make road big so tey five elephants dey waka side by side the same time, things no go better for we if the big people wey dey thief things wey belong to the land no stop. If all the wayos and jibitis wey dey our blood no stop, we no go make any headway for this land. So Honourable, the things wey we want be sey, make una stop wayo and jibiti for this land.(2013, pp.10-11).

Rhetorical/ Revolutionary Songs
Sequel to the simple language technique employed by the playwright, he further used songs that did not just ask critical questions that require active solutions but made outright revolutionary declaration thus charging the people to take their future into their hands by radical thinking that must ensure a better leadership class through a revolutions. The use of major ethnic languages from across the geo-political zones of the country (Nigeria) to embellish the songs further elucidates the revolutionary message intent of the play. Some are popular songs while others are product of his creativity. The use of created songs that further exemplify the Marxist radicality of the playscript is the song of the scavengers in the opening glee thus:

Lead: Yes, it's the dawn of a new morning but the Promised Land is still far away. Our destiny is in our hands, we must rise up now or else we perish
Chorus: Yes, it's the dawn of a new morning...

Lead:	Why do we shy away from civil struggle? The heavens help those who help themselves. Our destiny is in our hands. This is the time to fight all our oppressors.
Chorus:	Yes, it's the dawn of a new morning...
Lead:	Why do we shout God as if he never gave us brain? Why do we shout the devil like we are zombies? In the scriptures, all things were put in our hands. When we do nothing, the gods do nothing.
Chorus:	Yes it's dawn of a new morning...(2013,p.vi)

In movement One, the rap rendition of the scavengers while they bemoan the neglect of local expertise for unnecessary preference to foreign ones no matter how sub-standard, further elucidates the successful accomplishment of the playwright's mission thus:

SCAVENGER 1:	My name is Prof, suggesting I am schooled. I teach in the morning, in the noon and in the night. I studied in Ibadan and not in Toronto so, my papers can be screened. They are not obscured. But the men from Toronto are the gods of my land; they cheat, they brag. Indeed, their fakery is complete. (*Freezes*)
OTHER SCAVS:	(*chorusing*) We make them our gods and they loot our treasury.
SCAVENGERS:	I am a healer by talent and also by training, I love to heal so I went for knowledge; I was taught how to open and treat and close. My patients are amazed; they think I deserve an award. But here in my land, the awards are for jokers. The more you are fake, the higher your wage. The more sophisticated a rogue, the higher the respect and indeed awards in the land are meant for the crooked.

SCAVENGER 3:	Me, I am a farmer and I till to feed the land. I do all the sweating and they do all the eating. I asked for caterpillar, they provided me a ho*e,* for a fertilizer, they increased my tax. They carry all the money and buy Onfoloke yet they want my cassava for half a kobo. (*Freezes*)
OTHER SCAVS:	(*chorusing*) We make them our gods and they loot our treasury.
SCAVENGER 4:	I job with my hands, I be bobo technician. I tie all the screws and tighten all the nuts; I hawk all the spanners, the hammers and the scissors but the ,em of devil dem are plenty for we land, I work like a bull but they change all the figures. So I feed like ant and they consume like the bull.
OTHER SCAVS:	(*chorusing*) We made them our gods and they loot our treasury.(2013, pp.2-3)

The playwright's radicality in song creation is further manifested in the third movement where the market traders took up arms to protest the exploitative tendencies of the councilors by resolving to stone anyone who attempts to further defraud them thus:

SONG 3
A ma soko fun
Ouncillor to ba tugbowo leyin oja
A ma soko fun ooo

Anyi ga atu ya okwute 2x
Counciloors obula biara ina
Ina ego aka azu
Anyi ga-atu ya okwute

Agid ton enye ki tiat 2x
Councillors ndomokiet abogo
Okuk ke urua mi
Iya ton enye ki itiat (2013,p.25-26)

The zenith of his manipulation of song to suit the Marxist radicalist recast of the Ngerian national anthem into a rhetorical question thus:

O gods of creation
For how long shall we wait?
But they say you are gods of love
For how long you have shown us hate
You give us leaders who are rogues, you
make them milk us dry
We are waiting for the day when our help
Shall come down
Right from your abode(2013, p.5)

While in the eighth movement, he employs two very popular songs *"We must overcome!"* and *"We no go gree!"*, to drive home the revolutionary message he preaches.

The Play-within-a-play
Through the play within a play, the playwright recollects the tale of Odewale and Besija alongside the role of the gods in predestination which he refutes with a rebuff by projecting the end of the characters as being products of their decisions. Here the playwright shows the fact despite the supposed influence of the gods in the daily lives of men, the confidently analytical human can really change his fate for the better despite who and what the object of oppression is or seems to be. This view of the playwright is summed up through a revolutionary character thus:

ANDY: When we do nothing, the gods do nothing. We
          help the gods to either make or unmake us.

Imagery
The playwright severally made use of mental imagery from the the suggestive title of the play, which subjects one to pause and ponder on the possible relationship between the high-dwelling Gods and the earth-dwelling scavengers. Moreover, response of the scavengers to their several bemoaning tasks one to assess the

depth of the harm done by the privileged few to the majority. This cuts across even the songs that were used by the playwright.

Besides, the juxtaposition of the controversial Odewale and Besija in the play-within-a-play scenes, clearly shows the image of strength of decision to change one's fortune as contrary to any form of assumed will of the gods in justifying unnecessary human-induced suffering hence the call for revolt against an unjust system.

When the totality of capitalist orchestration that sustained the oppressive superstructure failed courtesy of the determination of the people, the dark past was recast through determination to achieve a better future with power I the hands of the people thus:

SCAVENGER 4: They were merry making, not knowing that we, the scavengers have taken our destiny in our hands and have started a struggle for the total transformation of the land of our birth. So, we moved into the Chairman's house and caught them like ordinary chickens.

SCAVENGER 3: So my people, these criminals have a common fate. They are rich and powerful. We also have a common fate, we are poor and hungry. It is a fight between the rich and the poor. Our differences are not in tongue or tribe, but the side of the ladder one belongs to. Hungry people from all homes should come together and confront their oppressors no matter the language the oppressor speaks. Brothers and sisters, you have an opportunity to change your destiny today, will you join the struggle?

CROWD: Yes! Yes!! Yes!!!

IYALOJA: Quiet, Quiet. (Silence) I thank una people. We ready to join una if na to better our lives. But look dead body don full ground

	from this senseless fight. How we go do? Also, this struggle, how we go struggle am?
SCAVENGER 1:	Thank you Iyaloja. We shall bury our dead, try to forget our losses and forgive ourselves for our ignorance. Two, these criminals shall not only cease to be our leaders from this moment, their blood shall wet our road to freedom and their children must never be allowed to take power in the future again.
MALLAM SHEHU:	(Addressing the audience) Tough talk by godless souls. Whatever these people have done, it is the will of the gods. We must not go against the will of the...
ANDY:	Damn the gods! Screw their will! When our ignorance, slot, greed and inertia hold us captive, we mutter "the will of the gods". We are either victim of our choices and thinking or the gods are mere robbers whose pre-occupation is to kill, maim and destroy. And let brothers and sisters tell one another that when men think and rise in action, their lives are affected and miseries flee. I say damn the gods and chose to be free.
SCAVENGER 1:	If the gods mean to force us into the destiny of Odewale, we should say no and refuse to die. I love the God of Besija. Remember, Besija destined to change his destiny for better and his God granted his request. Besija was not afraid. He did not sit down and succumb to a cruel fate. He did something and something good happened to him. Any god that ordains a cruel fate and seals all escape routes is a common criminal and must be blamed for the inevitable rebellion.(2013, pp.59-61)

Conclusion

From the foregoing, it is pertinent to observe that the nature of the Marxist radical playwriting experience in Nigeria having come of age can never be discussed wholistically without a vital reference to the celebrated playwright whose play-script is under study. It becomes very obvious that from his contribution, a lingering gap of communication mode, from the play-scripts of the ivory tower dons, to prospective readers and or audience members has been bridged hence demystifying the seeming obvious ambiguity characterizing previous Marxist radical playwriting experiences in Nigeria. This emanates from the fact that most previous scholarly playscripts whose messages either failed to be properly communicated in an intelligible language or are replete with somewhat abstract figures of speech that renders the entire decoding process much more difficult to the average reader and prospective audience. But, the celebrated playwright carefully created a work that took cognizance of individuals with varying levels of literacy and exposure who ought to be the target in the creation process of a Marxist radically oriented playscript since ideally power belongs to the people. Scholarly playwrights who subsequently utilize this *Bakarean* approach are most likely to record more success in terms of desired sociological impact of their playscripts.

Reference
Bakare, R.O. (2006). *The Gods and the scavengers*. Abuja: Roots and Books publications.
Cox, J.(1998). An introduction to Marx's theory of alienation. In: *International socialism quarterly journal of the socialist workers* party.(pp.65-83). Britain: International socialism.
Gbileka, S. (1997). Radical theatre in Nigeria .Ibadan: Caltrop publisher limited.
Ngugi wa Thiong'o. (1997). Writers in politics. In: Writers in politics. A re-engagement with issues of Literature and society. (Pp.67-77). Oxford: James Currey limited.
Osofisan, F. (2001).Literature and the pressure of freedom in Africa: A dramatist writes back In: *Pressure of freedom essays, speeches and songs*. (pp.28-43). Lagos: Concept publication Ltd.

Change And The Role of The Playwright in Bakare, Ojo Rasaki's *Once Upon A Tower*

By
Umenyilorah, Chukwukelue Uzodinma.

Change is the most constant phenomenon in life. The response that triggers change usually emanates as a response to previously existing flow of events that tend to encounter a new wave of reactions. The way it comes is made manifest in several ways according to time and place. In the myriads of multiple judgments and conflicting opinions, the playwright, especially in contemporary times stands as a bridge to fill the lacuna present in the lack of objective progression in contemporary societies The way diverse professions react and or adapt to changes tend to vary but for the purpose of this study, the advocatory role of a playwright as a catalyst to socio-cultural change process and the stylistics the playwright under study utilised informs the essence of this study. He stands as a sermonizer who having studied, knowing the truth, reveals to the common 'worshiper' ideals that if imbibed would transfigure such individual(s) presenting a more radiant person who would then stand boldly in his own office as a preacher also to guide the souls of men into realization of the ultimate truth which he himself has acquired. For the purpose of this study, the assessment of the aforementioned role of a playwright in his society, would therefore be done with Bakare, Ojo Rasaki's *Once Upon A Tower* in a bid to evaluate the situation that led to the change(s) as well as his own creatively ameliorative interpretation of change process would be exemplified subsequently.

Synopsis Of *Once Upon A Tower*
The plot revolves around the corrupt culture entrenched by mediocrity in the College of Medicine of a certain university(Mariapinto), where the old generation Lecturer (Prof. Kurumbete) replete with obsolete ideas persistently impedes the growth of a younger colleague (Dr. Akitikori) and an innovative younger generation (Pedro Omowaye). Rather, this same older

generation under the guise of being dogmatic encourages the enthronement of mediocre brains in the teaching profession of the academic community. The effect of this eventually leads to the death of Khadijat, the unfortunate young lover of an idealist, intellectual but frustrated young Pedro. This unleaches a wave criminal actions exposed via the vengeance mission of Pedro who had been incarcerated by the Khadijat's father whose conspiratorial actions ignored by the management aided the corrupt practices. The play ends by the murder of all the conspirators process.

Brief Review of The Concept of Change

Since this concept (change) form the essence of this study, alongside the ways in which the playwright under study utilized it; one would not be wrong to revisit some popular views on change.

In the words of E.U.M. Igbo and E.E. Anugwom (2002.p. 12) "Change occurs at a very alarming rate in the contemporary world and more often than not is a product of the crisis and chaos characterizing the contemporary social reality." From the foregoing, it becomes pertinent to observe that beyond the imaginative sphere which is subject to individual conceptualization, every other effect that cuts across all spheres of human endeavour has attendant impact on human society. This is via action or reaction, which affect the core existence of human beings in his society.

Social Change

Since the human society, as varying as it appears has its basic universality in the concept of change resulting from modification that are characterized by paradigm shifts, Igbo and Anugwom (2002, p. 12) opines that "social change is simply any variation from a previous state or mode of existence. It connotes something that is markedly different from its original version". This view practically centres on the emanation of newness of ideas that tends to overthrow a non-functional convention. The moment any phenomenon acts as a catalyst in the society, whether wholly accepted or revolted against, the reaction generates a whole new thought pattern that affects humanity. This lends credence to the assertion of Igbo and Anugwom (2002:p. 13) that... "social change is all about novelty and fundamental restructuring of the way members of a particular society relate or the manner a group in society function in relation to another group. It is against the above premise that the play-script under study be subsequently analyzed since its conceptualization and realization is a product of human actions and reactions thereby upholding the view of Ngugi wa Thiong'O (p. 4) thus:

> Literature (to which playwriting belongs) results from conscious acts of men and women in society. Being a product of their intellectual and imaginative activity, it is thoroughly social. The very act of writing even at the level of the individual, implies social relationships: one is writing about somebody for somebody.

Cultural Change

Having established the fact that humans and their societies are inseparable in terms of existential modus operandi; the vital question to ask then is how does the human race adapt to the innumerable survival challenges of life? The answer therefore is in the word 'culture'. Though its definition is not the essence of this paragraph, it is unchangeably perceived as the totality of a people's way of life. Then, when cultural change becomes the essence of the discussion, its further classification according to material and non-material attributes ought to be reckoned with since according to Igbo and Anugwom (2002, p. 16).

> The material culture are those tangible aspects of a people's way of life that can be seen and touched. (while) Non-verbal culture... refers broadly to actual human behaviour, cultural change refers mainly to culturally meaningful symbols produced by human beings in their attempt to survive within their societies.

From the above, it is paramount to observe that the totality of human existence in life is a reaction to one form of action or the other. These reactions in themselves cut across all spheres of human endeavour thereby triggering paradigm shifts in constituents of each society which in turn could lead to cultural change. These changes and how there were communicated constitutes role of preachers, reformers, financial experts e.t.c. with each exercising his claim through projections in indices/figures or mere literary documentation.

But for the purpose of this study, the role of the playwright through carefully selected words and suggested actions in reliving the quintessential aspects of a socio-cultural malaise to a larger society with the view of change would be assessed in the next chapter thereby corroborating Edith Hamilton (19, P.): "The way a nation goes, whether that of the mind or the spirit is decisive in its effect upon art". For purpose of precision in scope of study, the socio-cultural change role of Bakare, Ojo-Rasaki in *Once Upon a Tower* would be assessed under the following headings:
1. Thematic preoccupation
2. Stylistics
3. Institutional re-orientative essence

Thematic Preoccupation
The playwright chose to dwell extensively on the issues of corruption and mediocrity alongside their effects when purposely ignored in a system and the karmic implications of such actions. Under the corruption aspect, the playwright communicated through impeccable means to the minds of prospective readers and audience alike, the evils of stagnant senile mediocrity mitigating against the growth of the innovative younger generation's meritocracy. This is manifested in the Fifth movement when the provost prefers a submissive dullard(Yemi), as a prospective consultant compared to the assertive intelligent younger colleague (Akitikori), who he feels would usurp his position. The ensuing dialogues explain the situation:

UGOLO: Em... Prof, between you and me, he is not a trouble maker. Just that he is a downright non-

	conformist. He is too bold and vocal, can die for justice and never wants to be cowed. But the young man knows his job.
KURUMBETE:	You are only confirming the fact that he is dangerous. When a bold, justice-loving non-conformist also has the advantage of intelligence and professional relevance, then he is too dangerous. Look, that boy is dangerous to my future. He is in my area of specialization, well positioned to break my monopoly. He is also dangerous to your future. Brilliant and active, he is a threat to your long stay as the head of department. We have to get him out of the system fast! (pg 30 - 31).

When asked who would aptly replace such an experienced man whose absence would affect the system, he reacts thus:

KURUMBETE: To hell with the system suffering. I hope you are not fooling yourself thinking that you can help the system? Can't you see nobody care about the system? Everybody is just a hanger-on looking for how to survive via the system. Those who are in a position to make fat monetary rip-offs from the system do so. It is a merchandise. The system is not only suffering but bleeding. So what difference will another kick make? The system has seen nine hundred and ninety nine to hell with the millennium. (2000:p. 6).

To list the mediocre-based analysis of the characters in the play is simply to photocopy the play. That notwithstanding, one clearly sees the importance of this play-script since the playwright created characters in whom we see the typical origin of a negative socio-cultural change in the average ivory tower as a result of arrogance and fear-induced paradigm shifts in ideal values.

By such creative representation, the reader and prospective audience alike pause and ponder on the possible effects of such actions especially to a life-saving discipline as delicate as the medical profession. The height of mediocrity is further exposed through his response when told that his anointed candidate is not intellectually sound for the job thus:

KURUMBETE: Who cares? Is he going to teach your child? Look my dear, make no mistake about allowing your child to study in this country... I know we only compensated Yemi for being a long-serving junior staff of our, that was why we got him into the MBBS programme. But if his becoming a lecturer will be the way out to deal with a boy who is a potential threat, then why not? People like Yemi will pose no threat to us. He knows he is weak, so, he will be gentle, submissive, ask no questions and continue to be our good boy. (2000: p. 38)

The fact that such utterances emanates from a custodian of intellectual tradition simply reaffirms the extent to which the lacklustre attitude of the ruling class in all spheres of Nigeria who wish to cling tenaciously to power would go to remain unchallenged. The question is would a reader who after seeing the karmic end of this mediocrity not be compelled to re-visit his arrogant decisions (if any) so as to avoid such end?

The play-script, without direct approach, raises a lot of vital questions that dwell extensively on the integrity of leadership. Had people refocused on ideal socio-cultural values, the nightmarish end of the corrupt leaders in the play-script would have had no reason to have evolved initially.

But for lost ideal socio-cultural values, what else would make a vice-chancellor not take disciplinary action against a dubious contractor working for him and his institution and yet claim to be at the helm of administrative running of the same?.

Through the dialogue, the decadent culture that has enveloped an erstwhile soundly functioning system, one sees the effects which characterize the socio-cultural change the playwright repetitively shows and a reactionary one he judiciously advocates through creativity. The chain reaction that defies all forms of the typical African socio-cultural values of respect for the elderly and value for life, leads to the random killing of elders by Omowaye Pedro hence justifying the fact that all the characters involved in institutionalizing corruption in that institution paid with their lives and that of their loved ones. This stand to prove that all unconventional acts which constituted what became new cultures of the institution should be discouraged in preference to socio-cultural change that the playwright recommends.

Stylistics
Flashback
The playwright employed severally the use of flashbacks to juxtapose the causes and effects of injustice in the typical Nigerian society. He did a microcosmic representation of using the ivory tower supposed to be the base of knowledge and experience. The secret and public crimes of injustice against the principled happened in the past but the negative impacts upon the numerous victims eventually led to the disruption of what would have gone down in history as another colourful convocation party celebrating the entire management and deans of the school as super-humans whereas by their nefarious activities, talents were frustrated.

Chorus
Moreover, just like in the Greek theatre, the playwright made use of a very functional chorus christened Amebo band in his story-telling technique which suggests the archetypal gossip team. By their involvement, secret affairs are made public just like intentions. Theirs it was, to musically tell secret tales that exemplified virtually all the crimes of the play. The gradual process of moral decadence that enthroned mediocrity compared

to strict adherence to meritocracy initially in the University is encapsulated in the prologue song thus:

Solo: Once Upon a Tower
In our country Nigeria
The tower upon an ivory
On a gold on the marble ooo

Chorus: Later but later... the tower on the silver eee
Later but later the tower on the bronze / x2

Solo: Once Upon a Tower
The ivory on the marble
Na the citadel of learning
A place for civilization

Chorus: Small by small, the tower on the stone eee
Little by little, the tower on the wood / x2ce

Solo: Once upon a tower
The ivory upon the gold
E dey shine e dey glitter
A place for the high and mighty

Chorus: Now but now the tower in the dust eee
Now but now the tower in the mud
The high and the mighty
They are crawling, they are sleeping
Area men and women
They are winning, they are cheating
The high and the mighty
They are melting like jellies
Area bobos and girls
They are flying, they are kicking. (2000:p. 1-2)

Nemesis Nemesis Nemesis
Retributive justice (2ce)
The wickedness of today
Will be punished tomorrow
Nemesis, the seed that germinates

Nemesis Nemesis Nemesis

> Retibutive justice (2ce)
> Laziness of today
> Will bring poverty tomorrow
> Nemesis, the seed that germinates
>
> Nemesis Nemesis Nemesis
> Retributive justice (2ce)
> The corruption of today
> Will bring failure tomorrow
> Nemesis, nothing can stop its growth

But from the few selected songs, it is imperative to observe that the role of the Amebo band could best be likened to that of an omniscient narrator who knows the past, present and could even project into the future of the society via the play-script. From the above songs, one can easily deduce the concept of socio-cultural change being recommended by the playwright through a juxtaposition of past and present while leaving the reader or audience to figure out the rhetorics The songs are basically edutaining since melodious tunes were combined with informative lines with thought-provoking implications. So, from the above, it is evident that the songs used were instructive in an entertaining manner.

Institutional Re-Orientation
From this perspective, it becomes imperative to ask what formed the idea of the playwright's creative adventure if not the zeal to re-orientate the ideological foundations of every malfunctioning Nigerian establishment (not just universities). Now, if a leader has the interest of the larger society at heart courtesy of the ideal socio-cultural values of his people, he would not compromise the future of health practice on the altar of petty jealousy as shown thus:

UGOLO: Remember the extra-ordinary brilliant part 4 student, Omowaye Pedro whose genius we hope Akitikori will help to specially develop. Yemi will definitely not be able to offer the kind of stuff a brain like Omowaye needs to blossom.

KURUMBETE: There you go again. Who tells you I even support the idea of a well enriched special training programme for Omowaye Pedro? That Wizard? Even without any special training, he is already competing with part six students. People like him should be intellectually disempowered if we must own the future. And don't call me evil, I see nothing evil in what I am saying. Self preservation they say, is the first human instinct.

UGOLO: I agree with you completely sir.

Instead of engaging in institutional preservative actions, the leader stuck to mediocre decisions that would perpetuate him in office at the expense of the larger society. This situation had severe implications in the play as the playwright craftily shows the end of any leader who opts for personal preservation at the expense of institutional advancement.

Moreover, the vengeance mission of the Pedro-led hit men from a functionalist perspective actually acted to salvage the institution from future decay rather than encourage a lackadaisical attitude encouraged by mundane bureaucratic processes.

Finally, the play-script bore the challenge of re-orientating every institution already bedevilled by such obvious lacklustre attitude to leadership. This the playwright successfully achieved through the presentation of a violent present aimed at ensuring change alongside the past where criminal acts warranting such were committed.

Conclusion
This study has successfully attempted to highlight the role of human actions in shaping societal values in the process of change hence the role of the playwright in communicating this process

through a carefully crafted thought-provoking artistic masterpiece. Little or no doubt should be raised as to whether or not there are obvious leadership challenges facing virtually all spheres of Nigeria. Against a juxtaposition of a clean past that had a functional leadership system through a gradual corruption process, right down to victimization and karmic retaliation, one sees that attendant changes resulting from paradigm shifts characterizing optional choices and decisions influence human individual socio-cultural changes. This explains why Bakare, Ojo-Rasaki in a playwriting experience proffers catalytic solutions that would aid to change the fate of a nation with chequered leadership past, disorganized administrative present and an uncertain future.

References

Bakare, Ojo Rasaki. (2000). Once Upon A Tower. Uyo: Afahaide Publishing Company.

Igbo, E U .M and Anugwo, E.E. (2002). Social change and Social Problems: A Nigerian Perspective. Nsukka: AP Express Publishers.

Ngugi wa Thiong'o. (1997). Literature and Society. In: Writers in Politics. A re-engagement with issues of literature and society. Nairobi: East African Educational Publishers. (pp. 3 - 27).

Simon, Yves. (1986). Work, Society and Culture (ed.) Vukan Kuic. New York: Fordham University Press.

Voices of Power and Echoes of Moral Decadence in Bakare Ojo Rasaki's *Rogbodiyan*.

By
Olokodana, Oluwatoyin J.

Introduction

Power and decadence have bi- lateral affiliations. Power is a complex phenomenon and its definition varies according to its usage. Power may be associated with physical ability bestowed on an individual, group of people or institution to carry out behavioral regulation through the use of persuasion, pressure or compulsion (George- Genyi, 100). Nonetheless, power encompasses a lot more than just physical strength and ability because power speaks in different languages. The term may be used synonymously with other concepts such as wealth (money) as it may be used to gain social, political and religious prominence, brainwashing, not leaving out the supremacies of the super- naturals. Newman (51-52) agrees to the fact that "Power is to be thought of as a series of ongoing strategies and relationships rather than a permanent state of affairs" but Foucault (93) captures a more recognisable definition of the concept of power. He opines that "Power is everywhere...because it comes from everywhere". This implies therefore that power as concept transverses the physical ability acquired or bestowed on individual or centraliszed institutions because power may diffuse, disperse and reveal itself from different perspectives within each society. In reality, the search and desire for power and dominance will never seize until the physical world is extinct, this is for the reason that it is in human nature to acquire power and dominance. Emphasising that power, influence and money are great predators of the political system of many societies of the world today. It is also the crave for money and power that leads group or individuals to engage in demeaning acts thus, lowering the reputation of such individuals or membes of the society.

Unfortunately, it is upon the illegal or unconstitutional use of power that moral decadence rests. Moral decadence in its simplest form means a flight or divergence from ethical standards towards immoral values. It begins with making unprincipled or immoral choices and spreading same all over. In a morally decadent state, nothing is termed atrocious since the bad way of doing things is now described within the purview of the philosophical label "anything goes". One valuable way to measure the extent of decadence in a given society is to expose the strength and extent of corruption within the society. Mohammed (119) clearly declares that "One of the greatest threats to economic and political development of any nation is corruption" and this may also include buying of votes. Sha (123) is of the opinion that vote buying is a monetary persuasion technique employed by a candidate in the influence of another in favour of his choice. He reiterates thus,

> Vote buying is a corrupt act which usually takes the form of "a gift or gratuity bestowed for the purpose of influencing the action or conduct of the receiver; especially money or any valuable consideration given or promised for them betrayal of a trust or the corrupt performance of an allotted duty, as to a fiduciary agent, a judge, legislator or other public officer, a witness, a voter, etc.

Corruption in high and low places breed decadence and Nigeria as a nation is threatened by this specter because it is a worm that has eaten deep into the fabric of the Nigerian political and economic system. Unfortunately, and in most cases, the practice is fuelled by money bags and unscrupulous political leaders and their handymen. However, corrupt practices are detected amongst the mighty and the lows and the spread has led to Nigeria as a country, its leaders and citizens being indicted in foreign representations. As a matter of fact, Aiyede (39) records that "The general global perception about corruption in Nigeria is that it is a pervasive phenomenon. It is generally acknowledged that corruption and corrupt practices are endemic and systemic in both public and private sectors of Nigeria". Now, whether or not this perception is true and generally accepted about the Nigerian state and its people, corruption is widespread in Nigeria and this is evidenced in nearly every Nigerian society. Be it as it may, decadence not only rest it course on the lava of corruption because aside corruption, other unruly behaviors prevail within the society, and these may include political assassinations of the just and the un-just, assaults, bribery, injustice, religious hypocrisy etc.

"Rogbodiyan" in Yoruba context means cataclysm, suffering, ruins, tragedy etc. The play, <u>Rogbodiyan</u> places before the reader/ audience a satire of the Nigerian state, therefore the method adopted for the examination carried out in this paper "Voices of Power and Echoes of Moral Decadence in Bakare, Ojo Rasaki's <u>Rogbodiyan</u> is analytical. A critical study of our society through the lens of the play purely suggests that morality value within the societies is graduating paving way for decadence. The paper further appraises the work of Ojo Rasaki within the axiom of mimesis and concludes that the quest for power and wealth operate on the same pedestrian, and this may have detrimental effects on individuals and human community at large.

Power Illustration in <u>Rogbodiyan</u>
The quest for position and wealth is the preceding ground upon which selfishness, corruption, dishonesty takes its root, and it is also upon these that the political system of a community is destroyed. A solid background into Bakare Ojo Rasaki's submission may better be espoused through the face of reality and incidences within the various Nigerian states where the fate of the masses largely depends on the decision of the incumbent. No one dare question the position of the powers that be because the incumbent governor/power determines who rules next.

The play exposes the plague that ravaged a community though a self – imposed leader. First is the case of the Regent (Adebunmi) who in her mission to relinquish her position and regal authority still imposes two candidates (Gbadegesin and Asagidigbi) on the community under the pretense of submission and time constraint, ignoring the consequences of her action on the community. She believed that the power rests solely with her; therefore the decision also rests with her, consequently throwing caution to the wind and immersing the traditions and culture of the people in the dung. The voices of power is unveiled through many of the characters in the play such as the above mentioned, Adegbani, Agogo, who used his gong as the voice and power to gather people to the palace as instructed by the king saying "I have echoed the voice of her Royal Highness" (8). This signifies the transmission of power from the Regent to the Announcer (Agogo). In the case of 'Aloba' his power display was subtle and tactical, knowing fully well his choice of candidate, he gallantly played the other chiefs into believing that he is upright and just whereas his action was only a hoax.

In the play, different illustrations and voices of power abound and this is achieved through the playwright's discretion. The most obvious of the many illustrations of the use of power in this play was marked by Asagidigbi's action and in-action, seizing power through mischief, i.e. buying the votes and conscience of the council chiefs. This further buttresses Ojo's view that "'Money has, in fact, been made to become "the mother's milk of politics'" (117). Still, money cannot be relied upon in the discharge of honorable behavior. Asagidigbi, even after seizing the throne which the gods forbade him to, allowed himself to be power drunk, he then used his power to take possession of the votary maid whom the gods insist must be without blemish. He believed that "the pebbles the duck swallows never hurt its intestines" (37). In other words, he is immune to all forms of criticisms by his power, the power bestowed upon him by his financial status (money) and his social status as the king of the community. Regrettably, power can easily become a dangerous weapon of self-destruction in the hand of a fool. Asagidigbi's character displays the many voices of power. The power to rubbish human culture by defiling the "Arugba Oge" who was meant to be in seclusion and remain a virgin until at least after the festival. Asagidigbi not only defiled the votary maid in seclusion but further defiled himself due to selfish carnal gratification at the expense of the peoples' tradition. Being in power, he quickly detached the blame from his hands and sets it upon the head of an innocent man (Gbadegesin). With his powers, he directs that the innocent be seized and tied to Mogun with his head pirouetting to the drum of downfall. He is completely intoxicated by his power to the point that the traditional laws which had long existed before his existence became his play thing. Unfortunately for him, "… when laws are changed just to feed our personal appetites, the society dies even faster. The dog that swallows salt shall not live [sic] to tell the taste of its sweetness (37).

In accordance with the power of persuasive expression which Charteris-Black (143) describes as the "Conviction Rhetoric", 'power' which may be used as an element of dramaturgic characterisation is herein exemplified through persuasion and trickery. Adegbani, the son of the formal Regent had the utmost aim of seizing the thrown from Asagidigbi, this he systematically achieve through the use of the kind of power in his coffer. His tactics and power can be equated with Charteris- Black's description of Anthony Charles Lynton Blair of the United States' methodical persuasive skill. Adegbani understands the importance of constructing messages that are persuasive, that is, his possession of vital persuasive communication ability, constructiveness and trickery are the powers with which he eventually worn the throne. His power may also be likened to the deceitful wisdom of the tortoise. Using the method of simplicity, integrating ethos and the feigning the life of a martyr, he schemed the king and the town's people by presenting himself as a suitable candidate willing to take up challenges at his own peril for peace and sanity to return to Ilu Koroju. Adegbani's attitude is simply summed up by Salotin who says "Adebunmi, see your very son Adegbani has seized the throne. He has seized power despite those sweet promises" (57). Adegbani's character truly describes the attitude of Nigerian political leaders who will not publicly scramble for power but use that within their disposal to achieve their political intentions. Prior to his sojourn to the land of the dead, his voice is persuasive, beseeching the king and his subjects and offering his advice saying,

> If a child wants to punish the father by dying during the dry season when the ground is too hard to dig, the

> father should show his cleverness by burying him at the river bank ...let us fool the dead by making me wear the costumes of the king. I shall wear his Agbada and his sokoto, put the king's bead on my neck and wrists; but most important of all, I shall wear the crown on my head. Then I shall go for the healing water... I will be here back with the water and I will return the king's property back to him(48-49).

Within the space of 48 hours, having gone to the land of the dead and being in possession of the powerful healing water gotten from the land of the dead, Adegbani's action practically contradicted his first position. His mission of dethroning Asagidigbi and enthroning himself began to manifest. He emphatically reiterates that he should be made king having sojourned into the land of the dead. He says,

> People of Ilu Koroju, use your heads. I have the knife and I have the yams. I have already taken out of the water and I am healed. It is you who now needs the water and unless I am pronounced king, I will break the gourd and pour away the water and you shall go to your graves with your various deformities (56).

Just as humans possess power, money also has its own eloquent power; money can buy the most hardened hearted into conspiratorial acts and this Ojo Bakare gallantly articulates in his piece of work thus clinching Adetula's position that "Today, money drowns votes and voices in Nigeria"(xxviii). The chiefs all knew for sure that the decision of who succeeds the Regent rests with the gods and the gods, having spoken through Fadele that none of the two candidates should be enthroned; still, the chiefs presented Asagidigbi as the king. Asagidigbi used the power of wealth to his advantage to lure the chiefs into conniving and accepting him as the elected king. He believes that money can buy him anything hence his proposal,

> Money, man, money. Ego, wazobia! In each bag is contained what all of you combined cannot earn in twenty years. Give me the throne and take the money

or give the throne to Gbadegesin and die in poverty. The choice is yours (25).

Unfortunately or fortunately as the case may be, power exhibits itself from diverse perspectives. Just as human elements in the physical world possess power, the unseen gods/ Super naturals possess their own powers too and these powers may have counter effects on human's diverse power surges. This power cannot be equated with the power in human procession because god(s) possess infinite powers and wisdom to decipher and quickly rescue the innocent from the destruction placed on him by mere mortal. It is the power described above that Bakare, Ojo Rasaki captures in the Play, and that power that rescued Gbadegesin from the death sentence placed on him by the king. This shows the limitation of human power because, not a creature under the universe has an atom of power save for that which these Super naturals or God has bestowed on him.

The Echoes of Moral Decadence in the Play

...welcome to another season of laughter and merry-making. But most importantly, you are welcome to another season of meditation and sober reflection, as we bring you another story of the woes of a nation. The child, they say, needs not be stopped from growing protruding teeth. His foolishness would show when he finds it difficult to grow protruding lips to cover them. The crime of realization might be too late; the needle might have fallen from the leper's hand and picking it becomes impossible. ...Yes, catastrophe brought upon oneself. When the child does what he is not supposed to do, his eyes will see what they are not supposed to see. They are now victims of self-inflicted disaster, because the people dine and wine with injustice. Koroju, a land where merit is thrown to the winds, Koroju, abode of religious hypocrites and political sycophants, Koroju, where intelligence means nothing and the academically brilliant is a potential pauper. Koroju, a land where truth has been hindered and falsehood exalted. Ladies and gentlemen, a land of corruption where material and political wealth are worshipped and the false acquisition of them is encouraged is bound to be stricken by Rogbodiyan... (6-7). (Emphasis mine).

The above summation of the playwright best describes the Nigerian state, a state characterised by moral decays.

Morality is a phenomenon that must never be defiled, else degradation and level of decadence catapults. In every society, the need to maintain sanctity is bestowed on the ruling class or the elders of the land as well as the entire masses, with each playing his or her morally conducted roles guided by ethical principles. An imbalance may signal ruins and the presentation of a mere carcass of the society especially when all or an aspect of the society is tilted towards amorality or immoral acts. It therefore becomes the responsibility of the 'fore-seers' such as playwrights and artists to caution and correct these ills through their works. The playwright exposes the many echoes of decay from our past and present and the stench from the decay is now perceived as norms within our society. Moral decadence is paraded by the writer through many characters showing bribery and corruption, political sycophancy, bootlickers, religious hypocrites, etc.

As evidenced in the play, the decadence may be attributed largely to the leaders who exhibited compromise in their discharge of duties as well as the level of ignorance of the peoples' rights by the masses. First is a condition where action begets reaction, and then a decayed presence wherein a blind king is led into the presence of the people he governs by a hunch-back (Bakare). The blindness metaphorically symbolises lack of knowledge and realisation, stupidity, neglect, indifference. The hunchback on the other hand is an abnormal convex curvature of the upper spine, indicating the inability to bother about the concerns of others owing to the heavy burden of this deformity. The masses are also decorated with different deformities under a tensed atmosphere with tragic feelings (Bakare). These descriptions by the playwright purely epitomise the crippled state of the Nigerian nation characterised by blind and mischievous leaders as well as bad followers thus, showing the deplorable state of our nation. Bakare, Ojo Rasaki herein questions human morality principles especially in the character of Eto who could swim in different waters as long as he gets what he wants. Eto is regarded as a "bat of creature" that is "neither an animal nor a bird, neither here nor there" (20). On the contrary Eto believed that his gratification supersedes his position within the council, thus his response to Abere,

> ...Yes. That is how I get what I want, by belonging to all the camps. The only politics I play now is the politics of my stomach and probably that of my immediate family. How to continue remaining the number one citizen in my house and how not to give my wife the chance of overthrowing me in this era of women liberation. That is the politics I play now (20).

This in itself is a rape of human conscience and this reveals the attitude of some Nigerian leaders who place themselves before the needs of the people thereby putting the life of their people in jeopardy. The self-actualisation of personal integrity which Akanmidu (376) describes as "a state of completeness, uprightness and honesty" holds no ground here since dishonesty is much pervaded by the leaders and followers. 'Akigbe' despite his grey hair signifying his age, who should be a custodian of truth, misguides Kabiesi by leading him out of his supposed seclusion to late night carousal. Rather than conduct his performative role judiciously by offering tangible advice to the king when needed, his greed and selfishness led him to singing the praise of the king saying that "...the wind sends the leaf to where it likes. Do whatever you like in your land; you have our support (38). Knowing the implication of Kabiesi's action, he directs himself to be washed in the reprehensive showers of the rain and also aiding and abating Kabiesi's crime. In the same vein, the attitude of the other chiefs such as (Abere, Aloba, and

Salotin) cannot be expunged from the causal root of this shameful and monstrous act pervaded also by the chiefs. Clearly, their actions fall within the familiar culture of compromise in the Nigerian political structure. Instead of these leaders to guide jealously their own moral and behavioral disposition by electing or nominating a just and deserving king, their actions to a large extent contributed to the erroneous display of decadence in the play. As perpetrators, their conscience and votes were bought over by Asagidigbi through the power of money. This means therefore that in many societies, the level of decadence may be traced to the evils and unethical conducts of the ruling class as well as the inordinate ambitions of the lower characters that sometimes surround them.

In addition, one of the endemic sloughs described by the playwright that can further extricate a prestigious nation from the state of nobility is bribery and corruption. In line with Usman Mohammed's submission that "corruption continues to permeate and pervade every facet of national life in Nigeria"(119), and Nordstrom (58) opinion that corruption "is not merely about accumulation of wealth, but about creating strong foundations of patronage, of consolidating control over resources and thus governance…The more negative analyses label such pursuits cults of personality, megalomania, kleptocracies, and the supreme abuse of privilege", Bakare, Ojo Rasaki also divulge, through the characters of the chief, that the high societal chiefs which may include the Nigerian political gurus and leaders are also perpetrators of the moral decay. This also includes scrambling and diversion of public funds to their personal accounts at the detriment of the people they govern, and ceaselessly committing the act of homicide since human life is not much of importance, thus infringing on the right to life. They completely forget that free and fair election is prerequisite for good governance.

In the euphoria of his power, Kabiesi basks, bragging and exchanging words with Agogo who in his attempt to prevent evil and ruin upon the community ended up killing himself. Still Kabiesi boasts on his words and power saying "A cockerel which has been visited by the long knife cannot crow at dawn" This means that should Agogo not have on this day died, he won't live to see the next. Kabiesi, taking pride in killing an innocent man boastfully directs that Fadele should be seized and his head disengaged from his body. This further describes the level of decadence because violence is placed upon the pure and innocent. The height of defilement and moral decadence however is captured in the character of "Arugba Oge" who represents purity and wholesomeness on one hand, and holds the future of the community on the other. Now the question is, if purity, wholesomeness and future are defiled, what then is left for mankind? Isn't decadence a product of the rape of these vitals?

Conclusion
To say there is decadence and minimal level of morality in Nigeria is to say that which is obvious since writers and artists generally draw inspirations from their immediate/ physical environment. Playwrights, though may create fictional works, their works usually reveal certain aspects of their immediate society which discusses the ethical conducts of their society while also correcting the problems associated or evidenced within their perceived reach. In the play, *Rogbodiyan* which means catastrophe, suffering, ruins, confusion, etc. the writer exposes the different degrees and means of decadence. This decadence herein may be traced from factors ranging from poverty to selfishness and materialism and the trend keeps growing to the point that a great nation is been devalued. *Rogbodiyan* ascertains that people now live in decadent societies where morality exists overboard. People complain of bad leaders who do not represent their interest. Nonetheless, Ojo presents before us a question, "When power is given to you, what do you do with it? You squabble amongst yourself and mess up. You cheat and lie and play games" (57). The tendency usually follows that the bulk blame of incongruities and corruption within the nation is placed on the shoulders of the leaders and public office holders, but then, the question is not only directed to the rulers but equally to the followers who are quick to making judgmental assertions and slanderous statements. The fact remains that leadership is a

product of followership because leaders were once followers, thus, a society begets the leader it deserves.

Works Cited

Adetula, Victor. (Ed). "Money and Politics in Nigeria: An Overview."*Money and Politics in Nigeria.* Abuja: Petra Digital Press. 2008. Print. Pp. xxvii-xxxiv.

Aiyede, Remi. "The Role of INEC, ICPC and EFCC in Combating Political Corruption." *Money and Politics in Nigeria.* Abuja: Petra Digital Press. 2008. Print. Pp. 39-52.

Akanmidu, A. "Promises, Interest and Personal Integrity". *Dialogue. Issues in contemporary discussion.* Eds. Dopamu, A., Awolalu, O., Delamarter, S. G. Lagos: Big Small books. 2007. Print.

Bakare, Ojo-Rasaki. *Rogbodiyan.* Nigeria: Tamaza Publishing Company Limited. 2004. Print.

Charteris-Black, Jonathan. Politicians and Rhetoric. The Persuasive Power of Metaphor. New York: Palgrave Macmillan. 2005. Print.

Dung, Pam Sha. "Vote Buying and the Quality of Democracy". Money and Politics in Nigeria. Abuja: Petra Digital Press. 2008. Print. Pp. 123- 133.

Foucault, Michel. The History of Sexuality. Vol. 1: New York: Pantheon Books. 1978. Print.
_____ "The Subject and the Power". Michel Foucault: Beyond Structuralism and Hermeneutics. (Eds) Dreyfus, H. & Rabinow, P. Brighton: Harvester Press. 1982. Print

George- Genyi. *Gender, Power and Political Leadership in Nigeria: Lessons from Selected Plays of Tess Onwueme.* 97- 111. Web.04/07/2014.

Newman, Saul. Power and Politics in Poststructuralist Thought.New theories of the Political.London: RoutledgeTaylor& Francis Group. 2005. Print.

Nordstrom,Carolyn. Global Outlaws. Crime, Money, and Power in the Contemporary World. California: University of California Press. 2007. Print.

Ojo, Emmanuel. "Vote Buying in Nigeria".Money and Politics in Nigeria. Abuja: Petra Digital Press. 2008. Print. Pp. 109-122.

Usman, Mohammed. Corruption in Nigeria: A Challenge to Sustainable Development in the Fourth Republic. European Scientific Journal February 2013 edition vol.9, No.4 ISSN: 1857 – 7881 (Print) e - ISSN 1857- 7431 Web.118- 137

Leadership and Insensitivity in Nigeria: The Example of Rasaki Ojo Bakare's *Drums of War*

By
Fanyam, Joel Avaungwa and Gbilekaa, Richard K.

Introduction

Rasaki Ojo Bakare is aware of his environment as it is supposed to be in his role as a dramatist/playwright. Drama and Theatre are veritable tools for political education and national development. It has a symbiotic relationship with the society. Both drama and society either supply or feed from each other. The society provides issues through events or happenings both from human activities such as politics, marriage, crime or environmental/ecological activities while drama or theatre uses these issues through plays to inform, educate and entertain the society. Indeed, the society benefits from the plays by purging itself of certain habits showcased in a play and implements or enforces good suggestions to societal problems. Akinwale, asserts that theatre is an integral part of society and it is incumbent on society to promote its impact (109). That is why Drama and Theatre engages in intellectual and imaginative recollection and reconstruction of their societies.

In Nigeria, this succinct relationship between the society and drama or Theatre spread across the pre-colonial, colonial and post-colonial days when drama extensively served for entertainment, education and information purposes. Adedeji explains that in the colonial days, drama was the product of cultural nationalism which dates back to a period before the amalgamation of the protectorates of Northern and Southern Nigeria with the colony of Lagos in 1914 (3). Prior to this period, Nigerians were used to traditional performances that served for entertainment and religious purposes during festivals and naming ceremonies.

With the advent of colonial masters, stylized performances were introduced in churches and schools for selfish colonial objectives. However, this stimulated more artistic creativity as Nigerians who were part of these performances in the church and schools started experimenting with indigenous materials. Gbilekaa observes that the foundation of this brand of entertainment was laid by the more resourceful Abeokuta mission who started blending Yoruba indigenous material with European ones. The likes of Hubert Ogunde, Kola Ogumola, and Duro Ladipo became renowned names in the Nigerian Drama with plays based on Nigeria politics, religion and social life (14).

Drama contributed enormously in the fight for Nigerian independence. Hubert Ogunde, for instance, created a play entitled *"Bread and Bullet"* where he ridiculed the shooting of the Enugu miners by the colonial masters (Adedeji, 38). Drama was used as a tool to fight inhuman treatment by the colonial masters, and during independence it was used to fight for political cohesion. Ogunde used rhetoric of reason as a symbol of getting at the moral behind the political situation which developed among two Yoruba Political Wigs, Awolowo and Akintola (Adedeji, 39). He was telling the Yoruba people through Drama to think because the two were all Yoruba people and peace was above crises.

In the post-independence era, many political themes have manifested with different plays addressing them respectively. This period can be classified into the pre-military era, military era and post-military era. Despite the classification, basic elements have manifested in all the periods of dramatization. These elements include, corruption, crime, unemployment, poor economy, poor leadership, thuggery, election malpractice, greed, ethnic crises and poverty. Playwrights like Wole Soyinka, Iyorwuese Hagher, Femi Osofisan, Tess Onwueme, Bakare Ojo Rasaki, Ahmed Yerima, Saint Gbilekaa, Alex Asigbo, Tracie Utoh and Emma Dandaura, just to mention a few, have created plays reflecting the political state of the country. Gbilekaa, attests to this fact that,

A close examination of the literary production in Nigeria between the years just before the civil war and after shows that much of it is dedicated to political brinkmanship, particularly as it relates to the question of leadership. Different playwrights have approached the paucity of effective and pragmatic leadership and governance on the African continent (83).

It is in line with this, that this paper analyses the political situation in Nigeria as reflected in Rasaki Ojo Bakare's *Drums of War*.

Synopsis of Play
King Onome insists on his war of supremacy against a neighbouring village despite consistent protests from the village (including his own wife) and the warrior soldiers. Even his chief warrior resigns in protest and acceptance of the people's position against the war. Yet Onome did not cling to their idea. The onus of leading the reorganized troop to war now falls on his only son, the heir apparent to the throne. Regrettably, the son is killed in the war with other soldiers. Left without an heir, Onome is forced by tradition to take the calabash of abdication and dishonour.

Inter-Ethnic Crises in Nigeria
The play effusively explores the theme of inter-ethnic crisis that has engulf the body politic of the nation taking cognizance of the Tiv-Jukum crisis, the Zango – Kataf crisis, Jos religious crisis, Bauchi inter-religious crisis as well as the recent Boko Haram crisis. For quite some decades now, almost all the states in Nigeria have in one way of the other involved in inter-ethnic crisis as a result of bad leadership, arrogance, greed, pride and bad governance. This has led to the loss of lives of innocent citizens who have not reached their prime. 2nd woman captures this situation as she addresses the king in the following words;

2nd Woman: We told you to abandon this war. No, you must satisfy your ego. Now, see what you have done. Look all around

> you. See the body of young men who have not reached their prime. Do you know that the Ibujis have been destroyed and barns ransacked? Tell me why? (Bakare, 19)

The above epigram matches the Tiv Jukum inter-ethnic crisis of 2000 – 2001 where a whole village in Vaase thickly dominated by youth was besieged by militant soldiers sent by top Nigerian leaders. All the youth in the community were put on a firing squad, when the Tiv militants retaliated, the catastrophe became enormous as more people were killed including the Nigerian soldiers. The cause of this crisis is attributed to greed, betrayal of trust on the electorates and undue exhibition of power as well as atrocities committed consciously or unconsciously by our leaders which make some parts of the electorates suffer. This is evidenced in Jeje's response below,

> Jeje: People of our land, it is now obvious, that the gods are angry with our king, hence these strange calamities that have fallen our land. I suggest the king must vacate the throne and leave the land. It is obvious that there is a curse on his head (Bakare, 20).

The gods mentioned above signify the electorates (the society); it depicts strongly the Nigerian condition in crisis situation when the Tiv people became tired of the government in leadership, the situation is also synonymous with the Jos 1994/1995 and 2004/2005 crisis, where at one time, the former president Olusegun Obasanjo declared a state of emergency on the state. In order to ensure peace and stability, Dariye was suspended from office for a period of six months in order to pave way for peace to reign in Jos. Rasaki Ojo Bakare metaphorically envisaged a continuous crisis in Nigeria and the insensitive conduct of the leadership to the crises situation and likened it to a curse. In fact, most of the inter-ethnic crises in the country are characterized by poor leadership qualities which sometimes give birth to violence among youth who in most cases threaten to carve out sections of the town and declare it a sovereign. In this regard Jeje indicated his desire to carve out his supporters as is presented below;

> Jeje: No He must go, the land has never witnessed peace and prosperity since he became our ruler, instead we have been jumping from one problem to another. If he doesn't vacate the throne immediately, I shall lead my people and carve out my section of the town and declare it a sovereign town.

This idea reflects certain happenings in Nigeria. It is a depiction of the Niger-Delta crisis over the possession of the resources within their region and the campaign for the Biafra nation up to date in the country. The play having observed the society through its creative mechanism decides to showcase the meaninglessness and the senselessness of inter-ethnic crisis that is rapidly ravaging the nation. The entire war in the play ends without a meaningful result but a share expression of arrogance, pride and greed by the leaders at the expense of the populace. This didactic play is pungently a warning to all aggressors and agitators of wars in Nigeria. The play interrogates the paradox of Nigeria as a democratic nation suffering from bad governance as a result of arrogance and power drunkenness.

Insensitivity to the Plight of the People

Beyond the issues of crisis raised in *Drums of War*, there is an insincerity of political players whose interest is to serve their pockets at the detriment of the public, creating a tendency to engage in the struggle for survival by competing for limited resources and the national cake (Ubi, 90). Thus, hunger has taken over the society, aggravating mass misconduct, selfish aggrandizement, poverty, and jungle justice because the society is in a state of unruliness.

The situation where corrupt people are preferred to hold sensitive positions on behalf of the masses by a few people, who have perpetuated themselves in power using stolen wealth, is absolutely senseless. This is not to doubt that these leaders do not have some of the poor masses as their sycophants in the face of this misrule. In *Drums of War*, King Onome exhibited pride over the well being of his people. He valued his own peace but did not consider providing same conditions for his people rather he pushed them to war while his family remained protected. When Beleku raises questions, he is forced to keep quiet by the king's loyalist in the following discussion,

    2nd Chief: Patience, Beleku, Patience No matter how tall the neck is, the head is still sitting on top. Please, cool your temper, please.

    1st Chief: Jeje, why are you spending too much attention on a mere ringworm while leprosy is busy making a delicious meal of your limbs? Who should be begged, Beleku or his Royal self, the god personified (Bakare, 10)

Onome as the leader in Nigeria is personified or considered by his subjects as a god. He is so feared by his antics, such that Beleku's comment was simply considered invalid, although what he said was correct and with much relevance to the plight of the people of Abakpa. The situation in the play is a replica of the practicalities in the Nigeria's political firmament where the illiterate thugs are pushed to violence over the selfish ambitious of the leaders. The ruling class in Nigeria has forced a pretentious image on the masses to cover their greedy and corrupt intentions with fake promises claiming to better the lives of the citizenry.

It is in this regard that Mato asks below,

    Wait a minute; do you need to be told that Nigerians experience worst blackouts today than ever? Do you know that PHCN is simply not working? Does any government need to tell us that things are either working or not? All you hear from the power sector are meetings by one presidential committee or the other and frivolous releases of funds for contracts that if we are not careful may first end up like others before now. Nigeria is certainly in a very desperate situation that calls for concerted national attention. The worst part of the problem is that the leadership seems to be going deaf by the day (42).

The lines above present the precarious condition of the power sector in the society, as clear as they sound. However, they are not limited to the power sector alone; incidentally, the questions reflect the general condition of events in all sectors in Nigeria. The government seems to be deceiving the public by forming one committee or the other whose terms of reference are either limited in the face of the problems or their recommendations are never implemented and remain on paper. There is no light, no functional good health services especially at the local level, no good roads, as Mato rightly presents it above, even where they pretend to repair the roads, these facilities are given to incompetent, poorly skilled companies whose intentions are only to make money through giving of bribes and after executing shoddy or no job at all. Nothing that is really good in some states in the country, except in very few places and this has mostly been in the state capitals. Life is at its lowest level amongst the majority of the citizens in the rural areas and those who attempt to question these situations are seen as bad critics who do not appreciate anything. King Onome concludes Beleku's case in the following words:

King: It is ignorance that makes the rat challenge the cat for a fight (To his aides) take him and send him to the gallows (Bakare, 13).

Beleku's life ends like all other civil rights activists whose lives have long disappeared as a result of questioning government policies in Nigeria. Therefore, many atrocities have continued to stockpile. In March 2009 there was a Halliburton Nigerian LNG scandal where $30 million was claimed to have been shared to top Nigerians as bribe, the dailies carried the news until a national committee was set to look into the issue. These allegation has remained at that level, even when names of those involved were publicly disclosed.

Similarly, in April 2009 there was an alleged N1.5 billion fraud involving seven officials of the Nigeria Electricity Regulatory Agency (NERA), this information was also made public in the national dailies. By June 2009 and 2013 Academic Staff Union of Universities (ASUU) among several other unions went on strike action in protest over poor educational facilities and pay packages in Nigeria. These strike actions have become recurrent over the years with little efforts to solve them up till now, even when the government has agreed to implement the demands. There is also the issue of the Banks CEO saga of dolling out billions of naira for non-performing loans to their cronies, instead of their customers. These and many more, instances have become a clog in the wheel of the nation's development.

The current situation where Nigerian leaders sit on their own and decide what is good for the public whereas it is for their personal interests informs a system that impoverishes the poor and perpetually makes the rich relevant and important to at odds with all good sense and equity. Akogun laughs at the people of Abakpa in *Drums of War,* who decided that they refuse they no longer wanted war and sent him the chief warrior to the king in the following words,

>Akogun: (Laughs) If you think that like the cursed cockroach, I will extend my dance to the door step of the hen then your heads are not correct. I say if you think that like the foolish hen. I will trace my corn to the house of a butcher then you are thinking with your anus. I mean if you think I will carry my big mouth to the doorstep of his Royal Highness and deliver your suicidal message and let him bring down my head from my neck, then your skulls are empty (Bakare, 8).

This fear expressed by Akogun confirms the degree of intimidation and oppression by the king. It reveals lack of freedom of expression on the part of the subjects. Furthermore, it confirms the oppressive strategies used by Nigerian leaders to enforce what they want and think is a development for their people. Therefore, development strategies that are practiced in Nigeria are those that satisfy the individual needs of a selected few.

Conclusion

It is sad the way Nigerian leaders are continuously sagging with corruption and insensitivity. However, drama and theatre have been on the forefront of fighting corruption, bad leadership and violence in our society. Thus, Nigerian citizens should take drama serious and listen to the messages of the playwright so as to restructure the nation for a better development. Instead of what happens in instances where drama is considered simply as an entertainment tool during functions, the society should reconsider its position and use drama as an effective tool in giving voice to the voiceless in a morally corrupt society. Consequently, leadership positions in Nigeria should be given to people who have well proven integrity.

Works Cited

Adedeji, J.A and Ekwazi, Hyginus. *Nigeria Theatre: Dynamics Of A Movement*. Ibadan. Caltop Publications (Nigeria) Limited. 1998.

Akinwale, Oiu, Ayo. "The Social Influence of the Theatre on Contemporary Nigeria Society: The Education Factor". In *The Abuja Communicator*. Vol.1, No. 1. (2001) 103-110.

Amali, O.O. "Sustaining the Development of Theatre Practice in Nigeria". Being a Keynote Address Delivered at the I6th SONTA convention at University of Lagos. 2004.

Bakare, Ojo Rasaki. *Drums of War*. Zaria Tamaza Publishing Company Ltd; 1914.

Cleaver, Frances. Paradoxes of Participation: *Questioning Participatory Approaches to Development*. University of Bradford. Development and Project Planning Centre. 1999.

Gbilekaa, E.T. Saint. "Culture and the Democratic Experience in Nigeria: Wale Ogunyemi's "Langbodo" as example". *In The Abuja Communicator*. Vol.1, No. 1. (2001) 83-93.

Gbilekaa, Saint. *Radical Theatre In Nigeria*. Ibadan: Caltop Publications (Nigeria) Limited. 2012.

Mato, Kabir. "Is Nigeria Failing?" In *Daily Independent*. Vol.3, No. 1735. 2009.

Ubi. Abam, "Out. Ethnicity and Nation Building in Nigeria". In *Civil Society And The Consolidation of Democracy In Nigeria*. Calabar. CATS Publishers. 2000.

Nigerian Ivory Tower And The Human Development Dilemma: Bakare, Ojo Rasaki's *Once Upon A Tower* as a Paradigm

By
Idogho, Joseph Agofure

Introduction

Bakare, Ojo Rasaki is a versatile playwright cum dramatist, an academic, a scholar, a choreographer and dancer. He has done much to develop his society through his dramatic and performance oeuvre. He is a theatre director and a Professor of Theatre Arts. Although a liberal bourgeois intellectual, who could be described as Theatre all-rounder. Bakare is decidedly non-partisan in his vision. He encourages the oppressed and exploited peoples of the earth to strive to unsettle their oppressors as a first step towards achieving for themselves, freedom and respect specifically in his play, *Once Upon A Tower*.

Once Upon A Tower gives us a contrastive and double vision of social reality. In this text, Bakare Ojo Rasaki takes the academic world of the *MARIAPINTO, UNIVERSITY, NIGERIANA* as his focus, and principal locale. The creative imagination of the play may have been inspired by the decadence in the Nigerian education system, particularly the Nigeria University system. The play eventually manifest as a social commentary, an allegory of the social ills and anarchy emanating from the inherent contradictions in the Nigeria university system. The play is a political and satirical comment on the causes of disillusionment and disenchantment which characterised the Nigeria university system: a situation which has led to frequent violence, social insecurity, lawlessness, decay and sterility within the Nigeria university system. Not only has this decay destroyed the university system: it has also found its root in our larger society. Perhaps the University system is a microcosm of our society; most especially with its function of producing the manpower of the society.

Critics and scholars of dramatic literature have argued at different time and level that the socio-economic, political, material reality of the Pre and Post-Colonial Nigeria simply lend itself as readily material for dramaturgy. Playwrights thus utilise this phenomenon as a basis to produce plays reflecting the societal prevailing realities. In fact, "The continent of Africa is subjected to oppressive and exploit-forces very similar to the situation in Asia and Latin America. Colonialism, capitalism and imperialism have systematically impoverished Africa, plunging most of her countries into a crisis whose economic, political, social, cultural complexity (educational system, mine emphasis) makes the future very bleak" (Penina 67). Osofisan also asserts that, "art all art, was its very essence socio-telic, that its coming to being was dependent on, and determined by the surrounding social and political environment" (2). In other words, every art is a product of a society and its existence has been informed by the societal realities: cultural, economic, political, social and otherwise. To put it succinctly, the fundamental reasons theatre exists is to awaken in the audience, an understanding of the human condition they were previously unable, or unwilling to apprehend or change.

The above statements are germane to this discourse, in that Bakare Ojo Rasaki's *Once Upon A Tower* expresses the writer's disillusionment with the present education system in Nigeria, focusing on the University system specifically. Bakare in this play categorically asserts that if the university education system in Nigeria persists in its current, sterile and decay situation, the future of our country will be bleak. It will be merely expressing the obvious if we say that the Nigeria education system is in a state of shamble.

It is against this backdrop that this paper examines the aforementioned problems as captured in Bakare, Ojo Rasaki's dramaturgy, *Once Upon A Tower*, specifically, major problems affecting our university education that are explored in the play will be discussed to hone our initial remark that, Bakare, Ojo Rasaki is a critical satirist.

Theoretical Framework

Education has been described by scholars as the aggregate of all the processes by which a child or adult develops the abilities, attitudes and other forms of behaviour which are of positive value to the society in which he lives, that is to say, it is a process of disseminating knowledge either to ensure social control or to guarantee rational direction of the society or both. Education generally has been regarded, the world over, as a potent instrument for introducing and sustaining social change in human societies, as well as shaping its destiny. Apart from serving as a vehicle for enhancing upward social and economic mobility, "education is regarded as a key to social reconstruction and an instrument for conserving, transmitting and renewing culture" (Ukeje 9).

Consequently, the belief in the value of education as a powerful instrument of development has led many nations to commit much of their wealth to the establishment of educational institutions at various levels; America and Europe are good examples. However, the case is different in Nigeria. The fund allocated to higher education is just too minimal. Governments consider investing on higher education as mere expense, waste of fund: rather than to see it as a long-term investment of immense benefit to the society at large.

Going by these explanations in relation to what education is, the state of education and its process in Nigeria today as well as the attitude of its providers-Government at all levels and private investors; one with keen interest will be compelled to ask such questions as what has actually gone wrong considering the enormity of its effect on the output from the system in the aspect of productivity and the degree of acceptance in the labour market and educational institutions, especially outside the country. Response however, will be its militating factors stemming from the incidence of inadequate funding, poor facilities; cultism; examination malpractice indiscriminate mass promotion syndrome in schools, especially at the primary and secondary

level. As captured in Bakare's *Once Upon A Tower*. The causes of these could be traced to:
(i) Government insensitivity to education needs
(ii) Government and private institutions open encouragement of low productivity and
(iii) The lack of the spirit of hard-work among growing number of students.

The Dilemma of Human Development in Nigeria Ivory Tower
The concept of dilemma as used in this paper implies a situation with unsatisfactory choices, in which somebody must choose one of two unsatisfactory alternatives. It manifests in Nigeria society at large as follows: The politicians elected to rule the people turn the state to a business enterprise, enriching themselves through it. Later, they turn around to persecute the people rather than to protect their interests. The armed force personnel charged to secure lives and properties turn on the helpless citizens; brutalised, maimed and kill them. The police force recruited to enforced, maintained law and order in our society turn around to harass and terrorise the powerless and ordinary citizens. The medical doctor entrusted to safeguard lives, suddenly turn murderer: due to inexperience and lack of know-how, resulting from epileptics training received as a student. The teachers entrusted to teach the youngsters, inculcate moral values and ethics of the society, becomes a survivalist: the reverse becomes the case, destroyer of human resources.

The ivory towers instituted to train and develop its citizens; turn around to destroy its citizens consciously or unconsciously. Half bread (knowledge) is better than none suddenly becomes the watchword of Nigeria education system. According to Bakare, "Half education is better than none na de philosophy of our universities now. Half blindness dey risky katakata dey for front…" (*Once…*5).
Olujuwon also avers that:
> The tertiary institutions that are established to promote intellectual excellence, good virtues etc; have deviated. We are faced daily with reports of

students caught in armed robbery, rape, assassination: (cultism, abortion, examination malpractices, certificate forgery, bribery- sorting; within the university system etcetera, mine emphasis). The majority of these institutions have misplaced their goals and allowed social, political factors of their environment to create crises in their academic community. It is a known fact that tertiary institutions do not get their entire approved annual budget. (6)

We must bear in mind collectively that every literate Nigerian today is a product of Nigerian education system; directly or indirectly. It is important to consider the remark of a character in the play. **PEDRO**: "...Dr Yemi my teacher, permit me to wash ancestral curses off your feet...The anointed destroyer of human resources" (*Once*...61).

The above informs Bakare, Ojo Rasaki's *Once Upon A Tower*, if not his entire dramatic oeuvre: which has formed the nexus of this discourse. *Once Upon A Tower* by Bakare, Ojo Rasaki undoubtedly raises the complex issues that bothered on the Nigeria educational system. Significantly, the play highlights numbers of disturbing issues plaguing the Nigeria university system.

Thus the function of education as an instrument for promoting the socio-economic, political and cultural development of a nation is now questionable with regards to the present challenges facing Nigeria education system. Basically, a nation's growth is determined by its human resources. Thus, "the provision of the much-needed manpower to accelerate the growth and development of the economy has been said to be the main relevance of university education in Nigeria" (Ibukun 19).

The National Policy on Education highlights the aims of education, tertiary education specifically thus:
1. To contribute to national development through high-level relevant manpower training;

2. To develop and inculcate proper values for the survival of the individual and the society;
3. To develop the intellectual capability of individuals to understand and appreciate their local and external environments;
4. To acquire both physical and intellectual skills this will enable individuals to be self-reliant and useful members of the society;
5. To promote and encourage scholarship and community service;
6. To forge and cement national unity; and
7. To promote national and international understanding and interactions. (36)

Fundamentally, there are avalanche of problems to be solved in order to achieve quality education in our universities; specifically in order for us as a nation to achieve the aforementioned objectives. Three of the problems are primary in the sense that they are largely responsible for the other problems within the system. The primary problems are:
i. Inadequate fund
ii. The negative influence of a corruptive and valueless political system; and
iii. Planning and implementation problems.

These problems have led to the weakening of university administration; poor teaching and learning outcomes; diminishing research and consultancy traditions; and questionable service to the community. Cursory look at these problems; point to diminishing returns in the basic missions of universities. These problems are addressed extensively in Bakare's dramaturgy, *Once Upon A Tower*.

At single digit percentile of national budget, as against the United Nations Educational and Scientific Organization's (UNESCO) recommendation of 26 percent, the funding figures for universities, especially in the last three decades, explain the poverty of Nigerian universities and the concomitant dip in standards. Mostly affected are infrastructure (buildings, roads, power, and water resources); knowledge facilities (library accessions, computing facilities, and teaching aids); research funding; recreational facilities; and welfare packages for lecturers, administrative staff, and students. They are either inadequate or non-existent. Let us return to the play again:

PEDRO: I am the provost here…Now to you Mr Vice Chancellor, you had more hands in the process of making me professionally malnourished. I remember specifically, that most of the chemicals I started seeing in the hospitals after my graduation, were things I was not opportune to be familiar with when I was a student here just because the University couldn't make them available. I remember that at a time we were even doing what my H.O.D here called dry practicals. That is practicals without the required facilities. You just wrote chemicals instead of actually mixing them

VICE-CHANCELLOR: Not my fault… Not my fault.
I forwarded the necessary requests to the University Commission. The funds were approved based on my recommendation, but the Chairman of Senate Sub Committee on Education used his position to corner the contract of supplying the Chemicals and other facilities. And then we waited… and waited…and waited without any supply forthcoming.

PEDRO: And what did you do as the V.C? Did you protest or complain?

V.C: Protest? Who do I protest against? The man is a sacred cow, he is very powerful.

PEDRO: It wasn't the sacredness of that cow that stopped you from protesting, but your ambition to ensure a second term in office as Vice Chancellor. You didn't want anybody to work against your ambition so you compromised the future of those of us entrusted in your care. Anyway, that apart. You said the Chairman of the Senate Committee on education was this emergency contractor (*Once...*60).

In the case of students, for example, investment in university housing has been withdrawn, leading to sharp increases in squatting in the few hostel facilities available and off-campus housing for most students. As a result, many students these days go through the university without the university going through them, as the cliché goes.

Vice-Chancellors soon learnt the political act of defending their budgets and lobbying for subventions, the same way governors lobby for federal allocations and excess crude funds. The diseases of the political system diffused into the universities as professors began to migrate between government and university positions. In no time, the culture of scholarship gave way to the corruptive and materialist culture of the political system. The following conversation between the trio, Vice-Chancellor; Chief Executive Officer of the University, Chief Nosa Eguaben; the Chairman of Council and His Royal Highness Alhaji Sabo Abdella Katonga-Emir of Dogon Wayo; the Chancellor of the University affirms this reality:

V.C: I must congratulate you your Royal Highness and you Chief and of course my humble self for yet another successful convocation ceremony.

CHIEF: Mr. Vice Chancellor, I tremendous joy for the way everything went smoothly.

EMIR: I too. In fact, by the time the president reads those beautifully worded speeches of ours in the newspaper, I am sure he will give us another term. He will believe we are doing the job well.

V.C: This calls for celebration (Brings out a bottle of brandy and three glasses from the fridge. Each of the men fills his glass. Chief cracks a joke) (*Once...*7).

The government's poor planning and defective implementation of policies and projects has also adversely affected the universities. The Federal Government's education policies in recent time can best be described as "white elephant projects": policies structured to suit their incessant shifts. The situation has since worsened to the point that it is unclear which education policy is now operative.

The secondary problems within the university system captured in the play includes: witch-hunting, exam malpractices, mediocrity sponsorship base on god-fatherism / favouritism / nepotism, irregular school calendars, unnecessary monopoly of knowledge/ power tussle and inadequate mentorship within the system. For ease of discourse, we will take some of these problems and locate them within the critical lens of Bakare, Ojo Rasaki's *Once Upon A Tower*.

Mediocrity Sponsorship

The likes of Dr Yemi as portrays in *Once Upon A Tower* pervade the university education system: they lack the technicality and know-how of their discipline. Appointments are given without rational basis; the recent development within the system is to give appointment base on cult and club affiliations. Members of staff who are not in the good book of the authority/management or the head; suffers different kind of witch-hunting: ranging from ostracising, non-promotion, even outright pushing out of the system or elimination just as Dr Akitikori is frustrated out of the system in the play, *Once Upon A Tower*. The case of Dr Yemi's sudden elevation from mere laboratory attendant to a teaching staff, irrespective of whether he possesses the right knowledge and qualification or not: established mediocrity within the system.

Examination Malpractices
This manifests within the system. Examination malpractice could be defined as a deliberate wrong-doing contrary to official examinations / the university system rules designed to place a candidate at an unfair advantage or disadvantage. It comes in different forms: the leakage of examination papers prior to examinations, impersonation, external assistance, writing the answers on the blackboard, dictation during examinations, illegal candidates, electronic assistance using phones, papers etc, smuggling whitepaper into the hall, reproduction of another candidate's work with or without permission, inadequate space in the exams halls, lax supervision and inflation or reduction of a candidate original mark by those who grade the script. The aforementioned practices are noticeable within the university system. Another terrible example goes thus:

MISS JULIE: Gynae 307 to be specific. I told you I know I will never pass that course. It is too tough for me and you know Dr Akitikori, the lecturer-in-charge apart from being a non-push over is principled to a fault. <u>I have my way with other lecturers and get what I want</u> (mine emphasis). But … Akitikori is a principled stubborn he goat. He will never help me. (*Once...* 16)

The above underscores the degree of malpractices within the university system. Miss Julie had her way with other lecturers which must have manifested in any form. It could include given her body to the lecturers to get undue advantage just as she has being doing with Prof. Kurumbete:

PROF. KURUMBETE: Ha haa! Common make my morning…
MISS JULIE: (Still sobbing). I have always made your days but it is time for you to make my life now and all you are doing is promising heaven without…
PROF. KURUMBETE: (Covering his lips with a finger) Shhh…

> I will do not a thing but things (pulls her up and kisses her. A knock on the door they disentangle hurriedly. Dr. Akitikori, Dr. Yemi, Dr. Ugolo and two others enter the office, Julie exits). (*Once...* 17).

The underlined statements are emphasis to highlight the degree of decadence within the university system as captured in the play, *Once Upon A Tower*. As a female student, Miss Julie uses what she has to get what she wants, "bottom power", which is usually the parlance within the system. Perhaps, it is only the students who passed their examinations that are successful and Miss Julie has nothing upstairs: so she resorts to what she has to become a successful student too. What a moral decadence?.

Witch-Hunting, Unnecessary Monopoly of Knowledge, Power Tussle and Inadequate Mentorship

Movements Three and Four in the play create a sharp contrast between the characters of Prof. Kurumbete and Prof, Bola to establish the oppressive, domineering forces prevalent within the university system and the mentorship spirit, possessed by the later, which ought to dominate the system; in other to promote knowledge which is the primary goal of the university. Prof. Kurumbete represents an agent of retrogression within the system: while Prof Bola represents progressive agent within the system.

PROF. KURUMBETE: (Addressing these members of staff who have, by now taken their seats). I am definitely not going to stand akimbo and watch you rats turn that department into a lawless place... You mean talk like that? ... Impunite insubordination! ... You mean you talk like that to Prof. Kurumbete Ijakadi, first graduate of Gynecology in Nigeriana, Fellow, World Institute of Gynecology, ... Even in America, noboby ...nobody I say, will dare look me in the eyes. Because they know that in the field of academic gymnastic, I'am Primus Interparis. Even in Europe, they know that I am an institution and that everything about me is institutionally instituted... The Vice Chancellor cannot even talk to me this way... They respect my brain. They know that scholarly and professionally, I am the best-this country has and will ever produce in this field. (*Once...* 17-20).

The above extract establishes the person of Prof. Kurumbete, who sees himself as all-in-all in his profession. He would never have course to respect the opinion of others as far as his discipline is concern: neither would he mentor nor allowed his subordinate to grow. Prof. Kurumbete witch-hunts anybody who opposes his opinion and never willing to accept his subordinates' opinion: what an autocratic personality Below is the contrastive character, the meek, friendly and willing-to-mentor Professor, whose arms are open, always encouraging the subordinates to grow and cheerful:

AKITIKORI: I am fine sir. Let me help you with your bag

PROF. BOLA: Ha! No don't worry. Thank you. I am actually coming from your office. I met your door locked.

AKITIKORI: Oh! Hope no problem sir?

PROF. BOLA: No Problem. I only got information on the internet about a conference and workshop sponsorship for Mid-Level Colleagues in your area. It is being coordinated by an American Organisation. The information is on this sheet of a paper (hands paper over to Akitikori). Study it and give it a trial.

AKITIKORI: Oh Prof. you are ever kind-hearted and helpful. I am grateful. How I wish all Professor reason like you always do.

PROF. BOLA: Ha... this is nothing. I am only doing what I should be doing. (*Once...* 24).

Conclusion

Indeed, "the parents have eaten sour fruits and the children teeth are now set apart" This is the case of the Nigeria education system, the university system specifically. What a man sows, he reaps. The Nigeria society today mourns amongst others, the continual falling standard of education, the unemployability of the Nigerian University graduates and corruption pandemic. Meanwhile, we all started it somehow, directly or indirectly: just as we all are suffering it presently. The elite cannot shy away from it; the rich also cry maxim is at play in this our current predicament. Even if the haves possessed the wherewithal to send their immediate offspring abroad for studies: what about their extended family members that lack the means to do the same?. Or, would the elite progeny remain abroad forever. These and other reflections should be food for thought for every sane Nigerians especially.

The Senator in the play, being the Chairman House Committee on Education at the Senate: Upper House of the Legislator uses his office and position to siphon and embezzle money meant for education; making the system suffers:

KHADIJAT: You lie Dad, you lie. Your insistence that I marry that fool is… My Dad here is the Chairman House Committee on Education at the Senate. He uses his position and his party affinity with the minister to corner ninety percent of the contracts awards on education matters… (*Once*…44).

However things turn around and boomerang against Senator. He lost her only daughter to a quack medical doctor student, Pedro the product of the unavailable facilities and teaching materials in the university.

It is worthy to note at this juncture that the concept of poetic justice is a renaissance dramatic technique which aimed at punishing the evil-doer and rewarding the good person. This device is deliberately employed by Bakare in this play, to drive home his message in the play. The playwright cum play-director is thus sounding a note of warning to all the stake-holders within the education system to be up and doing, to stand up against corrupt practices, poor funding and all the vices within the system, because repercussion is imminent.

Works Cited

Bakare, Ojo Rasaki, *Once upon a Tower (A Play)*, Uyo: Afahaide Publishing Co., 2000.

Federal Republic of Nigeria. *National Policy on Education*. Lagos: Government Press, 2004.

Haralambos, M, & Heald R.M., *Sociology-Themes and Perspectives*. New Delhi: Oxford University Press, 2006.

Ibukun, W. O. *Educational Management: Theory and Practice*. Ado-Ekiti: Green Line Publishers, 1997.

Langer. R. "The Art of Teaching." *Teaching Agricultural Economics and Management in Asia*. (Ed.), Owen McCarthy. Canterbury New Zealand: Lincoln College. 1977.

Mlama Penina M., *Culture and Development: the Popular Theatre Approach in Africa*. Sweden Uppsala: Nordiska Afrikainstitutet, 1991.

Olujuwon, O.T., *Education in Nigeria: A futuristic perspective*. Lagos: Central Educational Service, 2004.

Osofisan, Femi. "The Political Imperative in Africa Dramaturgy and Theatre Practice." *Cross Currents in African Theatre*. (ed.) Asagba, Austin. Benin City: Osasu Publishers, 2001.

Ukala, Sam. (1996). "'Folkism': Towards a National Aesthetic Principle for Nigerian Dramaturgy". New Theatre Quarterly, 12(47), 279-287. http://dx.doi.org/10.1017/S0266464X00010277.

Ukeje, B.O. "Crises in the Nigerian Education System." *The Educator*. 13th Issue, University of Nigeria, Nsukka. 1978.

Corruption Syndrome in Nigeria, A Thematic Analysis Of Ojo Bakare's *Once Upon A Tower*: Challenges For The Director And Designers

By
Kingsley Oyong Akam

Introduction

Theatrical performance such as dramatic presentation is a reflection or re-enactment of life events on stage before an audience. This could only be achieved successfully with the involvement of various collaborators such as playwrights directors, producers, designers and actors, contributing their expertise in creating the imaginary world of the play. The dramatist plays a fundamental role in the collaborative process. Within this complex of artists, the playwright has a prime place because most often his work forms the basis of the project that finally crystallizes into a performance. The playwright's duty to this effect is best compared to that of a referee as argued by Emeka Nwabueze who posits that the dramatist is like a referee "who tries to correct those that violate the rules of the game and of life". He adds that; "the playwright enlightens the people and makes them aware of their situation in society" (161). Rasaki Ojo Bakare is a dramatist who has performed this role perfectly by using his plays like *Drums of War, Rogbodiyan, Once Upon a Tower* etc, to discuss topical issues as well as caution the society against the resultant effects of their actions such as war, conflict resolution, victimization, conflict, corruption and so on.

This, paper focuses on *Once Upon A Tower* where corruption with its negative effects in the society in general and specifically in the academic is skillfully treated. Corruption could be defined as misused of power or funds entrusted under the care of someone for his or her selfish interest, personal or private purpose rather than for the purpose it was meant for. Corruption according to Microsoft Encarta is; "wrong doing by those in a special position of trust. The term is commonly applied to self-benefiting conduct by public officials and others dedicated to public service" (2009). In their view, Ekanem, Okore et al see corruption as "an inducement to do wrong by bribery or any unlawful means. It is a dishonest behaviour by people who work for government and politicians" (448).

This paper is aimed at doing a thematic analysis of corruption syndrome in Nigeria as exemplified in *Once Upon a Tower*. The paper also highlights some challenges the would be director and designer may face in producing the play in term of scenery, lighting, costume and make-up.

Bakare and Musical Theatre
Bakare, Ojo Rasaki is today one of Nigeria's finest theatre practitioners per excellence who has made the country proud in his chosen profession. Born in Aramoko Ekiti on November 8th 1964. He started his theatrical practice as a trainee under the doyens of Alarinjo Travelling Theatre Chief Jimoh Aliu and late Hubert Ogunde. Bakare's parents like most parents who did not see anything good from theatre practice never wanted him to become a dramatist. In order to fulfill his dream and passion for theatre, he ran away from home to join Jimoh Aliu troupe where his theatre career began with the productions of *Fopomoyo, Agbarin* and so on. Due to his versatility in dance drama, Hubert Ogunde who saw him on a film location picked interest in Bakare. In an interview with the *Sun Newspaper* he discloses that;
> My parents didn't want me to become a dramatist I had to run away from home to join Jimoh Aliu with whom I did some plays…One day, I accompanied Jimoh Aliu to the location of a film where Ogunde saw me and instantly became interested in me because of my versatility in dance drama (*http://sunnewsonline.com/new/?p=39967*).

In *Nseobong Okon-Ekong's view, Bakare l*ived like an orphan even though his relatively affluent parents were alive and well. At the time, Bakare was holding on to a dream that his parents thought was a figment of his imagination. Their career preference was for him to become a lawyer. His passion was for something else. He wanted to study theatre arts and major in dance (*http://allafrica.com/stories/200911090517.html*). He is a holder of the following degrees: B.A (Hons) Theatre Arts, University of Calabar, M.A Play Directing and Playwriting, University of Calabar and Ph.D in Choreography and Dance Studies from Amadu Bello University, Zaria.

Bakare is today an international personality in Theatre Scholarship Practice. As a university teacher he has risen to the zenith of his career as a Professor. He is the first Nigerian to become Professor of Choreography and Performing Aesthetics. He is a Fellow, Dance Guild of Nigeria (FDGN), a multi-talented and award-winning Artiste-Scholar. Professor Bakare has directed over 200 major stage productions both nationally and internationally.

As a dramatist he has written over forty plays and books on theatre but only ten of his plays have been published. In Uche-Chinemere Nwaozuzu's views, Bakare Ojo Rasaki belongs to the respected group of multitalented and richly endowed artist/scholars in Nigeria. His rich vein of output and creative effort spans the genres of dance, directing, dramatic theory and criticism and playwriting (104). Some of Bakare's published works includes- plays: *This Land Must Sacrifice* (1991), *Drums of War* (1994), *Rogbodiyan* (1994), *Once Upon a Tower* (2001) and *Adanma* (2003) and non dramatic works are *Rudiment of Dance* (1995) and *The Artist- Intellectual: Sony Oti On Stage* (1998).

The playwright uses songs and music as a veritable tool to prompt the audience's mind and imagination on what they should expect from *Once Upon a Tower*. The play, however, is embedded with melodious and thought provoking songs and music that enhance the auditory aesthetic of the play. Instrumentals and songs serve as vehicles that help in driving home the message of the production by stirring the audience's emotion and evoking the feelings in their minds.

Like in most Bakare's plays: Like *Drum of War* and *Rogbodiyan* etc, songs and music play vital parts in heightening the emotions of the audience. The application and infusion of songs and music were very prominent in *Once upon a Tower*. The lyrics of the song in the exposition (proluge) and in movement one of the play creates an indelible mark in the mind of the audience and what they should expect from the play. The first, second and third stanza of the first song in movement one goes thus:

> Half education is better than none
> na de philosophy of our university now
> half blindness dey risky katakata de
> for front...
>
> Government go dey careless vice
> Chancellor go turn contractor
> The council go chop money
> Senate confusion galore...
>
> Dean na to play wayo
> HODs na politicians
> Lecturers turn survivalists
> Students na area bobo... (5-6).

The picture of the play as unveiled in the song became clearer when the main action opens in the Vice Chancellor's office few hours after the convocation. The playwright creatively employed the flashback techniques for sustenance of the suspense for effective communication of the dramatic message.

The Play Synopsis
The play x-rays and exposes the prevailing rates of corruption syndrome and the danger associated with it. It showcases the rot and decay caused by corruption in the educational sector with emphasis on the university system from the vice-chancellor, chancellors, lecturers, students and their associates. The playwright unravels the open-secret which has bedeviled our institutions of higher learning in a fictitious university-Mariapinta University, Nigeriana where some people in authority and

stakeholders conspire and aid the crippling of the standard of education in the country.

Corruption Syndrome in Nigeria: A Thematic Analysis of the Play

The play centres on Professor Kurumbete, as a scholar who monopolizes his field of specialization and out of sheer ignorance and fear of not wanting to lose this monopoly in Gynecology indulges in unpatriotic deals. His dominance in Gynecology makes him so relevant in the society. To him, however, losing such relevance is disastrous so he contributes greatly in frustrating the future of Pedro. Pedro, a gynecology graduate whose intellectual acumen and genuineness was destroyed before graduation because of corruption and greed *the dirty politics and the battle for supremacy* in the university system. In their arguments Ekanem, Okore and Ekpikem posit that; "in Nigeria, corruption has been a canker worm that has bedeviled all societies-universities inclusive" (448). It is very obvious that most people in the corridors of power are just there for their selfish interest. With their criminally minded interest for exploiting, siphoning, embezzling of public funds and overzealous ambition to find pleasure by employing all avenues to please their bosses through praise singing in order to remain their favourites. The chancellor in the play unveils how they have been using the praise singing strategy on the pages of newspapers to get undeserved favour from the government of the day either for appointment, contract or tenure elongation.

> **Emir**... by the time the president reads those beautifully worded speeches of ours in the newspaper, I am sure he will give us another term. He will believe we are doing the job well (7).

Corruption is like a two way traffic, in terms of bribery. As some of the lecturers and other staff in our Ivory Towers are corrupt, so are the students who are products of the corrupt system. Our universities today could be christened as breeding ground for all manners of immoral and corrupt acts such as examination malpractices, cultism, and prostitution. In his assertion, Priye S. Torulagha states that;

> Both male and female students are victimized by the corruption, deprofessionalization and the unethical behaviour that seems to dominate education today in Nigeria. Female students seem to suffer the most because it is alleged that some teachers, instructors, lecturers, professors expect female students to sleep with them, in addition to paying for grades (*http://www.gamji.com/article6000/NEWS7987.htm*).

It could be debated that, due to the high level of corruption which permeated every facet of human endeavour, where people perpetrated the act with impunity giving rise to Professor Kurumbete's romantic affair with his part three female student Miss Julie. This romantic relation is for her to pass all her examinations. Most students in the likes of Miss Julie who gained undeserved admission to the university due to the corrupt system and fail to pass any of their university examinations end up indulging in immoral acts with their lecturers. Chiedu Uche Okoye affirms that; "these class of students offer either their bodies or money to lecturers so as to score high grades in their courses" (n.p). One could be right to say that such immoral affairs between female students and their lecturers could lead to disrespectfulness and loss of moral standard on the part of the lecturers. Based on the loss of moral standard in professor Kurumbete, his evil tendencies and the fear of losing his profession monopoly he did not have the moral standing to rebuke Miss Julie's evil plot against Dr. Akitikori who was against corruption in the system and advocated for the right thing to be done. The dialogue below could throw more light on the above argument.

Prof. Kurumbete: Ha haa! Lady Jay...
Miss Julie: (sobbing) Prof. leave me alone
Prof. Kurumbete: Ha haa! Come on make my morning...

Miss Julie:	(still sobbing). I have always made your days but it is time for you to make my life now and all you are doing is promising heaven and earth without…
Prof. Kurumbete:	Are you talking about your examination?
Miss Julie:	Gynae 307 to be specific. I told you I know I will never pass that course. It is too tough for me and you know. Dr. Akitikori, the lecturer in charge apart from being a non-push over is principled to a fault. I have my way with other lecturers and get what I want. But, Akitikori is a principled stubborn he goat. He will never help me…
Prof. Kurumbete:	… With all the coercion? … Akitikori still left the result as it was?
Miss Julie:	Look, I even sent Black Hawk guys to threaten and if need be brutalize him. The bastard escaped all of their traps without a single scratch and there after remained adamant (16-17).

It is a fact that those who refused to compromise, support or encourage corruption are seen as the unwise ones in most cases. These incorruptible individuals sometimes are seen as threats to the corrupt ones who are always feeling insecure in the midst of the uncorrupt ones. Therefore, moving or plotting victimization processes against the uncorrupted individual(s) for advocating for an incorruptible system could be seen in movement five of the play where Dr. Akitikori who is known as a justice-loving, non-conformist is kicked out from the system.

Prof. Kurumbete:	…How is the trouble maker in your department?
Ugolo:	You mean Akitikori?

Prof. Kurumbete:	Who else?
Ugolo:	Em…Prof. between you and me, he is not a trouble maker. Just that he is a downright, non-conformist. He is too bold and vocal, can die for justice and never wants to be cowed. But the young man knows his job.
Prof. Kurumbete:	You are only confirming the fact that he is dangerous. When a bold, justice-loving non-conformist also has the advantage of intelligence and professional relevance, then he is too dangerous. Look, that boy is dangerous to my future. He is in my area of specialization, well positioned to break my monopoly. He is also dangerous to your future. Brilliant and active, he is a threat to your long stay as the head of department. We have to get him out of the system fast (30-31)

The level of corruption in the country has pervaded and crippled the educational system of the country drastically to the extent that most Nigeria graduates are half baked or quacks. Unfortunately, those who had benefited from the educational sector of Nigeria are the same people who had destroyed it because of their corruptible minds, greed and selfish interests. The playwright who is an advocate of social change, transformation and the watch dog of the society creatively exposes these satanic antics of some corrupt scholars in the academia in the likes of Professor Kurumbete, Ugolo, The Vice-chancellor, The chancellor, The senator and their cohorts who do not care if the system suffers in as much as they benefit from the corrupt system. They have reasons for their actions as it is revealed in the conversation between Professor Kurumbete and Ugolo.

Ugolo:	…But who takes over from him? He is too good in his area. If we get

Prof. Kurumbete:	him out, the system will suffer, our students will suffer.
	To hell with the system suffering. I hope you are not fooling yourself thinking that you can help the system? Can't you see nobody cares about the system? Everybody is a hanger-on just looking for how to survive via the system. Those who are in position to make fat momentary rip off from the system do so. It is a merchandise. The system is not only suffering already but bleeding...
Ugolo:	Sorry Prof... I understand.
Prof. Kurumbete:	Yemi will finish his housemanship some times next year. Akitikori is even his main consultant. So we get Akitikori out and Yemi take over his courses.
Ugolo:	Ha... Prof... Yemi is too weak academically. He is not a material to replace Akitikori.
Prof. Kurumbete:	Who cares? Is he going to teach your child? Look my dear; make no mistake about allowing your child to study in this country. If you don't have enough money to send your children to Europe, for university education, then send them to Ghana (31-32).

It could be deduced from the above assertion that, most unscrupulous individuals who have destroyed our educational system prefer to send their children or wards abroad to acquire university education. Torulagha affirms that:

> Due to the falling standards, quite a substantial number of Nigeria elite now send their children overseas for higher education. It is mostly the children of the middle and lower classes who remain in Nigeria to attend universities. It is unfortunate that the elite assisted immeasurably in destroying public education in Nigeria and after doing so, they send their children overseas
> (*http://www.gamji.com/article6000/NEWS7987.htm*).

It is painful that today, educational systems in Nigeria have become dysfunctional owing to the level of corruption. It is evident that those who are corrupt speak with both side of their month. In other words they are like double edges sword. This trait could be seen in the character of professor Kurumbete who denied to have given any support for a special training programme for Pedro. His refusal to support that special training programme is a trick to protect himself from losing his professional monopoly as he explains to Ugolo.

> … Well who tells you I even support the idea of a well enriched special training programme for Omowaye Pedro? That wizard? Even without any special training, he is already competing with part six students. People like him should be intellectually disempowered if we must own the future. And don't call me evil, I see nothing evil in what I am saying. Self preservation, they say, is the first human instinct (32).

The fear of not allowing anything to break the jinx of monopoly in any system among those who had monopolized the system is a threat to the growth and development of any country. These set of unscrupulous and unpatriotic people irrespective of their academic qualifications, and status because of their dead conscience, are not concerned about the enormity of their actions. Rather they are only concerned about their selfish gains. That is why a professor Kurunbete who is supposed to encourage, support and mentor his students and younger colleagues will rather plot for their downfall because he sees them as threats to his professional monopoly.

However, the issue of corruption has infiltrated also our families where parents out of their selfish interest and greed are pleased to be matchmakers for their children and wards without minding the resultant effects of such arrangement as seen in the play where Senator Alhaji Adbulraham Ike Anobi want his daughter Khadijat to marry Chief Ogbuefi Alexandra his cohort as third wife due to his selfish reason, greed and corrupt tendencies as exposed by Khadijat:

> ... My Dad here is the Chairman House Committee on education at the senate. He uses his position and his party affinity with the minister to corner ninety percent of the contract awards on education matters. But because of his position as a senator he cannot operate as a contractor openly. So he uses a dummy called Chief Ogbuefi Chukwuma as a front. And they share the proceeds fifty-fifty. My father feels cheated that a mere front is collecting as much as fifty percent... He wants me to marry Ogbuefi as a third wife so that I will function as the conduit pipe through which money will be siphoned from Ogbuefi's pocket into his pocket (44 - 45).

In another development, the high rate of unemployment in the country could be linked to high level of corruption in the country mostly in the academia. This is due to the fact that most graduates are products of a corrupt system where adequate training was not given to them while in school. Corrupt practices in our colleges, polytechnics and universities had negative effects on most of our graduates today who are more or less half baked and unemployable. In his argument Torulagha submits that; "the educational sector today, seems to produce graduates who are not sufficiently disciplined and equipped with the appropriate academic and professional skills ... ((*http://www.gamji.com/article6000/NEWS7987.htm*).) while Ekanem, Okore and Ekpiken opine that; "university education which is supposed to be the driving force for producing a desirable output for development turned out to produce outputs who lack employable skills". Sadly, based on corruption in the university system as mirrored in *Once Upon a Tower*, Pedro an aspiring and brilliant graduate of medicine and surgery who was described by his dean Professor Kurumbete as "the young man who won the best graduating student's award in medicine ... an eminent gynecologist ..." (12) ironically, is more or less a half baked graduate, a quack doctor and unemployable graduate courtesy of corruption syndrome in our educational system. Until he left the university, he did not see or use some medical equipments during his training. This inadequate training could also be connected to a lack of qualified and experienced lecturers in most of our Ivory Towers. Pedro who completed his studies under Yemi who is known to be "weak academically" (31) could be said to have contributed to the death of Khadijat whom Pedro administered a wrong dosage of drug in order to carryout an abortion in his friend's house Olusola, who is also a medical doctor. The dialogue below reveals how Pedro is more or less a quack doctor.

Pedro: ...I finished the operation, it is over fifteen minutes now.
Olusola: Which stuff did you use?
Pedro: Ketamine hydrochloride?
Olusola: Then there is cause for alarm. Ketamine has a rapid on set and lasts between five to ten minutes. If she is not up by now then... wait a minutes; what is her weight?
Pedro: I didn't weigh her, I only guessed she...
Olusola: Then how did you know the precise dose appropriate for her? Ketamine is dispensed at 1 to 4.5mg per kilogramme of body weight.
Pedro: No it is 14.5mg per kilogramme of body weight.
Olusola: Stop clowning Pedro!
Pedro: But I am correct. That is what my Ana 604 note says; I consulted my note before administering the drugs.

Olusola: Then your teacher must be crazy... (56).

Such a graduate like Pedro who is known for his brilliance in school, is rendered incompetent and inefficient in the field as a result of corruption. This could also be attributed to the fact that, he was trained by corrupt and unskilled lecturers to the detriment of the society. Bakare, Ojo Rasaki in an interview with Sola Balogun affirms that:

> An excellent medical system in the next ten years goes beyond a mere dream. Check out what is happening at the colleges of medicines in various universities: what goes around comes around. The play essentially harps on the dangerous politics in the university system and its terrible consequences on the society at large (n.p).

It is arguably that, despite Pedro's brilliant performance academically he relies so much on what he is taught without verification from other materials or sources. If Pedro had gone the extra mile to study on his own or confirm from Olusola, perhaps he would have known the right dose of drug for Khadijat. Pedro now has shifted the whole blame to his teacher's inefficiency and the corrupt system, exonerating himself from Khakijat death as he laments thus:

> If my teacher had done his job well, I would probably have been the proud husband of Khadijat today. But Mr. Teacher, you taught me nonsense and messed up my life (58).

It is a well acknowledged fact, that the system is corrupt and there are little or no materials, books, and equipment or adequate training facilities because they are diverted by those at the helm of affairs in the university system as is clearly stated in the play when Pedro was questioning the senator on his role in the corrupt system "... What do you know about chemicals... laboratory equipment when you cornered a contract meant for their being supplied to the university? Of course, you diverted the money into your bank account..." (63). The falling standard of our education could be linked mostly to lack of books, chemical, materials, laboratory and studio equipment emanating from the corruption syndrome which has caused a disastrous havoc in the society. Due to the rate of corruption which has bedeviled the system that most students in Nigeria tertiary institutions graduate without seeing most of the equipment and apparatus. In absence of these equipments and materials, they resort to dry practical.

Pedro: I remember specifically, that most of the chemicals I started seeing in the hospitals after my graduation were things I was not opportuned to be familiar with when I was a student…because the university couldn't make them available. I remember that at a time we were even doing what my HOD….called dry practicals. That is practicals without the required facilities… (59).

In a relative development, available equipments are diverted by corrupt Heads of department or other staff to their personal companies or organizations. As a result of this, students and some staff suffer and anyone who dares questions it is victimized like Dr. Akitikore in *Once Upon A Tower*.

Conclusion

This paper has attempted to examine corruption and its consequences in the society especially in the education sector.

It was argued that most corrupt people especially in the academia are of the belief that it is better to be a half baked graduate than not to be a graduate at all due to their corrupt mind set. Their views could be connected to the fact that people with such mentality are living human beings with dead consciences. According to Lere O. Shakunle; "where conscience is dead, the man is dead too" (*com/newsflash/film-theatre-and-society.html*). It is this dead conscience in human beings that could lead him/her into unpatriotic acts like corruption syndrome which has bedeviled the society generally and our academic environment in particular.

Corruption and all manners of ungodly acts easily thrive in an environment where people in that terrain see corruption as a norm without minding its ripple effect on the societies. However, as in most of Bakare's plays *Once Upon a Tower* was able to address universal themes of corruption, conflict resolution, violence, maladministration, man-in-humanity-to-man, insecurity and so on.

Works Cited

Bakare, Rasaki Ojo. *Once Upon a Tower*. Uyo: Afahaide Publishing Company, 2000.

_____ _____ _____. "I'll Remain a Restless Artist" in an Interview with Sola Salogun, *The Sun Newspaper* Reporter, 5th October, 2013. Web: http://sunnewsonline.com/new/?p=39967. Retrieved on Monday, 7th July, 2014.

_____ _____ _____."Theatre in Pursuit of Peace". An international Theatre Day Lecture delivered on 27th March, 2013 at Uyo. Web: http://www.nico.gov.ng/index.php/feature/89- theatre-in-pursuit-of-peace. Retrieved on Thursday, 3rd June, 2014.

_____ _____ _____."Dad disowned me for Joining Hubert Ogunde- Actor Dr. Ojo Bakare". Web: http://www.naijarules.com/xf/index.php?threads/"dad-disowned-me-for-joining- hubert ogunde-actor-dr-ojo.19078/. Retrieved on Monday, 7th July, 2014.

Bassey, Grace and Kingsley Oyong Akam. "The Relevance of Visual Art Designs In Theatrical and Film Productions for Sustainable Development in a Democratic Society: The Nigerian Experience". Unpublished Paper for Convention and International Conference of Society of Nigerian Theatre Artists- (SONTA), 2014.

Ejeke, Somomon Odiri. "Para-Linguistic Aesthetics in Ola Rotimi's Theatre" In Bakare, Ojo Rasaki (ed). *Ola Rotimi: Issues and Perspectives*. Abuja: Roots Books and Journals Nigeria Ltd., 2007:64-65.

Ekanem, Ekpenyong Ekpenyong, Egben Ogbonnaya Okore and William Etim Ekpiken. "University Education Policy in the Fight against Corruption and the Economic Development in Nigeria" Journal of Emerging Trends in Educational Research and Policy Studies (JETERAPS) 3(4): 2012: 448. Web: Retrieved on Thursday, 3rd June, 2014.

Microsoft ® *Encarta*. "Corruption" Microsoft Corporation, 2009.

Lasisi, Akeem. "Ojo-Rasaki Awakes the Stage in Oye Ekiti". *The Punch Newspaper,* 7th May, 2013. Web: http://www.punchng.com/feature/literary-punch/ojo-rasaki-awakes-the stage-in-oye ekiti/ Retrieved on Thursday,3rd June, 2014.

Nwabueze, Emeka. Drama and National Consciousness". In *Visions and Re-Visions: Selected Discourses on Literary Criticism (2nd ed.).* Enugu: ABIC Books, 2011: 161.

Nwaozuzu, Uche-Chinemere. "Nigeria's Political Leadershipand A Haunting Past: A Postcolonial Interpretation of Ojo Rasaki's This Land Must Sacrifice".
http:www.ajol.info/index.php/cajtms/article/view/89125/78683.
Retrieved on Thursday, 3rd June, 2014

Okon-Ekong, Nseobong. "Nigeria: Director General, Abuja Carnival Explains-Why They Call Me". Wed: http://allafrica.com/stories/200911090517.html. Retrieved on Thursday, 3rd June, 2014.

Okoye, Chiedu Uche. "Nigeria: Scourge of Corruption and Its Deleterious Effects", 2013.
Web:http://risenetworks.org/2013/04/nigeria-scourge-of-corruption-and-its deleterious - effects/. Retrieved on Thursday, 3rd June, 2014.

Panter, Howard interview with Vikas Shah on "*Theatre, Performance and Society*" Thought Economics, 2014. Web: *http://thougteconomics.blogspot.com/2014/03/theatre-performance-society.html*. Retrieved on Thursday, July, 2014.

Shakunle, Lere O. Film, "Theatre and Society", 2007. Web: http://www.nigeriavillagesquare.com/newsflash/film-theatre-and-society.html. Retrieved on Thursday, 2014.

Torulagha, Priye S. ''The Corrosive Effect of Corruption on Nigerian Educational System''.
(*http://www.gamji.com/article6000/NEWS7987.htm*). Retrieved on Thursday, 3rd June, 2014.

Factional Insurgency in Bakare, Ojo Rasaki's *Drums Of War* And *Rogbodiyan*

By
Idogho, Joseph Agofure

Introduction
That theatre mirrors the society, with the view of reflecting the socio-political, economic and religious reality of the society is a statement of fact. Over the ages, the theatre and its practitioners have served as a watch-dog of the society and mouth-piece of the oppressed. A critical look at Nigerian society today reveals class stratification: the rich and the poor, the haves and the have not, the bourgeois and the down-trodden. This stratification has doubtlessly engendered a class struggle that has consequently degenerated to insurrection, rebellion, factional insurgency, terrorism and insecurity. Subsequently the theatre and the dramatists have inadvertently or advertently depict this social reality for the society to reflect with the view of making changes.

The social imbalances in Nigeria that prompts the social unrests are perceptible; the ruling class in the Nigeria society subjects the poor masses to hardship and suffering. The poor people are treated with contempt; and are restive, yet helpless. However, at this point of this social injustices, the helpless and hopeless masses have one or two choices; either to fight to remain compliant to the oppressive over lord or to fight back to gain their political and economic freedom. Ousmane asserts that, "it is not those who are taken by force, put in chains and sold as slaves who are real slaves; it is those who will accept it morally and physically" (20). This statement implies that the masses have the right to choose to become free or remain in slavery. Conversely their choice relies greatly on their ability to evaluate themselves in the socio-political, religious and economic mirror- theatre, created by the creative artists.

Bakare, Ojo Rasaki is eloquent and pushy in his use of the seditious latent of the theatre to shape the audience's insightful alertness of the communal revolt which Nigerian masses are witnessing in contemporary Nigeria society. Bakare basically epitomises in his creative works, the intricacy of a selfish elucidation of society in Nigeria drama and theatre and proffers plausible solutions to these insurrections and insurgencies. Therefore, we will use two plays *Drum of War* and *Rogbodiyan* written by Bakare, Ojo Rasaki to examine factional insurgency and its effects in Nigeria.

Causes of Insurgency in Nigeria

Stability and national security are not possible in a political environment characterised by insurgency. Consequenctly, the following policies, tendencies, actions and inactions which constitute bad governance can lead to insurgency:

A. Lack of respect for the national constitution by political and military leaders who constantly amend the constitution or ignore the constitution in order to remain in power results in anger and frustration. The citizens begin to rationalise that their leaders only care about remaining in power and would go to any length to ensure that they remain in power. This leads to immediate insecurity because people begin to lose faith in the system. Countries like Libya, Egypt, Algeria, Tunisia, Ethiopia, Cameroon, Rwanda, Sudan, Niger, Chad, Ivory Coast (Cote ivory), Zimbabwe, Gabon, Togo, Angola etc. suffer from the fact that the leaders remain in power endlessly. On this score, Nigerians have been very fortunate, hence, President Goodluck Jonathan is the thirteenth head of state since the country gained independence in 1960. On the other hand, Cameroon has had only two heads of state since independence.

B. Lack of respect for the rule of law by political, military, police and business elites who violate the law with impunity without any legal consequences to them while those who are politically powerless are sent to prison for violating every imaginable act that can cause national insecurity.

C. It is bad governance when a country is characterised by too many security agencies. Quite often, in order to become relevant, security agencies and agents compete unnecessarily for attention from the political leadership. As they compete fiercely, they are unable to share and coordinate critical information, thereby, encouraging security breakdown to take place.

D. The refusal to listen to the moderate voices of opposition in the early 1970s led to the emergence of extremists who are now threatening the national security. The refusal to listen to those who expressed concerns about the deplorable situation in the Niger Delta resulted in armed opposition and other refusal to listen to ethnic militia with national agenda.

E. Problem of Corruption: Due to massive corruption in the last two decades, Nigeria has been reduced to a mere shadow of itself. It is obvious that the country finds it very difficult to move forward. The nation's wealth disappears into private pockets of the same officials who suppose to use the wealth to build the state.

Generally, it is quite easy to tell when a country is experiencing good governance. One of the signs that are readily identifiable is when the unemployment and crime rates go down. Another indicator is that the rate of inflation is down or manageable, thereby, affording most people an ability to live reasonably well. Similarly, the infrastructure is maintained, modernized and rehabilitated so that health care, public transportation, education and water and sewage management systems are functional. In addition, the government is responsible, transparent and accountable.

Synopsis of *Drums of War* and *Rogbodiyan*

Subversive and revolutionary intent regulate most of the dramatic works of Bakare, Ojo Rasaki, especially *Drums of War* and *Rogbodiyan*. In *Drums of War* (1995), Bakare combines music, dance and the human medium to reenact the tragedy of a self-centred, arrogance, dictatorial leader. This bothers on leadership and governance landscape of Nigeria. The play, *Drums of War,* explores the power drunkenness of king Onome, the fictional leader of Abakpa, an imaginary town in Nigeria. King Onome in his power drunkenness, dictatorial and autocratic leadership style defiantly ignores the yearning and welfare of his subjects, thereby leading to his tragic downfall. He meets his waterloo, through the lost of his only son Orighoye in the war and subsequently, his wife Queen Otubu as a result of his son's death in the war. The war which he palpably instigates and unashamedly refuses to stop, in spite of his subject plea and appeal leads to his subsequent banishment from the land. The creative imagination of the play may have been inspired by the incessant wars (inter and intra), religious and political wars and fracas instigated by our power-inebriated leaders, undermining the social welfare of their subjects, the masses who are the end receivers. The playwright hints this in the preface (Dedication) of the play-text: "To the victims of man's greatest expression of his bestiality. To those who perished in Somalia, Rwanda and Liberia, Bosni, Herzegovina and Yugoslavia, Biafra-Nigeria and the tiny village of Zango Kataf" (Bakare I).

In *Rogbodiyan* (1994), Bakare, Ojo Rasaki reenacts the corruption, power-drunkenness, intrigues and self-centredness of Nigerian leadership in Ilu Koroju, an illusory village, setting in the South-west, Nigeria. In *Rogbodiyan,* Ojo Bakare captured the intrigues of our leader to seize, or get into, clinch and the tendency to abuse power. Regent Adebunmi clinch to power more than necessary and when she eventually relinquish it, her son; Adegbani cunningly usurp the power from Asagidigbi, the undemocratically elected corrupt king, who abuse power within few days of his enthronement. He, Asagidigbi, is involved in extra judicial killing of his Special Adviser, Agogo and could not stay in seclusion for seven days as required by custom. He defiantly defies the Arugba-Oge who is expected to be in seclusion for seven days and a virgin until she carries the sacrifices in the Arugba-Oge Festival that is barely three days ahead. These atrocities resulted to chaos in the land and subsequently lead to Asagidigbi's downfall. The corrupt practices of the elders-the kingmakers in the electoral process in the land is also captured in the play. Also, the corrupt nature of Gbadegesin; Asagidigbi's opponent is also reenacted.

Functional of Insurgency in Bakare, Ojo Rasaki's *Drums of War* and *Rogbodiyan*

The leaders in Nigeria do not show respect to the rule of law, especially, judicial decisions. This hampers the judiciary to effectively discharge its duties. The predictability of the judiciary is not yet a reality in Nigeria, the political executives still undermine the independence of the judiciary through patronage appointments, and judicial administration is characterised by weak enforcement capacity. This is demonstrated by Regent Adebunmi in *Rogbodiyan*, when she infringes on the electoral process of the people of Koroju.

Regent: (Pause); A very important thing that quivers my liver gave birth to this call. (Pause)
> It has not been easy ruling this land since Adeakin, my father, left us to join his ancestors. That was seven years ago when I became the Regent. You all know that how we have tried since then to choose a new king but this has been impossible. Let me quickly tell you again that my lineage has ruled this land longer than any other lineage and I want my own reign to be the last of my lineage.

All: (Happy): Hee e.

Regent: I want others to be given the chance to rule. The land does not prosper when it is only one man that does the tilling.

All: Hee e. …

Salotan: (Stands). Your Royal Highness, we hear you, and judging from the reaction here, we
> are happy with what you have said. But oyibo people say "once bitten, twice shy". With all due respect, Your Highness, why may we believe you this time? In spite of several promises, your lineage has ruled this land for the last twenty- three years…

Regent: Thank you for that shower of pessimism, Salotin, but let me tell you, I am committed
> to what I am saying. I am sincere. To further show my sincerity, I have decided to hand over power before this year Oge Festival, which comes up in seven days time.
>
> **All**: (Surprised) Hen en.

Regent: Yes

Abere: (Squatting). Your highness, how do you intend to make this possible since we don't
    have contestants for the throne yet? How?

Regent: That has been taken care of. I have decided to choose two candidates who are not
    from my own lineage and out of these two candidates, the Kingmakers shall choose one and announce to the people in four days time while three days after the announcement, coronation shall take place.

Woman: (Stands) Long Live the Regent.

Agogo: She greets you.

Woman: (Furious). With all due respect, I am baffled by what is going on, Your Royal
    Highness

All: (Reproachfully). Eehn!

Woman: (Defiant). Yes. I insist on being heard! I must speak my mind. How can anybody
    wake up one morning and impose two candidates on us just like that? Aren't there established procedures for this sort of thing? Are we people without tradition? Wonderful things are happening in this land. (Sits petulantly)

Regent: I refuse to take your words in anger. As far as this issues is concerned I have spoken,
    and so it shall be. …

All: (With mixed reactions). Towalase e

Aloba: Your Royal Highness may the crown stay on your head and the beaded shoes under
    your feet. …

Regent: Now that you've heard from both men, I hereby order you Kingmakers to choose the
    next king. … (*Rogbodiyan* 8-16)

Lack of rule of law also manifests in the play, *Rogbodiyan*, (in Movement 7). The elected King, Asagidigbi is required by the law of the land to be in seclusion for seven days. While the Arugba Oge, the newly selected virgin who would take the sacrifice to the gods on the festival day is also required by custom to be in seclusion in the palace: unfortunately the king could not abide by these rules; he defiantly defiles the Arugba Oge, which in turn, into resulted catastrophe in the land. Therefore, the subversion of the electoral process and the choice of the people through disrespect for electoral law and rule of law in the land are responsible for factional insurgencies in the play, and in Nigeria at large.

Many observers of the development and governance crisis in Nigeria since independence agree that poor leadership has been a major factor. Most of the Nigerian leaders are not committed to development of their society. The conversation between 2nd Warrior and 1st Woman in *Drums of War* below captures this:
2nd Warrior: ... But the nation perishes where the leaders lack vision. The blindness of
>those that lead us has put us in a pit of death and destruction. We are people who have lost any direction, any goal.

1st Woman: ... we put you there, the chiefs and the King to be our light, to lead us aright and
>make the world a better place. But what do you do to us our leaders? You set us against our neighbours and make us fight senseless wars, instead of concentrating our efforts on meaningful development. We wake up every morning suspecting our neighbours, preoccupying our minds with the next strategy to use in bringing our so called foes on their knees... (*Drums of War* 10- 11).

The absence of development oriented leadership can, therefore, leads to factional insurgency.
In Nigeria, there is absence of transparent and accountable leadership. A government is accountable when its leaders (both elected and appointed) are responsive to the demands of the governed. Lack of accountability and corrupt practices are factors that can lead to factional insurgency.

Although corruption is a global scourge, Nigeria appears to suffer tremendously from this malaise. Every one appears to believe that the nation has a culture of corruption; Nigeria is a rich nation floating on oil wealth, but almost none of it flows to the people. The countless reforms and lack of ingenuity and integrity of our leaders have left Nigeria corrupt as ever. Politicians are expelled and later re-admitted into their parties. Then, what hope for good governance, when the leadership is deeply entrenched in corrupt practices. Corrupt practices manifest in varied degree in *Drums of War* and *Rogbodiyan*. For instance, King Onome, the protagonist in Bakare's *Drums of War*, is a symbol of corrupt leadership. Onome uses his power dishonestly, which is the thematic preoccupation of the play. It is important to return to the play again:

Akogun: But why must we continue instigating our people against our neighbours? Why
> must leaders always use their followers as cannon fodder for their own ambitions?

King: Why? Let me tell you. We must guarantee our security by annihilating all our enemies.
> Because, in this world, there is no room for the weak. We need to be respected and feared. And one more thing. You seem to be forgetting that the Ibuji people have refused to bow to our deity, the awesome Abasi Ibom, the Supreme God. Instead, they worship Agbeni. They must be converted by force, if necessary.

Akogun: But your Royal Highness, the laws of this land permit a man to worship whatever
> he chooses to worship and fundamentally no religion support the use of force. (*Drums of War* 26-27).

The play *Rogbodiyan* also captures the corrupt practices of Nigeria leaders at different level of Nigeria polity. Regent Adebunmi, her son Adegbani, who eventually usurps the throne; Asagidigbi the corrupt king, and his corrupt opponent, Gbadegesin are all epitomes of corruption. Apparently, every facet of Nigeria today is doubtlessly ridden by corruption; the homes and the place of worship inclusive. In this type of situation, factional insurgency is inevitable.

Electoral Malpractices has become a popular phenomenon in Nigerian politics. As a matter of fact, an average Nigerian believes that elections cannot be won except it is rigged. This is demonstrated by Asagidigbi and Gbadegesin in *Rogbodiyan*. In fact, electoral malpractice is the thematic preoccupation of Bakare in *Rogbodiyan*. Electoral malpractice is not a recent phenomenon in Nigeria, in fact, electoral malpractice has been part of Nigeria political system since independence and has continued to exist, even, in a modernised fashion. For instance, in the First Republic; the leadership of various political parties were accused and alleged of election rigging. The same happened in the Second Republic and even now. With this scenario, factional insurgency is inevitable.

Panacea to Factional Insurgency in Nigeria
Good governance, good political system, impartial judiciary, respect for rule of law and constitution of the land, security and protection of live and property, impartial electoral umpire, political stability and patriotism are some of the solutions that solve factional insurgency in Nigeria. The time votes are counting, the time corruption and bribery are forgotten, the time social unrest and favouritism are remained down, then factional insurgency will become history.

Thus, when people of a nation-state have organised their own human and natural resources to provide themselves with what they need and expect in life, and have learned to show patriotism in the larger national interest, then their resistance to disorder and violence will enormously increase.

Conclusion
This paper, has analysed and discussed causes and solutions to factional insurgency in Nigeria against the backdrop of Bakare's dramas; *Drums of War* and *Rogbodiyan*. We suggest viable means of generating transformational leaders who are capable of entrenching and sustaining good governance in Nigeria. It is advocated that candidates with clear visions and strategies for achieving such vision, strong commitment and determination for

development should be elected into political and leadership positions. In addition to this, the electoral system and process must provide citizens of every social status, the chance to hear question and receive answers from candidates on their vision, policies and specific strategies as well as timetables for implementing and achieving them.

On a final note, it is instructive at this juncture to note that Nigeria, since independence has produced a pattern of leadership characterised by coups, countercoups, corruption and instability, and stepping into the path towards another half century, Nigeria needs more than ordinary managers of national affairs. It should aspire for actors that push their people to achieve profound institutional changes. The latter is the role of transformational leadership. In fact the quality of leadership determines the nature of governance. Good governance inheres in good leadership. Without transformational leadership, Nigeria may continue to lag behind other nations.

Works Cited

Bakare, Ojo Rasaki. *Rogbodiyan*. Abuja: Tamaza Publishing Co. Ltd, 1994.

Bakare, Ojo Rasaki. *Drums of War*. Zaria: Tamaza Publishing Co. Ltd, 1995.

Osofisan, Femi. "The Political Imperative in African Dramaturgy and Theatre Practice." *Cross Current in African Theatre* (ed) Asagba Austin. Benin City: Osasu Publishers, 2001.

Ousmane, Sembone, *God's Bits of Wood*, London: Heinemann, 1960.

Mlama, Penina M. *Culture and development: The Popular Theatre aApproach in Africa*. Uppsala: Nordiska Afrikainstitutet, 1991.

Satirical Reflection of Social Stasis And The Reader/Audience Interpretation of Dramatic Text in Bakare, Ojo Rasaki's *Rogbodiyan*.

By
Cecil Ozobeme

Introduction

The threats to societal survival and national existence are not the social catastrophes witnessed in the society today but the continued perpetration of existing aberrant social trends that overtime generate such catastrophes. The severe and devastating socio-economic, political and developmental crises, threatening the core of our national existence and survival, be it increased crime wave, poverty, unemployment, social strife, religious intolerance, insecurity, hostage taking or the more recent and devastating wave of terrorism, are the by-products of a consolidated antisocial behaviours and practices of the individuals and structures in society. It is in this situation that the creative artist, using his art, tries to correct or caution society. Ebo (2008) rightly observes that in the use of creative writing to address societal problems, the artist is making an 'objective evaluation, exposition or the critical assessment of the socio-political conditions in society'. The aim is to save society from self-annihilation. Obadiegwu (2002) shares the opinion that in criticising, lampooning, satirising social vices, the playwright hopes to galvanise the populace into reflecting about their actions and instigate change. Surprisingly, the message of the playwright seem lost on the populace it tries to correct. Few seem to realise that they are the object of the writers scathing criticism. The reason for this is not farfetched. The fictive representation of social reality by the playwright makes the audience see themselves as far removed from the characters in a play. Some people find it difficult to read between the lines in a dramatic work and so they fail to get the message. It is such occurrences that raised doubts and fuels the controversy about the efficacy of the use of art in serving society. It is pertinent, therefore, for one to get an understanding of the various strategies the dramatist employ to serve society. One of such ways is through the fictive representation of societal shortcomings in a dramatic form. This paper seeks to use Bakare's play, *Rogbodiyan* to argue the functionality of the artist as a contributor to societal reconstruction through a reflection of social stasis so that remedial actions can be taken to ensure national progress.

Art in The Service of The Society
The controversy about the functionality of art in serving society dates back to the Platonian and Aristotelian era as cited in Dukore (1974). The relegation of art to the provision of entertainment and amusement for a viewing audience has tremendously dimmed in the face of the mammoth evidences that lends credence to the contribution of art to the development of several facets of society. As Ogundokun (2013) affirms: "It is possible to use art as a weapon or instrument to fight against repressive policies, blind cultural practices and other societal vices so as to develop the society since there is a deep relationship between art and the society which paves the way for its creation and eventual production".

It is an indubitable fact that creative writing has been used as a vehicle not only for culture preservation and transformation but also for instruction and the inculcation and uplifting of morals. Art, aside provision of entertainment, has been used for propagation of ideas and correction of societal shortcomings and a weapon "for fighting oppressive ideologies such as capitalism, fascism and other totalitarian hegemonic structures" (Vazquez, 1973).

Creative Work as a Product of Society
Before the era of literary documentation in Nigeria, drama was employed to lampoon social vices and ridicule some aberrant social trends in order to evoke change. Aberrant historical antecedents have found their way into the themes and subject matters of the works of several creative writers so that posterity can learn and avoid the mistakes of the past. Supporting the above position, Dandaura (2002) avers that the dramatist is "a

member of society, so naturally, his artistic sensibilities are shaped and sharpened by the socio-economic contradictions and political happenings of his time". Ngugi wa Thiong'o (1972) also believes that " literature does not develop in a vacuum, it is given impetus, shape and direction by the social, political, economic forces in a particular society". It is in the reflection of the decadence prevalent in society that the dramatist hopes to instigate the needed change for societal wellbeing.

Clear examples of the dramatists' contribution to society are replete. Several dramatist's have used contemporary socio-political situations as material for their plays. They include Ola Rotimi's *Hopes of the Living Dead*, a play that chronicled the heroic exploits of Harcourt Ikoli White and other patients of the lepers wing of the Port Harcourt General Hospital against their forceful relocation to the uncompleted leper's colony at Izuakoli, Ahmed Yerima's *Kafir's Last Game* (1998) is an exposé of Nigeria's flawed electoral programme and of society under a strangulating military regime. Others include Femi Osofisan's *Once Upon Four Robbers* (1982), a play that satirises and lampoons the attitudes of Nigerian leaders. Wole Soyinka's *King Baabu* (2000) satirises the arrogance and inhuman nature present in most African leaders. *The Trial of Brother Jero* (1966); a scathing swipe on several religious charlatans who once plied their trade in the Lagos bar beach. As Bakare (2013) right observes, "the work of art is either a reflection of the society that produces it or nothing". It is obvious that the socio- political occurrences in the country have consistently been source material for dramatic works but how the reader/audience receive and respond to such works is a question begging for answers.

Style And Audience Comprehension of Dramatic Texts

Dramatists' responses to social political events vary. Dramatists may employ commentaries, parodies, satires or other style of presentations to address prevailing social events. Some others present the matters as they are for the public to judge. It is noteworthy that their style and mode of expression may colour how the events are replicated in their works and how the audience receive it. The style of many writers seem to privilege aesthetics more that the message. Consequently, the audience derive pleasure from the artistic razzmatazz and miss the message they set out to express. Interestingly, every dramatists' work has to be couched in a dramatic form that is in line with the medium specific convention for artistic expression. In the play, *Rogbodiyan* the satirical form of presentation is employed needing appropriated decoding by the audience. The question is; Do the audience understand the dramatist's style of presenting important messages? Adeoye (2013) states that some playwrights "expect their reader-audience to have an ability to distinguish between the oppressive and dictatorial government of most of the leaders depicted in their plays. In this case, the reader-audience can relate these villainous characters to the political leaders in their own society". Bakare (2013) pushes this argument further when he states that satire has two parts; the encoding done by the artist and the decoding done by the audience to whom he particularly, leaves the task of encoding. One wonders if there is a lacuna in the decoding of the artists' work by the audience that could limit comprehension. Ibagere and Omoera (2010) claim that Nigerian theatre is mostly elitist, having no impact on a majority of the people. To have the pertinent impact, it has to move out of the elite environment to the people and influence them. Is this really the case? Many writers have employed satires as a form of dramatic expression which according to Bamidele (2001) are 'dramatic works' that aim at making caustic comments on society. He states further that satirical works aim at "hurting us so that we can amend." (Bamidele 2001). On the other hand writers like Ngugi (1982) sees the satirical artist as one who is "standing aloof, to view society and highlight its weakness" he urges the playwright to "try to go beyond this, to seek out the sources, the causes and the trends". If we go by this postulation, it follows therefore that the lacuna in audience comprehension of the dramatists work lie not entirely on the form used, but in the audiences' ability to decode them. To surmount this impasse Eghagha (2006) suggests "using a simple language, a simple method' for the dramatists to achieve "the change in values which both the leaders and followers of the country are currently clamouring for". He believes "that drama has the capacity to reach all strata of society". We shall at this point examine and attempt an interpretation of *Rogbodiyan,* a play that this writer believes is simple enough and fits roundly as a dramatic form.

The Playwright and His Work
Bakare, Ojo Rasaki is a dramatist who has penetrated the deep social political terrain of the nation. In the words of Uche-Chinemere (2011), he belongs to the respected group of multitalented and richly endowed artist/scholars in Nigeria who as a playwright treat themes as diverse as political instability, leadership question, social responsibility, the plight of the oppressed among many. In his work, *Rogbodiyan* the playwright makes a compelling and intriguing commentary on the Nigerian project. The work encapsulates the assiduous effort of an unrelenting visionary artist to brandish the aberrant social and political trends that has enveloped the Nigeria political landscape.

The Play *Rogbodiyan*
The play *Rogbodiyan* written by Bakare, Ojo Rasaki is a satirical exposé of the obdurate quest for power by the avaricious political class in the country. The play, set in the fictional Koroju community analogous to the Nigerian society, dealt with the dilemma of a land traumatised with the agony of self-imposed leadership. The search for a new king make two favoured but unworthy contestants to vye for the throne . Asagidigbi, using bribery, thugs and threats, outwits his rival Gbadegeshin and gets the throne. On ascension, his dictatorial and self-conceited nature coupled with his lack of moral rectitude make him to defill tradition. In a drunken spell, he had carnal knowledge of the Arugba Oge who is to remain a virgin in order to perform a crucial rite. Agogo, the court adviser paid with his life for trying to check the kings recklessness. Angered by the king's actions, the gods afflicted the people with different forms of deformities. The quest for a cure saw Adegbani volunteering to go to river Awogbaarun situated in the land of the dead to provide the sacred healing water. He comes back successfully but ends up

blackmailing the people into giving him the thrown in exchange for a cure. Left with no choice the ailing people agrees. He became king and Asagidigbi excommunicated.

Rogbodiyan as a Reflection of Social Stasis

The Oxford Advanced Learners Dictionary defines "social" as connected with society and stasis" as lack of development. Social stasis can therefore, be defined as societal retardation. The reflection of social stasis by the play becomes evident right from the opening sequence with the parade of the sick people of Koroju where the deformed led the blind. It is a situation that depicts the near hopeless situation of the Nigerian populace begging for salvation from several socio-economic traumas besetting the country. This becomes more succinct as the Narrator exposes the nature of the Koroju society as:

> ...*a land where merit is thrown to the wind...* an entity controlled by non-entities...abode of religious hypocrites and political sycophants...(a land) where intelligence means nothing and the academically brilliant is a potential pauper ...a land where truth has been hindered and falsehood exalted' ... a land of corruption where material l and political wealth are worshiped and false acquisition... encouraged {*Rogbodiyan* 7}

The above encapsulates the pervading circumstances in the nation's past and present where. merit gets sacrificed in the alter of mediocrity. A situation where those qualified for leadership task never get the chance to lead. The allusion to religious hypocrisy and political sycophancy bespeak of a society with a political landscape where appointments are determined by religious affinities, and political wealth bestowed on political party faithful irrespective of qualification. The pauperisation of the intelligentsia is a clear reflection of the society where semi-literate councilors earn more than a university professors. Qualified Lawyers, doctors, engineers, and some of the best brains in the nation roam the streets without jobs. The reference to the suppression of truth and the exaltation of falsehood is a clear indication of an era where the press and the judiciary suffer from the undue interference and subjugation from the leaders. The case of the assassinated celebrated journalist and the incarceration of his likes in the past are vivid examples. In addition, the negative outcomes of many election tribunal sittings, the suppression of justice and the granting of pardon to the high and mighty political criminals and treasury looters are clear examples of the exultation of falsehood and suppression of the truth.

One pertinent feature of the Koroju community that is akin to the Nigerian situation at that time and even, now is the animated jostle for political power, the gangling rape of all democratic principles, the abuse of our nascent democracy and the avid desire to either hold on to the reins of power or remain at the corridors of power. Okeke (2010) aptly describes the trend as "a self succession syndrome and planting of stooges.

The purposeless, sycophantic, and corrupt nature of electoral officers, typified by the elders of Koroju community, is brought to the fore. Despite the existence of a traditionally stipulated method of choosing future leaders (consultation with the oracle which is a representation of the electorate), the King makers are favourably disposed to manipulate the process. The eventual consultation with the diviner was a mere formality as his advise gets jettisoned. This underscore the mere formality of elections were votes do not count. It indicates the election rigging syndrome which we are all familiar with and the disfranchisement of the populace.

The greed, self-centredness, people's insensitivity and aridity of ideas displayed by some members of the political class is more evident in Eto who kept concurring to every motion and counter motion raised during the selection process. The following dialogue clearly elucidates the point:

      Aloba: You and I know that there is only one way of getting this thing done...ifa must be consulted
      Eto: Yes I support you Aloba

> Abere: ...For how long shall we continue to leave our fate in the hands of the oracle ... let us assess the candidates ourselves
> Eto: Its true Abere I support you.

Eto's stock in trade is plying on both sides which make Abere in anger to address him as a bat ..."who is neither an animal or a bat" (*Rogbodiyan* 20). Eto's reply, to this accusation puts matters to rest. He says ....

> "that is how I get what I want. By belonging to all camps... the only politics I play now is the politics of my stomach and probably that of my immediate family" (Rogbodiyan:20)

The above is reminiscent of the cross-carpeting witnessed in past democratic dispensation and which is prevalent in the polity today. The sheer absence of political ideology, the self centeredness, greed and gross irresponsibility are trends that characterise the nation's political experience.

From Movement 6, spotlight is thrown on the traditional declaration of a grand agenda by every new leaders when they come to power. On ascension to the throne Asagidigbi assures the people that he will solve their problem but he fails to do this.

As a result of official immunity which many political position holders wield, they display gross administrative rascality and flagrant disrespect for constituted authority. They taint and twist the law in the name of constitutional reviews just to serve their selfish interest. Little wonder that several reports of constituted committees never see the light of day. Again administrative rascality is a recurring decimal in our society today as portrayed in the play when the king gets himself drunk and defies traditionally constituted procedures for choosing the Arugba Oge and later defy tradition by sleeping with her during the period of seclusion. What this also depicts is decline in cultural values and normative behaviours which thrives in all aspects of society. Portrayed also is the fact that opposition or criticism is greeted with persecution. Anigala (2001) succinctly captures the position here when he say of the leaders:

> They succeed in wielding political power with the connivance of a few sycophants who constitute the pseudo-ruling cabinet. Such dictators further, perpetuate themselves in power through intimidation oppression and outright rape of justice (Anigala 2001).

In Movement 8, Akhigbe's antics represents another abnormality that is prevalent in our society. Reflected clearly in the play is the paucity of fearless patriots in society like Agogo who against all odds will be bold enough to say the truth. At the risk of losing his life, he still chose to uphold truth and justice in the face of administrative intimidation and tyranny. He also is a symbol for expressing the stranglehold on the press by the iron fisted tyrannical military regime of the recent past when there was suppression of freedom of expression. Those who were bold enough to challenge the despotic leaders got persecuted, incarcerated or killed. This trend is evident in the play when Agogo shows bravery while challenging the King.

The concluding scenes of the play, spotlighted one of the banes of Nigerian democracy which is the sit tight syndrome. Despite his blind state and his inability to steer the ship of the state, the King still hankers after the reins of power. Lastly, the antics of Adegbani, who blackmailed the people in order to seize power in the play clearly indicate, the coups and counter coup that has for long proliferated the political landscape of the Nigerian nation and indeed the African continent. It should be noted that the trend still continues with the spate of impeachment borne out of partisan differences and acrimony. Acrimonious politics as some political pundits observes, hampers reasoned policy formulation and implementation-a path way to administrative failure and eventual societal devastation.

From the fore going, it is obvious that the play *Rogbodiyan* is indeed a clear reflection of the society. It features several characters that are archetypes of past and contemporary political dispensation. The play preoccupies itself with the reflection of social stasis in order to elicit attitudinal change necessary for social integration and national development. One can clearly deduce from the play that we are the causes of our calamities and only a change in our attitudes and actions can alter the course to eventual national doom.

Summary and Conclusion

This paper set out to examine the role and contribution of the creative writer or dramatist to societal development. It revealed that by mirroring the society with his or her works the dramatist is able to elicit attitudinal change. Using *Rogbodiyan* by Bakare, Ojo Rasaki as a case study, the paper was able to show that there is a significant resemblance between the play and the Nigerian society. According to O'Cornel (2013), the play pictures the various hierarchies of corruption, maladministration, violence, misappropriation, terrorism in all strata of the country. It depicts the widespread level of bribery in all bureaucracies. Considering the allegory of the epidemic, the play reveals to us what happens when corruption has grown beyond its ostensible heights. The economy of the country is affected, thereby leading to mass hunger, poor academic environment, socio-psychological violence, inflation and suffering.

Recommendation

It is recommended that particular interest be given to the study of literature in this country so the audience will get acquainted with the communicative mode of the dramatist. Creative writers and dramatists should understand their role as the watchdog of society and so should live up to the task. It is recommended also that the attempt to correct social vices with their works, dramatists should lay more emphasis on the message than aesthetics. This way, the audience will not get caught in the maze of theatrics and lose the message.

References

Achebe, Chinua. (1988). An Image of Africa: Racism in Conrad's *Heart of Darkness*. In *Hopes and Impediments*: Selected Essays. New York: Anchor Books.

Anigala A. E (2001). Democratising a nation in crisis: The role of the theatre artiste. In: Austin Asagba (Ed.): *Cross currents in African theatre*. Benin City: Department of Theatre Arts, University of Benin, pp. 168-177.

Aziegbe. S. A.(1992). The political transition programme and the future of democracy in Nigeria. In: C.A. Gboyega, E. Osaghae (Eds.): *Proceedings of the Symposium on Democratic Transition in Africa.* Ibadan: CREDU, pp. 389-345.

Bakare, O. (1994) *Rogbodiyan* Zaria. Tamaza Publishing Company Ltd.

Bakare, O. (2013) I will remain a restless artist. *The Sun Online Newspaper* retrieved from http//sunnewsonline.com/new/oxct 5th 2013 accessed on 25/07/ 2014.

Dukore, B ed. (1974) Dramatic theory and critisicm: Greek to Grotowski. Holt Rinehart and Winston Inc.

Dandaura, E "Hagher, S.(2002). The playwright documentarist as a nation builder". *Theatre Experience.* vol.1 no. Awka: Penmark Publishers Inc, 2002. 177-194.

Dike E.V.(nd) State administration and acrimonious party politics. Retrieved from www.gamji.com 31st July. 2014.

Ebo, E. E. (2008) Social criticism in Nigerian drama: A study of Wole Soyinka's Opera Wonyosi. *Applause*: Vol 1 No 4. Enugu: AcademicPublishing Co.

Hornby A.S. (2010) Oxford advanced learner's dictionary (8th edition). Oxford University Press.

Ibagere, E. and Omoera, O. S. (2010) The democratisation process and the Nigerian theatre artiste. Retrieved from: www.krepublishers assessed 18/07/2014.

Julius-Adeoye, R J. (2013) The drama of Ahmed Yerima : studies in Nigerian theatre
Leiden University Centre for the Arts in Society (LUCAS), Faculty of the Humanitas, Leiden University. https://openaccess.leidenuniv.nl/bitstream/
handle/1887/20858/Julius-Adeoye%20Dissertation-printer%20.pdf?sequence=16.

Obadiegwu, C.O (2003). The search for ideal leadership and the evolution of Rotimi's Dramatic Heroism. *Theatre Experience.* vol 2 no1. Onitsha: Koly.

O'Cornel, A. (2013) *Rogbodiyan* by Bakare Ojo Rasaki: An Analysis of Forms. Retrieved from http://literatanish.wordpress.com/2013/06/14/rogbodiyan-by-bakare-ojo-an-analysis-of-the-forms/ assessed 25th July 2014.

Ogundokun SA (2013c). Literature as Instrument for Development: A Survey of Sembène Ousmane's Guelwaar. Int. J. English Lang. Linguist. Res. 1:1-9.

Okeke, T. J.((2010). Drama as a Tool for Social Commentary: An Example of Alex Asigbo's the Reign of Pascal Amusu Ujah: Unizik Journal of Humanities. Vol. 11 No.1 www.ajol.info/index.php/ujah/54028

Tomakint, (2012). Oputa Panel: A Tale Of A Neglected Supposed Remedy For Injustice. www.nairaland .com/1096075 oputapanel A-Tale- Of- A- Neglected- Supposed- Remedy- For- Injustice. assessed 28th August 2014

Uche- Chinemere, N. (2011) Nigeria's Political Leadership and a Haunting Past: a Postcolonial Interpretation of Ojo Rasaki's

This Land Must Sacrifice. AJOL vol 6 no 1 retrieved from www. ajol. info

Thiog'o Ngugi, (1972). Homecoming.: Essays on African and Caribbean Literature Culture and Policies in *Studies in African Literature*. London, Heinemann.

The Playwright And Commitment: A Study of Bakare, Ojo Rasaki's *This Land Must Sacrifice* And *Rogbodiyan*

By
Ekpenisi, Kingsley and Iyamah, Chijioke

Introduction
> In the movement towards chaos in modern Africa, the writer did not anticipate. The understanding language of the outside "birth pain", that near fatal euphemism for death throes absolved him from responsibility. He was content to turn his eyes backward in time and prospect in the archaic fields for forgotten gems which would dazzle and distract the present. But never inward, never truly into the present from which alone lay the salvation of ideals (Soyinka, 1988:18).

The above expression by Wole Soyinka captures the hopeless and helplessness of the writer where contemporary issue of politics are explored. This is because the polity is a bundle of contradictions. Secondly, it raises the question of commitment. Can the African writer be truly committed when the culture of reading literary works is limited to the ivory tower of learning, in Literature or Theatre Arts Departments? According to Yerima (2002:2):

> The art of playwriting is a very personal art, it is self-evolving, it is subjective, and no matter how conscious the playwright might be about his society and immediate environment... it start from self before it spreads into a sense of collective predicament propelled by a will to correct the ills or remain the gifted voice in any given society.

The above statement affirms the view that arts is a tool for self-expression and that any lesson derived is accidental. A writer cannot stay away from the society where he lives. In fact, it is the society that informs his experiences and sharpens his thoughts and ideas. According to Williams (1988:37), "a writer if he is true to his own calling must mirror the agony and desperation of his society". Literary artifact must play a functional role in the society or else it would be overtaken by events. It is against this background that the second generation playwrights moved away from the elitist nature of their predecessors and adopt contemporary issue of class struggle. Equally, Jeyifo (1981:419) re-echoes the functional role of drama. He writes that

> ...they (Nigeria plays) have not written for or about the popular urban and rural masses, these crucial groups plays passive and invincible role in these plays. And these plays have more or less been imbued with a mood and spirit of despair, disillusionment and sometimes with savage cynical misanthropic vision.

If Nigerian drama is to contribute its quota to the development of the society it must confront the harsh realities of human existence, it must eschew escapist tendencies and face contemporary issue with a view to proffering solution.

Textual Study of *This Land Must Sacrifice* and *Rogbodiyan*.
Bakare, Ojo Rasaki is undoubtedly becoming the most prolific among the third generation of playwrights in Nigeria. His plays depict a society torn apart by the painful reality that the leadership class has failed entirely. *The Land Must Sacrifice*, the first play published by the playwright as an undergraduate, explores in totality, the Nigerian nation that is balkanised along ethnic lines Ethnicity has become a hydra-headed monster threatening the existence of the country. The ethnic posture in the nation's politics is the handiwork of the British and when independence is achieved, election is polarised by ethnic strength. Based on this, the North has the Prime Minister while the South has the President. The play reconstructs history subtly. It presents the chequered history of the nation from the brutal slave trade through colonisation to eventual independence.

The play opens with the people struggling painstakingly to row the boat to the promise land and when they finally arrived, the land is divided into three. As they settle, leaders are selected and given instruction by Ayelala to live a just and egalitarian life. Wonbiliki Wonbia, who emerges as the king, amass enough wealth to himself through the state coffers and unleash hardship and suffering on his people. His reign becomes tyrannical to the extent that the people can no longer tolerate his high handedness and he is beheaded in the end. The characters are divided along social stratification related to Marxist ideological view. The rich is represented by the king and his chiefs while other characters, which constitute the majority, are poor. The struggle to free themselves from brutalisation and dehumanisation by the ruling class is a collective one. There is no gender divide in the fight. Therefore, the fight for better standard of living by the citizens requires a committed and concerted effort by all if a measure of success is to be achieved.

The play is a pointer that Nigerians and Africans in general do not learn from history. The Blacks who assumed the mantle of leadership after independence continue the oppression of their people from where the white stopped. All the promises made to the citizens before independence are abandoned for their selfish ends. Much to the people's chagrin, independence is not worth the fight. It is this pain and agony that Bakare mirrors in *This Land Must Sacrifice*. Sacrifice entails appeasement, amelioration and the beg for forgiveness but in the play it involves the sacrifices of the leaders by the citizens to the gods of the land. What is the economic explanation of a country that is blessed with vast natural resources and yet one of the poorest in the world. The people are impoverished that most of them are living below poverty line. The pity aspect of this situation is captured in the following lines by the Narrator:

> But my people can a pig be really made clean? You can wash a pig, a pig cannot be made clean, because after washing, the pig goes back to the mud. Come rain, come shine, a pig is a pig. That was the story of our past in the land of confusion (16-17).

The speech above is symbolic of the moral turpitude our leaders have degenerated into and with this crop of leaders that we continue to recycle; there is little hope. Various policies put in place are muddled up and the huge sum of money invested ends in individual's bank account. Even gloomier is the concept of revolution in Nigeria because it is most of the time dominated by the youths who are inexperienced and with no clear-cut vision on how to break even from the mistake of the past. They lack the collective will that is resplendent with radical change.

In simple moving language laced with indigenous languages drawn from major ethnic groups, the writer captures the humanisation of human spirit as seen in the activities the downtrodden engage in. Inhumanity against fellow man pushes the citizens to beg and steal. The law of the society is meant to protect only the rich. A poor man who steals is taking to the king's palace for punishment and the rich who steals large sum of money goes scot free. In every society, the youths are agents of change and desperate condition demands desperate solution. Wale begins the change but he is cut down in his prime but he has planted the seed of revolution which will materialise with time. The awareness has come. Ngozi says:

> We must do something to change the tide, things can't continue this way. Our salvation is in our hands. Wale's move must be backed up in a stronger way (42).

Revolutionary sentiments are whipped up by mass awareness and it is the main alternative to the decadent political system. The conflict in the play is between the young and the elderly, who represents the decadent system that is in dire need of change.

In *Rogbodiyan*, Bakare presents a sick and deformed society. The people of this community ranging from the King to the least person are all infested with various forms of deformities. The play opens with a female regent on the throne and time has come to select the real king who will lead the people. Despite the skeptism that greeted this idea, she gave the Kingmakers four days to select a king and another three days for the coronation ceremony. Asagidigbi alias "the big eagle" and Gbadegesin alias "the horse" are selected. As customary, the kingmakers decide to consult the gods to ascertain their wish in this matter. Intrigues follow the plot by the two candidates to ascend the throne. Asagidigbi, bent of ascending the throne buys and bulldozes himself to power. As a hegemonic leader, he needs to purify himself for the onerous task of fulfilling the functions as ascribed to his new status. In the process of carrying out this ritual, he falters. First, he is expected to go into seclusion for seven days but goes on drinking spree with one of his sycophants. Second, the girl who is expected to bear the ritual material is supposed to be a virgin, but he defiles her and bring calamity of unprecedented proportion on his people.

The play exposes the brazen arrogation of power by the rulling class. Asagidigbi uses money and political thuggery to achieve absolute power and uses it to unprecedented degree and undermines all voice of reason to satisfy his private fantasies. He surrounds himself with sycophants who tell him what he wants to hear and encourages him to circumvent tradition. The action typifies Nigerian political scenario where our executives surround themselves with professionally paid sycophants who deceive them and launder their image even when his policies are unpopular and meant to favour only the rich. The statement by Agogo points to this fact:

> Good advice, indeed! I know I am the one who gives bad advice. That is the way of our leaders. Good advisers are quickly sent packing because they tell the truth. Bad ones get promoted because they are professional sycophant (38).

The amusing aspect of our politics in Nigeria is that our leaders never admit their fault. They continue to wallow in stupidity and idiosyncrasy. Asagidigbi knows that he has defiled the gods of the land and the punishment, and hardship the people are passing through is caused by him. He begins to chase shadows and blames his opponent, Gbadegesin, for their woes. The leaders need to build trust and confidence of the people they lead. On the contrary, they inundate and feed the populace with lies. A good example is found in the King's speech:

> People of Ilu-kuroju, don't be swayed by the antics of my enemies. Can't you see what they are trying to do? Discredit me. They want my throne. The gods know… the gods know I never did anything like that.

> And you Aloba! You so- called kingmakers… how could you… after all the money I gave you (55).

The political scene in Nigeria is dominated by the highest bidder syndrome. Since the people are so impoverished by their economic policies they use money to buy prospective voters, law enforcement agents and electoral officers. The instrument of law and the thugs they have armed to the teeth are used to brutalise and scare their opponent or anyone who might oppose them. The electoral officers help to compute and falsify figures. They (leaders) have perfected their insidious way of getting to power and any attempt to resist them will be met with violence in the highest order. In this situation, the youths become willing victims to help out in the perpetuation of violence. Once it is election period, kidnapping, killing, arson, and all sorts of vices escalate and fear becomes the order of the day. This is akin to the Biblical assertion in the book of Mathew11:12: "from the days of john the Baptist until now the kingdom of heaven has suffered violence, and men of violence take it by force".

It is sad indeed to note that the primary duty of the government to protect their citizens is now becoming a mirage as recent happenings prove otherwise. The spate of bombings in the North and the kidnap of Chibok girls bear eloquent testimonies. People are no longer safe, there is disenchantment everywhere and violence has assumed ethnic and religious posture. Even the presence of foreign powers has not helped matters. Looking for external solution is only a deliberate perambulation in avoidance of the crux of the problems. The truth is that the solutions to our political woes are in our hands.

The issue of commitment brings to fore the functionality of Nigerian literature in responses to myriads of problems besetting our nation. Obafemi (2002:168) asserts that:
> The conscious ideological commitment of the younger dramatist in Nigeria is a significant point of departure between them and the first generation of dramatists in Nigeria.

The issue of commitment raises the question of how important is our literary artifacts in solving societal problems? Political motivated writings such as Bakare's works are targeted at the leaders and the led, at least to confront them with naked realities so that they can internalize pertinent questions and opt for solutions that will introduce progressive or radical change. Ekpenisi and Anyira (2010:127) lament the poor reception of literary works:

> Much to the writer's chagrin, all his creative energies to bring about a better society is wasted. He wakes up to the painful reality that the leadership class who is his target audience has to no time to read (or watch performances).

Be that as it may, there is an adage which says that "the old man must not fail to rebuke a wrong act even when his words are falling on deaf ears". The writer is like the old man who must constantly point out the ills of the society with a view to influencing others. Bakare has recorded the problem of leadership in our political landscape and he identifies it and advocates for change. Therefore, his commitment as a playwright is not in doubt.

The plays under scrutiny are couched in atmosphere of religion. This, of course, negates the Marxist denunciation of religion, which according to them is the opium of the masses. The interplay of the gods is used to show the outright disregard for established norms, customs, and conventions of the society by the leadership class. Their moral turpitude is exposed. The gods are also used as agents of change. Asagidigbi plunges his people into misery and agony and precipitates his own destruction and eventual removal from the exalted position as the King. Ayelala provides direction for a just and egalitarian society but Wonbiliki Wonbia arrogates much power to himself and continue to oppress his people. In the end, he is swept away by the force of revolution. The image of the plays is woven around sacrifice. The sacrifice the citizens must undertake to enthrone justice and fair-play in a society bedridden with corruption, abuse of power, injustice, hunger, deprivation, and all sorts of evil.

Conclusion
Bakare, Ojo Rasaki is a committed playwright who has recorded the anguish of Nigerian political system to the extent that he comes close to unraveling the situation and at the same time providing alternatives. This he captures in *This Land Must Sacrifice* and *Rogbodiyan*. He adopts the Brechtian alienation technique to distance his audience from empathising with the action to enable them read, watch critically and translate the dramatic actions into the society where change has become inevitable. He uses language, song and action to stir human emotions and catapult them as agent of change. This cannot be achieved individually but through collective actions of the majority for power belongs to the people.

References

Bakare, Ojo Rasaki. (1991). *This Land Must Sacrifice*. Enugu: New Age Publishers

(1994). *Rogbodiyan*. Zaria: Tamaza Publishers.

Ekpenisi, Kingsley and Anyira, Kingsley (2010). "Creative Imagination and the Quest for Peace". *Nigerian Journal for Development and Research* vol 1.No2.

Jeiyfo, Biodun. (1981). "The search for a popular Theatre" *Drama and Theatre in Nigeria*. Lagos: Nigerian Magazine.

Obafemi, Olu. (2002). *Contemporary Nigerian Theatre, cultural Heritage and Social Vision*. Lagos: CBAAC

Soyinka, Wole. (1987). "Wole Soyinka: Art, Dialogue and Outrage" *Essays on Literature*. Jeiyfo Biodun (ed). Ibadan: New Horn Press.

William, Adebayo. (1988). "Write and be Damned". Lagos: *Newswatch Communication* April 11.

Yerima, Ahmed (2002) "The Playwright as a Democrat: A Discourse" *Theatre and Democracy*. Akinwale, Ayo and Yerima, Ahmed (ed) Ibadan: Kraft Books.

The Aesthetics of *Performative Trinity* in Audience Engineering: A Study of Bakare, Ojo Rasaki's Directorial Device

By
Asuquo, Nsikan Bassey.

Introduction:
Bakare, Ojo Rasaki, a quintessential choreographer, theatre director, dancer, playwright, designer, songwriter, instrumentalist, scholar, professor of theatre aesthetics and choreography, is one of the most renowned Nigerian theatre practitioners; who's stage works have made success stories within Nigeria and abroad. Having worked closely with him both as a tutee and as a professional (for about a decade and a half put together), it is observed that with a mastery of craftsmanship, Bakare employs the "total theatre concept" - a blend of dance, music, and drama (as a technique) in most, if not all of his staged-plays; and this has always endeared theatre goers to his stage works. The total theatre is said to be "a performance that includes all or most of the theatrical elements – music, dance, songs, spectacles, and special effects."
(http://homepage.ntlworld.com/bradsweb/glossary.htm).

Having taken part in many plays directed by Bakare, a closer observation reveals that apart from the usual aesthetic effects that set designs, scenery, lighting, and or sound effects exude, Bakare's characteristic fusion of dance, music, and drama to form a whole performance also tacitly emits a great deal of aesthetic charm that audience may not immediately see but feel. This technique seems to be one of Bakare's "magic-wand" in keeping his audience enthralled and glued to his directed performances from the opening scene to the "curtail call". Bakare fondly terms the three genres (dance, music, and drama) the *Performative Trinity*". Therefore, in this study, the term *Performative Trinity* shall be used to mean dance, music and drama. In order to validate the claim on Bakare's penchant for total theatre concept, this study highlights some of Bakare's directed plays within a decade ago. Analysing all the performances could be an interesting challenge; but that would be too wide for the scope of this paper. Therefore, this study shall focus on one of Bakare's most frequently performed play, *Once Upon A Tower*.

Through interview, library/archival research, and the participant-observation methods, this study seeks to investigate the role and/or the impact of the *Performative Trinity* on the theatre audience; hence, provide a strong ground on which they are to be employed for effective audience engineering and education. Therefore, this study in addition, give a succinct account of Bakare's works and achievements as a theatre practitioner (to validate the positive impacts of dance and music in play performances).

A Brief Account of Bakare, Ojo Rasaki's Theatrical Walk And Works

The professional stage for Bakare's theatrical walk and works was set when he joined the Yoruba Travelling Theatre Movement at the age of 17 in 1981; under the tutor of Jimoh Aliu and late Hubert Ogunde, the acclaimed doyen of professional theatre in Nigeria. Rising from that humble beginning, today, Bakare is a multiple award winner (via his theatrical works). Apart from his works as a choreographer and playwright, Bakare has directed many plays; most of which were commissioned high-profile command performances; such as the ones for the three consecutive presidential inauguration ceremonies Nigeria has had since the third republic. These are: *Jagumolu* (during President Olusegun Obasanjo's inauguration in 1999), *Voyage* (during President Musa Y'adua's inauguration in 2007), and *Langbodo* (during President Goodluck Ebele Jonathan's inauguration in 2011).

In the area of competitive events, some Bakare's directed works include:

WORK ENTRY	COMPETITION	VENUE	YEAR	PRIZE WON
Sekai aiki (Dance-drama)	Spring Festival World Dance Competition	North Korea	1997	Gold trophy for Nigeria
Yemoja	Ceravantino International Festival	Mexico	2001	1st Prize
Dance, Drama, & Choral Music	National Arts Festival –NAFEST	Nigeria	2005	1st Prize
Dance, Drama, & Choral Music	National Arts Festival –NAFEST	Nigeria	2007	1st Prize
Dance, Drama, & Choral Music	National Arts Festival –NAFEST	Nigeria	2010	1st Prize

There is no gain saying that how good and successful a performance is, can be adjudged by those who watched the performance. Therefore, for Bakare's directed works to be adjudged worthy to win prizes as stated above, it will be agreed that the artistic/technical contents of the performances must have had the most of what is takes to enthrall and satisfy the audience/adjudicators; which further validates Bakare's artistic prowess for theatre audience engineering and sustenance. Bakare's other artistic works have also won laurels at other events such as the Abuja National Carnivals and at the Calabar Carnivals, to mention a few.

Plays directed by Bakare, Ojo Rasaki in the academic setting in the last decade
Below is a list of some of the plays directed by Bakare in some tertiary institutions where he has taught between 2005 and 2014:

S/N	PLAY TITLE	AUTHOR	INSTITUTION STAGED	YEAR
1	*This Animal Called Job*	Bakare, Ojo Rasaki	University of Abuja	2005
2	*Once Upon A Tower*	Bakare, Ojo Rasaki	University of Abuja	2005
3	*This Land Must Sacrifice*	Bakare, Ojo Rasaki	University of Abuja	2005
4	*Adamma*	Bakare, Ojo Rasaki	University of Abuja	2006
5	*The gods Are Not To Blame*	Ola Rotimi	University of Abuja	2007
6	Ovaramwen Nogbaisi	Ahmed Yerima	University of Abuja	2008
7	*Kurumi*	Ola Rotimi	University of Abuja	2011
8	*Hopes of The Living Dead*	Ola Rotimi	University of Abuja	2011
9	*Once Upon A Tower*	Bakare, Ojo Rasaki	Fed. University Oye-Ekiti	2012
10	*Adamma*	Bakare, Ojo Rasaki	Fed. University Oye-Ekiti	2013
11	*Langbodo*	Wale Ogunyemi	Fed. University Oye-Ekiti	2014

Each of the above listed performances was a composite of dance, music, and drama; which further establish Bakare's penchant for total theatre concept. It is important to note that each of these performances was well attended; but due to lack of proper documentation of audience attendance at these venues, it is difficult to state the exact figure of audience attendance.

The Concept of Total Theatre.
Total theatre is said to be "a performance that includes all or most of the theatrical elements – music, dance, song, spectacle, and special effects". The concept of total theatre was developed by Carl Orff (July 10, 1895 – March 29, 1982) – a German composer; but it was Serge Diagihlev who coined the term "total theatre", with his Ballets Russes. (http://homepage.ntlworld.com/bradsweb/glossary.htm).

An X-Ray of the *Performative Trinity* in the Performance of *Once Upon A Tower*
Once upon A Tower was staged as a Command Performance (in which this researcher featured as an actor) for the University of Uyo Convocation Ceremony in the year 2001. In 2005, it was also staged as a Command Performance during the University of Abuja Convocation Ceremony. It was also the very first full-length play to be staged at the Federal University Oye-Ekiti (one of the newly created Universities in Nigeria) in 2012.

Synopsis of *Once Upon A Tower*
Once Upon A Tower is a story that x-rays some corrupt practices perpetrated by some people in positions of authority in the society, the dangerous scheming in tertiary institutions, and the consequent negative effects on students and the society. Professor Kurumbete, out of his perceived threat to his monopoly of the position of the provost of a medical college, decides to frustrate Dr. Akitikori, a brilliant young Lecturer in the same Department (who had a special assignment of grooming Pedro – an extraordinary brilliant medical student) out of the system and decides to replace Dr. Akitikori with Dr. Yemi, a less intelligent old man (who is more or less Prof. Kurumbete's stooge). As a result of this, students of the medical college are stuffed with ignorance.

Khadijat (Senator's Daughter), who is to be forced by her father to marry Chief Ugboefi (for the Senator's clandestine motives) in the play decides to elope with Pedro, her true love. After a while in their hide-out, Khadijat becomes pregnant for Pedro; and for fear of their pecuniary standing and other issues, Pedro decides that the pregnancy be aborted. Meanwhile, Pedro (who as a student, had been inured to doing practical without the necessary facilities and chemicals), resorts to apply the abortion procedure that Dr. Yemi taught him. In the process, in the process of which Khadijat died. Pedro realises that this would not have happened if the right teacher, Dr. Akitikori is allowed to be his teacher. So, he resorts to avenge the death of his love on those who had hands in the cause of his professional malnourishment; worst of whom are: Prof. Kurumbete, Dr. Yemi and the Senator (Khadijat's father) who happened to be the person that diverted the funds meant for procurements of facilities and equipment for the Medical College. (Bakare, 2000).

Dance and Music in the Production of *Once Upon A Tower*
The performances of *Once Upon A Tower (*directed by Bakare) in 2001, 2005, and in 2012 all commanded a very high audience appeal; with each recording capacity-filled audience attendance and the request for "more" after each show. The three performances (each of which this researcher took part in) was a synthesis of dance, music, and drama. It is important to point out that the performance had a stand-by Orchestra which was not merely singing the songs but was actually performing some of them with some dance movements (especially at moments of scene changing; where they became the point of focus).

Each of the performances was made up of a Prologue and eleven Movements. At the prologue, the actions began with the musical band which played a high-life tune titled *Once Upon A Tower"* to reinforce the theme of the play, as well as to comment on the actions of the actors who were miming the construction of a university building. Immediately after the construction, the music and song changed to another song, titled: *"asewo campusi"* (which means: campus prostitute). The song, while evoking an atmosphere of gaiety, also reinforced the interpretative intent of the director; which was to portray Miss Julie as a prostitute; by commenting on the role of her character, as she moved Centre-stage, changed her dress into a body hug, swinging her waist invitingly as she smiles at two cult boys with whom she planned to deal with Dr. Akitikori).

In *Movement One*, another song titled: *"When Omowaye Dey Convoke"* is performed by the Band; to comment on the convocation ceremony which is being performed in mime. At *Movement Two*, *"Nemesis"* was sung; which prepared the audience mind of the impending action of Prof Kurumbete paying for his wicked deeds. When the scene ended and there was light out, the band sang: *"I Love My Provost"*; (a sarcastic song which further fed the audience of the undesirable persona of Prof. Kurumbete) was used to unveil his presence in the next scene (*Movement Three*). In this scene, as Prof. Kurumbete became piqued for being challenged by Dr. Akitikori, the scene ends and another song: *"Ofin Mose"* (meaning: the Law of Moses – "an eye for an eye") is sung to let the audience have a clear picture of the vile that Prof. Kurumbete is preoccupied with at that point in time. In *Movement Four*, when Christy informed Dr. Akitikori of how Prof. Kurumbete is fond of denigrating him (Dr. Akitikori) in the presence of students, another song: *"Block No Man's Way"*, was sung; this time by Dr. Akitikori. This song helped in portraying Dr. Akitikori as a victim and Prof. Kurumbete as the villain; thereby building audience's sympathy for Dr. Akitikori.

At the end of *Movement Five*, *"Asewo Campus"* was sung to herald the meeting between Miss Julie (the "asewo") and her ally, Prof. Kurumbete; as well as to re-echo the illicit affair between the two. The song *"Asewo Campus"* is repeated at the beginning of *Movement Six* to herald the appearance of Miss Julie (who was being projected as a prostitute) into the scene to falsely indict Dr. Akitikori of attempting to rape her. As Dr. Akitikori was to be wisked off by the security operatives, everyone except Dr. Akitikori became frozen, while the Dr. Akitikori raised an emotion-laden song: *"...Why Is the World Filled with Evil"* - a song which completely drew the audience empathy on Dr. Akitikori's side (and against Prof. Kurumbete).

At the end of *Movement Seven,* a high-life tune with title: *"Teacher Don Messi Messi ooo"* (meaning the teacher has goofed), was played; which in-turn announced and intensified on the intellectual paucity of Dr. Yemi, who was seen in a class room in *Movement Eight.* Apart from the song, dialogue and movements, the impact of this scene was beefed -up with dance movements that enthralled the audience. The song: *"Teacher Don Messi Messi ooo"* was played till the end of the scene amidst the choreography. This helped to ease the tension of the previous scene by eliciting comic relief.

Movement Nine featured Khadijat, Senator Abdul Rahmon's daughter, singing a love song; which apart being a stage business, actually prepared the audience's mind of the romantic scenario that subsequently ensued. At the end of the scene, the band raised a love song with the title: *Kiss Me before You Go".* Though the romantic bit of Khadijat's elopement was very brief, the continuous singing of the song during the scene change helped to build up and sustain the air of romance (to the enjoyment of the audience) for a while. Therefore, the next scene – *Movement Ten,* when Pedro talked about the love that existed between him and Khadijat and pain of losing (because of individuals' selfish interest), it was easy for the audience to identify with him and share his agony). Therefore, though Pedro took laws into his hands by killing Prof. Kurumbete and Dr. Yemi, the audience sympathy did not leave him. In the end, a dirge with the title: *"Oh! Mpa o"* permeated the atmosphere; leaving everyone in a sober for a deep thought about the entire scenario.

In a nut shell, the production which was made up of a Prologue and eleven Movements, was laden with dances and ten different songs (accompanied with instrumentation) – a synthesis of the *Performative Trinity.*

The *Peformative Trinity* – Bakare, Ojo Rasaki's Directorial Device

In juxtaposing the terms: *Performative Trinity* and Bakare's directorial device, this study implies: Bakare's fusion of dance and music in play to make a performance as his directorial technique in regaling, encouraging and sustaining wide audience participation for his play performances.

Bakare, in an interview conducted on the 26th of March, 2014, confirmed his penchant for the total theatre concept (or like he coins it: the *Performative Trinity*). The interview goes thus:

Interviewer: *Sir, I have observed that in most of your performances, you incorporate dance, music and drama ..., making it a total theatre...; why is it so?*

Bakare: Because that is my art really – I went to school to learn how to be a dramatist... I went to the university to study Theatre Arts. So, I acquired the training. But I was born with the operatic art. My art really is the operatic art. If you know the way the operatic art is, you will understand what I am saying – it combines the three (dance, music, and drama). In opera you sing you lines, you dance your movements (and there is accompaniment), and you act the parts. So, in opera, music, dance and drama are neatly webbed together. And that is my natural art... so, I'm a natural operatist. And when I got into theatre, what I just do is to adapt opera into all kinds of theatre modes. That is why you see that it is impossible for me to create without these three elements (dance, music and drama) being there...

Interviewer: *Sir, we know that when a manufacturer wants to manufacture a product, he considers the consumers; what they will like and the way they will like it. Do you consider your audience before making your performance a total theatre?*

Bakare: No. when I want to write, I want to write. But when I finish writing and creating, I now look for who can buy it. It is when you engage me as a director that I do what you have just talked about. In the selection of the work, I consider the audience. Number one: what does the audience need now? Which play can gel? What is the situation? Because you have to think of the performative exigencies - exigencies under which you are going to perform: the money available, what is at the front-burner in that environment, what is the mentality of the people, what is the kind of thing they want to hear that can move them; and all that. I consider all these before I choose the script.... I insist (more than the money I will be paid) on choosing the script. I do my research before choosing a script. The first step in making the audience to reject your performance is not to take them into consideration.

The Theatre Audience And The Impact of The *Performative Trinity*

In attempting to unravel the impact of the dance and music (in play performance) on the audience, it is important to find answers to questions such as: why are audience fascinated while watching actors and dancers move their bodies? Why are they thrilled when they hear melodious tunes? Why do the audience become amused, or moved by what they hear and/or see on stage; and become interested in coming to the theatre another day to watch and hear more? In addressing questions such as stated above, Ivar Hagendoorn, (quoted in
http://www.ivarhagendoorn.com/research/dance-aesthetics-and-the -brain), suggests the need for analysing the mental capacities that are exercised when people watch performances; thus, the need to evaluate the psychological effects of dance and music on theatre audience.

The Psychological Effects of Dance on Audience

Bakare defines dance as "the rhythmic movement of human body in time and space to make statements" (2). While the psychology of dance can be referred to as the set of mental states associated with dancing and watching others dance. (*http://en.m.wikipedia.org/wiki/psychology_of_dance*) It is argued in the field of phenomenology (that is: a philosophy based on the intuitive experience of phenomena, and on the premise that reality consist of objects and events as consciously perceived by conscious beings) and in the field of aesthetics that kinesthesia (sensation of movement and position) is central consciousness and to spectator response, and that dance audiences can experience physical and imaginative effects of movement without actually moving their bodies - that is spectators can react in certain respects as if they were moving or preparing to move. (*http://www.watchingdance.org/searchindex.php*). Daly (qtd. in http://www.watchingdance.org/searchindex.php), affirms the assertion above as he states that: "dance, although it has a visual component, is fundamentally a kinesthetic art whose appreciation is ground not just in the eye, but in the entire body". This is to say that when audience watch dance performance or dance in a performance, they can become so unconsciously carried-away; to the point that they begin to see themselves as the ones going through or doing what the dancers on stage are doing. Theodor Lipps (qtd in *http://www.watchingdance.org/searchindex.php*), also corroborates this assertion as he opines that: "when observing a body in motion, such as acrobat, spectators could experience an 'inner mimesis', where they felt as if they were enacting the actions they were observing." While Ivar Hagendoorn adds that dance is worthy of reflection because it "can be captivating, thrilling, moving and awe-inspiring..." (http://www.ivarhagendoorn.com/research/dance-aesthetics-and-the-brain).

Dance or dancing can also be seen as a means of endearing or overwhelming the targeted audience to respond in favour of the dancer. The Bible in (Mathew 14:6-7), has an account of how King Herod declared his willingness to forfeit half of his kingdom to a little girl simply because she pleased him (the king) with a dance. Even God the Creator was "moved" to act in defense of King David, by causing Micah to become barren for daring to mock king David when he (King David) danced before the God. (2 Samuel 6 verse 14-16, 20-23). All these point to the fact that (an interesting) dance has the power to command its audience interest.

The Psychological Effects of Music on Audience
Music can be simply defined as the sound people make when they sing or play instruments.

(*http://www.thefreedictionationary.com/music*). According to Brockett, "music can be used to evoke an atmosphere of gaiety or somberness, just as abstract hollow sounds can be used to evoke mystery or strangeness." Brockett continues by saying that sound in general can be used to evoke mood and atmosphere; reinforce the actions on stage; as well as to comments on the actions (415). According to a research carried out by Jeremy Dean (qtd in *http://www.spring.org.uk/2013/09/10-magical-effects-musi-has-on-the-mind.php*), the following are also listed to be "magical effects" music has on audience:

(1) It improves verbal IQ: according Forgeard (qtd inhttp://www.spring.org.uk/2013/09/10-magical-effects-musi-has-on-the-mind.php): a study of 8 to 11-year olds found that, those who had extra-curricular music classes, developed higher verbal IQ, and visual abilities, in comparison to those with no musical training.

(2) According to Nusbaum and Silvia (qtd in http://www.spring.org.uk/2013/09/10-magical-effects-musi-has-on-the-mind.php), music gives a feel of chill: over 90% of humans feel chill down the spine when listening to music.

(3) Ferguson and Sheldon (qtd in http://www.spring.org.uk/2013/09/10-magical-effects-musi-has-on-the-mind.php), also claim that actively listening to music amps up happiness: this suggests that engaging in a theatrical performance that has musical content(s), gives the participatory experience the extra emotional power.

(4) Singing together brings participants together; increases affiliation within the group and even make people like each other more than before.

The above points also suggest that theatrical performances that have musical contents (which the audience can identify with and sing along during the performance) increases audience affiliation with the theatre and performances – good for audience engineering.

(5) Music treats heart disease: it is discovered that music can at least help with the stress and anxiety associated with having treatment for coronary heart disease. According to Bradt and Dileo (qtd in http://www.spring.org.uk/2013/09/10-magical-effects-musi-has-on-the-mind.php), a review of 23 studies covering almost 1,500 patients found that listening to music reduced heart rate, blood pressure and anxiety in heart disease patients.

It could therefore be said that some theatre goers are interested in watching theatrical performances in order to ease stress and anxiety.

(6) Mood management: due to the cathartic effect of music, it can also be said that audience enjoy music (in performances) because it helps to improve their moods. Even sad music, according to Kawakami (qtd in http://www.spring.org.uk/2013/09/10-magical-effects-musi-has-on-the-mind.php), is enjoyable because it creates an interesting mix of emotions; some negative, some positive. Jeremy Dean adds that: "crucially, we perceive the negative emotions in the music, but don't feel them strongly."

The above perhaps, explains why a crying baby can change his or her mood to smiling and/or falling into sleep when listening to lullabies.

(7) Music creates mental aesthetics: Jeremy Dean (qtd in http://www.spring.org.uk/2013/09/10-magical-effects-musi-has-on-the-mind.php), states that "music naturally makes people think of certain colours. Across different cultures, people pair particular types of music with particular colours." Duller or darker colours are associated with sadder pieces of music while lighter, more vivid colours are associated with happier music.

From the above, it can be stated that with music in theatrical performances, certain auras of aesthetics pleasure are created; which the audience may not physically see, but feel; which could also be a luring factor in audience patronage of theatrical works.

Conclusion

An evaluation of the plays staged by Bakare in the last decade (as seen in this study), the analysis of <u>Once Upon A Tower</u> and the interview conducted with Bakare, has established the fact that Bakare has a penchant for integrating dance and music into drama to make a performance. This study also reveals that dance performance or dance in a performance has the power to create a vicarious experience in its audience; hence, it could function as a therapeutic technique for permeating into the sub-consciousness of the audience in other to register a director's or a choreographer's intent with a stronger impetus that mere words in its literal sense. This study also reveals that music has strong psychological effects on its listeners; hence, it has the potency to function has an alluring element in theatrical performances. In addition, drama (being an imitation of action) animates the lifeless characters in play scripts and consequently animates audience's interest for theatrical performances.

Some theatre goers are more fascinated by dance than by drama, while some prefer drama to dance, and/or music and drama than music and dance; but a well-crafted theatrical performance that has dance and music as its integral components, commands a strong audience appeal because it has something to appeal every theatre goer. Therefore, a well-crafted blend of dance, music and drama as a directorial technique yields wide audience appeal and should be encouraged. Bakare, Ojo Rasaki's *Performative Trinity* is a pointer in this direction.

Works Cited
Bakare, Ojo R. *Once Upon A Tower*. Uyo, Akwa Ibom: Afahaide Publishing Company, 2000.
Bakare, Ojo R. Personal interview. 26 March 2014.
Bakare, Ojo Rasaki. *Rudiments of Choreography*, Kaduna: Space Publishers. 1994.
Ivar, Hagendoorn. 7 August 2014 Dance, Aesthetics and The Brain. *http://wwww.ivarhagendoorn.com/research/dance-aesthetics-and-the-brain.*
Jeremy Dean. September 18, 2013 10 Magical Effects Music Has On the Mind. July 31, 2014 *http://www.spring.org.uk/2013/09/10-magical-effects-musi-has-on-the mind.php.*
Monkbot. 31 july 2014 Psychology of Dance. *http://en.m.wikipedia.org/wiki/psychology_of_dance.*
Oxford Advanced Learner's Dictionary
(*http://www.thefreedictionary.com/music*)
http://homepage.ntlworld.com/bradsweb/glossary.htm
http://www.thefreedictionationary.com/music
The *Holy Bible* King James Version. Dallas, USA: Jet Move Publishing Inc. 2004 watching Dance: Kinesthetic Empathy *ttp://www.watchingdance.org/searchindex.php.*

Language Use and Semiotic Appraisal of Bakare's *Rogbodiyan*

By
Miriam Stephen Inegbe

Introduction

Bakare's *Rogbodiyan* is a cultural product that promotes the traditions and cultures of the Yoruba community in Nigeria. The title of the play, *Rogbodiyan*, carries a semantic import with a high cultural content. As such, the play cannot be appraised or examined without proper meaning sharing from the interconnected pattern of linguistic choice of language, codes and symbols. The process of examining the codes and symbols as well as their relation to each other probes into semiotics. What then is semiotics? Fortier (1997:18) defines semiotics as:

> ...the study of signs: words, images, behaviour, human and animalarrangements of many kinds, in which a meaning is relayed by a corresponding outward manifestation.

Signs, like phonemes, function 'not through their intrinsic value but through their relative position' (Hawkes, 1977:28) As such, whatever distinguishes a sign from others constitutes the total mode of language. Language, as Blamires (quoted from *Cours de Linguistique Generale of Ferdinand de Saussure*) is 'a system of arbitrarily allotted signs which operate only in relation to each other in the total system' (1991:358-359). Language, therefore, is 'both a social product of the faculty of speech and a collection of necessary conventions that have been adopted by a social body to permit individuals to exercise the faculty' (Hawkes, 1977:21).

This work adopts the structuralist semiotic system of a Swiss Linguist, Ferdinand de Saussure, who holds that a sign is a meaningful physical object with two parts: 'the signifier' and 'the signified' (1974:66). The signifier is the material of a sign perceived, whereas the signified is the abstract or mental concept invoked by the signifier. Hawkes explains that the linguistic sign can be characterized in terms of the relationship which pertains between its dual aspects of 'concepts' (the signified) and of 'sound-image' (the signifier) (1997:25). He further adds that the structural relationship between the concept and the sound image constitutes a linguistic sign, and a language is made up of these. Language then becomes a system of signs that express ideas. Fortier documents Saussure's language belief to be 'the most characteristic semiotic system in as much as the relation between signifier and the signified is most arbitrary' (1997:18). The relationship of the signifier to the signified as Woollacot (1982:99) expatiates is analytically distinct in that there is no way to read a literal image neutrally, which is not in some way dependent on coding and cultural conventions.

Charles Peirce unlike Saussure is not so keen about the sign system. He works out his own classification of signs which sees the signifier and the signified not as 'monolithic in the arbitrariness of their relationship to the object but as related to the object in different ways and different degrees. A symbol- a word, for example has an arbitrary relation to its object. An index, a finger pointing to indicate direction,…, an icon- a photograph of someone…has a strong resemblance to its object (Fortier, 1997:20).

Roland Barthes, the French theorist, explains signification of Saussure as a concept using: 'denotation, connotation and myth' (Hawkes, 1977:133) as orders of signification. Denotation explains the simple meaning a word denotes as to what it says. Signs are determined by convention, shared code or nature. Connotation describes and presents things to be opposite of what they are said to be. Hawkes (1977:133) says that connotation is centrally characteristic of the 'literary or aesthetic' use of language. Myth explains a cultural way of thinking and perceiving issues about natural phenomenon with a veiled or abstract meaning as well as society's commonly held beliefs. Hawkes again explains that 'myths,…,have their grounding in the actual generalized experience of ancient peoples, and represent their attempts to impose a satisfactory, graspable, humanizing shape on it' (1977:13) However, these signs are all actively involved in the signification process. This essay, therefore examines the linguistic choice of the playwright in *Rogbodiyan* as well as the linguistic codes and symbols employed in the play.

The Use of Language in *Rogbodiyan*

Bakare Ojo Rasaki gives his characters appropriate language that suits each of them in the play. This phenomenon agrees with Hudson's (1980:24) assertion that ''what constitutes varieties of a language are the different manifestations or linguistic items which have different distribution''. Linguistically, the play *Rogbodiyan* is lucid and simple. The narrator uses free-flowing language which is one of the characteristics of realistic plays. The linguistic choice in the play is based on certain psychological issues like background and level of perception. This is evident in the statement of Aloba to the other elders in council:

"Go and choose the next king of this land and report
to me in three days time" so said the Regent
yesterday and we all hear it with our own ears. (p.16)

From the above statement, one notices the indication of inadequate mastery of the semantics of English language and direct translation from the speaker's mother tongue. Another example is seen in the statement of Asagidigbi:

My people ... by the time the end shall come and I
carry my gray hair to my ancestors, children yet
unborn shallhear of the eagle who once ruled this
land. (p.27)

King: The crown now sits on my head... (p.26)

The language use here emphasizes the speech pattern and thought processes of the society being portrayed in the play. This linguistic choice from the playwright has. to a great extent, expressed the ideas behind the statements to a lay-man from the society being portrayed.

The languages spoken in *Rogbodiyan* can be classified as English, Deformed English and Yoruba. An illustration of deformed English could be seen in the statement of Asagidigbi to the elders:

Money, man, money, Ego, wazobia! In each bag is contained…(p.22-23)

Asagidigbi is portrayed here as a polyglot who speaks other languages, other than his. The playwright also makes use of some loan words. They include:
   i) Agbada (p.43)
   ii) Sokoto (p.44)
   iii) Kabiyesi (p.30)
   iv) Oyibo (p.9)
   v) Ego, wazobia (p.22)
   vi) Mogun (p.48) etc.

The playwright's use of language has the syntactic structure of Yoruba language while its vocabulary is English.

The playwright also engages some of his characters in code mixing Yoruba with English. Examples are shown in these excerpts:

Regent: Ha! May Olodumare that owns heaven and earth continue to be our protector. (p.8)
Salotin: But Oyibo people say ''once bitten twice shy'' … (p.9)
Abere: … when a lady takes kumolu for a name … (p.38)
King: … seize him and tie him to Mogun (p.34)
Fadele: My Opele is here, kabiyesi… (p.34)

The playwright also makes use of high tonal diction. Some of his characters speak in high and harsh tones to heighten their moods. Examples are shown below:

Woman: (…) Yes. I insist on being heard! I must speak my mind. How can anybody wake up one morning and impose two candidates on us just like that? Aren't there established procedures for this sort of thing? Are we people without tradition?...(p.10)
King: Shut up! If I go down, you all go down with me! (p.49)
Adegbani: Enough of all this nonsense… (p.51)

The language in *Rogbodiyan* is also metaphonic and proverbial as demonstrated in the following statements:

Abere: (…) Eto, you bat of a creature. You are neither an animal nor a bird, neither here nor there (pp17-18)

Eto: (…) yes, that is how I get what I want, by belonging to all the camps. The only politics I play now is the politics of my stomach and probably that of my immediate family… (p.18).

The proverbs feature prominently in the dialogues of the Regent, King, elders and elderly people in *Rogbodiyan*. The Regent's address to the elders and people of Ilu Koroju commands interest and attention because of her use of proverbial language as stated here:

> The crown unworn is a crown smeared with dung, the staff unheld is a staff buried in the mud, the power unused is a power unworthy of being owned, …(p.11)

Bakare employs the proverbial language to evidently expatiate the insatiable greed of the aspiring kings in Ilu Koroju, when the Diviner warns that:

> No child of gun is a friend, the bullets kill, the powder maims (p.21)

One notices that, words are not spoken in plane language but in proverbial context. The playwright also uses proverbial sayings through Agogo to advice the newly coronated king who is about to defile the new Arugba Oge due to his greed and acquisitive spirit through this saying:

> The dog that swallows salt shall not live to tell the tale of its sweetness. (p.33)

And the stubborn king whose fate is already doomed rejects the caution and objects with another proverbial saying:

> The pebbles the duck swallows never hurt its intestines (p.33)

The employment of proverbial language has also given the play a cultural upliftment and the speeches brief and clearer.

The playwright also enriches his play with idiomatic expressions. Examples:

Regent:	I sent for u, without delay, eyes and feet are here complete. (p.8)
Regent:	A very important thing that quivers my liver gave birth to this call (p.9)
Aloba:	… Now, eyes are complete… (p.16)
Abere:	… Can't we as leaders knock heads together and choose he that wears the crown?... (p.17)

The phrase "eyes and feet are here complete" is an idiom which means "to have full attendance of the people" This is quite different from the group of words above. The second one "… thing that quivers my liver gave birth to this call" is an idiom which means "an important issue prompted this meeting" The third phrase "eyes are complete" means "we are all here" and the fourth phrase " knock heads together and choose he that wears the crown'" means "we can all access the candidates qualified and appoint a king".

Employment of simile is also observed in Salotin speech to Asagbidigbi as he bribes some of the elders:

> Your ascending the throne
> Asagbidigbi is as certain as
> milk in the breast. (p.23)

Here, Asagidigbi's ascension to the throne through dubious means is compared to the certainty of breast milk which is always present in the nursing mother's breast.

Semiological Features In *Rogbodiyan*
In the context of this analysis, the term "features" is taken to mean the necessary components or elements of something. Thus, semiological features in this essay are those sign elements of tradition employed in *Rogbodiyan* to create meaning and understanding which project the interconnected pattern of linguistic codes and symbols as well as their relation to the Yoruba society which the play is show casing. The semiotic appraisal of *Rogbodiyan* in this essay will take the following headings: Signifier, Signified and Symbols.

(A)   The Signifiers: This refers to all the physically perceivable elements found in the play. They include:

1) Rogbodiyan: The word, *Rogbodiyan*, can be seen as an icon with a strong linguistic caption that x-rays or photographs the confusion image in Ilu Koroju, the setting of the play.
2) Movement (scenes): movement (scenes) are index indicating the story details which cannot be condensed into the linguistic caption *"Rogbodiyan"* but directs the reader to the main text.
3) Crown, Staff, Beads: The special symbols used for identification and distinction of a monarch or a king in the Yoruba society. It is also the reflection of ideas pertaining to royalty.
4) Kabiyesi: The special name used as an icon of recognition to a king in Yoruba community.
5) Agbada and sokoto: These are icons which give the picture of the Yoruba cultural dress code. Agbada and Sokoto are objects of clothing or costumes show-casing Yoruba cultural attires.
6) Shrine: The special name and sign used as index for power centre where the people of Ilu Koroju gather to perform sacrifices during Oge Festival. The shrine alert on the people, the idea related to their beliefs and aspirations of the community.
7) Sacrifice: This is an index of appreciation shown by the Ilu Koroju people to Agboju, the sustainer of Ilu Koroju community.
8) Names: Names are more or less photographs of the bearers. They are used as icon which gives strong resemblance of the bearers.
9) Arugba Oge: A special name and title used as an index of purification for the choosen virgin maiden who is the only one qualified to carry sacrifice to Agboju's shrine.

(B) The signified: This implies the abstract and mental meaning which the signifiers invoke on the people. Its interpretation occurs in orders of denotation, connotation and myth significations.

1) Festivals, songs and dance: They depict celebration, happiness and joy. They also generate mythic feelings and sacredness. For instance when Asagidigbi says "... let the dance of the virgins commence at once" (p.28). The singing tones, rhythms and the dancing steps change from the celebrative one to that of spiritual enactment.
2) Arugba Oge: Her virginity denotes purity of body and soul. She signifies the saviour figure through which Agboju renews and blesses the people of Ilu Koroju spiritually. She symbolizes the eyes of Agboju their benevolent god.
3) Seclusion: It denotes solitude and communion with ancestral spirits through meditation for sustainable development in Ilu Koroju community. This act of secluding also generates mythical feelings.
4) Ara Orun: Ara Orun denotes death and bad omen. It reflects ideas pertaining to the dead.
5) gods (Olodumare, Orisa nla, Ifa, Ebu, Obatala, Ogun, Orunmila): These names invoke on the people of Ilu Koroju, the idea of sacred beings, which they hold as sacrosanct. They are also worshipped as spiritual entities with the myth of causing good fortunes and disturbances in everyday experiences as well as being responsible for misfortunes when cultural norms/taboos are not being held tenetly. These gods depict the Yoruba ancestral beings who have attained a high spiritual excellence of the soul. The people believe and relate these gods to certain facts and phenomena like creation, fertility, healing, wealth, thunder, etc.

C) Symbols: A word, ..., that has an arbitrary relation to its objects. (Fortier, 1997:20)

The play, *Rogbodiyan*, reveals that names in Yoruba community are not just arbitrary labels but are socio-cultural tags that have cultural meanings. Names in *Rogbodiyan* carry semantic imports; their meaning may be recoverable from simple rules of

lexical and syntactic analysis. These names have high cultural contents. Examples:
 a) Asagidigbi (p.12) meaning ''the big eagle''.
 b) Gbadegesin (p.13) meaning ''he that rides the horse with a crown''.
 c) Adegbani (p.42) meaning ''my crown has saved me''.
 d) Abere (p.16) meaning ''needle''.
 e) Ara Orun (p.43) meaning ''the people from beyond(heaven)/leader of the dead''.

The names above serve as reflections of the bearers' fortunes, hopes and aspirations. The playwright uses these names to reflect status, traits or attributes and these names are quite symbolic in the play. Giving symbolic names to characters agrees with Kaplan and Anne's (1997: 16) assertion that ''Names shape the language of the daily drama of gesture, a voice and inference that is part of our social life''. People from the royal/noble families in *Rogbodiyan* are known by the names they bear and such names convey ideas and general world views of the bearers. Such names include: ''Asagidigbi'' (p.12) which means "the eagle, a powerful bird". An eagle symbolizes strength and power. ''Gbadegesin'' (p.13) is another royal name, which means "he that rides on the horse with a crown". The horse is also a powerful animal. The horse is a symbol of strength and power too while the crown symbolizes kingship. Another name that denotes royalty in *Rogbodiyan* is ''Adegbani'' (p.42) which means "my crown has saved me".

The above names agree with the view that a name is a reflection of the bearer. The names also serve as a mark of identity to the bearers in the play. A name like '' Ara Orun'' (p.43) which means "the people from beyond(heaven)/the leader of the dead" is symbolic in nature. Ara Orun is a symbol for bad omen, and it explains the cultural belief of the Ilu Koroju people on matters of death, as a wicked and dangerous omen.

Conclusion

Appraising the sign system and the linguistic choice in *Rogbodiyan,* so far, has signalled some important facts about cultural practices and meaning-sharing. The analysis of this work in terms of language use in *Rogbodiyan* has revealed that the play has the syntactic structure of Yoruba language while its vocabulary is in English. This work has viewed language as a system of signs which expresses ideas as well as distinguishes codes and symbols through their relative position. It has also revealed that these signs are not independent of the context they signify. They are all actively involved in the signification process.

Works Cited

Bakare, O. R (1994): *Rogbodiyan*, Zaria: Tamaza Publishing Company Limited.

Barthes, R. (1992): *Mythologies*, London: Jonathan Cape.

Blamires, H. (1991): *A History of Literary Criticism,* London: Macmillan Press Ltd.

Ferdinand, de Saussure (1974): *Course in General Lingustics*, New York: Fontana & Collins.

Fortier, M. (1997): *Theory/Theatre: An Introdution*, London: Routledge.

Hawkes, T. (1977): *Structuralism and Semiotics*, London: Methuen.

Hudson, R. N. (1980): *Sociolinguistics*, Cambridge: Cambridge University Press.

Kaplan, J & Anne, B. (1997): *The Language of Names*, New York: Simon & Schuster.

Woollacott, J. (1982): ''Messages and Meanings'' In Gurevitch Michael ett al(eds): *Culture, Society and the Media,* New York: Methuen Inc.

PART TWO

DANCE AND MUSIC ON THE WORKS OF BAKARE, OJO RASAKI

Music And Songs in Bakare, Ojo Rasaki's *Rogbodiyan* And *Drums of War*

By
Ikibe, Solomon, Ph.D and Gabriel, Ojakovo

Introduction
Music is a veritable tool by playwrights and in play production. Apart from using music to set moods and depict scenes, music is used as a tool to enhance play productions by playwrights. In this paper, we examine the use of music in two plays of Bakare Rasaki – *Rogbodiyan* and *Drums of War*. This is to show the extent to which Bakare, Ojo Rasaki makes use of music in his plays. Although a dance scholar. Bakare has been a music enthusiast, a music director and a music conductor. In 2013, Bakare conducted an artistic performance of the Nigerian National Anthem which he had arranged himself, at the Benue State University, Makurdi. Although some of us musicologists saw the trend as an aberration to alter a country's anthem on the altar of artistic freedom, we also saw the ingenuity of Bakare Rasaki to "tread where the devils dread". Therefore seeing the enormity of Bakare's use of music and songs in his plays is not strange. Idolor, (2014, p.3) asserts that "in building a society, promoting people, creating meaning and imagining possibilities, music connects the individual to the society and the personal to the social". Retrospectively, most African playwrights such as Fugards, Soyinka, Osofisan, Wa Thiongo, Obafemi, Rotimi, Ladipo, Armah, Sher, Adeoye, Bakare, etc. adopt music and dance to actualise the concept of total theatrical performance which is predominately visible in their folk society. For instance, Abiodun (2013, P.95) avers that:

> Yoruba plays on stage or in movies often exhibit a total theatrical style- dance, music, action, mime, pantomime. The opening glees of early Yoruba stage performances of Hubert Ogunde, Duro Ladipo, Kola Ogunmola, Ade Love, Moses Olaiya and so on are evidences of musical performance within drama production. In addition to this, the soap opera and

folk opera of Hubert Ogunde are evidence of music in theatre or theatre in music.

The reason for the adoption of this ideology is to preserve and propagate their traditional styles of theatrical performance that is present in their diverse society. This is done to create room for audience participation and to sustain their interest during production. This process incorporates the audience by creating room for them to join in the chorus since they are familiar with most of the tunes, clap, yodel, and even dancing spontaneously to the rhythm of the song. Wade and Ukuma (2012, P.179) notes that "coming from a unique background of living oral traditions from which the performer draws his material, the audience can best be described as participatory and the performer only, thus revolves around the audience". This is achieved "through dramatic elements such as music, song, dance, riddles, proverbs, and dialogue…involves the audience in a participatory role (Awoyemi, 2012, as cited in Abiodun, 2013b, P.210).

This practice give the audience a sense of responsibility by being part and parcel of the production when the need arises. Music out of all these dramatic elements is the most characteristic element that moves the audience to different levels of artistic aesthetics (Abiodun, 2013b, P.97). Play production void of music, dance, and in some cases audience participation seems strange to some Nigerian audience who are grounded on the culture of total theatrical performance. In fact Nzewi (1981) affirms that "theatrical performance without music is alien to the Nigerian audience". For instance, in 2013, 'The Asylum' written by Ahmed Yerima was staged as an experimental departmental production with music and dance playing a passive role. The feedback received from the audience revealed 96% of them found the production boring, thus forcing them to leave before curtain call. The turn up of audience for day two production of the play was drastically reduced to 30% when compared to day one. This fact buttresses the need for music and dance in African dramatic performance.

Music in drama production is most times composed by the playwrights to add aesthetic and create effects for specific scenes. Some of the songs are borne out of the playwright's creative ability to portray the thematic essence and the settings of the play. In some cases, they also adopt folksongs associated with the given settings of the play to give it cultural relevance. Ikibe (2007, 2; 2011, p.3) made reference to Tobrise (1993:47) who earlier described Wale Ogunyemi as a playwright /artistic director who "used music to emphasize moods in order to create varying atmosphere of fear, joy, and gloom". Ojo Bakare is one of such Nigerian playwrights that composes original music and adapts existing folksongs in most of his works. This is hinged on the premise of his exposure to the Yoruba culture in which he was groomed in. He tries to maintain the legacy of total theatre as established by early Yoruba theatre practitioners.

Synopsis of *Rogbodiyan*

The play, *Rogbodiyan*, revolves around a town known as Ilu-Koroju where a Regent who had reigned for seven years needed to hand over to a substantive king. However, as no one was ready from the royal families, two people were nominated by the regent, Asagdigbi and Gbadigesin. Asagidigbi is chosen but defiled the Arugba – virgin maiden of the town who must carry the sacrifice of the people before the real coronation and festival is done. As a result of the defilement of the Arugba, Asagidigbi must go to Esumare to get the healing water with which to heal the people of Ilu-Koroju who had been under affliction of various sicknesses and diseases because of the sacrilege committed by the Asagidigbi. Asagidigbi refuses to go and Adegbami offered to go but must wear the King's crown. As Adegbami comes back from Esumare with the healing water, he refuses to surrender the crown back to Asagidigbi. Adegbami demands that he be recognised and accepted as the crowned king in place of Asagidigbi otherwise he pours the healing water on the ground. The people of Ilu-Koroju accepted the option and they got healed from their ailments.

Synopsis of *Drums of War*
The play, *Drums of War* revolves around a proud king who refuses to listen to the advice of people concerning the war of dominance. The play also centres on the senselessness of war and its consequences. No one is spared as it is portrayed in the play. The king at the end loses his only son, the heir apparent and his wife though he is warned by the women and his wife but fails to listen.

Music and Songs in *Rogbodiyan*
Music, defined by Mereni (2014, p.58) as the "art and science of sound" is an integrative element in play productions by many Nigerian playwrights. In his characteristic manner, Bakare Rasaki uses music and songs to spice the play from the tableaux through to movement 9 which is the last movement. Just before the play begins, music is played and the song on Rogbodiyan is sung thus:

> *Rogbodiyan oo, ee Rogbodiyan oo* (twice)
> *Rogbodyan tide oran sele, Ijangban ti de oran*
> *Sele, Iluoo roju kotun raye, awa bere ooo, eee,*
> *Awa bere oo kini ka ti?*

The song is sung from the beginning of the tableaux till when the narrator concludes his introductory narration.

Immediately after movement one begins with another song by the king's messenger with a musical instrument, the gong, his symbol of office which he rings whenever he is on an official errand. The song is taken over by the chorus twice. Agogo's song is:

> *Kee reek ere keere oo ee* (twice)
> *Odomode atagbalagba, lokunrin lobinrinpe*
> *Ipade **Ilu** di lola Laafin Oba*

It is after the song is taken twice by the chorus that Agogo delivers his message to the town people that had responded to the town-crier's call through his song and music made on the gong.

Movement two also begins with another song – *Ase etuwaa muroo*.

> *Ewu oye wa dabole*(twice*)*
> *Owa ran ni ipemi u a too oo.*
> *Ogbolori wee dide oo*
> *Ogbolri wee dide u a too*
> *Ogbolori wee dide oo*
> **Meaning**:
> No matter how wealthy you are,
> When the king calls,
> You must obey.

Apart from the main songs taken by the chorus and the king's messenger, the king's messenger also pulsates every speech the king makes with praise songs known as *oriki* in Yoruba. One of such *orikis* in Bakare Rasaki's *Rogbodiyan* is or "*o wi ire*" which means "you have spoken well".

Movement three is done entirely in songs as Gbadegesin and Asagidigbi with their followers enter the stage with political songs, trying to outdo each other. The songs they use for their campaigns are:

> *Asagidigbi o joba*
> *Nile yi ko o nile bomin ni, Asagidigbi ojoba.*
> **Meaning**:
> Asagidigbi wants to become a king,
> Never will that happen in this land.

> Asagidigbi' group sang thus:
> *Ta ni pawa oni baba kai ani oni baba.*
> *Asagidigbi baba wa kai ani baba*
> **Meaning**
> Who says we have no father?
> Asagidigbi is our father.

As movement three ends with songs, movement four begins with another song thus:

> *Afee moba waaa* (2ce)
> *Afee meni ti o joye yi*
> *Afee moba waaa*
> **Meaning**
> We want to know,

Who becomes king.
We want to know

The music and song on *Ejekamobawa* continues from the beginning to the end. On this song and rhythm, actors move rhythmically and at various intervals the song heightens to a crescendo especially where there are no speeches and gets diminuendo whenever dialogue is on.

Movement Five begins with the background music and songs like other previous movements while the Narrator does his narration.

Movement Six begins with a solo and chorus song thus:

(solo) *Aki in oooo*
(chorus) *Oke oke*
(solo) *Akolule*
(chorus) *Oke oke*
(Solo) *akalejo*
(chorus) *Oke oke*

Meaning

We greet you
We greet everybody here present
A second song taken in the sixth movement is:
Wa pe Kabiyesi o
Iw o yo fi da wajo
On e o a wa ma de

Meaning:
May you live long, Kabiyesi
You invited us for a dance
We are here.

A special music is played for maidens to dance to during the coronation ceremony of Asagidigbi.

Movement seven begins with the theme song of the play, *Rogbodiyan* as the Narrator appears onstage again to tell the audience what the problems in the town had been as a result of the misbehaviour of the new king that defiled a virgin in her exclusive state.

Movement eight starts with *bata* drum music as against the theme song. The bata drums music is accompanied with Akigbe's praise singing of the new king..

Movement Nine has five songs. The movement begins with a song and ends with a song. The songs are:

Song 1 in Movement 9
Ebo wa ree ebo ire
Ebo wa ree ebo ire
Ebo iye ree tiwa mati
da se yee
Agbojuu oo gbe bo wa
Agboru beye oo gbe bo wa
Agbouboye omo awo o
Agbouboye omo awo o
Agbouboye omo awo o
Agbouboye omo awoo o
Keboru ru keboda,
Kebo mori ire waye
Aboru boye omo awoo etc.

Meaning
This is our sacrifice,
This is our sacrifice for survival
Agboju, please accept our sacrifice
May our sacrifice bring good fortune

Song 2 in Movement 9
Aborub'oye omo awoo
Aboru boye omo awoo
Aboru boye omo awoo
Keboru keboda kebomori
Ire waye
Aboru boye omo awoo

Song 3 in movement 9
Orunmila gbawa aba wa
Se o Orunmila gbawa o
Ba wa se

Rogbodiyan eyi ti sun wa o
Bile aye se ndorikodo
Orunmila oo eee
Orunmila Baba wa bawa se
Orunmila gbawa o bawa se o
Orunmila gbawa o bawa se
Aburu eyi tit un poju
Afoju ilu oniye o Abuke Ilu otun lonka
Orunmila oo ee, Orunmila babawa bawa bawa se

Meaning
Orunmila, help us
This calamity is serious
Orunmila, our father help us

Song 4 in Movement 9
Rogbodiyan oo, ee Rogbodiyan oo (twice)
Rogbodyan tide oran sele, Ijangban ti de oran
Sele, Iluoo roju kotun raye, awa bere ooo, eee,
Awa bere oo kini ka ti?

Song 5 in movement 9
This is the last in the play.
Ologun gbawa o oni maroo
Ninini ni kun ini
Booba gbawa o a a se tire o
Nini ni ni kun inii

Music and Songs in *Drums of War*

The prologue begins with singers and drummers who formed the orchestra sitting and singing as one from the orchestra pit.

Hausa Song
Mutane kuso fadamaku labarin Nigeria
Kuso kuji labarin Nigeria

Meaning
People come from labour and listen to news about Nigeria
Come and hear the story of Nigeria

From the above song, one can deduce that the play is all about our country Nigeria, whose leaders quest for power are in most cases detrimental to the will of good governance. This song ushered in Ogbegun an old man who introduce himself as:
Ogbegun: ... Eriokan, the music maker. I am a musician by profession and my
> orchestra is ready to entertain you tonight. But ours is the music of the mind and not merely of sound or merry making... why don't you sit down, make yourself comfortable and listen to my kind of music.

This introduction set the pace for the drama performance. This was reflected in movement one where a warrior from Abakpa village ran into the stage singing and dancing to war songs from Igala to usher in his fellow warriors on stage. This was subsequently repeated by Ibuji warriors ready to engage in communal battle with Abakpa community. The singing characters form the core of the characters in Ojo Bakare's *the Drums of War*, the warriors, the villagers, the chiefs, the war leader are singers (solo or chorus) (Abiodun, 2013, p.211). No wonder Abraham (2013, p.57) rightly observes that Ojo Bakare is "highly musical and a natural dancer and so it is very difficult for him to do a play without dance and music".

Music: a Reflection of the Play Setting

The play is set in Nigeria, a society with over 250 multi lingua ethnic nationalities to mirror the ills of selfishness and greed of a tribe quest for political supremacy over the other. The setting allows the multi musical settings- the drumming and singing represents different settings (Abiodun, 2013, p.211). This creates room for the playwright to use music, dance movements, costumes and names of some tribes from South West (Yoruba), North Central (Igala) and South-South (Edo) region. This is done to reflect Nigeria and the instrumental music associated with the characters used in the production. Most of these songs are derived from existing folksongs that tends to promote war, peace, praise, unity, warning and even tears and sorrow. These claims can be seen from the song below:

Yoruba Song of Oneness and Patriotism

Nigeria kan n loni wa o (2ce)
We only have one Nigeria
Ibo, Yoruba ne e tabi idoma, Nigeria o
No matter your tribe and tongue, Igbo, Yoruba or Idoma
Eee, Nigeria Kan Lo ni wa
Nigeria is only one

This song is sung in movement one by women and warriors to celebrate the oneness of Nigeria irrespective of tribal affiliation. It is a clarion call for Nigerians to see themselves as one and for them to be wary of leaders who are set to cause disunity among them. It is also used by them to celebrate their triumph over setting war aside.

Edo Song of Praise to the King	**Meaning**
Oba oba oba	Our king, our king
Ogbo ghi ghi	Our king is great

This song is in movement two to praise the king whom the people believed to be their supreme leader. This is done to give the king their support in whatever the king so desires, by celebrating the king's daughter return when his soldiers are on the battle field fighting with the last drop of their blood to protect their kingdom.

Yoruba song of Warning	**Meaning**
Odele alagaa (2ce)	It is tough
Oyele mori nee (2ce)	It is tough
Eso fun oloye ko woro so o,	Tell the chief to mind what he says
Inu nbe nle niofe lofun	Death is not easy to come by here

This song is sung by the villagers present in the king palace to caution the excesses of Beleku who challenged the authority of the king over the war engaged by their warrior. To him, the king ought not to be celebrating why his subjects are in the battle field. This song is sang in a solemn mood as all characters on set freeze to stop Chief Beleku from engaging with the king in Physical combat. The people whom he tried to fight for warned him to tread with caution or risk being decapitated.

The use of folksongs by Bakare expresses the traditional settings of drums of war.

Music: a Reflection of the Theme of the play

The theme of drums of war is on supremacy of a leader over his subjects on sensitive issues of war with their neighbouring community. This could be blamed on for inter-tribal wars that have occurred between Offa-Erinle, Urhobo-Itsekiri, Itsekiri-Ijaw, Shao-Ilorin, etc., at local levels. The same could be said at national level between Nigeria-Biafra, Nigeria-Odi. These are amongst some few examples worthy of mentioning. This is as a result of man's inhumanity to others, to prove his political prowess and dominance over the minority for his own interest.

Music is used by the warriors from both villages to kindle their desire to carry out the instructions of their leaders to fight for their supremacy. This claim is reflected in song two, an Igala war song.

Igala	**Meaning**
Ogbo Ogwu Mamunedo	This is the war front
Ibuji enola wa mamunedo	Ibuji, this is the war front, we shall know who is stronger

This war diffused hatred and bitterness into the psychology of Ibuji and Abakpa, people who once lived in peace with one another. They considered each other an enemy that should be hunted with machetes and gun. This declaration for ethnic cleansing is seen in song three sang by Abakpa warriors in movement one.

Igala War Song	**Meaming**
Eju nudo kpa koko	Our eyes are red
Aja mo mayege	We know no friend neither brothers

The anger of these warriors was pacified by women from Ibuji Village believed to be the mothers and wives of their warriors.

These ladies are drained with the senseless war engaged in by both communities and begged the soldiers to shield their sword for peace to reign. This song creates a dynamic from hot tempo associated with warriors to celebratory song that reawaken in them the spirit of oneness among the soldiers. This was sustained with song seven, eight, and nine from Igala, Hausa and Igala setting.

Place of Music and Songs in Theatrical Performances
Music and songs are very essential in play productions. Akinwale (1998) and Nzewi (1981) have commented that that the Nigerian audience is used to plays with music and not just dialogue plays as seen in most European plays. Mereni (2014) makes mention of the importance of musicality in the society but that practical music must be well applied in order to let the hearer comprehend its essence. As good as music and songs are in play productions, they must be well applied so that the play is not turned into musicals. It is hoped that playwrights would continue to use music as a tool to enhance their plays just as Ojo Bakare has been doing.

References

Abiodun, F. (2013a). Quality control in choir management: A musicological pereformance in drama production. Gowon, A.D., & Ted, A. (eds.), *Quality assurance: Theatre, Media and the Creative Enterprises*. Makurdi: Society of Nigeria Theatre Artists.

Abiodun, F. (2013b). Analysis of musical styles and production techniques of yourba movies songs. *International Journal of Movie Scholars*. Maiden Edition, Pp.95-103.

Abraham, Tolorunju Johnson Adavi (2013). " An examination of directorial approaches in Barclays F. Ayakoroma's *Dance on the grave* and Ojo R. Bakare's *Drums of War* Unpublished M.A. dissertation presented to the Performing Arts department, University of Ilorin.

Akinwale, Ayo (1998). The impact of the theatre in contemporary society in Nigeria: a study in theatre sociology. Unpublished Ph.D. thesis, University of Ibadan.

Awoyemi, T. (2012). Historicity and protest in selected African drama. *Journal of theatre and Cultural Studies, Redeemers University, Mowe.*

Bakare, O.R. (N.D.). *Drums of war* Nigeria: Tamaza Publishing Company Limited

Bakare, O.R. (2004). *Rogbodiyan* Nigeria: Tamaza Publishing Company Limited

Idolor, E.G. (2014). *The traditions of Okpe disco and the challenges of modernism* a published inaugural lecture at the Delta State University, Abraka. University Printing Press, Abraka

Ikibe, S.O. (2007). "Isoko Performing Arts and culture: Music in folktales as paradigm" Unpublished Ph.D. thesis of the Performing Arts Department, University of Ilorin

Ikibe, S.O. (2011). *Isoko Performing Arts and culture: Music in Isoko folktales of Nigeria* Lambert Academic Publishers (LAP) GMBh, Germany

Mereni, Anthony Ekemezie (2014). *Theorising practice and practising theory: a phenomenology of music in Nigeria* a published inaugural lecture at the University of Lagos, Nigeria, University of Lagos Printing Press.

Nzewi, M. (1988). "State of literary music in Nigeria: A review" in Nigeria Magazine vol. 56, No. 3 & 4 pp. 5 – 24.

Nzewi, M. (1981). "Music, dance, drama and the stage" in Ogunbiyi, Yemi (ed.) *Drama and theatre in Nigeria: a critical source book* Lagos: Nigeria Magazine pp.433 – 456.

Wade, Z., & Ukuma, S. (2012). Tiv oral performance: An aesthetics rediscovery of function and style in Simeon Tsav's Songs. *Anyiba Journal of Theatre, Film and Communication Arts.* Vol.1, No.1, Pp.175-189.

Break and Mould the Dancer: Bakare Ojo Rasaki's Technique of Training.

By
Suru, Cyrus Damisa, Ph.D.

Introduction
"Everybody can dance, only a dancer can perform". This was the maxim that came from Bakare Ojo-Rasaki to us, the newly recruited dance artistes, as a Dance instructor/Choreographer and Cultural –Troupe-Builder (in conjunction with John Egugu Illah), of the the Kogi State Council for Arts and Culture, Lokoja where this researcher was a dancer (invited then from the Niger State Troupe – The *Gwape* International)in 1993. From those words, in spite of the experience gathered as a dancer, this researcher started to learn to draw a dichotomy between a dancer and a dance-performer. Also, reading Bakare (2007, p. 272)'s article, *Singing Old Tunes: Critical Comments on Welsh Asante's African Dance* he reference's Pearl Primus's comment on dance training in Africa that:

> There is a distinction between the trained dancer and somebody who just dances...the professional dancer must have been trained from childhood to be a dancer. Having shown special talent and skills, for rhythm and dance language, he is apprenticed to a master dancer who employs whatever methodology he feels is appropriate to take this apprentice through a rigorous dance training programme. The dancer-to-be then learns traditional dances of the people.

Reminiscent of Bakare's reference to Pearl, dancing is one of the most natural things to execute among the external prevalence and activities bestowed on man. In other words, the act of movement merged with feelings and emotions is paramount in the life of humans. That explains the "everybody can dance" and the other sub-quote "only a dancer can perform". It is predicated upon the skillful application of the natural and ordinary movements in an extraordinary manner through training, for entertainment, education and, information, also as a source of finance, which are regarded as the pivot of dance professionalism in the society. Shaibu Husseini (2006, p.296) comments that:

> Training is what separates a dancer artiste from say a club dancer. Because dance as an art form makes use of the human body, scholars have stressed that only a sound training in movement techniques can lead to a better manipulation of the body lines, curves, skeletal and muscular control and other variations in movement and velocity. This is where a professional dance artiste differs from those who can merely move to rhythm.

It then indicates that there are two types of dancers in the society; the born-dancers and the made–dancers. The born-dancer is a natural and talented dancer who executes rhythmic movements naturally and merely for self excitement or aggrandisement or for the delight of others – the informal spectator/audience. On the other hand, this study considers the made-dancer as that skilled and creative dancer who may be a born-dancer or not but, with adequate training, developed the techniques of performance-communication to entertaining, educating and, informing a formal or an informal spectator/audience. In the words of Suru C. Damisa (2012, p.1):

> Dance is concerned with the use of body gesture, body movements and other dance elements for expression. The elements being referred to here are: rhythm, time, space, dynamics, costume, props, make-up, music, drama, and so on. Dance messages are communicated using the elements mentioned above and through signs and symbols to impact on the life of the people.

Suru personifies dance as a living communication tool. This is where the dancer needs adequate training. Thus, this kind of dancer needs the expertise training of a professional and, this is where Bakare Ojo-Rasaki's didactic technique of training comes in handy; break, then mould the dancer.

Bakare Ojo-Rasaki and Dance

The title of this paper is borne from the flyer, Musing on Bakare, Ojo Rasaki @ 50, 2014 which was put out to scholars to contribute papers in honour of the great professor of choreography. The eulogy that x-rayed his contributions to the theatre world in the flyer notwithstanding, did not include his technique of 'Breaking and Moulding the Dancer' which this researcher is privy to, adopting the participant-observer methodology from the knowledge received through training by him as a cultural dancer in the Kogi State Arts Council added to secondary sources as support.

A cursory look at some of the lyrical movements of the write-up (divided into three parts for emphasis) serves to illuminate the above. The first part states for instance that:

> He joined the Yoruba Travelling Theatre movement. He consequently plied his trade under Jimoh Aliu's cultural troupe and the late Hubert Ogunde, who has been acclaimed the doyen of professional theatre in Nigeria. Rising from this humble beginning, today, Rasaki is Nigeria's first professor of Choreography... He is also the Artistic Director of Nigeria's National Carnival... In his career, Bakare has directed over 200 major theatrical performances. Over sixty percent of these were commissioned high profile command performances. In fact, three of these were for Presidential inauguration ceremonies.

The above is a laconic chronicle of Ojo Bakare's sojourn in the theatre world. He is privileged to have received his early theatre, dance and choreography training from popular theatre legends like Jimoh Aliu, Hubert Ogunde, including Arnold Udoka and a few others. They could have informed his didactic technique of impacting dance training on other naive dance artistes as a way to contributing his own quota to the society. Noorbakhsh Hooti and Nasser Meleki (2009) stress that "man cannot devote himself thoroughly just to his family, but he has equal responsibility to his own society. Though man's character is shaped by society, yet his impact upon society is inevitable as well." The flyer adds his achievements which have brought him to an enviable and respected position in the national and International theatre space.

The second part is an expository of his academic "onslaught" via the publications of plays such as *"This Land Must Sacrifice; Drums of War; Rogbodiyan; Once Upon A Tower; The gods and The Scavengers; Voyage; Sekere and The Parable of Many Seeds; Adanma; The Fate of Ejima; Etutu* and over thirty other unpublished stage plays that were produced and performed with rewarding and outstanding successes. (It is imperative to mention here that this researcher, apart from reading most of these plays also, played the character, Ogbegun, in the premier performance of the play *Drums of War*). The enumerated plays above have only explained to us that he is a dramaturge and a good scholar. And, that he has contributed to alleviate the dearth of African theatre literature and the demonstration of the performative art in the views of theatre enthusiasts.

The third part which aligns with the focus of this paper, in a seemingly similar note, is his dance and choreography accounts. The flyer on Bakare, Ojo Rasaki @ 50 stresses that:

> However, it is perhaps in Dance and Choreography that Rasaki has achieved his most enduring legacies. Today, *Dancerasaki* is the leading Nigerian dance scholar, the most sought-after Nigerian Choreographer and Dance Trainer and the most revered dance adjudicator. **He has worked directly with, and influenced most Nigerian dance practitioners, taught and trained many of those who teach and intellectualize Dance and Choreography today.** His numerous choreographed works are found in the repertoires of most dance troupes in Nigeria and beyond... His Choreography – Sekai Aiki won the First Prize for Nigeria at the Spring Friendship Festival, North Korea in 1997.

The alighted portion of this quotation is a truism of his immense contributions to dance and choreography scholarship in Nigeria and beyond. A quick addition is Bakare's scholarly battle for dance and choreography in Africa. For instance, Bakare (2007, p.267) challenged the lack of adequate knowledge of African dance thus:

> The popularity of dance as an art form in Africa notwithstanding, African dance has received limited scholarly attention. Even where such exists, apart from the fact that much of what exists came from Europe and the Americas, especially the Diaspora, it is largely anthropological and generic. Little scholarly attention has been given to the choreography of African dance and the technical devices proper to it.

The question is, where lies his technique of training the trainer in the act and art of dance and choreography?

Bakare's Techniques of Training

Bakare's technique, to my knowledge and to many that have been privileged to be trained by him, in one way or another, is that of allowing the 'talented' or 'professional' dancer or dancers to execute movements naturally or according to their dance knowledge and cultural dance experiences from which the most appropriate and suitable steps are chosen and are fine-tuned, for aesthetic sake, by him for the dance package or performance. One of the methods of actualizing aesthetics by Bakare involves moving around the rehearsals venue while the dancers execute free, talented or even earlier choreographed dance movements, trying to visualize or picture how the audience will appreciate the dance performance. As it were, aesthetic imperative is very paramount in the theatre be it in a drama, music or dance performance. Musa, Rasheed Abiodun (2001, p.92) captures it for drama in this manner, "be it professional or academic theatre, the essence of any dramatic or theatrical experience is aesthetic success of such performances. Interestingly, the importance of the theatre director in the art of directing cannot be over-emphasized if aesthetic experience is contemplated". Bakare's experience as a dancer and a choreographer has been instrumental to his aesthetic packaging of dance performance.

Another addition to his technique of training is the art of giving the technical know-how in dance for effective output of performance and the maximisation of energy and appropriate use of the body in dance to avoid dance related injury. As succinctly put by Sherbon Elizabeth (1975, p.23):

> All artistic expression is based on craft, the technical control of a given instrument of expression... there are two concepts that can be immeasurable value in learning the craft of dance. Probably the most important is the idea of striving continuously for complete efficiency in movement. Use only the amount of energy needed to perform the desired movement. The energy should be exerted in the desired direction and in the sequential order needed to accomplish the wished-for effect.

The above takes us back to the aphorism "everybody can dance, only a dancer can perform". Using the appropriate body movements in dance comes with the questions; Why? When? Where? and How? Why this movement? When should I apply it? Is it okay at this time, space and venue? And, how will it be executed? Which a trained dancer should answer in a sharp reflex manner. That explains why Bakare must break the dancer.

Breaking the Dancer
Breaking the dancer is one of the techniques of Ojo Bakare in grooming his dancers. A dancer may be talented in the act of dance but lacking the skills of performance (the dance art) and the proper way to sustain the energy needed for the performance. A dancer may be too stiff, and lacking the lubricant for malleability of body movements artfully. That accounts for the reason why Bakare (1994, p.7) explains that:
> There are certain fundamental principles guiding the preparation of dance and movement and without them

dance may not be accomplished. They prepare the body for its functions and they are fundamental to the entire process of dance-making and dance production. The dancer sustains his carrier with these principles and can only acquire them through training. These principles are: Centring, Posture, Rhythm, Gravity, Balance, Breathing, Grounding and Space.

A dancer or talented dancer must be acquainted with these principles to be a broken dancer Bakare concluded. In an attempt to break the Kogi State artiste-to-be, at the camp in Lokoja in 1993, Bakare, on a very serious note, warned the dancers to avoid heavy eating before rehearsals, drinking of beer which most Nigerian local artistes/dancers see as stimulants, better still, source for courage to face the audience and, baffling and puzzling too, was the non eating of fried meat, fish, plantain (*dodo*) and the likes which according to him could make the dancer weak, grow fat and heavy, even obese from the excessive oil intake. This last one was frowned at with the pessimism that he does not want the dancers to enjoy (but to endure) given the fact that, as at that time, we were not paid any salaries or allowances. Added to the 'punishment' were the everyday road and stage exercises and all-night rehearsals. The 'Ososa experience' under Hubert Ogunde one might say. At this point, we all saw Bakare Ojo Rasaki as a god, who does not sleep and never tired because as we all slept mid-rehearsals he was always awake and walking around only to wake us up again to proceed with the rehearsals.

Encouragingly, it was at that six months camp that many who were fat and bloated became trim light-weighted and flexible enough to execute hitherto difficult dance movements and also able to apply the principles enumerated by Bakare above in performances. Upon his departure, the artiste began to overdo the training. For instance, artiste dancers trained by jogging several kilometres during the day time, under the scorching sun, all in the bid to achieve stamina.

Sadly, Bakare's training was not sustained because after a few years, bad eating habits, lack of appropriate exercise and general laxity resumed and today, most of the artiste dancers are roundish, bloated and inactive. In addition, dancers, particularly in the arts councils, now eat uncontrollably and without caring about their health, body and the success of the dance profession. By so doing, they await re-deployment to other departments where they are no longer useful. Bakare's method of breaking the dancer is now better understood.

Moulding the Dancer
To mould the dancer is a germane procedure by a good choreographer. This is because the creativity of the dancer contributes, in no small measure, to articulating the message that the choreography is passing across to the audience through dance performance. Bakare (1994, p.2) puts it in this manner; "the dancer is to the choreographer what the actor is to the director. The choreographer creates while the dancer interprets what the choreographer creates, though the dancer himself needs some level of creativity to be able to interpret effectively." The dancer needs moulding, moulding through adequate, consistent and perseverance trainings. Bakare understands that the artiste dancer must first of all be helped to discover himself as a creative individual. This believability usually comes from a dance instructor or choreographer who instils self- confidence, sociability, self-reliance, personality, co-operativeness in the dancer to encourage, build or promote his/her ability and potentiality. Kane J.E. (1972) did not agrees less and affirms that:
> One explanation offered is that the environment in which physical abilities are displayed...constitute an ideal setting for the development of desirable personality characteristics such as confidence, sociability, self-reliance, co-cooperativeness and general personal adjustment.

The dancer is moulded to have a good and great figure, to exhume beauty in dance, to have the shape of a model with self-confidence devoid of low self- esteem and, courage to believe in others and to also, have confidence in them or themselves. These are some of the qualities of a moulded artiste dancer.

Conclusion

Breaking and moulding a dancer to carry on with the profession is imperative and should be the concern of every choreographer. While the businessmen in most fields give money to the graduating apprentice to begin business with, the professional dancer or choreographer should, as we have seen in Bakare Ojo Rasaki's technique, empower the dancer physically, morally, intellectually, financially and spiritually. Taking from the artiste dancer what rightly is due to him/her could be discouraging. Furthermore, as the doyen of theatre, Late Hubert Ogunde once advised dancers in 1988 at the Niger State Arts Council, Minna, "a dancer can only spend ten active years of his/her life on the stage, after which diminishing return sets in". In other words, all trained dancers and choreographers of today should not hide their skills but impact on trainee artistes or dancers to continue from and to keep the dance profession afloat. Furthermore, those who are blessed with the knowledge to intellectualise, commoditise and document dance through literary or practical means should not deter but rather persist in making dance in the society.

References

Bakare, Ojo Rasaki (1994). *Rudiments of choreography Part 1.* Zaria: Space 2000 Pace Publishers Limited.

Bakare Ojo Rasaki (2007). Singing old tunes: Critical comments on Welsh Asante's African dance. In Chris Ugolo (ed) *Perspectives in Nigerian Dance Studies.* (pp. 266-284) Ibadan: Caltop Publications (Nigeria Limited).

Kane J.E. (1972). Personality, body concept and performance. In Kane J.E. (Ed.) *Psychological aspects of physical education and sport.* (pp. 91-127). London: Routledge & Kegan Paul

Musa, Rasheed Abiodun (2001). Psychology as a factor in play directing. *The Performer. Ilorin: Journal of the Performing Arts Vol.3.*(pp.92-103). Department of the Performing Arts, University of Ilorin.

Musing on Bakare, Ojo Rasaki @ 50. 2014. Call for Paper. London: SPM Publications.

Noorbakhsh Hooti and Nasser Meleki (2009). The voice of conscience in the vortex of capitalism in Arthur Miller's all my sons. *Oye: Ogun Journal of Arts, Vol.XV June.* Ago-Iwoye: Olabisi Onabanjo University. pp. 46-51.

Shaibu, Husseini. (2006). From natural talent to professionalism: The challenges of a Nigerian dancer. In Ahmed Yerima, Bakare, Ojo-Rasaki and Arnold Udoka (Eds.) *Critical perspectives on dance in Nigeria.* (pp. 293-304). Ibadan: Kraft Books Limited.

Sherbon, Elizabeth (1975). *On the count of one modern dance methods,* 2nd *edition.* USA: Mayfield Publishing Company.

Suru, C. Damisa. (2012). "Marriage and funeral dance performances among the Ososo people of Nigeria." Unpublished PhD Thesis, submitted to the Department of Performing Arts, University of Ilorin.

Body Rhythmicity And Bakare, Ojo Rasaki's 'The Deformed Can Also Dance: Democratizing Dance Practice in a Democratized Nigeria'

By

Ufford-Azorbo, Ifure and Ufford, Ikike Inieke

Introduction

Dance in its performative stage brings to mind a whole lot of elements, paramount of which is the major instrument of the dancer – the body. Beyond dance, the human body is involved either as an instrument or an object of representation in all the art forms. The function of a fitting human body in dance cannot be over-emphasised. Being the whole physical structure of the human being, the human body is the central figure in any artistic expression. To Appiah (1996:21), the body is "alive, mobile and plastic; it exists in three dimensions". Every other aspect of theatre and arts comes after the person, who is the medium of or an instrument for expression.

Bakare's article "The Deformed can also Dance: Democratizing Dance Practice in a Democratized Nigeria" is one major influence in the advancement of a theory to back up the practice of dance with particular reference to the body. Emphatically, the requirement of a fitting body for dance should not limit the number of practitioners in the field; rather it should open up avenues for more bodies to be trained to speak in the language of dance. The article under study is one which holds that democracy is "a way of life: a principle guiding all human activities and interactions…". It is against the "capitalist mentality that it is only the fittest that must survive". Bakare goes on to describe the unfit or deformed as "people with physiological deformities" (2002:182).

This paper is a statement to the fact that all bodies interested in dance have great potentials in the practice of dance. They may be dancers, choreographers, critics, instructors, consultants and so on. It is, therefore, democratic and advantageous to the furtherance of dance practice to accept interested bodies and give them a platform to reveal their potentials. If the deformed can move, it means that they can be trained to dance.

Training
Dance practice demands rigorous training. Training has to do with the acquisition of knowledge, skills and competencies through a practical medium to empower one for the actualisation of any given task. It is necessary in the art of dance, as it is in any other endeavour, for the optimal improvement of capability, capacity, productivity and total performance. Potential dancers need to be trained in the technicalities involving movement rendition, body alignment, rhythmic appreciation, space awareness and communication processes. Through adequate training, a dancer acquires self confidence and builds high morale by developing positive attitude towards his career. This creates an enabling environment for career satisfaction and enhanced professional exploits and earnings.

Dance is revealed through movement. Movement in daily natural experience is free and is regarded as a normal occurrence. Some people do not even pay attention to the fact that they are moving, since they are already conversant with it as part of living. On the other hand, dance, as art, employs movement which differs in context and practice from natural everyday movement. To remake natural movements from their free state to an artistic product takes a lot of training and dexterity. The human body constitutes the instrument which is used for communication and so has to "transcend its traditional personal limitations... to become kinestically alive and kinesthetically aware..." in order to respond sensitively to the feelings and needs of the dancer and the spectator and also to the demands of his profession and the choreographer (Turner, 1971:23). Hawkins (1988: 3) therefore, concludes that,

> dance is one of man's oldest and most basic means of expression. Through the body, man senses and perceives the tensions and rhythms of the universe around him and using the body as his instrument, he expresses his feeling response to the universe.

The dancer goes through complex and uneasy techniques that are different from daily routines "extra-daily, non-habitual tensions are at work in the body" (Barba 1991:13). This is well represented in Brady's (1983: 136) submission that,

> A dancer's trick (is that of) defying...the natural order of things; like other tricks, once mastered, they give the performer an undeniable exhilaration, a sense of freedom from mundane things, a sheer, sensual joy in movement.

In dance, there is a transformative character in body rhythmic motion for communication. The dancer, through his body, reveals the spirit of life. This makes the body an end in itself regarding the arts of dance. Duncan, according to Thomas (1995:71), is of the view that the spirit of dance is firmly rooted in the human body and not in some transcendental beings. All aspects of life that stirs man's innermost being can be given form through his surging bodily rhythms. This is made perfect through adequate training. For Laban (1996: 146)

> Attitude toward or control over a movement is not necessarily a conscious act that the mover decides to do. However, the attitude which produces the movement quality is an aspect of behaviour and can be considered a product of learning, metabolism, perception of the environment.

This is a position which projects the importance of training in the realisation of the potentialities of dance and this has to do with all bodies. A perfect body with no deformity has to be trained for dance, likewise a deformed body. An untrained perfect body is as useless to the dance art as an untrained deformed body. Without training, a perfect body becomes deformed, considering its relatedness to dance practice. Therefore, training is the key word to a successful dance carrier.

Rhythmic Relevance To Dance Training

All through the ages, there have been rhythmic interactions in nature like the regular heart-beat, day turning into night and so on; and the arts in dance, drama, poetry, music and so on, as a powerful and binding force of unity and inter-personal connections. There is often a momentary experience of bonding when people undertake rhythmic group activities like dancing, jogging, singing, beat of the drums or work. Rhythmicity as a potent ingredient in everyday life, is, therefore a powerful force of linking people together and a vital force in the search for internal togetherness.

As an element which spans through all the arts, rhythm has the motion of periodicity or regular recurrence of events. It speaks of timing of any particular event which may be sound, silence, and meter of spoken language or dance movement. A perfect rhythm establishes a regular pattern of time and force (Ufford-Azorbo, 2011:45). It thus assumes a position of importance, just like the human body, in the actualisation of concord in any artistic endeavour. For Bakare (2002: 184), "...although the body is a fundamental instrument for dance, the most important instrument for dance is a good sense of rhythm".

Rhythm may be complex or simple, slow and even, fast or chaotic depending on the message to be communicated. In dance, Bakare (2002: 185) has defined it as "the underlying beat that animates movement" (2002:185). So a good dancer must possess three major attributes to enable him succeed. These are a good sense of rhythm in order to acquire the right synchronisation with movement rendition, a love for music, in order to re-enact that relationship where music moves "like the sound of the drum, through the dancer's body" (McIntyre 1996:131), and a willingness to learn in order to acquire the right skills and technicalities demanded for dance (Anne 1987:3). In corroboration, Bakare (2002: 185) avers that "for dance to occur, the executor of the dance movement must possess an in-built sense of rhythm. That is, he must have the capacity to execute his movements to a predetermined timing and sustain the process".

The element of rhythmicity in dance may occur in two major categories, the aural and visual. Aural rhythm is perceived through the sense of hearing which is mostly realised through instrumental accompaniment, song or any other sound from the human body, example, poetic recitation, calls, claps and so on, or electrical devices like the chirping of birds, gurgle of brooks, thunder and so on. Prospective dancers who are visually impaired may respond to the aural rhythm to execute movement. On the other hand, visual rhythm is that which is perceived through the sense of sight with the use of the eyes. It is a patterned repetition or sequential movement and gesture through physical space. Here, the rhythm is inherent in dance movement phrasing and is made manifest on the bodies of the dancers. This way, even the aurally impaired dancer maintains a steady rhythm throughout movement rendition. Both experiences of rhythm are integrated in dance practice. In watching a dance performance, the rhythm of the dancers is in some way transmitted to the bodies in the audience. This makes for a true communication between performers and the audience. The parallels between aural rhythm are very exact to the idea of rhythm in visual form. The difference, here, is that the timed beat is sensed by the eyes (in visual rhythm) rather than the ears.

Rhythm relies largely on elements of pattern and movement to be effective. Visual element can be created in not less than five major techniques. It could be linear, where such rhythm depends on the timed movement of the viewer's eye. Here, the eyes follow a regular arrangement of motifs to create predictability and order in a composition. It could be repetitive, which calls to attention repeated elements through numbers that relate to one another through a regular progression of movements. There is also an exploration in alternation where sequences of motifs are repeated in turns. For example, one could bring into dance, dull or bright, soft or hard movements; short or long duration, fat or thin dancers, light or heavy dynamics and so on. There is gradation which has to do with the employment of a series of patterned motifs and contrast of colour, texture, or shape, size or level. Contrast sets the point of emphasis apart from the rest of its background.

Aural rhythm manifests in musical sound elements like pitch, dynamics, tone colour and duration. Pitch defines what is high and low in aural perception of sound. This is determined by the frequency of its vibration. Dynamics is an element that determines how loud or soft sound is. Loudness relates to the amplitude of the vibration that produces the sound. Tone colour, which is also known as timbre is that element which distinguishes musical instruments. It has to do with the characteristics that will inform one that a particular instrumental sound comes from a drum or a gong, a piano or trumpet. Words like bright, dark, brilliant, mellow and rich are used to describe tone colour. Duration speaks of the length of time which a musical sound lasts. In rhythm, there are in characteristic display four major interrelated manifestations. These are beat, a regular recurrent pulsation that divides sound into equal units of time; meter which presents repeated pattern of strong beat plus one or more weaker ones. It is defined by the organisation of beats into regular groupings. Accent and syncopation are related terms which define the way individual notes are stresses and how they receive special emphasis. A note is emphasised most obviously by being played louder than the notes around it that is by receiving a dynamic accent. On the other hand, when an accented note comes where it is not normally expected and when a weak beat is accented, the effect is syncopation. Tempo is the speed of the beat, the basic pace of the music. A fast tempo is associated with a feeling of energy, drive and excitement while a slow tempo, more often than not, connotes solemnity, a lyrical mood and calmness.

With appropriate training, every dancer will appreciate the rhythmic demands of dance, relatively, considering the type of dance that best fits his physiological, artistic and mental condition. For according to Bakare (2002: 184), "…once a body is available, whether perfect or not perfect, once the body has a good reflex sensory to rhythm, it will be able to dance".

The Body For Dance
As rightly elaborated on, by Bakare (2002: 185-186), the human body, which is the body for the practice of dance is,

>...the outer frame that houses the internal organs of a human. It consists of the upper level of the head and the neck, the lower upper level of the shoulder blade, the arm and the torso, the middle level of the waist, solar plexus and the entire pelvic region, the upper lower level of the thigh and the knee and the lower level of the foot.

With the human body so segmented, one can only imagine the wide varieties and qualities of movements that a dancer could explore at different directions and levels, depending on the type of dance in display. There is no living human person who can be deformed in all the body segments. This means that with each of the segments illustrated above, several movement vocabularies can be developed and performed for the entertainment of the audience.

Dance happens with the human body on display. Without which it will not happen as it is the raw material which is manipulated artistically and coloured with other elements in order to communicate sensibly to the understanding of the audience. On a general note, it is a truism to say that in all manifestations of art, human beings are in focus. Artistic creations are done by humans and are meant for human consumption. This is why the human body is prominent in the actualization of artistic ideals. Dance involves the presence of the body as it is the body that has the first priority in any performance. The body unfolds in dance, in drama, in music, in poetry and in all other aspects of theatre. Being in a vertical position, the body is available for movement, ready to evolve and to adjust to all the shifts of weight as it is open to all metamorphoses. The deformed body does not have a different description or configuration, only an additional description which defines the kind of deformity a particular body has. The spectators, who may comprise of the fit and deformed, readily identify with the performing body or bodies as they, too, each have a body. There is an impression of recognition and strangeness too as the work is more stylised than daily routine. Counsel (2001: 138) puts it succinctly that "the spectator's pleasure is to contemplate himself in this body which always seems to have its own way, free from physical laws, malleable, and capable of shaping and being shaped at will".

The bodies which constitute the audience find pleasure in quoting with their bodies, the presentation of the performers on set and try to decipher the allusive characteristics of performance. As the major instrument of dance, the body sends direct felt messages to the audience and so with their body, the audience perceives the dancers movements. The spectator easily empathises with the physical body going through movement. This is the charm and beauty of live performances.

Dance produces genuine feelings as it does not go beyond the physical body in performance. It is not a reported event but happens in the 'now' before the live audience who are also present in the 'now'. It is therefore this "momentness of dance [that] is one of its most precious gifts" (Turner 1971:20). The human body in dance transcends its traditional and personal limitations and becomes kinetically alive and aware to respond sensitively to the demands of the Choreographer. This 'aliveness' is as a result of the stimulation by different elements of theatre like rhythm which spans through all the arts or dialogue in the case of poetry and drama. Without any means of stimulation, the body cannot react. Beck (1996:61), opines that "the body, if not stimulated by an inspiring impetus does not react with interest. The movements consequently, the expression, are empty because they are empty of meaning".

The body therefore undergoes training in order to extend its ordinary capacities, imagination and intellectual demands. With training, the body attains maturity and flexibility in the arts. It is Duncan's (1996: 160) submission that "the movements of the human body may be beautiful in every stage of development so long as they are in harmony with that stage and degree of maturity which the body has attained". It is the expression of the human body that determines the functional medium of performance.

The human body is involved either as an instrument or an object of representation in all the art forms. Its action rests upon four factors, all of which are integral in performance and makes for efficient presentation. They are the nature of the body as a moving entity, the space in which the body exists and moves, the time in which the movement takes place and the dynamic energies behind the movement.

Conclusion
Body rhythmicity emphasizes training as the basis of professionalism in the dance practice. The dance art brings to the fore, a congeries of bodies with different shapes, sizes, complexion, height, weight, levels of fitness and so on. The bodies manifest in two special groups that must be emphatically present for performance to take place – performers and the audience. The performing bodies have to undergo artistic training to communicate succinctly in the language of dance for the entertainment of the viewing audience. Democratically speaking, every willing body should be put through adequate training in line with the demands of the art and not thrown off as unfit because of certain parts seen to be unfit. Training for dance may even correct certain abnormalities of a dancer's body as reflected in Bakare's (2002: 135) assertion that "…the opportunities some of the deformed people would have had to benefit from the therapeutic effect which dance activities can offer and therefore aid their physiological and mental recovery is denied them as a result of non-involvement in dance. The classification of a fitting or unfitting body for dance is relative, considering the type of dance. A fat body may be unfitting in a dance which speaks of the slim and a slim body will be an unfitting representation in the dance of the fattened maiden. This paper corroborates with Bakare's (2002: 186) submission that

> If choreographers can, therefore, approach composition for the deformed with the same principle of de-emphasizing the limitations and emphasizing the strengths and extend dynamic dexterity instead of contempt and condemnation, to the dancing of the

deformed, the deformed will not only dance but be spectacular at it.

References

Anne, M. (1987) *Lets disco.* (1st Edition). London: Western Publishers.

Appiah, A. (1996) Actors, space, light, painting'. *The twentieth century performance reader.* Michael Huxley and Noel Witts eds. London: Routledge. 21-24.

Bakare, O. (1994) *Rudiments of choreography.* (Part 1). Zaria: space 2000 Publishers.

Bakare, O. (2002) The deformed can also dance: Democratizing the dance practice in a democratized Nigeria. *Theatre and Democracy in Nigeria.* A. Yerima and A. Akinwale Eds. Ibadan: Kraft Books Ltd. 182-189.

Barba, E. (1991) *Theatre anthropology: the secret art of the performer: a dictionary of theatre anthology.* R. Gough Ed. R. Fowler Trans.. London: Routledge

Brady, J.(1983) *The unmaking of a dancer: An unconventional Life.* New York: Pocket Books.

Beck, J. (1996) Acting exercises. *Twentieth century performance reader.* M. Huxley and N. Witts Eds. London: Routledge 61-63.

Counsel, C. and Laurie, W. Eds. 2001. *Performance Analysis: An Introductory Course Book.* Canada: Routledge

Duncan, I. (1996) The Dancer of the Future. *Twentieth Century Performance Reader* ... 157:163.

Hawkins, Alma (1988). *Creation Through Dance.* (Revised ed.) New Jersey: Princeton Books Company Publishers.

Mclntyre, D. (1996). A Twentieth Century African American Groit: Cynthia S'thembile West. *African dance: an artistic, historical, and philosophical inquiry.* K. W. Asante Ed. Trenton: Africa World Press Inc. 131-143

Thomas, H. (1995) *Dance, Modernity and Culture: Explorations in the Sociology of dance.* London: Routledge.

Turner, M. (1971) *New Dance: Approaches to Non-Literal Choreography*. London:
University of Pittsburgh Press.

Ufford-Azorbo, Ifure (2011) Form and Content of Canoe Dance Theatre of Peoples
of The Niger Delta. A Ph. D. Thesis. Department of Theatre Arts, University of Ibadan.

Willis, C. 1996. Tap Dance: Manifestation of the African Aesthetic. *African
dance: an artistic, historical, and philosophical inquiry*. K. W. Asante Ed.
Trenton: Africa World Press Inc. 145-160.

A Synergy of Musical and Theatrical Works as Exemplified in Bakare, Ojo Rasaki's *Once Upon A Tower*
By
Ekong, Grace E., Ph. D. and Udoh, Ukeme A.

Introduction
The blend or juxtaposition of music and word in drama has been an age long practice, from operatic theatre in Western music to African oral literature. For example, in the Ancient Greece, Ferris (1995) claimed that "music, which was included in the general education system, constituted an important part of Greek drama and certain religious rites" (p. 97). To the Greeks, the word music meant "the art of the Muses" (the goddess of all the arts), and had much more general meaning than is ascribed to music today. Whereas, music to the contemporary Africa as Idolor (2007) has observed, "suggests the relationship between music and humanity" and *'humanity* denotes mankind and the characteristics that evolve in the interaction of human beings; and as a study in the performing, creative and liberal arts, it is directed at people and their cultural activities" (p. 13). For instance, indigenous folktales have a synergy with folksongs creating audience participation. A quick elaboration of the principles and blend between music and words in drama reveals Ojo Bakare's portrayal of his utmost desire of a total theatre in Nigeria.

According to Akinwale (1997),
> By total theatre here, we mean a theatre in which Music, Dance and Drama are presented in an interwoven manner, such that each of them is a necessary art within the total ambium of the performance. This in essence shows a situation where the three areas of the performing arts are integral to the production and not one sub-servient or merely a cosmetic aspect of the production (p. 245).

The explanation above summarizes the intentions of Bakare's *Once Upon a Tower*. The use of a musical band placed at a conspicuous location in the stage is very important, while the songs are selected from traditional, contemporary gospel, *kegite/gyration* (palm wine) club, and popular styles. The lyrics of these songs are very apt and portray the thematic occupation of the drama beginning from the prologue to the dirge. Our intention in this paper is to present the songs, their texts or lyrics, and both the textual and structural examination of all the musical items in the play.

Musico-Dramatic Works in Nigeria

According to Omojola (1997), musical practices in traditional Nigerian societies are generally conceived as part of a multi-media experience. The association of music with dance, religious, and social activities in traditional society is a common feature of musical activities in the Nigerian culture. Of the imported European musical forms to Nigeria, those which provide the most effective means for the transmission of the multi-media concept of African music within a contemplative tradition, are the opera, the cantata and the oratorio. The emergence and popularity of religious musicals and consequently the modern folk opera, in the first half of this century in Nigeria, is symptomatic of the Nigerian fascination for combining music with drama. A good number of Nigerian composers have written works which are multi-media in conception. They include Sam Akpabot (*Verba Christi* - an oratorio and *King Jaja of Opoba*- a folk opera), Adam Fiberesima (*Opu-Jaja,* an opera), Meki Nzewi (*Lost finger* - an opera), Ayo Bankole (*Festac Cantata*, a cantata), Okechukwu Ndubuisi (*Vengeance of the Lizards* - an opera) and Bode Omojola (*Ode for a New Morning* - an opera). Of course, this is a musicological purview. In the theatrical perspective, Akinwale (1997) asserts that "in all theatre traditions in the contemporary times, the place of music has become clearly defined. In the indigenous theatre tradition, and the popular theatre tradition, music had been seen to play a prominent role"(p. 254). In his description of popular theatre, Akinwale has observed that popular theatre traditions have made effective use of music; their opening and closing glees contained songs that philosophically touch on the socio-political and economic lives of their huge audience. He went on to stress that

> Music was also used in the productions to comment on a passing action or to announce what to expect next. Such music are both within the context and mood of the play. Their music is thus used to put the audience and the actors in a spiritual experience which both the performers and the audience lives (sic) to remember for a long time (254).

Hence, Bakare's *Once Upon A Tower* is best examined as a popular theatre tradition that is set within the ambience of the literary theatre tradition of educational institutions. *Once Upon a Tower* had its premiere production at the Department of Theatre Arts' studio, University of Uyo, Nigeria on the 15th and 16th January, 2001 respectively.

The Music in Ojo Bakare's *Once Upon A Tower*
The man, Bakare, Ojo Rasaki has been described as the quintessential Choreographer, Theatre Director, Dancer, Playwright, Designer, Songwriter, Instrumentalist, Arts and Culture Administrator, Scholar and Professor of Theatre Aesthetics and Choreography. In this paper, Bakare, Ojo Rasaki is an astute creative writer, whose perceptive prowess has been displayed in the subtle encapsulation of the decaying academic environment in Nigeria. He has, in *Once Upon A Tower* presented an ideal play, intending to achieve the perfect marriage of music, dance, and words in drama. Thus, Bakare, Ojo Rasaki is a songwriter and an astute musician by all creative standards as seen in the examined synergy he has created between music and drama in *Once Upon A Tower*.

Strumpf, Anku, Phwandaphwanda and Mnukwana (2003) have opined that "songs of all types derive their impetus from song-text as it generates melodic interest as well as the aesthetic quality of songs" (p. 132). In *Once Upon a* Tower, Ojo Bakare has written ten songs. They are: *Once Upon a Tower, Asewo Campusi, When Omowaye Dey Convoke, Nemesis, I Love My Provost, Ofin Mose, Block No Man's Way, Teacher, Kiss Me,* and

O Mkpa. The emphasis in this study is on songs and not on the entire elements of music used in the play. This is because songs carry certain ascribed verbal messages and meaning intended in most performances.

It is worthy of note that the study of the structure of music from whatever framework begins with the classification of all aspects of music into five basic categories: *sound, harmony, melody, rhythm,* and *form* - the structural elements. The *sound* of the music in this write-up is limited to the human voices and/or instruments (Band) used. *Harmony* has been completely omitted in our discourse as the songs are presented in melodic patterns only. However, any musical band intending to perform songs in *Once Upon a Tower* may choose to present the songs using simple harmony that are symbolic of the different styles of music in the play. The *melody* of the songs in Bakare's composition includes the prominent melodic lines and their repetition and variation, the range and contour of melodic material, the phrase structure of the melodic lines, the scale basis for melodic materials, and the relationship and relative prominence of the various melodic ideas that appear together in a work. The evaluation on *rhythm* in Bakare's works includes the nature of rhythmic activity, and the tempo markings in the transcription provided. *Form* refers to the larger shape of the composition, thus, the shape of the songs are examined (*cf.* Benward and Saker, 2009, p. 95).

Different Musical Styles in Once Upon A Tower
  i. Highlife Music (*Once Upon a Tower*)
  ii. Afro-beat music (*Teacher*)
  iii. Kegite (Palm Wine) Club Music (*Asewo, When Omowaye Dey Convoke, I Love My Provost*)
  iv. Afro-American Gospel Music (*Ofin Mose!*)
  v. Traditional Folksong (*Mkpa O!*)
  vi. Popular Style (*Nemesis, Kiss Me* (Juju) and *Block No Man's Way!*)

Agu (1999) has identified the main structural forms of African songs to include Solos, Call and Response, Solo and Chorused Refrain, Mixed Structural Form, etc. (p. 15). Bakare has made use of strophic melodies in his songs, with short, repetitive, non-modulatory phrases, which hover around a tonal centre. He has applied extensively the call-and-response pattern (solo and chorus) in his songs, except in few cases where the song is intended for solo performances. The melodies in Bakare's songs are very simple and tuneful with no accidentals, chromatic note and modulation. The songs are presented below as they appear in the play.

Presentation of The Songs
Song 1

Structural Analysis

Key: A major
Tempo: q = 78 (i.e. 78 crotchets per minute)
Scale: Diatonic
Time signature: 4/4
Form: Solo and Chorus
Length: 32 measures

Textual Presentation

Solo: Once upon a tower
            In our country Nigeriana
            The tower upon an ivory
            On a gold on the marble ooo

Chorus: Later but later… the tower on the silver eee
            Later but later the tower on the bronze/x2ce

Solo: Once upon a tower
            The ivory upon the marble
            Na the citadel of learning
            A place for civilization.

Chorus: Small by small the tower

On the stone ee little by little
The tower on the wood/x 2ce

Solo: Once upon a tower
the Ivory upon the gold
e dey shine e dey glitter
a place for the high and mighty.

Chorus: Now but now the tower
in the dust eee now but
now the tower in the mud.
The high and the mighty
they are crawling they are sleeping
area men and women
they are winning they are cheating
The high and the mighty
they are melting like jellies
Area bobos and girls they are flying
they are kicking

Song 2

Asewo

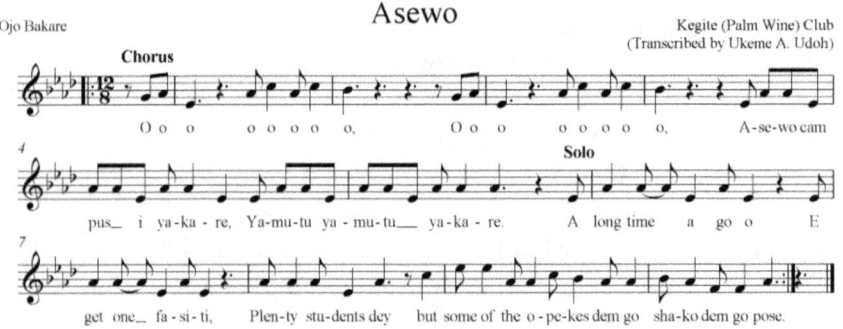

Structural Analysis

Key: A Flat major
Tempo: q = 90 (i.e. 90 crotchets per minute)
Scale: Hexatonic

Time signature: 12/8
Form: Solo and Chorus
Length: 10 measures transcribed

Textual Presentation

Chorus: ooooo   ooooo
           Ooooo   ooooo
           Asewo campusi yakare
           Yamutu yamutu yakare

Solo: A long time ago
           E get one fasiti
           Plenty students dey
           But some of the opekes
           Dem go de shako dem go pose

Chorus: ooooo   ooooo
           Ooooo   ooooo
           Asewo campusi yakare
           Yamutu yamutu yakare

Solo: Some of these Alan posers
           Dem brains na tomatoes
           Na to waka corner corner
           When exam don come dem
           Go do anything to get marks.

Chorus: ooooo   ooooo
           Ooooo   ooooo
           Asewo campusi yakare
           Yamutu yamutu yakare

Solo: Dem go enter this office
           Enter that office
           Dem go use gossip, gossip
           To come cause confusion
           Dem go knock heads together
           Bo ba ye kori e o

	Obatorun mi wo e.
Chorus:	ooooo ooooo
	Ooooo ooooo
	Asewo campusi yakare
	Yamutu yamutu yakare
Solo:	Asewo campusi yakare
Chorus:	Yamutu Yamutu Yakare
Solo:	Asewo campusi yakare
Chorus:	Yamutu Yamutu Yakare

Song 3
When Omowaye Dey Convoke

Ojo Bakare
Kegite/Gyration (Palm Wine) Club
(Transcribed By Ukeme A. Udoh)

Structural Analysis

Key: A major
Tempo: q = 100 (i.e. 100 crotchets per minute)
Scale: Heptatonic
Time signature: 4/4
Form: Solo and Chorus
Length: 16 measures transcribed

Textual Presentation

Chorus: When Omowaye dey convoke
         When Pedro dey do induction
         Mama and Papa happy

Solo:	When Omowaye dey convoke Half education is better than none, Na de philosophy of our universities now Half blindedness dey risky katakata dey for front
Chorus:	When Omowaye dey convoke
Solo:	Government go dey careless Vice Chancellor go turn contractor The council go chop money Senate confusion galore
Chorus:	When Omowaye dey convoke
Solo:	Dean na to play wayo HODs Na politicians Lecturers turn survivalists Students na area bobo.
Chorus:	When Omowaye dey convoke When Pedro dey do induction Mama and Papa happy When Omowaye dey convoke Once upon Ivory Tower Done turn to house of mess Igedegede too dey smell Ee wo palaver dey come.

Song 4
NEMESIS

Ojo Bakare

Ojo Rasaki Bakare
(Transcribed by Ukeme A. Udoh)

Structural Analysis

Key: A major
Tempo: q = 92 (i.e. 92 crotchets per minute)
Scale: Heptatonic
Time signature: 2/4
Form: Solo
Length: 16 measures transcribed

Textual Presentation

Nemesis Nemesis Nemesis
Retributive justice (2ce)
The wickedness of today
will be punished tomorrow
Nemesis, the seed that germinates

Nemesis Nemesis Nemesis
Retributive justice (2ce)
Laziness of today will
Bring poverty tomorrow
Nemesis the seed that germinates

Nemesis Nemesis Nemesis
Retributive justice (2ce)
The corruption of today will
Bring failure tomorrow
Nemesis nothing can stop its growth.

Nemesis Nemesis Nemesis
Retributive justice (2ce)
The envy of today will bring
curses tomorrow
Nemesis the seed that germinates

Song 5
I Love My Provost

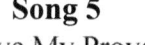

Ojo Bakare   Kegite (Palm Wine) Club
(Transcibed by Ukeme A. Udoh)

Structural Analysis

Key: C major
Tempo: q. = 100 (i.e. 100 dotted crotchets per minute)
Scale: Diatonic
Time signature: 6/8
Form: Solo and Chorus
Length: 64 measures

Textual Presentation
Chorus: I love my Provost
                I no go lie

	Na inside fear
	He dey sleep and wake
	if you good for brain
	E go fear your reign
	Na men like chicken dey be im friend

Solo: E get one man
Na Baba Kukuru
Im name na Provost
Im beards goatee
If you see am for dark…
You go answer Ben Johnson
Because the man E look like demon.

Chorus: I love my Provost etc.
Solo: As the man been brief
Na so Im brain
Na so Im temper
Na so Im heart
Even sef for house
E burn Im Orchard
Because the shade they reach in the neighbourhood

Chorus: I love my Provost etc.

Solo: Im foolishness plenty
Na true I talk o
Im say for d world
Na im be the best
Im talent na to stop
the young from growing
Di man E sick
E need Neuro-surgeon

Song 6
OFIN MOSE

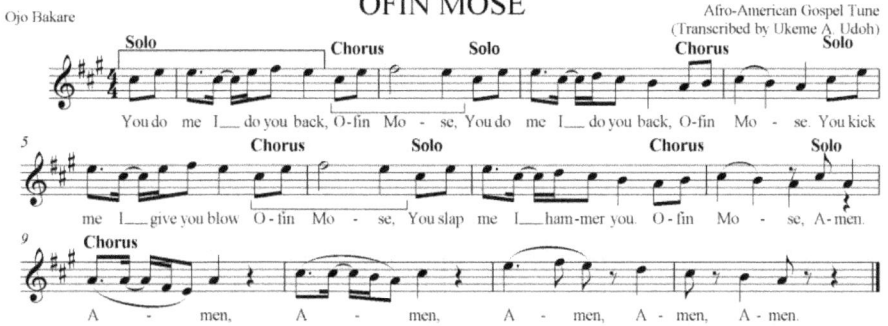

Ojo Bakare — Afro-American Gospel Tune (Transcribed by Ukeme A. Udoh)

Structural Analysis

Key: A major
Tempo: q = 80 (i.e. 80 crotchets per minute)
Scale: Heptatonic
Time signature: 4/4
Form: Solo and Chorus
Length: 12 measures transcribed

Textual Presentation

Solo:	You do me I do you back
Chorus:	Ofin Mose
Solo:	You do me I do you back
Chorus:	Ofin Mose
Solo:	You kick me I give you blow
Chorus:	Ofin Mose
Solo:	You slap me I hammer you
Chorus:	Ofin Mose
Solo:	Amen
Chorus:	Amen, Amen, Amen, Amen, Amen
Solo:	You pinch me I pinch you back
Chorus:	Ofin Mose
Solo:	You bite me I bite you back
Chorus:	Ofin Mose
Solo:	Just spit on me you're drowned in sea
Chorus:	Ofin Mose

Solo:	Use your nails on me and feel my sword
Chorus:	Ofin Mose
Solo:	Amen
Chorus:	Amen, Amen, Amen, Amen,
Solo:	Forgiveness where was it born?
Chorus:	No Idea
Solo:	Forgiveness is foolishness
Chorus:	In your own head
Solo:	Comfort, for me alone
Chorus:	Professor Stupid
Solo:	Amen
Chorus:	Amen, Amen, Amen, Amen.

Song 7
Block No Man's Way

Ojo Bakare

Ojo Rasaki Bakare
(Transcribed by Ukeme A. Udoh)

Structural Analysis

Key: D Flat major
Tempo: q = 85 (i.e. 85 crotchets per minute)
Scale: Diatonic
Time signature: 4/4
Form: Solo and Chorus
Length: 32 measures

Textual Presentation

Solo:
I will never block anybody's way
I will never block anybody's path,
Let them live and let me also live
Let them live and let me also live
That only is my crime,
that only is my crime,
Jehovah mi ooo.

Chorus:
Hear my prayer, Jehovah
Nissi you are my banner
thou knowest I do no evil
You are my witness I seek
Nobody' downfall

	Rock of Ages I hide myself in thee.
Solo:	One day I went to buka
	Over there I met one good friend
	I say friend will you give me love
	After two days the love turned to hatred
	Only Jah gives one true love
	Jehovah mi ooo.
Chorus:	Hear my prayer Jehovah Nissi (etc.)
Solo:	Why is the world filled with evil?
	Why is the heart of man wicked?
	Why will a dog eat a dog?
	Why will a Cain kill an Abel?
	Why will my blood another take?
	Jehovah Lord….

Song 8
Teacher (Teaser)

Ojo Bakare

Afro-Beat Tune of Fela's *Teacher*
(Transcribed by Ukeme A. Udoh)

Structural Analysis

Key: A Flat major
Tempo: q = 68 crotchets per minute
Scale: Diatonic
Time signature: 4/4
Form: Solo and Chorus
Length: 9 measures transcribed

Textual Presentation

Note: Teacher is pronounced "teaser" for chorus section only.

Chorus:	Teacher don messi messi ooo
	Teacher don fumble fumble ooo
	Teacher don messi messi ooo
	Teacher don yab yab ooo.

Solo:	(*Dr. Yemi*) Okay you are ready
Chorus:	Teacher!
Solo:	You are bloody ready
Chorus:	Teacher!
Solo:	In the field of teasing (*teaching*)
Chorus:	Teacher!
Solo:	I be Pedagogy
Chorus:	Teacher!
Solo:	In the file of Shurgery (*surgery*)
Chorus:	Teacher!
Solo:	I be master butser (*butcher*)
Chorus:	Teacher!
Solo:	You get a Pasient (*patient*)
Chorus:	Teacher!
Solo:	With Pelptic Ulcer
Chorus:	Teacher!
Solo:	E swallow codine
Chorus:	Teacher!
Solo:	E swallow pheldine
Chorus:	Teacher!
Solo:	And de Ulcer stubborn
Chorus:	Teacher!
Solo:	Just carry the pacient (*Patient*)
Chorus:	Teacher!
Solo:	And put am for table
Chorus:	Teacher!
Solo:	(*Pick prunner for demonstration*)*!* And Yanka the tommy.
Chorus:	Teacher!
Solo:	The Pacient (*Patient*) go wake
Chorus:	Teacher!
Solo:	And sout (*Shout*) Halleluya
Chorus:	Teacher don messi messi ooo Teacher don fumble fumble ooo Teacher don messi messi ooo Teacher don yab yab ooo.
Solo:	Sometimesh (*sometimes*) ago

Chorus:	Teacher!
Solo:	For a certain shity *(city)*
Chorus:	Teacher!
Solo:	E get one bobo
Chorus:	Teacher!
Solo:	E get one shickness *(sickness)*
Chorus:	Teacher!
Solo:	the shickness im name?
Chorus:	Teacher!
Solo:	Na insect-eye *(greed)*
Chorus:	Teacher!
Solo:	If e see your cow
Chorus:	Teacher!
Solo:	Or e see your ram
Chorus:	Teacher!
Solo:	Na to thief and carry
Chorus:	Teacher!
Solo:	When de people tire
Chorus:	Teacher!
Solo:	Dem send for me
Chorus:	Teacher!
Solo:	To come cure the shickness.
Chorus:	Teacher!
Solo:	As a master shurgeon *(surgeon)*
Chorus:	Teacher!
Solo:	I catch the patient
Chorus:	Teacher!
Solo:	*(Picks the cutlass for demonstration).* And yanka im limbs.
Chorus:	Teacher don messi messi o.
Solo:	Teacher don fumble fumble etc.

Song 9

KISS ME!

Ojo Rasaki Bakare
(Transcribed by Ukeme A. Udoh)

Structural Analysis

Key: C major
Tempo: q = 68 (i.e. 68 crotchets per minute)
Scale: Heptatonic
Time signature: 4/4
Form: Chorus and Section refrain
Length: 24 measures

Textual Presentation

KISS ME
(Taken in chorus)
Kiss me before you go x2
My darling my darling fami
Mora, gbogbo ohun to n se mi wa lara e
Kiss me before you go.
Oh darling sweet, you are the
only one that comforts me I will
never depart with you,

	Dear, Pedro is the name of the boy I love,
	When I kiss his pillow to represent Dear
	When I kiss her picture to represent Darling
	Pedro is the name of the boy I Love.
Refrain:	Eni tan tori e na mi
	ni ng o Pada fe
	Khadijat Oloro mi jojolo ooo.
	Dhadijay majaje n jiya yi pe
	Kiss me Kiss me
Chorus:	Kiss me before you go x2
	My darling my darling
	Fami mora

Song 10
A DIRGE
Mkpa O

Efik/Ibibio Folksong
(Transcribed by Ukeme A. Udoh)

Structural Analysis

Key: A major
Tempo: q = 78 (i.e. 78 crotchets per minute)
Scale: Heptatonic
Time signature: 6/8
Form: Solo or Chorus
Length: 35 measures

Efik/Ibibio	English Translation
Oh! mkpa o x2	Oh, death O (2x)
Oh! mkpa amanam manam o	Death you have done, done, done o
Mkpa amanan ayara re	Death you have beyond revelation
Ewongo edioo ndito eka Iba kesit Ikot 2x	All come out o, two *ekesine* brothers in the forest
Ewongo edioo ndito Eka Iba ete ke enyene	All come out o, children of Same mother, They say that the house owner

Ufok enyene Idang esen	Owns the bed, the visitor
Akama unyong	Holds the departure
Edi se senku Mioo	Come and see what I have seen here

Textual Analysis

Adegoju (2009) presents the opinion that contemporary Nigerian musicians use their lyrics to reflect on happenings in society. As such, they become chroniclers of events, recreating the history and culture of their people, commenting on aspects of societal values that have diverged from historical reports, and suggesting ways by which society could be restored to the normal order. In so doing, the musical social critics cannot but resort to employing the tool of satire to deride the prevalence of social ills in a bid to correct them. This brings to the fore the didactic function of music. Idolor (2002) explains:

> The didactic function of music is affected through logical organisation of lyrics and performance practice. Some lyrics are presented in direct or indirect satire through such speech figures as simile, metaphor, alliteration, allusions, and even short anecdote to convey an observation or/and opinion to a witness-audience. In other situations, other activities in performance teach both viewers and participants the coded lesson(s) (p. 6).

Bakare, Ojo Rasaki as well as other artistes can be seen here as 'town criers' who satirize social foibles in order to make human society and living worthwhile. In fact, this is an important cultural element of developing countries that face extreme social and economic hardship. They make use of several techniques in the presentations like *yabis*. Olatunji (2007) defines *yabis* as 'a biting satirical song that is deliberately composed with the aim of correcting an atrocity, a misdemeanour or sacrilege committed by an individual or a corporate body within a particular society' (p. 27). He notes that this brand of music was pioneered and propagated by the Fela Anikulapo-Kuti who, during his friday night musical show known as Yabis Night, criticized the government for corrupt practices and insensitivity to the suffering of the people. Olatunji points out further that satirical music is not new among many African societies. Thus, Ojo Bakare's adoption of this technique has helped to present his disapproval of the decaying situation in the Nigerian universities.

In a different examination showing the indigenous cultures, Akpabot (1998) has presented five categories of song with non-ritual connotation, they include "songs of social control, philosophical songs, songs of protest, educational songs, and entertainment songs" (p. 74). Songs of social control are designed to regulate good conduct in the society. Philosophical songs are conceived in a style that contributes to the moral and spiritual well-being of a community. Most songwriters make use of proverbs and cryptic references in their songs. Protest songs can be defiant, insolent, scandalous and irreverent depending on the situation of performance. Educational songs are those that teach the community about their historical and cultural past and bring them face-to-face with legends, myths, and symbols associated with their ancestors. Entertainment songs comprise children songs, women's songs, nonsense songs, work songs and cradle songs. Bakare has encapsulated all the five categories in his ten songs presented above. The last song in Bakare's play is a dirge (a slow song that expresses sadness or sorrow). He has explained that the play ends in death but that it is not a tragedy. He comments, "The dead characters deserve what they have got and the society can (sic) breath a little better. Without being sentimental the play has muted punishment to whom it is due" (Bakare, 2000, vi)

A Socio-Linguistic Study of Bakare's Song-texts in *Once Upon A Tower*

Oyeleye (2007) in Ayodeji (n.d.) asserts that it is always interesting studying the relationship between language and the society. This is interesting because it is always rewarding to look at the obvious relations between language and the situations within which we use it. In *Once Upon A Tower*, Bakare has

created a peculiar ambiance typical of a Nigerian university environment through language. The sociolinguistic studies available in these dramatic songs include:
(a) The Nigerian English (Pidgin)
(b) Efik/Ibibio Language in *Mkpa O!*
(c) Yoruba Language in Kiss Me!
(d) English Language, and
(e) Kegite/Gyration (Plam Wine) Club Language.

We are interested here in explaining the esoteric nature of the Kegite language because it is the most coded in all the sociolinguistic languages listed above. Ayodeji (n.d.) explains that the Kegites Club or the Palm wine Drinkers Club is the most popular socio-cultural group in the Nigerian tertiary institutions. It is very difficult to classify the Kegites language as indigenous. This is because the languages are clipped and borrowed from English, French, Yoruba, Hausa, and Igbo. There are some words that one cannot really classify as belonging any language. The Kegite language also permits and parades a great deal of code-mixing and code-switching and yet, communication is achieved because the language users make use of non-verbal communication cues while 'vibrating'. For example, Bakare's *Asewo* (song 2) has demonstrated the many-sided nature of Kegite/Gyration songs. A word like *Okpeke* from South-South Nigeria is literary translated as – *ready for tapping*) or just a coincidental coinage to represent females. While *Okpekerization* includes the addition of a suffix -*rization*, derived from English meaning a man having an intimate affair with a woman. Then, if the woman (*Okpeke*) is pregnant, then holy water (palm wine) has filled her belly.

Challenges of Musical Documentation in Nigeria
A major challenge to assessing the development of the musical arts of Nigeria has been poor documentation, where there are presentations of musical ideas in text or lyric format without any form of transcription or notation. African and Nigerian musicologists have, over the years, continued to seek ways of creating a historical relationship between the music of the present and the oral music of the past. Such efforts have not yielded

much effort, as the songs of the past (orally transmitted) have in most cases been presented without any form of notation or transcription. Thus, the songs presented in this paper were collected through interviews conducted by the authors with Sunday Umanah who acted as Senator Emeka Ekwelem in the premiere presentation. Also, Ifure Ufford-Azorbo of the Department of Theatre Arts, University of Uyo, Nigeria was interviewed, and she helped in the confirmation of tunes provided by Sunday Umanah. The songs were recorded and the transcriptions thereof are provided in this paper.

Conclusion
This paper has examined the synergy between musical and theatrical works in Nigeria using Bakare, Ojo Rasaki's *Once Upon A Tower*. Emphasis in the examination has been laid on the songs and the song-texts. Ten songs were examined in the study. These songs have been transcribed and a summary of the textual analysis also presented. This study recommends cooperation between music composers and Playwrights as well as the directors of Nigerian theatre. The Playwrights can write lyrics or poetry and let the composers of music find suitable melodies for the lyrics. The paper also recommends a presentation of total theatre in theatrical works, where songs, dances, and words in drama are presented together. There is also the need for a joint collaboration between musical and theatrical experts through conferences, workshops, and symposium that are jointly organized by both practitioners. Finally, contemporary Nigerian society is in dire need of works like Bakare's *Once Upon A Tower,* which encapsulates a total theatrical experience.

References

Adegoju, A. (2009). The Musician as Activist: An Example of Nigeria's Lagbaja. In *Itupale Online Journal of African Studies,* Vol. 1: 1-23.

Afolabi, O. A. (n.d.) A Sociolinguistics Study of the Kegites (Palm Wine Drinkers Club) language. At www.bukisa.com *An online paper.* Retrieved on 2[6th] July, 2014.

Agu, D. C. C. (1999). *Form and Analysis of African Music.* Enugu: New Generation Books.

Akinwale, A. (1997). Music and the Nigerian Theatre – The New Social Dynamics. In Bode Omolola (ed.) *Music and Social Dynamics in Nigeria.* Illorin: Department of Performing Arts, University of Ilorin, Nigeria, pp. 245 – 258.

Akpabot, S. E. (1998). *Form, Function and Style in African Music.* Ibadan: Macmillan Nigerian Publishers Limited.

Bakare, O. R. (1999). *The Artiste-Intellectual: Sonny Oti on Stage.* Ibadan-Nigeria: Jofel Books.

Bakare, O. R. (2000). *Once Upon a Tower (A Play).* Uyo: Afahaide Publishing Company.

Ferris, J. (1997). *Music: The Art of Listening.* U.S.A.: Bown & Benchmark Publishers Ltd.

Idolor, E. (2007). Music in the Contemporary African Society. *Journal of Social Science,* 14 (1): 13-18.

Olatunji, M. O. (2007). Yabis: A Phenomenon in the Contemporary Nigerian Music. *The Journal of Pan African Studies,* Vol. 1 No. 9, 26 – 46.

Omojola, 'Bode (1997). Compositional Style and National Identity in Nigerian Art Music. In Bode Omolola (ed.) *Music and Social Dynamics in Nigeria.* Illorin: Department of Performing Arts, University of Ilorin, Nigeria, pp. 209 – 219.

Strumpf, M., Anku, W., Phwandaphwanda, K., and Mnukwana, N. (2003). Oral Composition. In Anri Herbst, Meki Nzewi and Kofi Agawu (Eds.) *Musical Arts in Africa –Theory and Practice.* Pretoria: UNISA Press, University of South Africa, pp. 118 – 141.

Functionality of Music And Dance in Bakare, Ojo Rasaki's *The Gods And The Scavengers*

By
Ufford-Azorbo, Ifure Ph.D and Azorbo Tam Gordon, Ph.D.

Introduction
Most dramatic works of literature and performance from the Nigerian setting have an ancient history of being coloured with music and dance. It is the tradition of most Nigerian cultures to elaborate on the entertainment values of storytelling using these spectacular arts of the theatre. Music could succinctly be defined as an audible art of time for expression of emotion, group sentiments and concerns of a people either for entertainment, protest, ritual and other celebrations. Nwadigwe describes this phenomenon as "the harmonious composition or presentation of sounds in a…. rhythmic sequence to entertain or communicate" (2002:205). Music could, therefore, be seen as that which is produced by audible movements that act as accompaniment to dance which is manifested through visual movement. Music is extremely elusive. It has an abstract and formal character and is like other arts, a social phenomenon as it functions in all aspects of life as a social commentary. Music is a stimulant for dance because "it accompanies and efficiently supports dance "(Ufford, 2004:21). The correlation between music and dance is that the two arts share the organising or unfolding of events in time.

Zallman sees dance and music as a combination done because of the "demands of artistic usage if not inevitability" (1971:71). This also re-establishes the fact that dance happens with some form of music in its enactment. Possibly, this informs Umukoro's submission that
> Dance and music are twin arts of the theatre…although it is generally claimed that dance is the oldest art of the theatre, it is inconceivable that it could have developed entirely independent on some form of rudimentary music, if only by way of rhythmic pattern of feet, the clapping of hands…in all

> probability, dance and music evolved simultaneously as complementary arts. Dance is the visual translation of music, while music is the aural translation of dance...both are transient and ephemeral; but while music exists only in time, dance exists in both time and space (2002:72).

Jones in corroboration with Umukoro opines that "dancing is the principal way in which musical pleasures become realised in physical movement and in bodily grounded aesthetics" (Willis et al, 1990:65). The most fruitful relationship is often one in which an element of collaboration exists between composer and choreographer; it all depends on the basic medium of expression. There are no set rules regarding this collaborative manifestation. To Langer, "whether a dance is accompanied by music or not, it always moves in musical time. The recognition of this natural relation between the two arts underlies their universal affinity (1953:198). For Limon, he hears "music with the muscles and bones and blood and nerves: in short, with all the human facilities for movement" and so music is woven inextricably into his fibre (1978:189 – 190).

> Therefore, "the categories of music and dance must be discarded when entering a discussion about African culture" (Asante, 1996:2007). The drum talks to the dancer and the dancer talks back to the drum in the body as a result music moves "like the sound of the drum in the dancer's body" (McIntyre, 1996:131). Nicholls observes that "African dance is conterminous with the music that accompanies it and the visual art that embellishes it" (1996:157).

For Kinni-Olusanyi (1996:29) "the dance to drum (and other percussion) is a potent and vitalising element of African culture...drumming and dancing are almost synonymous projections as ardent, driving rhythms, pungent complexities of form and consonant, articulate expression". Though there are many distinctions and separations to be used in the presentation of music and dance, those distinctions are internal and interrelated within the entity as opposed to outside of it. Both impact on each other. The play has a prologue and a total of nine movements

Prologue of the Play
Music style is a song rendered by two singers, on taking the lead and the other playing chorus. It takes after the style of music which utilises a call and response. This is a major characteristic of the African music genre. The song which is a projection of the theme of the play that of revolt pre-empts what is to be seen later in the play. The music goes steadily and then goes into a persuasive, frustrating wailing manner to emphasise the urgency of the revolt for attainment of freedom. The song in this play which speaks of dawn of a new morning is used as opening glee for the revelation of the circumstances in the play. The song is also rendered in an operatic style as the chorus is a comment of agreement on the initial speech-song of the lead.

Movement 1 (A Refuse Dump)
Song at refuse dump. This song speaks of the miserable state of the scavengers. This has rhyming lyrics which are rendered in a specified time to a beat. Here Bakare uses rhymes
>We are the scavengers, we the <u>main men</u>.
>When those rogues eat their <u>beans,</u>
>we comb their <u>bins.</u>
>They <u>cheat</u>, we <u>lift</u> their <u>shit</u>.
>We are the scavengers, we the <u>main men</u> (1-2)

This music serves as a definitional model for roles. This is so because the music is utilised by the playwright to demonstrate, summarise and establish characteristic traits of the Scavengers.

The second song serves as the dialogue of the Scavengers. Here, the lines of the Scavengers are rendered in a sing-song chant which is called Rap. This rap occupies a gray area between speech, prose, poetry, and singing. It is a rhythmic style of chanting. This music is often seen as that of revolt associated with the people seen to be societal dregs of the low class who are always clamouring for change and complaining of oppression.

This is very functional in relation to the characters of the Scavengers.

The song-dialogue rendition acts as a commentary on the qualifications of the scavengers. They communicate the fact that they are qualified professionals in their different fields of endeavour but are suffering from societal malfunctioning. We see a teacher, a doctor, farmer and technician in action.

In this Movement, the first dance is initiated and is functional as ritual. This is done by Scavenger 5. The description of costume given in the script is suggestive of the kind of dance it is.

> ...costumed in a long white robe. Her right hand clutches a cross while a large Islamic chesbi adorns her left hand. On her head is a black cap decorated with beads, charms, cowries and assorted shells. She dances towards other Scavengers in ritual posture (2006:3).

Again, the songs which accompany the dance reflects the ritual situation. This is enunciated through such wordings like, "Osun de e olomo...", "we are the Scavengers...", "song of forgiveness" and a mimickry of the second verse of the Nigerian National Anthem. This last song brings to mind the real words and suggests through the situation of the Scavengers how futile and meaningless they are.

Movement 2 (Market Place)

The song used in this movement is functional in the introduction of the characters present in this scene. They come from different cultural settings which make up Nigeria. They also employ the use of their traditional dances to emphasise their heritage. We recognise in this movement, the Hausa, Ibibio, Igbo and Yoruba people through their songs rendered in their different languages and their peculiar dance steps. The situation in this movement is a market and the people gathered captures a true market situation where you find people from different backgrounds assembled. Again, in Nigeria, the Igbo people are well known for their enterprise in business. This possibly explains why the song used to welcome the Chairman is rendered in Igbo language. At the end of the Chairman's speech, giving the people some hope of freedom even when it is just a smokescreen to further deceive the people, they send off the Chairman from the market with a Yoruba song of praise. Here, the Yoruba setting of praise singing is realised. We see it in experiences of their having praise singers attend to dignitaries during important occasions. The song, " tanilawaoni baba…" is thus functional in capturing the true picture of that scene in the light of natural experiences.

Against the Chairman's promises and reassurances, Mallam tramples on Hadiza for not paying tributes to him. Hadiza then raises the song " inazamuje…" (15) with others singing in their own dialect to reflect their state of hopelessness and lack of faith in their leaders. This angers Iyaloja who snaps them out of that state with the song, "we no go gree…" (17). With one voice, they sing and are poised up to seek redress. On page 23, we have the song repeated at the meeting. This war song acts as a commentary on the situation of the citizens. After the councillors have tried to calm the citizens, they swing into a song\chant form of rendition in the Yoruba language to mock the councillors and state their resolve to stone the councillors who disturb them by extorting their monies.

In this movement, Bakare succinctly captures the cultural environment and setting of the play through the use of music and dance to synthesise, project and propel cultural themes from the Nigerian environment. Movements Three and Four (Conference Room and Outside the Conference Room) have no songs and dances but enhance the understanding of Movement Five (Desert). The song in this Movement, on page 33 is a Yoruba song of agony as the Scavengers are left in the desert land with nothing to fall back on. On page 34, Scavenger 2 sings:

> Chant: sometimes I feel like the motherless child 3xs
> Chorus: a long way from home, a long long way from home.

Scavenger 5 and the Orchestra sing a song of hope as there are crumbs to munch where they had nothing.

Movement 6 (Bush Path)
Music in this movement takes a different turn as there is an instrumental music running at the background. After this comes two songs. The first reflects the Igbo girl who is killed by the gunman and the second girl in frustration. As the corpse of the first girl is carried out, there is a dirge that accompanies this action. The music here possesses an anticipatory import through a suggestion on the nature of dramatic activity, giving clue to what the reader should expect. The change to instrumental music accompanying mime creates dramatic tension. This movement reveals through the aid of music, the major conflict in the play between the ethnic groups. The dirge emphasises the mood herein as it defines and sustains the dramatic action.

Movement 7 (Anago's Shrine)
Here, Yemoja dances in accompanied by six beautiful maidens. Ritual song and music are functional here to represent the mood of presentation as Yemoja magically opens the locked cellgate, unchains Anago's hand and places a crown on his head. Music becomes louder and they dance off with their ritual movements. At Anago's freedom, song and music changes with increased intensity (43). There is a presentation of a full mime and dance in this movement done by the Chief Hunter who feeds fat to the detriment of the people. There is also a dance of romance as the Chief Hunter lusts after the alluring beauty of Yemoja and ends up being swept away. This narrative piece summarises the full text of the play even as it furthers the plot of the main play. The dance here functions as a commentary on the situation of the play. Everything here happens in the extra-mundane realm, a suggestion on what is to be physically.

Movement 8 (Desert)
This movement again brings in the familiar song of the Scavengers which speaks of their hopeless state but this time, Andy has a song for his story which conscientises the Scavengers

on the need to rise up and fight for their freedom and not wait for the gods. Here, Bakare re-writes Odewale'sexperience in Ola Rotimi's *The Gods are not to Blame*. Odewale is not to blame but the gods. The Scavengers now rise with a resolve to overcome their travails with the song, "We must overcome ..." (56). This is a cardinal song in the play as it proposes a turning point in the hopeless situation, the Scavengers found themselves. The songs here are used to realise the conflict situations in the play and resolutions elucidated.

Movement 9 (Market Place)
This is the last movement of the play where the issues are resolved. At the peak of lawlessness with killings and maiming, the Scavengers enter with their corrupt leaders who they have arrested. They conscientise the people on the need to be united for development and the need to punish their corrupt leaders. Here, the crowd begins to sing in one voice "yes its dawn of a new morning..." (63) in affirmation of their resolve to do a fresh start and taking their destinies into their hands. This song facilitates the realization of a climax in the play under study and functions in this movement as the closing glee.

Conclusion
This paper has attempted to delineate the functions of music and dance in Bakare's The *Gods and The Scavengers*. It has discovered that music and dance carry the correct mood of the play in relation to the different situations enunciated and in consideration of the playwrights experience and style. They function emphatically in the development of the plot as audible and visual dramatic extensions, comment on important events and the revelation of the locale. They play presents a very rich communicational technique through the use of music and dance in an exemplification of various themes like socio-religious, socio-political and socio-economic concerns of the people. The writers hope that this modest contribution to the analysis of musical and dance functions in drama will provide a spring-board for further postulations.

References

Asante, K. W. (1996) The Zimbabwean dance aesthetics: senses, canons and characteristics. *African dance: anartistic, and philosophical inquiry*... 203-220.

Bakare, O. R. (2006)*The Gods & The Scavengers.* Abuja: Roots Books & Journals Nigeria Limited.

Kinni-Olusanyin, E. (1996) Panoply of African Dance Dynamics.*African dance* ... 29:38.

Langer, S. (1953) *Feeling and Form: A Theory of Art*. New York: Scribners.

Limon J. (1978) Music is the Strongest Ally to a Dancer's way of Life. *TheDance Experience* ... 189-196.

Mclntyre, D. (1996) A Twentieth Century African AmericanGroit: Cynthia S'thembile West. *African Dance* ... 131-143.

Nicholls, R. W. (1996) African Dance: Transition and Continuity.*African Dance* ... 41-62.

Nwadigwe, C. (2002) The Piper and the Tune: The Dynamics of Popular Music in Nigeria. *Theatre and Democracy inNigeria.* Ahmed Yerima and Ayo Akinwale (eds). Ibadan: Kraft BooksLtd. 205-213.

Ufford, I. I. (2004) Interrogating the Past and Forging New Identities: A Study of Ndem Dance Theatre of the Efik People.An M.A. Dissertation, Department of Theatre Arts, University of Ibadan.

Ufford-Azorbo, I. (2011) Form and Content of Canoe Dance Theatre of the Peoples of the Niger Delta. A Ph.D Thesis, Department of Theatre Arts, University of Ibadan.

Umukoro, M. M. (2002) *Drama and Theatre in Nigeria Schools: A Blue Print of Educational Drama and Theatre.* Ibadan: Caltop Publishers.

Willis, P. (With Jones, S.; Canaan J. and Hurd, G. (1990) *Common Culture* (1st Edition). Milton Keyness: Open University Press.

Zallman, A.(1971) Music and Dance. *New Dance: Approaches to Non-Literal Choreography.* M. Turner Ed.. London: University of Pittsburg Press, 71-75.

The Choreographer as a Teacher: Analyzing Ojo-Bakare's Impartation Method
By
Onyemuchara, Casmir E.

Introduction

The history and origin of dance in Nigeria dates back to pre-historic times. It has been a way of life of the people because there is no activity that is marked without one form of dance or the other - child birth, puberty rites, initiation into different social and ritual positions, achievements, installations and death. Even when these dances are performed, they are stylized and patterned for aesthetic purpose and to communicate or pass an idea. Although it is difficult to ascertain/ account for the creators of these dances which today are owned by different communities and societies, the fact still remains that the movement and patterns were arranged by somebody or a group of persons. The dances were either learnt from neighbouring villages or created from myths and legends of the land. This group of people can be regarded here as residual choreographers or Dance masters who are choreographers in their own rights. As Bakare succinctly puts it, if choreography is the creation and designing of bodily movements to rhythm in time and space to make statements then the creators and designers of the various traditional/ ethnic dances in Nigeria were and continue to be choreographers in their own rights (66) Writing further, he affirms that choreography is not new in Africa (Nigeria inclusive) but that what is new is modern choreography where the "choreographer is engaged in the business of making personal statements in accordance with the social, theatrical and aesthetic demands of his contemporary audience (66).

Today, dance has grown from simple to complex movements with its attendant challenges in the area of arrangement and design to make statements. Moreso, it is no longer an exclusive preserve of communities and societies that own it and does not only end up in the village squares, shrines and so on. Dance has taken a different dimension both in practice and pedagogy and requires creative minds and intellectual might.

Modernization and globalization have contributed in no small measure to the growth of varied forms of dance in Nigeria, these include; African contemporary dance, creative or dance theatre, salsa, walza, hip hop, folk dances to mention but a few. Again, dances are no longer performed just for the entertainment sake but themes and topical issues are addressed through dance medium which is a non-verbal communication.

To achieve the above mentioned requires expertise, hence the attention of a choreographer. Someone with great compositional use of organic unity, rhythmic or non-rhythmic articulation, theme and variation, and repetition.(www.en.m.wikipedia...), to actualize the desired result effectively and efficiently.

In this paper, effort will be made to explain in detail, the meaning of some key words in the context for which they were used. These will include, choreographer, teacher and impartation. Bakare's model of teaching dance will be highlighted through some selected dance projects (production) which this writer had participated in to buttress our point for choosing impartation method as a veritable model of passing knowledge because of its effectiveness and efficacy.

Conceptual Definition of Terms
Choreographer
Dance, generally speaking, is a creative venture. Like music, drama and any other performative art, it relies on the creative ingenuity of people and accomplished in bodily movements and gestures. These movements and gestures do not just happen, they are usually composed and arranged. The person charged with this responsibility is called choreographer. Simply put, a choreographer is one charged with the responsibility of putting movements and gestures together to form a dance. According to the online dictionary, a choreographer is "a person who creates dance compositions and plans and arranges dance movements

and patterns for dance" The oxford dictionary of dance defined a choreographer as one who makes dances. The person responsible for creating and arranging the steps and pattern of a dance work (104).

It is worthy of note here that choreography, which on its own is an art, is a contemporary concept and only appeared in the American English dictionary in the 1950s and the word "choreographer" "was first used as a credit for George Balanchine in the Broadway show *On Your Toes* in 1936" (en.m.wikipedia.org).

The word choreography is derived from two Greek words choreo and grapher meaning dance and writing. Hence choreography in the 19th and 20th centuries is seen as the art of creating and arranging dances. Prior to this time, in the 17th and 18th centuries it meant the written record of dances but the emergence of dance notation has significantly changed this view. Ugolo 1998, quoted in Iyeh assert to this when she writes that:
> Choreography involve the composition of dances, the structuring and arrangement of movements, writing of dance scripts and dance notation (137).

Choreography and or choreographer have become a universally accepted concept among scholars and practitioners of dance art today.

Teacher
A teacher is one who teaches in a bid to pass on knowledge especially in a school. The mastery of the `subject matter is a pre-requisite of a good teacher. Usually organized and articulate in his/her approach to impart knowledge to others. A teacher is a demonstrator who uses creative skills to make understanding easy, effective and efficient. According to Longman Active Study Dictionary 5th Edition, to Teach means "to teach or show someone how to do something" (918). A noble profession that leaves people under the watchful eyes or guidance of somebody. Teaching involves active participation between the teacher and the learner. It is learner friendly because the teacher tries the best

possible ways of imparting knowledge to the learners. The teaching method is also universally accepted best approach in education unlike the lecture method which gives the learner little or no opportunity to participate actively during learning. It is the clear opposite of teaching method in the sense that, it is the teacher that lectures without allowing the learners/student to contribute. An approach that is non-participatory and makes the atmosphere of learning boring. This is referred to as the improvisational method in choreography.

Impartation
Impartation is the art of sharing and communicating knowledge. It connotes giving part of what you have to someone in terms of knowledge, ideas and legacies. To impart means to give quality information to someone or somebody. There is an intimate relationship during the period of impartation because the person imparting the information or knowledge takes his or her time to bequeath or bestow the knowledge to the person(s) involved. In most cases, this could take rigorous practical examples.

The Choreographer as a Teacher

> The choreographer should be a good teacher. He should acquire the techniques of imparting knowledge. He should device a simple way of putting across what he wants the dancers to do (Bakare, 55)

The above submission by Bakare is a clear indication that a choreographer is indeed a teacher. The creative abilities of the choreographer enable the dancers to comprehend movements and gestures easily. Using his body as the instructional material, the choreographer performs and/or exhibits the movement and gestures that he wishes to pass down to his dancers. He does not seat to watch them make mistakes or wallow in ignorance, he brings to bear his creative ingenuities and skills to perfect the dance. He displays his wealthy of experience and mastery of movements to his /her dancers who he sees as his students. This

invariably earns him/her respect among the dancers. Bakare is in agreement with this ascertion when he echoed that:
> Though, the choreographer may not be a fantastic dancer himself, he still needs to be above waters in the art of dancing because if he is a dancer himself, it makes his job easier (54).

Bakare's words above affirm the fact that a sound knowledge of dance art is a prerequisite if one must assume the office of a choreographer. His continuous hunger and quest to improve himself through training, good observation and research becomes imperative in his/her chosen career. As a teacher, a choreographer is responsible and accountable to his dancers (students) by way of giving them directions, studying their psychologies, taking care of their welfares and motivating them if he/she must achieve his or her desired result. This indeed is lacking among most Nigerian contemporary choreographers who only see themselves as gods that must be honoured. The inabilities to study the learning capabilities of their dancers is a big challenge to them, the dancers and dance art in general. As a teacher, the choreographer must know that there are slow learners and fast learners. The slow learners must be carried along to avoid frustration and giving-up their talents. The ideal thing is to be patient with them, encourage them, praise them where necessary to boost their moral.

The choreographer must as a matter of fact make him/her rehearsal session a lively one. Dancers (students) do not learn well in a tensed condition. However he/she should draw a line between when there is seriousness and when there is fun or play. A combination of these makes an ideal scenario. The choreographer in essence is the life wire of dance, which means, a good dance production is dependent upon the creative abilities of a choreographer. He/she analyses, composes and arranges the movements and gestures to the delight of his/her audience by communicating an idea or message. Arnold Udoka quoted in Bakare opines that "a choreographer needs special intellectual qualities, a quick study with intelligence, artistic humility and aesthetic judgment" (57). Bakare attests to this when he writes that a choreographer's "role as a story creator, an imaginative thinker, a transformer, a model, a designer, a teacher, a manager, a critic, and a coordinator require him to be inclined to analysis (56).

Analyzing the Impartation Method of Ojo Bakare

Ojo Bakare is a household name in the performance industry generally and dance in particular. Apart from being a teacher in school, he has been a consultant to many Arts Councils in Nigeria and beyond serving in different capacities as dance teacher, choreographer, Director, and many more. His works in Gambia and Jamaica are landmarks of his dance exploit which till date are used as reference points in those countries. In Nigeria, Ojo Bakare's dance projects speak for themselves because they are master pieces. This section analyses his impartation method by x-raying his approach and methodologies which will also enable the study to arrive at the reason why his model in dance teaching and choreographies is an ideal approach to dance.

There are two basic choreographic methods adopted by choreographers in teaching and choreographing dances. These include;

    (1)   The improvisation method
    (2)   Planned choreography

Improvisation method

The improvisation method of choreography involves the dancers directly. In this method, the choreographer gives instruction about an idea, sequence or motif and allows the dancers (students) to grapple with it. Wikipedia online captures this when it writes that "improvisational scores typically offer wide latitude for personal interpretation by the dancer" (en.m.wikipedia.org).We can relate the scores here to the information passed on to the dancer(s) by the choreographer during the process of dance creation. In most cases, the dancer's imaginative thinking and creativity becomes the materials -

movements and steps, which he (choreographer) arranges or puts together.

In big and/or commissioned projects that require a handful of artistes (dancers), Ojo Bakare only introduces this method during the first two days of rehearsal to keep the dancers 'on their toes'; awaken their creative instincts.

During this period, he narrates the story and divides the dancers into Segments to work out movements and ideas. The voyage, a dance drama production commissioned by the Federal Ministry of Information and National Orientation in 2006 is a point of experience here. Using what the writer calls the pouching method of selection, he (Bakare) assembled great dancers across the length and breadth of the federation to execute this project tagged "The Heart of Africa Project." This project was toured the world starting from United Kingdom in order to reconstruct the Nigeria's battered image abroad. Poaching here implies a selection method where the Choreographer knows where to pick an artiste for a particular role and knowing his/her abilities without calling for an audition.

The improvisational is quickly discarded by Bakare as his rehearsals progress because he says the method usually impede the speed at which the desired result can be achieved. This, according to him, is because, the choreographer is reliance on the dancers and his continuous directive without practical examples is a major challenge. The improvisational method is usually used by "Arm Chair" Choreographers. Arm chair meaning, seating at a place to give or dish out information and directives.

Planned Choreography
The planned choreography is regarded as a direct teaching method in choreography. The Choreographer here is fully in charge of the dance in terms of movement creation, gestures and arrangements. He dictates motion and form in detail, leaving little or no opportunity for the dancers to exercise/express personal interpretation. This method is holistically adopted by Ojo Bakare

in his Choreographic works. Here, Bakare turns his dancers into students and assumes the office or position of a teacher. He performs/displays the movement and interprets same to the students (dancers). This can be seen in most of his works during the National Festival of Arts and Culture competition packages in Nigeria, hence the avalanche of his dance assembles or choreographies in most state Arts councils which have become part of their repertoires till date. The planned choreography method has been adjudged as an efficient model in choreography because of its direct approach. @Smallbizperson assert to this when she opines that; The best way to teach dance is demonstration and repetition (answers.yahoo.com).

In large group which is usually the case in most of his dance projects, Ojo Bakare divides the dancers into segments to enable him teach the movement and see or monitor the dancers well or clearly. The National Sports Festival tagged "Abuja 2004" is also a case in point here. At his disposal was a huge number of dance artistes, about one thousand two hundred in number. His ability to impart his ideas, concepts and movements to them when creating the dances is unimaginable. This takes him into several hours of rehearsals which he also achieves through his camping technique. He brings his dancers into a camp where they can be monitored in terms of food, hygen, discipline and above all accessed. Although planned choreography as adopted by Ojo Bakare is effective and makes impartation easy, it is enormous, tiresome and may hamper speed at which result can be achieved. Impartation, which is a core teaching method -learning by examples is teacher/student oriented. This is because the dancers (students) pay good attention and concentrate to pick the technique and observe the shape of the instructor/teacher (choreographer).

Ojo Bakare and the Choice of Impartation Method
Human nature is characterized by choice. This choice whether positive or negative is usually necessitated by ones background. Ojo Bakare is no exemption to this fact. His rise to stardom is traceable to his decision and choice to be an artiste (dancer). May

be a cursory look at how he started, will enable us treat this section and arrive at why he chose the impartation method in choreography.

First, Bakare refused to bow to parental influence in career choice. He followed his instinct against all odds even when he was told to his face that he has been disowned by his own father. At a tender age of seventeen, young Bakare left home without telling anybody his where about, only to join Jimoh Aliu cultural group of Nigeria in Ado Ekiti 1981. He later moved and became an apprentice under the tutelage of chief Hurbert Ogunde, the man described today as the doyen of professional dance and theatre in Nigeria. His hunger for education and in theatre endeared him a recommendation from Ogunde himself that helped him to secure admission into the department of theatre arts of University of Calabar even with National Certificate in Education (NCE) for a direct entry course.

Arnold Udoka was another impact factor in Bakare's dance career having taught him in the university as a dance major of Calabar and later was employed by the university to teach dance upon graduation. Between 1985 and 1996, Bakare was the choreographer of the old Ondo State Council for Arts and Culture. The list of his artistic exploits and endeavours is endless. From the above brief background it is possible to deduce where Bakare is coming from. First, he is a teacher by training having acquired the National Certificate in Education (NCE) he knows various teaching methods and skills, how they can be used and applied.

Secondly Bakare is a trained and practicing dancer and actor having performed with Jimoh Aliu, Hubert Ogunde and Ondo state council for Arts and Culture till date. Bakare apart from being a scholar of note, has in his kitty, 33 years of dance and theatre practice experience. Bakare's background has made it impossible for him to separate dance teaching from choreography. Although these two can be separated and handled by different individuals, they can also be handled by one individual depending on his or her dance proficiency. This has informed his (Bakare) choice of choreographic method and technique called impartation. Dancers own movements are better informed after seeing some one else perform. This means that having dancers (students) sit and watch you demonstrate a full phrase may actually help their muscle pick up choreography more efficiently (Julia, 2). It is also deducible that Bakare is practically oriented, a situation that makes his impartation method realizeable and effective.

In a chart with this dance maestro, he revealed that it is impossible for him to be on seat and watch his rehearsal without climbing the stage especially when there is something new to teach his dancers. According to him (Bakare) the instinct is just spontaneous. One understands the correlation between his experience and training and his choice of teaching method called impartation.

Conclusion
In conclusion, the essence of choreography is to make or create body movements to rhythm; in time and space to make statements (Bakare, 66). The choreographer who is charged with this responsibility has the right to choose the best method that can serve him/her effectively. It is a fact from this study that Bakare is choice of impartation which involves direct teaching method is informed by his background and experience. In a general sense therefore, it is safe to state that the background and orientation of an individual affects the way he/she see things or put in a different way affects his/her life philosophy. From this study of Ojo Bakare's journey through life in dance and theatre practice and being privileged to work with him in several dance projects, one can ascert that Bakare employs the impartation method to achieve the following: to
1. Impart on his dancers the right technique and movement coordination.
2. Imbue Self confidence among the dancers .
3. Learn by watching and practicing.
4. Build a good sense of body usage and attitude.

5. Demystify choreography /choreographer. And
6. Build in the dancers a sense of humility.

Conclusively it is the opinion of the writer that the two choreographic methods be applied in teaching dances and/or choreographies. This is because, both of them (Improvisation and planned choreography) give and accommodate different learners and give them the sense of belonging. In this case, those that understand movements more when it is explained those that understand it when it is demonstrated and those that understand when they are asked to practice it can all be carried along. As Lauren Warnecke writes:
> In order to best your chances of the dancers picking up movement quickly, you should accommodate for all three learning styles. Say what it is, demonstrate it and allow ample time for practice(2).

Works Cited.

Bakare Ojo Rasaki. Rudiments of Choreography. Lagos. Dat and Partners Logistic Ltd. 2004.

_____The Contemporary Choreographer in Nigeria a Realistic Culture Presever or a Harmful Distortionist Critical Perspectives on Dance in Nigeria Ahmed Yerima Bakare Ojo Rasaki and Arnold Udoka (Eds) Ibadan Kraft Books Limited. 2006. 64 -75.

Iyeh Mariam A. Modern Choreographic Approach to Dance Adaptation: The Example of Break a Boil(a Drama Text) Perspectives in Nigerian Dance Studies Chris Ugolo (ed) Ibadan Caltop publications (Nigeria)Limited. 2006. 136 -148.

Debra Graine and Judith Mackrell. The Oxford university Dictionary of Dance.New York. Oxford University Press Inco. 2000

Longerman Active Dictionary 5th Edition . England Pearson Education Limited 2010.

Julia Diana. Make it stick Dance Teacher Magazine Online. www.dance-teacher com./2013 Retrieved 15th August 2014.

Lauren, Warnecke. Teaching Choreography. www4dance.org/2013. Retrieved 13th August, 2014.

Small biz person. What is the Best Method to Teach a Dance Choreography. https://anwers.yahoo.com. Retrieved 13th august 2014.

www.dictionary.reference.com Retrieved 14th August,2014.

http//en.m.wikipedia.org. Retrieved 14th August ,2014.

The Choreographic Style and Techniques Of Dancerasaki

By
Dosumu–Lawal, Yeside.

Introduction

A creative person in the arts emerges through his ability to bring forth an identity for himself through his creative prowess that he presents and known for his creativity, does not emerge out of vacuum but most times through the observation and participatory method that he gets involved in both consciously and unconsciously as a member of a community and society at large.

His sense of belonging enables him to participate as a member of a community, either as a member of a community, as a member of an age group cum performer, or an audience that plays his part. This creative person, in his prime is unconscious of what has been bestowed on him as he participates and observes different activities that constitute culture, which is a way of life that man represent until he starts creating and bringing to life all he has acquired. On the other hand, creativity, a process associated with freedom and psychological phenomenon, becomes part of his existence bringing him into it.

This paper examines the contribution of Prof. Ojo Rasaki Bakare as an erudite Professor of dance and choreography through one of his stage performances, with his choreography style and technique as a major focus. His biography will be highlighted to give a background and understanding of his works and achievements.

The place of dance and choreography in African culture is enormous and its usage is encompassing. Dance in the African cultural context could be said to be holistically embraced. Primus (1997) personified the African dance experience and explained that through an encounter with it, the magic of life is experienced, eternity captured, an initiation, a belief and a voyage into before and beyond. Dance is one of the most dynamic art forms which in African context expresses the heart of African life that ranges from birth to death. It creates a feeling of dynamic trust and resistance, like a strong magic with a sense of urgency, direction and purpose. Dancing is education; it tends towards exceeding the imitation of the body as they are experienced in everyday use. Dance is a natural expression of united feeling and action, expresses the geographical location, religious belief, political and historical experience, biological, social practice and economic peculiarities in a simple language;

> "The rhythmical movement of human body in time
> and space to make statement" (Bakare 1998:2)

Bakare submits that, dance does not exist in a vacuum, there are other factors responsible for its existence, which are; Time, Rhythm, space, body, intention and communication with the audience. Dance draws from life and contains only the essence of real life like abstractions from it. Dance is a vital tool of communication, used extensively by Bakare in most of his works. The choreographic style and technique in one of his works would be analyzed later in this paper.

The Biography of Bakare, Ojo Rasaki

Born on 8th, November 1964, to a Muslim family in Ekiti State, he left home in 1981 at the age of 17 to join Jimoh Aliu cultural troupe, a Yoruba travelling theatre despite the disapproval of his parent. His love for theatre enabled him to forge ahead. He acquired his training under Jimoh Aliu and later Hubert Ogunde, whose choreographic style reflect so much in some of Bakare dance compositions.

Bakare's Philosophy And World View

Understanding the man called Ojo Rasak Bakare is like studying a man with a mission, which many fail to understand. He is an apostle that has the mission of proclaiming the gospel of dance according to his forebearers "The Alarinjos".

The "Alarinjo", the Yoruba traveling theatre style of performance is to move from one locality to another, bringing the theatre to the door step of the people. Bakare has imbibed this performance style in his quest for Academic excellence, as he moves from one institution to the other leaving behind him a mark, which till today serves as a point of reference and contribution to knowledge and achievement. Unconsciously, Prof. Bakare may not know that his ability to move is as a result of being bitten by the bug of Alarinjo travelling tradition. In the organization of this traditional theatre, their focus and function is to teach and entertain, but if they are not accepted, they move on. Though from a Muslim background, he fell in love with the traditional theatre which was opposed to by his father, making him to leave home for some years. His experience later became the foundation on which he built his dance style and technique and a stepping stone to greater achievements.

He shares almost the same world view with the late Ogunde, whose root is in the tradition of his people and the zeal to preserve and improve on our culture (which is in line with the concept of syncretism as a philosophy and choreographic device). Also, Bakare, believes in the philosophy of "live and let others live" by training students in the area of dance and encouraging them to work hard and believe in the ability to stand. He takes care of his dance students by looking out for them but never pampers. This is responsible for his long chain of disciples, even outside the academic environment because he has a way of convincing one that he can make it and he will make sure you get there.

As the first professor of dance in Nigeria, his mission is complete and with many disciples behind him, his philosophy worldwide is well accepted with various achievements, as he has proved that it is possible to achieve the impossible if the passion is there and the mission is focused upon.

Performance Style And Technique of Ojo Bakare
In the performance of one of his works; Drums of war, he employs diverse ethnic dance movement forms and style in a medley to add to the aesthetic value in the play, with a modern

creative approach in the area of technicalities using special sound effect, make up, properties and light.

The play, Drums of war, is a satire whose thematic trust hinges on power tussle to the detriment of the masses. Bakare's treatment of the socio political issue using theatrical elements makes communication pleasant. His directorial approach in the realization of the play production makes theatricalities interesting. His dual role, as a Director and a choreographer shows the versatility embedded in this energmatic personality. My first experience with him was the play ***"Drums of War"*** staged at the Obafemi Awolowo University between 1995 – 1997 (twice) first as a departmental production and later as a convocation play, which left the audience in a confused state of mind, as who the director of such a magnified production could be due to the large (cast) a style which late Prof. Ola Rotimi was known for. The auditorium was agog when Bakare was introduced as the director. His dexterity as a director /choreographer couldn't be over emphasized, as he embellished the entire production with all theatrical elements at his disposal.

His choreographic style and technique left no stone unturned as he adopted the Alarinjo style, which Ogunde theatre passed unto him, under the tutelage of Jimoh Aliu theatre troupe, where Bakare started his training. His style evolved from the Alarinjo style of casting where dancers are chosen after solo performances and the ability to follow him as an instructor. Bakare's style of demonstration helped him in testing the ability and capability of the dancers. He used diverse ethnic dance movement technique to test the strength, dexterity, energy, dynamics, concentration and interpretation. The casting of dancers was done first before other cast members are picked because the play requires lots of dancers that must constitute seventy percent of the cast.

Though in an academic environment, it was not easy getting enough dancers and this created a lot of challenges for him. Also his ability to demonstrate as an instructor, breaking down the technique of different dance styles in the simplest way, encouraged students to believe in the study of dance. He teaches by forming a synergy between theory and practice. His method of teaching does not end in the classroom, he teaches all the time when present at rehearsal grounds, all you see is his versatility as a director, choreographer, drummer, composer, designer etc and failure to understand him in any capacity, what you would hear him say is "NO now, no now, it is not like that but you have to do it this way" he profers solutions and does not take impossibility as a challenge.

The Concept of Style and Technique in Ojo Bakare's Drums of War

The whole concept of style and technique in performance has been discussed extensively by historians, theorists, choreographers and critics. The likes of Cohen[1983] Wollham (1987) Adshead [1988] champlain/Blum[1989]Mcfee (1992) while coming out with different views and opinions on dance style and techniques all agreed that dance techniques are related but style could be individualistic, or depend on cultural background or a particular group and a specific period. The definition of style is a method adopted by an individual or group, as a pattern or system of operation for productivity, while technique is method adopted in getting things done or a particular pattern in actualizing a goal. Dance style and technique of an art work cannot be divorced from culture.

Blum and Chaplain support this claim that cultural style reflects the social customs, religious beliefs and philosophy of people, in their notion of beauty, power, virtue, etc, it is their identity.
Bakare as an individual is identified by his choreographic style and technique, which is inflicted in his casting, choice of movement and the execution of movement and this is supported by Amankulo (1980:85) that dance in theatrical expression is so fundamental to the concept of dramatic performance. This is the main medium inculcated by Bakare to communicate. Also, Peggy Harper (1974:210) succinctly puts this; "that in Africa, dancers dance with the whole of themselves; they respond to music physically, emotionally and intellectually". All these are part of

the attributes of Bakare that make him to stand out as a unique dance scholar for his concept of style and technique. His music cannot be divorced from his dance. In the choreographic style of Bakare, he exhibits the mastery of traditional music in both oral / lyrics and musical instruments, an organic, creative talent evident in him. As the first Nigerian professor of choreography, he has excelled not only as an academician but as a trainer of many dance scholars and dance artistes, he has professed a guide to African choreography in his book, Rudiments of choreography, which has become a handbook for dancers. However, he has adopted the Ogunde choreographic style as a philosophy of integration, collaboration and synthesization Ugolo[1998] whose result in eclectism and syncretism in the performance of most of his works especially in *"Drums of War"* where he uses the philosophy of multi-culturalism to solve the problem of ethnicity and cultural pluralism.

Bakare borrowed largely from the traditional African theatrical form in the preparation of his performance, by combining traditional elements; dance, music and drama in his artistic expression. So, in the packaging of Drums of War staged at Ife, 60% of his time was given to dance. His choreographic approach, like Ogunde can be found in a typical African festival performance, where traditional elements were merged for artistic result.

According to Ugolo[1999] Ogunde Choreographic approach borrowed extensively from the African traditional style of performance and this method has helped in solving the problem of ethnicity through the creation of what we referred to as a national choreographic style. One can boldly say that Bakare's experience under Ogunde, the acclaimed doyen of professional theatre in Nigeria, has contributed a lot to his choreographic style and technique. In his movement vocabulary, he has a vast knowledge of traditional dance movement all over Nigeria, from their theatrical framework to their practical components.

The choreographic style and technique of Bakare in ***Drums of War*** is categorized into three: casting, choice of movement and execution of movement.

Casting
In the area of casting, dancers are tested on the ability and capability to use the body according to the dictates of the choreographer. Though a choreographer does not need to be a good dancer, but Bakare's ability to demonstrate the dance movement for the dancer to initiate makes his choreography easier and interesting. The dancers are taken through the journey of understanding different technique of dance through the demonstration of dance movements of different tribes in Nigeria. This exercise enables him to choose and cast them into two categories; good and upcoming dancers. Bakare never condemns outrightly, but encourages one to strive.

Choice of Movement
The choice of movement is determined by the kind of work at hand. Virtually all his plays have infusions of dance and if the production is purely dance, the dancers are given the task of interpreting on their own before he starts polishing. Creating the opportunity is to help the dancers in making use of their movement, vocabulary, understanding dance composition and acquiring dance skills.

The Execution of Movement
The play ***"Drums of War"*** depends mostly on music and dance which constitute seventy percent of the production. The play starts on a high note, with a war dance as the opening scene, showcasing it as *compact*. Bakare uses the parallel line formation which is confrontational to establish the war situation, followed by stunts of different magnitude.

The stunt performed was as a result of technique taught by Bakare which does not leave even females dancers out of the stunts.

The music, the dance and stunts, dictate the pace and establish the play on an interesting note and end same.

The execution of movement in the play is as a result of rigorous, and energy sapping rehearsals that puts all casts and crew on their toes. From casting to reading of lines, to dance rehearsal, to the tryout of property built for the production, to the set construction and light rigging, the execution of Dance movement is involved. Choreography is like a second skin to Bakare, which makes his choreographic works to be a rewarding and outstanding success.

Conclusion
The promotion of dance and Choreography in Nigeria is highly commendable. This was made possible by Professor Bakare, a multiple award winner for his choreographic works both within and outside the country. His brilliance is prodigiously fore grounded in academic essays, published plays and choreographic works, which has influenced many dances and made him a role model for his peers and upcoming dance scholars.

References

Adshead (1988) (ed), Dance Analysis: Theory and Practice London: Dance Books.

Bakare O.R. (1998) Rudiment of Choreography, Zaria Space Publishers Ltd.

Blom A.L & Chaplin T. (1982): The Intimate Act of Choreography Pittsburgh: University of Pittsburgh 1982.

Clark, Ebun (1979) Hubert Ogunde, The Making of Nigeria Theatre, London OUP

Harper, P. (1999) "Dance Studies" in a Handbook of Methodology in African Studies Dele Layiwola (ed) pp. 43-70. Ibadan: John Archers Publishers Limited.

MCfee, G. 91992) Understanding Dance, Rutledge, New York.

Primus, P. (1997) "African Dance": in Africa Dance:An Artistic: Historical and Philosophical Inquiry. Kariamu Welsh Asante (ed): pp. 3-11: Eritrea. African World Press Inc.

Ugolo, C.E. (1999) "The Nigeria Dance Theatre: Agenda for the Next Millenium" in Nigerian Theatre Journal. Mabel I.E. Evwierhoma (ed) 85-89.

Dance Practice and the Choreographer's Creativity through the Lens of Bakare, Ojo Rasaki.

By
Peter Adeiza Bello

Introduction
Dance as an art form and mode of expressive communication has since the emergence and development of modern theatre become a viable field of the performing arts that individual or group of persons under a registered company engages in as a career and source of livelihood. Dance practice, therefore, simply refers to regular dance performance activities as a theatre form to represent and portray issues of life by means of relying on the application of series of purposeful and symbolic movement of the body set to a given arrangement of functional music. While the amateur dancers practice dance as part of cultural and extracurricular activities, the professional dancers are fully engaged in the art of dance as a means of livelihood.

Beside the academic dance scholars with various specialisation such as dance criticism, dance technology, dance history, dance therapy to mention but a few. The professional field of dance practice is primarily composed of two major complementary fields of specialisation; namely dance and choreography. However, a professional dance practitioner can combine the two specialisation doubling as a dancer and at the same time a choreographer. Also, some professional dancers and choreographers specializes in the area of creating and designing dance for children composed of pure dance, mime, pantomime and games to instruct and teach morals. This aspect of children theatre can take the form of what is known as dance repertory theatre whereby a dance theatre company engages in the performance of dance theatre treating various issues of concern from time to time or within a stipulated period or season. Usually, such repertory is targeted at creating awareness, educating a targeted society with the aim of proffering recommendable suggestions and solutions to certain matters. In other words, it is a practice that involves a fiesta of a theatre company repertoire (stock of a theatre company's creative works) designed to hold within a given period of time in a place. Bakare, Ojo Rasaki being a dance academic and practitioner, a librettist, choreographer and dancer, in his book, ***Rudiments of Choreography***, view the role of the choreographer as an encompassing art of creation. He likened the choreographer to a creator who sourced his creative materials from his imaginative power and environment. Thus, the choreographer relies on the dancer if he must actualise or represent his imagination to communicate a particular motive via dance. In view of applying the right communicative indices into every given dance performance, Bakare classified dance performance into six types of genre which include pure dance, study dance, abstract dance, dramatic dance, dance drama and comic dance. (7). Essentially, the classified genres could aid a choreographer's creative ability to be focused on packaging and delivering a purposefully content-conceived performance.

In Bakare's view, pure dance is a product of kinesthetic stimuli that explores a wide range of movements. In other words, the genre of pure dance performance accommodates series of innovational and improvisational movement patterns. On the other hand, dance genre is not open to a wide range of movement material as the dance performances under this category usually focuses on the specific movement pattern of the type of dance that is being explored. Bakare's view of abstract dance genre debunks notions that a given dance performance can be considered abstract when it is void of a story line or lacks a logical sequence. He submits that "A dance is abstract when the dance creator has abstracted some ideas about a particular object or group of objects". (8). Examples of an abstract dance can be a symbolic representation or portrayal of emotional concepts such as love, beautiful, pain and natural phenomenon such as rainfall, sunrise/shine, moonlight and sparkling galaxies. Jonathan Burrows reflects that "Sometimes working consciously in the abstract is the best way to arrive at another subject". (135). This implies that series of abstract dance could be harnessed into an experiental journey that will at the end of the day give birth to a given concept permeating certain matters of interest. Furthermore, the thin line between dramatic dance, dance drama and comic dance genres is that while dramatic dance refers to the application of rhythmic movement to represent a particular mood or to emphasis a notion within a play, a dance drama is simply a narrative dance performance with a story line, plot and characterization. On the other hand, comic dance can be described as exaggerated manipulation of the dancer's series of body gestures in conformation to series of arranged music to provoke excitement and laughter.

Choreographic Process
The art of choreography is the creative process of designing and patterning of dance movements to communicate certain ideas and to create aesthetic appeal. Bakare affirms that "Choreography is the structuring of movements in time and space to make statements". (1). In like manner, Ugolo also asserts that the art of choreography involves "the composition of dances, the structuring and arrangement of movements, writing of dance scripts and dance notation". (70). Ajibade Debo view choreography as the art of transforming emotions into images with logical arrangement of gestures. He concludes that choreography deals with the "ability to create and arrange dance movements by the power of one's imaginative prowess, sensitive by nature to visual impressions cum environmental observation, emotional feelings using series of rhythmic body gestures as the vehicle of its carriage to form images". (33).

The essence of choreography is to create visual aesthetic appeal with the arrangement of the dancers whose calculated movements portrays chains of motives in a sequence to make a complete non verbal statement. Therefore, every given choreographic process starts by conceiving or imagining an idea which is further developed into a picture. The pictured imagination is then actualised by representing the ideas with the employment of dance composed of series of rhythmic gestures, mime and pantomime. A well structured choreographic process is expected to sail on the basic elements which Bakare itemised as line, space, mass and coherence(29) to arrive at creating a logical floor pattern and symmetrical and asymmetrical design in a dance sequence. Hence, it is important that onlooker or audience should be able to identify the characteristics of the basic principles of composition comprising the elements of unity, transition, variation, contrast and repetition in a well choreographed dance sequence or performance. However, in some instances especially in African setting, the traditional root of a given dance may dictate the pace, pattern and formation of a sequence which may not always accommodate the exact measure of modern choreography. Bakare recaps that choreographic appeal depends on the setting of every given dance by his classification of two major types of choreography namely; residual and emergent choreography. He insists that

> Residual choreography being traditional and communal oriented is restrictive while emergent choreography being modern and individualistic advocates and allows for freedom of expression. This is the case all over the world. Every culture world over had its own traditional dance form out of which the modern dance or emergent choreography has evolved. (2).

In essence, what is known as modern dance or emergent choreography draws its materials from a combination of indigenous dance movements and series of the rejuvenated and prevailing style or fashion of the moment in every given setting or society.

The Choreographer and His Creative Role
The choreographer is a creative personality in the theatre, most especially in the field of dance art. The choreographer is the equivalent of a play director who may also wear the shoes of a playwright. He is a creative artist vested with the responsibility of designing dance movement and interpreting a given libretto by harnessing human and material resources in performance. The choreographer's major tools to efficiently carry out his creative

work involves the power of imagination, good sense of rhythm, repertoire of series of movements which can be derived from culture and environmental influences. He is required to be a patient artist with a listening ear and observing eyes. To achieve the functional use of his tools, he needs the services of dancers (human resources) without which his creative ability will be dormant.

Bakare describes the choreographer as "a creative thinker whose creative thoughts are expressed not verbally but through body movements called dance"(1). In the same vein, Ugolo is of the opinion that "The choreographer is one who is not only a master dancer but should have an in-depth knowledge of the human body and personality. He is a designer, organizer of human resources, director and musician. He is a person who is able to translate ideas and emotional impulses into visual symbols and form"(71). However, it is worthy of note to state that though the choreographer as described by Bakare, champions the creative process of the sequential arrangement of dance and dancers but the expressive interpretation of the choreographer's thought lies in the hands of the dancers. On this, Bakare asserts that "Though, the choreographer may not be a fantastic dancer himself, he still needs to be above waters in the art of dancing because if he is a dancer himself, it makes his job easier". (54). That is, a choreographer will be perfect at his job if he is equally a dancer, though this may be debatable in other climes.

The Dancer's Place in a Choreographic Process
Dance is an expressive, non-verbal communication that can be identified in the day to day lifestyle of humans and even animals. Dance is usually associated with rhythm or music and it can either be exhibited to express excitement, to entertain and to meet socio-cultural and religious obligation. A dancer is a performer who communicates through the calculated or motive oriented manipulation of his body gestures set to a given rhythm without verbal utterances. In other words, a dancer is like a vehicle that helps to transform imaginations and ideas into meaningful patterned human body motion. Dancers are the live wires of a

choreographer's creative efforts because the absence of dancers means that the choreographer will not be able to actualise his imagination in pictorial movements. Consequentially, the success or failure of any given dance performance depend on the dancer's creative expression and his ability to play along and adhere to the necessary instructions and promptly conform to the rhythm with accurate precision, transition and apply the right measure of energy at every point. The dancer is simply a performing artist whose job is to represent an idea or feelings by the rhythmic manipulation of his body. He is the equivalent of the actor and his major instrument of expression is his body, imaginative power, and sense of rhythm, experience and a repertoire of varieties of movements. He must be flexible with a teachable and team playing spirit. He must be a good observer of his environment and must be able to convert pictures into meaningful dance movements. Hence, there is simply no dance without the dancer who could equally double as a choreographer.

Choreographing a Dance Drama
Certainly, the realization of a dance drama from the conception ideas to the actualisation of thematic issues of life could be a challenging task because of the complexity of conveying and transmitting narrative messages without verbal dialogue. Therefore, a choreographer must be versatile and must understand how to perfectly apply and set signs and symbols to a purposeful music. Hence, a good choreographer must avoid unnecessary application of verbal utterance. Also, the continuity and transition of the dancers' movements and communicative indices must not suffer any iota of slackness else the audience will lose track of the storyline. The term, dance drama is known as a narrative dance. That is, a dance performance designed to narrate a plotted story. Bakare explains this by stating that "the intention of a dance drama is to narrate a coherent story and do it through a sequence of actions and movements. In the same view, Ajibade define dance drama as an "art form whose graceful and expressive movement of the body takes proportions of dramatic plot devoid of verbal words" (41). Mariam Iyeh also affirms that dance drama pays attention to characterization and mood to

adequately address thematic issues of life that are arranged into logical plot(35). Hence, dance drama is a juxtaposition of the elements of specialized dance movements, characterization / acting, storyline and symbolic communication.

The Choreographer as a Librettist
In some instances, most professional choreographers are usually the creator of their stories. In essence, the choreographer also performs the duty of a librettist as he sourced his materials from human experiences and even natural occurrences to create an experimental piece or thematic issues of life designed into plots. A dance libretto is a dance performance script designed in descriptive pattern giving a would be choreographer the opportunity to task his or her creativity to interpret the storyline in performance. Therefore, a librettist is the equivalent of a playwright; he or she is someone who creates, writes or designs a dance drama script for performance. However, a librettist could also go beyond description to put down his own creative floor pattern, design and interpretation. i.e his personal concept, interpretation and performance structure. It can be segmented into either movement one, two and three…, or sequence one, two and three….or whatever descriptive subheading one chose to adopt. Creating and developing a dance libretto requires a great deal of creative ability to harness imaginative ideas with experiences and related happenings that could be recreated for performance. Moreover, a seasoned librettist or choreographer needs to weave his storyline around a collection of theoretical framework that should include a theme, choreographic interpretation, choreographic concept, technique/style and a given setting that will define the unique features of his work. Core issues that affect and influence the choreographer below will be considered to drive home the fact that the choreographer is a critical factor in dance creation and interpretation.

What is a Theme: Theme is the central focus or subject matter by which a librettist, choreographer and dancer develop his ideas; interpret his perception concerning an issue of life. In other words, deriving a theme propels a choreographer's approach towards addressing a particular issue with the employment of appropriate movement design and all other elements of dance performance.

Choreographic Interpretation: This is a witty expansion of the subject matter in few words based on the plot of the storyline and flaws of the central character or characters. In other words, it is an interpretative conceptualisation of the subject matter.

Choreographic Concept: This is usually a one word phrase that captures or compresses the prevalent riding factor that permeates the storyline.

Choreographic Style/technique: This is a systematic mode of delivery that is peculiar to a given choreographer in a particular choreographic work. In other words, technique or style is a particular way of doing something (performance) which encompasses the totality (packaging and delivery) of the performance ranging from the representational movement pattern and all the composite elements and paraphernalia of performance which include sound cues, music, costume, props, lighting, scenic design. For example, a choreographer could characterise his style with the employment of eclectic innovation and improvisation; eclectic innovation refers to sourcing materials from various sources to achieve a given interpretation. This involves a wide range of experience, imaginative and improvisation power to harness and harmonise movements recreated from diverse sources. Both the choreographer and dancer must be highly equipped with the ability to tap from diverse sources.

Setting: Setting in a theatrical dance performance refers to the background, culture, place, time/ period and context upon which the performance is developed. To a great extent, setting determines the choreographer's decision on the total package and final outlook of his performance. This is because; setting dictates the application of appropriate instrumental music and songs, costumes, props, scenographic design and lighting and most importantly the dance movements, gestures and symbols. In the same vein, Yerima Ahmed is of the opinion that "Dance represents the identity of the people. Through the body, dance uses the emphasis of areas of the body as metaphors and symbols. Specific parts of the body are used to reveal the history of the people, their occupational engagement, and their environment" (124).

Conclusion
Dance is an expressive medium of communication and the choreographer plays the foundational role of creating the communicative indices to aid the dancer's creative, interpretational and representational abilities with the use of their body. In essence, the choreographer and the dancer are both involved in the dance creation and interpretation of concepts. It will not be out of place to also state that every versatile dancer is a potential choreographer who constantly engages in the art of choreographic recreation as he or she dances. In fact, the dancer's kinesthetic-sense must always be at par with the kine-sphere to appropriately and precisely represent his intentions in conformity to his given music and within a given space. As a creator, the choreographer cum dancer depends on his imaginative power; and his ability to study nature and environmental occurrences. Every given choreographer is nurtured by his cultural root, environment, experiences and exposure. Therefore, the choreographer who will live above limitations in his creative role should endeavour to sustain his relevance in the traditional and contemporary choreographic dance performances by interplaying his socio-cultural influences with the emerging trends.

References

Ajibade, Debo. "A Personal View of the Tenets of Dance & Dance Drama". *Rutajib Dance Arts*
Services, Ibadan, Nigeria. 2010.

Bakare, Ojo-Rasaki. *Rudiments of Choreography*. Dat & Partners Publishers, Lagos, Nigeria.
2004.

Bakare, Ojo-Rasaki. "The Contemporary Choreographer in Nigeria: A Realistic Culture
Preserver or a Harmful Distortionist?". *Critical Perspectives on Dance in Nigeria*, (Ed)
Yerima, A., Bakare O., Udoka, A., Kraft Books Limited, Ibadan, Nigeria. 2006.

Burrows, Jonathan. *A Choreographer's Handbook*. Routledge; Tailor & Francis Group, New
York. 2010.

Iyeh, Mariam A. *Introduction to Choreographic Analysis: The tragedy of a People in Focus*.
Freedom Press and Publishers, Kaduna, Nigeria. 2011.

Ugolo, Chris. *Perspective in Nigerian Dance Studies*. Caltop Publications, Ibadan, Nigeria.
2007.

Ugolo, Chris. *The Choreographer and the Dance Art in Contemporary Nigeria. An*
Encyclopedia of the Arts. Vol. 11(1). 2006.

Yerima, Ahmed. *Symbol and Images in Nigerian Dances. Critical Perspectives on Dance in*
Nigeria, (Ed) Yerima, A., Bakare O., Udoka, A. Kraft Books Limited, Ibadan, Nigeria. 2006.

Postmodern Dance In Bakare, Ojo Rasaki's *Drums Of War* And *Rogbodiyan*

By
OLALUSI, Kehinde Adedamola

Introduction

The process of writing a play is considered creative yet technical. It involves a whole lot of processes that are germane to the essence of playwriting. This is done through a thorough research into the culture intended and equally into the society in order to identify the problems and comfortably reflect such in the script. It is not unusual for playwrights to identify with dance in their plays perhaps because of the seriousness of their thematic preoccupation. Many have stayed glued to the use of music as a linkage of scenes and for setting the mood of the play. However, the African richness of culture and tradition and the strong influence of music and dance in it, canvass for a strong use of both in the processes of writing plays. African dance scholars have situated types of African dance to include ceremonial, invocation, war, social, acrobatic, elders, property, occupational, masquerade, maiden, and cult dances. It is almost impossible to write plays without one of these occurrence. This presupposes that identifying with dances in the process of playwriting is a matter of choice and convenience and not that of appropraicy. Abbe (2007, p10) believes that "Dance has always being with man. It has always been part of religion, ritual, drama, education and recreation. As an expression of the doings of man and his society, it documents man's tradition and the changes that occur in a society". Abbe's opinion means that dance should be part of a playwrights' weapon of presenting tradition and culture and the changes that occur within them. Bakare Ojo Rasaki is adept at this, as he creatively weaves music and dance into his plays and thereby creating the consciousness of the need for choreography. Over the years, several theories have been used to interrogate the functionality of dance within its performance mould. Postmodernism as one of such theories becomes the crux of analytical discourse in this work. In essence, this paper discusses the use of postmodern dance in Bakare Ojo Rasaki's selected plays.

Literature Review

The term postmodern dance has come to mean the utilisation of the body parts in actualising movements that are basically fashioned out of every day activities. According to www.wikipedia.com (2012), "postmodern dance is a 20th century concert dance form. A reaction to the compositional and presentational constraints of modern dance, post modern dance hailed the use of everyday movements as valid performance art and advocated novel methods of dance composition claiming that any movement was dance and any person a dancer (with or without training". This perhaps emphasised the efficacy of pure movement as against heavily stylised and complicated movements which were considered bogus and ambiguous to suitably express some intended messages to the audience then. Stressing the notion of postmodern dance further, Banes (1983, p.113) avers that:

> Perhaps even more important than the individual dances given at a Judson concert was the attitude that anything might be called a dance and hooked at as dance; the work of a visual artist, a film maker, a musician might be considered a dance just as activities done by a dancer, although not recognizable as theatrical dance, might be reexamined and 'made strange' because they were framed as art.

The above is considered true because postmodern dance entails envisioning and experimenting various visual components as artistically suitable to the artistic and choreographic intention and purpose. That is why Kaye (1994, p.23) believes that "postmodern moment is not the property of any particular discipline". It is a notion that cuts across disciplines and its usage is adaptably used as indices of communication across board.

Postmodern dance existed as a result of a reaction to modern dance. Many choreographers and dancers felt that dance ought not to be compulsorily stylised for it to be dance, and therefore based their dances primarily on pure movement of the body which individual choreographer may explore or not. That is why Banes (2001, p.31) believes that,

> In the theory of post modern dance, the choreographer does not apply visual standards to the work. The view is an interior one: movement is not preselected for its characteristics but results from certain decisions, goals, plans, schemes, rules, concepts, or problems. Whatever actual movement occurs during the performance is acceptable as long as the limiting and controlling principles are adhered to.

The above stresses that the component of postmodern dance is a result of plans and schemes which are guided by rules. This is why it is necessary to state the four categories of postmodern dance that were utilized by the Judson theatre choreographers:

1) Dances that are comprised entirely of ordinary movements and/or activities, including tasks.
2) Dances that incorporate ordinary movement and/or activities along with perceptibility dancerly movement.
3) Dances that employ movement that is neither straightforwardly ordinary nor dancerly, notably dances with game-like structures.
4) Dances whose movement is so category-defying that the only way to describe it is as movement simplicity. (Banes and Carrol, 2006, p 59-60).

While the above was the genesis of postmodern dance features, performance praxis over the years has enabled a wide range of practices, styles and structures of dance to develop. For instance, in Nigeria today, dance practices are geared towards experimentation. In fact, to be postmodern from an artistic and choreographic/dance purview, means to be experimental, and at some point deconstructive. This is because within the choreographic and dance creative process, the lacuna to be filled is the yearning to generate new artistic/choreographic concepts rather than continue to feed on the existing practices of dance and the hybridisation of a variety of dances to make them look new. Postmodern dance has been one of the vehicles of creativity.

Postmodern dance, therefore, is a veritable medium of practice that uniquely allows for an integration of simple yet creative dance movements with artistic embodiment.

Bakare Ojo Rasaki's Contribution to Traditional, Modern and Postmodern Dance in Nigeria.

Having headed numerous theatre companies and National Troupes of Nigeria and the Gambia, Bakare's wealth of theoretical and practical experiences are vast and unquantifiable. His book, *Rudiments of Choreography* is an important document and one of the few dance books in Nigeria. Equally, his choreographic experience has brought to fore, a number of new trends in dance and choreography. It is our concern here to point out some of such strides in dance and choreography.

First, to be comfortably involved in the teaching of dance theory in a Nigerian University and actively involved in the creation and choreographic process of different traditional, modern and postmodern dances is a great sacrifice and contribution to the development of dance in Nigeria. Also, his development of dancers and choreographers is a proof of his intense passion for dance practice in Nigeria, particularly from its sustenance point of view. For instance, Bakare (2006, p.74) believes that "the modern choreographer is trained to understand both the dynamics of the society and the nature of these dances. He is thus skilled enough for the task of adapting the dances for preservation and survival and makes them conform to the mechanisms of contemporary living". It means that Bakare's training and development of dancers and choreographers are to enrich them with a multi-varying perspective of theory and practice of dance specifically for functionality.

Again, because of his background in theatre practice, Bakare has been at the forefront of packaging, exhibiting, preserving, performing and showcasing the various cultural and traditional dances in Nigeria on the local, national and international stage. He is a passionate cultural exhibitor and this is evident in his elaborate organisation of the Abuja Carnival which is a conglomerate of dance, costume parade, music, carnivalesque etc. In fact, he strongly believes that " for any culture to survive, it must be dynamic and integrative. For the dance culture of Nigerians to survive, therefore, the contemporary Nigerian choreographer, as a matter of reality must in the words of the Tanzanian social scientist, Mohiddin examine carefully his traditional heritage, and see how best it can be adapted to modern conditions" (2006, p.74). It then posits that Bakare's experiment with the different Art Councils across the nation, the National Troupes of Nigeria and Gambia has been solely for the purpose of adapting the age long traditional dances to modern conditions that would appeal and excite.

From the postmodern dance genre, Bakare's impact is also felt in the Nigerian dance scene. He is adept to choreographing medley of variety of dances as a performance for the contemporary audience. Most notable of this is the Unity Dance which is a medley of major ethnic groups in Nigeria. Bakare's choreographic endeavour also reflects the postmodern dance. Even in his writings, he has utilised the postmodern trends such that directors would require choreographer's expertise in creating the dances which are to enhance the message of the play.

Postmodern Dance in *Drums of War* and *Rogbodiyan*
It is no mean feat to combine the artistic prowess of playwriting, choreographing and dancing. Certainly, this artistic combination is an advantage to scholarship and creativity. Bakare, in the process of writing his plays has weaved postmodern dance into the fabrics of his plays. This intentionality may be borne out of his desire to allow for the blend of the total theatre aesthetics even as he disseminates his intended messages. What the dances do to this plays is that it gives it the needed variety, it helps intensify the culture attached, and in some cases, it is in itself the medium of actualising major aspects of the play.

For instance, *Drums of War* which is one of his most performed plays is a metaphor in its writing and performance. Analytically, it is evident that when drums roll, what accompanies it is dance.

The metaphor is, therefore, reflected in the fact that while the drum is lively and pleasant, war in its meaning is bad, evil and negative in approach. The play revolves around a war hungry king whose quest for war and dominance is far greater than the love of his people and even his family. His urge for wanton destruction of a village led to the collapse of his family and kingdom. From the dance interpretation, a considerable part of the play entails the use of simple basic movements to exemplify war movements and fighting. To make this effective, the choreographer must consider the four components of postmodern dance as practiced by Judson Theatre (see page 6). The reason for this is because war like movements is not to be highly technical movements, they should be simple yet stylised to conjure the feelings of a battle and to create the atmosphere of wanton destruction. In some cases, the choreographer may employ the use of slow motion in dance in order to capture the movements in its slowest form and, therefore impress more on the audience the effects of war. This confirms Cohen-Stratyner's (2001,p.122) opinion that, "The post modern choreographers also use social dance as a source for pedestrian movement, since it, like walking, can be done by anyone."

From another point of view, and particularly taking a cue from the 2005 dance adaptation of the play in the Department of the Performing Arts, University of Ilorin, an artistic/choreographic ingenuity of the creation of another movement added more meaning and further contributed to the success of the dance production. In the dance theatre, the choreographer and other crew members added a movement of celebrating King Orighoye's third year on the throne where singing, dancing and marrying was prevalent. This movement was created to further deepen the futility in war by presenting the celebration after the King had unrelentingly sent his warriors to fight with the Ibuji town. The dances done were from different cultures in Nigeria to reflect more on the playwright's setting of contemporary Nigeria. From the angle of experimenting and deconstruction which are indices of postmodern art form, the playwright's utilisation of different tribes like Igala, Yoruba, Ebira, Hausa, Igbo, Edo etc is an experimentation in creativity. Equally, its easy adaptability to dance theatre is a huge reflection of it being postmodern in design.

In *Rogbodiyan*, the intrinsic design of post modern dance is evident. *Rogbodiyan* in translation means calamity. As the title suggests, its undertone is negative and calls for solution. In the prologue of the play, the playwright begins by writing that "a voice rings R-o-gb-o-d-i-y-a-n". This, from the choreographic perception could be interpreted in a way that captures the message of the play. For instance, a choreographer could create simple dances from running, hoping, jumping, and limping etc to showcase the effect of trouble and chaos. The movements will be rapid and fast but basic movements that are only designed to reflect the message. With the song Rogbodiyan being echoed by the orchestra in a fast tempo, the array of dancers, moving fast in their confused state would have a huge impact on the intended meaning of Rogbodiyan.

The playwright's stage instruction immediately after is another avenue for exhibiting dances. It reads:
> Follow spot pick townspeople coming from the audience in different Directions. They are all deformed, carrying all sorts of physical deformities. e.g. Blindness, Paralysis of the arms, legs, hunchbacks, etc. Those who are blind are led by those who are lame or hunchbacked. The entire picture is nightmarish and horrible yet, somehow, it is grotesque funny. They sing to the accompaniment of music as they come on stage. Their movement is rhythmic though it cannot be said that they are dancing. (P. 6)

This writer disagrees with Bakare within the expanse of postmodern dance because Movements in its simplest form is one of the qualities that enrich postmodern dance. The physical deformities mentioned above clearly gives room for the exploration of movements, in any case, the instable nature of their bodies would require the choreographer to work more on their movements to make it neater and in order. In Movement Six, Bakare's stage instruction reads *"Coronation scene. This is mostly enacted in dance. Towns people dance wearing colourful attires. They are apparently in a festive mood. They take their positions and form a big arc"*.(P.28) The above is an open check to a choreographer to limitlessly explore the multi-dimensional aesthetics of dance. Being a celebration scene, the dances are fast and lively and therefore open an avenue for different choreographies.

Conclusion
The use of postmodern dance in these plays is of great value to the dissemination of the intended messages. It is certain that with the involvement of a choreographer, the work of the director would blossom. By design, the art of playwrighting is literal, yet it involves conceiving, generating and developing ideas that are completely geared toward performance of such plays on stage. Dance being a vibrant artistic tool is one of the elements needed. This opinion is vibrantly supported by Adeoye (2014, p.ix) who opines that "Dance has the trusted crown of honour because of its paradoxes and multidimensional complexities of flexibility to rigidity, seriousness to ribaldy, feminity to masculinity, grace to greif, absurdity to logicality, supplication to demonstration and joy to sadness in the celebration of the culture in man and the man in culture". His declaration above is a pointer to the need for playwrights to willingly subject themselves to the alluring nature of dance and its ability to positively enhance the meaning in their plays. Like the USB cord, dance can be a connecting channel between playwrights, their plays, actors and the audience.

References

Abbe, J. (2007) "The Dance Art in Nigeria". In *Perspectives in Nigerian Dance Studies.* (Ed) Ugolo, C. Ibadan. Caltop Publications (Nigeria) Limited.

Adeoye, A. (2014) "Forward" for *Dance Scripts for the Stage.* Vol.1. (Ed) Akinsipe, F. The Department of the Performing Arts, University of Ilorin.

Bakare, O. (2006) "The Contemporary Choreographer in Nigeria: A Realistic Culture preserver or a Harmful Distortionist?" In *Critical Perspectives on Dance in Nigeria.* (Ed) Yerima. A Et.al. Ibadan: Kraft Books Limited. Pp 64-75

Bakare, O. (1994) *Drums of War.* Nigeria: Tamaza Publishing Company Limited.

Bakare, O. (2004) *Rogbodiyan.* Nigeria: Tamaza Publishing Company Limited.

Banes, S. (1983) *Democracy's body: Judson Dance Theatre, 1962-1964.* Michigan: Ann Arbor.

Banes, S. and Carrol, N. (2006) "Cunningham, Balanchine and Postmordern Dance" In *Dance Chronicles.* Taylor and Francis ltd. Vol.29, No. 1. Pp. 49-68.

Cohen-Stratyner, B. (2001) "Social Dance: Contexts and Definitions" In *Dance Research Journal.* Congress on Research in Dance. Vol.33, No. 2. Pp. 121-124.

Kaye, N. (1994) *Postmordernism and Performance.* London: Macmillian press.
www.wikipedia.com ® (2012)

PART THREE
PERFORMANCE AND DESIGN AESTHETICS ON THE WORKS OF BAKARE, OJO RASAKI

Reconstructing The Democratic Environment In The Dramaturgy and Performance Of Bakare's *Drums Of War*

By
Ejue, Olympus G.

Introduction

Literature cannot escape from the class power structures that shape our everyday life. Here a writer has no choice. Whether or not he is aware of it, his works reflect one or more spects of intense economic, political, cultural and ideological struggles in a society. What he can choose is one of either sides of the battle field. The side of the people or the side of the social forces and classes that try to keep the people down…Every writer is a writer in politics. The only question is what and whose politics. WaThiongo (101)

In a nation like Nigeria where celebrated saboteurs or over-ambitious political enthusiasts make the most of religious pluralism, political instability, tribalistic sentiments to perpetrate complicity in the polity, then actions that bespeak the need for political orientation and education through theatre become pivotal in harnessing democratic ideals. Playwrights on their part must indulge in "shaping attitudes, perspectives and understanding of the populace as they address corruption, exploitation, ethnicity, tyranny and other ills which create breeding grounds for war, within the country and at the global level" (Yakubu and Iyav, 124) In other words, playwrights' must contemplate democracy as a prototype for galvanizing best living conditions for members of society. Yet over time, there has been the proliferation of artistic quackery. The disinclination to explore and tackle the socio-political and cultural situation in contemporary times, due to lack of creativity amongst particularly young dramatists in the industry is becoming worrisome. How far have these playwrights been able to change the sensibilities of the people? Are the dramas simply portrayed as just intellectual configurations?

Regrettably, this seeming lethargy is because a lot of writers are until now still locked in a passionate embrace with colonialism and its psychological consequences. Gbilekkaa (314) supports this claim as he reasons that; "Nigeria may have broken from the leash of British imperialism 49 years ago but the question of defining what broad national values and consensus must drive the country's sociopolitical life is still a spectre in the imagination of the country's political gladiators". In this regards therefore, theatre must use this social experience to interpret a new image that would drive her main political actors and citizenry to achieve national development. In fact, "there is the need to move rapidly away, in our theatre-making, from colonial, political and economic canons and Eurocentric cultural hegemonies, which we ought to have dismantled since independence, but which still stand, as cliffhangers, over our theatre aesthetics." Obafemi (4-5) The allusion here is that we must jettison any artistic form to reimperialize the nation and its subsequent transfer of such to budding dramatists, as it might foreclose their imaginative ability particularly in a society that is yearning to becoming a global political economy. Be that as it may, how has the enabling or non-enabling environment affected the artistic capabilities of the Nigerian dramatists in terms of a political option that is in existence within a distinctive period of history?

> When a patriotic, highly educated person sees the fate of the country decided by the whims of corrupt, incompetent and often barely literate leaders, silence is impossible. Passivity would be tantamount to a betrayal of the people and a lack of principled integrity. Only those insensitive to the misery of the people can lock themselves up in a room full of flights of imagination. Mustapha (6)

It was WaThiong'oand Mugo who in their preface to *The Trial of DedanKimathi* asserted that; "African writers are either fighting with the people or aiding imperialism and the class enemies of the people" (preface) In this wise, evaluating the three stages of development in the growth of an African artiste as conceived by

Franz Fanon in his book-*The Wretched of the Earth* becomes pertinent. It is a situation where the artiste first strives to indulgence in assimilating the culture of the colonialist-saying he too can be like the white man. And when he encounters rejection, which is the second stage, he comes back home to exalt his past-saying he too has something good. All these are still enshrouded within an artistic context that smacks of colonial tendencies hence the artiste still appears to be addressing the colonialist. Then the third stage, which to Fanon is the most appropriate, is that which jolts the writer into reality hence he begins to look inwards with a view to addressing his own identity problem and seeking a way forward for his society.

In a democracy or any other type of governance, it will depend on how one views a government vis-à-vis the artists. Nonetheless, drama deals with socio-political issues in a tendentiously contemplative manner so as to arouse human passions among society members. In a less apprehensive environment therefore, a deep dramatic reflection about society should enable ones curiosity see what kind of society that may be least tyrannical in a given condition. This is in relation to society, politics and even the playwright himself and how drama could swing into X-raying the basic necessities of human existence. For example, in the Spring of 1999, *Horse and Bamboo Theatre* of Rossendale, Lancashire in the United Kingdom and Sam Ukala in an artistic collaboration created *Harvest of Ghosts* to offer a graphic representation on the atrocities of the Abacha led regime in Nigeria. It is a theatrical statement that reveals the circumstances that led to the killing of Ken Saro-Wiwa and other Ogoni activists in 1995, coupled with the deplorable landscape of the Niger Delta region as a result of the unprecedented oil exploration activities in the region. Although these events transpired in a military regime yet the playwrights;

> Could not resist the attraction of such an internationally topical subject, especially as it held out the opportunity for us to also highlight the plight of ordinary people, about whom and for whom we created our apparently different theatres. Ukala (158)

Revealingly, in a genuine democratic dispensation the expectancy level is to have a proliferation of the most patriotic and exciting creative activity with less or no iota of government repression on the artists as a performer. Surely, and in this circumstance, a creative writer whose society reflects stable institutions and respect for the rule of law would certainly enjoy conditions which are conducive to challenge the establishment. Unlike in a monocratic regime, the repercussion of the global changes and the impact of democracy in Nigeria provide a platform upon which theatre, playwrights and creativity can operate with at least modified suppression and harassment.

Mainstreaming Theatre into Democratic Practice in Nigeria
Grappling with the concept of governance in a democratic dispensation is to some extent a complex bewildering puzzle, particularly that the country is still battling with redefining itself after thirty five years of military dictatorship. It is clear that since May 29, 1999 the post-military democracy in Nigeria and it's so called 'democratic dividends' is still eluding us as a people. There has been a lot of contending socio-political, religious, economic and ethnic forces that have remained unfathomable until presently. Doki succinctly captures this socio-political and economic backwardness of Nigeria. Hence he asserts that;

> Upon the attainment of independence, Nigeria has been plagued with one crises to the other: civil war in 1967, sharia crises in 1977, *maitatsine* crises in 1980, the oil crises in 1986, the declaration of jihad in Kaduna state in 1996, the Kaduna andAbia religious riot in 2000, Tiv/Awe communal clashes in 2001, Tiv/Udam crises in 2002, and a host of other sporadic attacks at different times and places. (142)

Nonetheless, the obvious connector of theatre integrating democratic principles and ideals in Nigeria is essentially to steer the concept of accountability as well as the most widely accepted views or tastes of a nation or culture within the politics and governance of Nigeria. Accountability at this instance means "holding public officials responsible for their actions." Adamolekun (3) This involve politicians and their administrative appointees (bureaucratic or technocratic) all occupied with governance of a particular society. Interestingly, it is these people (politicians and technocrats) that are later transformed into dramatic personages upon which the dramatists most times could draw his brainwave from. It is simply to say in the words of Etherton that; "the art of drama cannot be separated from the greater political task, and its function, from social reality". (27) This tends to be agreeable with Gbilekaa's estimation of the relevance of Nigerian literature and social experience. He acknowledges that: "one of the major ways which the image of a new Nigeria can be constructed and reinforced is through her literature." (315)

After all, "art can raise man up from a fragmented state into that of a whole integrated being. Art enables man to comprehend reality and not only helps him to bear it but increases his determination to make it more human and more worthy of mankind." (Fischer, 20) Nigerian writers, just like Aristophanes and other ancient Greek playwrights, must through their creative endeavours' engage their society and the authorities into competing and proffering conduits for nationhood.

Albeit, the consequences of conceiving a politically motivated objective through a creative process can be grievous for a writer, yet the quest to still use the power of the art, which transcends several dissections to stimulate the masses social consciousness and liberal democracy is still a preferable alternative. We do know that most politically committed writers the world over have lived in exile or been outlawed at one point in time or the other in their various countries for their artistic commitment to the peoples' cause. For example, Soyinka was incarcerated during the Nigerian Civil War (1967-1970) and as if that was not enough, his book *The Man Died* was outlawed. At a point, he also lived in self-exile in Ghana. The ban of Ogunde's *Yoruba Ronu* in 1964 which triggered off a frightening chain of violence that led to the rejection of the unpopular and corrupt government of chief S. L. Akintola the then premier of the Western Region forced Ogunde to relocate to Lagos in order to avoid more crises.

Others like NgugiWaThiongo, Mongo Beti, Bessie Head, Athol Fugard, AimeCesaire suffered whilst writing for their people too. All these examples shows that perhaps their artistic postures lie within a revolutionary socio-political manifesto for generations yet unborn. It is indeed, a frame of mind and attitude that disagrees with politics that is not guided by principles of scientific and philosophical outlook.

This is because, to some people, who are not grounded in a comprehensive understanding of the objective nature of social being and social consciousness, democracy is still considered a colonial legacy. It is against this background that Ogundowole (25) warns against not taking into account the historico-material regularities and leaning of the political development. He believes that "under such a condition the management of political live-activity of the state and society is haphazard and riddled with crises." Thus, an active playwright must therefore demonstrate a high degree of leadership and passion that is all encompassing in terms of giving hope and inspiration to the people. This model of democracy and its quality of leadership as described by Iorapuu must be paramount on the playwright's psyche, hence;

> It takes a leader with clear vision, passion and integrity emblematic with a high sense of maturity to radically democratize democracy and uplift hitherto tragically submerged voices (24)

Nevertheless, the state of theatre in a democratic dispensation should be seen taking the posture of a crucial personal diary of a playwright and how his artistic psychological dramatic presentations re-establish anew the universe of being for his people. In other words, he prepares the masses of Nigeria on the need for the sustainability of democracy as a form of government that would be more beneficial to Nigerians as a people. Therefore, the playwright as artists in society should realize the importance of making a people once colonized to be more thoughtful and conscious of their earlier state of slavery and the opportunity of an alternative (democracy) that is presently within their purview. These politically committed playwrights have to resort to using literary diplomacy that consist in creating characters that are analogous to those already in existence in any democratic society to underscore their point.

According to Agbada (7)
> It must be a theatre to which the entire people can respond because they see in it their inner lives, the imitation of their daily existential situation, their useful tradition, their progressive customs, their essential metaphysical beliefs, their linguistic and expressive repertoire; and in it an effort to educate, inform, organize, influence and incite them into life-saving and mancipatory actions.

The increasing literary works therefore should apply a customary approach where the socio-political observations of the playwright can no longer be portrayed as a behind the scene phenomenon. This is particularly as playwrights' also view nations under authoritarian rule democratize themselves either genuinely or ostentatiously. After all, "most scholars agree that democracy, on some level, is desirable and necessary in a cogently governed society." Johnson and Lee (38) Consequently, and in this instance, the playwright bothers himself with why the sub-saharan African region still flounder in authoritarian rule. This is true because, democracy as a phenomenon should be able to engender Nigerian playwrights with a view to finding solutions to our seemingly intractable socio-political setback. The playwright must be able to diagnose the causes of our lack of national coercion through investigating certain subtle shades of the Nigerian democratic predisposition in order to ascertain the pulse of the nation as well as present a thematic focus. He (playwright) must strive to redirect the wavering socio-political and monolithically characterized Nigerian culture that is already eating up the nation. Sufficing to say that, "the creative artist, by his training, is knowledgeable about the psychology of preference and products or service intended for a target audience in a given environment." Emeji (94) More importantly, that playwrights have taken their findings depending on the themes that affect them most to different states of the Federation for presentation. This would be practically the same as to either publicizing democratic dividends or on the other hand, presenting a discontent as the case maybe.

One of the ingenuity of the playwright from the cultural point of view could be seen from the dramatic adaptation of Chinua Achebe's *Things Fall Apart* which the Nigerian Television Authority (NTA) serialized in 1986. This act would no doubt be considered as an innovative thought, hence it revealed a lot about the socio-cultural temperament of the Eastern people of Nigeria to not only Nigerian, but to the rest of the world. This again is to show how creativity in dramatic presentations could enrich and at the same time unravel even the political history that characterized and bound a particular group of people and their society.

This frame of thought appears to be the reason why Ukala's discourse on the Challenges of Nigerian Cultural Revival in the face of Modernity encouraged governments all over the federation to;
> Encourage modern Nigerian writers of prose fiction, plays and poetry to draw on and adapt the published indigenous sources, for example, history, folk tales, proverbs and songs (57-58)

Ukala goes further to hint that good adaptations as text for educational institutions with a view to instituting a national and state competition would no doubt serve as a creative and profitable means of reinventing the nation's true identity. The strength of drama in this regards can be seen as a veritable medium through which participation, critical consciousness, dialogue and understanding of the issues can be inculcated amongst the citizenry. Idegu citing OyinAdejobi observes that; theatre artists are regarded as;
> Practical journalists because they may be some issues of public importance which the government wants to publicize but which the people may not care to write about. And of course many people cannot read in our society. Through special plays we can publicize such issues and interest the people in them. (18)

It becomes obvious therefore that the theatre artist and the democratic environment must find themselves in a mutual relationship that would contribute to the reaffirmation or devaluation of the democratic ideals. The playwright's creativity could be in form of using "theatre performance as a platform for reaching the society, for shaping their attitudes and even their consciousness." Jeyifo (109) It is in this regards that Boal in his *Theatre of the Oppressed* has used theatre not only to address the marginalization syndrome of the ordinary Brazilian, but has used the theatre as a platform for political education to theatricalise politics. He actually formulated a legislative theatre whose ideology held politicians accountable for their actions or inactions. Therefore, in this moment of national emergency, "Nigerian playwrights will show that there is an urgent need for Nigerian playwrights to join the voice of democracy and national unity" Musa (47). On a similar note, Uzoji whose discourse lies on how Nigeria's democracy and its political transition have been bedeviled by lots of crises has this to say;

> In Nigeria alone, a large group of writers, artists and musicians Have played prominent roles in placing the arts at the forefront Of the nation-building, democratic struggles of the last five decades. The group includes among others, Ola Rotimi, Fela Anikulapo-Kuti, Sunny Okosuns, Molara Ogundipe, Femi Osofisan, Femi Fatoba, Niyi Osundare, Festus Iyayi, Bode Sowande, Iyorwuese Hagher, Funso Aiyejina, Tunde Fatunde, Esiaba Irobi, Olu Obafemi, Tess Onwueme, Salihu Bappa, Ogah Abah, and Ahmed Yerima. (215)

To him the list can be enlarged in order to accommodate more radical intelligentsia in the political way of life of a country like Nigeria.

Plot of *Drums of War*
Bakare's *Drums of War* is a daring proclamation against the evils of wars generally. The play which is dedicated "to those who perish in Somalia, Rwanda, Liberia, Bosnia, Herzegovina and

Yugoslavia, Biafra-Nigeria and the small village of Zango-Kataf" condemns the option of war as a means of settling disputes. It calls on the human conscience to consider the millions of people killed over avoidable conflicts and sue for peace.

The play begins with an introductory prologue by the ninety years old musician and story teller, Ogbegun, who speaks of how he has continued to search for an end to the cycle of man's inhumanity to man, howbeit unsuccessfully.

In Movement I, series of war chants rent the air as charged warriors from Abakpa and Ibuji engage themselves in a fierce and vicious battle, in defense of their kingdoms. Amidst those noisy chants of war, kill, and destroy, a group of women appear from the inland singing songs of peace, unity and tolerance. The Abakpa warriors are forced to listen to voices of reason as they begin to lay down their arms. Seeing this, the Ibuji warriors saw no point in furthering the battle

Otubu, Queen of Abakpa, wife to king Onome and bearer of his children, unexpectedly shows up at the battlefield to congratulate the women for their decisive action in bringing to an end the unjust war declared by her hot-tempered husband. She declares her support for the women and encourages the warriors to listen to the voice of reason. Hearing this, the soldiers were inspired and resolve to stand against the king's decision for the war.

Based on this, the women begin singing and dancing to songs of solidarity, peace and unity as Otubu "dances round, giving each of the people a small flag of Nigeria." (Rasaki, 59) Akogun, the chief warrior of the armies of Abakpa comes in seething with anger and fury almost immediately as Otubu leaves. He chides the warriors for their 'chicken-hearted' behaviour of abandoning the war and allowing a group of harmless women to disarm them. He orders them in the name of the king to pick up arms and resume battle, but they all responded in the negative, with one voice. He attempts forcing them, but is rather attacked, and manages to escape lynching.

Movement II begins in a very light and merry-making mood in the king's palace. The chiefs sing to usher in the king and his family while another chief-Beleku, is conspicuously uninterested. He accuses the king of being insensitive to the plight of his people and wonders why the king should be celebrating and making merry while their sons perish in the battlefield. This angers the king who orders that Beleku's hands be tied up. To further show his anger, the king slaps Beleku for insulting and challenging his authority and thereafter orders that he be taken away and killed.

Just then, Akogun rushes into the palace like a man being chased by a hundred vexed lions. He tells the king how the soldiers have refused to fight and how he was attacked when he insisted that the 'war must continue'. The king's anger is once again rekindled beyond reason as he commands Akogun to return to the battlefield and resume battle. Akogun then enquires for the first time, the reason for the war from the king and is told that it was because "the Ibuji people have refused to bow down to our deity, the awesome AbasiIbom, the supreme God". Akogun therefore argues that the law of the land permits its people to worship "whatever" they chose to worship and besides no religion supports the use of force. In the midst of this disagreement, Akogun offers to resign as chief warrior of the land. The king then orders that Akogun be banished and stripped of all his titles, lands and place in the "Society of Lions". Otubu's attempt to advise the king against such hasty decisions is rebuffed.

The mood in the palace becomes tense as the king appoints Gbeje as the new Akogun of the land, but Gbeje humbly declines for reasons of fear. King Onome then calls on Jeje to take up the mantle and attack Ibuji, but he too would not. Just then, like a man inspired by something innately evil, Gbeje suggests that the king's only son-Orighoye, be made the Akogun. The king protests, but Orighoye accepts and so the decision is reached. Orighoye, the prince of Abakpa and heir apparent to the throne of Onome, girds up and leads his father's army to their waterloo.

In Movement III, the battle between the Abakpa and Ibuji becomes fierce and terribly bloody. The soldiers of Abakpa people are outnumbered, outfoxed and understandably defeated. When king Onome and his wife discover that their son, Orighoye is killed in the battle, he is embittered whereas Queen Otubu commits suicide. The people of Abakpa, in revolting against him, demand that he vacates the throne in accordance with the custom as he now has no heir. The townspeople offer him a calabash which by interpretation means suicide and on that note, the play comes to an end.

Bakare's *Drums of War* and The Nigerian Democratic Space
There is no gainsaying the fact that if playwrights' align or realign their plays and stage-craft with positive leadership qualities, they would be on their way to not only conscientizing the populace, but providing an exposé on the unwholesomeness of appalling and negative leadership. Qualifying theatre therefore as a potent social and moral force in society, Odelami (111) believes that, it can be "guided by the precepts of the interrelatedness of art and society on one hand and of art and politics on the other hand". It is this sociological thrust that should give impetus to a playwrights' search for ideology and democratic order in his society.

Bakare has used his play as a vital tool upon which a resurgence of positive leadership and the democratic environment in Nigeria is being mirrored. In it, the democratic principles tend to have been placed side-by-side with harshness, threats, unnecessary intimidation, bestiality and general autocratic rulership. It is a situation where positive leadership vacuum is created and its consequences even on the so called leaders. It is rather lack of democratic principles that we are being reminded of as indicated in the opening lines of Ogbegun;

> For four scores and ten have I traversed through the tunnel of our nation and for four scores and ten have I hoped to see the glittering light at the end of the tunnel. For four scores and ten have I seen dog eat

dog, mortals chase their own shadows and the darkness deepens each day that passes. (57)

Bakare is simply referring to the terrible state of our nation here and how hopeless and bastardized things had become for us as a people. The resentment between the egocentric leaders and the led even in a democracy is so glaring that the led are left out in the scheme of nation-building. Presenting the play to Nigerians at this time of our emerging democracy presupposes that Nigeria is in dire need of purposeful leaders, especially in a democratic dispensation. Therefore, Bakare's incisive utterance is to use drama to mobilize society towards sustaining and achieving democratic principles for the growth and development of society.

The principle behind *Drums of War* lies between illusion and reality. Bakare uses contemporary situations through his use of diction and language, characterization and images. *Drums of War* serves as a timely warning for the modern Nigerian politician who must realize the importance of good governance to the people. The play draws from diverse ethnic beliefs within the Nigerian state to buttress the age-long cycle of hostilities among its populace. Bakare quickly recommends a swift return to the principles and dictates of democracy as the surest way out of unnecessary bloodshed and cycles of unproductive wars.

Democracy as it is has been defined as a system of government chosen by the people, to be entirely made up of the people for the advancement of the people's goals and objectives. If this is true of democracy as accepted and practiced all over the world by the people, then there are certain accompanying principles which every democratic system must measure up to in fulfillment of their democratic mandate. These principles are given prominent thematic posture in Bakare's *Drums of War*.

It is indeed worthy to note that, in every democracy, elected and appointed officials are responsible for their actions and inactions and must as a matter of necessity be accountable to the people. In *Drums of War*, King Onome failed in his responsibility to the people by assuming himself a demi-god. It is a situation whereby he made himself inaccessible, incorrigible and unquestionable.

He demeaned the people without whom he would have been a nobody. Hear him;

> The people, the people, who are the people? A group of common, poverty stricken rabble who do not know the left from the right hands. Look, we are here to direct their affairs and guide them. The people must have leaders who will make decisions for them. (68)

King Onome showed his undemocratic traits in more ways than one. Of course the people must have leaders who will make decisions for them, but not when the people wished otherwise. For example, the people told Akogun-the king's chief warrior to;

> Tell the king and his chiefs that we women, the mothers of the land insist that this war should stop and we have come to the battle field ourselves to stop the soldiers, our husbands, sons and brothers from fighting. Tell him we no longer want war but peace and tolerance. (62)

The women warned him (king), the soldiers did, the elders and chiefs in his palace also tried to caution him, his wife-Otubu even attempted to dissuade him from going against the wishes of the people, but he remained adamant, unthinking and stubborn. This is like defying the age-long Italian maxim of; 'Voxpopuli, Vox Dei' meaning 'the voice of the people is the voice of God'. Instead he rebuffed; 'the war must continue'. Knowingly or unknowingly to king Onome and his cabinet members that they had drifted too far away from the people at the grass-root as their viewpoint on issues of communal bearing appear to be failing to match with the people's expectations. The people's message of "tell the king and his chiefs" is a pointer to the fact that they (people) had disowned their king and his chiefs even before the war began.

It is a known fact that most democratic countries have a list of their citizen's rights and freedoms. This helps to limit the powers of the government and prevent possible abuse as well as spell out the extent of the freedom guaranteed to all citizens and members of that democratic setting. However, in the script under review, King Onome fails to understand this, and as a result, lost the right to commandeer his subjects. Despite the king's insistence on having his way, which he did, the people still had their say and in the most resounding manner too. Judging from the queen's distribution of the Nigerian flag to all women and warriors of the land, one would assume the queen to be a unifying personality in the play, whereas the king who distributed arms and ammunitions to the people is divisive in nature. The Nigerian constitution recognizes freedom of speech, but when Beleku aired his views on the happenings in the land, he was not only beaten, but manhandled and eventually murdered. Consequently, everyone else took caution and great care to always say what the king would love to hear. Freedom of expression was suppressed, and even when the people spoke, mindless of the fact that it could be God, his *Abasilbom* speaking through them, he silenced all voices of reason and proceeded to war.

Besides, citizen's participation has been adjudged the single most important basic ingredient of a democracy anywhere in the world. In fact, citizens of a given democratic setting can take part in the administration of their affair by running for an office in an election, voting in an election, debating issues of governance, attending community meetings and even protesting in order to build a strong democracy. In Bakare's *Drums of War,* the people chose to participate by means of a peaceful protest and the king considered their actions as treacherous. He fails to recognize the rights of the people to protest against his decisions; hence he took every necessary measure to truncate their efforts. The townspeople on the other hand refused to be intimidated by the Kings' egocentric mind-set. The soldiers played their part at least by participating in the war with the Ibuji until the women talked them out of it. Conversely, the women chose the part of peace as a panacea towards building a democracy. Otubu upholds this view by saying that;

> Like the water from the snail shell, our job as women has always been to cool the heat that runs in our men's veins and melt the rock in their hearts when it matters. I am not surprised that you women of the land have taken this giant step and I want to let you

> know that I am solidly behind you (jubilations). Don't be surprised that I, Otubu, the king's wife is supporting you in stopping this war declared by my husband, the king. I have always told my husband that he should promote love and Peaceful co-existence with our neigbours instead of instigating us against our fellow mankind. (58)

However, the king's obdurate stance of basking in the radiance of his inestimable authority caused his followers to abandon him when he needed them most. Gbeje and Jeje for example, rejected the offer of an exulted office such as the *Akogun of Abakpa kingdom* when the king stripped and de-robed Akogun of the position. This rejection is borne out of fear that they may not live long enough to enjoy the benefits accruing from occupying such an exulted position in the land. Thus, king Onome's face-off with Akogun plainly denies the people their democratic right to political participation and only letting them participate only in a way that pleases him. He brought to the front burner ethnocentric issues like religious intolerance and other vices inimical to democratic principles. He wanted the Ibuji people utterly destroyed simply because they do not subscribe to his own definition of God. For him, the 'awesome *Abasilbom* is the Supreme Being who must be worshiped by all. Although this does not seem to go down well with some members of his cabinet, yet they cannot challenge their god-king. In fact, the king does not only believe himself an equal with the gods, but also think that the worship of his own *Abasilbom* is a constitutional matter that must be enforced. This action is rather undemocratic, and since the playwright draws inspiration from his immediate environment, it would be safe to assume that he used this pointer to condemn the spade of religious crises in Nigeria over the years.

Still basking in arbitrariness, king Onome in a show of shame, partiality and selfishness rejected the people's suggestion that his son- Orighoye and heir apparent takes over as Akogun (chief warrior) and resume hostilities with the Ibuji people. He argues that his son, Orighoye "cannot be exposed to unnecessary danger" simply because he is the son of a king and as a result, is destined to becoming a king too. He must sit back in the palace celebrating and feasting with his family, whereas other people's families are in the battlefield fighting themselves to death.

In a democratic system of government, no one is above the law, not even the king. But contrary to expectations, king Onome violates the most sacred of all laws. He murdered Beleku for reminding him that his reign (king) does not only impel crueltyand carnage, but that the war is futile and senseless. He endangered the lives and properties of the people he swore to protect. King Onome is hot-tempered, incorrigible and unfit to rule in a democratic setting.

Staging *Drums of War* in Abuja
It is assumed that; "theatre is not shaped only by playwrights, directors, actors, but also by audiences and by the cultural norms of the society to which all belong". (Bradley ettal, 16) Therefore, as part of 2005 activities lined-up for celebrating Nigeria's *Democracy Day* at the seat of government-Abuja, was the command graphic presentation of Bakare's*Drums of War* at the Cyprian Ekwensi Centre for Arts and Culture, Abuja. The performance was sponsored by the former F.C.T. Minister-Nasir El Rufai and organized by the Abuja Arts Council. The presentation of *Drums of War* couldn't have come at a better time than this as government functionaries were also expected to be part of this dramatic experience.

The staging of the play by the playwright himself revealed a lot of innovations arising from the director's artistic commitment and political exigencies of his time. Assessing the circumstance surrounding the performance of *Drums of War* as a protean encapsulation of the organic image of the Nigerian polity, the director needed to carve a suitable approach towards its realization on stage. Considering the fact that; "the directorial approach, the cast, the effects, the nature of the audience and the degree of sponsorship, are all elements that contribute to the success of the production." (Johnson, 40) Bakare as the play director simply transforms his personal vision as author of the play into a public performance in which interaction and exchange of gestalt between the artist and audience could take place. Bakare's vision in presenting the play using a realistic directorial style recorded his maturity within the socio-political environment, the sensibilities of his audience and of course achieving the purpose for the production.

Therefore, as most directors, he considered it expedient to tinker with the original storyline in order to capture the mood of the nation and her leadership crises and strategies. The performance qualityamongst other factors was carefully handled by the director. First, the choice of the play in which "he has to choose a play that is relevant to the social and moral conditions of his environment." (Bell-Gam, 105) From his choice of play, auditioning, casting, rehearsals, to the public consumption of the play, Bakare maintained a friendly atmosphere in which all other production elements like sound, lighting, set design/scenery, costumes, make-up, even the special effects unit were all harnessed tolerably. Indeed, his directorial approach assumes that of a democratic director in terms of blockings, ground plans and character-actions.

In staging the play, Bakare's realistic settings is enhanced with a lot of theatrical elements like dance, music, spectacle, dialogue to create a masterly-mix for his audience appeal. This left the audience with the impression of one who has a compact initiative of the aesthetic super objective of the play. Scene- after-scene, the play maintained a particular steady rhythm, mood and motion-action. In casting the play for example, Bakare as it were, exemplified creativity as he had envisioned the best actors from within and outside Abuja for the performance. Despite the different casting methods like 'assignment technique', 'volunteer technique', 'traditional technique' confronting Bakare as the director he rather settled for the assignment technique which is the same like 'stock character method'. His reason is simply that he already knows the capabilities of most of the actors based on his previous knowledge and performance experience with them.

Hence as a result of his proclivity for verisimilitude he matched the actor's heights, physiognomy and vocal strength with those of the characters in the play. Actors with remarkable physiques type, carriage and resounding tonal inflections were given roles. Indeed, the physiognomy, carriage, and vocal inflections of KayodeAiyegbusi were a perfect match and the best character portrayal as he played King Onome. In the same vein, the likes of Esther Omale playing queen Otubu; Awake Ogoh playing Beleku; Zulu Adigwe as Akogun and Joe Wenna as Orighoye amidst others were best seen as stock characters for the roles they played. The features of their body's, face, psyche and aura were used by Bakare as perfect indicators of their character and temperament.

Bakare's penchant for very elaborate settings was at its best as the massive stage of the Abuja Arts Council and its conditions provided the opportunity. The set was constructed in a manner that revealed a realistic picture of king Onome's palace. It was well structured that the entire stage represented the king's palace. In fact, the mass set and painted sceneries, sound effect and perspectives created a sense of realism and make believe in the minds of the audience especially through the use of Ellipsoidal, Fresnel, Floods, Follow-Spot, crystallized jells and Strobe lights. It made the illumination of the set-design and the various costumes worn by the actors create aesthetical configurations of the production by way of weaving the visual and sound effects into the verbal text in every scene. For example, the costumes and make-up depicted not just the culture and locale of the play, but revealed a good sense of character portrayal in term of status and social personality of the people who wore them.

The significance and handling of lights in a performance of this magnitude cannot be overemphasized. The lights for the performance were quite strong and well handled. As the play begins, Ogbegun is made known to the audience by a *follow-spot* in order to show his importance to the performance as the Narrator who bears the message of the play. Also, in the well choreographed war scene for example, Strobe lights interspersed with red and yellow colours was used to heighten the scene. It was like a perforated disk rotating in front of a high-intensity light source, at the same time producing sparks of lights on stage. This technique did not only enhance the convincing movement and dance patterns of the warriors, but also the conveyance of danger, tensed mood, uncertainty and anxious moments in the play. In fact, as the war raged on, we witnessed a dramatic stunt where one of the warriors cut off an enemy's hand and proceeded to drink the blood gushing from the severed hand. From the make-up properties and lighting effect, Bakare's creative technicalities no doubt amplified the situation as very realistic. He also incorporated certain ritualistic displays which he heightened through lights as we see in the grand conferring of war ornaments on Orighoye in preparation for the battlefield as the new *Akogun of the Abakpa*. The use of these various lights contributed greatly in creating aesthetic value that was pleasing in appearance as the performance unfolded.

Conclusion
Theatre is regarded as not only a roadmap to raising the issues associated with democracy, but as a platform upon which round table discussions on such issues can be tackled. It becomes apt therefore to see the structure of actions in *Drums of War* as conceived in thoroughly theatrical terms hence tone and gestures and the ideology of the play repeatedly parodied the 'majestic sadness' associated with war and other social vices. Bakare's *Drums of War* reveals that there is no clear distinction between the democracy that is purported to be practiced by Nigerian politician and the manner of military control of yesteryears. He critiques the extreme mentality that go on in a democracy by our leaders. By the actions of Akogun, Beleku, Otubu, 1st Women, 1st and 2nd soldier and a few others, Bakare demonstrates certain Marxist ideology where the masses do not resign to fate, but could take their destinies in their own hands. This is seen as characters questioned existing obnoxious belief system afflicting the land, hence their rooting for social change.

In fact, the central message lies within encouraging the ordinary working class individual to be more proactive in tackling the 'stumbling block' or rather, bad leaders in any democracy. Through a brilliant crafting of characters, he uses war as a metaphor to satirize the notion of wanton violence (political, religious, communal) and destruction of innocent lives and properties in our nation due to unprecedented display of snail-speed development and egocentric leadership instinct by some of our leaders. The performance ensures through the various characters that even those in government are not above the law. They too must act in accordance with the dictates of the laws of the land. This is succinctly captured as king Onome is handed over Agbeni'scalabash;"the calabash of death" indicating suicide.

The creative artists should be seen organizing the Nigerian society through his writings with a view to mobilizing people and/or rejecting saboteurs or over-ambitious political enthusiasts who would rather subscribe to an oligarchy than a democracy. Invariably, it is only a creative artist that can project the corporate existence and identity of a nation that could leave a lasting cultural impact on the life of the people who even recognize themselves in those dramas.

Dramatic text and performances must exude great theatrical relevance and need for change in the wake of increasing violence and corruption in Nigeria. Through the instrumentality of literary objects, the playwright must deploy a transformative role in society. For example, one of the most passionate and profound statement against war is Bertolt Brecht typifying of the seventeeth century European war in *Mother Courage and her Children* in which Brecht reaffirms the absurdity and senselessness of war. In this wise, the carnage of war as also expressed in Yerima's*Little Drop* and a host of other playwrights' is what has become the fulcrum of Bakare's dramatic thrust in some of his plays like *Rogbodiyan*and *Drums of War*.

The role of theatre therefore in reconstructing the democratic environment must rely on awakening consciousness mechanism and coercing of society. In fact, African dramaturgy and performance in the thinking of Traore,(91) must "bring about a certain solidarity; it is a means of creating a common consciousness" . Therefore, the imaginative power to reflect the goals and aspirations of the leaders of that period must be captured succinctly by dramatists. In other words, the theatre through its performance should strive to develop as well as bringing to the fore, the spirit of innovating social reforms and comradeship in nation building.

Works Cited

Adamolekun, Ladipo. *The Governors and the Governed: Towards Improved Accountability for Achieving Good Development Performance*. Ibadan: Spectrum Books Limited, 2008

Agbada, Nwachukwu. "Drama and Theatre for Rural Emancipation in Nigeria: A Modest Proposal" *Nigeria Magazine, vol 57 Nos 1 and 2* January-June 1989. Pp 5-9

Bell-Gam, Henry Leopold. "The Role of the Artistic Director in a Democratic Environment: What Prospect for the Nigerian Theatre". *Nigerian Theatre Journal*. (Ed) Ayo Akinwale. Ilorin: Folly Publishers, Volume 6, Number 1, 2000. Pp. 105-110

Bradley, David, Thomas Philip and Pickering Kenneth.*Studying Drama: A Handbook*. London: Croom Helm Ltd, 1983.

Crow, Brain. *Studying Drama*. Essex: Longman Group Limited, 1983.

Doki, Ama Gowon. "Culture, Theatre and the National Question: A Critical Appraisal of Saint Gbilekaa's Prized Chickens are not Tasty". *Nigerian Theatre Journal* (Ed) JenkeriZakariOkwori. Abuja: Madol Press Ltd, 2004.

Emeji, Josiah M. "Exploring Corporate Subsidy and Participation in the Arts in Nigeria" *Nigeria Magazine, vol 57 Nos 1 and 2* January-June 1989. Pp 94-99

Etherton, Micheal. *The Development of African Drama*. London: Hutchinson University Library for Africa, 1982.

Fischer, Earnest. *The Necessity of Art*.Harmondsworth: Penguine Books, 1986.

Glilekaa, Saint. "Nigerian Literature and Social Experience: The *ZakiBiam* Episode" .*Culture, Identity and Leadership in Nigeria*.

(Eds) Emmanuel Samu Dandaura and AbdulRasheed Abiodun Adeoye. Ibadan: Kraft Books Limited, 2010.

Idegu Emmy U. "Between Theatre and Society: The Question of Understanding". *Theatre, Politics and Social Consciousness in Nigeria.*(Ed) EgwugwuIllah. Jos: Leadership Production Press, 2002.

Iorapuu, Tor. "Democratic Innovations in Nasarawa State: Participatory Leadership Paradigms of Alhaji Aliyu Akwe Doma".*Culture, Identity and Leadership in Nigeria.* (Eds) Emmanuel Samu Dandaura and AbdulRasheed Abiodun Adeoye. Ibadan: Kraft Books Limited, 2010.

Jeyifo, Biodun. *The Truthful Lie.* London: New Beacon Books Ltd, 1985.

Johnson, Effiong. *Play Production Processes.* Lagos: Concept Publication Limited, 2001

Johnson, Patrick and Lee Chris. "Political Liberalisation and Democratic Change in Sub-Saharan African, 1970-1995: A Cross-Sectional Analysis". *Democracy and Development: Journal of West African Affairs. Harmattan Edition.Volume 3 Number 2,* 2003. Pp 37-50

Musa, RasheedAbiodun. "Sustaining Nigeria's Nascent Democracy: Playwrights and the Need for Content Reappraisal".*Theatre and Democracy in Nigeria.* (Eds) Ahmed Yerima and Ayo Akinwale. Ibadan: Kraft Books Limited, 2002

Mustapha, Khalid Al Mubarak. "From a Playwright's Notebook".*African Theatre: Playwrights and Politics.* (Eds) Martin Banham, James Gibbs and Femi Osofisan. Indiana: Idiana University Press, 2001

Obafemi, Olu. "Making a Difference through Theatre in a Democracy".*Theatre and Democracy in Nigeria*. (Eds) Ahmed Yerima and Ayo Akinwale. Ibadan: Kraft Books Limited, 2002

Odelami, Victoria. "Theatre and Democracy: The Need for the Resurgence of Positive Leadership Model in Nigerian Plays". Nigerian Theatre Journal (Ed) Ayo Akinwale. Ilorin: Folly Publishers, Volume 6, Number 1, 2000. Pp. 111-118

Ogundowole, Kolawale E. *Philosophy and Society*. Lagos: Correct Counsels Ltd, 2004

Rasaki, BakareOjo. *Drums of War*. Zaria: Tamaza Publishing Company, 1994

Traore, Bakare. *The Black African Theatre and its Social Functions*. Ibadan: Ibadan University Press, 1972

Ukala, Sam. "*Harvest of Ghosts*: The story of a collaboration". *African Theatre: Playwrights and Politics* (Eds) Martin Banham, James Gibbs and Femi Osofisan. Indiana: Idiana University Press, 2001

----------------. " Politics of Aesthetics". *African Theatre: Playwrights and Politics*. (Eds) Martin Banham, James Gibbs and Femi Osofisan. Indiana: Idiana University Press, 2001

----------------. "Challenges of Nigerian Cultural Revival in the Face of Modernity".*Culture, Identity and Leadership in Nigeria*. (Eds) Emmanuel SamuDandaura and AbdulRasheedAbiodunAdeoye. Ibadan: Kraft Books Limited, 2010.

Uzoji, Emmanuel E. "The Prophetic Power of Drama: Nigeria's 2007 Elections in Soyinka's Beatification of the Area Boy". *Theatre, Culture and Re-Imaging Nigeria*. (Eds) Emmanuel Samu Dandaura and Alex Chinwuba Asigbo. Proceedings of the 23rd Conference of the Society of Nigerian Theatre Artists

(SONTA) Held at the Nasarawa State University, Keffi June 2nd-6th 2010. Pp 214-225

Wa Thiongo, Ngugi. *Writers in Politics*. London: Heinemann, 1981

Wa Thiong'o, Ngugi and MugoMicereGithae. *The Trial of DedanKimathi*. Heinemann Books Ltd, 1976.

Yakubu, Angell Nguemo and Iyav Ben Due. "Culture and Global Peace: Lessons from Playwrights". *Theatre, Culture and Re-Imaging Nigeria*. (Eds) Emmanuel SamuDandaura and Alex ChinwubaAsigbo. Proceedings of the 23rd Conference of the Society of Nigerian Theatre Artists (SONTA) Held at the Nasarawa State University, Keffi June 2nd-6th 2010. Pp 123-129

Artistic Direction and Directorial Exploration in Bakare, Ojo Rasaki's *The Gods and The Scavengers* and *Once Upon A Tower*

By
Arinde, Tayo Simeon, Ph.D.

Introduction
Plays, which are the intellectual product and the artistic creative invention of a playwright, can be made unambiguous when directions are provided. This is because, providing direction promotes transparent synergetic relationship between the playwrights, the artistic directors, the audience and the society at large. We have observed that lack of synergy has been responsible for why playwrights stage a walk out of theatres because of the "bad way" their creative works was handled by play directors. There is no doubting the fact that most of the 'celebrated' artistic works of many playwrights' today have suffered from poor patronage because they lack direction. This perhaps is the reason why the works of a few playwrights are recycled year in year out. In this study, we examine the concept "direction" as well as the concept "exploration" and how they have helped our understanding of the two play texts under review: *The Gods and the scavengers* and *Once upon a tower*. We interrogate the work, using Graham Hitchen's *Directional thinking theory*. *The Directional thinking theory*, which was propounded in 2006, is: "a *dynamic* approach to strategy and project development – focusing on the longer-term, by helping to create new programmes, projects and future plans which can test the appetite for change and to help make it happen".

This theory is apt considering the predominantly directionless approaches that mars Nigerians focus on issues. Nigeria with her abundant human and material resources, still gropes in the forest, without a visible direction. These selected theatrical pieces provide a dynamic approach that would engender new directions toward positive change. The theory emphasises amongst others; leadership development, relationship and stakeholder engagement, team building and change management. This we consider as a welcome approach to complimenting numerous efforts of scholars, socio critics and human right activists who have devoted their lives and resources to seeing Nigeria advance in a purposeful direction.

In this paper, we shall examine the issue of 'direction' from two perspectives; one from sociological standpoint and the second from the artistic directorial exploration perspective. By sociological direction within the content of this work, we refer to the direction for achieving egalitarianism and objective socio-political standard. These we found in the two plays under examination. On the other hand, an exploration of the artistic directions, which we refer to as directorial exploration, is to educate us on how the playwright wants his concept in the interpretation of their creative works to be sustained when play directors put the plays on stage for performance.

As we engage in the analytical dissection of the two play texts, we are overwhelmed by the direction provided by the playwright as he addresses the realities of the events around him and us. Bamikunle (2001, p.v) in his forward to the play *Once upon a tower* identifies these when he describes Bakare's work as reacting to the "very stark realities of events around [him]…presented in an artistically significant way". This will be one of the directions that we intend to explore in the two play texts. We are not oblivious of the fact that playwright don't just write, they are induced by the happenings in and around their environments. They capture, using their artistic view lenses what they have seen, heard or read. In *Once upon a tower*, we see the muse in Bakare pointing to the decays that have enveloped our citadels of learning, which he puts together in a most compact and down-to earth manner. In the same direction, in *The Gods and the scavengers,* we were confronted with the stark reality of the degree of corruption that the Nigerian society has had to contend with; orchestrated in different metaphors of dramatis personae that run through the play. Having critically examined the two plays, which we describe as didactic pedagogic artistic works, we observe that the two play texts also shocked us into the realities of the menace of the societal ills in our society. It is also gratifying that the playwright made significant attempt to provide directions towards eradicating them.

Some concepts will run prominently in this work, we consider it apt to illuminate on them. The concepts are; *'Direction'* and *'exploration'*.

Direction and Exploration are very common concepts, which should not be subjected to any misinterpretation.

Direction, according to *Webster Dictionary* retrieved from *Webster*.com (2014) is "the course or path on which something is moving or pointing". It also defines it as: "a statement that tells a person what to do and how to do it; an order or instruction". However, for the purpose of this study, we shall adopt the latter definition. Bakare's artistic packages in the two play texts made statements that tell us what to do and how to do them.

Exploration that we made reference to reveals how one (a playwright, director) intends to discover his literary and artistic directions. Therefore, 'exploration' as defined in the *Wikipedia, the free Encyclopedia* (2014 np), is "the act of searching for the purpose of discovery of information or resources" In this work, we shall examine direction and the exploratory approaches adopted in bringing the content of the art work to the fore.

Digests of the play: *The Gods and the scavengers* **and** *Once upon a tower The Gods and the scavengers*
The metaphor of the scavengers employed in the play; *The Gods and the scavengers*, portrays the pathetic characters that citizens of Nigeria are turned into by the leaders who they elected into office with their votes. The scavengers, who are turned to the wretched of the earth and social outcasts, because of the greed and the corruptible dispositions of the leaders they elected. They decide to take their destiny in their own hands by revolting against the corrupt leaders, who are epitomised in the elected

local government Councillors, representing the three major ethnic groups in Nigeria. Bakare, in demonstrating Uka's (2006) as well as the conclusion of Etop Akwang (2006), a critic/dramatist comments at the back page of the script describe the play as: "Bakare's artistic rebellion" and the play which "lampoons the political gangsterism in Nigeria" respectively. Truly, we found this artistic rebellion uneconomically demonstrated but with positive intention's in the play.

Also, in *Once upon a tower*, Bakare presents starkly, the rot in our citadel of learning. He exposes in an unambiguous term the kinds of leaders that our society breeds as epitomised in the antecedents of the Provost, College of Medicine of the Mariapinto University Nigeriana. Three students whose careers are cut short in their primes decide to take their pound of flesh from the provost on the day of the school's convocation ceremony and this buttresses the misnomer in our institutions of higher learning. The students, armed to the teeth, on a vengeance mission made their way to the office of the Vice Chancellor, where the Chancellor and the Chairman governing Council and of course the Vice Chancellor are basking in the euphoria of the success of the Convocation Ceremonies of the Mariapinto University Nigeriana. The armed students, who after manhandling the trio, demand that the Vice Chancellor should produce the atrocious Provost or else, they will be made the sacrificial lamb, have their request met. The atrocities of the provost and his crony lecturers, the corrupt Chairman, Senate House Committee on Education are blown open, before the Chancellor, the Chairman of the school's Governing Council and the Vice Chancellor. Little did these atrocious fellows know that their corruptible tendencies, which they perpetrated, perhaps at a time that they thought no one will know, will later in their lives result in cycle of terrible events. This are the directions that Bakare points us to in the two works under review.

The Playwright, Bakare, Ojo Rasaki
Bakare, Ojo Rasaki was born fifty years ago in Aramoko Ekiti, precisely, on November 8th 1964, Professor Rasaki Ojo Bakare

became the first Nigerian Professor of Choreography and Performing Aesthetics, having drawn his artistic inspiration from his mother. He started his theatre career from being a theatre apprentice under Chief Jimoh Aliu and late Hubert Ogunde. Rasaki took a leap in the pursuance of his theatre career by attending University of Calabar where he obtained his B. A. (Hons.), Theatre Arts and M.A, Play Directing and Playwriting. He had his Ph.D. in Choreography and Dance Studies at Ahmadu Bello University, Zaria, Prof Bakare's career as a University Teacher and a theatre practitioner has earned him many awards. He has handled over 200 major command performances both nationally and internationally amongst which include the command performances for the presidential inaugurations of Chief Olusegun Obasanjo, Alhaji Shehu Musa Yar'Adua and his successor Dr Goodluck Ebele Jonathan. The opening ceremonies of National Sports Festival 2004, Under 17 World Cup 2009, NUGA 2008, NAFEST 2005 and many others were also in the track of his directorial exploits.

Exploring the Direction in *The Gods and the Scavengers*
The truth that playwrights do not just write from a vacuum, but in reaction to situations around them, is made manifest in the artistically woven dramatic piece in, *The Gods and the scavengers.* The play incises the corruptible tendencies that are deeply entrenched in the socio-political and economic diversities in our land. The play definitely, is an eye opener to the ugly leadership misnomers that have made our political system look like it is a government without direction.

The first two words in the prologue "total darkness" (p.vi) present the Nigeria situation as it was and still is. One would imagine that since 2006, when the playwright identified that Nigeria was in darkness, up till now, the situation has remained, if not darker than what the situation was in the past. The first stanza of song raised by the lead singer below, which captures the essence of the dark nature of our nation blazed the trail:

> Lead: Yes, it's the down of a new morning but the promise land is still far away, our destiny is in our hands, we must rise up now or else we perish (p.vi)

When one looks at the period when the play, *The Gods and the scavengers* was written, in 2006, it is clear that the period being referred to was the Alhaji Shehu Shagari, era (1979-1983) the Nigeria first republic era and the military regimes of Major General Buhari/Idiagbon (1983-1985) and subsequently, the Ibrahim Babangida/Shonekan and the Sanni Abacha/Adulsalam regimes between 1985-1999. The reason advanced by the various military regimes that took reign of government from their preceding governments, then, was hinged on the fact that the nation was plunged into barrages of corruption. This situation, the play text under review tries to recall. The story reveals the political travail of a Local Government Chairman, who intends to be transparent but is smeared by his supervisory Councilors on one side and by his own chameleonic tendency to amass wealth. His Councilors who are to be the eyes of the people in his local government administration happen to be the ones extorting from people that they are representing.

The people of the land of Nigeriania, as Bakare describes the setting are presented citizens in the metaphors of the market men and women. Invariably, they represent the three major ethnic groups in Nigeria who congregate in the market square to protest the corruptible tendencies perpetrated by their councillors who are supposed to be their representatives at the Local Government. The people whose businesses were almost wrecked decide to rise to the challenge with the charge from the Iyaloja (Head of the market men women)

> Iyaloja: Yes, that some hoodlums in the name of councilors try to perpetrate irregularities, fraud and long throat should not make us hopeless. We have hope in our Chairman, we have a chairman that listens

> ...let us rise and complain to our Honourable he has ears he will listen.

My people this is not the time to sit and mourn, this is the time to rise and act. (p.16)

Jean-Jacques Rousseau (1712-1778) a French philosopher and writer philosophically describes how corruption crept into our societies when he observes that: "everything is perfect coming from the hands of the Creator; everything degenerates in the hands of man". Bakare in the play under examination, exploring <u>Graham Hitchen's</u> directional thinking provides us with a direction, charging that sitting down and folding our arms is definitely not the way out; rather, we should take action by crying aloud and protest to the appropriate quarters, barring violence and wanton destruction of properties. On many instances, Nigerians have taken the latter in their actions to protest against what did not go down well with them. They have implored the means of arson and all sorts of violent approach, thinking that when such approach is explored we will make responsible leaders out of our leaders but it has not worked. The Bakare's option of a violent free protest seems to be the right action in the right direction as he enumerates in Iyaloja's submission.

In another direction, the Chairman, of the Local Government, Hon. Anago, who demonstrates that that there could be leaders who have exception to corruption, Bakare exemplified this in the Chairman's refusal of gifts offered him by the market women. He tries to demystify the culture of bribing our way to the heart of our leaders before getting their attention as he expounds in the dialogue below:

Anago: Why? Why that? That dispensation has come to an end. I am your Chairman. Why are you giving me gifts for doing my job? I am only doing what I am supposed to be doing, sharing thoughts and sweat with my

> subjects. Why must you go hungry because of that? Why starve yourselves because you must give the Honourable gift? I appreciate your gift but take it away and sell it (p.13).

This prescribes the direction that true leaders should toil. As if that is not enough, the Chairman (Anago) also shows his exception and zero tolerance to corruption, when he openly disagrees with his councilors who pleaded that he forgives the night-watchman that he personally set a trap for and caught red handed collecting bribe from a stage managed armed robber. The Chairman (Anago) uses the scenario to demonstrate his vehement opposition to acts of greed, cheating, stealing and other unbecoming tendencies of his councilors thus:

Anago: (*Rises fiercely in anger*) No way! No way! Gentlemen, I told you, dishonesty will not have a way in this dispensation. Insincerity, greed, love of wealth, love of power, desire to amass wealth at all cost ruined this land during the days of my fathers. I am here to stamp these vices out, no matter what it takes. Zaki, take the man into the underground cell. There he shall spend the rest of his life. (p.23)

The plea of the councillors prior to the Chairman's antiphon, accentuate the caricature of the dispositions of our leaders to issues of corruptions in Nigeria. It reveals how those that we call leaders of the people celebrate pleasure of milking dry their citizens. It also lays bare the different approaches they deploy to perpetrate all kinds of misdemeanour, which manifest in stealing and looting the resources of the country. To get out of our predicaments, Bakare made the above speech in the character of the chairman to engender change in our leaders and point them in a new direction.

Scavengers in the play text under examination denote the metaphors of the hard-working citizens, the downtrodden who, in spite of the very unpleasant economic situation, which the nation is confronted with, take pleasure in scavenging left-overs from garbage bins, to make ends meet. They jettisoned their skills and qualifications, swallow their prides, and take their destiny in their own hands to become relevant in life. For instance, Scavenger 1 reveals the stuff that some of the scavengers we see around are made of in his self-description thus:

Scavenger 1: My name is Prof, suggesting I
am schooled. I teach in the
>morning, in the noon and in the night. I studied in Ibadan and not in Toronto so, my papers can be screened, and they are not obscured. But the men from Toronto are the gods of my land; they cheat, they brag. Indeed their fakery is complete (p.2).

So also are Scavengers 2, 3 and 4 who are healer (Doctor), farmer and technician (pp.2-3) respectively but who our corrupt leaders, cheaters, liars, looters of our treasury and the so called political leaders turned to scavengers. Sometime ago in Nigeria, we recall with nostalgia the different investigation panels set up to confirm the authenticity or otherwise of certificates presented by some major key position holders in our land.

Bakare, in his nine movement play shows how we allow ourselves to be used against each other. We blindfold ourselves to see reason, whereas we allow those that we call politicians whom we elected with our own votes to set us against one another. As he laments this unfortunate situation, he opens our eyes to what should be our disposition to the antics of our corrupt leaders in the speech of scavengers 4 and 2 respectively thus:

Scav 4: How can you make yourselves so
>cheap for these rogues to manipulate? They come telling you stories of how they have been fighting for your rights and how it is the other man who is

	frustrating it, and you draw daggers at one another. Come on! These folks are common thieves, they are not fighting for anybody's interest (p.59).
Scav 2:	If you doubt what we tell you, listen to this; didn't they pretend to you that they were enemies of each other over there? It is a lie. Look we caught them a couple of minutes ago dining and winning together in the Chairman's lodge. It was there we arrested them (p.59).

No doubt, the two dialogues above present the stark prototypical sarcastic political comedy that we experience in Nigeria. In the same direction, Essi, (2014, p.195) observes that "the maladies of corruption and bad leadership have continued to impede our country's march to progress" The question that keeps ruminating in our minds would be, shall we fold our arms and watch these situations? Definitely not, rather we shall be guided by the submission of Scavenger 1 who submits thus:

Scav 1: …We shall burry our dead, try to forget our losses and forgive ourselves for our ignorance. Two, these criminals shall not only cease to be our leaders from this moment, their blood shall wet our road to freedom and their children must never be allowed to taste power in future.

This is a bold initiative, a wise counsel no doubt, but who will bell the cat? The Nigerian political terrain has been one that is full of the most unpredictable summersaults that have not brought any tangible dividend to its citizenry. Since we have tried a few political policies that do not seem to be beneficial, the time has come to redirect our focus towards egalitarianism. It is however, gratifying to observe that in this theatrical piece, Bakare Ojo

Rasaki has provided a direction that our destinies are in our hands, and we are in a position to change it for the better.

In the *Once upon a tower,* Bakare deploys another approach to expose the rot in our citadel of leaning. Of course, one can always appreciate the truthfulness in the power-packed theatrical piece in *Once upon a tower* when one counts the number of years that Bakare, as a University lecturer has had with students. No one could better enumerate the rots that have enveloped Institutions of higher learning in Nigeria. He stripped naked the garbs of pretence that most lecturers robed themselves in, by revealing how some university teachers in the euphoria of self centeredness, delight in murdering the eminence in some promising students. Professor Kurumbete Ijakadi stood proxy for such numerous foxes that devour the flowers of promising students at their prime.

Omowaiye Pedro, by all standards, is a promising eminent gynaecologist who studied Medicine at the Mariapinto University Nigeriana. He graduated after ten years of studentship due to incessant lecturers' strikes and the syndrome of putting the square peg in a round hole - employing incompetent teachers to teach students. Pedro unveils this when he sharply sarcastically rebuffed the consoling interjection of the Chancellor who ignorantly says "it is the will of Allah" thus:

Pedro: The will of Allah? Is it also the will of Allah that a professor who was supposed to nuture (sic) my growth should play politics with my future and as a result stuff me with ignorance? Professor Kurumbete *(Points to him)* wouldn't mind whatever becomes of the future of an innocent student as long as his professional monopoly is permanently guaranteed and his imagined enemies ruined (p.13).

Professor Kurumbete actually did all that Pedro accused him of as he further reveals how the Professor uses his dull, academically backward Girl-friend to set up and expel Dr Akitikori. Dr Akitikori is an innocent but very hard-working and brilliant lecturer who any serious student would have yearned to come across as a lecturer. Pedro reveals below how he is unceremoniously relieved of his job, exposing the role played by Professor Kurumbete:

Pedro: Through the Bandleader of Amebo voices (*points to Band*) Miss Julie, the then girlfriend of yours, the very girl that was used to set Dr Akitikori up? She is the bandleader. Remember she could not complete her medical studies and opted for a combined honours in Music and Drama (p.14).

As highlighted above, Dr. Akitikori's appointment is eventually terminated on the recommendation of the almighty Professor Kurumbete, the Provost, paving way for a mediocre lecturer, one of his cronies, to teach a course he has little knowledge about. The result of the bad teaching is what led to Pedro's misapplication of medication on a patient, his girlfriend on whom he performed an operation on. The misapplication of drug eventually led to her death as Pedro reveals in the dialogue that ensue below:

Olusola: How did you know the precise dose appropriate for her? Ketamine is dispensed at 1 to 4.5mg per kilograrnrme (sic) of body weight.
Pedro: No it is 14.5mg per kilogramme of body weight.
Olusola: Stop clowning Pedro!
Pedro: But I am correct. That is what my Ana 604 note says, I consulted my note before administering the drug. (p.56)

Indeed, an outcome of a bad foundational teaching and the result of the evil done in the dark as it is later revealed in the cycle of effects that manifests later as Pedro narrates in his story below:

Pedro: I was taken to court after several months in the remand home. The presiding Judge was lenient. He handed me a seven years jail term. That was two years ago. However, there in the prison cell, my mind continually tells me that if the minor evacuation had been successful, I wouldn't be a prisoner today. If my teacher had done his job well, I would have been the proud husband of Khadijat today. But Mr Teacher, you taught me nonsense and messed up my life. My liver raged for revenge and I got in touch with my hitmen outside the prison. I escaped in the night and got connected to my men and here we are to accomplish one mission; snuff lives out of all those who made me a half-baked Medical Doctor (p.58).

The father of the late Khadijat, Pedro's girlfriend is the Chairman, Senate House Committee on Education who cornered the contract to supply laboratory equipment to the University but would not. His daughter happens to be the one on whom Pedro uses an overdose sedation drug before performing an evacuation operation on her. Pedro points to the senator his own faulty area thus:

Pedro: ...Now Mr Senator, I need no psychiatrist. You were not my teacher, but you constrained my teacher from teaching me properly. Tell me, what do you know about contract? What do you know about chemicals...what do you know about laboratory equipment that you cornered a contract meant for their being supplied to the University? Of course, you diverted the money into your bank account and supplied nothing. After graduation, I was still a stranger to some facilities I should have been familiar with even as a student. Do you know that was partly responsible for my using the wrong stuff to sedate your daughter and she died in the process? The reason for which I was sent to seven years imprisonment…(p.63)

Overtly or covertly, we tend to downplay the likely negative future effect of our action as Arinde (2013, p. 29) observes that: "we pretend to be oblivious of the negative effects of these incongruous attitudes. We also downplay the attendant harm that they bring to our society". Professor Kurumbete is a prototype of some very senior, self-centred, self glorifying, and outdated academics that litters, our universities and other institutions of higher learning, who take delight in sacrificing merit for mediocrity, just to pad their egos. We note that when these kinds of lecturers sneeze, their cronies catch a cold, which is the reason why they have the effrontery to witch-hunt anyone who stands up for the truth and challenges their turpitude.

Bakare, as a social critic, theatre director and a non-verbal art communicator, exposes the ills in our society and provides direction of identifying them, invariably pointing us to the direction that we can explore to avoid making the same mistake.

Bakare Ojo Rasaki's directorial exploration
All through the two plays under examination, we are bold to say that Bakare explores both artistic direction and directorial elements that navigates us into the ethics of egalitarianism. He made manifest his directorial exploration in the application of the fundamentals of play directing; composition, picturisation, movement, rhythm, pantomimic dramatisation and lavishly embellished the two plays with total theatre idioms with spices of technical effects.

Explicating on his composition, Bakare faithfully applies features of composition picturisation, which Dean and Carra (1965, pp. 109 and 173) describe as "the structure, form, or design of the group…visual interpretation of each movement in the play". For instance, in *The gods and the Scavengers,* Bakare manifests his composition and picturisation exploration as he compose his stage directions that usher in each movement. We shall illuminate on a few of them. For instance, he directed the composition of this scene thus: (*At upstage centre, the other scavs kneel in prayerful position facing stage left as they sing while scav5 became the choirmaster*) (p.4). The placement of the actors reveals the composition of the scene while their action (praying) tells the picture of the action. Also, in *Once upon a tower*, we benefit from Bakare's compositional skill and his picturisation thus: *A bare stage in a dark auditorium. A musical band placed at a conspicuous location in the auditorium play highlife tune and sings* (p.1). Bakare did not only lead readers to direction, in this instance, he grants liberty to any would-be director of the play, the choice to place on stage the musical band at any place on stage that he may consider conspicuous.

Also in movement one, Bakare, shows the composition of a convocation arena in *Once upon a tower*. He showcases this in the stage direction as follow: *The stage is flood lit. A University convocation ceremony. Mid stage right is a podium on it stands the Vice Chancellor and the Registrar who mimetically reads a list of names from a document.* These various directorial explorations run through the two plays.

Bakare also showcases movement and rhythm as part of his directorial exploit. For instance in *Once upon a tower* in Senator Abdul Rahamon Ikeanobi's sitting room in the stage direction on (p. 46) movement is indicated that: *Senator runs inside and re-emerges with Khadijat. Ogbuefi had moved to the left of the room where he is admiring a work of art...* In movement eleven, Bakare dictates the movement in character, Khadijat when he indicates in a part of the stage direction that: "... *She moves furiously towards the exit.* Showcasing what Dean and Carra (1965, p.18) describe as "the stage picture in action".

In analysing Bakare's exploration of rhythm in the plays under examination, a lot of rhythmic elements run through the work providing what Dean and Carra (1965, p.234) call "aesthetic pleasure". One of such is found in *The gods and the scavengers* where it is indicated in the stage instruction: "(*The volume of singing and instrumentation reduces drastically as they speak. The following lines are rendered in the singsong chant called rap).* This situation indicates the aesthetic pleasure that one can derive from departing from a noisy situation to a lower, sonorous, satisfying and pleasing pitch.

Bakare also made it artistically clear that it is not only through the use of dialogue in plays that message could be passed, he underscores pantomime. In the stage direction that ushers in movement one in *Once upon a tower*, during the school's convocation ceremony, he indicates that: ...*On it stand the Vice chancellor and the Registrar who mimetically read a list of names from a document*". (P.5) and in movement eight he also explores mime when he directs that: ... *This scene is purely enacted in mime and dance movements. (*P.36) The use of this element makes the enjoyment of theatrical performance more appreciated, which is in tandem with Dean and Carra's (1965, P.257) observation that "most people are visually minded and therefore are more deeply impressed by what they see than by what they hear".

In analysing his total theatre idiom, we can submit, without prejudice that Bakare, uneconomically employs songs to accentuate mood, which is one of the idiom of total theatre. The songs run through pages vi, 1, 4,5,7,13,15, 16, 33-36,45, 51 and 52 in forms of singsong, chant, rap, richly in operatic nuances in *The gods and the scavengers.* As well as on pages 1-3, 5-614-15,22-23, 27-28, 36, 49 and50 in *Once upon a tower.*

Conclusion
We have in this work examined direction as a guide to achieving egalitarianism in our society, especially in bringing good governance to the people of our nation. We have also examined a few directorial skills that are exhibited in the plays; *The gods and the scavengers* and *Once upon a tower,* which the playwright, Bakare, Ojo Rasaki employed to bring his message to the people.

It has became crystal clear that our society needs to collectively, in one voice, irrespective of our race, creed, position or affinities, imbibe and embrace the concept of zero tolerance for corruption if we must make our society a better place to live. We also found in Bakare's display of artistic skills, warming directorial explorations, which we realise bring aesthetic pleasure to his audience, considering the way he used music, dance and dialogue to accentuate moods in the plays. We, therefore, recommend that playwrights should take a clue from Bakare by writing plays that will show direction to the path of equality, social justice and respect for the opinion of others.

References

Akwang ,E. (2006). A critic/dramatist comment on Bakare, Ojo Rasaki's *The gods and the scavengers*.

Arinde, T.S. (2013). The creative theatrical oeuvre in Sunnie Ododo's *Hard choice*. In Adeoye A.A. (Ed) *The Performer*. (15) Pp26-36. Department of the Performing Arts, University of Ilorin.

Bakare, O. R. (2000) *Once upon a tower*. Uyo: Afahaide Publishing Company.

Bakare, O. R. (2013). *The gods and the scavengers*. Abuja: Roots Books and Journals Nigeria Limited.

Bamikunle, A. (2001). A Professor of Literature's forward to the play; *Once upon a tower*.
Carra, L.and Dean, A (1965). *Fundamentals of play directing*. New York: Holt Rinehart and Winston, Inc.

Essi, D. A. (2014). Issue of fate, corruption and social vices in selected works of James Atu Alachi. In Sunday Enessi Ododo and Jonathan Desen Mbachaga *Theatre and sociocriticism: The dramaturgy of James Alachi*.(pp. 192-204) Society of Nigerian Theatre Artists (SONTA) National Secretariat, University of Maiduguri.

'Exploration' retrieved from *Wikipedia, the free Encyclopedia wikipedia.org* (2014)

Hitchen G. (2006). Directional thinking. Retrieved from http://directionalthinking.net/about/ on 2nd September 2014.

Jean-Jacques R, (1712-1778). Corruption. *Microsoft Encarta Premium* 2009. Redmond WA Microsoft Encarta

'Direction' retrieved from Marriamwebsterdictionary.com on 24 August, 2014

Uka, K (2006). Critique as a professor of drama and socio commentator on the message in Bakare Ojo Rasaki's *The gods and the scavengers*.

Interrogating Dance Drama as a Total Ensemble: A Study of Ojo Bakare's Production of *The Voyage*.

By
Mbara, Nnamdi C

Introduction

The purpose of any dance is the motivation behind such dance. Dance has always been with man; it has always been part of religion, ritual, drama, education and recreation. As an expression of the doings of man and his society, it documents man's tradition and the changes that occur in a society. Dance as we know, is not only a carrier of cultural signs and symbols, rather it also reflects individual and group identity. The dance of a people has been a potent medium through which information regarding geographical, environmental, religious, philosophical, political and social life styles of the people can be sourced. This is because the human body, which is the basic tool and medium of the dancer is endowed with producing and ascribing meanings to dance performance. This is apart from the other theatrical elements and paraphernalia like costumes, props and music that carry symbolic meanings.

The texture of dance is the movement of the dancers and no other media are necessary to reveal expression, symbolism, and eventually poetry non-verbally. Perhaps nowhere else has man ever expressed himself so directly and completely as through dance? Dance is life expressed in dramatic terms. Important events in the community have special dances to enhance their meanings and significances. It is a language, mode of expression, which addresses itself to the mind through the heart using related, relevant and significant movements to musical, poetic stimuli for a deeper insight into our ways of life, our labours, material culture, religious beliefs and disbeliefs, etc. that makes us the people that we have been and at present are revealed to the serious seeker in our dance. Dance in our traditional context is a "total performance". This is evident in our festivals and ceremonies which are usually a meaningful event in the lives of the people and during which the gods are said to be present either as observers or performers.

In the Voyage as a dance drama, the singers intermittently play the role of dancers at the same time, while dancers also play the role of singers as the performance goes on. Like any other African art form, dance is not for the sake of dancing, it commits the individual as it becomes the vehicle for projecting the norms and values of the people. It therefore becomes an onus on the dancer to carry out this responsibility to the society, through dance movements/art. One social characteristics of dance is that, it is functional-integral with life and the rhythm of life.

The concept and definition of dance is a very controversial subject matter, as most scholars have offered various definitions and explanations on this it. The anthropological works by Meek (1925) and Talbot (1926) shows that Nigeria has at least 250 languages, which expresses or define their various environments as ethnic groups. Essien Edet defines dance as "an art by means of which the individual expresses himself and so a method of expression which makes use of the body" (1). Nwamuo Chris explains that:

> As the expression and transference through the bodily movement of mental and emotional experience which as individual cannot express by rational or intellectual means. It is calculated movement, movement with measured steps or a celebration of organized movements (3).

He goes further to argue that dance is a "pure movement in space and time which has theoretical values like any other art form. As a new technique in body language, it is a visual communication medium which embodies a peoples culture and which is a response to music and sound"(3). Bakare, O. R. also shares similar view as he defines dance as "the rhythmic movement of the human body in space and time to make a statement"(1). All the afore-mentioned scholars share a common opinion where they see dance as a means of expressing one's emotions and feelings, rhythmic movement of the human body as well as being a means of communication.

Dance Drama

Dance drama entails telling a dramatic story in dance. In other words, it would be executing drama using dance or the configuration of dance movements. The term dance drama, presupposes the infusion of the artistic genre viz, the dance genre and the drama genre. Narrative dance or dance drama is not the same as opera or a musical dance as most people imagine, rather it is a distinct art form that finds its roots in ritual primitive rites and non-verbal communication where actions speak louder than voice. The primitive man is practical and not theoretical in his interactions with the gods whose speech he did not understand. He uses dance sequences to express his fears. In doing this, he told a story in mime but stylized it through dance. Note, there is necessarily a third genre for the effective co-ordination of the first two (dance and drama), and this is 'music'. Music binds the dance and drama genres, and dictates the movement and footwork. The obvious features of dance drama actually lie in stylized dramatic movements, dance and music. Non-verbal communication is the spirit of dance drama, in the sense that few words or total dumb silence is used, gestures, body movements and use of space are all involved as means of communication.

For dance drama to be visible there must be **plot,** which is the accumulation of indicants, it is that which happened. Dance theatre also communicates ideas through the accumulation of incidents. It tells a story which is simple since dance cannot communicate or convey sophisticated ideas or concepts. The simplicity of the story encloses or envelops the subject matter. This is essentially satisfactory because dance drama is specifically for entertainment and because of its stylized movement and accompaniment of music as well as its largely ritual origin, it concerns itself more with the spiritual rather than the mundane, the sacred rather than the banal, the esoteric rather than the ordinary. All these subsumes/diffuses in a healthy intoxicating atmosphere of rhythmic drumming or music and gyrating dance. The story remains apparent but at a simple level.

Dance drama also requires **Characters** who embody the message. The characters can be human, spirits or animals, depending on the story being told. The theme of the production is exhumed from the interactions between the character and the others, the character and himself and the character and his environment. There is also **Movement** in dance drama, which is stylized motion designed in patterns that are identifiable signature of ideas, imprints of motion aesthetics. **Song** is also an element of dance drama, but not a central element. Africans like songs because most of the songs for a dance deals with folklores. However, song/music for dance drama aids in the conveying of the mood/emotion behind the production.

Ensemble:
An **ensemble** is made up of cast members in whom the principal actors and performers are assigned roughly equal amounts of importance in a dramatic production. The structure of an ensemble cast contrasts with the popular centralization of a sole protagonist, as the ensemble leans more towards a sense of "collectivity and community. According to Harper Douglas, ensemble is:

> all the parts of a thing taken together, so that each part is considered only in relation to the whole... the entire costume of an individual, especially when all the parts are in harmony... the united performance of an entire group of singers, musicians, etc. ... a group of supporting entertainers, as actors, dancers, and singers, in a theatrical production(1).

Other forms of narrative for productions with ensemble casts having equal amounts of importance is demonstrated in the production of the Voyage, where the cast have already been established in their individual performances. In the Voyage, there is no need for a main protagonist in the story as each character shares equal importance in the narrative, successfully balancing the ensemble play. Referential acting is a key factor in executing this balance, as ensembles, 'play off each other rather than off reality'. Lending support to this, the English World Dictionary defines Ensemble as:

> ... all the parts of something considered together and in relation to the whole ... the cast of a play other than the principals; supporting players ... a group of soloists singing or playing together ... the general or total effect of something made up of individual parts ... all together or at once ... involving no individual star but several actors whose roles are of equal importance.

Ensemble casting also became more popular because it allows flexibility for writers to focus on different characters in different scenes. In addition, the departure of a cast is less disruptive to the premise than it would be if the main actor of a production with a regularly structured cast were to leave the performance. Ensemble casts of 20 or more actors are common in big productions like the Voyage, a genre that relies heavily on the character development of the ensemble.

The man Bakare, Ojo Rasaki:
Born on 8th November 1964, Bakare, Ojo Rasaki hails from Aromoko-Ekiti in Ekiti State, Nigeria. He is the first child of Alhaji Sule and Mrs. Sidikatu Bakare. Bakare, O.R. attended A.U.D Primary School Ado-Ekiti, United High school Ilawe Ekiti, after which he had a brief spell with Jimoh Aliu cultural troupe and Late Hubert Ogunde theatre, during which he acted in some Yoruba films. He later attended Ondo State College of Education, Ikere-Ekiti, after which he had another brief stint with Ondo State Centre for Arts and Culture before going to the University of Calabar and later Ahmadu Bello University (ABU), Zaria, where he studied Theatre Arts and Choreography. Apart from his choreography works, which are conspicuous in the repertories of many Nigerian Troupes, Bakare, R.O. was the choreographer in charge of the Gambian National Troupe from 1994-1996.

He has performed and worked with dance troupes in the continents of the world. One of his work's, the Sekai Aiki won the first prize for Nigeria in the group dance category at the world dance competition, Friendship Spring Festival, North Korea in 1997. Also his training workshop with the National dance and Theatre Company of Jamaica in 2003, continues to be a reference point in that country. He has offered training services to most state dance troupes in Nigeria and has had a stint with the National Troupe of Nigeria as an Assistant Director. Bakare, R.O. has taught dance and theatre in the universities of Calabar, Ahmadu Bello, Uyo, Abuja and currently Ekiti. He has over sixty full length productions and more than thirty scholarly publications to his credit, among which are: "This land must sacrifice", Rudiments of Choreography", to mention but a few. He is an embodiment of the performing arts, a professional choreographer, an accomplished playwright, a powerful actor, a talented drummer, flutist, poet, songwriter, and a complete artiste to the core. No wonder he once described himself as a "theatre addict".

The Voyage

Voyage as a production, was performed for the opening and closing ceremonies of the 2004, 14th National Sports Festival hosted by the Federal Capital Territory (TCT) Abuja. The project was choreographed and directed by the renowned choreographer, Prof. Bakare, Ojo Rasaki. The "Voyage" is a satire of the political history of Nigeria. In about twenty five minutes of performance, it summarizes the history of Nigeria from the colonial era to the present leadership. The events of the drama took place in a boat known as Uwa-aghara,(city of confusion). At the beginning of the drama, the white men (who represents our colonial masters) were seen harassing and subjecting the citizens to series of punishments and hardship, flogging and forcing them into captives in their own land. As this arbitrary way of life persisted, there was a revolt led by a woman, which later bought them freedom by the white men who granted them their request for self rule. After being granted freedom, they started their journey to the promised land.

During the journey to the promise land right inside the boat, there were changes of Master Paddlers (representing former Nigerian leaders) at each point in time. As the boat rolled on, there were complaints upon complaints by the citizens on the way and manner in which the Master Paddlers were paddling the boat. After much complaint from the people on the inefficiency of the Master Paddlers, the military struck, killed the civilian Master Paddlers and then took over. There were coups and counter coups by the military till the last coup which led to the sinking of the boat. This was due to the most wicked rule and handling of both the citizens and affairs of the land by the MMP(Military Master Paddler) who represents the late Sani Abacha. The people cried and prayed unto their God/gods to save and rescue them. Their prayers were answered as the military master paddler died while in service. The people organized a democratic process of choosing a leader for themselves. An election was held and a leader was democratically elected.

Having seen that the boat had already sunk before he took over the paddle of leadership, the newly elected leader attempted to bring the boat up alone without seeking for the help and advice of others. This of course he tried but failed on several occasions, until a voice of caution came to him in form of a song telling him that the task is not just for one person alone, that others should be involved so that they can work together. He listened to the voice and invited others to join him, this they did and the boat was able to rise again.

Artistic / Technical Influence:

Cast
Cast for the production of the Voyage were gotten from all parts of the country. The invitation and selection of casts was not limited to a specific sect of group(s) or individual(s) as local troupes, individual free-lance, workers, students, artisans, private

troupes, as well as arts council artistes were all invited. It was a total mix-up of artistes, as it calls for talent development and exposure also to disabuse the monopoly by the arts councils.

Rehearsals

The choreographer brought all his teaching and training experiences to teach the artistes as a teacher. This made his job of choreography easier. Also to add to making his work much easier for him, the choreographer employed the services of creative assistants who helped him teach the other artistes the dance movements, after they (creative assistants) might have finished learning the movements from the choreographer. The artistes were also exposed to very rigorous and hectic rehearsals for them to achieve the goal.

Choreography

The movements used for the production of the Voyage were derived from the existing movements in the various cultures of the country. The choreographer also used his own movement vocabulary. The movement vocabulary comes in to portray what the choreographer wants to communicate to the people/audience. This could be witnessed in some of the scenes like the opening of the drama, where he made use of stress and anguish movements to depict suffering and hostility, the struggle for freedom, he made use of combat movement, during the election, he used a mimed race to determine the winner, etc. Also some of the dance movements of the various cultures of Nigeria like the Atilogu (from the south-eastern part of Nigeria), Bata (from the western part of Nigeria), Jarawa (from the northern), Akoto (from middle belt), Ekombi (from the south-south), Koroso (from the north), Bede (from Bayelsa), as well as the contemporary dance movements were used. The production was a sort of wonder and surprise to the audience at the main bowl of the National Stadium Abuja, as the artistes delivered to a very large extent, their talent and skills adorned in their glaring and beautifully designed costumes and props.

Costume

Is defined, as clothes worn by actors during a play. It is also seen as a broad spectrum that covers anything worn by man to cover unpleasant weather and environment. Many writers have over the years made submissions concerning costume, hence it is an essential aspect of theatre and an indispensable element in theatre practice. According to Ohiri, I.N. he defines costume as:

> live scenery worn by an actor in a particular role in a particular play... it is the exterior reflection of the actors impersonation, which assumes that the person portrayed is someone other them the actor himself.

Costume is believed to have very powerful ways of talking about people's culture and traditions. This also contributed a lot to the dramatic effects of the Voyage. This is evident in the production as the artistes especially the dancers on show outside the boat, interpreting the dramatic happenings in the boat with their stylized dance movements, adorned various kinds of traditional costumes depicting the tribes/ethnic groups of our country Nigeria. The aesthetic view of costume in the production of the Voyage, which has to do with beauty and artistic taste, is simple and colourful.

Welfare

For a perfect rehearsal and performance, a choreographer must have perfect control of his artistes, especially in a production of this nature where there were over four hundred artistes performing. The choreographer was able to conquer this as he made sure that the welfare of the artistes was placed on high esteem. There were provision of first-aid services as well as medical assistance for the sick and injured artistes, the artistes were well accommodated in fully air conditioned rooms at the National Games village Abuja, there was a central feeding point for all the artistes, as they were served with three square healthy meals each day, as well as free transportation to and from the rehearsal ground. Meanwhile, both the artistic director of the project, the crew, as well as the entire artistes left for their various destinations happily as they all received their entitlements, including their transportation fare.

Music/Sound
In the belief of the creationist school of thought, the universe came into being through sound in the 'word', or the evolutionist view which states that life evolved after the great explosion, itself a sound. This therefore established the fact that sound, in one way or the other is an emotive and creative force. The symbolic relationship between musical sounds and movements in the African sense is adequately reflected in the performance of the Voyage. For example, the lead drummer in the production, to commence the actions of the performance calls the artistes unto the stage by codified drumming patterns. Dancing in Traditional Nigeria is a response to the compelling sound of music and a way of life, deeply rooted in the dynamic culture of the people, which in every aspect, is vibrantly imbued with affective colours, sounds and movements, expressive of the people's mood at any given time.

In reflecting the cycle nature of the African world view of existence, the African man begins life with music and dance, traces his developmental stages through music and dance in various initiation rites, and ends that life with music and dance. This is also demonstrated in the performance of the Voyage, where the interpretational abilities of the dancers of various tribes dance to the response of musical sounds with comprehensible movement patterns to all the actions and events in the boat. The legacy of musico-dance drama therefore, lives with us in all forms of our traditional life and theatre.

Light
Stage lighting is the most rapidly expanding phase of scenic art. It is taking the place of paint in many productions because white backgrounds can be instantly transformed by light in response to changes in mood, action and location. There is no more intriguing phase of play production than working out truly effective lighting for different scenes, whether there is the availability of the simplest or the most sophisticated equipment. Without doubt, lighting is the most important element in scenic design, for it

affects the creation of mood and atmosphere. All these came to play in the Voyage, as the production was well lit and the beautifully built and designed boat, costumes and scenic designs were aesthetically appreciated by the audience.

The lighting plan was well plotted according to the instructions of the director, and various kinds of lights like the ellipsoidal reflector spotlight, fresnel, follow spot, strip lights, border lights, ellipsoidal leko, etc. of different shapes, watts and sizes were put to work to enhance the realization of the production. It will be worthy to note that, the production would have been in shamble as some technical effects like light and sound were almost hampered, owing to the refusal of the managers and contractors of the stadium(Julius Berger Plc) to grant the technical crew access into the light and sound room. But for the professionalism and technical expertise exhibited by the technical director, his assistant and their crew, who worked tirelessly and unrelentlessly both night and day, the story would have been different.

Conclusion
In concluding this research work, it must be noted that dance reflects the society which it has created. Like all art forms, dance cannot be created in a vacuum. It must paint the mannerisms, attitudes, styles, codes(visual), values and other behaviors of the society in which it is produced. Dance or the art of dancing has been a means of sociological communication to the old and the new generation, both in Europe, Asia and Africa. Dance has been used throughout history not only for glorification but also as a means of satirizing the events of the society as was seen in the production of the Voyage. The creative ingenuity of the artistic director and his crew to the successful production of the Voyage was also x-rayed, as the attempt of this research was to give an analytical interrogation into dance drama as a total ensemble play, using the stage production of the Voyage as a case study.

Works Cited.

Ojo Rasaki. Rudiments of Choreography (An Introduction). Lagos: Dat and Partners Logistic Ltd. 2004.

Collins English Dictionary: Ensemble. Complete and Unabridged.10th Edition, Harper Collins Publishers 2009. In *Online Etymology Dictionary*. http://dictionary.reference.com/browse/ensemble. Accessed: July 29, 2014.

Edisua, Oko-Offoboche. The A-B-C of Dance Arts. Calabar: Uptriko Press, 1996.

Essien, Edet. Space, Rhythm and Design. Calabar: Unpublished Lecture Handout, p. 1.

Harper, Douglas: Dictionary.com, "Ensemble", in *Online Etymology Dictionary*. http://dictionary.reference.com/browse/ensemble. Accessed: July 29, 2014.

Nwamuo, Chris. An Introduction to Dance. Owerri: AP Publications, 1993.

Ohiri, Innocent. Introduction to Media Arts. Owerri: Lilino Publishers, 2001.

Theatre Design in Bakare's Drums of War: an Evaluation of Nigeria's Diversity

By
Adeoye, Aderemi Michael

Introduction
Nigeria is made up of numerous tribes, within which are obviously many conflicts. Some of these conflicts have degenerated into serious national and international issues, the flashpoint of which, for instance, is the current poignant and ethno-religious (Boko Haram) insurgency in the Northern part of the country. The scenario in question has been engendered by the hasty and arbitrary amalgamation of the so-named Northern and Southern Protectorates of Nigeria by the colonial masters in 1914, which has lasted for about a century now. Hence, Okwori thus asserts:

> The historical beginning of the Nigerian nation is intertwined with colonial incursion into Africa. The portion of West Africa being referred to today as Nigeria is the natural home of some two hundred (200) different ethnic groups like : the Hausa, Fulani, Yoruba, Igbo, Ibibio, Efik, Tiv, Edo, Nupe, Kanuri, Igala, Itsekiri, Kalabari and others ... (88).

There is diversity in the cultures of the Nigerian nation. This has manifested through dissimilar historical backgrounds, language heterogeneity, contrasting theological convictions, divergent political ideologies, inconsistent administrative principles and extremely opposing ethical standards. It is therefore a logical assumption that *Nigerians are not one* people, contrary to internal governmental propaganda and Western diplomatic insinuations. The impact of this diversity is mainly negative because Nigeria failed as a nation when it failed at managing its diversity, whose positive attributes would have been maximised to orbit the nation out of poverty and insecurity. Ratnapala, cited by Omilusi, thus opines, "The modern state has become, among other things, a provider of goods and services, social insurer, wealth distributor, moral guardian, entrepreneur, keeper of the currency, banker, and economic planner. But it has been an abject failure in each of this roles" (456).

Different attempts have, however, been made at proffering solutions to the problem of diversity in Nigeria. For example, Nigerians have been forced to take solace in coup d'état, about seven of which have interjected the peace of the country since its independence from Britain. The country has also witnessed civil wars especially the Biafra War in the early seventies, when the people of Eastern Nigeria sought political autonomy from a country they considered dysfunctional. Electoral riots (from early 1980s till date), terrorism and many other unconstructive, sub-cultural and antisocial reactions, have become rampant on the Nigerian street with no hope for a solution.

The amalgamation topic often posts a significant challenge for Nigerians; hence, this discourse will continue to breed reactions of seminal importance among scholars, especially in the arts and humanities. The findings, analysis and propositions of this research would avail scholars and the entire society with materials of historical value. While, it is positioned within the theoretical framework of aesthetics, this research also applies an unconventional problem-solving technique in understanding the Nigerian socio-political process; vis-à-vis cultural peculiarities, diversities and complexities.

Therefore, this research is concerned with the relationship between art and society and focuses on the technical realization of the play, *Drums of War* by Bakare, Ojo Rasaki (1993) as a creative demonstration of how the African theatre addresses the African problem, with particular reference to Nigeria. The Nigerian amalgamation saga, hence, comes to the fore in this instance, as an age-long, unresolved puzzle, urgently begging for critical analysis which can only be offered by the arts and specifically under the aegis of Theatre Design. This position has been further accentuated. Hence, "The relevance of an artiste is subsumed in his ability to project without ambiguity the events, problems and issues of his time. Thus an artistic work is never separated from societal happenings that touch on the social challenges of the masses" (Oshionebo and Mbachaga, 1).

Culture, Theatre and The Nigerian Society

The concept of culture is interestingly broad. It encompasses the society's entire life including artistic manifestations. Nigeria as a society engages in cultural expressions of symbolic codes that are direct derivatives of art thereby validating the relevance of the artiste to the Nigerian society. Theatre, therefore, as an art, is one of the most potent means through which the society understands, reflects, analyzes, expresses and records its values as well as activities, behaviours and events. Man communicates culture though art. This is established in one of the earliest definitions of culture, offered by Tylor (1871), who defines it as "that complex whole which includes knowledge, belief, art, morals, law, custom and any other capabilities and habits acquired by man as a member of society" (Ojo, 1986: 2). Tylor's definition of culture is anthropological and represents art as one of the major elements included in the "complex whole" of culture. It has therefore also been pointed out that "his usage of culture is synonymous with civilization."

Hence, it is logical to say that theatre, as an art form, including Theatre Design, is capable of capturing, expressing, recording and analyzing the historical, political and sociological life of the Nigerian society. Theatre, therefore, is an integral element of culture and an indispensable instrument of cultural expression. It is one of the most fundamental cultural processes under which all expressions of thoughts, feelings and ideas are governed and it has often been an important resource in understanding the Nigerian society. By implication, all verbal, theatrical and plastic (literary, performing and visual) codes, are classified as theatre arts and have been central to the process of culture and its diverse manifestations in Nigeria.

Theatre as an art has a composite affiliation to the society. One necessitates and validates the existence of the other. Suffice to say without theatre arts, the society is not complete because the society is based on culture, whose major expressive attributes are found in the performative and material contexts of the arts. To understand Nigeria as a society, therefore, theatre art has often played a major role as a principal ingredient of culture. Piddington (1950), as cited in Ojo 1986 has argued that "forms of art, ceremonial and recreational are to be found in all societies, these are not necessary for biological survival."

Drums of War: **An Analysis.**
In his attempt to use art to address Nigeria's problems, Bakare has directed a number of plays, which include: Wale Ogunyemi's *Langbodo,* Femi Osofisan's *Women of Owu,* Ola Rotimi's *Kurunmi,* and *the Gods are not to Blame,* as well as his own plays such as *Drums of War, Rogbodiyan, Once Upon A Tower* and *This Land Must Sacrifice* and others. However, for the purpose of this study, emphasis would be placed on the stage production of *Drums of War,* which took place in July 2012, at the Kogi State University, Ayingba, Nigeria. Through Participant Observation as a research methodology, the technical realization including the extreme designs and special effects has been observed and thus, data collected and used in this study.

Synopsis of the Play
The *Drums of War,* a ninety-minute stage play by Rasaki Ojo Bakare (1994), narrates the story of a dictatorial king who rules without adequate commitment to existing tradition. This autocratic ruler is also extremely thirsty for power. This brings about one serious war after another. At a time, his son becomes one of the victims of one of such wars. This devastates his queen who subsequently hangs herself thereby bringing the king to the realization that the last and bitter option is the royal tradition of opening the white calabash, which translates to the imminent death of the king. The king now allows the people to direct their destinies in their own hands as he heads for his doom.

Technical Analysis of the Play

Bakare has employed six principal aesthetic elements, demonstrating in the theatrical process that Nigeria is an amalgam of diverse ethnic interests. All these six aesthetic elements namely *Dance, Extreme Design, Poetry, Music, Comedy, Emotion* are often present at the same time in almost all Bakare's works, hence they have become the hallmark of his directorial methodology. Using art as a pragmatic instrument of communication, the *Drums of War* satirises the problem of ethnicity and culture in Nigeria. This is an indication that a play in the form of a text or script is not tangible or substantial because it remains inert and weak and does not assume the enabling environment for communication unless it is visually concretized through the creation of the three-dimensional performance space. Enabling the communication of meaning is the whole essence of design.

The technical approach visible in the play could be evaluated on a tripartite pedestal as is often characteristic of Bakare's style. The first stratum of this principle is primarily informed by the concept of *Interpretive Anthropology* which capitalizes on the need to place premium on the native or original point of view. Here, cognisance is given to the playwright's intention as the original or native point of view which informs design and upon which performance is built. *Interpretive Anthropology* accepts the theatrical art as being anthropological because it is entirely centred on man. It is a social phenomenon, and therefore a key element of culture, particularly responsible for expressing man's *other conceptions* (artistic content) for which he has no verbal words.

As earlier indicated, the use of diverse or assorted artistic fragments in the play is basically eclectic and thus constitutes the second stratum. The third is the theoretical principle of Aesthetics which emanates from the opinion that *what constitutes beauty has relative interpretation in different cultural situations and environments*. Objective universality is not applicable in aesthetics. A major branch of philosophy aside, of ethics, epistemology, metaphysics and logics, aesthetics is the only philosophical principle that relates entirely to the broad concept of beauty. It releases the audacious freedom to appropriate beauty from a relative viewpoint.

While ethics deal with the concept of good-and-bad or what is acceptable as good or bad in a particular culture based on cultural complexities, epistemology is to do with the concept of knowledge. Basically epistemology relates to how one knows and what one knows. In other words such philosophical ideologies as idealism, realism, pragmatism and autodidacts are offshoots of epistemology. Aesthetics is mainly about the human subject matter which involves many variables and controversies. This is an indication that the human subject matter involves certain variables which arise in the process of communication as justification for the subjectivity of the arts. The *Drums of War* as a work of art obeys the holistic principle of aesthetics as observable in the following ways:

i. **Subjectivity:** aesthetic thinking is based on the opinion there is no universally common way of measuring experience. An aesthetic experience is not specific or measurable. It tends to suggest that the qualitative research instrument is better than the quantitative. Quantitative research instruments are too statistical and therefore not good for the humanities.

ii. **Emotion:** emotional experiences are not objective and can never be accounted for. Emotion is put into the narratives for the audience to empathize with the play. (E.g. in the last scene where Orioye's body is carried amidst tears; some members of the audience sometimes also cry here).

iii. **Culture:** Aesthetics is culture-based and subject to cultural variables. It thus leads us back to our roots to create alternative reasoning. Many critics quarrel about the universalism of aesthetics. Attempts have been made to universalize some elements of culture especially in the twenty- first century which has witnessed some similar cultural features, around the world under the concept of globalization, thereby penetrating every community with new global colonialism or capitalism. The *Drums of War* relies on the different cultural forms in Nigeria to preach harmony.

iv. **Time:** is also a variable in aesthetics. This implies that form, nature and disability are changed by time. King Onome is a powerful war monger in the first scene. He however becomes helpless in the last scene in which he is banished.

v. **Morality:** aesthetics is tied to the issue of morality. An aesthetic phenomenon that lacks morals also loses its aesthetic appeal. Onome's attitude is considered immoral, therefore despite that this role is often played by a talented actor, the actor is often disliked by the audience who may sometimes attack him.

vi. **Ethics:** the theatre in aesthetics tends to suggest that a good play must end or come to something generally known as "good."

Conclusion
Theatre as art can help Nigerians to better understand themselves; the challenge of diversity and ways in which to surmount it. Theatre Design particularly possesses the capabilities to interpret the artistic statement in the playwright's work and to communicate sociological messages. The *Drums of War*, through the use of six principal aesthetic ingredients; *Dance, Extreme Design, Poetry, Music, Comedy, and Emotion*, appeals directly to the mind of the average Nigerian on the need for peace by romanticizing and exaggerating the negative tendencies and "evil" nature of "war."

The theoretical principle of aesthetics as applicable in this study also demonstrates that a good work of art must coherently hang together, as one main idea. This reveals the essence of design, in the theatre which goes beyond construction of the stage, props or costumes but includes the symbolic use of colour and other audio-visual codes, at the physical and mental levels to make social statements. Therefore, Nigerians should be more receptive to art with a view applying its suggestions to their social and intercultural challenges with seriousness. They should seize benefits offered by the intervention of the arts for socio-political development of the country.

Works Cited

Adebayo, T. A. A Critical Appraisal in of Eclecticism in Ben Enwonwu's Works. Arts Courier: African Journal of Arts and Ideas, 9. 15–127. 2011.

Adejemilua, M. S. Ulli Beier and Instigation of Creative Revolution in Contemporary Nigerian Art. Arts Courier: African Journal of Arts and Ideas, 9. 86–114. 2011.

Albert, I. O. "Techniques for Collecting Oral Data in African Culture History" A Handbook of Methodology in African Studies. 90-100 1999.

Bakare, O. R. Drums of War. Zaria: Tamaza Publishers 1994.

De la Croix, H. and Tansey, R. G. Gardener's art through the ages. San Diego: Harcourt Brace Jovanovich Publishers. 1986.

Ejeke, O. S. Creating the Performance. Abraka: Masterpiece Prints and Publishers. 2012.

Ojo, R. O. Traditional African art and anthropology (Unpublished paper) 1986.

Omilusi, M. Democratic Governance in Nigeria: Key issues and Challenges. Akure: Adex Printing Press. 2013.

Oshionebo, B. and Mbachaga, J. D. "Introduction" Literary Perspectives on Corruption in Nigeria. Oshionebo, B. Mbachaga, J. D. (Eds.) Makurdi: Bookmakers. 2010.

Pogoson, O. I. "A Visual Arts Methodology" A Handbook of Methodology in African Studies. Ibadan: Institute of African Studies. 19-30. 1999.

Ukala, S. "Folkism: Towards a National Aesthetic Principle for Nigerian Dramaturgy" New Theatre Quarterly xii, 279-287. 1996.

Jagunmolu: Dance Battle in Nigeria and The Triumphant Dancerasaki

By
Thompson, Victor.

Introduction

Dance has always been a core condiment of culture and celebrative icon of the Nigerian and indeed African society. It has continued to serve as group representation of the people's collective world view, borne out from their folklores, their memories, their rituals, their fears and aspirations. The dancers demonstrate feelings and plunge others into the ever-glowing fire of feelings. Both dancers and the audience, at the instance of dance enactment, share a deeper experience which is mythical and real, religious and secular, pleasant and "unpleasant". Consciously or unconsciously, our society has become a dance society. Dance is creatively employed in the expression of the people's communal ethos and pathos. Whether the movements are pulsating, slow, martial or languid, Nigerian dances are 'picturesque' socio-cultural event abounding in vitality and beauty (Ebewo, 2). From a creative perspective, the Nigerian dance experience is a eurhythmic cultural metaphor. Study shows that from the origin of man to man's imponderable future, the human body is civilization's most poetic and aesthetic asset when it communicates in dance as a transforming state of beingness. Nigeria is a gold-mine of this body-poetry and body-aesthetics. The artistic and organizational characteristics of Nigerian dance forms derive from its utilitarian conceptions. Whether such usefulness is religious, physical social or therapeutic, dance culture in Nigeria is "conceptually a process of socialization of the individual through participation in group ethos and expression" (Nzewi: 5). Thompson observes that "it is on the whet stone of traditional dances that the Nigerian people sharpen and re-discover, more realistically, their cultural values, break the palm kernel of indigenous technology and are brought body-to-body with authentic meaning of identity" (1). The inference from the above underlines the fact that Nigerian dance culture is the performative summary of Nigerian socio-cultural matrix. Culture and dance continually confluence and share molecules in their manifestations. Significantly, the Nigerian dance is continually engaged in survival battle against the frontiers of the society.

Dance Practice In Nigeria: Perception of The Society
The tribulations of dance art in Nigeria are the woes and cries of the practitioners. The Nigerian society is circumstantially preoccupied with hydra-headed challenges in politics, economy, corruption and sundry crisis. Modern science and cutting –edge technology, oil and gas, telecommunication, football and banking industry seem to have a firmer hold on every sphere of the human space. Little or no opportunity of survival or attention is envisaged for the Nigerian dance practice. Dance is viewed as a mere intangible, non- material art, a thing of entertainment that should not demand serious attention. Dance practitioners therefore are disdainly regarded by the society as loafers, drop-outs vagabonds and paupers who lack the aptitude to join in the current materialistic and professional race. In fact the practice is considered a pigment of philistinism even by the very class of elites found in position to offer the dance art a leg-up in the socio-professional spectrum. Udoka observes that "the professions native to Nigerian indigenous cultures are pottery, carving, pestle and mortar making, etc… and no matter how long the list may be, one thing is clear: dance will not appear on it as a profession" (2). One predominant question resonates at every discourse of Nigerian dancer thus; is dance a profession? Sad enough, some up-coming and practicing dancers ask the same question; wondering how dance could possibly shift emphasis from its traditional status as a celebrative idiom of culture to a profession. The utilitarian essence of dance art is greatly misunderstood in Nigeria. Susanne Langer corroborating this assertion posits that:

> No art surfers more misunderstanding, sentimental judgment, and mystical interpretation than the art of dancing. It critical literature, or worse yet its uncritical literature, pseudo-ethnological and pseudo-

aesthetic, makes weary reading. Yet this very confusion as to what dancing is – what it expresses, what it creates and how it is related to the other arts, to the artists, and to the actual world – has a philosophical significance of its own (169).

Langer's observation above on the treatment of dance in Europe and America is even more approbatory when compared to what Africans and indeed Nigerians feel for or towards and about dance. This is because of the basic belief that dance is taken for granted… it belongs to our natural consciousness… a common aspect of our cultures, it is not bought or sold, it is just there, so what is the big deal about dance (Yerima, 1). Significantly, the big deal about dance is: dance is the central part of the performative aspect of our cultural heritage and has the ability to compliment development and assimilate, infuse, adapt to the new developmental trends, be they social, political or socio-political. The study of and patronage of Nigerian dance culture is an attempt to understand further, the essence of the Nigerian existence because even when the dance vocabulary defers, the magic or mystic of dance (in rhythm) and the communal aesthetic of the dance is one and the same.

The Nigerian dance artiste is a vibrant and pragmatic cultural communicator. He remains the constant scale with which the cultural equilibrium of the nation is measured. The dancers are always there when all else fail. They remain sane when politics and politicians display absolute insanity. They are always at work when others go on strike action. When others are entitled to minimum wage, they are entitled to maximum work. They are always in control when others are out of control. Noticeably, of all the organs in the cultural sector, it is dance art and the dancers that remain the most used and exploited. While other culture-oriented arts enjoy reasonable acceptance and patronage, the same cannot be said of dance. The dancers even at State Art Councils have been reduced to the ignominious standard of Airport Entertainment, performing on rough surfaces under the

scorching sun. Incidentally their take-home pay cannot really take them home. Sharing this view, Oduneye states:
> "These dancers continue to provide entertainment. They take us on historical and cultural excursions. In their performances, they educate and inform us about Nigerian cultures. Their remunerations are disproportionately low and not reflecting their contributions to our history, literature, performing arts, philosophy and leisure" (7).

Shaibu Husseini, a former National President of Dance Guild of Nigeria opines that "year by year, we wail collective dirge of advocacy, we have chanted songs of advocacy, we have rolled drums of advocacy, we have exhibited dances of advocacy, yet the society continually breath hostility against our practice" (3). Husseini's position above connotes the desperation of a community of people in search of self-worth, acceptance, patronage, socio-professional and economic relevance and integration. This is the dance battle in Nigeria. Apparently, there are very few warriors in the battle front and fewer triumphant warriors are on record. Mis-perception of the utilitarian essence of dance is one of Nigerian's greatest pit falls, for it is on the stages and performance squares of Nigerian dances that Nigerians (irrespective of diversity of cultures) are re-assembled and collectively immersed in the fire of cultural rhythm.

It should be noted by the Nigerian society that dance, like in other parts of the world, has arbitrarily shifted emphasis from it original status quo as an exclusive ethnic activity or entertainment excursion. In its new role, dance and dance artistes are veritable catalysts capable of socio-cultural and political re-engineering, global peace initiative among other roles. There are two basic categories of dancers within the holistic; Nigerian dance culture: the primordial and civic dancers. The traditional, ethnic dancers belong to the primordial dance category. The dances here "include those performed on religious and communal festivals" (Hall, 1). Dances in this category hardly change within its environment. They follow a strict kinetic vocabulary and rarely done out of context. Udoka describes Nigerian traditional dances as:

> The collage of dances that owe their origins to and were created, performed and handed down without written records by culture of the nation states that now constitute what is geographically known a Nigeria (5).

The common feature of this dance form is that it is kin-group-specific and built around substantive conceptions of tribal groups. Some practical examples are *Ekombi, Swange, Bata.* These dance are unmistakably typical of *Efik, Tiv* and *Yoruba* tribes respectively. On the other hand, the civic dancer is the one involved in the evolving nation-wide Nigerian dance experience which relatively comprises plural and inter-cultural traits within the Nigerian society. Unlike the ethnic group-line segmentation of primordial dances, the civic dance form has single movement trend per time for all Nigerians. It collates elements from western and modern sources for its contextual and aesthetic significance. The Nigerian civic dance genre is dynamic. In the 1960's for instance, the *highlife, Palango* and the western *Twist* dominated the social dance scene in Nigeria. In the 70's the *Sowambe* and *Cyncro* styles dominated the *Juju* scene, Fela Anikulapo Kuti and Orlando Julius popularized the *Afro-Beat.* In the 80's the *Talazzo*, the *Fuji* Raggae and Break dancing took the stage and dance floors. From Ajegunle, a popular ghetto in Lagos, Baba Fryo and Daddy Showkey (two Nigerian musicians) invented and made popular the *Galala* and *Swoor* dance styles in the 1990's. By the middle of 2000, so many civic dances have been introduced including *Yawuze* and *Alanta*. Today, *Azonto* and *Etighi* saturate the Nigerian dance space. Whether the dance artiste is primordial or civic in his style, he is consciously or unconsciously, directly or indirectly caught up in the web of the Nigerian dance battle.

Jagunmolu: Significance And Signification

The term, *Jagunmolu* is a combination of two Yoruba words. "Jagun," meaning to fight a war and 'Molu', meaning to gain bounty and victory. It could be inferred from the foregoing that

Jagunmolu means victorious warrior. In the Yoruba culture, Jagunmolu is a para-military title given to a victorious fighter, a successful community war lord. In this module, the concept of Jagunmolu will be discussed phenomenally as a performance and create-artistic description of Ojo Bakare in line with his mileage and conquest in dance scholarship and practice.

The Dance-Theatre
Jagunmolu as a dance project was conceived and choreographed by Ojo Bakare in 1999 as a central command performance to mark the swearing-in ceremony of Chief Segun Obasanjo as the President of the Federal Republic of Nigeria. Though the performance took place at the International Conference Centre, Abuja, the star-studded production was managed by the United Artistes for Nigeria. Frontline Nigeria theatre performers like Kola Oyewo, Jide Kosoko, Kayode Idris, Ernest Obi, et al, took part in the project. *Jagunmolu* is a story of Nigerian political history; from pre-colonial to colonial and post colonial dispensations. The gist of the tale hinges on political characteristics of the different leaders in Nigeria – their attainments and challenges. Remarkably, the dance theatre dramatizes the leadership and political activities of Segun Obasanjo; from military rulership to the dark moments of his incarceration and post-in carceration civilian governance. The Lead character in the dance act, Jagunmolu, (christened after the project title) was kept in the prison. Upon his freedom, he participated in, and won an election in his community. It was his successes and giant strides and achievements as a military leader that earned him the people's support and the title *Jagunmolu*.

Bakare paints a vivid choreographic visual of Obasanjo as a triumphant warrior who fought the civil and political wars of Nigeria with phenomenal character and determination. As a "political prisoner" he was not lackadaisical in taking active decision to join the presidential race. It is obvious that President Obasanjo and his involvement in the 1999 Nigerian election was a conspicuous display of guts, ebullience and tenacity. Metaphorically speaking, it is such guts and tenacity that drive

Bakare from the playground of theatre apprenticeship of the foremost Nigerian actor-manger, Hubert Ogunde, to his present spectrum of scholarship and dance practice

Dancerasaki And Jagunmoluism
The dance and choreography brand of Ojo Barkare is Dancerasaki. Bakare is a dance Scholar, Choreographer, Art Writer/Director, Songwriter and perhaps the first Nigerian Professor of Dance. Born in Aramoko, Ekiti State on November 8th, 1964, he served as an apprentice of a popular theatre experience under Chief Hubert Ogunde and Chief Jimoh Aliu. Rasaki obtained his Bachelor and Masters degrees in Theatre Arts from the University of Calabar and proceeded to the Ahmadu Bello University, Zaria where he earned his Doctorate in dance and drama. For over twenty years he has dutifully combined dance and theatre scholarship with outstanding dexterity. Bakare Ojo Rasaki is the Director and chief Executive officer of the Abuja National Carnival. He has been part of various dance and theatre projects in different capacities within and outside Nigeria. A multi-award winner, art administrator and culture communicator. Currently, he is the Dean of Humanities and Social Sciences of the Federal University of Oye Ekiti.

Unarguably, Bakare has formalized an amiable, formidable trademark for himself in the dance and theatre industry. He has dignified himself via dint of diligence and commitment to education, professional resource development and core practice. This is the battle he has fought over time, triumphed and become the *Jagunmolu* (triumphant, warrior) of Nigerian dance profession. He combated various frontiers militating against the very survival and liberation of Nigerian dance practice. This is the basis for the concept of jagunmoluism of Nigerian dance. Bakare, Ojo Rasaki is considered in the work as the pathfinder, the nucleus and subject of metaphor. This emerging concept or theory is concerned with the holistic development of the Nigerian dance practitioner. The development must take into cognizance his professional, academic and economic emancipation. The theory equally aims at re-positioning of the Nigerian dancer and his art at the global creativity market as well as equipping him with the aptitude, penchant, and intellectuality to interact and re-shape traditions in order to find new meanings and fulfillment in his chosen profession. The theory discourages the Nigerian dancers from bemoaning their under-developed state.

The theory of Jagunmoluism is not silent over the issue of dearth of professional infrastructure. It recognizes the importance of dance/choreography training and training facilities; well-equipped dance studios and well intentioned dance exchange programmes with artistes from other parts of the world. Inter-cultural choreography as a means of globalized art should be encouraged. The Nigerian dance profession must embrace choreo-technology. For instance, e-dance should be employed to improve choreography, dance training and preservation. In a frantic bid to mobilize audiences for the Nigerian industry, concerted effort should be put in place to extend dance performance venues from live stage to the electronic media such as film and television. The Nigerian dance makers should shift emphasis to dance movies and create dance mega stars on the screen.

Conclusion
The facts that dance is a celebrative heritage and a pragmatic idiom of our culture, indirectly gives the society the impetus to debase and take dance for granted. The art of dance is not accorded the respectability it deserves not even by government. The common belief, which has actually grown into derogatory statement, is that "everyone can dance, so what is so special about dance". Even within the academia milieu, most non-theatre scholars and students question the rationale of enlisting dance in the University academic curriculum. To them, dancing is a common entertainment that should be employed to provide emotional support for the Medical, Engineering and Law programmes. This erroneous perception of dance art by society encapsulates the socio-professional battle of the dance art and artistes. Few Nigerian dance practitioners have prevailed over this hydra-headed challenge of societal hostility towards their

profession. Bakare is the lead character in this regard. Thus, jagunmoluism is a celebration of his courage vision, tenacity and triumph.

Works Cited

Ebewo, Patrick. "Dance Art in Hausa culture: Problems and prospects". Paper presented at the National Symposium on Nigerian Dance, Ibadan, 1986.

Hall, Babarinde B. "Nigerian Dance: Development Through Technical and Academic Training". Paper presented at the National symposium on Nigeria Dance, Ibadan, 1986.

Husseini, Shaibu. International Dance Day keynote Address in GOND News vol. 1 No 4, 2003.

Langer, Sussane. *Feeling and Form:* The theory of Art. New York: Charles Scribner's sons, 1953.

Nzewi, Meki. "Dance, Music and Curriculum Development". Paper presented at the National Symposium on Nigerian Dances, Ibadan, 1986.

Oduneye, Bayo. Keynote Address at GOND National Dance Summit, Lagos, 1999.

Udoka, Arnold. "Is Dance a Profession?" Paper Presented at GOND Annual Dance Lecture, 1998.

Udoka, Arnold. "Promoting Nigerian Cultural Dances as Instrument of National Unity". An Article in *The Mask*, vol. 1 No 11, 2010.

Yerima, Ahmed. "Dance Art: A Machinery for Political and Socio-cultural Development in Nigeria." Keynote Address at National Dance Summit, Lagos, 2001.

Aesthetics of Body and Floor Patterns in Bakare, Ojo Rasaki's Choreography: The *"Sai Ka Yi Aiki"* Example

By
Tume 'Tosin. K.

Introduction
One of the most comprehensive definitions given dance is that, "it is a language which expresses the geographical locations, biological temperament, religious beliefs, political and historical experiences, social practice and economic peculiarities of the people that own it." (Bakare, 2005:76). The recognition of dance as language, makes it useful for encoding and decoding information. However, Damisa asserts that "dance in its peculiar nature has no language but those of expressing itself. It can become a language only when it is adopted for that purpose by the dance composer or choreographer." (Damisa, 2012: 220)

The onus then lies on the choreographer to employ dance in making meaningful statements, because even though dance is self-sufficient as means of communication, it needs the manipulation and dexterity of a competent choreographer for it to come alive in performance. Dance is made up of expressive efforts of the inner impulses from which movements originate. Laban (1988:13) posits that "...the components making up the different effort qualities result from an inner attitude (conscious or unconscious) towards the factors of movement: weight, space, time and flow". Since the body is an instrument of expression through movement in space, the use of floor patterns to aid understanding of dance intentions become essential. Thus, if well employed, dance could reveal all the traits and characteristics of a given culture or people e.g. their food, way of dressing, norms, beliefs, and occupation.

Over the years, choreography has evolved to mean the art of writing, creating or designing dance movements. Since dance is first and foremost a form of communication using the body as medium, the job of a choreographer then is to craft and design sequences of movements in which form and motion are specified, using the bodies of dancers as raw materials for visual patterns and information dissemination on the stage. The visual patterns in dance are also referred to as shapes. Shapes are the strongest visual component in dance actions, because they are used to convey meaning. Floor patterns are also very vital to dance choreography because movements and shapes are symbolic actions. Floor patterns are produced through locomotion which stimulates progressions in space.

In principle, a symbol may not mean anything definite but it can conjure up a variety of images in the spectator. To this end, Tume agrees that "floor patterns of dance movements are (usually) of significance to the ceremony (involved)" (Tume, 2012: 179) Hence, floor patterns are not only created to avoid monotony or stagnancy of movements, they serve as underlying determinants of dance in terms of context and content. It is against this background therefore, that this chapter discusses Bakare, Ojo Rasaki's use of floor patterns for functional and aesthetic purposes in his "Sai Ka Yi Aiki" choreography. It should be noted also that researcher was the Assisstant Choreographer to Bakare, Ojo Rasaki during a Departmental production at the Theatre and Media Arts Department of the Federal University, Oye-Ekiti, tagged "Festival of Dance". "Sai Ka Yi Aiki" was among the dances staged. This paper borrows extensively from that unique theatrical experience.

Aesthetics in The African Worldview
In the African worldview, art is not something that can be dealt with as a separately existing subject. It has no autonomy, and it permeates life. There are three main angles to the African aesthetic theory, namely: metaphysical, communal and social morality. For the fact that Africans view art and beauty from a metaphysical perspective, the contents of African artworks are therefore symbolic. Accessories such as masks, or hand-props such as horse-whisk, apart from their physical beauty as objects, are seen as mythical symbols.

Ruth and Anyanwu (1981:16) explain that "the African artist lays emphasis on symbolic representations... not on proportionality. So we do not look for the beauty of his works in their proportional nature but in their symbolic meaning." Though, this can be achieved only by keen observation, Africans appreciate works of art with an inner eye, as they search for their deeper meanings.

The African artist is not left out in his communal way of life. Nwala (1985:38) agrees with this when he says:
> The urge to create...might be basic for individual artists; but the urge is inseparable from the social and communal motivations which depend on the function of traditional art, since the artist does not create for himself alone but rather serves as the bearer of communal values."

In Africa, both extrinsic and intrinsic values are assessed in the evaluation of art. Thus, the concept of beauty is in the positive values of an object or subject. In many Nigerian languages, the same word is used to mean 'beauty' and 'good'. Hausas call it 'Kyakyawa' or 'Kyau', for the Ibos it is 'Mma', the Yorubas refer to it as 'Ewa' or 'Dara', while the Tiv people call it 'Doo' or 'Mdoom'.

To clarify any form of confusion between the two concepts of good and beauty, Kariamu (1994: 203) asserts that the fusion of beauty and good does not denote a lack of distinction between the two. It is instead an indication of the perennial multiplicity of concepts that occupy equal status and dominance. He further states that it becomes clear however, that a real understanding of African Art and African value systems lie in the very recognition that the two concepts overlap. According to the African concept, to be able to appreciate beauty or external harmony of artworks, one must possess an artist's insight, discerning inner eye and perceptiveness. This is what the Yorubas refer to as: 'Oju inu' or 'Oju ona'.

Africans believe that not all beautiful things are good, but all good things are beautiful. This accounts for the origins of some appellations and nicknames in Yoruba land. On one hand, if someone is tall and well behaved, they call him "a gun t'aso o lo" which means – "tall enough to exhibit the volume and beauty of a wrapper" but on the other hand if the person is ill-mannered, he or she may be referred to as "a gun ma n'iye" which means "tall but senseless".

Both names reflect on the height as a quality, but at the same time they extol or condemn the positive or negative attributes of the subject as the case may be. It also applies to "a kuru y'ejo" which means – "short and cute to manipulate the art of dance", and Kukute which means – "short devil", the former is affectionate while the latter is derogatory. Kofoworola (2004; 12) submits that, "…the appreciation of beauty among the Yoruba ethnic group or Africans in general, is not based solely on the manifestation of beauty which is derived from the physical features of presentation. Thus, the physical appearance or the tangible texture is not the main (or only) criterion of evaluation."

Judging from various African cultures, one can say that aesthetics is fundamentally moral. For the Yoruba people, honesty, good name, self-control, kindness, goodness, hard-work lead to beauty. To them, beauty is innate and virtues of the heart are held in high esteem. To corroborate this, they have a saying which goes thus; 'Iwa lewa', the direct translation of this is- "Character is beauty", but what they actually mean is that no matter how outwardly beautiful or handsome you may think you are, only your character or behaviour determines your good-looks. Another of their sayings is; 'Ise loogun ise' meaning 'hardwork is the antidote for poverty'. Poverty of course, is ugly and can be cured with hardwork which is beautiful.

"Sai Ka Yi Aiki" as An Occupational Dance

"Sai Ka Yi Aiki" is a farming occupational dance created by Bakare, Ojo Rasaki. Occupational dances are dances performed by guilds of craftsmen or professionals who are bound together by their work experience. Members of these guilds frequently celebrate their affinity through the performance of dance movements which are mostly derived from the various nuances of their common work experience. According to Felix Bergho, "...there are special dances for blacksmiths, hunters, and some other traditional professional guilds. These are the dances the guild-members resort to in the expression of their guild's character on eventful occasions in the guild's particular life." (Bergho, 1988: 168) Usually, the aim of occupational dances is to provide encouragement for the workers while they work, and also to stress the importance of their profession. The dance, "Sai Ka Yi Aiki" re-enacts the processes of planting and other agricultural activities in details.

"Sa Ka Yi Aiki" which literally means 'Until you work' in Hausa language, buttresses the quote from the holy book which says "...if anyone would not work, neither should he eat" (2 Thessalonians 3:10). As the name suggests, it is an occupational dance which advocates the dignity of labour, hence, the inherent sub-themes are resilience, team work, division of labour and professional fulfilment. This is one of Bakare's most popular choreographed works, and it can be found in the repertoire of many State Councils of Arts and Culture. It won the First Prize for Nigeria at the Spring Friendship Festival, North Korea in 1997.

Aesthetics of Body And Floor Patterns in *Sai Ka Yi Aiki*
In appreciating a work of living art such as dance choreography, there is a need for focus on its relevant aesthetic properties. James Shelley outlines three propositions in appreciating works of art:
(a)　Artworks necessarily have aesthetic properties that are relevant to their appreciation as artworks (proposition R);
(b)　Aesthetic properties necessarily depend, at least in part, on properties perceived by means of the five senses (proposition S);

(c) And there exist artworks that need not be perceived by means of the five senses to be appreciated as artworks (proposition X) (Shelley, 2003:363).

In line with Shelley's propositions R and S, "Sai Ka Yi Aiki" choreography will be appreciated via the various components such as; movements, floor patterns, costumes and musical accompaniment. These elements are usually imbued with the thematic pre-occupations of any dance choreography. It is important to note that the two senses of sight and hearing are thoroughly engaged in dance appreciation or criticism.

Key for Floor Patterns:
△ - Male dancers
◯ - Female dancers
☐ - Instrumentalists
⁞⁞⁞ - Audience

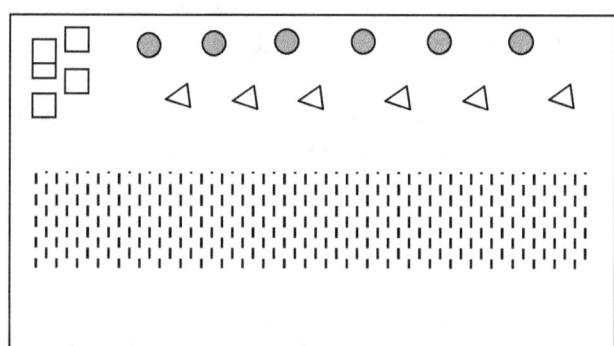

Fig. 1: Some of the linear floor patterns which dominates the "Sai Ka Yi Aiki" choreography.

The dance starts with the entrance of women garbed in the typical work clothes of the Nigerian female farmer; a wrapper tied above the bust with a supporting scarf around the midriff. The women come bearing baskets and small calabashes in centrifugal position as they bounce their baskets while executing agile feet-tapping and leaping movements. The flow of this movement explodes outward from the hip, as the leg moves from the hip instead of from the knee. This movement is done in a linear pattern to indicate their strength and determination to commence the farming process. Bakare, (2004:37) rightly states that straight line floor patterns "gives a feeling of boldness (and) communicates strength and determination". The heavy percussion instrumentation and fast-paced music adds gait and rhythm to their activities.

The dancers later break into two lines, move towards opposite directions and meet to form a single line again. This pattern illustrates that even though there is division of labour among the farmers in the farming process, all hands are on deck for the overall success. The men arrive wringing their hoes in forward strokes while executing the same feet- tapping and leaping movements as their female counterparts. They are also in a linear pattern as they crouch while slashing and flicking their hoes forward and backwards in four counts. This movement is a parody of the ridge-making process in preparation for planting. The ladies who have been floating their baskets sideways, take over from the men, planting into the ridges in pressing effort action and gliding their feet across the earth to seal up what they have planted. This they do in the same four counts and crouching movement as the men. The men recline and sway their hoes sideways as they wait for the women to get done with their planting chores.

Fig. 2: The men reclining with their hoes swayed sideways while the women plant.

The men do acrobatic moves punching their hoes underneath their legs and raising them up above their heads intermittently as they swirl and circle themselves in pairs. The planting aspect done, the women tap-leap across with free flow movements to serve drinks to their men. As the men attempt to drink, they open and clasp their legs in four counts sideways while rubbing their free hand at the back of their heads as they savour their drinks. While this is going on, the women crouch with their knees flexed, and bodies bent at the waist; to rock their knees and waists from side to side. When the men are through with the drinks, the women sway their hips as they wipe sweat off the men's brows with their scarves.

Fig. 3: The women wipe sweat off their men's brows with scarves.

After collecting the scarves from the women, the men leap sideways in four counts while tossing the scarves sideways as they see the women off to carry their baskets. The women hold their baskets in place on their heads with their right hands while the left hand swings in gathering and scattering gestures.

Fig. 4: After planting, the women carry their baskets and seek out a partner each from the men.

Both male and female dancers meet centre-stage in symmetrical design to celebrate the successful completion of their farming activities. They rejoice with more dancing and singing as the rhythm of the music becomes more vigorous. This makes the dancers jerk their bodies hither and thither, clasping their legs intermittently while their pelvis rock from side to side. At this point, they pair up as man and wife, with each couple doing duet displays of scintillating dance movements to the propulsive rhythms.

Fig. 5: The dancers performing the duet displays.

The men hang their hoes on their right shoulders with their right hands while their left hands are clasped around their women's shoulders. The women hold their baskets with their left hands while their right hands are clasped around their men's waists. After their duet displays, the dancers dot the stage in pairs and do a harmonious dance routine dabbing their tummies, arms and heads in unison. This dance action sequence which is punctuated by the drum to symbolise their fulfilment in their chosen profession, and their gratitude to their creator, captures the essence of the choreography. Each couple dance off the stage clasping and opening their legs in a centrifugal position as they disappear into the wings with their full-front to the audience while waving at them.

Conclusion
As Snipe (1988:65) rightly observes, "...the style of dancing in Africa is dynamic and demands stamina... African dance also involves repetition with an emphasis to the earth... That the majority of the dances are focused into the earth emphasizes its importance because (African) men and women till the soil to survive and at the time of death, their remains are laid there to rest". This symbiotic relationship between Africans and the earth is clearly evident in "Sai Ka Yi Aiki" choreography. Since the dance is anchored on agriculture as a thematic preoccupation, the choreographer places emphasis on footwork. Throughout the dance, the dancers' feet display a cordial relationship with the soil while their arms move toward the earth in gathering and scattering motions. On the whole, "Sai Ka Yi Aiki" is a typical African choreography which demands agility and features a variety of footwork that depict an affinity with the earth unlike the Western dances which seek to defy gravity.

To affirm that rhythm is at the core of African aesthestics, "Sai ka yiAiki" is steeped in rich music. With the accompaniment of heavy percussion instrumentation, the dancers' bodies express a wide variety of emotions, rapid rhythmic patterns and aesthetic floor patterns which communicate efficiently, the message of the dance. In spite of the plethora of complex dance movements executed, asymmetrical juxtaposition of equilibrium, balance and control are displayed throughout the choreography. The dancers display a variety of rhythms with great flexibility, intensity, virility, speed and agility. This gives the dance a vital aliveness and spontaneous quality. n a nutshell, the clear; though complex body and floor patterns in "Sai Ka Yi Aiki" choreography reiterate that farming is a vigorous yet rewarding communal labour in Africa. This creative work also confirms, once again, that Bakare, Ojo Rasaki is choreographer par excellence.

Works Cited

Bergho, F. (1988). "Traditional African Dance in Context" in *Africn Dance: An Historical and Philosophical Inquiry.* Kariamu, W.A (ed), Asmaria: Africa World Press, Inc. Pp.163-182.

Bakare, O.R. (2004). *Rudiments of Choreography.* Lagos: Dat & Partners Logistic Ltd.
-----------.(2005). "Towards a Choreographic Theory of Indigenous West African Dance Movements" in *Critical Perspectives on Dance in Nigeria.* Yerima, A.(eds), Ibadan: Kraft Books. Pp.76-91.

Damisa, C.S (2012). "Choreographic Possibilities inSunnie Ododo's *Vanishing Vapour* (A Dance Libretto) in *A Gazelle of the Savannah:Sunday Ododo and the Framing of Techno-Cultural Performance in Nigeria.* Osakue, S.O (eds), Kent, UK: Alpha Crownes Publishers. Pp. 219-227.

Hume, D. (1971). *Three Essays: Moral, Political and Literary.* Indianapolis, Literary Classics 5.

Kariamu, W.E. (1998). "The Zimbabwean Dance Aesthetics: Senses, Cannons and Characteristics "in *Africn Dance: An Historical and Philosophical Inquiry.* Kariamu, W.A (ed), Asmaria: Africa World Press, Inc. Pp. 203-220.

The Holy Bible, (King James Version, 2000). 2 Thessalonians 3:10.

Kofoworola, Z. (2004). "Aesthetics of Performance: An Exploration of Concepts in African Theatre" in *The Performer: Ilorin Journal of the Performing Arts.* Vol.6. Pp. 1-19

Laban, R. (1988) *The Mastery of Movement,* Tavistock, UK: Northcote House Publishers Ltd.

Nwala, T.U. (1985). *Igbo Philosophy.* Lagos: Literamed.

Ruch, E.A. and Anyanwu, K.C.(1981). *African Philosophy*. Rome: Catholic Book Agency.

Shelley, J. (2003). "The Problem of Non-Perceptual Art". British Journal of Aesthetics, Vol.43, No. 4.

Snipe, T.D. (1988). "African Dance: Bridges to Humanity" in *Africn Dance: An Historical and Philosophical Inquiry*.

Kariamu, W.A (ed), Asmaria: Africa World Press, Inc. Pp.63-77. Tume, O.K. (2012) "Music and Dance as Emoticons of Bridal Processions: An Assessment of the Obitun Performance of the Ijumu People of Kogi State", *Gender politics: Women Writings and Film in Northern Nigeria*. Ahmed Yerima (Ed.). Ibadan: Kraft Books Limited. Pp.165- 180.

Multi-Dramatic Aesthetics in Bakare Ojo Rasaki's *Rogbodiyan* and *The Gods & The Scavengers*

By
Adenekan, Lanre Qasim

Introduction

In the cotemporary Nigerian literary sphere, most writers especially playwrights wittingly or unwittingly deposit their plays, promoting not only an ideology but a form or style of writing. This notion can be further buttressed going by different published plays by Nigeria playwrights which are in lieu with a particular style or form of writing. It is unarguable that the plays of Wole Soyinka in terms of language are complex while that of Ola Rotimi is a sharp contrast in analogy. Aside this elementary obvious submission, Femi Osofisan's writing is consistent with the full embellishment of songs and audience awareness forcing them to reason out the situations of the play.

Not quite long, specifically through his doctoral thesis, Sam Ukala posits that plays in Africa should surface in a folkloric form, thereby he coined and wrote plays with the theory of folkism. Through this theory, he wrote plays among which are *Akpakaland* and *Break a Boil*. The purpose for these plays is to define a style of playwriting that is true to Africa. Ukala (2007, p. 33) says

> In my PhD thesis, entitled Folktale to Popular Literary Theatre: A study in theory and practice, I introduced into the world theatre scholarship the word "Folkism", which is both a theory and a dramatic aesthetic principle. I also developed a model "Folkist" play entitled "The Placenta Soup". I subtitled at a folkscript because it reads a folktale performance script.

The position of Ukala makes it crystal clear on the need for a model of playwriting in Africa, which he called dramatic aesthetics. So far so, he has been able to confirm this with his propagated model in his plays.

In another vein, Obafemi (2001, p.109) explains the dramatic aesthetics in the writing of Ola Rotimi that:
> Rotimi proficiently employs element of traditional theatrical performance language as in incantation, proverbs, an unabashed translation of stock Yoruba sayings, music, dance, songs, mimes and acted narratives to achieve meaning and dramaturgy.

It is no mist that the assertion above, explains the dramatic techniques in the plays of Ola Rotimi. This is not just documented after critical reading and proper digestion of his plays but a number of his intellectual pouring.

To this effect, on dramatic aesthetics, it is imperative to understand the word "aesthetics" which will therefore serve as a pointer to our position in this paper.

Concept of Aesthetics
According to Oxford Advanced English dictionary seventh edition, "aesthetics is the branch of philosophy that studies beauty, especially in arts. The definition looks at aesthetics as a fusion of both art and beauty. This means art constitutes beauty. Kofoworola (2004, p.3) cited Hegel that "aesthetics is a form of beautiful experience by which the rational rendered sensible, which the sensible appearance being the form in which the rational content is made manifest". Hegel's standpoint on aesthetics contends that for something to be termed beautiful it must conform with our rational principle of beauty, meaning it should be scrutinised in human mind.

In addition, Kant quoted in Kofoworola (2004, p.3) discloses "aesthetics as that branch of philosophy that criticises the taste of an art analysed by spiritualising it to a divine plane and giving it a metaphysical meaning". The position of Kant about aesthetics is that taste is paramount in the evaluation of beauty. The taste comes from human mind which determines the attraction or distraction something can generate in the mind. Succinctly,

Kant's opinion on beauty places aesthetics at the pedestal of human judgement.

The need to clarify the meaning of aesthetics emanates from our intention to demystify the choice of using multi dramatic aesthetics in the selected plays for our analysis. Aesthetics to us is the identification, judgment and evaluation of beauty in art.

A Summary of *Rogbodiyan*

The regent of ilu-koroju having waited for several years with no avail for the enthronement of a new king, decides to transfer power to either Asagigigba or Gbadegesin. Both are from royal families in the land. Therefore she orders the chiefs to select the best candidate among the two for the throne. Her decision, according to her, was to stem the long rulership of the land by her lineage.

After dimensions of controversies and intricacies, Asagidigbi is enthroned. On his coronation, he unwittingly defies the norm of choosing the Arugba but the Abore however gives it a nod. Aftermath, he continues to deliberately show recalcitrant positions to the tradition, more so when he defiles Arugba who was supposed to remain a virgin till after the Oge festival.

As a result, problems surface in which all villagers become deformed including him. Hence, the need to cleanse the land is necessary and Fadele, the diviner is then invited. He submits that the king needs to bring water from River Awogbaarun situated after the Land of the Dead as Ifa demands. Asagidigba refuses, attributing his refusal to his blindness. However, Adegbani, a son to the immediate regent accepts to bring the water with a bid to disguise as the king. His proposal was accepted and he embarked on the journey and later emerges with the water. He however refuses to deliver the water until he is made king. At this point, the people succumb to his stand coupled with the revelation that Asagidigbi is the cause of their deformities.

A Summary of *The Gods and The Scavengers*

The play unveils oppression, corruption, killings, disunity and self-aggrandizement in a nation. The play uses the characters of scavengers to project poverty and oppression in a land where the ruled are maltreated by the rulers.

Anago, the chairman feigns statesmanship by rejecting the gift offered to him by the market women during his visit to the market. This gives the market women the impression of a good leader in Anago, who ironically orders his aid to relocate the scavengers to the desert. Anago also criticises and vows to punish his councillors - Chief Olowokere, Madunagwu, Abasi and Mallam Mai Angwa for collecting royalties from the people as well as diverting into personal pocket, funds to construct roads and market stalls.

Chief Andy, a personal adviser to Anago decides to terminate his appointment after all his advices to Anago for good governance were jettisoned. Therefore, he challenges the scavengers to protest against the government to better their lives and society. At the end, the people heed the advice and dislodge Anago and other councilors from their positions. They then resolve to choose a leader amongst themselves.

Multi Dramatic Aesthetics In The Selected Plays
Aesthetics of Prologue

The acclaimed genesis of theatre, the Greek theatre employed prologue in the structure of their drama. It is the first elements of Greek drama while others are parados, stasimon, exodus and epilogue. Prologue introduces the play. It gives a clear insight into the content of the play. In the selected plays, Rasaki uses prologue to introduce the plays. This can be equated to tableaux in the performance context. It owes to the fact that tableaux beams light to the embedded actions or events in the unfolding performance.

In Rogbodiyan, prologue is applied, taking the form of music perhaps song using a character, which is portrayed as a narrator to introduce the play to the audience. The song as well is an eye opener to explain the inherent meaning of the title, through the mouth of the narrator.

>
> (Darkness in the theatre. A voice rings)
> Voice: Ro-gb-o-d-i-ya-n
> (Follow spot picks towns people...)
> Song: Rogbodiyan, oo, ee rogbodiyan oo (twice)
> Rogbodiyan tide oran sele, ijangba tide oran sele,
> iluoo roju kotun raye, awa bere oo,..
> (...Narrator appears)
> Narrator: (To the audience) welcome to another season of laughter and merry making. But most importantly, you are welcome to another season of meditation and sober reflection. (2004,p.6)

Similarly, in *The Gods and The Scavengers*, prologue is used to inform the readers perhaps the audience about the dramatic experience using chorus and (Total darkness. Two sonorous voice begin a song)

> Lead: Yes it's dawn of a new morning but the promise land is still far away,
> our destiny is in our hands, we must rise up now or else we perish.
> Chorus: Yes, dawn of a new morning... (2013, p.vi)

Aesthetics of Song Opening Movements
Similar to the use of song in the prologues of the selected plays is the adoption of songs to open the play. This is apparent in both plays for this discourse i.e the use of song to start the movements. The playwright believes in using song to foretell the story of the scenes before dialogues ensue. To our understanding, the employment of songs for opening scenes also assists the reader to decipher the mood and atmospheric condition of the scene in lieu with the characters.

> The opening movement in *The Gods & The scavengers* opens thus (...A song begins from the

background and we see four hungry looking, gaunt and unkempt people... They sing as they move towards the refuse dump...)

Song: we are the scavengers, we the main men.
when those rogues eat their beans, we comb their bins.
They cheat, we lift their shit...(p. 1)

In the same vein, Rogbodiyan follow suits in "Movement 1":
(Agogo, the kings adviser/ messenger enters...He sings)

Agogo: kee ree kere keere o ee (twice)
odomomode atagbalagba, lokunrin lobinrin pe
ipade ku si lola lafin oba. (p. 8)

Aesthetics of Script Directing

Lange, cited in Arinde (2012, p.100) points "directing requires creativity, imagination, vision, and a clear concept to bring playwrights work to life for a cast and crew and ultimately the audience" Directing as perceived by the scholar above corroborates our understanding of Rasaki's dramatic techniques in directing script using elucidate stage instruction. Script directing is obvious in the selected plays for this research. This is immensely showcased in the stage instruction and the overall actions in the plays. The events or situations are coordinated, organised and harnessed to ensure the flow of happenings, coupled with the infusion of songs, entrance and exit as well as starting occurrences through stage areas. This means the playwright compromises with Musa (2001, p. 47) that "directing can also be described as the organisation, management, interpretation, coordination and manipulation of human and material resources towards the sole purpose of creating an artistic whole for the audience". Though this disclosure when critically checked, expresses more of stage performance, yet the application is made manifest in the manner Rasaki weaves the plays.

In *Rogbodiyan* or opinion is supported:
(Darkness in the theatre. A voice rings)
Voice: Rogbodiyan

(Follow spots pick towns people coming from the audience in different directions... Their movement is rhythmic though it cannot be said that they are dancing (p.6)

(...A group of people - Gbadegesin's supporters storm the auditorium through the left crash door... as they are about to exit through the right crash door, Asagidigba supporters enter through the *right crash door*. (italicise mine) p.17

(...song and music continue at the background. Narrator comes forward to address the audience) p. 28

Similarly, The Gods and The scavengers shows (At upstage centre, the other scavengers kneel in prayerful positions facing stage left...) p. 4 (They stand, hiss, kneel again facing stage right with their faces toward the sky...) p.4 (Sudden blackout. Light returns and we are back in Anago shrine) p.45

Aesthetics of Detribalized Language
This is a unique portrayal of Rasaki as a detribalised playwright. This can be attested through his plays, in which he blends confidently other languages to express his ideology. Apparently, his plays adhere to functionalist ideology through which social problems are exposed. He uses his plays as a form of metaphor to disclose the maladies in the Nigerian society with a view to changing the society for better.

As a result, in the Gods and the scavengers, Rasaki heavily uses the three major languages in Nigeria; Hausa, Igbo and Yoruba. He does this, through the characters representing the three tribes; Chief Olowookere, Chief Madunagwu and Mallam Mai Angwa. These characters speak their dialects as well as English in order to confirm their tribes.

Chief Olowokere: wa n' bi arabinrin moti n wa e lataaro. Why haven't you brought to me those

	things that are meant for the honourable? (P. 13)
Hadiza:	Haba Mallam! Mai ya faru? Ranka dede just left this place.
Mallam:	mai ki ki nufe? (p 15)
Chief Madunagwu:	Machie onu! Are you asking me? (p.14)

These indigenous languages are also used for songs in the play.

SONG 1

IGBO
Nne nne udu mara puta mu o du 2x
Udu nji chu miriri
Ama magbi in udu awa udu (p.35)

SONG (YORUBA)
Iyayi male ra mio
Eleyi male yeye o
Oluwa mafebi pa'niyan (p 44)

SONG (HAUSA)
Ina zz muje 2x
Ina zamu koma yaruwa ina za muje
Anche duniya babu dadi
Anche latira kuma da zafi
Iwa zamu koma yaruwa ina lamuje (p. 15)

The beauty of these songs is that it sets the moods as well as explains that the playwright understands the society in which the play is located. He relates the play to the tribes without given undue priority to his tribe, understandably Yoruba.

Aesthetics of Eclectic Drama
Eclectic simply means subsuming varieties to make a whole. Oxford advanced learners dictionary seventh edition (p. 465) sees "eclectic as not following one style or using a wide variety". Adopting this into the discourse, apparently pronouncing the

plays of Rasaki, involves varieties ranging from songs, music, instrumentation, dance, drama, technical etc.

This idea can be related to total theatre looking at it from performance angle. Adeoye (2012 p. 52) quoting Reilly and Phillips says total theatre is "usually a production style that makes free use of all the many resources of the stage and theatre in general; drama, music, dance, song, film, slide projection, advanced technological effects etc". Adeoye adds "Kofoworola...will introduce the functional use except in his play"...

The earlier citation especially on total theatre gives a clear insight on our choice of eclectic drama, owing to Rasaki's employment of this aesthetics in the script not on stage. Rasaki vigorously weaves songs, instrumentation, perhaps music's, dance, mime etc in his plays as seen in the case of *Rogbodiyan* and *the Gods and the scavenger*.

In the two plays, songs are conspicuously engraved and cognisance is attached to mime, dance alongside dramatic dialogues. Evidently, this can confirmed in page 6,17,23,24,39 etc of *Rogbodiyan*. In the same vein it is obvious in page vi,1,4,15,23,43,45, etc. of the Gods & the scavengers.

Aesthetics of Technical Aids
Technical in the theatrical sphere ranges from the use of lighting, costume, scenery sound effect, instruments, properties among others. In the course of the research, we discovered in *Rogbodiyan* and *the Gods and the scavenger* that technical aids are properly harnessed in the use of lighting and instrumentation.

The playwright expresses himself through the plays as having good knowledge of lighting. He announces in the stage instructions when and where lights will be projected as well as giving basic information on the type of lantern needed for the lighting.
    In *the Gods and the scavenger* he explains

(...Dim light reveals assorted types of containers filled up with discarded materials...) p.1
(Stage lights come on gradually showing scavs kneeling...) p.5
(Dim Light. Anago is seen in his shrine consulting Yemoja...) p. 41
Also in Rogbodiyan lighting is dictated
(Follow spots pick townspeople coming from audience in different directions) p.6
(Floodlight in the auditorium ...) p. 17
(...The narrator appears in the auditorium. Follow spot picks him...) p.39

Aesthetics of Multiple Characters
It is no news that some plays emerge with few characters. Such is the case of Sizwe Bansi is Dead which experiments with three characters. However, Rasaki in *Rogbodiyan* and *the Gods and scavenger* employs multiple characters. The use of multiple characters in these plays could be borne out of the functionalist ideology propagated in the plays. This is also prominent in the plays of Osofisan who is believed to be a leading figure among playwrights of political drama, radical drama or Marxist drama in the country. That is why Obafemi and Yerima (2004, p.132) speak of Osofisan characters in reference to his radical ideology:

...osofisan plays..........thrive on the faith of the character..........to be liberated. In variably, it is the necessity to live that controls and motivates characters into organised revolutionary action to confront the necessity to change their situation and find new solution to their predicament.

Having noted the plays call for societal change against plaguing issues within, Rasaki's use of multiple characters is understandably justified. The presence of multiple characters is in similitude to the presence of large audience which the plays intend to address about problems in the society.

Aesthetics of Song Closing

Song is the beginning and ending in *Rogbodiyan* and *the Gods and the scavengers*. Songs are used at the closing scenes of the two plays in order to give a clear understanding of the situation of the characters. This is done in two dimensions particularly submitting totally to two functionalist schools. The critical realism and social realism; critical realism calls for the readers or audience to embark on a critical reasoning to solve their societal problems. On the other hand, social realism points the way forward to the readers or audience.

In *Rogbodiyan*, the playwright ends the play with a song that declares the people in a continuous struggle.

Song: ologun gbawa o ni ma roo
      Ninini ni kun ini
      Booba gbawa oaa se tire lo
      Nini ni ni kun inni (p. 59)

However, *The Gods and The Scavengers* shows the closing song as a liberation song. It declares the people as victors after a series of turmoil. (...the songs in the prologue "yes it's the dawn of a new morning..." is repeated. Singing continues as the stage light gradually fades into total blackout.)

Conclusion

Our sojourn in this research allowed us to critically and analytically examine what we termed the "multi dramatic aesthetics" in the selected plays. This is borne out of our comprehension of the dramatic techniques the playwright uses in stirring his artistic deposits in the playwriting parlance. It will be no naivety on the part of any reader to comprehend the songs, mimes, instructions and the plot of the selected plays having worked through this research.

The style of an individual distinguishes his works from others. With this notion, we believe Bakare Ojo Rasaki wittingly crafts his plays especially taking cognisance of the African realities in terms of societal issues and culture of songs, music, dance, pantomimes, acrobatics among others. It is also noteworthy at this point that Bakare's dramatic techniques will give easy room for any yearning director to put on stage for physical manifestations his plays.

References

Adeoye, A.A (2012). Aesthetics, dramaturgy and directorial poetics of Ayo Akinwale's theatre. In: *The dramaturgy of a theatre sociologist: festschrift in honour of Ayo Akinwale.* (ed.) Abdulrasheed A. Adeoye pp. 26-60 Ilorin: Department of the performing Arts

Arinde, T.S (2012). Directorial style and skills of Ayo Akinwale in the mountains of wealth. In: *The dramaturgy of a theatre sociologist: festschrift in honour of Ayo Akinwale* (ed.) Abdulrasheed A Adeoye pp. 98-107 Ilorin: Department of the performing Arts

Kofoworola, Z.O (2004) Aesthetic of performance an exploration of concept in African theatre. *The perfomer: Ilorin journal of the performing arts* 6:1 -19

Musa, R.A. (2001). Play directing and directors. An evolutionary documentation in the Nigerian theatre. Retrieved from http://www.unilorin.edu.ng/facultyofarts/departmentoftheperformigarts/AdeoyeAbiodunAbdulrasheed

Obafemi, O. (2001). *Contemporary Nigerian theatre cultural heritage and social vision.* Lagos: CBAAC

Obafemi, O. And Yerima A. (2004). *Ideology and stage craft in the Nigeria theatre.* Ikeja: bookplus Nigeria limited

Oxford advanced English dictionary seventh edition

Rasaki, B.O. (2004). *Rogbodiyan.* NP: Tamaza publishing company limited

Rasaki, B.O. (2013). *The gods and the scavengers.* Abuja: Topklass

Ukala, S.U. (2007). *African theatre beast of no gender?* Abraka: delta state university

Riddles and Ripples in Bakare, Ojo Rasaki's Works: A Directorial Perspective

By
Ugala, Best B.

Introduction

At the Nigerian Universities Theatre Arts Festival held at the University of Port Harcourt in 1987 (NUTAF '87), one strong idea that was canvassed was that NUTAF plays should be written and directed by students. The purpose was to encourage theatre students to deepen their training as a catalyst for grooming the future generation of playwrights. In 1988, the Tosin Ayoola-led Executive of the Nigerian Universities Theatre Arts Students' Association (NUTASA) gave a welcome fillip to the idea, and opportunity was open to students of Theatre to start writing plays for NUTAF. Students struggled to make the NUTAF '88 entry, but most of the plays did not accord with the theme of 1988 festival which was "Theatre as a Forum for societal reflection and projection into the future". Because of this, many universities came to University of Ilorin which hosted the festival with plays written by their lecturers or by the Ngugi wa Thiong'os and the Ayo Akinwales. The institutions that were able to meet the new challenge were University of Calabar with Ojo Bakare's "This Land Must Sacrifice", University of Ibadan with Debo Sotuminu's "The Fractured Dream" (both unpublished then) and perhaps one or two other universities. Although Bakare had had some stage apprenticeship under Jimoh Aliyu and Hubert Ogunde, *This Land Must Sacrifice* marked the beginning of his literary pilgrimage.

If one may reminisce further, *This Land Must Sacrifice* ran for three nights at the New Arts Theatre in UNICAL, but could not be staged at NUTAF '88 because the festival ended abruptly as a result of the closure of Nigerian universities occasioned by the nation-wide student riot/demonstration against the Babangida Administration. However, the play was repackaged for NUTAF '89 held at the University of Jos. It was adjudged as one of the most outstanding performances at the festival. After the three-night run in UNICAL, Prof. Charity Angya (then Dr. Chairty Pever-Ge) sent in a note to this writer who was then the President of the Departmental Students' Association. In the note, she remarked that in the play, Bakare sought to historicise and address socio-political issues by harnessing folk and Marxist aesthetics. The result, according to her, was both shocking and absorbing. Indeed, *This Land Must Sacrifice* is the first born, the first product of Bakare's creative genius.

Bakare's Social Vision
Social vision implies an imaginative guide or aspiration to the development of one's society. Nigeria as a nation has since her independence been scorched by the flame of bad leadership, corruption, injustice, dishonesty, impunity, arrant lawlessness and other variants of abhorrent tendency. Nigerian writers and artists in all the genres have always deployed their literary and artistic arsenals to tackle these evils. Bakare is no exception.

Bakare's ideological commitment is distilled from Marxist dialectics of right and wrong, of light and darkness, of wealth and penury, of grandeur and squalor. As he set out at dawn with *This Land Must Sacrifice,* he declared eloquently: "Socialism is good for us" (27). It is a song that bears the imprint of an anthem and which presages the divine injunction that "everybody must be equal... Everything should belong to the Land... Everybody must share anything in common" (28). This is Bakare's recommendation or redemptive programme which he envisages for his society. However, it was unknown to him that socialism which he so forcefully adulated would, three years later, collapse inexorably.

With or without socialism, Bakare remains undaunted and unshakeable in his belief that the brutal, squalid environment that offers nothing but harrowing experience must be destroyed and replaced with an egalitarian system. His approach is in tandem with Soyinka's belief that "A book, if necessary should be a hammer, a hand grenade which you detonate under a stagnant way of looking at the world" (Agetua, p.48). Thus, his major desire or sacred wish is to use his revolutionary plays to provoke heaven and earth to unleash a revolution that would terminate the woes and malediction of his native land.

All in all, Bakare is absolutely a man of peace. In all his plays, his quest for peace is profound. With *Drums of War*, he makes a statement on the meaninglessness and futility of wars; in *The Gods and the Scavengers*, revolutionary campaign led by the messianic figure - Andy brings about the reconciliation and unification of all the ethnic groups and contending parties; in *Rogbodiyan*, The conflict and tension heighten to a boiling point but full scale hostility is painstakingly averted, and in *This Land Must Sacrifice*, the fatality is allowed only to the extent of its purgative and restorative essence.

Directing Bakare's Plays
As furnished by history, the director is a new comer to the theatre, but since the days of the Duke of Saxe-Meiningen, his functionality has proved beyond equivocation that he is of "tremendous importance in shaping the destiny of modern theatre" (Whiting. 213). As Whiting also notes, the present day director ranks second in importance only to the playwright in the process of presenting a living play on the stage (207).

To ask the researcher's question, who is the director? The *Batsford Dictionary of Drama* simply defines director as the one who "envisages and creates the dramatic text in space" or the one who "harmonises the craft of acting with the demands of pictorial staging" (96). Cameron and Gillespie (1989:99) take a broader perspective of the director and his role: The director, as a unifier, is saddled with three responsibilities – interpretation, presentation and management. As interpreter, presenter and manager, he not only analyzes the dramatic text, but also evaluates the nature of the expected audience and assesses the abilities and potentials of the other theatre artists (155). Archer (99) explains it perfectly: "Ideally, directors determine their own intention for each production, engage the other artists and filter all of the other creative work through their own vision, welding all effort into a smooth, cohesive whole".

Like practical prophet, a serious director should be able to predict the kind of audience that would grace his production and their kind of responses to his staging styles and procedures. He is also a critic of some sort because, as part of his creative procedure, he has to appraise or criticise both the playwright and actors. As Archer contends, during rehearsal, the director evaluates, modifies and tries to improve the over all production (99). He does all these according to his aesthetic taste and artistic vision.

Now, let us examine how Bakare, Ojo Rasaki plays can be approached from directorial perspective. As usual, it is advisable that a director have his directorial concept before he commences rehearsal. The concept, according to Wilson (282), "comes from a controlling idea, vision, point of view, or metaphor, which will result in a cohesive production and present the spectator with a unified artistic experience". It is the concept that will determine whether the director will exercise his license to tamper with the script or not, or how to periodize the play or whether to transpose or adapt it. However, Wilson warns that in developing his concept, the director should not allow his desire for originality or showy style to distort or violate the integrity of the script (284).

In order to formulate a valid concept of Bakare's play and begin the directorial process, the director must read and re-read the script to distil the general impressions about the theme, the dramatic situation, the artistic construction, and even the events in the structured society that Bakare draws his materials from. Because his plays are socially engaging, it becomes obligatory for the director to adopt scientific approach of enquiry to unravel the causes and effects.

After these preliminary procedures, work starts in earnest. And what the director is most likely to see are critical elements that will put his proficiency to the test. For the purpose of analysis, we have chosen to label these elements "Riddles" and "Ripples".

Riddles and Ripples in Bakare's Play

In common usage, a riddle is a kind of puzzle, a conundrum or difficult question that creates some amusement when correctly solved. Bakare is a multi-talented artist with dance and choreography as his special forte. Dance presupposes the presence of music. It is therefore not surprising that Bakare's plays overflow with music and dance. In this paper, these two insparable elements are discussed under the imageries of riddles and ripples in which they have appeared under direction.

The Riddles

As stated earlier, the three-fold business of the director is interpretation, presentation and management. The focus of this paper is on the first – interpretation. To interpret Bakare's vision on stage, the director must first crack the riddles. The riddles are the critical challenges which the director has to tackle and surmount, and they range from the task of staging the playwright's intentions, and realising the various dramatic techniques to the rigours and exertions of the production.

Anyone who has directed Bakare's plays would confess that it is only through rigorous rehearsals that the production could be realised. Almost all his plays fray the nerves with rigours and stress on one hand and titillate with thematic beauty, spectacles, profound histrionics and celebratory values on the other. The reason for this is not far-fetched: Bakare is first and foremost a dancer and choreographer of the finest stock. It is not surprising therefore that music, dance, expressive mimes and oral narratives are organically fused into the texture of his plays. These are serious elements in the theatre which only "the strong breed" can take on. Emasealu (97-98) vividly pictures an instance of such rigorous performance in Daniel Kpodo's direction of *Drums of War*:

> As the prologue opens with a flute and a chant, eight Ibuji warriors bearing cutlasses and clubs emerge from up-stage right and engage in a highly physical and elaborate choreographic movement using the

> entire stage in different formations...., as the eight Ibuji warriors exit, eight Abakpa warriors emerge from stage right (?) to engage in equally highly physical two-minute choreography that suggests their preparedness for war.

In fact, to realise the circular dance movements, the energetic display of bravado and the stylised, choreographic combat is not a task for an untested hand.

This Land Must Sacrifice offers a greater rollercoaster of overwhelming challenges. See what the director faces in Movement 1:

> There is a fast tempo music. A man dressed in the colonial master's attire dances in. Another man in shorts and bare-bodied dances in from the opposite direction. His movements suggest agony... They dance and meet at the stage centre. The bare-bodied man worries the colonial lord persistently until the colonial lord mimes "You HAVE BEEN FREED" and removes the chains... (p.7)

In this scene, the entire history of Nigeria's struggle for independence is re-enacted in music and dance. In Movement 3:

> People are seen inside three canoes on a river. In front of each canoe is a leader with long sticks paddling and directing the canoes. The "passengers" hold one paddle each painted in green, white, green colours. They are paddling, singing and dancing to the accompaniment of music... (p.9)

In this scene, the director is expected to replicate the spectacular boat regatta of the popular Argungun Fishing Festival. For the director, it is not just enough to choreograph these dance movements; he has to ensure that the music, dance, dialogue, artistic setting, props costumes are harmoniously blended under his directorial superintendence.

It is a known fact that dance scenes are problematic in the hands of a director who has no knowledge of choreography. The matter is worse if the theatre company or department has no trained choreographer. Cameron and Gillespie affirm that there are instances of when directors found themselves complaining before the actors: "Do I have to do everything"? (173). Yes, there are instances of where directors were frustrated and compelled to "cut" the choreographic scenes or get their actors to contrive something near it. This is escapist!

Emasealu declares: "No text may be regarded as sacrosanct", and therefore can be reworked" for reasons of "shifting historical winds" (88). This is correct, but it is important to explain that any form of reworking that vitiates the integrity of the script or that borders on escapism is unholy and unacceptable. Just as Cameron and Gillespie contend, a production is not necessarily bad because it fails to stage the 'playwright's intention, nor is it necessarily good because it stages the playwright's intentions precisely. What is important is that the director should try to understand the playwright's approach and "evaluate it for what it is" (189).

Another thorny riddle is the use of music and songs. Music is a universal art, and it constitutes the fabric of African art and culture. As (1974) explains:

> Music making in African may be organized as a concurrent activity, that is, as incidental or background music for other events as games wrestling matches, walking parties, processions, beer parties and feasts (Awodiya, 180)

Bakare draws extensively from oral literary devices salient among which is music and songs. The traditional Yoruba society has a profoundly rich and complex cosmology which is the source of his creative inspiration. As a composer, Bakare writers songs in different languages and infuses them into his dramaturgy. These songs serve three basic functions in his plays: as background, as incidental music and as intermission between scenes. As incidental music, they are used to enrich the performance, heighten mood, deepen the thematic thrust and achieve purgative or cathartic effect.

Ordinarily, written song texts are gratuitous provisions from the playwright. But the problem is that the songs are not furnished with musical notations, and this makes it difficult for the director to utilize them in his production. This writer has directed a couple of Bakare's plays and shudders to recall the difficulty he had in searching for anyone versed in music and in Yoruba language to turn the lyrics into songs. The most recent experience was when he directed, *This Land Must Sacrifice* for the Fourteenth Convocation of his institution in July, 2014. Of the eleven songs in the play, five were in Yoruba, four in English, one each in Esan and Aniocha. Among the entire cast and crew, none could speak Yoruba, let alone teach us the Yoruba songs. Some suggested rendering the songs in English since the translations were in the glossary, but that would have yanked the play off its cultural base and subverted its "integrity". The saving grace was that the Technical Director's wife hails from Yoruba, and she came to our rescue.

The Ripples
Ripples are a series of gentle and rhythmic movement or waves that a pool of water exhibits on the surface when disturbed or unsettled. It is our chosen metaphor of Bakare's plays in motion; it symbolises the rhythm, colour, the flowing tempi and fluidity that constitute "movement" or the theatricality of his plays. The plays are remarkable for their richness and lucidity in language and density and grandeur in movement. As the actor uses "body" language, so the director employs "movement" language. Terry Hodgson (1988) confirms this when he explains that "successful plays seem to have a characteristic tempo with rhythmical variations of movement between and within the acts and scenes" (230).

Rhythm is marked by regularity of repetition, and the elements of rhythm are movement, tempo, words and timing. With regard to movement, Emasealu contends that movement which is used
> to express the mood of a character, to emphasize a character, to evaluate characters and to suggest sub-textual meanings as well as convey other vivid

>   pictorial images has been of tremendous significance
>   in picturization which in itself is an important factor
>   of theatre directing (9)

Generally, in theatre, movement complements words and actions and in Bakare's plays, movement operates across vertical and horizontal lines.

Perhaps, it is important to explain here that in theatre, movement is not action but part of action. Action is a very broad concept; it covers the cognitive, affective and psychomotor domains, the internal and the external, the mental and the physical of the stage activity. Movement, words and silence are part of stage action, but movement is basically physical or exterior. It consists of visual and auditory activities (Hodgson, 230).

With Bakare's plays, the task before the director is how to weave movement into ripples in which lie the thematic essence and aesthetics' of the play. Without rhythm there are no ripples and without timing there are no rhythms. The director, therefore, should know how to time every stage activity. Cameron and Gillespie advise that in designing a performance, the director should know when to deliver a laugh-getting line and how long the laughter will last; he should work out how "a quickening of tempo will increase tension or a slowing will enhance a feeling of ponderousness or doom" (182). Wilson (288) shares the same view: "The director must instill and implant in the performers such a strong sense of inner rhythm in rehearsals that they have an internal clock which tells them how they should play". Generally, in the progression of performance, quickness in tempo presupposes urgency or tension and slowness, relaxation.

Because of his social commitment, Bakare's plays are community-based. Most often, a whole community is put on stage. Osofisan (20) declares that there is no other playwright or director who equals Ola Rotimi's mastery of crowd management techniques and the use of space for spectacular climaxes. From all indications, Bakare is irreversibly inching his way to that highest rung of the ladder on which Rotimi has been standing lonely. For example, in Movement 3 of *This Land Must Sacrifice*, we see an exodic movement involving three major ethnic groups and some minorities; in *Rogbodiyan*. Movement 6 features the coronation scene in which the entire people of Ilu-Koroju assemble to inaugurate a new epoch.

It takes a crack director to handle such an assemblage of actors on an average proscenium stage. It also takes a director of Duke Georg or Ola Rotimi's caliber to realize the mounting excitement and swelling crescendo of jubilation in such scenes. And to achieve this, Wilson counsels that "The director should established the proper pace and rhythm in the movements of the scenes and the dynamics of the production as a whole" (293). The director should also strive to underscore the essence of such assemblage through stage pictures, visual composition and clear definition of the spatial relationship of the actors on stage. Emasealu observes this in the production of *Drums of War* as directed by Daniel Kpodoh. According to him, "One technique that Bakare employed in *Drums of War* is making his characters to freeze at the height of a tense moment of dramatic action thereby eliciting a strong mental propensity to think and/or act on the part of the audience" (86).

One thing that is worthy of note is the cross-cultural and transnational element in the working of Bakare's social consciousness. In almost all his plays, he employs the integration theory to advance his nationalist cause. The theory expounds the principle that the success of a whole can only be achieved through the functionality of its derivatives. It is based on the operation of bringing together of the constituent parts into a whole as opposed to the differentiation theory. In *The Gods and the scavengers*, there is reference, albeit impliedly, to the various ethnic groups through the professions of the scavengers – the cattle rearing, fishing, blacksmithing and the farming groups. The scavengers are ejected from their slummy community, their right of occupancy is revoked and the slum is reclaimed by the "gods", the powers that be. Meanwhile, Andy, the Special Adviser to the Chairman ditches his master and decides to lead a revolutionary campaign that culminates in the reconciliation and unification of all the ethnic groups. The same nationalistic fervour runs through *This Land Must Sacrifice* and *Drums of War*. Aborishade (18) notes that in Drums of War, Bakare garbs Onome, the King of Abakpa as a symbol of national politics and unity: "Onome's dress portrays Yoruba, Hausa, Edo, Fulani and Igbo traditions. He wears Hausa cap, Igbo shirt, Yoruba trousers and Edo royal beads". The director should take note of this ethnic and national dimensions in formulating his directorial concept, metaphor and approach

Conclusion
Bakare, Ojo Rasaki has became a leading light among the third generation of Nigerian playwrights. With over ten full length plays, he has set the theatre firmament aglow and offered directors some palm nuts to crack. Any director of Bakare's plays must have the wherewithal to crack the hard shells which are the riddles before bringing out the Kernels which are the ripples. Ripples represent the total aesthetics of a performance which are expressed in the fluidity, transition and movement of the performance.

By his works, Bakare has carved out for himself an image of a Marxist, and directors may want to consult Marxian or Brechtian manual before taking on his works. This may not be necessary, not because Marxist scholarships is suffering untold regression, but because Bakare, from the onset, took liberties to break some of the Marxist taboos By that, he has since reached the final stage of dissonance with Marxism. He writes with absolute sense of commitment, not in defence or furtherance of any ideological dogma, but in pursuit of a just, open, equitable and egalitarian society.

In his avowed mission, drum is his creative symbol, and music and dance are his special medium. Music and dance are the most exciting aspect of performance but the hardest to realize. Thus, they are the director's terror. When faced with such terror at rehearsal, the director finds himself in a state of confusion and creative stasis. At such a point, the director should heed Bernard shaw's advice.

> But don't say..."We must go on at this until we get it, if we have to stay here all night...." If it goes wrong, it will go wronger with every repetition on the same day. Leave it until next time. (9)

Bakare's plays have the tendency of overwhelming the director and drawing him into a kind aporia. But with hard-work, with rigorous rehearsals that feature physical drills and vocal exercises, with audition that identifies the ability, creative imagination and special attributes of the actors, the challenges can be overcome.

References

Aborishade, Akinwale. "War Agianst War". *Tell Magazine* No. 19 Lagos: Tell Communications, May 13, 2002

Angya, C.A. "Revolutionary Night in UNICAL", A Note on the performance of *This Land Must Sacrifice*, 1988.

Archer, Stephen M. *How Theatre Happens* (2nd ed.). New York: Macmillan publishing Co, 1983

Bakare, Ojo Rasaki. *Rogbodiyan*. Zaria: Tamaza Publishing Co. 2004

.... This Land Must Sacrifice. Enugu: New Age publishers, 1991

Cameron, K.M. and P.P. Gillespie. *The Enjoyment of Theatre*. New York: Macmillan Publishing Co., 1989.

Emasealu, Emmanel C. "A Study of Bakare Ojo Rasaki's *Drums of War* as Text and performance". The Crab (Vol. 1 No. 2). *A Journal of the Dept of Theatre Arts,* University of Port Harcourt, 2006

Hodgson, Terry. *The Batsford Dictionary of Drama*. London: B.T. Batsford Ltd, 1988

Holy Bible, The. Acts of the Apostles, Chapter 9

Uka, Kalu. "Foreword" to Bakare Ojo Rasaki's *This Land Must Sacrifice*, op.cit.

Novikov, Vassily in Kemi Illori, "Book Review" in *Theatre Forum* No. 1. A publication of Nigerian Theatre Arts Students' Association (NUTASA), 1987

Osofisan, Femi. "Beyond Translation: A Comparatist Look at Tragic Paradigms and the Dramaturgy of Wole Soyinka and Ola Rotimi". Ife Monographs on Literature and Criticism. 1985.

Soyinka, Wole in *Interview with Six Nigeria Writers* (Agetua ed.). Benin City: Bendel Newspapers Corporations, 1974

Symons, Arthur. In Suzan Khin Zaw et al, *Beginings of Modern Drama*. Great Britain: The Open University Press, 1977.

Wilson, Edwin. *The Theatre Experience*. New York: McGraw Hill Book Company, 1976
Whiting, Frank M. *An Introduction to the Theatre* (4th edition). New York: Harper and Row Publishers, 1978.

Yeats, W.B. In Suzan Khin Zaw et al. op. cit.

The Abuja Carnival and Bakare Ojo Rasaki's Directorial Imprint

By
Isijola, Oluwatayo

Introduction

The need to harness the vast cultural and artistic resources that manifest in the ethnic plurality of the Nigerian state for the purpose of social engineering dates back to 1970, with the advent of the All Nigerian Festival of Arts. As part of the post civil war reconciliation efforts, the festival was intentioned for national reintegration and reunification (Ben-Iheanacho, 37). This, in present-day has begotten the annual event that summons thousands of participants as contingents; the National Festival of Arts and Culture (NAFEST). Established by Decree No 3 of 1975, and amended by Decree No5, 1987, NAFEST is billed to coordinate cultural activities across the country for the purpose of developing, preserving and promoting the "living art and culture" of Nigeria at national and international fora" (NCAC *Handbook*, 2).

In 1977, the Second World Blacks and African Festival of Arts and Culture, famously known as FESTAC '77 held in Nigeria, as a Pan-African celebration, and it recorded good success (Wikipedia[1]). The instance of FESTAC signalled possibility of further exploration of the nation's ethnic plurality for the purpose of culture tourism and cultural diplomacy (Ben-Iheanacho, 37), but this possibility remained unattended for many more years. Thus, the need to explore the abundant cultural resources in the Nigerian society, to fashion a huge scale and home-grown cultural tourism project, aimed at promoting Nigeria as a safe tourist destination, informed the imitative Abuja Carnival. Since inception in 2005, Abuja Carnival has grown in leap and bounds towards fulfilling the purpose for which it was set up, and becoming a paradigm for previously existing and newly emerging state carnivals, as well as other cultural festivals within the federation.

The national carnival is becoming an international brand that assembles some thirty six (36) State troupes, including the Federal Capital Territory (FCT), and troupes from friendly international communities annually. Ajimotokan, reports concerning the 2013 edition, thus;

> Abuja Carnival reinforced the spirit of unity and high expectation as people came out singing and festooned in colourful costume. They partied on the streets of Abuja from dawn to dusk regardless of social status and age difference (*Thisday live*, web).

He refers to the Street Carnival, a compulsory contest entry for all participating state troupes, as the "big stage where contesting and visiting international troupes display". This is the major highlight of the carnival, which attracts a mammoth crowd consisting of residents of the FCT and environs, as national and international tourists take to street, either flanking the eighteen (18) kilometres long carnival route or standing on bridges along the carnival route. In what seems like a street theatre, contingents are engaged in a moving and continuous stretch of performances with the express road as stage, and the endless crowd of spectators as audience. The focus of this paper is to analyse the qualities that the director brings to bear in harnessing and achieving the desired result in the performance on the "vast stage" of Abuja National Carnival Street Party.

Abuja National Carnival

> A Carnival typically involves a public celebration or parade combining some elements of a circus, mask and public street party. People often dress up or masquerade during the celebrations, which mark an overturning of the norms of daily life (Wikipedia).

The foregoing aptly describes the nature of the Abuja National Carnival, as it is true of other world class carnivals. The overturning of norms of daily life, at least, is felt by all and sundry in Abuja, including residents who show indifference or disinterestedness to carnival activities. That carnival day is declared a public holidays for civil servants, and certain roads mapped out as carnival route are shut down on commuters. For Lillian Bakare, the carnival is "a street dance and a loud and boisterous parade of colours (169). She observes that the coordinating ministry (Federal Ministry of Culture and Tourism), declared that: "The design of Abuja Carnival clearly marks it as one of the most diversified carnivals in the world, and it is said to be Africa's largest parade of glorious cultural extravaganza" (qtd in Ojo Bakare, 170).

Furthermore, the Ministry states that:
The Abuja National Carnival has continued to reflect the original ideals of the concept of the carnival, and as follows:
- A platform to demonstrate our unity in diversity, bridge building and enhancement of friendship amongst Nigerians and our friendly countries;
- A unique Nigerian experience and a veritable tool for tourism development;
- A tourist product that celebrates Nigeria's warmness and hospitality;
- A brand that will contribute to the economic growth and transformation of the nation;
- A brand that is designed for the development of the creative ingenuity of our people thus boosting several aspects of the creative industry in Nigeria; and
- Promotion of micro, small scale and medium enterprises. (FMTCNO, 11)

In the same vein, Ojo Bakare declares during a workshop session that his concept as director is that of "a national carnival that is colourful and grandiose for a world-class content package that does not lose its local flavour and unique identity" (2011). This concept is gradually coming to realisation, as the carnival is beginning to enjoy the participation of more international troupes. Record has it that

> "The international participation is increasing every year. In 2011 four (4) countries participated viz: Egypt, India, Ghana, and Trinidad and Tobago. This year some countries participating are: China, Trinidad and Tobago, Egypt, Cameron, Sudan, Cuba, Namibia, Ghana and Senegal etc. This is an indication of its growing acceptance as an international brand" (FMTCNO, 11).

The Abuja National Carnival is a four-day event which holds in Abuja, Nigeria's Federal Capital Territory, and its competitive nature makes the troupe's participation a breath-taking entertainment event to spectators, as every troupe strives to win. The major contest events include the following:
1. Street Carnival
2. Masquerade Fiesta
3. Children Fiesta
4. Boat Regatta
5. Cultural Night
6. Traditional Cuisine and Bush bar

All contest events designed for the carnival are open to public free of charge, but observably the mammoth crowd turn out mostly for the street carnival. Although, some critics have identified certain hitches and challenges and also blamed the Government for poor funding of the carnival, this study seeks to assert that if participants comply to carnival directives sincerely, Abuja Carnival can evolve as self-sustaining and a robust brand.

The Street Carnival

The Street Carnival event of the Abuja National Carnival is a procession that employs the use of motorized floats. Floats were first unused in the theatre by churches in the medieval era, as mobile stages for religious drama where pageant wagons; movable sceneries were used for passion plays. Brockett refers to this as a "movable stage" on which "mansions were mounted and moved from one location to another" (76). Studies show that "those wagons were most noticeable during Corpus Christi (festival) established in 1264 by Pope Urban IV where 48 wagons would be pulled through town with each one representing a play in the Corpus Christi Cycle" (Carnival Arts, web). In the Street Carnival event of Abuja Carnival, each troupe is provided with a flatbed lorry bearing a 40ft by 10ft space.

Each state troupe is expected to transform the lorry into magnificent floating scenery, by decorating it to interpret a theme and to compliment the accompanied spectacle by the troupe's performers. Each float, bearing a banner that identifies the troupe, is designed to convey a carnival king and queen. The peculiarity of floats is that they do not carry troupe members on the float, outside the King and Queen. The floats themselves play significant role in supporting the troupe assigned, by volunteering information about the theme, mood, era, style etc of the performance to be displayed.

For proper coordination, there is a limit to the number of performers accompanying each float, which also includes drummers, dancers, musicians and masquerades. The ensemble of performers accompanying each float is duty bound to sustain a steady display of spectacles on the stretch of the Carnival route. Over and again, it has been observed that most troupe that emerge with woeful performances suffer from of the following:
- Technical inadequacies occasioned from inappropriate engagements
- Inadequate preparations
- Insufficient performance content through the stretch of

carnival route
- Non compliance to carnival theme

Ojo Rasaki's Directing Qualities in Abuja Carnival

Ojo Rasaki Bakare is a Professor of Dance with unequalled exhibition of creative ingenuity who has mastery of all aspects of performing arts. He was appointed the Artistic Director of Abuja Carnival in 2009, and he had since remained the longest serving Artistic Director since the inception of the carnival. His approach to duty, directing the affairs of the National Carnival for the organizing ministry is admirable, as it has made carnival management, in this regard, an easy task. While exhibiting the qualities of a theatre director, he brings to bear with ease, his directorial vision on the carnival project. In a workshop for facilitators, he remarks that he envisions "an indigenous performance that is apt and refined with breath taking spectacle and aesthetics art forms, while interpreting the thematic thrust" (Workshop, Bakare)

The approach of Bakare to directing Abuja National Carnival consists in the exhibition of the all-important functions of a theatre director as posited by Harold Clurman: "The director must be an organizer, a teacher, a politician, a psychic detective, a lay analyst, a technician; a creative being... and above all he must inspire confidence" (14). This study shall analyse the above qualities, as manifested by Bakare in directing Abuja National Carnival.

i) <u>An Organizer</u>: A massive event such as the Abuja National Carnival requires elaborate mobilization for grass-root participation and thorough sensitisation to avoid the instances of inadequate representation at carnival or misrepresentation of the ideals of the carnival. For instance, in past years, there was a huge concern against the presentation of masquerade in their sacred overtone, on the street carnival. Though, Bakare, with his approach to theatre performance seem to belong to the school of thought that upholds the evolutionist thinking that Nigerian Theatre and Drama evolved from rituals, he however agrees with Ossie Enekwe's argument that "a ritual" only "becomes entertainment once its outside its original context or when the believe that sustains it has lost its potency (qtd in Ogunbiyi, 5).

Therefore as Artistic Director Abuja Carnival, he insists that every state troupe should make effort to seeing that masquerade displays on the street carnival would be a presentation of 'art forms' and should not capture its religious nuances. To ensure that the regulations and directives for carnival, such as this are communicated effectively, Bakare holds meetings with all stakeholders from the states, such as Commissioners, Permanent secretary and Directors of the Ministry of Culture and Tourism and Director of the state's Council for Art and Culture. He also organises a team of facilitators whose duty is to communicate the details of the regulations, directives and themes etc, to the grassroots in order to engender desired result.

2) **A Teacher:** Any artist who has worked with Ojo Rasaki Bakare is quick to reveal that he is indeed a teacher and a teacher at heart, whose passion for teaching comes to play outside the classroom. As a teacher, his insistence on discipline is evident in the level of order achieved during the all-day performances display at the Abuja Carnival Street Carnival event. For him, the discipline of the theatre is imperative for carnival directing, giving the nature of the people composed in the various state troupes. Aside from the artistes who come from the state Council of Arts and Culture, constituting only about fifty (50)% of a certain state troupe for carnival, other contingents are sourced from the traditional societies within the state, either as masquerade players and their accompanies, or special performers who do not possess the training and discipline of trained artiste.

With the instrumentality of team coordination, Bakare insists and enforces discipline among contingents, so seriously that discipline and team coordination takes a good proportion in contest adjudication. Contingents know that as a matter of rule, that appearance in procession is ordered alphabetically, from the first troupe to the last, and that as no one troupe should overtake or overrun the other, none should break the chain of flow with internal indulgences. The end result in the audience's view is the synthesis of an aesthetic ensemble.

3. <u>A Politician:</u> We also see the director of the national carnival as a politician. Here he functions diplomatically and acts as the go-between for his team, stake-holders and the coordinating ministry, in order to engender the smooth running of carnival activities. Anything more than that, Bakare will refute, as he has characteristically announced in many instances "I am not a Politician" in the normal sense. However, his duty as Artistic Director of the national carnival puts him in a position to manage relationships and issues with parties that are politically conscious , in order to facilitate and process necessary approvals, at all levels. In this consideration, Bakare brings to bear a high level of diplomacy, patience and sometimes compromise in order to achieve his directorial vision.

4. <u>A Psychic Detective:</u> Bakare is psychologically conscious as a creative director with high sensitivities to the plight of his team members, and little wonder he has built a base of dedicated individuals, who work on the national carnival project, year in year out. This has in turn led to dedication, commitment and passion, with constantly improving delivery capacity. As an astute manager of human resources, his approach to human engineering is largely connected to his ability for psychic detection. Hence, this quality puts Bakare at an advantage of attracting the best hands for the execution of his directorial vision.

5. <u>A Lay Analyst:</u> Every edition of Abuja Carnival is tagged by a theme, and all state troupes are to ensure that their entries for the national carnival reflect the year's theme. Hence, compliance to theme is of huge concern during adjudication. Bakare, as a lay analyst, put forth themes that are digestible and straight-forward for interpretation. He settles for a theme that reflects the ideals of

the National Carnival, and would apply in context to all states of the federation. The theme for Carnival could be likened to a theatre director's concept for a play production at hand, in which he shares the interpretation with the performers and collaborators in the course of rehearsals. In like manner, Bakare makes a lay analysis of the theme and shares with his grassroots facilitators, who in turn impart same to the participating state troupes ahead of the national carnival.

6. <u>A Technician:</u> The technical aspects of the street carnival involve a set of acidulous tasks, which are very demanding. There is a float garage, which opens some four days before the Carnival activities, where low-bed lorry are assigned to states and visiting tropes, and from there all floats are to be designed, fabricated and decorated. Bakare, the technician artiste will always visit the garage, in the course of preparation, ahead of the Street Carnival contest event, just like the theatre director will monitor the course of progress of the scene designer. There, he offers technical advice on what the various troupes have already set to do, in the interest of the overall carnival. He inspects compliance to rules, observance of safety precautions and accesses the viability of designer's experiments, in order to forestall danger in the course of on procession.

7. <u>A Creative Being:</u> There is no gainsaying that it takes none less than an embodiment of creativity to occasion success on the task of directing a carnival of the magnitude of Abuja Carnival. The continuous improvement of the carnival outlook in all ramifications, as attested by the increased participation of the international community and the attraction of tourist to Abuja on account of the Carnival, expresses Bakare's creative ingenuity. He also inspires and demands the same level of creative commitments form team members and state troupes from all around the nation.

8. <u>Understanding People:</u> Only a few creative artistes can be said to have built an itinerant career as Bakare did over two decades. Apart from being trained in various part of the country, he has

lived and worked as a creative artist in all regions of the country, his creative works reside in the repertoire of most state's Council for Arts and Culture across the country, and he is proclaimed to have staged performances in all continents of the world (Bakare, Author's Biography). By virtue of Bakare's vast relationship and interactions with diverse peoples and culture, he will naturally understand people, and given that he has an adroit insight into managing people to achieve the defined goal, he exploits this to achieve a directorial vision.

9. <u>Inspire Confidence:</u> From observation, Bakare's warm disposition simplicity and humility, in spite of his stern and insistence on professionalism, have inspired confidence in many who encountered him. Not considering his high level of creative ingenuity, being regarded as "one of the most versatile, and multitalented theatre practitioners on the African Soil" (Bakare, Author's Biography), Bakare will always shares his personal experience with his team members, facilitators and contingents during carnival, like he does with theatre workers. Often this inspires confidence in them, and challenges them to greater heights of creativity.

Conclusion

Much as one may agree to the fact that Government funding of the National Carnival it is also important to note that a Carnival is people oriented, and more than anything else should be owned by the people. By that, passion and sincerity of purpose, rather than obligations and duty should be the new attitude of all contingents from the states troupe, if Abuja Carnival must evolve as a globally renowned international event. In spite of Ojo Rasaki Bakare's great commitment and qualities as director, it is expected that state troupes will apply themselves and comply with all directives and regulations in order to take the carnival to a point where the director's vision completely comes to bear. At that point only, can the national carnival become a self-sustaining brand that attracts the attention of more and more people from within and outside the country.

If all state troupes will imbibe Bakare's insistence on professionalism and accept his recommendation towards engaging experts such as Choreographers, Art instructors, Kinaesthesia experts, Physical fitness trainers, Production designers, etc, to groom and prepare participants ahead of the National Carnival, the overall output will be very robust and greatly enhanced. Such enhancement, can be made possible, not just only by Government's increased subvention, but by the commitment of state troupes and individual contingents to fully comply with the carnival directives and regulations. It is only when this is done that the Abuja National Carnival can attract investors and benefactors who will need to leverage on the robustness and visibility of the event to grow their own brands.

Works Cited

Ajimotokan, Olawale. "Thrills, Glamours of Abuja Carnival." *This Day Live*, 30th Nov 2013. Retrieved from Web on Mon Sept 15 2014. http//www.thisdaylive.com/articles/thrills-glamours-of-abuja-carnival/165527. Web

Bakare, Ojo Rasaki. ed. *The Artiste-Intellectual.* Revised Ed. Ibadan: Jofel Books, 2004. Print.

Bakare, Lillian E. "Dance Costumes in Abuja Carnival: The Contradictions of Social-Political integration International." *Journal of Innovative Research and Development.* Vol.3 Issue 5. (169-174) www.ijird.com

Ben, Iheanacho, ZZ. "Cultural Tourism and the Nigerian Economy: Synergy for Improved Creative Industry Products Consumption." *Perspectives on Cultural Administration in Nigeria.* Ed. Barclays Ayakoroma and Olu Obafemi. Ibadan: Kraft Books Ltd, 2011. 37-48.

Brockett, Oscar G. *The Essential Theatre* 2nd Ed: New York: Holt, Rinehart and Winston, 1980.

Clurman, Harold. *On Directing.* New York: The Macmillan Co., 1972

Denja Abdullahi, "Quality Assurance in Playwriting and Production at the National festival of Arts and Culture (NAFEST) 2011." *Nigeria Theatre Journal.* Vol. 13, No 1. Maiduguri: *SONTA,* 2013. 110-121.

Federal Ministry of Tourism Culture and National orientation (FMTCNO). *Abuja National Carnival 2012 Event Brochure.* Abuja: FMTCNO, 2013.

Carnival Arts Portal. "Carnival Floats Design." Retrived from Web on 15 Monday 2014.

http://www.carnivalarts.org.uk?portals/o/carnival%20%floats.pdf

Ogunbiyi, Yemi. ed. *Drama and Theatre in Nigeria: A critical Source Book.* Lagos: Nigeria Magazine, 1981.

Wikipedia. "Second World Festival of Black Arts." Retrieved form Web on Mon 15 Sept. 2014. http://en.m.wikipedia.org/wiki/world_festival_of_black_Arts

"Carnival" Retrieved form Web on Mon 15 Sept. 2014. http://en.m.wikipedia.org/wiki/carnival

PART FOUR
BAKARE, OJO RASAKI ON THE MARBLE OF HISTORY

Interview i

Abinibi And Ability: An Incursion into Nature and Nurture in the Art of Bakare, Ojo Rasaki
By
Adeseye, Bifatife Olufemi Ph.D.

Introduction

Abinibi is a Yoruba coinage of the term hereditary. This paper investigates the link between talent and arts; juxtaposing hereditary factors and environmental influences to situate the seemingly complex talents of drumming, dancing, singing and acting; found in the person of Bakare, Ojo Rasaki. This paper employs a historical approach in unveiling family and environmental influences on the subject. Oral interviews with Bakare, Ojo Rasaki and selected associates are used to crystallize the focus of the paper. The study design combines biographical notes with critical analysis of the manifestation of the potentials of the Alarinjo Theatre Tradition, which provided cover for the 'fugitive' son of an Imam to flourish in the arts of the theatre. That artistic inclination and talent are arguably encoded in genes or resident in environmental influences has been the subject of controversy for ages. Talents do contribute immensely to excellent disposition in arts, but raw talent may never create excellent art. This is the crux of the discourse here. That it helps to be in an environment that fosters arts for innate tendencies to manifest is perhaps undisputable. The situation becomes more challenging for a child born into a family whose religious tenets do not patronize arts, especially the arts of the theatre. This was indeed a challenge that our subject had to contend with.

During our interaction with the man; Bakare, Ojo Rasaki, we unveiled how *Abinibi and Ability* combined to make the man. For convenience sake we shall refer to Bakare Ojo Rasaki as *BOR* and the interviewer referred to as *ABO*.

ABO: Usually, a first child has no forerunner to learn from, but the parents. What were the peculiarities in your childhood about your growing up? Let us start with your pre-elementary education days.

BOR: I am a first child in the family of thirteen children. Nine from my own mother and four from my step-mother. We were thirteen children by the same father, and i am the first. My mother had had her nine children before my father married the second wife; who also gave him four children. Now, of the thirteen, ten are alive today. My mother lost two of her nine, while my step-mum lost one of her four.

As a first child in that kind of set up; especially since my father had scanty education, as you may call it; he didn't go beyond standard six. My mother is better educated. My father was a policeman, who later left the police force and became a security operative for a couple of companies around the South-West. He later left security services and went back to the job he learnt, which is plumbing, and that is what he is still doing to date. He is presently the oldest plumber in Ekiti State, still active, taking jobs and executing them.

My mother is a petty trader and deals in provision. She is also a textile artiste; my mother is a specialist in 'Adire' – what you call 'tie and dye'. I grew up assisting her, fetching all the water, helping to get the dye of different colours and getting the materials for her and watching her design the patterns on the fabrics. So, whatever my mother was able to make from her 'adire' and provision trade plus the income from my father as a policeman was what was available for the entire family to live on. In that kind of environment, I grew up learning to sacrifice for my younger siblings because I knew early in life that as a first child, people expected me to help my younger ones grow and I cultivated that attitude right from when I was young.

ABO: The Police discipline from your father must have impacted heavily on you. Relate that to when you were growing up and perhaps later in life.

BOR: Definitely, my father was a disciplinarian to the core and that is seen in me everywhere I go. Of recent, somebody wrote that I am misunderstood by a lot of people because of my insistence on discipline always. In any situation I don't compromise discipline. That is one of those things I grew up with having grown under the tutelage of a very stern policeman. He brought me up that way while living in the barracks. You know the kind of situation in such homes, the fear of my father was the beginning of wisdom. And so, today my kind of life was shaped by the level of discipline that I grew up with. That is why today, I am your friend if you are disciplined, I am your friend if you like things to be done the way they ought to be done. The moment you are breaking the rules, we are enemies, no matter who you are. And that is why I step on people's toes, you know, because to me; what is right is just right – there is no other name that we can call it.

ABO: Let us examine your relationship with your grandfather – your maternal grandfather. Living with him in the palace definitely had some cultural implications on your development; what are they?

BOR: At a point in my life, I had to stay with my maternal grandfather who was a king. That was in my pre-primary school days. My maternal grandfather was a traditional ruler. My father came to Ado-Ekiti as a policeman and met a princess and married her, so we stayed in Ado-Ekiti where I grew up. My maternal grandfather was the Akitipa of Odo. Odo is a small town under Ado-Ekiti and it is a prince of Ado-Ekiti that is sent to become king whenever there is vacancy in the palace. (This is similar to Uselu Quarters in Benin City, where the crown prince of the Oba of Benin reigns. The difference here is that the prince does not stay in Odo in the hope of becoming the Ewi. He becomes Akitipa and that is all.).

My maternal grandfather, being a prince of Ado Ekiti was sent to Odo to become the King. I had the privilege of staying with him.... in the palace. Even before staying with him, I was already close to him. My mother was from a deeply traditional home; both from her paternal and maternal sides. They were experts in masquerade festivals, traditional religion and all related cultural things. I lived with them more than my own paternal relations because my father is from Aramoko Ekiti, which is far from Ado-Ekiti. We were born and raised in Ado. Today, when I want to speak Ekiti language, I speak Ado dialect; I cannot even speak Aramoko dialect.

I was introduced to the traditional lifestyle by my maternal relatives. But I was most influenced by her father, because being a traditional ruler. He directly introduced and initiated me into the masquerade cult before I was even four years old. By the time I was four I knew everything about his masquerades; their secrets, their dances, their music. I was already imitating the guttural voices with which they spoke. In fact, after the age of four, people would stop me on the street and ask me to speak like the masquerade for a fee. My mum would always feel angry and embarrassed over that and would spank me sometimes. But that didn't stop anything. In the neighbourhood, people knew I was already deep in those things in spite of my very tender age. Apart from being a traditional ruler, and a traditional worshiper, my maternal grandfather was also a mystic of some sort. Even today, I jokingly say it that, if papa had not died when he did that I would perhaps have not gone to school. He died when I was in primary three and that helped me. Because if he had lived longer, it was obvious I would not have gone beyond primary school because his vision for me was to take over his mysticism and his traditional worship.

He trained me to be everything he was. In fact, till he died, he never called me Rasaki, he called me Adeyemi, which was the palace name he gave me. A name which alluded to *the crown fits me*. The man almost vomited himself into me.

Looking back now, I think that my love for culture, my love for tradition, my love for the arts and some of the natural endowments I have today artistically, were the things that I picked up from the palace.

ABO: No wonder you were never afraid of masks.... You are always at home coordinating masquerade programmes from all over the country at national events like the Abuja National Carnival.

BOR: Exactly .I grew up in the midst of masks. How can I be afraid of them now.

Talents and the Arts.

ABO: Some parts of your artistic disposition perhaps bear some semblance of heredity that is traceable to your mother. In fact, you look more like her... even your gait, the way you walk.

BOR: Yes, I am almost a male version of my mother in almost everything. I have my father's face, but every other thing, my height, the body type, my complexion, my hair, the way I walk, the way I gesticulate, the way I even talk; I am a carbon copy of my mother.

Again, even talent-wise too; today, my mother, owing to the fact that she got married to a Muslim; she is now the 'Iya-Suna' (Godmother General) of the Muslim community in Aramoko; my mother was actually a Christian. Her Christian name is Eunice. My mother was the head of the choir at the First Baptist Church, Ado-Ekiti. She was the lead singer and the lead dancer.

At every spare moment with my mother today, you will find her singing. She is a fantastic singer. I have no doubt, that apart from the influence of staying with her father, who was a traditionalist and well versed in masquerade systems; in terms of natural endowments, I have no doubt in my mind that I inherited a lot from my mother.

As we speak, my mother is about 73, she still sings excellently. Her voice is tenor; but oscillates between tenor and soprano. If you close your eyes and listen to my mum sing, you will think that you are listening to a twenty year old singing, but in reality she is 73; same thing when it comes to dancing. So, when I grew up and I saw more of that from her, I knew who I inherited these talents from.

ABO: Juxtapose talent and professionalism from a critical perspective as a Professor of theatre practice.

BOR: Our field is talent driven, no doubt about that. You are a theatre artiste first because you are a career of the seed of creato-performative theatrics. If you don't have talent, you are just wasting your time. It is like being a footballer and you don't have the talent. Then, you are in the wrong profession. Even in becoming a professor, you write and you analyse, but what do you analyse? If the creators do not create, what do you analyse? If the performers do not perform, who are you as a theatre professor, you have no job. Those who create and those who perform are the real employers of the theatre professors.

What do you profess, if all the writers don't write, the choreographers don't choreograph; the dancers don't dance, the actors refuse to act; the designers refuse to design; what will you profess? What will you write, what will you publish your papers on?

So, talent and scholarship, of course, a symbiotic relationship does exist between them. One feeds from the other to grow. The scholarship feeds from the practice. Also, the practice gets better, benefitting from the works of the scholars.

Without criticisms, nothing will put the creative artists under pressure to do better. Professionalism is about your talent; you may have the raw talent and you are not a professional. So, knowing exactly what to do with your talent; being able to order your talent; being able to order your practice; being able to order yourself and applying your talent in such a way that gives you livelihood, puts food on your table, places you on the social strata you are supposed to be in society. That order enables you to conduct your affairs in such a way that you are respected and your art is respected in the society. All these come together to make you a professional. You may have the raw talent and you may never become a professional; it depends on how you apply the talent, that's what makes you a professional.

The Rebel in Bakare, Ojo Rasaki.

ABO: Respect your father and mother so the Bible says; especially their opinions about upbringing. You are not a conformist. How did the radical ideological choice impact on your development? First, let us hear about the distractions resulting from your non-conformist stance.

BOR: That is the one I don't know who I inherited from. I think I was just created by the creator like that. I can trace my artistic influences to some people but that aspect of me being a constant rebel.... I don't know; I get that from the Creator. I just find it difficult to change my mind about things that I am convinced are the correct things to do. It takes me time before I take a decision. I am the worst critic of myself. In fact, a psychologist once told me that I self-censor myself too much and that it is not good, he said i am just lucky that i am normal.

The moment I have searched my mind and my conscience does not tell me that I have an ulterior motive, that this effort is self-serving; I feel right and divinely correct about it, I go ahead and do it. I don't conduct my affairs the way other people conduct theirs. I don't believe in what other people believe in. When the time comes to take a decision, I simply analyse the issue critically, make sure that I am not myopic about it, and that i am not unfair. When I do all of these things and they add up to convince me that I am right, I just go ahead with the action. That is why people will say that I am a rebel; am a non-conformist, because people expect you to conform....

ABO: Actually, there are two ways to living; either conforming or rebelling.

BOR: People expect you to do what they want you to do, how they want you to do it. Also, they want you to think like them. Naturally, when you are pushing me into those things I become rebellious because it is not part of me and I can't just pretend.

My parents will tell you that as a child, 'he was very obedient', as an adolescent, I did not give them any problem. As a teenager, I was never a rough boy. You cannot even try any nonsense with my father anyway. But at each point in time, that I was expected to take a decision about my life, I was extremely rebellious. I never compromised. There is nothing that I am today, that is as a result of what my father or mother told me. I took my decisions myself.

When the time came for me to choose a profession, I was fresh from Secondary School. At sixteen plus, I had completed my secondary education. Then my father said, I should go and study law, and i refused. At the age of two, everyone in the neighbourhood knew me as an artist. My Dad was influenced by the status of his boss when he was a security officer at Textile Mills, Ado-Ekiti. The late Royal Majesty George (Adelabu) who later became the Ewi of Ado, was the general manager of Ado Textile Mill – when my father was a security officer at the place. My dad liked the man so much and wanted his son to be a lawyer like his hero – Adelabu, and so, he tried to force me to study Law. But I knew who I was; *at age two*.

The Baby Masquerade – *Atori Ijo Gbagbe Omu.*

BOR At the age of two, my maternal grandmother died. Due to her chieftaincy titles, masquerades performed round the entire town of Ado Ekiti for seven days as part of the burial rites. For those seven days, I followed the masquerades round the town. I was just two. It was wherever they stopped to rest for the night that I would sleep.

At two, I was still breast-feeding. My mother had employed all the traditional methods to stop me. She would use bitter leaf to rub the nipple; but I was so cunning that I would gather saliva in my mouth and use it to clean the bitter taste, then spit it out and continue breast feeding. Everyone was helpless, they didn't know what to do to make me stop breast feeding. So, when her mother died and the masquerades had to perform for seven days, I left my mother and followed the masquerades for seven days. I knew all of them and they knew me. When I got tired, one of them would carry me on his shoulder. For seven days, I slept whenever they stopped to pass the night.

At the end of the seventh day; the masquerades returned to their original grove, and I returned home to my Mom. Until I became a University lecturer, I was calling my mother by her palace name; the name I met everybody calling her when I was a child; Oja. (Oja is the name for the princess in Ewi palace, Ado-Ekiti). I said to my mom, 'Oja, sit down I want to suck breast'. And then, everybody laughed. And she said, for seven days, you did not suck breast, you were following masquerades, my friend, go away. And i smiled, and that was how I stopped sucking breast. That is why people today will tease me singing; ' *a tori ijo gbagbe omu*' '....one who because of dance, abandoned breast milk.

When I remember those things, it continually reminds me that I am an artist. So as a teenager at sixteen plus, when I left secondary school, and my father told me to study Law, I kept telling myself that I am an artist, and that It was not my destiny to be a lawyer.

Beyond Mere Drama

BOR An episode happened when I was in primary four. My father was still in the police force. I took my father's service rifle to school to use in acting a play. I didn't know that the rifle was loaded. I was on stage, and I fired it. I played the role of a hunter in our end of year drama and I was chanting *Ijala*... and these are things nobody taught me. I never sat under anybody to learn the instruments I play today. They just came to me naturally. I am not from Oyo and I know how to chant this *Ijala* which Oyo people are known for... then I fired the rifle. You can guess what my father did to me that day. I did all these just to build my artistic instinct.

By the time I was in the secondary school, I was the leader of the Dramatic Society. We did plays such as Macbeth, Julius Caesar, Othello and many others. I often played lead roles in these performances. And so, when my father was telling me about Law, I knew what my instinct was saying, and where my strength in life lay. So, I was resolute about what I wanted to do.

Apprenticeship Under Jimoh, Aliu.

ABO: What were your experiences and what did you pick up from your stay with Jimoh Aliu?

BOR: I ran away from home and approached Jimoh Aliu, I told him that I wanted to enlist as an apprentice. He looked at me and said, 'but you looked like *ajebota*'. He said, go back home. But I told him I'd rather kill myself than go back home and that my father had already disowned me.

One point to note however, is that whoever was working under any theatre leader at that time ran away from home. Even the leaders themselves ran away from home to form their troupes. You must have been a 'vagabond' of some sort to venture into theatre practice. I told Jimoh Aliu that my father had already disowned me and I had no home to go back to. So the man kindly took me in and I started under him as an apprentice.

So, for the first time, I started learning how a theatre troupe is organized, administered, managed and run for both artistic success and financial success. It was no longer the school dramatic society which we were just doing for the fun of it and for reasons of academics.

All of us were his staff. The troupe must make money, be able to pay its bills and all that. More importantly, what i learnt was the organization and then the fact that in this kind of theatre, unlike the modern Western oriented theatre, there is no compact-mentalization of talent. You are an actor, a dancer, a drummer, a costumier. You are in the set; all rolled together.

ABO: Let us quickly talk about your sojourn at Ogunde.

BOR: I was with Jimoh Aliu, and my mother traced where Jimoh Aliu's house was at Ado Ekiti and met me there she started crying. She was pregnant then. She started to roll on the floor crying and begging Jimoh Aliu to release her son for her. I sympathised with her and said, 'but your husband had said I should leave the house, that he is no longer my father, I had no house to go to, but because you have done this, just go home, trust me, let me collect my stipend at the end of the month, I will come back home and see how I will go back to school, with the little money I have'. I was just deceiving her and so she believed me and went back. That night, I packed my things from Jimoh Aliu's house and disappeared. I ran to Hubert Ogunde as I already had an insight into the strength of the Hubert Ogunde theatre, because while with

Jimoh Aliu, we had gone to Ososa to do some collaboration with Hubert Ogunde on the *Aropin ni teniyan* film of Hubert Ogunde. If you look at *Aropin niteniyan* film very well, I think I was the second youngest, apart from the baby actor, who was about three or four years then. When we were on the set of that movie, I discovered some things about Hubert Ogunde, I discovered that he uses more of music and dance in his works than Jimoh Aliu and I liked that, so when I was thinking of where to run to, Ogunde became the natural target.

ABO: Here you were no longer a new green-horn..?

BOR: Exactly i already had some experience. At Ogunde's place you also train to become everyrhing. You are a tailor, a costume designer, you are everything, you must learn everything together. The good thing however, is that as I was doing all of these, with Aliu and Ogunde, gathering all the experience and sharpening my talents and learning from those who were my seniors in those places, something kept telling me to go back to school.

ABO: To study drama and theatre?

BOR: Yes, I knew I had to take it beyond their level, I knew I had not reached my bus-stop. I was only doing that because I needed a place to go and learn this thing and perhaps earn some money with which I could send myself to the University to study theatre arts since my father would not spend his money on me to study theatre arts. Finally, one evening I packed my things and left Hubert Ogunde's place and came back home to Ekiti. I told my mother that I was back and wanted to go to school, but that I didn't need my father's money I have my own money and to prove this point, I did not wait for JAMB, I was just looking for any higher institution that was willing to admit students. I Then read in Daily Sketch that College of Education Ikere Ekiti was selling its admission forms, so I went to that school and asked questions about the course I could do that will enable me study theatre arts in the future, they didn't have theatre arts in the school then. The teacher I met picked two arts subjects that would enable me study theatre arts in the future. The subjects were religious studies and Yoruba language. My sojourn there led to an N.C.E

ABO: So the NCE was a springboard?

BOR: Yes, not because I wanted to be a teacher but I needed to go to school then to prove to everybody that I did not hate education, because that's what almost everybody was saying in my village then, that ' how could this brilliant boy decide to go to theatre", did he no longer wanted to go to school'. But just to convince everybody that I knew what I was doing, i went in and became a student at the College of Education Ikere-Ekiti. I stayed there for one year and wrote JAMB to enter the university and study theatre arts. However, I started liking the things we were taught in the education courses, and as a result, decided to finish the course and get the N.C.E. It was after this that I proceeded to study theatre arts. I didn't know that providence was pushing me to those decisions, but looking back now I know better. Today, people compliment to me saying, 'you teach well'. I actually learnt the rudiments of teaching and acquired the skills from my three years stay at the College of Education, Ikere Ekiti. So I left Ikere, taught for a while, and worked briefly with the Arts Council and had other cameo jobs here and there with the state radio and television before proceeding to the University of Calabar to study Theatre Arts.

ABO: In University of Calabar you studied theatre arts and today you are a professor. I know you have been a very mobile person . I would want you to react to the changing platform of arts marketing, especially considering the effects of the new media on arts patronage.

BOR: Talking about arts marketing in Nigeria, you know it's unfortunate that the things that work in other countries, most often don't work in Nigeria, because as we speak, live theatre is still very much alive in other parts of the world, but what happened in Nigeria that killed that heritage has a long history to it that am not willing to go into now, but given where we have found ourselves now, I think we have to make use of the opportunity that modern technology has availed us of to better our lot as entrepreneurs in the creative industry. Those in music are already doing that anyway, you will not come and pay and enter the hall to watch their shows if you will pirate their CD's and DVD's and deny them of their financial gains. What they do now is to partner with the network providers, they just release a new track and then you receive a text message from your network provider, Dbang has just released his song. If you now want it to be downloaded into your phone, fifty naira will be deducted from your credit, if a million people do that, the artist is better off financially.

ABO: Can you please enlighten us more on this.

BOR: Out of the several million of Nigerians, Dbanj has made fifty million naira, just through that, so he might not care about the CD's you are pirating or the DVD you are pirating, he won't even go and pay for a hall and organise any shows that he knows you will not buy a ticket and watch. He is making his money by just keying into those opportunities that modern technology especially at the level of ICT has delivered on our door steps. Who says a theatre producer cannot do the same? Who says a theatre director cannot do the same thing? Who says you cannot, direct your play and do a tight and very entertaining thirty minutes extract of the play and go into partnership with Glo or MTN and they send it to peoples' phones and then do the same thing that the musicians are doing. For instance, Femi Adeseye has just produced and directed BRING BACK OUR GIRLS or whatever is the name of the play. If you don't want to watch it, send No to 85104. If a million people do not delete it or send No, they pay unknowingly. For every play you direct or produce, and go into partnership with the network providers, you are smiling to the bank with your millions. This is an example

ABO: of some of the things we can key into now using these new platforms.

ABO: That's good, thank you very much sir, it won't be nice to end this without my doing some soul searching about Alhaji, please I have some questions on him that I would want us to quickly go through. Do you not see your picking his character, in a way helped in forming who you are? Or do you see yourself as a male version of Alhaja please resolves this conflict.

BOR: My Dad was a normal youth because his own circumstances were quite different from mine. My Dad never knew his mother, his mother died when he was eighteen months old, and his own father was a chronic polygamist and my father was the first child of his father from the first wife, and then when he was barely eighteen months, his mother died and so he was left alone without any sibling from the mother.

So as a baby he was taken away by his father's younger sister, who was also a struggling ordinary woman. She managed to raise him. By the age of five he was already cooking for himself and learning how to survive by himself. He was a sober and extremely humble child, so by the time he now left home to carve a future for himself, he naturally would do all other things that young men do and he was very sociable. The only thing I know I could have picked from him within the context of being rebellious is the fact that my father would die for his honour, and he remains like that up till today. He is still alive, and is about seventy seven years old now. He will never ask you for assistance even when he is dying, he would rather keep his problems to himself. He is a ruthlessly self-reliant fellow, and would do anything to a child that breaks those principles. He believed that whatever you are able to fend for yourself, you live with it, so you will never see my dad asking anybody for assistance. You don't see my father borrowing money from anybody. When he has, he will spend it on what he wants to spend it on, when he does not have and there are challenges he will tell you those things can wait till when he has money. Today, we are the best of friends, i am his confidant, and he is my own. As is am telling you now, my father will be broke and he won't tell me, if I see his car now, and I see his tyre is no longer good, he will say '*ehn*' he can still manage it, that when he has money he will buy. If i offer him money, he will say no, don't bother and I will force him. So it's been like that and I want to allude that to the kind of experience he had when he was growing up. He really had nobody to cry to, he had to learn how to survive by himself and so today he is an extremely independent person and he is blunt to a fault. There is nothing my father cannot say to anybody, in fact he will tell you that the person he cannot bare his mind the way it is, has not been given birth to yet. So these are strands of being a non-conformist that I can say yes I picked from him.

ABO: You've answered my question sir. Let's quickly discuss Alhaja. The *Oja* from the palace in Ado, the Eunice from the church got married to an Islamic scholar, how was she able to cope with that transition and how did this impact on you growing up?

BOR: Thank you again. You know when you are a princess in this part of the world, you are expected to be a model, you don't do those things that will bring dishonour to the palace. My mother was trained like that, so whatever she puts her mind to, and whatever she wants to do, she does it very well. She got married to my father who is a Muslim cleric and it was purely for love. Religion was not part of it, my father was not a serious Muslim then, he had not become a cleric then, he was just a young boy doing his work, enjoying himself, so my mother never thought that religion would become an issue. When they got married, the two of them agreed that if in future, my father became serious with religion, he will continue to practice his religion, while she will continue to practice her Christianity. While I was growing up, it was my mother I was following to church. The first twelve years of my life I was a church goer with her, every Sunday I would go to church with her, she was going to her church while my dad was not into any religion then, it was around the time I was twelve that that my father suddenly saw the need to be closer to God and he came home and he said he wanted to go to Mecca. The way he put it then was that he had become a born-again Muslim, and he wanted to get serious with God. So he now said that as an Alhaji's wife, my mother should stop going to church. It was a thug of war for three years, because my mother said no, there was an agreement and I won't become a Muslim. However, my mother's father, my maternal grandfather now called my mother and said, you knew him to be a Muslim and even though he was not serious with his religion, you know he was from a Muslim family when you decided to marry him, so you will not bring dishonour to this family. You can't divorce him, because my mother wanted to divorce him. She had packed her things back to her father's palace and so the father said no, none of my daughters would get a divorce, it's a shame, so go back to your husband's house and do what he has asked you to do. It was because of that admonition from the father, as my mother was brought up to be very obedient, and she couldn't say no to her father, came and accepted to convert to Islam and changed her name from Eunice to Risikatu. The commitment that she had for the activities in the church was the same commitment she brought to the mosque and Islamic activities and all the clerics in the state saw that commitment in her and in spite of the fact that she was not from my father's town Aramoko, she was installed as Iya Sunna.

ABO: So *Oja* Adetokumbo became *Iya Sunna*?
BOR: Yes
ABO: Thank you very much, you have made my day. I now see what hitherto i couldn't. My eyes are opened beyond what I knew. Before now I didn't know you were a

typical *Olojede* who had the real training from the beginning, thank you once again.

Summary

We are dealing with the biography of a critic who self-censor his dispositions often times to a fault. This fluid narration is perhaps the least we can expect from an orator. It must be noted that this can only be a slice of the man's life story because a complete rendition of all the essential departments of a man of many parts will naturally occupy a very big volume of many chapters. This is therefore a biography on a specific subject matter – seeking to unveil the muse responsible for the creative spring in Bakare, Ojo Rasaki.

The name Rasaki sounds 'rascally' and the positive rascality in the man began to show at such a tender age as it was his love for dance that made him abandon his cherished breast milk from a mother who had tried unsuccessfully to wean him.

This is a metaphor on the fact that man can let go almost anything to pursue his dreams. Alhaja, the mother confirmed that he was actually three years plus when he went dancing with masquerades and that was what helped her to wean the young Rasaki. Pursuing his dreams at all cost has taken him round the universities in the six geo-political zones of Nigeria, which earned him the nickname 'itinerant/nomadic' scholar. He has also been a globe trotter, visiting every continent with dance and cultural scholarship.

Conclusion

This little slice of history extracted from Bakare, Ojo Rasaki makes so many statements about destiny and determination, about raw talent and professionalism and about clearing the rough edges that usually trail the road to success. This piece further affirms that every theatre leader worthy of the title began the race as a vagabond minstrel.

It is a truism that destiny may never play itself out unless the man involved has a clear vision to accomplish the inherent mission of the divine essence. We can also conclude that the name Ojo was not a mere co-incidence for Rasaki Bakare; because Ojo in Yoruba cognomen paints a picture of a stubborn fighter; never deterred from achieving his goal. The primary muse that propelled Bakare, Ojo Rasaki resides in Princess Oja Adetokunbo, the Eunice that became Alhaja Risikatu Bakare.

Interview ii

How to Develop Nigeria's Culture – Bakare, Ojo Rasaki.

Interview by
Balogun, Olusola Kayode.

Preamble

For five consecutive years (2009- 2013), Professor Bakare, Ojo Rasaki, Nigeria's first professor of Dance and Choreography has served his country as Artistic Director of the Abuja International Carnival. He has also worked as a leading scholar in many universities before recently relocating to his home state, Ekiti, where he is currently serving as Dean, Faculty of Humanities and Social Sciences and Head, Department of Theatre and Media Arts at the Federal University, Oye-Ekiti. This erudite scholar, teacher, dancer, choreographer and culture activist who turns 50 on November 8, 2014 recently expressed his anger about how Culture is being relegated to the background in the country. He also called on the Federal Government, and all those who are in positions of leadership to first see Culture as the bedrock of development; hence they must ensure that all what they do to improve the conditions of the people and the nation in general have cultural undertones. He therefore called on government and the people of Nigeria to use culture to revamp the economy, launder the country's image and re-launch it on the path of development and growth. He spoke to **Sola Balogun** *on a number of issues bordering on culture:*

Current State of Nigeria's Culture Administration

As a stakeholder, practitioner and teacher in the sector, I really can't compare our cultural agencies with their counterparts in other countries of the world. The different chief executives of the cultural agencies may have been trying their best. They may have been doing their work but you see Nigeria is fundamentally a country without an ideology; a country without a philosophy.

And a country without ideology and philosophy is going nowhere because it has no mission. In other words, Nigeria as a country has not determined what it wants to achieve with these agencies. Those agencies were established for a particular purpose. But from what we have seen them doing, the agencies are merely being run to give an impression that government is doing something about culture and our identity. First we may ask ourselves, what does Nigeria want to use the sector to achieve?. For example, in the field of sports, every nation chooses what it hopes to achieve when it participates in international competitions like the World Cup. In Nigeria, we just hear that people are going for World Cup, and we too must go. But nations don't just go and play in the World Cup. When they are going, there is something they would want to use their presence at the World Cup to achieve. So going for the football tournament is not an end in itself. It is a means to an end. Most of the time, the end is diplomacy. Sometimes too, the end could be economic, politics or culture.

But in Nigeria, government just appropriates funds to projects, but it does not usually bother about how those projects are executed or for what purpose the projects were conceived in the first place. It thus becomes the case of 'Let it be said that we allocate funds, and let's keep those who have been appointed busy'. So it is not because there is a philosophy, or an ideology which government wants to use that platform to achieve. That is what is happening to the culture sector in Nigeria. Everything is basically superficial. And that is why up till now, we do not have a cultural policy yet. There have been major attempts by government to put the cultural policy in place and set in motion the process of implementing it, but up till now, government is yet to give us an identifiable cultural policy.

Why Nigerians Neglect their Culture

In every country, there is always a constitution, but a constitution does not solve problems, it does not lead to development on its own, what leads to development is a sound ideology, philosophy as well a sense of mission. If we take the example of North Korea today, if America barks once, North Korea will bark ten times. It is not because North Korea is richer than America but that it is a country with a sound philosophy and right ideology. The last person in South Korea is ready to die for the honour and pride of the country. That is the work that culture can do and that is what is happening in North Korea. The people have been so oriented culturally that culture has become their religion. It has become their life, and that is what they demonstrate through their sense of patriotism.

One of the reasons why people are not patriotic in Nigeria is because government has relegated our culture to the background. We do not have an identity. Identity plays a role in self pride and it is out of self pride that one can experience or demonstrate patriotism. If you are not proud of your country, you cannot be patriotic. And the reason why you are proud of your country is because do not you love the things that are of your country. And the reason why you cannot love the things of your country is because you are not cultured.

Creating Culture Awareness Through My Stewardship As Artistic Director Of The Abuja International Carnival

The carnival is not an agency but a national project. The Federal Government has not established a carnival commission. So we just handle it as a major cultural project for now. It is like the Federal Ministry of Culture and Tourism's project which I handle as a professional. So what I have been doing is more or less to consult for the ministry on the project. I direct the carnival artistically, so it is like being a technical director to a local organizing committee (LOC). It is not an agency. That is why I am still working fully in the university. All what I have been doing at the carnival office is to promote Nigeria's culture diversity through the carnival. And I am not being paid for it; although many people don't know this. I only put into creative use, my talent, experience, knowledge of the country and my professional sector in order to promote and showcase our culture.

Meanwhile, the carnival has grown far beyond what we inherited. We inherited a traditional festival procession that was limited to Eagle Square. Today we have a proper carnival performance stretched along an 18 kilometer route. More tourists now come in to the country to witness the carnival. More foreign countries troop in to participate it on a yearly basis. These are some of the indices to measure the growth of the carnival over the years. Now all the schools in Abuja and all members of the armed forces and paramilitary formations participate in the carnival.

The usual delay in the decoration of streets has always been caused by the Federal Ministry of Finance which has not always released the token budget for the carnival on time. They often force us to start preparations late.

On how the carnival is funded, the truth is that we keep squeezing water from the stone. The funding of the carnival is really frustrating because we always keep rationing our meager resources hoping that someday, things will get better.

So the major challenge of the carnival has always been poor funding and we've always tried to overcome this challenge by being over prudent.

Last year (2013), a total of 28 states participated in the carnival. Six foreign countries were also part of it. That was not quite low and all the events of this year's carnival such as street parade, floats, boat regatta, durbar, command performance, etc were better delivered too.

If I Were Made Head of a Cultural Agency

If I have the opportunity to head an agency in the sector, the first thing I would do is to make sure that we work on government to align culture properly. The mission would be to consider what constitutes Nigeria's national ideology or philosophy. As people in the cultural sector, it is our duty to force the country to yield a national ideology and a national philosophy. You see, if you don't have a guide, you don't have a direction and you won't have a sense of direction. That means you are heading to nowhere.

So the first thing would be to make sure the culture sector works with the politicians to evolve a national ideology and a philosophy for Nigeria. It is not about constitution as I said, it is deeper than that. And only the sector can push government to evolve a national ideology. So we would be talking of developing culture beyond just projects and events. We would be talking of developing culture to the extent that it would become a lifestyle for Nigeria. When culture becomes a lifestyle for Nigerians, Nigerians would change. What is wrong with Nigeria today is that a lot of things are wrong with the minds of people that make up Nigeria. So there is need to change people's mindset because as you know, the man is what his mind has made him. And the country is what the man has made from his environment. My mission would then be to develop the sector beyond events and programs and activities to the point that an average Nigerian lives a cultured life, a cultural life. When that happens, Nigerians would start identifying with their country, and their cultural life would yield patriotism, because a cultured man would never be corrupt. The traditional culture is against corruption. We grew up in the days when on your way from the farm, you meet tubers of yams by the roadside; and you would just put six pence on a leaf and put on top of the yam to indicate your willingness to buy the yam. You know that a tuber cost six pence. You would take just one tuber of yam while you put the six pence there and nobody would touch it. Anytime the owner of the yam comes, he would meet the remaining tubers and the six pence there. That is culture. If we had all our people today conscious of their culture, nobody would steal in Nigeria. So what we need in Nigeria today is to develop our culture to the point that it becomes the lifestyle of every individual. We should live it on a daily basis until it changes us, until it changes our mentality, our consciousness and our mindset.

Reviewing And Implementing Nigeria's Cultural Policy

The first assignment would be to dust up the Cultural Policy document and work on strategies of implementing it. The first strategy is to work with the politicians. You cannot implement the policy without the politicians and let them realize its benefits. They should be made to understand its principles and buy into it. There would also be need to hold series of meetings and workshops with politicians. This may involve bringing people and experts from other countries of the world who can teach our politicians about what America is achieving through culture. Many people don't even know that America achieves a lot of things through culture. The American culture is reflected through their football, military, security and in all their ways of life. So there is need for experts from other countries of the world to let our own politicians know what the country is losing because our culture is relegated to the background. They should work with the experts so that proper policies are put in place, and eventually ensure that a national philosophy; or a national ideology emerges through culture.

Why We Need Cottage Theatres in Every Local Government in Nigeria

This lends credence to what I said earlier on, that government is not exploring culture to solve national problems. If they had been conscious of this, they would have encouraged our local communities to build their cultural centres and theatres a long time ago. If you have cottage theatres all over the country, it would curb restiveness among our teeming youths. The absence of such theatres at the grassroots level is strongly responsible for the current security challenges in the country. The situation now is that the devil has found job for our idle youths. If we have good sporting facilities and good theatre halls in every local government, most of the youths who have nothing doing would not take to crime but would have something creative to do.

Today, Nigerian universities are producing thousands of graduates of Theatre Arts every year, but these graduates don't have a place to work. If we had community theatres at the local level, these graduates can work at the grassroots level by coordinating community theatre troupes. These community theatre troupes would have the opportunity of performing in these cottage theatres for people at the grassroots level to watch. By so doing, they would have created employment for themselves, or kept themselves gainfully busy. Also, government would have succeeded in taking the youths away from the streets, and of course taking them away from crime. This is what should have been done some 30 or 40 years ago in this country. If in the days of SDP and NRC, Nigeria had money to build two offices for the two parties in each local government in this country, then what prevented the country from building just one cottage theatre in every local government to empower artists at the grassroots level and make the youth positively busy and keep them away from crime? Only wickedness and lack of vision have prevented our successive governments from thinking about improving the lot of our artistes and creative people in this country.

My Life as a Theatre Artiste, Scholar And Culture Practitioner

I started this career about 32 years ago in 1981. That means I have been in professional theatre practice for over three decades. I started combining lecturing with theatre practice about 24 years ago. So for twenty four years, I have been a university teacher and for thirty three years, I have been a theatre practitioner. Within that period, I can't count how many plays I have directed, or how many dances I have choreographed. I don't think there is anything I would have done to be able to arrive at an accurate figure. What I know today is that I have been in charge of over 250 major productions in my lifetime; both as a play director and as a choreographer. As a playwright, I have written over 40 plays, out of which about10 have been published, while some are in the process of being published. Many of these plays have been performed because I always write my scripts and make sure that they stay with me, I perform them over and over again, and ensure I put them on stage severally before I decide to publish them.

I am grateful to the almighty God, my creator for the opportunities He has given me to use my talents positively. As a director, I have directed three presidential command performances, all of which were commissioned for presidential inaugurations. I know quite well that it is not every theatre director that would have such opportunity. I have also been involved in major national assignments, such as directing the national carnival (Abuja Carnival) - a very delicate national assignment at that, in a country, I mean, in an environment like Nigeria where everybody is just waiting to pull you down and take over whatever you think you are doing. I cannot but be grateful to God that in the same country of over 160 million people, I have had the opportunity to be in charge of the same carnival for the fifth consecutive year under three different ministers.

With all these achievements, I definitely have reasons to thank God. But having said all these, all I know is that my best is yet come. At 49, I believe that age is still on my side and it is now the work and the service to my fatherland would start. I believe that all of those things that I have had opportunities to do in the sector in the past have not ended. They have essentially made me stronger and positioned me for greater achievements in the future. I consider the experiences and knowledge I have gathered over these years as the ladder that God wants me to climb to reach the apex of my career. I don't know how I have made all these possible, but I believe that if God was not preparing me for something greater, he would not have given me the ability and opportunity to get loaded with as much experience and knowledge that I have now.

Interview iii

Bakare in The Spotlight: In Conversation With Ugwu, Agozie.

By
Ugwu, Agozie

What is your definition of Carnival Theatre?

One of the ways of describing what carnival is is by saying that carnival is theatre on the street. This is because most of the things that characterize a theatre performance are also obtainable in a carnival performance. So it is an imagined performance culture in Nigeria. If we look at what Raymond Williams calls the emergence and the residual culture, Carnival as a performance genre is one of the emergence culture but that is speaking of Nigeria now but it is derived from the residual culture of the people. Nigeria as a country has come to adopt this mode of performance to power the tourism business in Nigeria. It is a known fact that Nigeria cannot compete with the tiny east African country of Tanzania in terms of eco-tourism. But it is also a known fact that most of the country of the world cannot compete with Nigeria when it comes to culture tourism. One thing with culture tourism is that it survives on activities, events and therefore you have to create events that will lure people into your domain which is what Nigeria is now doing using carnival as a mode of performance. In Nigeria today you have Abuja carnival which is the national carnival, the Cross River State Carnival which is called the Calabar carnival. Kanuri which is Rivers State carnival, the Lagos State carnival that takes place every Easter, Kogi state started their last years, that is 2013, since 2012 Enugu State has been doing its own. Imo wanted to start their carnival this year but because of the Chibok adopted girls, they have not been able to roll out the drums. You can see that most of the states of the country are now cueing into this kind of performance genre as a mechanism to drive our tourism industry in Nigeria.

To what aspect of Theatre would you classify Carnival Theatre?

No aspect of theatre can be called carnival theatre. It is that carnival could qualify as a genre of theatre. This is because a carnival is a modernised version of the traditional African festivals. Our festivals on the streets for instance. Actually the idea is African. It is from here that our brothers when they were catered away to the new world began as a way of managing themselves psychological began to play back those things they left behind at Africa and so while working in the plantation farms they will sing the songs and do the dances they left at home here. Subsequently, they started meeting during certain days of the week or month when they are free. They will come to town from the farm and meet and dance on the street and all that. That was how the whole idea of carnival started. It was later that contemporary governments now felt that this thing that these people do could be turned into a business, so they organised and it became better organised and thus hence metamorphosed into what we call carnival today. It is not that there will be an aspect of theatre that will be called carnival. It is that a carnival can be argued to be a form of theatre. This is because most of the elements of theatre are present in a carnival performance.

Do Teaching Methodologies and Curriculums In Nigerian Institutions Promote The Concept of Carnival Theatre?

No it is just because when most of these curriculums were designed, carnival theatre was not known in Nigeria. There have not been conscious attempts to teach it but what is going on is that since at the national and different state levels people are embracing carnival, different departments of theatre arts or whatever they are called are not teaching some aspects of carnival theatre as part of sub-theatre courses. A few of the departments have gone ahead to review their curriculums and they have included events management, as some of their courses. Under such courses as event management, they squeeze in carnival management. It has to be more than that and I believe that very soon, most if not all the departments, will catch the bug. And consciously make sure that at least three to five courses in carnival planning, carnival design, carnival execution and carnival management would become part of the courses in theatre studies.

What Does it Entail to Manage and Produce a Carnival Both Financially and Otherwise?

It requires a lot. A carnival is very massive because it involves a lot of people. So, it must be someone good at handling logistics because there are lots of logistical needs in a carnival performance. Secondly, you must be an expert in multi-tasking. You must be this chap who can handle about ten or more things at the same time and yet succeed in achieving all perfectly. At the level of funding, carnival is cost intensive because of its nature. The source of funding will be good, otherwise you will have problems. Also at a level you have to be somebody who is very security conscious and can handle difficult matters because a lot of risks are also involved.

What Plans Are on Ground to Foster The Development of Carnival Theatre in Nigeria?

On daily basis, the different levels of government, state or federal produce carnival performances, produce carnivals and these carnivals are getting better. Abuja carnival is not the way it used to be in 2005 when it started. Calabar carnival is growing in leaps and bounds. The same thing with Kanuri in Rivers state and the Lagos state carnival. The natural thing when you are handling a project is to want to improve every year and that is happening to carnivals. The environment affects whatever entertainment package you offer. The security situation that has made both the government and the masses to be sober is the major factor affecting carnival theatre in Nigeria. Before now, it was only the masses that are sober and angry. The government are excited as there will be money for government to spend. They will roll out the drums and you will be looking for people to come and participate in the carnival and be begging them. What we have now is that both the governed and the government are all sober. That is bad news for the entertainer because it is when people are happy that the entertainer can entertain.

Besides Dance What Are The Other Performance Arts That Thrive In Carnival Theatre?

Mostly it is craftsmanship because carnival is a celebration of what we can be. A cultural festival is a celebration of what you have but a carnival is a celebration of what you can have. Carnival plays more on weird and wild designs. At carnivals you want to create the impossible, the unthinkable. At the carnival you are celebrating what you can possibly have. At the level of design and creativity, the carnival is more esoteric and so that is one thing that makes it different from other things we are used to in the theatre world. Carnival is where you come and you want to show what people have not seen before. That is the nature of carnival but at the cultural festival you use what is natural. For instance a red cap for an Igbo man and a Yoruba man's agbada. Carnival is talking about how your creativity can make the impossible possible, like someone creating a cloth with pieces of broken bottles and the person is wearing it. Is it not wild? That is a carnival. It celebrates the impossible. It makes the impossible happen. Those who really make money working for the carnival are the craftsmen.

Can You Compare The Nigeria Carnival Theatre With That of The Other Parts of The World?

There is no point comparing because when you do that then you kill your carnival. What do I mean? If you say you compare, we are likely going to end up imitating them. Once you imitate other carnivals of the world, this one will die. The selling point of Nigeria carnival is that there is no carnival that looks like it. If we want to compare or imitate what the Jamaicans do, what they do every August on the street of London, and in Brazil, what will happen is that nobody in China will have reason to come and watch our carnival in Nigeria. The reason is simple. Tourist, will have any reason to come to Nigeria just to see performances they have seen in other parts of the world. Nigeria in Abuja carnival has the largest variety in the world. Ordinarily there are 520 languages with about 32.... Cultures. So when each representation of this avalanche of cultures puts out its own repertoire to the audience there is variety and that variety is our selling point to the world, so there is no point comparing.

What Are The Contributions of Theatre Art Practitioners to The Development of Carnival Theatre in Nigeria?

It is theatre artists that comes to represent their states. You can have a theatre carnival without the theatre practitioners. From the set constructors, the drummers, singers, to the foot soldiers that is those who wear the costumes and display on the street are all theatre practitioners. Without the theatre artiste there will be no carnival.

Explain the concept of "new thinking" in the Abuja carnival. A conception you introduced at your resumption of office in the carnival

The carnival I inherited as the director was cultural festival. There was no was difference between NIFEST and Abuja carnival so we have to change the thinking. Somebody will come and wear the traditional and cultural Igbo or Yoruba attire and be on the street and say he/she is doing carnival. Is it a carnival costume? We have to let them know. Even as we speak some people are still fighting it. They don't understand. Carnival is about looking forward. What can you create from what we have?. If we are holding unto what we have in the 14th century or there about, there will be no development. Where development comes is when we use what we have in the 14th century to create the new thing to survive on in 2014. That is what life is all about.

You Have Been Involved in The Establishment of Many Art Councils But at The State And Federal Level. What is The Experience Like?

At the level of experience it has given me the opportunity to understand the nature, challenges, capacity, limitations, possibilities, strength and weaknesses of the Nigerian artiste. It has also in the same vein helped me to understand the challenges and the prospects of artiste and culture administration in the country. Those are the things I have experienced. I have also benefited from working in various art councils all over the Federation because I am one person that can situate whatever I have learnt, be it dance, songs, drama or musical performance in any culture in Nigeria with ease because I have worked around. I think that is the greatest thing I benefited from the experiences I have had from the various art councils.

Why Are The Art Councils Especially At The State Level Not Flourishing in Practise?

The art councils are established by the government to research, propagate, document and transmit the different cultures of the states that own them. The same government that establishes the art councils have failed to empower them. They are not funded. It's like when am employer refuses to give the employee the empowerment needed to do the job. So what will these employees do? They stay in the office and collect salary. This is what is happening to the art councils. The same government that employs them to research, package, propagate and transmit our culture is the same government that is not giving them what they need to do those jobs. These people are human beings and they want to survive. This means they cannot resign and be looking for job that is not available. So they keep quiet, seat in their offices and collect their salaries. That is what is happening.

Working With Hubert Ogunde is a Life Opportunity Any Nigerian Theatre Artiste Will Like to Have. Tell us About How Those Moments Spent With Ogunde Have Influenced Your Career.

Everything I am doing is gotten from those moments. Except that people know that I specialise in dance I am an all-rounder theatre person. This is because if you attend the school I attended. The University of Calabar, you must specialise in an area. So I specialised in dance because that was when Nigeria was really suffering and I guess is still suffering. We still do not have enough people in dance but then there were less than three people teaching dance at the University level in the country. I decided I will go into dance. Apart from the fact that people know that academically I major in dance, people would have found it difficult to actually know what I am in theatre because I write, create, direct, design, light, costume, and I am into sounds. I have over eighty million Naira investments in sound alone. So if it is performance, in any area by the grace of God my two feet are strong on the ground. What is the reason?

This is because in the Alarinjo theatre where I trained, there is nothing like area of specialisation. What Soyinka called compactalisation. The Alarinjo theatre derives heavily off course from traditional African model, where if you an artiste, you are an artiste. As an artiste you perform, create, drum, dance etc. You must know how to do everything and that is why even though Ogunde practised contemporary theatre, his model was derived heavily from the traditional African models. So under Ogunde, the artiste learns how to be a costumier, he got a sewing machine for everybody, you learn how to decorate, make up, the artiste will even learn publicity, dance, act. The artiste learns virtually everything. There was nothing like compactalisation of the art. Like if you are an actor, you just stick to that. It is not like that in the traditional African model. It was like that in the early Nigerian theatre that borrowed directly from the traditional model. I have carried it on to even the contemporary practise that I am involved in. This is why today they will just say Bakare is in dance because academically you must define your area of specialisation. They also know that Bakare does any other thing that is there to be done in the theatre. I am a playwright, song writer, dancer, designer, critique, director and many others. These are the legacies picked up from training under Ogunde. It has made me to be a complete artiste.

Bakare is Known For Both Lecturing And Taking The Theatre Practice Outside The Four Walls Of The University. How Have You Been Able to Strike a Balance Between Both?

So many things are involved. It is not easy to manage the two. I have been able to manage the two because naturally I am a multi-tasking person. That goes back to my training under people like Ogunde and Jimoh Aliu. Jimoh Aliu is about the oldest living theatre practitioner in Nigeria today. He was one of the followers of Ogunde then. Ogunde was their boss. There were seven in the whole of the country. It was part of my training under them. I grew up being multi-tasking. In the University, I will be Head of Department, belong and head many committees in the University, teach my classes very well and yet I will be running three different productions in three different states of the country simultaneously. This has been possible because I have given up time to spend on myself and family. I don't have time to do any other thing apart from work. The extra time I am supposed to have for myself and social activities has been devoted to the practice outside the four walls of the University. If I must do my work at the University and also be a full time practitioner on the street, something must suffer. What is suffering in this situation is time for me and family.

Also I have been able to manage well because I have never given the University system room to say otherwise because I have always done my job in the University satisfactorily. So the University had never had any reason to ask me to choose between the University job and the practice. They see me teaching more than those who are not even practising. I give more to the university system than those are not practising. I have also suffered in the process. I am a victim of professional envy and jealousy. If I don't practise I will die. I was first an artiste before becoming a scholar. I started out as an artiste. It was because of that, I now went to the University and the institution says that this guy is intelligent let him come and teach. I am an artiste who later became a scholar. That original nature you cannot kill, If you kill it, it is me you kill. What has been happening to me in the last five months is that I have been using my University Salary to run a production where I am not making any money and now my two children that are left in secondary school have been sent home because of non payment of school fees. Meanwhile in the past four months nothing less than two million has come to my hand as salary. I have spent all that taking Langbodo on tour performance. We have been going round schools and the students pay ₦100 so how will you make the money. To move one hundred and eighteen persons alone from one location to another for performance is a huge sum. The production has not been able to pay any bills for us but I am happy. If you check my blood pressure now it is too low. It doesn't bother me. I am just happy we are doing productions everywhere. So the day I do a production and there is money fine, and if I do another and there is no money, I am okay. I am just expressing myself, my nature. It is for the purpose I was created.

It is now that my colleagues are beginning to understand. Before they thought I was making some millions from practising and envy and jealousy was so much. For four years my submission for professorship was denied. The University sat down and assessed my submissions and I scored 236 points as against 60 points I needed to be a professor. It was envy and jealousy that held my confirmation as a professor for four years. Practising and teaching has also exposed me to the deepest level of victimisation. I was a part of the Alarinjo and what that did to anybody that was part of that set up is that it makes you rugged. So I am rugged with a very thick skin so things don't bother me.

Why Are Theatre Arts Graduates Not Going Into Practice?

The reason is very simple. Most of those graduates of theatre arts are not artistes. They were not given admission because they are artiste. Everyone knows him/herself. You cannot go into practice when you know you came and managed to get certification. It takes an artiste to go and practice. So the admission procedure is faulty. People should not be admitted into theatre arts department because they are able to pass jamb and post-Ume exams. People should be auditioned. That has been my recommendation. If the University system begins to audition before admitting over eighty percent of the graduates will go into practise because they are artiste before coming to study theatre.

Another reason is that even some of those people who are talented, who are artiste, because they are looking for quick money do not practise. Theatre practice does not give you quick money. What is gives you is a lot of work to do but at the end of the day it will compensate you. You cannot die poor. Money will come. You may waste the money but it will come. Most of those theatre artistes that have died poor is not that money didn't come their way at a particular time but they wasted it. They were not organised to invest the money that came to them wisely. Some of these young people are so much in haste to make money without necessarily committing some years to labour. This is another reason why many will not practise because the practise will not give you quick money rather is will give you quick fame.

Most of Your Plays Are Known for their Creation Of Dramatic Spectacle Through Dance and Songs. What Informs Your Style?

First and foremost my art is opera. I am very operative naturally. The entire fabrics of my body, my nerves, every muscle in me swims in rhythms. This is my art really. It reflects in every play I write. I send powerful messages through music, songs, and dances. In fact it was that nature that sent me into theatre. I grew up as kid singing and dancing everywhere, following masquerades. I am from a strong Islamic background. My parents are Muslims and we don't even do those things. I was a rebel as a child. What drove me into masquerading as a child was the music and dances involved in it. My maternal grandpa was a king. I spent some years with him in the palace. I found what I was looking for. I will follow his masquerades, his place drummers and chants, acolytes and will be performing. I am someone who is passionately drawn by music and dance. So it is myself I am expressing when you see those things in my plays. I joined palm wine drinkers clubs when I got to the University. It was because of the singing, drumming and dancing that lured me into it.

The Prophetic Essence Of Your Play *Rogbodiyan* Has Attracted So Much Interest to The Play. Were You in a Kind of Trance When You Wrote The Play or Some Voodoo Rituals Helped In The Creation of The Play?

International Conference for Arts, Literature and Language was holding in Calabar and I was commissioned to write a play and direct it for the opening ceremony of the conference of that year. I was still doing my masters then. I thought of what to write and I looked at what was happening then which was Babaginda transition program. I sat down and picked up my pen. All the thoughts that came to my mind on the transition program was that military was not saying the truth and that they will not go. I wrote it as a satire exactly the same way it came to my mind amd it happened two years later. That was how everything happened in 1993 and I wrote in 1991. I titled it *They Shall Return* that was the first title. To me I just created an art. I left Calabar in 1992 by 1993 when everything happened with June 12 and all that and everything played out the way I had written it. I was a staff of ABU Zaria then. I was to believe that every genuine artiste is a prophet. One way or the other the things we write come to add up.

What are the emerging trends in contemporary Nigerian dance?

Contemporary Nigerian dance practice again began with Ogunde. He used dance as opening and closing glees. Acrobatics were the major patterns of his glees. Some part of the performances also comprised of dance as well. Later with colonial influences and post-colonial influences more foreign influences came into our dance practice. There was a strong level of persistence from African dance practitioners themselves and so people adamantly and deliberately want to do a kind of contemporary dance that borrowed heavily from Nigeria's indigenous systems. The influence of the foreign cultural agencies like Alliance Francais' to an extent, USIS (United States International...) and even Goethe Institute, but mostly Alliance Francais'. Their dance project in Nigeria heavily dealt a devastating blow on our indigenous dance systems because most of our dance practitioners who are not ideologically aware fall prey easily especially because money is involved. Ordinarily it should be participants paying to attend a workshop but these foreign agencies will come and organise dance workshop in Lagos and they will pay you for coming. By so doing they captured and brain washed our own people. Instead of those one continuing with that trend of creating contemporary dances that derive basically forms, indigenous forms they abandoned it for the foreign forms.

Contemporary dance is a nomenclature that shows nothing but unintelligence. There is no dance form that is called contemporary form. When you say contemporary form of dance, what it means is that that environment has created for themselves at the moment. What they are doing now is nothing but copying what is done in Europe and America. Coupled with the fact that we as Nigerians have been influenced by the consumer mentality, we sleep and snore and wait to consume what other people have created. We never create our own. When you go to Lagos and see most of those people who call themselves contemporary dancers, it is nothing but copying what is done in France, America and other western worlds.

The continuation of this innovation is where various organisation uses dance as advertising mechanisms for their products. So you have things like Maltina Dance All and the rest of them. If you look at what they are all producing there is nothing in it that is Nigerian. All they are promoting is American street dance genre. That is the trend presently. Those who are doing those kind of dances, they only do them when they go for their own competition and world cups. Nobody is patronising them. For instance it is not possible for one to invite someone to come do ballet at a wedding ceremony in your village. This owes much to the fact that the level of ignorance in the dance sector in Nigeria is high because most of the people who practise dance in Nigeria are not schooled. They don't even know about ideological issues and identity issues.

In Nigeria Arnold And Bakare Seem to be The Most Popular Dance Practitioners, Can You Tell us More About Some of Your Contemporaries
Arnold trained Bakare in the University. I have other teachers before I got to the University, the Ogundes and all that but in the University, Arnold was my teacher. He trained me before he left the University system. I have been going round to train people myself. i have trained the likes of Yestide, Yestide is in Lagos state University. I have trained the likes of captain and Cosmir. He is in Alvan Ikoku College of Education teaching dance. I trained Suru even though he was not my student in the University. I trained him and instructed him to go to school and get a degree. Esther Ogbale and more. They are in the hundreds. Almost 99% of those who teach dance in Nigeria are trained by me either directly or indirectly.

Can You Tell us About The Multi Awards You Have Been Wining in Your Career?

Dance guild of Nigeria admitted me to their fellowship. That is the highest level in any profession. On 23rd of May the Chartered Institute of Administration will be admitting me to the fellowship of that body. They said they followed me as an administrator for eighteen years. Even though I didn't train as an administrator but their report is that I am a good administrator. In October last year I was awarded as Ekiti State Cultural Ambassador. The Nelson Mandela African Leadership Award for Integrity and Transparency came from the Nelson Mandela foundation in South Africa. There have been series of awards even those that I do reject. A fellowship is not an award really. It is a professional investiture or recognition. SONTA (Society of Nigerian Theatre Artistes) also last year during the annual conference at Benue State University Makurdi also gave me honorary Fellow of the association.

Notes on Editors and Contributors

Editors

AbdulRasheed A. Adeoye, Ph.D is an Associate Professor and the immediate past Ag. Head, Department of the Performing Arts, University of Ilorin, Ilorin, Kwara State, Nigeria. His areas of academic interests include Play Directing, Playwriting, Dramatic Theory and Criticism, Cultural and Performance Studies. He has edited eight volumes of *The Performer; Ilorin Journal of the Performing Arts* and *The Dramaturgy of a Theatre Sociologist: Festschrift in honour at Ayo Akinwale at Sixty.* This is the third book that he will be co-editing with other seasoned scholars in the Nigerian theatre. He is the current Events Manager of the Society of Nigeria Theatre Artists, SONTA. This is an organisation he has once served as Public Relations Officer and Financial Secretary. He is also a contributor to this book.

Uche-Chinemere Nwaozuzu, Ph.D. is the immediate past Head, Department of Theatre Arts and Films Studies, University of Nigeria, Nsukka. A well-published and well-travelled scholar, before this work he had edited about three other books in Theatre Studies. He is also a contributor to this book.

Solomon Ejeke, Ph.D is a Senior Lecturer and former Head, Department of Theatre Arts, Delta State University, Abraka, Nigeria. He is a scholar in Play Directing and Media Arts.

Etop Akwang, Ph.D is a Senior Lecturer and the immediate past Head, Department of Theatre Arts, University of Uyo, Nigeria. He is also a contributor to this book.

Contributors

Michael A. Abiodun, Ph.D. is a Professor of Linguistics and the current Dean, Faculty of Arts, Ekiti State University, Nigeria.

Stephen Inegbe, Ph.D. is an Associate Professor and former Head, Department of Theatre Arts, University of Uyo, Nigeria.

Bifatife Olufemi Adeseye, Ph.D. is a Senior Lecturer in Media Arts at the Department of Theatre and Media Arts, Federal University Oye-Ekiti, Nigeria.

Lanre Quasim Adenekan is of the Department of the Performing Arts, University of Ilorin, Ilorin, Nigeria. He is a young scholar in Play Directing.

Michael Aderemi Adeoye is a lecturer in the Department of Theatre and Media Arts, Federal University Oye-Ekiti, Nigeria.

John A. Afolabi, Ph.D. is a Senior Lecturer in the Department of Dramatic Arts, Obafemi Awolowo University, Ile-Ife, Nigeria. He is a scholar in Dramatic Theory and Criticism.

Foluke Aliyu-Ibrahim, Ph.D. is a lecturer in the Department of English, University of Ilorin, Ilorin, Nigeria. She is a scholar in Feminism and Gender related issues.

Kingsley Oyong Akam is of the Department of Theatre and Film Studies, University of Nigeria, Nsukka, Nigeria.

Tayo Simeon Arinde, Ph.D. is a lecturer in the Department of the Performing Arts, University of Ilorin, Ilorin, Nigeria. He is a scholar in Play Directing and Acting.

Nsikan Bassey Asuquo is a lecturer in the Department of Theatre and Media Arts, Federal University Oye-Ekiti, Nigeria.

Tam Gordon Azorbo, Ph.D. is a lecturer in the Department of Theatre Arts, Niger-Delta University, Amassoma, Bayelsa State, Nigeria.

Peter Adeiza Bello is a lecturer in the Department of Theatre Arts, College of Humanities, Redeemer's University, Mowe, Ogun State, Nigeria. He is a scholar in Dance and Choreography.

B. J. Balogun is a lecturer in the Department of English, University of Ilorin, Ilorin, Nigeria. She is a Language expert.

Jide Balogun, Ph.D is an Associate Professor in the Department of English, University of Ilorin, Ilorin, Nigeria. He is a scholar in Dramatic Theory and Criticism.

Yeside Dosumu-Lawal is a lecturer in the Department of Theatre and Music, Lagos State University, Ojoo, Nigeria. She is a Choreographer and Dance scholar.

Kingsley Ekpenisi is a lecturer in the Department of Theatre Arts, College of Education, Agbor, Nigeria.

Chidiebere Ekweariri, Ph.D. is a lecturer in the Department of Theatre and Media Arts, Alvan Ikoku Federal College of Education, Owerri, Nigeria.

Olusola Kayode Balogun, Ph.D. is a lecturer in the Department of Theatre and Media Arts, Federal University Oye-Ekiti, Nigeria.

Igwe Ezinne, teaches at the Department of Theatre and Films Studies, University of Nigeria, Nsukka, Nigeria.

Olympus G. Ejue, Ph.D. is a lecturer in the Department of Theatre Arts, University of Abuja, Abuja, Nigeria.

Grace E. Ekong, Ph.D. is a Senior Lecturer in the Department of Music, University of Uyo, Uyo, Nigeria.

Chidi Jonathan Ezeh is a lecturer in the Department of Theatre and Film Studies, University of Nigeria, Nsukka, Nigeria.

Joel Avaungwa Fanyam is a lecturer in the Department of Theatre Arts, College of Education, Katsina-Ala, Benue State, Nigeria.

Joseph Agofure Idogho is a lecturer in the Department of Theatre and Media Arts, Federal University Oye-Ekiti, Nigeria.

Yankson, C. Iyamah is of the Department of Theatre Arts, College of Education, Agbor, Nigeria.

Chijioke Y. Iyamah is of the Department of Theatre Arts, College of Education, Agbor, Nigeria.

Richard K. Gbilekaa is a lecturer in the Department of Theatre Arts, College of Education, Kastina-Ala, Benue State, Nigeria.

Solomon E. Ikibe, Ph.D. is a Senior Lecturer and the current Ag. Head, Department of Performing Arts, University of Ilorin, Ilorin, Nigeria. He is an Ethnomusicologist and a committed scholar.

Nnamdi C. Mbara, teaches Dance and Choreography at the Department of Theatre Arts, Alvan, Ikoku, College of Education, Owerri, Nigeria.

Ubong S. Nda, Ph.D. is a Senior Lecturer and the current Ag. Head, Department of Theatre Arts, University of Uyo, Uyo, Nigeria.

Torti Nelson Obasi is of Department of Theatre and Film Studies, University of Nigeria, Nsukka, Nigeria.

Jonathan Desen Mbachaga, Ph.D. is a lecturer in the Department of Theatre and Media Studies, Federal University Oye-Ekiti, Nigeria.

Oludolapo Ojediran, Ph.D. is a lecturer in the Department of the Performing Arts, University of Ilorin, Ilorin, Nigeria. She is a scholar in Dramatic Theory and Criticism.

Kehinde Olalusi is a lecturer in the Department of the Performing Arts, University of Ilorin, Ilorin, Nigeria. He is a Choreographer and Dance scholar.

Gabriel Ojakovo is a lecturer in the Department of Visual and Performing Arts, Kwara State University, Malete, Nigeria.

Paul Olarewaju Ojo, Ph.D. is a Senior Lecturer in the Department of Religion and Cultural Studies, University of Uyo, Uyo, Nigeria.

Oluwatoyin J. Olokodana is a lecturer in the Department of Creative Arts, University of Lagos, Akoka, Nigeria.

Casmir E. Onyemuchara is a lecturer in the Department of Theatre and Media Arts, Federal University Oye-Ekiti, Nigeria.

Cecil Ozobeme is a lecturer in the Department of Theatre Arts, College of Education, Warri, Nigeria.

Cyrus Damisa Suru, Ph.D. is a lecturer in the Department of Theatre and Cultural Studies, Nasarawa State University, Keffi, Nigeria.

Ifure Ufford – Azorbo, Ph.D. is a lecturer in the Department of Theatre Arts, University of Uyo, Uyo, Nigeria.

Ikike Inieke Ufford is a lecturer in the Department of Theatre and Media Studies, University of Calabar, Calabar, Nigeria.

Ukueme A. Udoh is a lecturer in the Department of Music, University of Uyo, Uyo, Nigeria.

Best Ugala is a lecturer in the Department of Theatre Arts, College of Education, Agbor, Nigeria.

Agozie Ugwu. He studied Theatre and Films studies at the University of Nigeria, Nsukka. He is the Artistic Director/Chief Executive Officer of Mozaic Theatre Productions, Lagos, Nigeria.

Christopher E. Unegbu is a lecturer in the Department of Theatre and Media Arts, Federal University Oye-Ekiti, Nigeria.

Chukwukelue U. Umenyilora is a lecturer in the Department of Theatre and Media Arts, Federal University Oye-Ekiti, Nigeria.

Oghenevize M. Umukoro is a lecturer in the Department of Theatre Arts, College of Education, Warri, Nigeria.

Joseph O. Umukoro, Ph.D is a Senior Lecturer in the Department of Theatre Arts, University of Uyo, Uyo, Nigeria.

Ifeyinwa Uzondu is a lecturer in the Department of Theatre Arts, Alvan Ikoku Federal College of Education, Owerri, Nigeria.

Victor Thompson is a lecturer in the Department of Theatre Arts, University of Uyo, Uyo, Nigeria.

Miriam Inegbe is of the Faculty of Education, University of Uyo, Uyo.

Tosin K. 'Tume is a lecturer in the Department of Theatre and Media Arts, Federal University, Oye-Ekiti, Nigeria.

www.ingramcontent.com/pod-product-compliance
Lightning Source LLC
Chambersburg PA
CBHW050157240426
43671CB00013B/2155